☆

Mr. SAM

☆ MR. ☆
SAM

C. Dwight Dorough

RANDOM HOUSE

New York

Thanks are due for special permission to quote material from the publications of the following:

The Bell Syndicate, *Washington Merry-Go-Round,* by Drew Pearson, March 15, 1955; August 31, 1959.

Crowell-Collier Publishing Co., *American* magazine, "Mr. Speaker, the Dynamo of Capitol Hill," by Edward Boyd, CLIX, 99–100.

The Hall Syndicate, Inc., *Allen-Scott Report* (nationally syndicated column), by Robert S. Allen and Paul Scott, January 9, 1960; and *Inside Labor* (nationally syndicated column), by Victor Riesel, June 9, 1959.

Harcourt, Brace & World, Inc., *Behind the Ballots,* by James A. Farley, 1938.

King Features Syndicate, *Washington Scene,* by George Dixon, August 9, 1960; June 20, 1961.

Bela Kornitzer, "The Untalkative Speaker Talks—About His Father," from *American Fathers and Sons* (Hermitage House).

Louisiana State University Press, *The South During Reconstruction, 1865–1877,* by E. Merton Coulter.

The Macmillan Company, *The Age of the Great Depression,* by Dixon Wechter, 1948.

The New York Times, article by James Reston, January 4, 1959.

Valton J. Young, *The Speaker's Agent* (Vantage Press).

FIRST PRINTING

 Published in New York by Random House, Inc., and simultaneously in Toronto, Canada, by Random House of Canada, Limited.

Library of Congress Catalog Card Number: 62–14442

MANUFACTURED IN THE UNITED STATES OF AMERICA

by Kingsport Press, Inc., Kingsport, Tennessee

Design by Tere LoPrete

TO

"Ninety-eight and a half per cent"

of the people in the

Fourth District

☆ ACKNOWLEDGMENTS ☆

When the author of a book like this, filled with reminiscences and testimonials, comes down to the point of expressing his appreciation, he hardly knows where to begin, since so many for so long have helped. Individuals and sources referred to know the extent of my indebtedness. I think I should first express my gratitude to the city of Bonham itself for providing me with a type of atmosphere and symbolism to see my subject with perspective and sympathy. But people make a town. I must hasten to thank the many individuals for information, encouragement, and the use of their research facilities. The repeated question "How is our book coming along?" informed me of their interest. I think that Mr. Sam was aware that the people would be helpful to a home-town product when he granted permission for this type of book to be written.

To my father (Deets Dorough), mother (Maude Scott Dorough), and brother (Robert E. Dorough), I express my thanks for the many personal things of which they are aware. To the staff of the Sam Rayburn Library and the people who provided their photostating equipment, I am indebted. To Director H. G. Dulaney and Buster Cole (Attorney and Treasurer for the Foundation) I am indebted. To my wife, Ivy Anderson, who assisted with some of the research and read the manuscript, I owe a special debt. She and my daughters are also to be commended for their tolerance during the past two years of my isolation.

To those who established the Rayburn Research Fund—Will Clayton, Mrs. S. M. McAshan, Jr., Walter G. Hall, Sr., J. R. Parten, Mr. and Mrs. Fagan Dickson, and James S. Abercrombie—I feel real appreciation. Without this kind of assistance, the book could not have been completed for several years. Some of these also gave interpretations of various problems in my research.

There are many others, especially in Houston, of persuasions different from Mr. Sam's, who helped me to see another side of a question and to balance an inevitable prejudice. To Neal Pickett of Houston, I owe special thanks for his assistance in the planning stages of the research. I pay tribute to the congressmen and senators who responded to my questionnaire with such detailed biographical data. I want to mention particularly D. B. Hardeman, Speaker Rayburn's research assistant, who sent files as I needed them.

To the University of Houston, I am most grateful for the use of its facilities. Universities should not reflect partisan views, for they by necessity are non-partisan. While I am aware that the politics of Mr. Sam was not entirely acceptable to some of my associates and fellow citizens, they agreed with me that I should tell the story authentically. There was never any attempt by anyone to direct my thinking. The book was written in a friendly atmosphere.

I should like to thank the research assistants in Bonham and Houston, especially my daughter Elaine for reading the chapters tangent to her field of specialization. I particularly wish to express appreciation to Marjorie Deyoe and Fleta Fisher for secretarial assistance, to White's Studio, the Brady Studio, and Atnip's Photos of Bonham for their photocopy work.

The bibliography will speak for itself; however, there are many obligations here which I cannot define or begin to include. The book has been too long in the making and is too closely integrated with other phases of my professional interests for me to separate some things which have unconsciously become background information.

Although the principal source was Sam Rayburn himself, as revealed in interviews, correspondence, the proceedings of the Texas Legislatures, *Congressional Records*, speeches, and testimonials, a great deal came from secondary sources. The bibliography and notes will reflect to some extent my indebtedness to others, but there are many more. For example, since 1948, I have pursued political histories, biographies, have collected articles by more than one hundred newsmen, columnists, etc., whose ideas have undoubtedly been added to my own store of knowledge. Space, however, will not permit their names to be listed, but where their articles were referred to in the preparation of the original draft, they have been included. Besides these, I had at my disposal a number of clippings from newspapers and magazines, that were provided by clipping bureaus, friends, and the

Rayburn Library. Some of the more ancient were fragmentary and without the proper identification as to source and, sometimes, dates. Associated Press items and Fourth District newspapers reported ideas of columnists, a fact which complicated paying tribute where it was sometimes due.

The sources of numerous quotations from Mr. Rayburn himself posed the most difficult problem in the entire study. He repeated himself so frequently to so many, who quoted each other, that I could not know who was originally responsible. Anyone who interviewed Mr. Sam knew the workings of his mind. He had a most remarkable knack for telling a story repeatedly, using the same wording. He always told what he considered to be the truth and never deviated from it.

In several instances, I have taken the liberty to fuse what Mr. Sam told me with what he told someone else in order to give a more complete report. I have leaned heavily on Valton J. Young's *The Speaker's Agent,* where problems in agriculture were concerned, because no one else better understood this side of Mr. Sam. Young's field notes are authentic and specific. They were superior to other accounts more general in nature. However, I have tried always to inject new materials whenever possible, especially from Mr. Sam's correspondence. I also want to mention that Walter C. Nash's thesis was helpful for background and information he collected from Lucinda Rayburn.

Finally, I want to thank Bascom Timmons for his timely articles in the *Houston Chronicle.* Though my manuscript was essentially finished at the time they appeared, he did provide reassurance and helped straighten me out at times on chronology.

☆ CONTENTS ☆

☆ INTRODUCTION ☆

The book *Mr. Sam* had its beginning long ago, before I was even aware that it was in the making, because my grandparents, as well as my father and mother, were either voting for, or associated with Sam Rayburn before I was born. Some of the unidentified comments and generalizations about Mr. Sam were made by these folk or their friends before I realized they would later have any significance.

With a father who entered politics himself when I was two years of age and who has been Chairman of the Democratic Executive Committee for thirty-five years, I was oriented very early toward the profession. I can remember handing out campaign literature when I was four. I cannot remember a time when I did not know Sam Rayburn because the date of my birth coincided closely with his decision to make the race for Congress. Hence this is the type of book that a man with my heritage is compelled to write. He must get it out of his system before he can turn to anything else.

My first inspiration came in 1935 when I encountered Mr. Rayburn on the train from Bonham to Austin. I had only recently worked in the campaign of William McCraw, who made a successful race for Attorney General. He had appointed me as a legal investigator, and for several years I was to combine politics with Ph.D. studies.

Another student from Fannin County came up to me on the train and whispered in my ear that "Uncle Sam" was several cars back. My generation was practically grown before we discovered that there were two Uncle Sams, the image of our "Sam" being ever before us. As we grew up we began to perceive that Mr. Sam of the Fourth District came rather close to the embodiment of the very soul of America and was a splendid example of what our type of civilization could produce.

When I entered the parlor car where he was sitting, he was staring in serious reflection across the countryside of winding gullies, eroded land, and waist-high weeds which seemed to stand like ghosts among the scrubby cotton stalks. His thoughts appeared to be of the future and not of the past. I saw something in his expression which made me recall an identical situation that had inspired the lines by Carl Sandburg as he too gazed from a "crack train" at the prairies—"into the blue haze and dark air." Sandburg projected himself likewise into the future when "all coaches [would] be scrap and rust and the men and women laughing in diners and sleepers [would] pass to ashes." Then the poet turned and asked a man in the smoker next to him where he was going, and he replied, "Omaha." I had scarcely shaken hands with Mr. Sam when he asked, "Where is the farmer going? Where is America going?" From the looks of the countryside, I wanted to reply, "Omaha," but I waited for him to answer his own question, and he did, with a sincere exposé on conservation.

As the subject drifted around to the House of Representatives, I asked a very harmless question. "Mr. Rayburn, to what do you attribute your success?" But instead of waiting for him to reply, I added tactlessly, "Horsetrading?" When the top of his head turned pink, I knew that I should have waited. He replied, "NO! A knowledge of parliamentary procedure!" Then he went on to explain how a bill gets to be a law. When he had finished, I felt somehow that he had not told the whole story.

Then he talked about his school days at the old Mayo Normal. He told about his financial struggle to get an education and how lonely he felt at times when he looked ahead at the obstacles:

"I know what it is to want things, and I haven't forgotten. I haven't forgotten. There's not a boy or girl in America that I wouldn't like to put my hand on their heads and say, 'I am for you and go to it.' I wish in those dark, blue days that someone would have come along and said, 'Sam, we've got confidence in you; we believe you're going to make a great one.' "

Two hours with Sam Rayburn were gone before I realized it. He made a profound impression upon me that day with his respect for the soil, insight into government, and love of people, especially those who needed help. He made me feel confident and secure. This was my hour of commitment, for I left him that day feeling that his hand was on the heads of all the boys and girls in the Fourth District. When he became famous and we shared him with others, he never removed that hand from all our heads. It remained there until it fell limp by his side on November 16, 1961, in the Joe Risser Hospital.

The longer he lived the deeper became this love of people. In his later years he had only a hate of "hate" itself and fear of "fear" for what these abstract qualities could do to people.

By 1948 I was collecting the story of Sam Rayburn in a somewhat unsystematic fashion. The files grew with the years. At this time I wrote him that I wanted to do a biography, quite aware that he had turned down three or four requests, because, as he liked to say, "the dead cannot talk back." He wanted to be fair with those whose arguments would also have to be presented. I felt also that his modesty and lack of appreciation of his contributions were reasons for his unwillingness to authorize such research.

In 1959 when I sent him an offprint of an article about Thomas Jefferson and asked him whether I could proceed with my idea for a book about him to emphasize something of the Jeffersonian motif, he promptly replied, "I should be pleased."

When the word got around that I was writing a biography of Mr. Sam, some of his friends—Walter G. Hall, Sr. (Dickinson), Will Clayton, James S. Abercrombie, Mrs. S. M. McAshan, Jr., J. R. Parten (Houston), and Fagan Dickson (Austin) established a Rayburn Research Fund at the University of Houston to defray expenses for salary, travel, photostating equipment and assistants. Within a year's time I had read and photostated everything of significance—speeches, letters, newspaper files, references to him in the *Congressional Record;* I had corresponded with or interviewed numerous people in Washington and elsewhere. These voluminous materials were added to my previous collection of clippings and reminiscences. Mr. Sam was also very generous with his time, submitting to hours of recorded conversation which followed the outline of a brief that he had studied prior to the sessions.

When I looked at the material before it was put into chronological order, I had an uneasy feeling. Two problems stared me in the face. There was more than I could possibly use and there was an inescapable, almost monotonous, pattern about the man's life.

He was elected to Congress in 1912 and twenty-four times thereafter, nearly always with opposition. When Congress adjourned he came home to relax on his farm, campaign for re-election, and every four years to serve the Party and National Ticket in several capacities. His speeches numbered into the thousands, reflecting a conspicuous consistency of philosophy that evolved with the times so gradually that it was scarcely recognizable. He was opposed to foreign travel, preferring to see America first. Most of it he saw from behind the microphone at a political rally or through the window of a parlor car or airplane. Yet this man whose life seemed to have only two poles—Washington and Bonham—was known all over the world, as was evidenced by the scope and volume of his correspondence. His renown never seemed to shake his equilibrium; he was just as pleased, maybe more so, about getting a letter from an old crony around Bonham as a communication from, for example, Winston Churchill.

Hence the life of Sam Rayburn seemed filled with thousands of people in the Southwest whom the rest of the world did not know or could not have cared less about. These people seemed important, not so much for their achievements in world affairs, but because they were made out of the same stuff as Mr. Sam. He wanted these folk to be identified with him, and I was quite in agreement, particularly since I felt the same way about them. These people are in this book because that is the way Mr. Sam wanted it. They were his constituents. In 1960, when asked if they bothered him when he came home for relaxation, he replied, "Bother me? I have been bothering them for almost fifty years."

When I scanned my files again I found further repetitious materials. He was eulogized on birthdays and for breaking more records than any other congressman on Capitol Hill. He was bipartisan in foreign affairs and highly competitive on domestic issues, piling up an inconceivable legislative record.

In October, 1960, when I organized the mechanics of my research, it was the skeleton of Sam Rayburn which I saw; but I very shortly realized that beneath it all was a soul—an ideal—one of the founding fathers of a new America.

This book was conceived among Mr. Sam's people in the Fourth District and has been written with their interests and tastes in mind. They represent, however, a fairly broad cross section of America. Yet there is a consciousness that any frank presentation of "Mr. Democrat's" ideas and political wars will reopen a few old wounds. Some perchance may smart from their reminiscences or transgressions, but so long as their consciences do not haunt them, the pain of this brief reminder should be soothed by pleasant recollections of the man who inspired this work. The universal concern and grief for Mr. Sam were authentic; hence it is the hope that this recounting will not disturb these sincere emotions.

I am quite aware that there are some who know far more than I about isolated incidents but I hope that my comprehension of the whole will offset the inadequacies. "Many of the original information sources, indispensable to the story," states John W. McCormack, "have already passed from the scene." Perhaps, though, this biography will serve to set in motion those impulses and insights which will lead to a more profound treatment, when Mr. Sam has settled back among his companions in American history.

When I asked him if he planned to read this sizable manuscript, he paused for some time, then said:

"Ninety-eight and a half per cent of the people are good folks. They are the best judges I know. You are the only one who can destroy the faith they may have in you. Tell the truth and you will have nothing to fear."

He gave me my answer and my challenge, but I left him on that day not completely satisfied because I could not keep from worrying a little about the other one and a half per cent.

C. Dwight Dorough

May, 1962
Houston, Texas

☆

Mr. SAM

☆ I ☆

Mr. Sam's Last Frontier

THE first week in January on Capitol Hill, for more years than some can remember, belonged to Mr. Sam. It was the week containing his birthday, when friends near and far paid their respects—at a reception, at a dinner, by spoken word, by written communication, or by silent tribute. In two respects January 6, 1961, was no different from all the rest because Mr. Sam merely added another year to his long string to make it seventy-nine and attended a series of receptions and a dinner given by friends, who had been honoring him for twenty years. In another way this birthday was unlike the rest, for the fatigue on his face seemed an ill omen, when he had passed his seventy-ninth milestone. President-elect Kennedy appeared as a surprise visitor at one of the celebrations—that given by the Ed Connallys. Rayburn was reassuring:

"I may be old in years, but I am young in spirit. I have hope I will live a while longer to be of service to my day and my generation and perhaps will be able to leave the world a little better than I found it."

This was cheering news to the "New Frontier."

The week began, as had been the custom since 1940, except for four years, with Mr. Sam sitting on the rostrum. On

January 3, he called the Eighty-seventh Congress to order. He noted that he had seen many changes since that historic Sixty-third of the New Freedom and now, after forty-eight years, he was still looking forward with his eyes focused on the horizon at a New Frontier. The country's geographical frontiers had apparently been reached, discounting the talk of a fifty-first state in Puerto Rico, and now America was stretching her energies toward new landmarks—goals in science, human relations, and economics—challenges to body, mind, and spirit. The grand old man of the Democratic Party was full of enthusiasm and was prepared to throw his talents and energy into the quest of a world order where free men could live without fear and with a sense of economic security.

As an expression of their appreciation of this faithful public servant, Representative James Fulton (R., Penn.) had introduced a bill to name one of three buildings on Capitol Hill for Sam Rayburn. The other two Speakers to be honored were Joe Cannon and Nick Longworth. Mr. Sam, however, had the kind of modesty which led him to sidetrack such measures, especially when more urgent business was pending. He showed a similar lack of enthusiasm on September 7, when Senator Ralph Yarborough proposed that the Treasury Department coin a gold medal to honor the Speaker. Mr. Sam objected to such a symbol to commemorate a living man. But late in November a saddened Senator revived his idea and coupled with it a recommendation, supported by Vice-President Johnson, to issue a commemorative postage stamp in honor of the Speaker. Other gestures were then forthcoming, including the establishment by the Touchdown Club of Washington of the "Mr. Sam Award" and the sale of the "Speaker Sam" rose bush. This is a yellow rose with a red tint around the petals.

Sam Rayburn said, in opening a session of Congress, "I love this House. It is my life." On this particular day in January, he might have added, without offense, "It is *my* House," because he had presided over it fairly and firmly for longer than anyone else. He had been a leader as well as a Speaker, "affixing his signature," as Jim Wright said in his nominating speech, "to more important legislation than that of any other man in history."

At these opening sessions and at Mr. Sam's birthday parties, congressmen of persuasions different from his were on their good behavior. Thereafter the atmosphere could change. Even Sam, soft-spoken and kind, could throw off a holiday manner very quickly. On January 9, in no uncertain terms, he let the people who bolted the Kennedy-Johnson ticket, and all the other obstructionists, know that they were headed for trouble if they tried to set up a roadblock against the New Frontier. Among those who were so honored by his reference were the six ultra-conservatives on the Rules Committee.

Robert S. Allen and Paul Scott on January 9 reported the following conversation between Rayburn and Minority Leader Halleck:

"Charlie, you had better think twice before you attempt to interfere in the selection of the Democratic members of the Rules Committee. That's a game two can play. You are asking for trouble if you try to do anything like that, and I want you to clearly understand you'll get it. I don't have to remind you that the Speaker of the House has a lot of authority. And I won't hesitate to use it if you force me to."

"What do you mean?" demanded Halleck.

"For one thing," retorted Rayburn, "I'll use my authority as Speaker to select the Republican members of all special and joint committees. I have that power, but I haven't used it. I have allowed you to designate the Republicans on these committees. But if you meddle in what we Democrats do about our members on the Rules Committee, then I'll give you a dose of your own medicine on the special and joint committees."

There was a long silence as the two men looked at one another. Halleck then replied, "You know I have to follow whatever our caucus decides. This matter isn't only up to me. The caucus will vote on the course to pursue, and I'll be bound by that."

"Yes, I know all about that. But when you told Howard Smith you would back him if he would lead the floor fight for Colmer, that was no caucus decision. That was your own, and some of your Republican colleagues are publicly saying they don't like it," declared the Speaker.[1]

Representative Joe Martin had already been to see Mr. Sam, and before he left the Speaker he informed his friend of his stand on the forthcoming Rules issue. "I'll line up as many of our people as I can to help you, and I think you will be surprised by the number who will." Martin valued Rayburn's friendship, recalling particularly his sympathy in 1959 when the new order in the Republican Party had unseated him as Minority Leader.

Though the Speaker had temporarily pacified the liberals in the House by his action in the Eighty-sixth Congress, he knew that he had reached no permanent solution with respect to the problem within the Rules Committee. A coalition of two Democrats (William Colmer of Mississippi and Howard Smith, Chairman, of North Carolina) and the Committee's four Republicans had frequently prevented liberal legislation from reaching the floor.

No sooner had the Democrats been assured that their November triumph was authentic than the Speaker's mail to Bonham increased in volume. As soon as the first round of congratulatory and victory epistles slackened he began receiving communications portending trouble. The liberal plan to revamp the Rules Committee became evident and the conservative resistance likewise. Two types of advice crossed Mr. Sam's desk: "Purge Colmer" and "Don't revamp the Committee." The first came from Party loyalists and the latter predominantly from supporters of Richard Nixon, or people in the Southern states where he had many friends. The problem immediately became quite complicated for the Speaker. The closeness of the popular vote did not inspire him with enthusiasm one way or the other. In the final analysis he knew that he would be faced with a value judgment, a decision he would have to make. For six weeks he read his mail and listened patiently. He struck matches, puffed away first at his favorite brand of cigarettes, then at filtertips or at any kind, drummed his desk with that famous finger, and quietly worked at his problem. He smiled even less. He became more serious and melancholic. The initial joy over the Democratic victory faded into silent reflection.

The following excerpts from correspondence reveal some of the reasons for his seriousness. "We want Colmer." "Viva Economy, Conservatism and Patriotism." "Down with inflation and Communism at home." "Start those nuclear tests now." "The enemies are *here,* promoting strikes—wage–price–profit race which will soon price us out of foreign and domestic markets causing mass unemployment." "Stop the union goons and Red mouthpieces and big-spending and tax-boys in and out of Congress." There were also unsavory remarks about some of the New Frontier appointees, the "egghead and theory-crazy professors," all of which confirmed Mr. Sam's belief that he had some constituents who were too distraught to listen to reason.

After two weeks of bombardment he made a statement: "Yeah, it's a pretty big problem." This was all—not one word as to how he proposed to solve it. When probed for hints as to his course of action, he said, "I plan to wait until the caucus and see how the boys feel before I say anything." This was his mind on

December 26, but the twinkle in his eye had replaced the pensive stare of late November. Sam Rayburn had a plan, but he was keeping his own counsel.

On the surface this appeared to be a liberal-conservative battle for control over legislation and a showdown between two old Democratic political warhorses—Rayburn and Smith—but it was bigger than this and one that had its origin in the remote past. For years the Rules Committee and the presiding officer of the House had been laboring over the question as to who should direct legislation. The Committee has frequently been referred to as the "Third House" with its Chairman in a powerful position. He could control the House and reduce the Speaker to a mere figurehead since he determined what legislation should be cleared. Such authority could have a paralyzing effect upon any Administration whose philosophy was incompatible with that of the Committee. For two Congresses the Speaker had been forced to resort to strategems and personal appeals. Mr. Sam and the White House had now decided that only a showdown could resolve the stalemate.

The Committee was established in 1789 and for a century performed the routine duties of simply formulating parliamentary procedures for the House. With an increase in the volume of business and the retarding effect of the two-thirds rule upon the flow of legislation, the Rules Committee acquired its power of selectivity, its power to determine the length of debates, whether simple majorities would suffice, and whether amendments could be proposed from the floor. By 1880, it had become a standing Committee. With rule changes, the Committee increased its power further. From 1858 to 1910, the Speaker was a member of the Committee, during which period the procedures of the body became solidified and under Joe Cannon's firm hand a weapon of power. The Committee worked cooperatively with the House leadership because he was a member of the body. The story has been told many times about the expulsion of Speaker Joe Cannon from the Committee for exploiting its function to build his own legislative empire.

By 1961, the Committee possessed the power to determine the rule for each bill. The time limit on debate is customarily several hours, but it can be fifteen or more hours. The rule also sets the nature and number of amendments that may be offered from the floor. If it adopts a "closed rule," there can be no amendments, if an "open rule," any number of amendments. This procedure was an efficiency measure, established to clear up time-consuming problems before the full House had a chance to begin debate.

A bill on the Consent Calendar may be brought up only on the first and third Mondays, but requires unanimous consent for passage under suspension of the rules, without debate, the first and third Mondays, but needs a two-thirds vote of the House of Representatives for passage. A bill under the "Calendar Wednesday" procedure has to be completed the very same day, being subject to stalling techniques after it has reached the floor.

Privileged bills, such as appropriations, revenue measures, veterans' pensions and a multitude of others, may be called up to the floor at any time but are subject to the "open rule."

Thus a Committee which was designed to simplify, and cooperate with, the will of the majority evolved into an isolated and autonomous group. The change in attitude and mood was the result of philosophical differences between the White House and an entrenched minority in Congress. In 1961 it was a group of Southerners who were defending their ideas and way of life. National sentiment visioned it as a cliff-hanging stunt.

Under the New Deal the Committee functioned as an aid or arm to the Speaker in speeding up favorable bills. During the first four years of his Administration, Roosevelt made the most of an overwhelming majority and staged his much discussed "crash program." But during Roosevelt's second term a coalition of Southern Democrats and Republicans resorted to the panel in an effort to slow the stream of liberal legislation. Roosevelt's effort to pack the Supreme Court and his forty-cent-an-hour minimum wage fomented the coalition within the Committee, of which Smith was a member.

According to existing procedures, a measure can bypass the Rules Committee and reach the floor under "suspension of the rules," which allows only forty minutes of debate and no amendments. Since a two-thirds majority is required for this procedure, important bills stand little chance where a coalition exists.

Bills so blocked could circumvent the Committee in two ways. There was the discharge petition, which had to be signed by a majority of the members in the House, a cumbersome and unattractive procedure particularly in the eyes of the minority party. Already handicapped it does not want to incite the hostility of a committee that can exercise vindictive powers upon its own legislation. Only two bills—the Federal employees' pay increase and Fair Labor Standards Act of 1938—have ever succeeded by means of the discharge petition.

There is the "Calendar Wednesday" technique, already mentioned, which permits a committee chairman, during a roll call of committees, to bring up a measure without the approval of the Rules Committee. At this time bills and resolutions not otherwise privileged may be taken up. A committee recognized for this purpose may choose one of its so-called emergency items. Prior approval from the Speaker and floor leaders must be secured and a motion of unanimous consent must be granted. Suspension of the rules is required, however, before a vote can be allowed. Though it is possible to give a day to such a bill, there is the time limitation which a strong opposition can exploit to stall a measure to death. Rayburn did use this technique once, in 1959, to circumvent Smith in the depressed areas legislation.

As long as Eugene Cox of Georgia was Chairman, Rayburn had little trouble because of a personal relationship. The death of Cox in 1952 elevated Smith, who became the mouthpiece of a section which appeared more and more on the defensive. Smith's resistance was not so much to Rayburn personally as to his symbol of power and identification with a trend toward federalization. More and more he questioned Rayburn's basic loyalty to his section. The drift of the times drew the men apart ideologically, though there was more cordiality than one would expect. Professional politicians know how to isolate their personal feelings and responses from the bitter feuds in the House.

Even after Smith became Chairman of the Committee, Rayburn had found ways of succeeding, thanks to Republican Joe Martin. However, with the rise of Charles Halleck, who would not compromise as did Martin, came a new order. Halleck never threw away an opportunity to cultivate Smith's strong opposition to the Democratic majority on important legislation, where partisanship became the order of the day. Rayburn's inability to get the "middle-of-the-road" Carl Elliott labor reform bill out, until the Republican supported Landrum-Griffin bill was called for by public sentiment, is a good example of the widening breach between Speaker and Committee. The special session of the Eighty-sixth Congress, specifically, opened Rayburn's and Kennedy's eyes to what had to be done—Smith's power had to be curtailed, either by a "purge" or by "packing," as the terms came to be loosely used.

Howard Smith had assured Rayburn that he would allow

about five of the New Frontier bills to clear, but the Speaker pointed out that there could be as many as forty. During the days before the Eighty-Seventh Congress convened, Smith proudly affirmed: "My people didn't send me to Congress to be a traffic cop." And he also inferred threateningly that even a "packed" committee can fail to meet near the end of a session when "log-jams" occur, and that the machinery of getting a chairman to call a meeting can consume valuable time. Rayburn recalled the Eighty-fifth Congress in this connection.

When the Speaker arrived in Washington shortly after the beginning of the new year, a great deal of Party advice was awaiting him. He disappeared into the smoke of tiny conference rooms.

Representative John Blatnik of Minnesota, who had assisted Rayburn on any number of occasions in breaking through the Rules block of liberal measures, advised the purging of Colmer. Blatnik said that he had been in communication with Richard Bolling of Missouri, Sidney Yates of Illinois, Chet Holifield of California, Frank Thompson of New Jersey, and other liberals. They were united in their plans and wanted to know Rayburn's views on the Rules Committee problem. Some of these people had already reached Rayburn by telephone. Mr. Sam said he had a plan but that he needed a little more time before making it public. Blatnik then reported that he, too, "had a plan" and was prepared to put it into effect if Rayburn had not found a solution by the time of the Democratic caucus. He stated that he was going to offer a resolution to prevent Colmer and three other Mississippi Democrats, along with Louisiana's Otto Passman, from participating in the caucus as Democrats because of their desertion of the Party. Blatnik added that he was going to make an attempt to negate the seniority rights of these men on committees as Democrats. Rayburn assured Blatnik that he would have a plan on Monday morning and would present it to them in his office immediately before the caucus.

Vice-President Lyndon Johnson, fresh from the battlefields of Dixie, where he had encountered some guerrilla bands of marauding Democrats, also wanted Colmer's scalp. Carl Elliott of Alabama was suggested as a replacement, appearing to be the Southern liberal best suited to break this conservative strangle hold. Rayburn deliberately stayed away from his office and conferred with many by telephone. He talked to Howard Smith and explained that he was forced to take action on Colmer since the coalition with Charlie Halleck foreshadowed trouble for Administration legislation. He also explained that Colmer, a Democrat, had denounced the Kennedy-Johnson ticket.

There was a brief silence in the Speaker's office after Congressman Blatnik and his delegation took their seats. Mr. Sam cast his eyes around the room from one to another until he had surveyed the men. Then he proceeded to state that for two months he had been under considerable pressure. Effort had been made to prevent his reaching the decision he was about to announce. The Party had been hurt by some fellows who were being carried along as Democrats and were enjoying the rights and privileges of such. He then announced that he was compelled to make the decision to help the assembled delegation to remove Colmer from the Rules Committee and to urge that other disloyal Democrats should lose their seniority rights.

Blatnik then made a statement to Mr. Rayburn that he was pleased with the type of leadership demonstrated and that, as far as he was concerned, there was no violation of seniority rights because these men had "jumped the Party" that had put them in their positions. Men like Colmer, he said, had by their actions invited this decision and the Party was now accommodating them. The meeting adjourned shortly before the caucus was scheduled to begin; however nothing definite was settled at this first caucus.

At another Democratic caucus, held on January 17 behind closed doors, there were three approaches to the problem which received consideration: 1) to proceed as in the past, 2) to purge Colmer, 3) to increase the membership of the Committee. The conservatives urged the first, the liberals were divided on the last two since either one would achieve their purposes. When Mr. Sam came to Washington he appeared to lean a little toward the latter because it was not vindictive and had a precedent.

He made this statement during the caucus:

"I have received thousands of letters opposing this change in the Rules Committee. About eighty per cent of the letters, I might add, came from people who voted for Richard Nixon. Most of them believe either in maintaining the status quo or in turning back the clock.

"I've talked with hundreds of people who have traveled the world and they tell me how the United States is looked upon today by foreigners. Their reports have not been very encouraging at a time when it is vital that, to maintain our position of leadership, we have the confidence and respect of other nations.

"The reason is that the last Administration failed to live up to its responsibilities, failed to do a good job.

"At the same time, we must not look for miracles by the new Kennedy Administration in the next hundred days. There's a lot of work to be done by all of us and I intend to give the new Administration the tools it needs to get the work done. That's why I am convinced that this change in the Rules Committee is imperative."

For nearly two weeks Rayburn had nursed the two propositions, considering the effect that each would have upon the 100-vote Southern bloc. Certainly he did not want to make a martyr out of anyone and solidify an opposition for the entire session.

On January 18, Rayburn stated in a twenty-minute meeting that he was opposed to punishing or purging. At this time he announced that he was now prepared to propose an expansion of the twelve-man Committee by three—two Democrats (one a Southerner) and a Republican—so that on most issues this should give an eight to seven vote in the Rules Committee. The two Democrats would be members who "voted Democratic in the precincts and the counties and the states, as well as in the House." Rayburn made an effort to keep the fight on an impersonal plane and to contain the intra-party friction behind the closed doors of the House. Chairman Smith agreed to meet with reasonable promptness and report the proposed new rule. Smith had one last chance—to defeat the measure on the floor.

On January 23, the Republicans held their caucus and voted overwhelmingly to resist Rayburn's move. Speculation was that on a voice vote Rayburn could win, but on a roll call the issue would be close.

In a press conference Rayburn stated dogmatically, "I think we are going to win." He knew he was laying his own prestige as Party leader on the line. It was a winner-take-all proposition. In fact, he knew his position as Speaker could be jeopardized if he lost. It took a great deal of courage to bring to a head an issue which could possibly have rocked along for at least another session before an explosion.

All thoughts of purging Colmer vanished on January 24, when the House renamed the personnel of the Rules Committee as it had been previously constituted. The following day at 10:00 A.M. Smith called the Committee together and voted the question out for House consideration. Rayburn had tentatively set it up for January 26.

In a press conference Rayburn announced that the White House was keeping hands off since this was something for the House of Representatives to settle. White House sources confirmed Rayburn's statement. Developments of the next few hours, however, called for a change in plans in the Administration's position and in the date for final action.

Joe Martin was called out of town and was not expected back before Thursday, and a poll of Republican strength showed 154 against and only 20 for Rayburn. When Carl Vinson of Georgia reported to McCormack that he was making little progress with the Southern bloc, the Majority Leader told Rayburn that he was not sure of the outcome. Most of the ninety-nine Southerners, Vinson reported, were making it a Civil Rights fight. Economic conservatives, they also were holding back on the Rules change, according to Smith, "to prevent Congress and the Kennedy Administration from spending the country broke." The coalition was pushing the belief that the least government is the best government and implying that in view of the country's critical fiscal condition the expensive legislation should not even be considered.

The stage was set for the showdown vote, but on January 25 Rayburn suddenly announced that it was being postponed until Tuesday, January 31, with the statement that some members were ill and others would have transportation troubles in the bad weather. Washington had been having some of its worst weather in years. Republican leader Halleck vigorously protested the change on the grounds that many had rearranged their plans to make the Thursday meeting. The day before, Rayburn had called for a head count which showed he had a margin of three votes, but two of these were suffering from pressure back home. Letters were pouring in, particularly from the Southern and Southwest sectors. The National Association of Manufacturers, the American Medical Association, the United States Chamber of Commerce, and the American Farm Bureau were exerting all their influence against Rayburn. The liberals were getting help from organized labor and school lobbies. Several members of the Texas delegation had already received considerable fan mail. Tuesday now seemed a better day to Rayburn, for President Kennedy would have his Monday's State-of-the-Union message behind him. On the sudden change of the date Rayburn stated: "I don't think we will be in worse shape Tuesday than we would be tomorrow and I think we'll win."

Smith said, "They must be afraid they haven't the votes." He was reported also as saying that he would win by one to five votes, but there was considerable switching around. Richard L. Lyons of the Washington *Post,* whose account of the above supplements Rayburn's quite well, reported that one member had changed his mind four times. Committee assignments versus the ill-will of a powerful Rules Committee had some congressmen in a dilemma.

It was a week-end of rumors. Some had heard that Smith was trying to make a deal to let every Kennedy "must" bill go through, in exchange for the status quo.

The Speaker, however, quieted all reports by announcing on January 28 that the Tuesday vote would be a winner-take-all fight. "There never has been any basis for compromise between Mr. Smith and me," he affirmed. Mr. Sam had developed a sort of contempt for professional Southernism since the last Congress. "The issue is boiling down to whether President Kennedy has a right to have his recommendations considered in the House."

Over the week-end both sides worked feverishly. To hold his people in line, Halleck had deliberately withheld his recommendations on committee assignments until the votes were all counted on this major issue. On Monday morning the White House decided to call off its neutrality. Vice-President Johnson and Attorney-General Robert Kennedy went to work in their efficient manner. The Presidential telephone was also called into action. Four Republican Senators—Cooper of Kentucky, Javits of New York, Scott of Pennsylvania, and Case of New Jersey began telephoning congressmen from their states.

The battle in the House began at 12:28 P.M. when the Speaker recognized Representative James W. Trimble (D., Ark.), his only Southern supporter on the Committee, to call up "Resolution Number 127." The Speaker had his say, in which he pointed out that back in 1933 Howard Smith, who was protesting the so-called "packing," was put on the Committee by this very procedure, and in 1939 Colmer got on in exactly the same manner. There were others who made their pleas.

Clarence J. Brown (R., Ohio) gave the lead-off argument for the opposition; Howard Smith then denied any "quarrel" with the Speaker and offered his compromise. Halleck then threw in his support.

The Speaker resumed his place on the rostrum at 1:37 P.M. Although both sides had counted and recounted the votes the day before, the twenty-five-minute roll call was filled with suspense, since people under pressure do not always "stay hitched," Sam said. The roll call was taken amid an unusual quietness with the members remaining in their seats making notations on their tally sheets. Some observers in the galleries, which contained a predominantly Rayburn crowd, also kept score and watched for any changes. The clerk then called the roll of the absentees, and only six of the ten showed up, three voting "aye" and three "no." The final count was announced by the Speaker as 217 for the Rules change and 212 against. Then followed the applause after moments of tension.

Smith promptly took sanctuary in the cloakroom and remarked, "Well, we done our damnedest."

Rayburn's joy was profound. "We won and I am satisfied," he stated laconically. It was a victory comparable only to that of securing the extension of the Selective Service Act. The White House was also well pleased, considering it as being virtually of the same value to the country's welfare. But both Rayburn and Kennedy knew that this was only the first engagement, although a decisive one, in a series to be witnessed in the Eighty-seventh Congress, because 64 Southern Democrats had joined with 148 Republicans. The margin of victory actually came from 22 Republicans in the Northeast, where Joe Martin had influence.

As far as the Speaker was concerned, this was a bitter fight and affected him more directly than any had previously. His leadership of the House and the Party was at stake, and the issue became personal with him. Ordinarily he remained composed and left personalities out of his comments, but this time some of his barbs found a target in such men as Republican Bruce Alger, with whom he generally managed to stay miffed. Rayburn was bragging about losing only four of the twenty-two votes in the Texas delegation when the reporter corrected him. "The tally, Mr. Sam, shows you lost seven, counting Alger."

"Hell," growled Rayburn, "who counts Alger?"

Rayburn may have also felt irritated with the six other members of the Texas delegation who resisted the elder statesman. Like all those who lost they were the beneficiaries of a "bucket of ashes." They were on the losing side in the House; they were challenging, he believed, the Party and House leadership; they were also expressing their lack of confidence in the new Administration.

There was some immediate retribution for those Texans who tried to break Mr. Sam's "political back." In choosing House members to attend the first Mexican American Interparliamentary Union in Mexico, Rayburn selected only J. T. Rutherford of Odessa from the Texas delegation. He bypassed Joe Kilgore of McAllen, and Clark Fisher of San Angelo, whose districts were also along the border. Kilgore had authored the Texas Legislative bill creating the Texas Good Neighbor Commission. Mr. Sam went down the subcommittee seniority list through six congressmen before finding his supporters in the Rules fight. With some eight hundred such honorary appointments each year which have bearing upon a congressman's prestige back home, a Speaker can give some very practical demonstrations to prove the value of loyalty.

The Republican Party, by virtue of its almost solid opposition, declared that it would resist change. The sixty-four men from Dixie also expressed the same desire to keep the status quo. Together they attempted a roadblock to check the social and economic revolution which had begun in 1933 and which, they believed, was destined to get out of hand during the next four years.

The New Frontier concept came into being as a philosophy of progress to continue exploration in democracy, social amelioration, natural science, and technology. It was defined by the young man in the White House as the only way civilization could move forward, for standing still meant moving backwards in a world torn by competing ideologies. This was the philosophy to which Mr. Sam had declared allegiance. For these concepts he laid his own personal prestige on the line and won. Since there was so much at stake, those who resisted him lost, because he would have lost had the issue gone the other way. But victory on an individual as well as a national basis is sometimes relative, and the player who picks up the chips may have to put them back on the table before the game is done.

There is the old saying which is very common in Mr. Sam's District that what goes over the devil's back will someday come around under his belly. The closeness of the vote would make Mr. Sam and the White House keep a watchful eye on future developments. Some tried to draw a parallel between the career of Joe Cannon and Sam Rayburn, but Mr. Sam's case was slightly different. He sought dictatorial powers not for self-aggrandizement, but for the expediting of a program where the public welfare was involved. However, some of the arguments advanced by Rayburn were used by Cannon in securing a tight grip on legislative procedures. Cannon finally fell a victim to the inability of President Taft to get his program moving and Cannon's unpopularity increased until Administrative wrath found its scapegoat.

On the streets of American cities people in discussing Mr. Sam's triumph asked many questions. Of course, the hand of fate has now made them unanswerable. Had liberalism exploited the loyalty of a friendly elder statesman? Which way will it strike if it goes sour? Had Mr. Sam gambled Congress's most brilliant career on a philosophy whose success is yet unknown? Does Howard Smith belong to a lost cause? Would Mr. Sam become the beneficiary of another? Should the New Frontier lose its glamor and fail to achieve its projected goal, some feared the Speaker's prestige and image could suffer in this failure. Not vindictive by nature and given more and more to love rather than wrath, some also made predictions, repugnant to those who knew the affection between the Speaker and leader of the liberal movement, that he, like Cannon, could be made a scapegoat when frustration began to take a toll. But the success or failure of the functioning of an enlarged Rules Committee cannot be adequately measured without the Speaker who kept the unsheathed sword on the table at his right hand and the olive branch at his left.

Fully aware of his own precarious position after the victory, Sam Rayburn moved quickly and appointed two "good Democrats" to the Rules Committee—Carl Elliott of Alabama and B. F. Sisk of California. The Republicans, with two vacancies on the original Committee as constituted and the new position just created, proceeded more slowly.

On most issues Mr. Sam believed the Administration could count on at least an eight to seven vote. He did not expect assurance on every measure, but with the new enlarged Committee he thought the New Frontier had a chance to be heard.

Chairman Smith, who possessed an impish sense of humor, immediately revealed his intention of cooperating. Willard Edwards of the Chicago *Tribune* press service reported Smith's behavior thus: "We are on the New Frontier. The Administration calls for action. The wagon train must roll." Then he promptly called up two measures which were objectionable to Rayburn—the authorization of television hearings of House proceedings and the outlawing of "back door spending," a procedure whereby certain Government departments are able to bypass Congress in spending. Aware that these two measures were very popular in the House, the eight liberals promptly voted to keep this legislation from reaching the floor. Smith then mockingly reminded the group that there had been serious objection in the past to a committee's having the power to block a House vote on legislation with popular support.

It was an incident like this which prompted the following conversation, as reported by Edwards:

> "Who won the fight?" a freshman congressman inquired of an older member. "The Judge looks happy, the Speaker, sore. I should think it would be the other way around."
>
> "Sam Rayburn and Judge Smith both know only too well," replied the older, "that Sam has won the first two skirmishes but the Judge may win the war. This one is going to be fun to watch."

This uninterrupted account of the Rules problem passed over and beyond that which Mr. Sam believed would prove to be the most significant event in the second half of the Twentieth Century—the Forty-fourth Inaugural Ceremony which ushered in the thirty-fifth President: a man who possessed the intellect, understanding, and vitality to give America and the democratic countries the kind of leadership and example which the philosophy of free peoples demanded, to restore the West in world esteem. Rayburn also pointed out that the new President would have in his Vice-President one of the most able understudies in history to help him carry out his program.

Speaker Sam Rayburn began to get into the spirit of the approaching event when the Texans, who had suddenly descended upon Washington, took over the Mayflower Hotel on the night of January 16. They were paying their respects to the Speaker and his two sisters—Mrs. W. A. Thomas of Dallas and Mrs. S. E. Bartley of Bonham. The Roland Boyds of McKinney, Texas, had engaged the East Room for a reception and buffet.

The reception for Vice-President Johnson in the Statler-Hilton Hotel on January 18 was one that the hotel officials will remember for a long time. Several thousand people from everywhere stampeded the doorkeepers to shake hands with Johnson and Rayburn. The arrival of the President-elect, and then of President Truman, set off further agitation.

The following night Rayburn and Johnson went to a reception given by the chief executives of forty-four states. Afterward the Presidential party attended the traditional inaugural concert by the Washington Symphony Orchestra. At the intermission the dignitaries eased out to go to a $100-a-plate affair.

Inauguration Day was sunny but cold after an eight-inch snow the day before. Mr. Sam was very much in evidence in the Presidential party, from the White House to the Capitol, then out to the new east front, "his east front." At the swearing-in ceremony it was Rayburn's privilege to administer the oath to the Vice-President. Hatless and coatless the Senator stood before his proud mentor. This was a great moment but not a new experience for the Speaker because he had already administered this same oath to Johnson three times while he was a member of the House during the war years. Johnson faltered a bit when Rayburn gave him too much to repeat, omitting several words and improvising. Rayburn used the Bible given to Johnson by his mother. At the end of the brief ceremony Rayburn's solemn expression changed to a joyful smile. He clasped the new Vice-President's hand and said firmly, "God bless you."

After the invitation luncheon in the Capitol, Mr. Sam rode in the parade. He was in section number five in the vehicle following the President's. With him rode the Vice-President, Mrs. Johnson, and their two daughters—Lynda Bird and Lucy Baines. The crisp afternoon air caused Mr. Sam to crouch in his seat, but he smiled and waved to the admiring throngs.

When Governor Daniel's automobile passed by the reviewing stand in front of the White House, followed by the University of Texas Longhorn band, the majorettes, the Fisher County Sheriff's Posse, and the band from Southwest Texas State College, Rayburn was profoundly moved. He knew they were honoring him as well as their favorite son. He had long ago realized his personal ambition. His people had been good to him and had given him everything he had ever wanted, and now he had placed the mantle on the shoulders of a man he loved as a father his own son. A long, successful career was behind him; an heir to his own political throne in Texas and the nation was gracefully taking over the reins. The Texans in Washington on this day were well pleased with their Mr. Sam and his selection of an heir apparent.

During the months when this drama of a man from the Fourth District was reaching its yet unknown denouement, the people back home were writing the text of another one. For several years two actors had been rehearsing their script—

Representative James A. Turman of Gober and Senator Ray Roberts of McKinney.

The people of Fannin County liked to believe that history would repeat itself, and since they were fearful that their Mr. Sam might not endure forever, they had already begun to look around for a young man to step into his place. Since Mr. Sam pioneered the course to political glory they picked one who followed the same pattern—one born of rural folk in a humble setting, who served in the schoolroom, and was elected to the Texas House. In the summer of 1960, they decided that they had better get him elected Speaker of the Texas House so that he could duplicate exactly Mr. Sam's apprenticeship. This young legislator had a long visit with the old master at his Speaker's office in the Memorial Library. Mr. Sam told him how to get the job done, and then Turman went forth to seek his political fortune. The third generation of Rayburn men started raising funds and seeing the "big wheels" in Texas politics.

The campaign was reminiscent of that back in the early days—as far as tenseness and occasional bitterness were concerned. By January 10, 1961, the wheel of Fannin County's political fortune had made a complete turn.

Representative L. Dewitt Hale of Nueces County placed in nomination for Speaker of the Fifty-seventh Legislature the name of thirty-three-year-old James A. Turman. Hale made the following comparisons:

> "Fifty years ago today, on January 10, 1911, the distinguished gentleman from Hill County, the Honorable Luther Nichols, stood on the rostrum to extol the virtues of and to place in nomination for Speaker of the House of Representatives of the Thirty-second Legislature the name of a young man from Fannin County who was destined for greatness in the world of politics.
>
> "Trust in this young man was not misplaced.
>
> "The race for Speaker was won in a close vote after a long, bitter and hard-fought campaign. The skill and ability of the new Speaker soon earned for him a place of high esteem in Texas politics. The following year he was elected to Congress and is now beginning his twenty-fifth term as member of that body. He has served as Speaker of the House of Representatives of the United States Congress longer than any other man in history. His contributions to our country and the world have been monumental. In the presence

> of the Great he stands without peer. The people of Fannin County can and should take justifiable pride in the achievements of their most famous native son, the Honorable Sam Rayburn of Bonham."

Hale then proceeded to show that the fertile soil of Fannin County had fifty years later "produced another young man destined for greatness in politics." In his presentation of James A. Turman, he revealed the similarity of the two men.

The votes being cast and counted, the Chief Clerk certified to the Secretary of State the following results: James A. Turman 83 votes, Wade F. Spillman 66 votes.

As further evidence of strange coincidence and Fourth District determination, at this very moment, Ray Roberts, one-time assistant to Mr. Sam and Senator in the Ninth District (State), was being elected President pro tempore of the Texas Senate. He too had been tutored by the master.

Though both men had written across their brow the sign of V, the fact that they had rubbed shoulders with the champion of champions gave them the encouragement young men need. Both aspirants had Rayburn's blessings and sound advice; however, he hoped their swords would never cross, because they were from the same District. This is what he told them as they launched their political careers: "Tell the truth, never violate your nature, and my people will be good to you."

Mr. Sam inspired these two gentlemen with the desire to be public servants. Others in the District also came under the Rayburn spell, because he gave a practical demonstration that politics was an exalted profession. He had mastered the "techniques of the machinery of democracy." Men who dream of filling his shoes, though inspired by a noble example, may likely be awed by any such undertaking. They know that public judgment can be both ruthless and humiliating when a man exceeds his grasp.

By the end of February the Congressional hoppers were full of New Frontier bills. Mr. Sam seemed well pleased with the way House committees were going about their work. "Congress is making good progress on bills," he told Ralph H. Johnson of the Lindsay-Schank Newspapers in a February 26 interview. Rayburn explained that there was no crisis like that in 1933 when Roosevelt took office, but nevertheless, there was a need for action. A depressed areas bill and a feed grain farm plan, with higher support prices and more controls, were two measures that he considered to be urgent. When questioned further about the farm bill measures, he stated in his usual abrupt way: "I never did believe in the soil bank—too much fraud. I'd rather support prices a little higher than pay a man for the poor land he takes out of cultivation."

The son of a Confederate veteran, who, a century earlier, had fought to divide the Union, joined in a ceremony on March 4 to honor Abraham Lincoln, who had dedicated himself to preserving it. The occasion was a re-enactment of the Inauguration of March 4, 1861. Carl Sandburg was one of the star performers in the dramatic and poetic portrayal of this era in history. Sam Rayburn was carried away, along with the many school children, by the prophetic words of the Lincoln biographer:

> "What the young people want and dream across the next hundred years will shape history more than any other motivation to be named. Youth now living and youth as yet unborn hold the seeds and secrets of the folds to be unfolded in the shapes to come." [2]

While this was a program to honor a great man, Rayburn was particularly impressed by the accent on youth and its part in the shaping of the future. Already Rayburn had felt a new atmosphere around Washington with a youthful President in the White House, and he was getting the feel of the new order himself, despite his seventy-nine years. He could feel the vitality of the times in the phrasing and type of legislation which was coming from the new Administration. The New Frontier, Mr. Sam felt, was more than a slogan: it was the heartbeat of a new age which was trying to be born—to the more cynical only an ideal, but to a realist like Mr. Sam a necessity if the free world was to survive and its economy to endure.

As he sat in the Cathedral Parish Church to assist the new President at the traditional Red Mass, a seven-hundred-year-old ceremony for the purpose of invoking God's blessing on the administration of justice by law, Sam Rayburn undoubtedly sensed that a new age had dawned. Here he was participating in a ritual which was a manifestation that a man's religion would not bar him from the White House. The concluding paragraph of the prayer, observed reporter Sarah McLendon, was written in 1790 by Bishop Carroll for George Washington:

"Let the light of thy divine wisdom direct the deliberations of the Congress, and shine forth in all the proceedings and laws framed for our rule and government; so that they might tend to the preservation of peace, the promotion of national happiness, the increase of industry, sobriety and useful knowledge, and may perpetuate to us the blessings of equal liberty."

Mr. Sam recognized in these words some thought for every facet of the New Frontier program—international problems as well as sectional issues.

Back in his District at a luncheon in McKinney on April 4 he predicted: "We won't get everything in all of the bills but we are going to get a large majority of the measures through that the President has asked for." A strong believer that America's problems could best be solved by the media set up in the framework of government, he warned against "strange rostrums." He was eager to talk about the John Birch Society, without using any names, but the occasion and time allotted did not permit him to do so.

At the Walter Hotel, Raleigh, N.C., on April 15 in a Jefferson-Jackson Day Dinner Address, he gave his most comprehensive analysis of the state of the union in 1961 and the New Frontier program. Some of the legacies from the previous Administration he mentioned were these: 1) five billion dollars of gold reserves siphoned away in the preceding three years; 2) farm income and parity ratio down; 3) automation ignored; 4) depressed areas and surplus labor; 5) decline of America in missile and space programs; 6) loss of prestige in Latin America; 7) foreign aid fumbled in many areas.

These were only a few of the challenges, Rayburn said, that faced the "lean, blond young fighter as he arose in the bitter cold of January 20 to deliver one of the greatest inaugural addresses—and one of the greatest speeches—in all history."

The elder statesman then described how the young executive went to work:

"He promised action, and I am here to report to you that he is giving us action.

"He promised progress, and I am here to report that we are making progress. Once again America is on the move. Our people are beginning to stir, our friends are being reassured and encouraged, our sinews of defense are being bolstered, and our economy is being reinvigorated. We are beginning to lead, not drift. We are beginning to work out problems, not postpone them. We are beginning to face unpleasant facts rather than trying to wish them away."

Sam Rayburn expressed satisfaction with the way the new President was performing his duties and marshaling the best brains in the nation to help him. "We take new heart at his broad offensive on all fronts, aimed not just at patching up the old order, but planning and building the new order." Then Mr. Sam proceeded to list a few of the things President Kennedy had already accomplished after only three months, by means of executive decree, negotiation, and a great mass of legislation, some of which was already as far along as the conference committees.

Sam Rayburn reminded the Democrats that they had an awesome responsibility—"one in which we cannot fail, for if we fail, the lamps of freedom will go out all over the world, and mankind will be plunged into a new Dark Ages, perhaps forever." He called upon Democrats and Republicans alike, men and women who treasure freedom, to give the young President "their confidence, their active support, and their prayers."

This April 15 address was Mr. Sam's most complete and eloquent dedication to the New Frontier. During the next four months he expressed broad approval, as he had done through all Democratic administrations; he took a long look at issues which did not jibe with his own philosophy.

Mr. Sam made a trip to Bonham over the week-end early in May. Saturday he spent on his ranch and Sunday with his family at the home place. As sole possessor of the title "Mr. Democrat" he was quizzed rather sharply on his interpretation of the outcome of the U.S. Senate race in which John Tower, a Republican, defeated William Blakley, a Democrat. Blakley, who had held two interim appointments, one by Governor Shivers and the other by Governor Daniel, perhaps in each instance with the assumption that he would not seek a full term, had faltered in two races. Senator Blakley had been against so much of the liberal legislation that the Texas liberals "went fishing" on election day. For years Blakley and Rayburn had been rather close personal friends, despite the Senator's recent voting record. Mr. Sam during the campaign tried to offer advice, but frankly admitted that "Blakley was the hardest fellow to help he had ever seen. He never did say what he was for, only what he was against." When queried about Tower's victory, he remarked that one half of the two million registered voters did not go to the polls. These, he said, were people who would have supported someone else less conservative. Tower and Blakley merely divided up the conservative vote. "If the Republicans think they have achieved a two-party system in Texas, let them try to elect a governor."

While he was on the subject of politics, he commented on the recent article in *Time* which reported that he was planning to retire. The article reported that because Mr. Sam's eyes were getting so bad that he could not recognize people he had decided to quit. He stated that he was feeling fine, though busy, and that he had no time to even think about retiring. In fact, he accepted an invitation to attend the 1961 Texas-Oklahoma Fair, September 25–30, which was to be dedicated to him; however, this was an activity which his doctor later told him he should cancel. Rayburn also accepted an invitation to be the commencement speaker for the May 29 graduation exercises at the Ladonia High School, in his District. If there were any thoughts of retirement on his mind, he certainly did not reveal them when he went to Birmingham the second week-end of May for a $25-a-plate Jefferson-Jackson Day dinner for 1200 Democrats. Here he was the same firebrand who had ignited the party loyalists at Raleigh a few weeks earlier. Nor was there any indication of sparing himself when he spoke to the graduates of Woodward School for Boys in Washington, D.C., June 7. "To make knowledge worth while," he told them, "it must be used properly and that requires just plain elbow grease."

The older Mr. Sam got the more set he became in his ways. He went to Washington in 1913 as a full-time, dedicated congressman, who liked to put in a good day's work and feel satisfaction with the closing of each session that the country's business had been completed. To him finishing the nation's business was like getting a cotton crop out and the land laid by. He worked hard and kept his mind on his job, expecting the same of the 436 others in his House who shared in his responsibilities.

During the second week in May, Mr. Sam heard about a petition that the congressmen's wives were circulating. What was contained in the document violated his routine way of running the House. Seventy-nine Republican wives and a greater number of Democratic spouses, mostly younger ladies with children of school age, wanted Congress to recess for August and September so that the families could have some time together. The way Congress operates, the children are away from Washington in the summer and the father is back home in the fall, after adjournment, to look after his political interests. The weaker sex received moral support from Senators like Hubert Humphrey, who affirmed:

"I have always felt strongly we should operate as a better Congress and that we could get more constructive work done; and it would make for happy homes if Congressional families could take vacation trips like other people. But the Senate and House must operate at the same time, and that is that."

When the Speaker had the proposition presented to him, he was in no mood for a "vacation while school was out."

"That is the greatest nonsense I have heard of, and I wouldn't mind being quoted on that. If we recess and come back in the fall we may be here forever. I don't want it—I don't believe in it. If Congress sticks to the business at hand we can clean up and get out of here in two or three months. Nobody with any sense would attempt to put a time limit on it now, but we will get through faster than some people think."

Rayburn was a master at whipping legislation through during the waning days of a session when congressmen were suffering from fatigue. If he gave them a chance to rest and get their "second wind they would harangue until Christmas," he thought.

Humphrey disagreed with the Speaker, but he admired his fearlessness. "It takes a courageous man to stand up against the organized opposition of the womenfolk. The Speaker is always a brave man."

Mrs. Frank Church, wife of the Democratic Senator from Idaho, expressed the disappointment of her Committee in these terms:

"I hope Speaker Rayburn will give further consideration later on and that he will change his view. At least, members of Congress should talk about it. We are just wives thinking of the health and welfare of our families and of how we feel Congress can do its work best."

After hearing Mr. Sam blight their hopes, Mrs. John Sherman Cooper, wife of the Republican Senator from Kentucky, stated, "It is still a good idea."

The older congressmen on the House side tried to appease their younger colleagues by reminding them that the air-conditioned Capitol quarters were more comfortable than the facilities back home. They had worked with Mr. Sam too long not to know that he was immovable when he made up his mind about something he believed was correct. A constituent, laughing about the incident, remarked, "I have known Sam a mighty long time, and I could have told the lady folks they were wasting their time. He won't even argue about things having to do with running his own business. He's the boss. Period."

Although this controversy between Mr. Sam and the ladies of Congress might have appeared laden with fuel for bad feeling, such was not the case. Mr. Sam was one of the most popular men on Capitol Hill with the wives. At a social function he was frequently seen off in the corner of the room talking with several, not about politics, but about their children, their favorite recipe for a dish, and so forth. His correspondence is conspicuous with references by congressmen and others to something the wives have said about Mr. Sam. The following paragraph out of a letter (February 28, 1958) from Harry Truman to Rayburn reveals a typical example of the esteem in which the Speaker was held:

> You made quite a hit with the Madam when you refused to have any more pictures taken. The two of you share the same attitude about photographs, and I have a dickens of a time with her. She says you are the greatest man she knows, and that makes me just a little bit jealous.

Though he was doing considerable traveling on week-ends during these months, particularly to speak to the youth at commencement exercises, he did not fail to gavel the House into session on a Monday. He had the reputation for being on the job. Administrations came and went but the one permanent member of our Government was Sam Rayburn. People around Washington came to regard him as such. This attitude is quite clearly revealed by Robert C. Albright in the Washington *Post* for June 11. President Kennedy tells the story of a call received at the White House switchboard one day while he was in Canada, Vice-President Johnson in Asia, and Secretary of State Rusk in Geneva. "Who's keeping the store?" demanded the frustrated caller after trying to reach each one of them.

"The same man who's always kept it, Sam Rayburn," reported the operator. She was aware of the fact that Mr. Rayburn had been keeping the store off and on for four Democratic Presidents.

On September 16, 1940, Sam Rayburn first took the oath as Speaker. He served continuously, with the exception of the Eightieth and Eighty-third Congresses. Then on January 31, 1951, the House of Representatives saw Henry Clay's 3056½-day record broken and on March 5, 1959, that of Joe Cannon. For two years Mr. Sam enjoyed the satisfaction of being the "Sultan" of all gavel handlers, each day breaking a record—his own. When June 12, 1961, arrived, following the invocation and roll call, Sam Rayburn asked the Republican Charles Halleck to take the chair as Speaker pro tempore. The Chair then recognized

John McCormack, who asked for consideration of a resolution, which the clerk read. The first paragraph follows:

> "Resolved, That the House of Representatives hereby extends its heartiest congratulation to its beloved Speaker, the Honorable Sam Rayburn, who, today, has served in the high office of Speaker of the House of Representatives for sixteen years, 273 days—more than twice as long as any other Speaker in the history of the United States. . . ."

McCormack then read this communication from the President:

> "Dear Mr. Speaker:
>
> "It gives me great pleasure to offer my congratulations today when the length of your service as Speaker has doubled that of an earlier Member, Henry Clay.
>
> "Attention will be called today to other records which you have equaled and exceeded, to other measurable accomplishments. Immeasurable, however, is your devotion to cause and country; and immeasurable is the respect, esteem, and affection which all of us who have served with you hold for you today.
>
> "With warmest regards and best wishes,
>
> Sincerely,
> John F. Kennedy"

For a man who had seen World War I, an era of normalcy and prosperity, the Great Depression, World War II, Reconversion, the Korean Conflict, the dawn of the Atomic Age and the Space Age, the doubling of Henry Clay's record was about as exciting as the Yankees' winning the American League pennant. But Mr. Sam had served continuously the longest of any member in the country's history, and during these fifty years his colleagues on both sides of the aisle had used up their repertoire of adjectives and compliments many times before. On this June 12 the lawmakers again paused to pay their homage. Carl Vinson, who had served with him for forty-seven years, expressed the thoughts of everyone when he said, "It is becoming increasingly difficult to describe the very distinguished Speaker of the House of Representatives." To those who try to laud him or write books about him Vinson's words have a special relevance, for his long career almost proved that he was "indestructible, imperishable, and indomitable." The man from Georgia added the qualities of "integrity, wisdom, loyalty, friendliness, fairness, and leadership." "I can truly say that my life has been enriched by my association with this distinguished man, who has become an outstanding symbol of representative government to the free peoples of all the world," Vinson added.

Some eminent men who served in the House paid tribute to the most eminent. They saw his fingerprints on every important bill passed during half a century. He was portrayed as the balance wheel in the Government of the United States. Though incomparable achievements lay behind him, he always believed that his biggest job lay ahead because of the perilous times through which America must pass.

This June 12 ceremony was by no means restricted to Democrats. Republicans also asked to be recognized that they might extend their respects. Arends of Illinois, for instance, expressed the hope that Rayburn would serve for many more years in Congress and he wished for the Speaker everything he could desire, except one—another term as Speaker. Smiling as he continued, he assured Mr. Sam that his failure to vote for him to be Speaker in the past had nothing to do with a lack of affection or respect.

Jensen of Iowa revealed another Republican tribute when he told how Mr. Sam once saved him from defeat and humiliation. A housing bill was before the House of Representatives, and Jensen, with a background in the lumber business, offered an amendment to correct a flaw that one with his experience could see.

> "A point of order was raised against the amendment on the ground that it was not germane to the bill. Our Speaker, Mr. Sam Rayburn, a Democrat, I a Republican, vacated his Speaker's chair, put another Member in his place, and came to my side while I was standing here, red-faced. I did not know what to say or what to do because I had not anticipated that a point of order would be raised against my amendment. Mr. Sam said then, 'Ask unanimous consent to withdraw your amendment to this section of the bill and offer it to section nine. It will be germane to section nine. You have a good amendment, and I want to see it passed.' "

Jensen then reported that Rayburn took the chair again and that the advice given resulted in the adoption of the amendment. This was the example Jensen cited to show how a Democrat like Rayburn won a permanent Republican friend.

The qualities most frequently in the minds of House members on this June 12 were Rayburn's warmth, humaneness, and capacity for friendship. Amidst his abruptness, reserve, sternness, seriousness, and commanding efficiency, this affection for people—individuals and the mass—stood out particularly. Congressmen responding to a questionnaire listed these qualities most frequently. This is Rayburn's tap root which supplied strength in political crises. Herein lay a source of his power. His humaneness, Thornberry remarked, kept him from using his awesome power to bend and crush people to his own desires, but enabled him to lead them in the ways that his wisdom directed. Representative Auchincloss of New York made reference to his friendliness, and the regard the House had for him: "The respect and real affection that members have for him, whatever their party affiliation, is beyond measure. . . . He is a man's man—and all the ladies love him." Auchincloss's final remarks could have been a fitting finale to the ceremony, before Mr. Sam expressed his appreciation:

> "Personally, I consider it a great honor and privilege to count him as a friend. I have met and known many men serving in various capacities in my lifetime, but I have never known one who is more true to his friends, who can be counted on at all times for wise counsel, for sympathy when the going gets rough, and for honest and helpful criticism when one gets off the track. May he enjoy many more years of good health and of opportunities for service so others may catch somewhat of the aura of his personality and be better citizens because of him."

Representative of the sentiments of the Texas people who expressed themselves on that momentous occasion is the following letter (dated June 13), to Congressman Rayburn from the Houston Democratic Women's Club:

> Congratulations, Mr. Sam, and too, we feel that congratulations are due the United States of America. For your brilliant leadership of Congress has steered our country through some very trying times—and always, you have kept paramount the interests of the United States and the interests of humanity.
>
> The Lone Star Flag of Texas flies higher, brighter,

and stronger because of the strength, the luster, and the character reflected upon its folds by our Mr. Sam. We are so proud of the wonderful chapter you have written in American history, and join Senator Ralph Yarborough in regretting that the tide of history did not sweep you into the White House, where, undoubtedly, you would have served the United States of America, and the world, as gloriously as you have served in the Congress and as Speaker.

We salute the greatest of Democrats: Mr. Sam.

Respectfully,
The Houston Democratic Women's Club
Mrs. Harry C. Austin, President
Mrs. Chattie Slayton, Secretary

Congressman Wright Patman once remarked that he hoped, when the time came for the academicians to write about Sam Rayburn, that they would not overlook the quality of humaneness. The Congressman's words were unnecessary, for Mr. Sam's life is inseparable from his work. His daily activities were filled with a multitude of services. There are fully twenty four-drawer filing cabinets in the Memorial Library filled with the evidence. There is perhaps no other man in public life who has done so much for so many. He showed no preferences. The obscure veteran with a fractured foot from injuries received at Perrin Field received just as much attention as a war hero like Sergeant Alvin C. York. If the case was worthy, Mr. Sam gave it his undivided attention.

The incident of Sergeant York attracted attention because he was a World War I hero who came from the hills of Tennessee, the land of Mr. Sam's birth. The press remembered Rayburn's earlier utterance that:

"There was something in the elements there . . . which caused men to grow into rugged stature. The soil and vegetation put something into the flesh and bones of the people of those hills that is found in few other places."

For many years Mr. Sam had been an admirer of this Tennessean. He believed that the Tennessee hills did give the Sergeant a special trait. Rayburn again revealed this quality of humaneness when he came to York's rescue on March 18.

The Sergeant had been in trouble with the Internal Revenue Department since 1942, when he received $150,000 for the book and movie rights to his life's story. The Government billed him for $85,000 in taxes, and York fought a losing battle in the courts. In 1961 the bill had increased to $172,000, which included the original sum with interest. Bedridden, the seventy-three-year-old Tennessean was unable to pay. Uncle Sam by necessity was cold and indifferent but Mr. Sam was warm and attentive. He had several conferences with the Internal Revenue Service and the Justice Department and got them to agree on a compromise offer of $25,000 to pay off the debt. Commissioner Mortimer M. Caplin was explicit in stating that York "was given no special advantage." Representative Joe L. Evins (D., Tenn.) was selected as treasurer of the fund-raising campaign, and Mr. Sam, its chairman, started the drive by giving a personal check for $1000. Within a few days there was a surplus of $2000. The additional money was put in trust for York to use as he needed it.

But Mr. Sam was not going to let Uncle Sam outdo him in this business of forgiving. His opportunity came during the third week of June, 1961. George Dixon, who has collected many anecdotes about the Speaker, tells the story of his visit to Mr. Sam's outer office to find that the desk nearest the private sanctum was unoccupied. Miss Martha Freeman of Bonham should have been sitting there. John W. Holton, the administrative assistant, looked as if the red-haired assistant had passed on to her reward. When Dixon questioned John he learned that she had suffered a fate worse than death.

> "She has gone to work for a Republican," he said.
>
> "Not Martha!" Dixon protested. "You mean she's deserted Mr. Sam—Mr. Democrat himself—for the enemy?"
>
> "She's been raided by the GOP," said Holton. "She's been carried off by the new Republican Senator [Tower] from Texas."
>
> "This is unthinkable," Dixon exclaimed. "Why, I remember when Mr. Sam hired her nine years ago. She'd been in a terrible automobile accident, and could barely move around on crutches. But she was from Sam's home town of Bonham so he gave her a job. Do you think he will ever forgive her?"

While this dialogue was taking place Mr. Sam had quietly stepped behind Dixon and was listening. Then, a soft voice came from behind the newspaperman, "Yes, I told her, 'It breaks my heart to have you working for the GOP but I forgive.'"[3]

Dixon expressed his sympathies to the Speaker and went to room 142 in the old Senate Office Building, where William A.

Blakley, the interim appointee and defeated candidate, had his headquarters. At first Dixon was told by the receptionist that Miss Freeman was out, but when he said that he was sorry he had missed her as he brought the news that Mr. Sam had forgiven her, the climate changed. Dixon was ushered in through two rooms before he reached the new office manager. Miss Freeman was trying to avoid publicity for fear of hurting Mr. Sam, but now that she knew it was all right and he had forgiven her she was willing to talk about the change. Miss Freeman knew Sam Rayburn was a practical man and understood her need for a $4000 raise in pay, but she could not bear the thought of hurting her venerable employer.

Though neither Miss Freeman nor Dixon mentioned the subject, they must have recalled Mr. Sam's appraisal of Tower during the campaign. "He's a pip squeak." Whether the Speaker revised his opinion of Tower is unknown. He met the Senator-elect in the corridor near his dining room the day before he was sworn in. Rayburn would not commit himself to anything in particular when questioned, but Tower reported, "We chatted amiably. The Speaker was very nice and gracious."

Mr. Sam had phenomenal health, having maintained a consistent weight of 176 pounds for forty years. When asked how he manged to maintain his physical and emotional stability with his tremendous responsibilities, he remarked, "I guess it's just the way I'm put together." Dr. George Calver, physician to Congress, through the years, had not ignored Mr. Sam despite his good health record and habits. He knew that Mr. Sam continued his routine of stretching and bending exercises before breakfast, but some had observed that in 1961 the brisk walk in front of the Capitol sometimes did not take place. Instead the Speaker, while Congress was in session, would slip out on an obscure balcony where he could stretch his muscles by shifting his weight up and down on the balls of his feet, all the while inhaling and exhaling. George Dixon found Mr. Sam here one day during the spring of 1961. This was his way of "getting the kinks out of his back," Mr. Sam said.

Though he did not diet during these months, his meals continued to be simple—luncheon in the Capitol's House Restaurant, where he had a bowl of soup (often the famous bean variety) and a dessert, preferably green apple pie with ice cream. His dinners consisted of a main dish, with vegetables (preferably fresh, green string beans and potatoes). His taste for Mexican foods still prevailed. More and more during these strenuous months, he liked a quiet evening in his apartment with the radio and television, watching sports events, Westerns, and programs that did not tax his mind.

Then suddenly, during the latter part of the summer, he began to lose his appetite. His energy declined and the pounds slowly dropped away. Several times while he was sitting in his big chair on the rostrum he felt a dizziness. By early August he was complaining more and more of pains in his back. Finally he went to physicians in Washington and they examined him just about as thoroughly as any doctor could a person like Mr. Sam, who did not know how to be sick. He helped the House physician in his diagnosis and came away with "a bad case of lumbago."

Finally, the pains became so intense that he telephoned Dr. Joe Risser, the family doctor in Bonham, to get a good home remedy. Joe knew the type of patient he had so he flew to Washington prepared for an argument; but Mr. Sam had already made a decision—to leave for Bonham August 31, with the idea of getting some tests at Dallas.

Several days before Risser was telephoned, Rayburn asked Joe Martin to come to his office as he wished to see him. Martin reported that his friend wanted to have some pictures made of the "two living Speakers." However, this was only an excuse to see Joe, for he knew that there was still a third Speaker down in Uvalde County. What Mr. Sam wanted to say to Martin was that he had decided to go home, and he wanted his friend to be the first to know. The next day the Speaker told the House of his plans.

Rayburn's decision came as a big surprise to his colleagues who immediately felt concerned, knowing how conscientious he was about his duties in the House of Representatives. There were some major pieces of legislation hanging in the balance, but he assured everyone that he would be back. "I want to die with my boots on and with my gavel in my hand. They are going to have to carry me out of here, God willing. I love this House." So he left Washington on August 31 and went home to the big white house, where he could be near Dr. Risser's clinic. The people who believed he would not be back in January, he said, were just "damned fools."

When the home folks heard that Mr. Sam had left Washington before the end of the session and that he had come home for treatment, they were disturbed. He had left an area where he could get the best medical assistance in America because he was afraid the doctors would put him to bed. Washington was such a lonely city, he thought, for a country boy to get sick in, and his first impulse was the normal one—to go home.

Joe Risser took him to his hospital for daily treatments to build him up for an examination of the area where the pain was worst, the pancreas and liver. After two days, Dr. Risser had checked the heart, lungs, stomach, and intestinal tract to find no problems. After each day's treatment he made a report to the White House, as he was instructed to do when Rayburn left Washington. Mr. Sam was a jovial and congenial patient. There were several occasions, however, when the Rayburn and Risser ideas clashed. One day Mr. Sam wanted to drink a toast to the New Frontier, but Risser said, "No." To make a long story short, Mr. Sam cussed out Risser and Risser cussed out Mr. Sam. But the conference was terminated in favor of the Speaker.

On September 8, Mr. Sam graciously gave some time to the author of these pages. By the stream of people going and coming one would never have suspected that the Congressman was a very sick man. Mr. Sam was lying on his couch but remarked that he believed he would like to sit in a rocking chair.

There are rocking chairs throughout his house, nineteen someone counted. Mr. Sam liked to say:

"People need rocking chairs in their homes. I like to see a man make a decision from a rocking chair. I wish we had more on Capitol Hill. But I am glad Kennedy has put a few in the White House."

Replying to questions about his health, Mr. Sam remarked, "My back is giving me hell. I just decided that I wasn't going to stay up there in Washington any longer and take that beating."

The conversation was mainly about the achievements of the Eighty-seventh Congress. He knew the New Frontier had taken a beating since he left, but he did not say so. He was especially pleased that old folks could look forward to decent retirement and live in some degree of dignity. Of course, he was none too happy about the failure of the medical-aid bill and he was thoroughly disgusted with some of his colleagues for ruining the school bill:

"Everybody rushed in and tried to get aid for their own schools. It's just ridiculous for the Federal Government to give money to all these institutions. Things just got out of hand, but I'll try again in January to straighten it out."

The last prediction seemed to be casual, merely from habit. He persisted in his fears relating to Federal aid for teachers' salaries:

"Just let the Government get its nose in and it will tell us what should be taught. We must not come to this. Of course, we did something for the distressed areas. What has me bothered is this international situation. I have told the President, though, that he must get tough, and I believe he means business. This is serious. Do you know that if a nuclear war should get started the entire white race could be wiped from the face of the earth?" [He meant that the members of this race could use it on each other.]

While he talked he continued to finger his cigarette nervously, repeatedly spitting in a wastebasket by the side of his chair. Finally he said he wanted to lie down, but would not hear of terminating the conversation. He continued to puff away at the cigarette but never realized that the wastebasket was no longer by the side of his couch. Moments of such conversation were too precious to worry about a rug. His voice was weak but contained the Rayburn determination when he spoke of the January session.

After a while a visitor arrived who seemed to have an urgent problem and the conversation came to an end. Mr. Sam painfully struggled to his feet. The handshake was a bit prolonged. "Dwight, may God bless you." There was something in his voice that made one feel that he was moved by instinct like the king of the elephants who came back to his burial ground to die so that his elements could mingle with those of his kind. There was a smell of tragedy in the late afternoon air. The author stood in dejected silence before he spoke to his assistant, waiting in an automobile. He sensed that an era was about to close. Not even the Weather Bureau's excited warnings about Hurricane Carla could tear his mind away from the image he had left behind.

On September 16, after his morning treatment, Mr. Sam asked to be driven to the home of Columbus C. Baker, his barber of forty years. Though he had retired, Mr. Baker had set up a chair on his front screen porch where he continued to cut a few heads of hair each morning for his favorite customers. Perhaps a Sam Rayburn haircut would not appear to require any particular skill, but, Baker said:

"There was a special ceremony. On September 16, as I had been doing through the years, I ran the clippers over the top of his head. There was still a little fuzz. Then I clipped around his ears and along the side of his head with my scissors. Then I shaved his neck. Afterward I always massaged his neck, and he would smile and say, 'that does me so much good.' When he got out of the chair he reached in his pocket and pulled out three one-dollar bills.

"He always paid me with the money in his side pockets, nickels, dimes, quarters, half-dollars, bills—never counting it, but quietly and inconspicuously cleaning out his pockets. Once he had only a five-dollar bill, but I could not make him take his change. A haircut in those days was only fifty cents. Now it's a dollar. Mr. Sam was a man of modest means, but he had a way of giving enormous tips. Buck Hunter, who shined his shoes for twenty-five years would sometimes get two dollars for one shine, in addition to money for his church. Mr. Sam believed that money had no value if it was out of circulation. 'Keep it moving,' was his motto in public and private finance.

"September 16 was just like old days when I cut Mr. Sam's hair, but now [November 18] I can see it was different. I walked out to the car with him, seeing that he was pretty sick, and said, 'I would be glad next time to come out to your house and cut your hair at any hour, day or night.'

"Then he replied, 'All right Bake (this was what he always called me). If I need another, I'll call you.'

"Today, I understand what he meant, what he was trying to tell me."

Dr. Risser at last persuaded Mr. Sam that the time had come to go to Baylor Medical. On Monday, October 2, he walked into the hospital and told the doctors to get started. By late Wednesday his spirits were improved, for he was beginning to joke and gripe about all the "poking and prodding" tests. On Thursday, October 5, Dr. Robert F. Short, Jr., in charge of the examination, telephoned President Kennedy's personal physician of the findings, advising him that a biopsy had revealed a metastatic malignancy.

John Holton, stunned by the report, told friends, "It may be just a matter of days. It's all over him."

The President, in expressing his sorrow, asked the nation to join with him and Mrs. Kennedy in prayer for Speaker Rayburn, "who has served his nation so well and so faithfully for so many years."

The following day Vice-President Johnson was at Rayburn's bedside. He told reporters that Rayburn's condition "is a great personal tragedy to Lady Bird and myself and every other American."

Two days later, October 9, the President, returning from a week-end at Newport, Rhode Island, made a three-thousand-mile detour to Dallas. When the President left the hospital he told reporters:

"We had a good conversation. I was happy to have a good chance to talk with him. He's sick, of course. I was glad I could be with him. He was in good spirits and showed enough courage for anybody."

Rather suddenly, shortly before noon on October 11, he developed pneumonia, went into a coma, and was reported to be dying. However, within twenty-four hours there was a complete change. His rugged stamina had enabled him to ride out the storm. The daily injections of five-fluoruracil, an experimental drug used to slow the spreading of cancer, were stopped until the pneumonia process was fully under control.

Ex-President Truman had telephoned Dr. Short on October 9 to find out when he might see the Speaker. Truman arrived at the hospital on October 13 for a five- or six-minute visit. At this time Rayburn expressed to Truman the hope that he would be able to go home by January 1. There was no reference to a return to Washington. Mr. Truman was not cheered by what he found, but in leaving Baylor Hospital, he tried very hard to make an appropriate remark. He expressed relief that Sam was in good hands at a Baptist institution, subtly reminding everyone of his own and Sam's religious persuasion.

Though the press reiterated that Mr. Sam was not informed of the nature of his illness, Joe Risser knew he had cancer on September 23. Mr. Sam was never a man to dodge the truth about anything, and he could recognize it from a long way off. Mr. Sam had followed the symptoms of the same disease in his sister, Miss Lou, and had seen several close friends die of it. He had his fears when he left Washington on August 31, and undoubtedly knew intuitively by September 15.

The illness of Sam Rayburn produced a tense hospital drama at Baylor Medical. Visitors, knowing they would not be admitted, came to Dallas merely to inquire about Mr. Sam and to stand around the reception room where John Holton, Mrs. W. A. Thomas, and Mrs. S. E. Bartley tried to see them all. Newsmen throughout the United States descended upon the clinic and there were between fifty and seventy-five who covered the President's visit. The major networks and wire services were given a room on the first floor, where their equipment was installed. Rows of typewriters and telephones were set up for top newsmen from New York, Washington, Chicago, Los Angeles, and elsewhere. Daily press conferences in the hospital library attracted as many as twenty correspondents. The room also housed overflow television and sound equipment. The Associated Press and United Press International staffed the Baylor press room on a twenty-four-hour basis. One weary wire-service reporter said he had been on duty fifty-five hours without a break and when relieved he would report for active duty with the Texas Forty-ninth Armored Division of the National Guard.

Letters and telegrams poured in daily by the thousands from all over the world. Mr. Sam told John Holton to have his staff acknowledge every one of them and express his appreciation.

When adversity strikes the Rayburn family it seems to hit hard, for while he was in the hospital his seventy-seven-year-old brother Dick and Dick's wife were both patients in the Risser Hospital at Bonham, ill with pneumonia. The couple's son, Dick Tom, was also in Baylor Hospital with his fifth operation for a kidney ailment.

On Tuesday, October 31, Mr. Sam was taken from the Baylor Hospital to the Joe Risser Hospital. The decision was made on the afternoon of October 30 by his two sisters out of deference to the Speaker's often-expressed desire to end his days among "those friends and neighbors who for so long have given me a love and loyalty unsurpassed in any annals." His great-nephew Robert Bartley, who flew home on emergency leave from the Army in Korea, reported, "He seemed to perk up when he realized he was home." Earlier Mr. Sam had made a somewhat typical remark when Bartley first visited him in his hospital room in Dallas: "Robert, this the damnedest thing that has ever happened to me."

For two weeks Bonham was a solemn town. Never have any people anywhere been more grief-stricken. They drove slowly around the hospital, stood in the street outside, on the public square, huddled together in the places of business—praying, but with dwindling faith, that the periodic bulletins would bring some news on which they could pin their hopes. They felt some little comfort in learning that he could still "crack a few jokes," or had eaten a roast quail for lunch; but then they learned that he was becoming less alert. Day by day, hour by hour, minute by minute they watched the dark cloud as it slowly descended upon the tiny hospital and enveloped the man who, once strong of mind and body, had shepherded them for so long.

At 6:20 A.M., Thursday, November 16, 1961, Mr. Sam died. Dr. Risser in his official bulletin to the White House stated:

> "He died quietly. His respiration stopped. His heart continued beating for four minutes. There was no evidence of pain lines in his face. He seemed as one in sleep. The cause of death was a paralysis of the breathing muscles in the central respiratory system. The respiratory center of the brain ceased to function."

The actual announcement to the nation came from the President. Speaker pro tempore John McCormack, after being notified by the White House, designated 105 members of Congress to fly to Bonham for the funeral.

That which transpired during the next two days could well fill the pages of another volume, and the eulogies from men of high and low degree, the pages for its sequel. The theme of these eulogies could be summed up, however, by a conversation between two men standing on the southwest corner of the town square, one a native of Bonham and the other from Washington. The first remarked sadly, "We have lost a great congressman."

"Yes, you have, but the Fourth District can replace its representative. We in Washington, though, cannot replace him. The nation's and free world's loss is greater than yours."

His body was removed to the Wise Funeral Home and later to the foyer of the Sam Rayburn Memorial Library. Just a few feet from the foyer is a replica of Mr. Sam's office in Washington which he occupied for more than twice as long as any other man.

The city of Bonham was invaded by state police, Texas Rangers, and Secret Service men. As early as Thursday afternoon all truck traffic was routed fifty miles around the city. All day Friday and through the night there was a procession of automobiles moving toward Bonham bringing Mr. Sam's friends. At times there were as many as a thousand people lined up in front of the library, waiting not to say "farewell," as Elder H. G. Ball phrased it, but "only to say good night." From 9:00 A.M. Friday until 10:00 A.M. Saturday, admirers from all over the United States moved slowly by to pay their last respects to the Speaker. At periods they came three abreast by the bronze casket and occasionally the state police had to step up and say, "Move along!"

Before Mr. Sam died he made two requests: first, that people not spend their money on flowers but send it to the Rayburn Foundation as a part of the sustaining endowment and for student scholarships; and second, that his best friends stand by him until his body should be removed to Willow Wild with his family. Despite his request the foyer was walled with flowers—one arrangement was sent from Tennessee. His friends did not desert him, for they stood by two's throughout the night, and the last couple trailed the hearse Saturday morning to the First Baptist Church where they awaited the hour of 1:30 P.M.

His friends in Bonham had agreed in advance to surrender their seats in the sanctuary to visiting dignitaries—presidents, cabinet members, ambassadors, senators, congressmen, state officials, out-of-town visitors, and others. "We have paid our tribute through the years, and he would want you to have this last opportunity."

Airplanes and helicopters descended upon the city. Black limousines brought saddened dignitaries—President Kennedy, Vice-President Johnson, former President Eisenhower, and former President Truman. The latter came early, he said, "to walk around the square to shake hands with Sam's friends." People from all walks of life were there. Despite the weather people just stood around the courthouse square. They were well-groomed and quiet. Farmers who had not buttoned up their shirt collars or put on ties for years were dressed like ushers in a city church.

At 10:05 A.M., on this raw, cold day, an aged Negro man, Eddie (Buck) Hunter, with his wife and family passed in front of the house where the author's parents live. "Where are you going, Buck?" he was asked.

"I'se on my way to Mr. Sam's funeral. I want to be sure I gets as close to him as I kin." Buck trudged on up the street two blocks and squeezed into a crowd of several thousand that had already gathered at the west front door, where Mr. Sam would be brought in. The side entrance was reserved for the people in limousines.

A crowd of fifteen thousand stood quietly outside the church with bowed heads, listening over the public address system, as Elder H. G. Ball of the Primitive Baptist Church at Tioga gave the eulogy to twelve hundred within the sanctuary and almost an equal number in the Sunday school rooms. As the organist, Mrs. J. C. Christian, Jr., played "America the Beautiful," a white pigeon, which had sat perched on top of the high gabled roof up to this point in the service, flew away into the afternoon haze.

The services were carried in full by national television. Simultaneously there was a memorial service being held in the Washington Cathedral, in a city which Vice-President Johnson had earlier described as "a lonesome place without Mr. Sam." While the body was being taken to Willow Wild Cemetery, the Chicago Symphony Orchestra played appropriate music.

For the brief committal rites Chaplain Bernard Braskamp of the House of Representatives led the prayer at the opening of the service. The new grave was beside that of Miss Lou in a plot with his father and mother and other members of the family. With the words, "He has finished his course . . ." the ceremony was concluded. At this point there were spontaneous farewells from some in the crowd, "Goodbye, Mr. Sam."

When the second session of the Eighty-seventh Congress opened on January 10, 1962, there was another Speaker on the rostrum, because, as the late Mr. Sam proudly uttered many times, "the wheels of this great body, the greatest institution ever conceived by man, must turn and move forward." Yet John McCormack, the new Speaker, in the Commemoration Ceremony on January 18, voiced the sentiments of the entire Congress, when he said:

> "For me, it will be impossible to rise at the podium where he stood for so many years, to wield the gavel he held in his hand, to address this House without somehow, through the chemistry of memory, deriving a spiritual and an intellectual substance from this extraordinary American."

What manner of man was Sam Rayburn to have accomplished so much for so long? Each member of Congress tried to answer this question. Men from the North, East, South, and West offered many ideas, all seeming to express a sort of gratitude for the privilege of having known him, and a prayer that some of his qualities might become interfused with their own beings to make them better representatives of a people and a country that Mr. Sam served with such religious devotion.

☆ II ☆

Parental Roots and Influences

AMONG the many holdings and displays in the Rayburn Memorial Library the most cherished of them all to the Speaker was not the 3,000-year-old Grecian urn, the numerous gavels and symbols of his trade, the many citations, honorary degrees, or books, but the packet of letters from Martha Waller Rayburn, his mother. He was not a man to talk about such personal things, but the fact that, for years, he quietly carried this correspondence in his brief case, back and forth between Washington and Bonham, would indicate something of his feeling and attachment. Worn from frequent perusal, these simple and warm expressions of maternal wisdom became a source of inspiration and strength to Mr. Sam, as they lay in his brief case among the penciled drafts of unfinished bills and speeches. For years after her death in 1927, he carried around among his papers only the last letter she wrote. When asked if he would permit it to be photostated along with the rest, he replied, with the most pained expression, "I lost it!"

The many references to his parents in the Rayburn collection and in his conversations indicate something of their formative influence upon the Congressman's character and his firm belief that the blood of kin is thick. The Rayburn family very early became a closely knit clan.

In the Speaker's office, on the mantelpiece behind his red leather chair, rested the photographs of his mother and father—Martha Waller and William Marion. She wore a high-collared silk dress with a tiny brooch. The simplicity of her costume and general appearance would suggest that she had been lifted out of a seventeenth-century Puritan setting to pose for this late nineteenth-century Sunday portrait. The thoughtful eyes behind her glasses inevitably remind one of the son's characteristic expression, save when his dry and homespun wit brought a twinkle to his eyes.

The other photograph portrays a gaunt, raw-boned frontiersman, with a bony and bearded face. The heavy mustache, fashionable for the period, concealed a solemn appearance. Dressed in his "Sunday-go-to-meetin'" suit, the coat buttoned at the top, he seemed ill at ease staring at the camera, which he appeared to distrust. Suggested here is the origin of his son's shyness before cameras, a trait which gave news photographers great uneasiness, for after one or two shots, he was known to say, "That's enough, boys," or, "Did you snap it when I was licking my lips?" William Marion bears a somewhat pained expression. He even gives the impression of a man whose inner self and hopes for material prosperity have been scarred by the unpredictable weather—the basis for a farmer's anxiety.

Those interested in genealogy will have to work a long time to find out much about the family of William Marion Rayburn, but the absence of fact about his father's forbears made little difference to Mr. Sam. He did establish a kinship to an eighteenth-century painter named Raeburn. He knew that his grandfather, John Rayburn, came from Virginia to East Tennessee when he was a small boy, as an orphan, with an uncle of another name. John Rayburn died when his son, William Marion, was six months old. Absorbed in the problem of digging a bare existence out of the rocky soil in East Tennessee, this mountain family had little time for recording family histories. Mr. Sam did know his father had two brothers—James and Charles—and two sisters who died when they were very young. James Rayburn never married but Charles moved to Coffee County, Tennessee, and reared a large family. The Congressman was told that he was named after an uncle who was the husband of one of his mother's sisters.

To those correspondents who have tried to establish kinship with his family, Mr. Sam has written graciously that there were two families of Rayburns, of no relation, in Roane County, Tennessee. The other family spelled their name Rayborn. To his knowledge there were three other men named Sam Rayburn—a man with Lord and Taylor, the New York department store, who was at one time a successful lawyer in Arkansas; an evangelist; and the one-time mayor of Philadelphia. To Mr. Sam this was not particularly important information but it amused him personally.

Although the Congressman actually knew very little about his father's people, he was confident that he had nothing in his past that would ever bring him shame. What was important to him was the realization that his grandfather was just a typical American pioneer who followed the frontier line, as defined for historians by Frederic Jackson Turner. His people, of Anglo-Saxon heritage, settled along the Atlantic seaboard. Desperately poor, they moved with the frontier westward over the mountains armed with axes, crude rifles, seed corn and potatoes. With these simple tools Marion's father, in 1802, secured a foothold on the frontier to subdue a sinister wilderness.

The agrarian philosophy of Jefferson, combining the worth of the individual man with the dignity of honest toil, became transformed by Jacksonian attitudes and mores. In the log cabins in the hills of Tennessee was born a coonskin and shirtsleeve democracy, which was the culmination of a political idealism in conflict with an unsophisticated frontier. The spread of this democracy produced a strong people and a way of life which gave the South its strength and the western expansion its impetus.

This is the background of which Mr. Sam was proud. This was the source of his faith in common people and the background for a legislative program designed to improve their lives and enable them to compete with a metropolitan economy. This was the basis for the Southern Democrats' faith in him personally, and his triumph when the Dixiecrat revolt almost destroyed Party harmony. This was the background of a loyalty to Party and common man, inseparable in his mind from the spirit of America.

Mr. Rayburn was more fortunate in putting together the family history on his mother's side of the house, sketchy though it was. Martha Waller Rayburn was a descendant of an old Virginia family. On May 6, 1951, at the dedication of the marker over the graves of his great-great-grandfather, Colonel George

Waller, and his wife, Ann Winston Carr, in Oakwood Cemetery, Martinsville, Virginia, Mr. Sam paid tribute to this heritage. First he made a casual reference to the past, in the Waller history, and then extolled the values of genealogy itself:

"In an early edition of the Poems of Edmund Waller, Poet Laureate of England during the reign of Charles II, published in the year 1705, there is a short life of the poet. The author, whose name is not given, says 'The antiquity of his family, and the services they have rendered their country, deservedly place it among the most honorable in England.'

"Many people do not know who their grandparents were. Heredity, however, is a fact which must not be forgotten. We owe a great deal to our forefathers whether we know who they were or not. If they lived evil lives we must suffer; if they were decent and well-ordered, we start in life with great advantages. It is pleasant then, for one reason, to be able to look back for centuries and feel you have nothing to fear and nothing to blush for, and that honor and respect may be freely given. The pedigree of the Waller family is not merely a list of names of which nobody ever heard; they have been distinguished in the church, the law, and in literature.

"Again, we know the importance of a knowledge of history, the reason for things being as they are, how we obtained our liberties and privileges, the great names to whom we owe gratitude and whose memory we delight to honor. Some of the most interesting things in the world are its antiquities and its ancient buildings, with their associations and connections with the past.

"Genealogy has always been an important subject and has played a part in the history of the world. Among the nations who have not known the true God, reverence for the departed has formed part of nearly all different forms of religion. The Chinese worship their ancestors; and with some savage tribes it is the only sort of religion practiced. In the great book of records of the past—the Bible—genealogy occupies a prominent position. Several lines of descent of immense antiquity and importance are found here. The children of Israel were most careful in preserving the names of their fathers and forefathers. How often we read of some reward or promise being given to an individual, that it should be not only for himself, but for his seed forever; thus greatly increasing the value of the blessing. How they loved to think that their bones would rest and mingle with the ashes of those who had given them life."

According to Speaker Rayburn, the family of Waller goes

back to Alured de Waller of Newark, Nottingham. He lived during the reign of Henry VII and died in 1183. Since Alured was of Norman origin, his grandfather probably came to England in 1066, when William the Conqueror invaded the island. The name of Waller is recorded in the Doomsday Book, a listing which would have been justified by the receipt of a grant of land from William following the Battle of Hastings. The family adopted a coat of arms. The crest was a sprig of the walnut tree fastened in the helmet, from which was derived the "walnut tree proper" of heraldry. The shield was black with a "Bend engrailed argent," a band slanting across it on which was embroidered or painted three golden walnut leaves. In all probability the number "three" would suggest the Holy Trinity. The fact that Alured may have participated in one of the crusades would suggest the reason for the religious emphasis.

In 1405, Thomas de Waller, six generations removed from Alured de Waller, purchased the estate of "Groomsbridge" in Kent from Lord Clinton. For the next two hundred years this was the seat of the eldest branch of the family. At the end of this period the *de* was dropped from the name.

Richard Waller, a grandson of Thomas, distinguished himself on October 25, 1415, at the Battle of Agincourt. He was later knighted for the achievement of capturing Prince Charles, Duke of Orléans, who was one of the French generals. For twenty-four years he held the Duke in "honourable restraint" at Groomsbridge waiting for a ransom to be paid. (Prince Charles, during his sojourn in England, made gifts to the parish church of Speldhurst and to the chapel of Groomsbridge, over the porch of which his coat of arms was carved in stone. Also reminiscent of the Prince's years in England is an oak-paneled apartment in the house, and the ducal arms, the lilies of France, over the fireplace.)

After Richard was knighted, the King granted the addition to his crest of a shield with the arms of France suspended from the walnut tree and the motto "Agincourt—*Hic Fructus Virtutis.*"

In 1650, William Waller came to Virginia, where he married Mary Allen and patented land in 1669.

Three generations later George Waller, born in 1734, married Ann Winston Carr, the daughter of Captain William Carr and his first wife, Elizabeth Winston. He moved from his native Stafford County to Pittsylvania County, which became subdivided, his section later being named Henry County. Shortly after, he acquired a large estate on Smith's River. His brother-in-law,

Mordecai Hord, bought a similar estate adjoining the Waller plantation, which he named "Hordsville," where one branch of the Hairston family has lived for a hundred and forty years. This family and the Wallers helped establish the town of Fieldale.

George Waller was one of the first justices of the new County of Henry in 1777. He was an active member of the Court, sheriff, collector of public funds and exchequer. In addition he held many honorary positions.

On May 11, 1781, as major of the militia, he was commanded by Colonel Abraham Penn to lead sixteen companies from Henry County to join General Adam Stevens at Hillsborough, N.C., to prepare for the battle of Guilford Court House, which was fought four days later. Promoted and commissioned a colonel of the militia, he was ordered southward for further duty.

Colonel Waller was active during the Revolution and was at Yorktown with George Washington to witness the surrender of Lord Cornwallis. Following the war, he returned to the plantation, where he lived the life of a planter in all the atmosphere implied by such. He died on November 18, 1814.

His wife, Ann Winston Carr, survived him by many years. There were eight children (see Appendix). She died in 1839 and was buried beside her husband in the family burial plot on the plantation. In October, 1951, their remains were removed to Oakwood Cemetery, Martinsville, Virginia, where a monument had been paid for by contributions from George Waller's descendants in Virginia, Tennessee, and Texas.

Mr. Rayburn pointed out that Colonel Waller belonged to that group of "grand old patriots whose service and sacrifice are without a parallel in the history of mankind." He said, "They fought well, wrought better, and laid the foundation of the greatest government the world has ever seen, and while they bequeathed to us many blessings, they also laid upon us the obligations to carry on as they carried on."

Almost by accident the Speaker discovered, on a piece of yellowed paper, fragmentary information about George Waller's descendants. George Waller's grandson was John Barksdale Waller (born November 28, 1803), Mr. Sam's grandfather. He married Katherine Pickle Waller (born December 29, 1808), and had thirteen children (see Appendix)—six boys and seven girls—the eleventh being Martha Clementine (born August 26, 1846, died February 21, 1927).

She came to be a sort of symbol of this vital and living heritage which he commemorated at Martinsville in 1956. He saw in her a synthesis of ancestral traits and achievements. These persevering forbears he proudly acclaimed "fought well, labored diligently, helped lay the foundation of the greatest government on earth, and bequeathed to Americans an obligation to carry on with a keen sense of dedicated responsibility."

In his Martinsville commemoration of this vital and living heritage, Mr. Sam unconsciously wrote his own eulogy. Most Americans a decade later eulogized him as he did Colonel Waller: He, too, fought well, labored diligently, helped lay the foundation of the greatest government on earth, and bequeathed to Americans an obligation to carry on with a keen sense of dedicated responsibility. His type of consistency and personal integrity were qualities he liked to attribute to his heritage and virtues he hoped he could bequeath to posterity.

Mr. Sam's interest in public service was, he liked to believe, hereditary. He was of the opinion that he owed more to his mother's people than to his father's. The precedent for concern about public affairs lay with the Wallers. Martha Waller's father had been a justice of the peace for thirty-two years in Roane County, Tennessee, and also a member of the County Court. Hence Martha Waller was a woman who had lived among civic-minded people from whom she developed a social consciousness. After they came to Texas, she tried to impart public-spirited attitudes and a social conscience to the members of her family, but her husband's preference for solitude and the soil seemed to pull the family in the other direction. William Marion's legacy and influence, however, must not be underestimated. A love of horses, cattle, the out-of-doors, good soil, and the integrity of one's own silent thoughts were deeply implanted in the son who learned early how to carry alone a heavy political burden without showing physical or emotional strain.

Some may find two inherited tendencies and two Sam Rayburn's—statesman and squire. But there was in reality only one Sam Rayburn, who stripped life to its simplest denominator and learned how to be at peace with himself, whether on crowded Pennsylvania Avenue or in the most remote corner of his beloved rural hideaway. His nature contained the best qualities from the past.

Mr. Sam at seventy-nine reached the stage in life where he could view things and people in retrospect. He was truly, as

D. B. Hardeman, his research assistant, wisely said, a legend in his own day! In the realm of politics he had developed a sort of cosmic consciousness.

Before he went to Washington he was "Mr. Rayburn"; then under the New Deal he became "Mr. Democrat" and subsequently "Mr. Congress" and "Mr. Speaker." During his last ten years he was generally called just plain "Mr. Sam." He received mail so addressed. Finally, with the emergence of a transcendental view of life and politics, he was even referred to as "Mr. Everything."

Always proud of his consistency, Rayburn was not fully aware of his own evolvement, but, nevertheless, he grew with his country—it never left him behind.

As he reflected on the difference between the man who left Flag Springs and the man he was when he opened the Eighty-seventh Congress, he liked to recognize the changing attitudes in himself and in the country at large. The old "forty-acre farm" concepts, he knew, were gone, whether the people liked it or not. This was the age of bigness, and he believed that Americans as individuals should stretch themselves to reach a philosophy that would help them adjust to a changing world.

However, some of the biases, or beliefs of his father's age never quite forsook him. The geographical distance from Flag Springs to Washington may seem relatively short in an age of jet airplanes, but it always seemed a "fur piece" to Mr. Sam. He continued to marvel about a country that would allow a prairie lawyer to reach the White House or a tenant farmer to hold the Speaker's gavel. This was to him the miracle of the American system. Once he remarked, "I came within a gnat's heel of remaining a tenant farmer."

Of course, many saw him through the same nineteenth-century frame of reference which they had stubbornly retained. While they prided themselves on "being able to read him like a book," they were strangers to his mind, continuing to parrot the platitudes of the Rayburn who was born during the Depression but had long since expanded his sectional-consciousness into a human and international consciousness. Although he became an exponent of the enlarged function of the Federal government, he revealed some views on occasion which clearly defined him as a Southerner. But reasonably consistent in his beliefs, he evolved a political philosophy out of a Jeffersonian agrarianism in opposition to that which stemmed from a Hamiltonian federalism. Perhaps the best portrayal of what happened to Mr.

Sam is contained in a letter from a Negro, employed by him for twenty-two years, and his wife. This was their birthday present to Mr. Sam.

Bonham, Texas
Jan 1st 1960

To the Speacker:

Thru, all these changes, that you have witnesed, which have come with such rapidity as to be almost confusing to the human eye, and mind, you have maintained that calm spirit and vigorous body which have readily adapted themselves to conditions, making use of the best and rejecting that which was worthless.

We congratulate you and extend to you our good wishes. May the world still have in store for you many thrills and much happiness

Charlie and Willie

Call Mr. Sam what one may, the fact remains that at least the early Rayburn was a Southerner. He came by his early sectional views naturally enough. A student of history and biography, he indulged in some of his father's favorite topics. He may have learned much about his country from books, but his father ignited his imagination with the grim accounts of the Southern holocaust after 1861. At his father's knee he learned about his section's history. It was there that he became a Democrat and fell in love with the common people.

The story that William Marion Rayburn told, which impressed Mr. Sam, was that of the South's destruction as a military power and the liquidation of its economy. Painful to him, and frightening to the young folk about the family fireside, were his descriptions of the aftermath of the war. This is the picture he painted, the same one which historians have portrayed.

The lone chimneys, among the burned debris, which dotted the path that General Sherman took as he forged his way through Georgia to the sea, stood like shattered ghosts against a background of burned countryside. The General's efficiency, Marion agreed, was undisputed, for not a building was left on the railway from Macon to Savannah. In the Rayburn family there were only two names more offensive than the devil's—Sherman and Judas. However, by the turn of the century men like Marion had grown more tolerant, for some of them had partly forgiven Judas.

With some echoes of regret, Sherman in the *Weekly Con-*

stitutionalist (Augusta, Georgia), November 27, 1867, reminisced to his veterans about his experiences:

> "Look to the South, and you who went with me through that land can best say if they too have not been fearfully punished. Mourning in every household, desolation written in broad characters across the whole face of their country, cities in ashes and fields laid waste, their commerce gone, their system of labor annihilated and destroyed. Ruin, poverty, and distress everywhere, and now pestilence adding to the very cap sheaf to their stack of misery; her proud men begging for pardon and appealing for permission to raise food for their children; her five million slaves free, and their value lost to their former masters forever." [1]

What happened in Georgia, Rayburn learned, was only a sample. South Carolina, Virginia, Alabama, Mississippi, and Tennessee also felt the destructiveness of the torch and indignities of a haughty conqueror. An atmosphere of gloom hovered about every Southern home. Poverty threatened all classes. Perhaps the poet Paul Hamilton Hayne best defines these years and expresses something of the feeling William Marion imparted in his reminiscences. Hayne's impassioned feeling and embittered soul are clearly defined in his poem "Poverty" (1882), a metaphor of awesome beauty in its portrayal of the grim Reconstruction years:

> *O Poverty! I behold thee as thou art,*
> *A ruthless hag, the image of woeful dearth*
> *Or brute despair, gnawing its own starved heart.*
>
> *Thou ravening wretch! fierce-eyed and monster-lipped,*
> *Why scourge forevermore God's beauteous earth?*

War brought about the destruction of Southern economy; and the absence of controls over unscrupulous groups, that had perfected exploitation and created dissension between classes, slowed the region's recovery to almost a halt. Horace Greeley, also a name well known to Mr. Sam, wrote at the time that the carpetbaggers "steal and plunder many of them with both arms around Negroes, and their hands in their rear pocket, seeing if they cannot pick a paltry dollar out of them." These were the sentiments in Rayburn's campaign speeches for the first twenty years.

William Marion Rayburn was a product of this era. With

time on his hands during the crisp winter evenings, after the land was laid by, the father told of his experiences and the mother reinforced them from the literary record. Though the accounts about the war always had the tragic conclusion of Appomattox, they made good listening to the children. They excited the small boy but angered him as he grew to manhood. There was not much recreation on a farm where hard work was the order of the day. They heard these stories in Tennessee and again in Texas.

The inspiration for these reminiscences is not hard to find. Sam's father enlisted in the Confederate Cavalry at the outbreak of the War between the States. He rode with Nathan Bedford Forrest on some of his daring raids. Accounts of these cavalry skirmishes led by this "Swamp Fox" of the Confederacy stirred the young masculine blood in the Rayburn household. There was not so much cutting and slashing with sabers, said the father, not firing from the saddle; instead there was the dismounting and fighting like infantry. Like Marion Rayburn, Nathan Forrest was untrained in military affairs, but had tremendous courage. Rayburn told how his fearless commanding officer was wounded four times, had twenty-nine horses shot from under him, and killed more Yankees with his own hand than any other Confederate soldier. These daring exploits stirred young Rayburn's sectional pride. Here began Mr. Sam's loyalty to the Democratic Party.

The most lasting imprint was made by the stories of Robert E. Lee, about whom Sam Rayburn collected a small library. The accounts of those "heart-breaking months" of 1864 reveal that he rode with Lee to the bitter end. He was recommended for a captaincy because of his popularity among enlisted men and because of the esteem of his commanding officers. The offer of a commission was declined since, being unable at the time to read and write, he could not have handled the paper work accompanying the responsibility. He also served with a regiment under Colonel Turner Ashley and with the company of Captain Joe Wheeler.

The Rayburn fireside talk also revealed the events leading up to the fateful April 9. The father recalled the loss of Petersburg, the abandonment of Richmond, of their frantic march along the roads from Amelia Court House toward Danville searching for rations but finding only Union opposition. With starvation and annihilation facing the Confederates, Lee, on the morning of April 9, sent for General Grant.

The older Rayburn reported that the hearts of fifty thousand Southern men beat with new hope because of the liberal terms of the surrender. When Grant noticed Lee's dress sword at his side, he wrote into the articles of capitulation a provision that the officers might keep their side arms. However, the most important and most generous provision made by Grant was that the Southerners could retain their horses. With the South on the verge of famine, the men realized that the horses would be invaluable in planting a spring crop to ward off what seemed inevitable starvation. Lee paid special tribute to General Grant's generosity, and this moment of noble behavior, as communicated by Marion Rayburn, swelled Mr. Sam's boyish heart with respect. Mr. Sam's photograph of Grant perhaps implied some of the Speaker's own respect for fair play to an opposition, whether on the battlefield or in the House of Representatives.

The Army disbanded and the war-weary men made their way to their wrecked homes, scattered families, and crushed hopes. The infantry had only the inevitable means of transportation. But the cavalry, thanks to Grant's generosity, turned their backs more quickly on the ceremony where they had interred half a century of ambition and faced a future with little promise of a resurrection.

William Marion Rayburn started back on his dappled-gray mare to the hills of East Tennessee. With the war now over he had only one concern—to get back to the little forty-acre, bottom-land farm on Clinch Creek. His thoughts were of his widowed mother and getting the corn in the ground before the season was gone. Marion told his children years later that his mother once had a dream in which she saw him riding his horse. This was explained to the young folks as God's way of answering his mother's prayers and communicating to her tidings of his safety.

Sam Rayburn, very early in life, learned to put faith in Divine guidance, though he rarely expressed his beliefs to any except immediate members of his family. Sam Rayburn's constituents almost never discovered this piety because he flavored his conversation with a rough masculine vernacular. His utterances were filled with expressions that led them to see only a salty, militant politico instead of the more reverent conformist to spiritual patterns of behavior and thought.

In Knoxville there occurred an incident which the paroled soldier could never forget, but the passing of time brought forth some measure of forgiveness. Marauders took away his horse and left him without transportation or the means of getting his crop in the ground. Tired and footsore, he walked the rest of the way to what had been a comfortable house. His mother was safe, but plagued by anxieties. Nearly all the property had been destroyed by bushwhackers and guerrillas who fought for neither the North nor South, but plundered both. Marion, however, accepted the challenge, as did thousands of other returning Southern veterans, to recreate a way of life which had been reduced to rubble. He naturally had no affection for Yankees, and it took years for his experience of the horse to wear away.

Many years later the Speaker said, "Father did not like Yankees, [but] I want to emphasize that the stories written about Father's 'hatred' of the Yankees are pure nonsense. Father was a Baptist with deep religious feeling and he could not nurse hatred in his heart." The Speaker's evaluation was somewhat colored by his own maturity and serenity, for with the passing of time a man in his position will generally rise above such sectional feeling. The Speaker said that he would not suffer himself to experience the degrading effects of wrath because the very process of hating relegated the hater to a position lower than the object of his animosity. "I have never hated any man, but I have been temporarily provoked with several." The incident of the horse, nevertheless, left an impression upon the whole family, although the realization that the action of the marauders did not reflect the intentions of Northern leadership made the indignity easier to bear. His deep religious faith did cool the emotion of young wrath and helped the older Rayburn to see the incident in its proper perspective. It was a valuable lesson in forgiveness for Mr. Sam.

The Speaker, in the same connection, also silenced another rumor. The story had gone around that the father left Tennessee and went to Texas because the horse had been stolen. Some attached great significance to the incident, seeing it as the basis for the family's ultimate move and the motivating force behind Mr. Sam's career. In quieting all such beliefs, the Speaker remarked, "There is no truth in the connection between Father's move from Tennessee and the actual horse theft, since father lived in Roane County, Tennessee, for twenty years after the horse was stolen."

The incident was only one of many financial adversities, but the father, an orphan who was brought up by a kind uncle, learned early in life to face reality. He imparted this attitude to his children. It was a young, but rather mature William Marion

Rayburn, who married Martha Waller on May 14, 1868. He built his own log cabin near Lenoir, Tennessee, in the Clinch Valley. Children came along fast in those days—ten before not many more years had passed. In the order of their births they were as follows: John Franklin, Charles, Katy (Mrs. W. A. Thomas), Lucinda, Jim and Will (twins), Meddie Bell (Mrs. S. E. Bartley), Samuel Taliaferro, Richard Ashby (Dick), and Tom. The eleventh child, Abner, was born after the family moved to Texas.

Samuel Taliaferro, born January 6, 1882, was the eighth. He was given this middle name out of respect for an old uncle who was living with the family at the time. In later years he chuckled when he thought about this "highfalutin brand." "I had to shed this thing, because so many of my friends couldn't spell it."

Rockwood and Kingston were towns where the father sometimes went for supplies. The log cabin in which Mr. Sam was born saw the family off to a slow start economically. "My parents, especially in the early years," said the Speaker, "were faced with all the real hardships of farm laborers. They were healthy, thrifty, industrious and upright folks, who worked hard on the little farm, but opportunity was limited in the Clinch Creek district of Tennessee, ravaged by the Civil War." The principal crop was corn, from which came the only money they ever saw. They tried to survive by good management and by raising their own food.

Mr. Rayburn said he did not remember too much about the years in Tennessee, but occasionally he had flashes of insight, impressions of his parent's reminiscences, which they repeated many times after moving to Texas.

To George Stimpson he once mused about his mother one rainy afternoon in connection with the Tennessee homeplace, as the large drops of water splattered outside between the marble columns of the Capitol building. He had just picked up her photograph which rested on his mantlepiece, and his thoughts had gone back half a century as he commented on the strength and courage she must have possessed to handle a family of ten children so efficiently under their circumstances.

"Have an apple," said Sam softly, waking from his reverie and pointing to the large hamper near the door; "they make me think of those leather-coat apples on the old Clinch Creek farm in Tennessee." For a moment Stimpson was unable to come out of the past, to realize that Mr. Sam had offered him a real apple. On other occasions Rayburn commented on the smell of those "leather-coat" apples from the trees that grew near the house.

Besides the odor of apples he also remembered the wood smoke from the steamboats carrying produce up and down the Clinch. The tall smokestacks with their ruffle-like funnels excited his boyish imagination, and even years later the very sight of a steamboat brought back a whole chain of associations. The steamboat seemed to cast the same type of spell over him as it did over the youthful Sam Clemens, so intimately portrayed in *Life on the Mississippi,* a book which had thrilled Mr. Sam. In later years when quizzed on this, he remarked, "Yes, I have old Mark's works over there on the shelf. I have read them."

The decision to transport a family of twelve from Tennessee to Texas—a distance of more than a thousand miles—required forethought and courage. Sam was only five and there were two children younger than he. The parting from friends and relatives, the picking up of personal belongings, and the leaving of the countryside itself was like pulling generations of roots from the hills.

Bill Waller, a first cousin, who at one time lived in the same house with Sam Rayburn, and in 1960 resided on Buttermilk Road about a mile from the Rayburn homestead in Tennessee, gave some interesting facts about the family and the day of the departure for Texas. He said that the home in which Rayburn was born was razed in 1958 but that the house in which Martha Waller was born, and in which many members of the family lived, was still standing, though finally vacant after two hundred years of use. Sam, he said, attended briefly the old Acme log cabin school near Wallerton:

"The morning they left, Sam came out on the porch barefoot and got into the wagon with the rest of the family. They went to Lenoir City to get a train. There were ten children in the wagon, and one of them fell out and they didn't find it out until they had gone a long way."

Most of the journey to Texas was made by train, explained Sam's sister, Mrs. S. E. Bartley, because the connections were not too bad. Information about this trip is rather meager. Sam did not recall too much about it himself, except his interest in the train—the first one he ever saw. He faintly remembered seeing the wagon trains from the coach window. "I was fascinated by the people I saw on their trek West, all their earthly belongings heaped on covered wagons, men in plainsmen's outfits with wide-brimmed hats and guns on their shoulders, leading the oxen." With ten children, including two babies, a thousand-mile train trip in 1887 must have been a memorable experience—certainly to the parents. They arrived in Dodd City by the Texas and Pacific railroad.

The Rayburn family stayed briefly in the homes of their Texas kinfolks—the Dickeys and the Wallers—who had come to Fannin County a few years earlier. For years Newt Waller enjoyed telling how Sam and the other children were amused by the railroad trestle and became "goggled-eyed" when a train passed.

With his savings in his pocket, William Marion Rayburn began looking at land. He liked his relatives and was welcome there, but at nightfall he became impatient to stare up at his own roof. He found a forty-acre tract three and one-half miles south of Windom, Texas, where, boasted Mr. Sam years later, the waxy black soil was forty feet deep. The transaction was consummated on November 2, 1887, when Marion Rayburn paid $600 cash, and gave notes for $550, $250, and $262 at 10 per cent interest, to be paid to J. P. Griffin on each November 2 for three successive years. From G. W. Wigly on July 18, 1890, he purchased a small, triangular piece of land for $50 and gave one note of $35 at 10 per cent interest. On December 31, 1897, he sold this piece of land to C. W. Anderson for $160 and took a note for $100 at 10 per cent interest. Martha Waller Rayburn signed this document "M. C. Rayburn" to use a signature which does not appear anywhere else. The "C" stood for Clementine. Historians will refer to this area of Fannin County as the Flag Springs Community.

In Tennessee the Rayburns had known only corn farming. In Texas they tried their luck with cotton, a crop that was relatively new to this section of North Texas. In fact, no one seemed to understand very much about the cultivation of the crop. The first cotton in Texas was actually sown broadcast. This was back in 1866, and the yield finally became so good that gins were built. Even had the Rayburns been experienced, they could not have surmounted the cotton farmer's greatest hazards—rain and the inevitable boll worm. That first year the floods came and the crooked creeks made lakes out of the miles of bottom lands. In the wake of the torrents came the boll worm. Then arrived the omnipresent "Billy Boll Weevil," who sat on the barnyard gate and hurled carefree taunts at the harassed farmer.

The Rayburns made only two and one-half bales this first year. The family could not remember any hardships in Tennessee that equaled these adversities. How Marion Rayburn paid the

$550 note, with the 10 per cent interest, and kept the "wolf from the door" remained, to Mr. Sam, an example of ingenuity and frugality. The parental faith in the Almighty's beneficence saw them through these grim months while they were attempting to sink their roots into Texas soil.

Their faith was well founded, for Providence began to smile on them. They learned more about planting and chopping the cotton, and the seasons became dry at the right time so that the bolls matured without being stung by insects. Sam grew older and watched his parents adjust to a more prosperous and comfortable life.

Another son, Abner, was born. Then there was a further addition when Uncle Jim came to live with them. Fourteen Rayburns were crowded under the one little roof. But they were a congenial group. "The bigger the family the closer they get together, in my opinion," Mr. Sam remarked years later. "And those of us who are living now are just as close brothers and sisters as we were when we were fighting out on the little farm down there in North Texas." "The blood of kin is thick," he liked to say as he reminisced about the bond that formed between him and the other children in the family.

By this time Marion Rayburn had learned to read well enough to sample some of the books his wife had already introduced to the family. He began to break his customary silence with critical comments about the politics of the Civil War period. However, when Sam was asked years later by Bela Kornitzer if his father possibly influenced his public career after all, the answer was:

> "No! Father's political activity started and ended with the War between the States. His interest in politics was casual and inconsistent. He did like to talk, however, about the great political issues of his time, frequently about General Lee, and occasionally about Lincoln and Grant. My admiration for Lee is probably the result of the magnificent stories Father told us about his great military genius. Lee's army may have surrendered in the shattered battlefield of Appomattox, but Father's unquestionable hero of the war remained Robert E. Lee. His framed picture occupied the prominent part of our living room. Aside from Lee, no other American public figure attracted his attention. Consequently, my interest in politics arose from elements outside the family environment." [2]

As already observed, the father's "magnificent stories" about the war no doubt had their influence upon the impressionable children and helped give Sam an unconscious sense of dedication and loyalty to the Democratic Party, later referred to as his "crowd." His Party became synonymous with his country and a particular way of life.

The habits and attitudes of the parents had an indirect influence upon him. He remembered his father in these early years as a not too sociable fellow; that is, as one who would not feel at ease in the "smoke-filled rooms" where political deals were made. He was not the gregarious sort. Instead he possessed a frontier trait of incredulity and silence. A tight lip and vigilance, supported by an alert trigger finger helped him preserve a type of independence and security that characterized the atmosphere along the Red River—in those days the boundary line between civilization and lawlessness. Immediately following the War, before Union troops were withdrawn, the Oklahoma territory was referred to as a "sanctuary for those who resisted tyranny." Perhaps Sam's quietness and alertness had a legitimate source. He was referred to by his colleagues as "the untalkative Speaker," as evidenced by the brevity of his more typical speeches made during debates.

Sam's parents were not given to a show of sentiment and affection for the children; however, the restraint did not blind him to an awareness of parental love. Puritan attitudes against frontier conditions made life a serious and solemn affair. Keeping the many mouths fed and bodies clothed consumed the parent's attention. Merriment and light-heartedness had their place more frequently in the holiday season, and then curtailed by good sense and restraint.

On one occasion Mr. Sam defined his parents as believers:

"First of all in a fairly rigid Constitution, but not an unchangeable one; in order, in self-discipline, in a rather hard but fair justice; in the utmost of personal freedom wherever it is accompanied by personal responsibility—and personal responsibility is the greatest article in the credo. They took no great stock in money for itself, or property for itself, except for the proper maintenance of one's family and connections and a proper station in life, and therefore they did not really fear economic reform, not even sweeping economic reform."

The influence of these ideas were definitely visible in his lack of concern about material things and his preoccupation with legislation that might improve the lot of those who would sound the depths of good family living.

His parents, however, questioned, according to a colleague, any social reform which seemed "to abridge innately personal rights, even the not very pretty right to be a little prejudiced, as opposed to mere money rights. They were strong in the works of mercy, but very weak in the sufferance of those they considered to be fools." Such ideas are implicit in Mr. Sam's responses to the issues and problems of his day.

The mother, he told Kornitzer, was undoubtedly the predominating influence in the family. Sam said:

> "It's true that Mother was the stronger of the team. Father was a quiet and modest man who never talked loudly, never had an argument, and never laid a hand on us children. We used to call Father 'Easy-Boss,' and we were completely relaxed with him. With Mother, it was different. I think she spanked me more often than I deserved. She was very energetic, and highly intelligent. . . . My sister Lou once said, 'Mother had good judgment about everything. There was no subject remote to her, because she read everything printed!' "[3]

Sam gave credit for an early interest in books to his mother. He became a voracious reader of political science, history, and biography in his early years even before he went to Congress. His Extension of Remarks in the *Congressional Record* reflect quite a repertoire of background information, which his iron memory held secure in a body strengthened by good living and high thinking.

☆ III ☆

School Days

ACCORDING to Mr. Rayburn's own account of his early life, his first formal instruction began in 1890 under J. Ilan Moreland at Burnett (twelve miles from Bonham), to whose school he walked a mile and a half, many times through the mud. The teacher described his pupil as a "wiry little fellow who wouldn't stay still in the classroom or on the playground. A sister and a brother came to school with him." He began to study the *Blue Back Speller* and *McGuffey's Reader* while sitting on Moreland's lap. This teacher, who retired after fifty-seven years in the classroom, recalled his student's visits to see him after his return from Washington. Once he remarked, "You never can tell what a little boy is going to be."

Mrs. Sam Payne picked up the story at this point. She lived near the schoolhouse where some one hundred children received instruction from C. C. (Charles) Farley and she recalled something of educational conditions in this early period (1891). "I think Sam went over to Burnett to school the first year," she said. "To the best of my recollection, we didn't have a school at Flag then. We just had one room at first and Mr. Farley taught all of us. A few years later they added a second room and Miss Kate [later Mrs. W. A. Thomas, a sister of Sam's] taught some after that." The rest of his grade-school training was received at Flag Springs, three miles south of Windom.

Mrs. Payne added, "Sam was always smart. In the spelling

bees, he was usually the winner or one of the last to get spelled down. Of course, we didn't study all the things they do in school today, but Sam always knew the answers to any questions on any of our subjects Mr. Farley would ask him."

As to the equipment, she stated, "Of course, there were no chairs or desks in the first school. We all sat on long benches, about ten or twelve of us to the bench and there wasn't much running around the room during classes."

Since there were more than one hundred students in the one room, Farley was compelled to rule with an iron hand to keep order. "He had," Mrs. Payne remembers with amusement, "a stack of good bois d'arc switches in the corner and he knew how to use them. I don't recall whether Sam ever had to have one used on him or not as he was a pretty well-behaved boy and always knew his lessons."

In this connection she continued, "We had the bumping block—blocks on which the women would climb to get on the horse to ride—and when the boys felt that another one needed a bit of punishment, four or five would catch him and bump him against the block. I don't know if Sam ever got bumped, but I expect he did, as just about every boy around got bumped at one time or another."

As to the extracurricular activities and recreation, Mrs. Payne had some illuminating reminiscences. "Sam," she recalled, "liked to play just as did the rest of the boys when he had the time." She reported that though his father had only forty acres he was constantly in need of all the Rayburn boys to help in the field, because in those days farm work moved slowly, everything having to be done manually. Sam did not have much time for pleasure under these conditions. Mrs. Payne marveled at the good job he always did in the field, whether he was plowing, hoeing, picking cotton, or harvesting oats. She also recalled the times when if neighbors were helpless to get out their own crops because of illness, Sam was on hand to do the job without any financial reward. He enjoyed helping those in distress, his kindness and humaneness being quite conspicuous even in those early days. Though he was always very serious and conscientious about helping his father and friends, he was capable of having fun when permitted; but he never shirked his duty, to indulge in boyish fancies or impulses.

Mr. Payne supplements his wife's recollections about the extracurricular life:

"Sam liked to play just like the rest of us boys when he had time. He was out with us nearly every Sunday riding calves and would go rabbit hunting with us in the winter when the snow was on the ground and we could find them in their nests or set the dogs after them. We had a couple of swimming holes where he always went swimming in the summer. One was known as 'Buck Hole' and the other 'Doe Hole' because deer frequented them for water. We played in the water and swung on the grapevine swings over the holes every chance we had."

In recalling these favorite swimming places of forty years ago, Payne said, "I have been down there recently and you can hardly tell where these holes were. They have filled up with dirt through the years."

He also reported that "Sam was a pretty good baseball player. He was an outfielder, but his brothers, Dick and Tom, were pitchers. Dick was a left-hander while Tom was a right-hander." There was also the game called stink ball. "In stink ball, we'd choose up sides with each side having a base. A player would make a dare and if he was caught by the other side he'd be put on the stink base and would have to stay there until rescued."

Records on those who attended the old Burnett school at the beginning of Rayburn's educational career are incomplete, but there have been references in the correspondence to Sam Payne's brothers—Dick Payne of Gainesville, Will Payne of Bonham, Ed Payne of Crowell, and Pleas Payne of Durant, Oklahoma. Payne's sisters, who knew Sam in the classroom, were Mrs. Sid Berryhill of Dodd City, Miss Pale Payne and Mrs. May White—both of Flag Springs. Ed White, son of H. S. White, was another who remembered with some degree of feeling these early educational experiences.

The story of how Mr. Sam was first bitten by the "political bug" has been repeated many times. Sam Rayburn, the boy, aged twelve or thirteen, after finishing his early morning farm chores one Saturday was permitted by his father to go to town. Sam said he washed his feet at the pump and turned his thoughts toward the county seat:

"My first impulse for public affairs came when Joseph Weldon Bailey, my Texas predecessor in Congress, was speaking to a gathering of his constituents at Bonham, Texas. I remember it was a rainy day and I made the several miles from our farm at Flag Springs on a mule over a gummy mud road to hear Bailey's magnificent speech, which he delivered in a covered 'tabernacle' of the Evangelical church. The place was jammed.

It was raining and when I saw all those rich townfolk in store-bought clothes, I decided to stay outside. I found an open flap and listened attentively for two hours. I can still feel the water dripping down my neck. I slipped around to the entrance when he was through, saw him come out, and followed him for five or six blocks until he got a streetcar. Then I left, wondering whether I'd ever be as big a man as Joe Bailey. It must have been under the spell of Bailey's oratory that I decided to become some day a Speaker."

When the stocky farm boy reached home he went in to the fire to dry out his damp clothing. After relating his experiences, he announced calmly and firmly to his brothers and sisters that one day he too would sit in the halls of Congress. Apparently they trusted his sincerity, for no one ever questioned his prophetic statement. This truly was his hour of dedication, for every action and dream from this day forward seemed to bring him a bit closer to the fulfillment of the prophecy. A secondary ambition, he said, developed very shortly—to become the Speaker of his country's legislative body.

The image of Bailey accompanied him about the farm as he did his chores and guided him around the turn row before he set his plow into the fragrant earth. Mr. Sam would have blushed had he known that his brothers hid in the loft and at the corner of the barn to hear him hold forth from the top of the feeding troughs. He hurled short and powerful statements at the farm animals and chickens in an eloquence that pleased the small children, for he talked about doing great things which would relieve hardships. As he grew older, stronger of will and conviction, his mind became more active and his emotions explosive. The thinning of cotton was only a springboard for his thoughts. As the hoe whispered to the earth about superfluities, his imagination visioned a better world for those who were deserving but had been denied opportunities. Here in the North Texas cottonfield was born the concept of rural electrification, farm-to-market roads, and securities legislation in the mind of a boy still clothed in homespun. Here also, was conceived his dream for better social security coverage and medical assistance for the aged. That his childhood concern for humanity never faded is implied in his own statement on the afternoon of September 8, 1961, shortly after his back ailment had forced him to leave Washington:

"I am so happy that our people in America can now grow old with a sense of security, can live in some degree of dignity, and, I hope, have bodily ills administered to. I just can't understand doctors who do not have the heart to want these things for our people. They want to call it socialized medicine, but it isn't."

Though these were busy years, filled with hard work and the companionship of his brothers and sisters, they were, nevertheless, lonely ones. In looking back on this era around the turn of the century, he recalled that it was a dull life on the Texas farm, one of isolation and bitterness and often discomfort for a growing boy or girl. The least break in the monotony of the daily routine brought great relief, and a trip to Bonham provoked ecstasy.

Although these may have seemed solitary and bleak years, they were a catalyst for the period of public service. He knew the daily grind of the chores and the challenge of endless rows of cotton. He learned that mud, sweat, and dust were realities. Yet he perceived that they were only a part of farm life, not the sole reward for honest toil. History will record that this was Mr. Sam's hour of commitment, as his later defense and fight for the farm folk of Texas and the nation will testify. He championed their way of life and justified their luxuries, as the following incident reveals.

One early evening in the mid-Thirties when a group of fellow congressmen and other Capitol cronies were gathered in his apartment at 1900 Q Street, just off Connecticut Avenue, the topic of Government grants to farmers for not planting cotton was mentioned. Nearly everyone spoke in a rather disparaging manner. Rayburn remained silent throughout the conversation until someone objected to the farmers' owning automobiles and burning up gasoline going to town. Then he leaned forward in his chair with elbows on his knees and fingers interlocked. Silence followed! They observed his displeasure. They awaited, with a feeling of uneasiness, the cogent rebuke which their sense of justice knew they were about to receive:

> "When I go home to Bonham to see farmers' cars parked in the courthouse square, while the womenfolk walk around window-shopping with their children or talking with their neighbors, I'm glad to see it even if they haven't got a dime in their pockets. Many a time when I was a child and lived 'way out in the country, I'd sit on the fence and wish to God that somebody would ride by on a horse or drive by in a buggy—just anything to relieve my loneliness. Loneliness consumes

> people. It kills 'em eventually. God help the lonely. That's why I'm glad to see farmers have cars and use 'em."[1]

In this brief moment Rayburn relived the long, lean, and more unpleasant aspects of his childhood. He was positive in his determination to do whatever he could to prevent the recurrence of such an atmosphere to mar the memories of America's rural people.

There was perhaps no farm boy in Texas who had fewer opportunities, or greater ambition and will to succeed. Perhaps there has never been another Texan who has come so far from such a humble start. Sam Rayburn knew he had little chance of ever being anything except a tenant farmer, if a change was not made. At what point he reached his decision, or how long he was in arriving at it, is not known; but a Rayburn decision was not arrived at whimsically, and when once reached, it was irrevocable. Only Andrew Jackson's tenacity equaled his. "Neither hell nor high water," one constituent remarked, "would ever make Sam turn back when he set his head." Congressmen discovered this quality many years ago and either came to admire it or learned how to live with it, recognizing his unselfish motives.

But one day at the age of seventeen, he checked the stroke of his hoe, leaned on the handle, and told his father that he did not want to continue farming. He asked if he might leave the farm and go to school in Commerce, Texas. He explained that he did not want money, that there would be no trouble with the cotton picking, and that he would manage somehow to take care of his own expenses. He asked only for his father's permission to go, and for his blessings. As William Marion Rayburn looked across the forty acres of cotton, there came to him the realization that his model of success was not sufficient to inspire a son like Sam to follow in his footsteps. He knew that a good argument should be based upon a strong premise, so he granted Sam his wish.

The fall of 1900 was a milestone in the Rayburn household. The preparation for Sam's departure did not consume very much time, for he had few material possessions. He rolled his clothes up in a bundle and tied them with a piece of rope. As he pitched his belongings behind the seat in the buggy, he came back to the gate to receive his mother's farewell; the father fumbled tensely with the harness. It was a brief and unsentimental parting, which revealed the depths of this mother-son relationship. There were no doubts, no regrets, no heavy hearts. The future posed uncertainties and problems, but nothing so insurmountable, they believed, that a Rayburn could not overcome it.

The trip from Flag Springs to the Ladonia train station by buggy over country roads took several hours. Sam was to board the train for Wolfe City, which was the junction to Commerce, actually only fourteen miles from Flag Springs. The father bought the train ticket. Then he handed his son $25. He had previously told Sam that he had nothing to give him except character, and the boy knew that this was all the money he had. There had been little talk along the way, and the parting instructions of an old Confederate soldier to his son was perhaps one of the shortest speeches ever recorded. Certainly it was an injunction that was meticulously realized—as most people will agree, whether Democrat or Republican.

The father shook his hand warmly and said, "Sam, be a man!" These words became indelibly stamped into his emotional and rational faculties. Years later, after he had achieved national and international fame, he confessed that this statement from his hard-working, devout Christian father had been his beacon light through half a century of public service. When called upon to make a decision involving ethical values, he said he remembered the image of that man standing there on the station platform with those serious eyes peering into his very soul. Rayburn also acknowledged that the experience gave him a devotion to duty.

In that brief moment of farewell a pattern of behavior and ethics was defined. Choices on political and moral issues became mechanical for Rayburn. He could recognize right from wrong instantly. He mastered the technique of evaluating ideas, things, and people—good and bad. Though he considered people to be essentially good, Rayburn believed in absolutes, not in relative values. He never bothered with ideologies or shades of party philosophies. A man was a good American or he was not; a man was a Democrat or he was not. His empirical and intuitive approach in making such clear-cut distinctions bothered the reformists and idealists, in and out of his Party, for he left no place for splinter groups or what appeared to him to be fuzzy intellectualism. One fact remained supreme. This $25 was the first and only gift of money ever received personally by Sam from Texas' Fourth District, according to his own testimony, which he reiterated many times. Money for congressional races, the little that he received, was sent to campaign chairmen who handled all the finances which did not come out of Sam's pocket. The Chairman of the Democratic Executive Committee in Fannin County states, "Mr. Rayburn never saw any of this money. It was all spent carefully and there was rarely enough." Contributions to the Rayburn Foundation were handled by the Secretary or Treasurer of the Board of Trustees under the provisions allowed for such gifts.

The decision to attend the Mayo Normal School at Commerce was a logical one as the older people in Northeast Texas will agree. The school had a very appropriate slogan: "Ceaseless Industry, Fearless Investigation, and Unfettered Thought." Like Mr. Sam, there were many who never spoke of William Leonidas Mayo except with a sort of reverence. His inspiration and influence upon college-age people in the agrarian section of the State has never been equalled. The schoolmaster frequently reproved Sam for his dogmatism on issues involving ethical and political problems but the boy refused to compromise his convictions on anything. Mayo's efforts, however, did have an effect on Sam's intellectual development and attitudes. He learned early that the other person has his convictions also. In fact, there have been few educators in the whole State, affirmed Rayburn, "who ignited more souls to learning and kept alive more the sparks of ambition than 'Professor Mayo,'" as he was affectionately called. Present-day students of East Texas State College continue to perpetuate the tradition. His invitation was simply, "Come one, come all."

This respect which East Texans bear for Mayo is well founded because other students, who were Sam Rayburn's contemporaries, report that he touched many lives and had a part in training young people for various types of careers. Besides Rayburn, who was a janitor in the high-school building at the time, there were the following classmates who in later years had only praise for Mayo: F. B. Caudle, attorney at Mount Vernon; Miss Ola Price, who later married Ralph Edmonson and moved to West Texas; Miss Lillie B. Pate, who taught at Graham for a number of years; Clyde Pharr, a Ph.D. and head of the Foreign Language Department at Vanderbilt University; E. E. Holmes, real estate man at Los Angeles; the Reverend W. L. Tittle of Wichita Falls, formerly pastor at Dallas, Bonham, and elsewhere, and presiding elder of the Methodist Church at Nacogdoches; A. P. Barrett of Fort Worth; E. P. Mangum, real estate man at Greenville; and N. A. Coston, Attorney at Waco, Texas.

The fact that Sam had only $25 did not bother Professor

Mayo, for nearly everybody was poor who came to his Normal in those early days. His room and board came to $8 a month. Sam received credit for a room in the dormitory, and Mayo gave him a job the first year (1900–1901) as bell-ringer. He and another student formed a partnership to sweep up the North Ward school building about a mile from the campus, for which they received $8 a month. Sam's share as the junior partner was $3. In addition he earned another $3 per month extra for spending money by milking a cow for W. A. O'Neal, one of the early settlers of the Commerce community.

At one time Sam lived just north of the main building in a one-room shack with B. J. (Buck) Alexander. Since there were no cleaning shops the boys pressed their pants between the mattresses. Of course, pillow, bed linen, and cover had to be furnished by the boys. D. E. Denny, later an insurance agent at Wolfe City, in describing Sam's life at East Texas, when he returned in 1902 after a term of teaching at Greenwood, remembered that, "we studied by coal oil lamps for the most part, had our axe and chopped our own wood for the little sheet-iron stoves that one could make red hot with a newspaper, and freeze the next moment." He added that "Sam used to be the first one to enter a room for the next class and poke fun at the girls when they came in. They all liked that."

The curriculum at the Mayo Normal was not as diversified as it is today at East Texas State, but it was sufficient for Sam to secure the kind of education he was after. He called it a "horse block" education. The term "horse block" already referred to as "bumping blocks," came from the custom, then prevalent, of setting up large blocks provided with steps at just the proper height to enable a lady to mount and sit down upon her side saddle without having to expose so much as an ankle in the whole process. Sam Rayburn wanted the type of education which would enable him to mount with propriety upon the wildest horse in the world, figuratively speaking, and bring the animal back to the corral a gentle steed.

He studied hard, continuing his interest in history and biography. From time to time he bought a book—not without some sacrifice—by skipping a meal or doing his own washing. "Many a time," he said, "I pulled down the shades in my room and got out a washboard and tub and cleaned my own clothes." Such frugality made possible the purchase of books like Ralph Waldo Emerson's *Representative Men*, Philip Gilbert Hamerton's *Intellectual Life, Outlines of English History,* and J. Dormon

Steele's *Popular Physics*. About these items and others he commented, "I read all of my books, because I saw no point in buying a book and putting it in my library if I had no intentions of reading it." Years later he said he kept one book at his office and another at his apartment which he would work at until completed, at which time he would put the initial SR on page 99. In such a fashion almost one thousand books in the personal collection of the Rayburn Library became identified.

When questioned one afternoon about Hamerton's *Intellectual Life*, he revealed some very fond and almost painful memories. He had turned down the corner of page 259 at the essay "To a Student in Great Poverty." Almost sixty years had passed since he had read this essay about the way a poor man can overcome difficulties and achieve an intellectual life, but he remembered something of its ideas. The recollection of this experience in the realm of books set him off on the long discourse about his own financial troubles in college and how he overcame them. He said he took the regular three-year course in the equivalent of two years, but he admitted, "I was mighty worn out when I finished."

The incident of the books also brought back other reminiscences of college. "During the morning exercises Professor Mayo was the most inspiring man I ever knew. He made a student feel like a criminal if he did not work, and not only that, but work to his utmost capacity." Here, Mr. Sam had admitted, was his inspiration for hard work and his trademark of "Let's do it now." He refused to put off anything until tomorrow which could be done today. When he ran out of work, he went around looking for something to do.

His punctuality in ringing the school bell that first year was commended by Mayo. It was at this time that he developed an almost fanatical insistance upon promptness. Rayburn's connection with this bell helped formulate a tradition on the campus. He climbed up the belfry every forty-five minutes to ring it and waited five minutes to ring it again, the signal for the new classes to begin. This ancient-looking old bell has become one of the most treasured relics on the broad campus. Though it has long since been replaced by a modern system, it remains as a sort of bridge between the old order and the new. Perhaps it is such a symbol as this which has enabled the younger generation to hold in high regard the achievements of its college when it existed as a Normal and turned out men like Mr. Sam.

Sam worked hard in these days, but he had his fun. Baseball

was his favorite sport. He also liked to escort the ladies. One Sunday Sam and E. C. (Tubby) Hopper borrowed a one-horse surrey, with a square top and a six-inch fringe all around. They drove out in the country to see two girls. After picking up the ladies, they rode along admiring the countryside. Though peach orchards were quite common, the girls saw a tree of choice fruit at one place which was so inviting that they dropped a hint. Sam and Tubby wasted no time in climbing over the rail fence to oblige. The farmer saw them coming and waited until the boys were engrossed in finding the largest peaches. Then he turned his dogs loose on them. They were normal boys, so they ran toward the fence. Tubby, whose legs were longer, was able to reach it in time, but fortune was against Sam. Just as he reached for the top rail one of the dogs reached for Sam. "The dog unroofed the seat of his pants and Sam had to stand cautiously the rest of the afternoon, facing the gals when out of the buggy," mused Denny. Years later, Mr. Sam, smiling, tried to pass the incident off as just a "romance."

"On another occasion," recalled Denny, "a bunch of us boys were down on the railroad west of the school about a mile, and a freight train came along. As the train slowed down on the grade, we all made a run to catch on and ride into town. Sam was a bit short, and he stubbed his toe and fell, bursting across the knee the only good pair of pants he had. That broke up the ride for some of us, and we came in. Sam was worried, for he had a date that night and his pants were torn. One of the boys had a sister and he took her Sam's pants to mend—so the date was kept on schedule."

After one term at Commerce, Sam Rayburn had exhausted his funds, but he had made some progress toward the achievement of his goal. With a teacher's certificate he qualified for an assignment at Greenwood in Hopkins County. The building was three miles east of Commerce on the old Cumby road at the intersection of the present Commerce-Sulpher Springs highway. He carried into the classroom a great store of information and an enthusiasm for his subject which inspired his pupils to study. He knew that he learned more than those he taught, but where methodology was lacking, conviction made up the difference. The patrons were satisfied.

The next year he returned to Commerce with sufficient savings to supplement his income from several part-time jobs such as washing dishes and waiting tables. He was then able to continue without interruption until he completed his B. S. degree.

During these remaining years in college he spread his wings and got the feel of the type of life he planned. There is a photograph in the Rayburn Memorial Library, taken in Commerce on April 24, 1912, of ten members of the Oratorical Association as constituted in 1902. Mr. Sam was a leader in the group. A classmate reported years later that Sam was a good mixer and made friends wherever he went. "Sam gained his reputation as a speaker before he ever got into politics. He went around to picnics and would speak on just any subject. He was a good speaker, too, even then and has improved through the years." As a member of the Philomathean Literary Society, he gained poise and self-confidence. Later when he was attending the University of Texas Law School, he was on a team which was runner-up in a debating contest.

In 1901, a barber by the name of E. K. Freeze, while clipping Sam's hair, made a prophetic suggestion which had its influence. "Sam, I heard you debate last night. I want you to get out of school and into politics. I want to vote for you for Congress."

Sam Rayburn received his B. S. degree in 1903. In his graduating class were Clyde Pharr, Charles Strickland, Charles Swearington, Charley Hamilton, J. Edgar Finley, N. A. Coston, John Puryear, Rebecca Swearington, Lanora Jones, Nova Smith, and others.

In the fall of 1903 Sam again turned to the classroom, for there were the usual debts to pay. He took an assignment at Dial, then after two terms (1903–1905) he went to Lannius, a two-teacher, two-story structure. Both were not too far from Burnett and Flag Springs, where he had begun his own education.

Perhaps the fondest memories were those he had of the people in whose homes he chanced to spend a night or visited. He recalled the evenings with the parents and the joy expressed by the grateful children who felt honored to have the schoolteacher under their roof. Some of the people around Bonham who were in Rayburn's classes were Eugene Bailey, Virgil Caldwell, Joe Caldwell, Bertie Cobb, W. H. Coppedge, Myrtle Coppedge, May Cosgriff, Isom Duke, Bessie Gravely, Edna Newsome, Cornelia Palmer, Neal Palmer, Eugene Renfro, Bert Tabor, Ernest Wallace, Sula Willis, Walter Willis, Mattie Bell Wolfe, and Bud Wolfe. Years later Joe Caldwell sent Mr. Sam into quite a fit of laughter when he reported how Myrtle Coppedge and May Cosgriff put pins in the erasers of their pencils and gave him gentle nudges at the most inopportune moments. Their desks were immediately behind Caldwell's.

Half a century later, at a home-coming on the site of this old Lannius school, Mr. Rayburn took occasion to remind some of his assembled students of the good times they had had. Joe Caldwell of Paris and E. E. Cross remembered particularly the long treks through the woods and other events which country children enjoy. Before the Bois d'arc Creek was straightened and much of the timber cleared away, the lowlands were appealing to small game hunters. Mr. Sam recalled some of these hunts which took place in the late fall of the year after the persimmons were just right for boy and 'possum. "On those 'possum hunts, we didn't catch many 'possums, but we did have lots of good exercises in the outdoors as we tramped through the bottoms all around here." A full moon would inevitably bring boy, man, and yelping hound into the woods. After the hunt they would all congregate around a bonfire, where the old timers would rehash the hunts of long ago or give garbled renditions of stories like "The Big Bear of Arkansas" or "A Coon Hunt in a Fency Country."

It was on these invigorating jaunts that Sam began re-examining his status and boyhood ambitions. His life, however, was temporarily satisfying, for he continued to make his home under his father's roof. At this time he said he became more appreciative of the philosophy of Thomas Jefferson. He admitted in December, 1960, that he had loved teaching but had had no intention of staying with it longer than was necessary to pay his debts. The death of one of his brothers brought sadness into the Rayburn household, but friends reported that the experience seemed to cement the family together into a unit which remained solid. One of William Marion Rayburn's greatest pleasures was derived from having the children all together, and as Sam looked back on this period he remembered that he was contented in the congenial family atmosphere. The children had a feeling of security.

Sam's salary from teaching was modest but he paid his college debts. The parents had taught their children to pay cash, and he had a very good feeling deep inside when he owed no man and felt a little extra change in his pocket. These were rewarding days, despite the fact that he was only marking time and waiting for his big moment—to enter politics.

☆ IV ☆

A Young Representative

IN 1906, at the age of twenty-four, when Sam told the Board of Trustees at Lannius that he planned to make the race for the State Legislature and that he would not be back for the next term of school, no one was surprised. They had heard about the prophecy of the thirteen-year-old boy, had been given a sample of his public speaking, and had seen his eyes sparkle with even a casual reference to politics. Sam's entry into the public arena seemed inevitable, his decision being merely a confirmation of his father's "Hard-Shell" Baptist beliefs in predestination. Shortly before he paid his filing fee, Sam discussed his future with a friend who swears that the following were Rayburn's exact words: "I'm going to get myself elected to the State Legislature. I am going to spend about three terms there and then I want to be elected Speaker. After that I am going to run for Congress and be elected."

A man in Sam Rayburn's economic bracket did not make decisions like this without some financial assistance from friends. Dr. J. C. Carleton, Ben and Charles Halsell, Anse Moore, H. A. Cunningham, Tom Steger, and a man from England, referred to as Mortimer, were among the first to contribute to his campaign fund. Others responded shortly afterward, the list growing to include quite a number of Bonham's leading citizens.

Shortly after Rayburn made his announcement, D. E. Denny saw him at the Leonard Picnic passing out cards and soliciting votes. Sam was wearing a black suit and a black wool hat. He already had the appearance of a politician many affirmed. His campaign attracted considerable attention, especially in the communities where he was known. A. K. Lee, one of Rayburn's students at Dial, reported a conversation he overheard between two neighbors. One of them asked the other, "Are you going to vote for Sam?"

"Certainly. What is he running for?" was the reply.

On the back of a little brown pony he traveled through the county visiting with the voters. He had no platform, but his affable smile and complete sincerity would stop a farmer in his tracks and keep him from his work until Sam had said his piece. In Fannin County a man with Sam's ready store of information, who talked cotton, hogs, and farm problems with such conviction, was a cinch to win. He had enough book learning to bring out the best from his knowledge of practical politics. Rayburn's campaign was simple but efficient. He went from one farmhouse or cotton field to the next. He would ask, "Who lives at the next house up the road?" He wrote it down and, at the same time, a brief comment about the man who supplied him with the information. Hence he moved through the county learning names and calling them. Knowing people became a profession and the longer he called their names, the better he liked them—"ninety-eight and one-half per cent of them good folks," he frequently remarked. His Baptist upbringing, good living, and complete temperance were written all over his countenance as he talked to both individuals and groups. Although he was not a man to sway crowds with eloquent oratory, he was very effective in winning people one by one, with the left hand on the shoulder, the firm handclasp, and honest eyes that inspired confidence. In his first campaign he won not only votes but friends for the future, and the more campaigns he made, the more loyal they became.

Sam Rayburn conducted a part of the race with his opponent, Sam Gardner, as his companion. They went together in a one-horse buggy. "They'd ride into a small town," recalls Mrs. S. E. Bartley, "gather a crowd together, and one, then the other, would stand at the back of the buggy and talk. Sam's opponent got sick during the home stretch of the campaign. It was an ideal opportunity for him to hustle some votes his opponent had no chance to reach. But Sam nursed his opponent for three days, sticking by his side until the other man was able to hold up his end of the speaking."

As the later years reveal, Mr. Sam continued this caliber of sportsmanship and formed some of his closest friendships with those across the aisle, who could be professional and honest with him in their differences. Sam Gardner seemed to Rayburn such a man. They fought a spirited but clean battle and became friends for life. In later years Sam Gardner was appointed permanent postmaster of his home town Honey Grove upon the recommendation of Sam Rayburn. In 1906 Honey Grove may have failed to send a representative to the State Legislature but the people gained something more important—a citizen who held Rayburn's confidence and ear in later years. And those who have worn themselves to a hoarse whisper trying to attract his attention will confirm that having Rayburn's confidence could be quite important. His imperviousness and insensitivity to pressures from sources he did not trust are well known to some who lost his confidence and respect somewhere along the line.

News traveled slowly in 1906, for there was no radio or television coverage of an election. It was held on Saturday, but not until Tuesday were the sealed returns and ballot boxes all collected at the clerk's office in the courthouse. The Rayburns waited quietly, every member of the clan gathered in Martha's sitting room. The courier from Bonham finally arrived with the results, and when he announced that Sam had led the field by 163 votes, pandemonium broke forth. The group was not too carried away in its celebration, however, to pause for an expression of gratitude to the omniscient hand which was believed directly responsible for the good fortune.

Sam Rayburn entered the field of politics in Texas at a time when the tendencies and activities of its citizens were taking on a more definite direction. The Terrell Election Law in 1905 had provided for the selection of party candidates for state, county, and district offices through primary elections. Although the method of choosing officials had changed, the voters remained loyal to two major issues—"Baileyism" and prohibition. With the voters divided thus they could scarcely reflect an unbiased judgment upon the relative merits of candidates for public office. In the absence of a functioning two-party system, political struggles then, as today, too often degenerated into an unwholesome type of guerrilla warfare, with sometimes even brother against brother. Years later Sam looked back upon this phase of his career—three terms, the last one as Speaker—with amazement that he weathered the crises. "I got through it all," he said, "by God, by desperation, and by ignorance."

Sam Rayburn had fallen under the spell of Joseph W. Bailey, who campaigned first as a prohibitionist but later realized that it was a mistake. "This Adonis of a man with massive brain," said Rayburn, "captured my imagination and became my model." On the question of prohibition, which attracted the greatest interest during the Administrations of Governors Tom Campbell and O. B. Colquitt, 1907–1915, Rayburn made his position clear, for personal reasons and very practical ones. He was from conservative Fannin County, which became one of the strongholds of local option.

Colonel E. L. Doheney of Lamar County, which joins Fannin on the east, was the father of the local option concept, which entered the Texas Constitution in 1876. Local option, as originally conceived, allowed each county to determine as a unit whether it would be wet or dry, but in 1891 the law was amended to allow a subdivision of a county to declare for prohibition. Not until statewide prohibition in 1919 was the State Constitution changed. With the repeal of prohibition on a national basis, however, through the nullifying of the Eighteenth Amendment, the Texas electorate ratified an amendment approving the sale of liquor, but provided for local option elections by counties.

By means of these early loopholes Fannin County had known with chagrin the swinging door and brass rails, but the churches finally became sufficiently organized to vote down the "wets," and there is no evidence today to support the belief that the climate of opinion will ever change.

If Sam Rayburn had believed in 1906 that prohibition was not a sound approach to the liquor question, it would have meant political suicide for him to have said so. Yet, there were two distinct camps in Fannin County, and fortunately for Rayburn, he was born on the side of those who triumphed, else he might have returned to the classroom. The Texas Local Option Association had been formed at Dallas in 1903 and the Anti-Saloon League entered the State in 1907. The Texas Brewers' Association and then the Retail Liquor Dealers' Association joined forces on the opposite side. These organizations made the liquor question a political issue and quickened the tempo in Austin legislative circles. As Rayburn's later correspondence will reveal, the man was emotionless in dealing with this issue, for he declared that the people should be given the opportunity to vote on it and that all should abide by the mandate.

Few public servants have been more attentive to the wishes of the people and very few have possessed greater faith in their innate goodness and sound judgment. The combination of a strong will and inner strength, a high regard for people and a positive outlook, made Sam Rayburn good material for the State Legislature.

When Sam Rayburn reached Austin in early January, 1907, for the opening of the Thirtieth Legislature, he received a quick indoctrination into a type of politics which has made many neophyte statesmen in Texas question their choice of careers. But not so with the man from Flag Springs! The political future of his idol, Senator Bailey, was at stake. Sam remembered him for his nineteenth-century eloquence when he first championed the cause of prohibition and the Southern Democrats, and he put little stock in those charges which identified Bailey with the railroads and corporations like Standard Oil. Rayburn was never given to listening to rumors about his friends. The large trusts were looked upon in rural Texas as enemies of the interests of the common people. Bailey had won in the July election and had been declared the nominee at the State convention, but the rumors of his relations with oil companies provoked an inquiry by Attorney-General R. V. Davidson. Upon learning that the Legislature might attempt to select another Senator to replace him, Bailey announced from Washington his intention of returning to Texas for the purpose of driving "into the Gulf of Mexico the peanut politicians" who were trying to smear his name. Indignant over the activities, Bailey declared that even the best replacement would "rattle around in his seat like a mustard seed in a gourd."

In speeches throughout the State, Bailey explained that he had been in a retaining capacity for his clients only when the Senate was in recess. With the strongest opposition to Bailey in the State Capitol, the stage was set for an exciting investigation. After several weeks of invective in smoke-filled rooms, the Committee finally approved Bailey, but not until some of the brilliance of the Senator's halo was gone. And for the next ten years, every candidate for public office was compelled by the voters to declare his stand not only on prohibition, but also on the Bailey issue. So after the investigation, the Thirtieth Legislature resumed its business, split on two major issues.

The new Governor, Thomas Mitchell Campbell of Palestine (Anderson County), was from James S. Hogg's section of the State, where the red land had become celebrated, the natives bragged, for producing peas, peaches, peanuts, pumpkins, persimmons, 'possums, preachers, and politicians.[1] However, Campbell, a lawyer, was not a politician as the concept was understood in the old days, for he relied more on horse sense and business judgment than upon duplicity. At least ten of the planks in his platform anticipated areas of special interest to Rayburn after 1913: the curtailing of lobbying, eliminating free passes by railroads, preventing big trusts from contributing to campaign funds, eliminating insolvent corporations, requiring telephone and telegraph companies to transmit each other's messages, eliminating nepotism, establishing a uniform textbook law, enlarging the scope and benefits of drainage and irrigation laws, supporting eleemosynary institutions, enacting laws relative to public roads, reforming the jury system, providing homes for wives of Confederate veterans, removing the occupation tax from useful occupations, providing for a just rendition of property, establishing a state department of agriculture, and providing for a minimum six-month school term. There were four called sessions in which the Governor tried to enact his program.

Rayburn moved about quietly and skillfully. As the House Journals reveal, he made few public utterances, for while he was "learning the ropes" he preferred to be guided by the old adage that "it is better to be silent and pretend dumb than to speak and remove all doubt." Reticence came to be a trademark with Mr. Sam, but he kept his mind on his business or was preoccupied with someone's problem.

The Rayburn collection in the Memorial Library has countless pieces of correspondence which reveal his acts of thoughtfulness, kindness, and understanding. The porters, clerical help, and pages were also quite responsive with their oral evaluations. Upon the dedication of the Memorial Library on October 9, 1957, Bryan Blaylock, brother of Colonel Myron G. Blaylock, wrote his congratulations and appreciation to Mr. Sam for his fatherly assistance back in those early days:

> I well remember the first time I ever laid eyes on you. You were a young member of the Texas Legislature, 'the Gentleman from Fannin,' and I was a green, 11-year-old country boy who had just completed my first train ride from Marshall to Austin to become a page boy.
>
> The Legislature had been in session only a week when I became desperately homesick, as most boys do

> on their first trip away from home. I let out a loud cry on the floor of the House and you came to me, led me to an anteroom and quieted me with kind words as a father would his own son.
>
> From that day in Austin many, many years ago until today, I have followed your career and admired you for your simplicity, honesty, and devotion to public service.

Recognizing that he needed greater knowledge, at the end of the session Rayburn registered at the University of Texas Law School, where he continued to take courses until he passed the bar examination in 1908. This additional expense on the $5 per day in the regular session, and $2 per day when the session went overtime, called for rather frugal living, but Sam had already learned the value of a dollar.

The voters of Fannin County returned their young representative to Austin for the regular session of the Thirty-first Legislature, 1909. Campbell was re-elected Governor in the primary on an anti-saloon platform; so the "drys" took this victory as their cue to work for a State constitutional amendment favorable to prohibition in the general election.

Rayburn's usefulness was now beginning to be recognized. Speaker A. M. Kennedy appointed him to the Committee on Constitutional Amendments, a type of assignment on which he showed real astuteness. Rayburn was also appointed as Chairman of the Committee on Banks and Banking, was placed on the Committee on Education, and the Committee on Private Corporations.

The Thirty-first Legislature seemed preoccupied with investigations. On February 25, 1909, Representative Gaines offered a resolution which proposed censoring the behavior of A. M. Kennedy. He was accused of paying money out of the treasury for equipping the Speaker's office with furniture and for excusing absences and paying certain employees in a way unprescribed by the rules of the House.

Rayburn recognized immediately that the Speaker was being punished for a prior, undefined political affront to the Administration; and to circumvent the hostile forces, he offered a substitute resolution. Kennedy, early in his Administration, had promised a thorough investigation of the manner and methods adopted by the textbook board in the selection of textbooks for the public schools. He had also expressed the desire to look into a certain waste of funds in the penitentiary system. Rayburn's resolution stated that, from the evidence at hand, the Speaker had no connection with the selection and purchase of the furniture; instead it was purchased by others duly authorized and approved by the Superintendent of Public Buildings and Grounds. The purchase, he affirmed, was made for all future Speakers and was quite in line with similar expenditures for the Senate. As for the payment and excusing of certain employees, Rayburn found that only in one instance did the length of absence exceed that time allowed by regulation, and that Speaker Kennedy was not guilty of an intentional wrongdoing, but had erred in continuing a policy which should never have been tolerated in the first place. He then proposed that the particular account of the salary be audited and adjusted so that the State would not lose the amount of money involved.

Rayburn's resolution was designed to bring about harmony, but a vindictive substitute amendment was promptly offered and was passed. The second one required that the Speaker apologize to the House and assume responsibility for reimbursing the State for $120, the amount in question. Kennedy had no other choice but to offer his resignation before the session ended.

Because of the peculiar circumstances, the customary presentation of gifts to a retiring Speaker was held over until the opening of the first called session. Representative Crocket of Mitchell County presented Kennedy with a gold watch from the House membership; Representative T. W. Blake gave a punchbowl on behalf of the clerks and stenographers; and Representative Morgan Wright, a suitcase on behalf of the pages. Then the ceremony was climaxed by Rayburn, who was asked by the Negro porters to present a chafing dish. After paying tribute to the "little woman" (Mrs. Kennedy) who would preside over a punchbowl containing a liquid, he would hope, "as pure as she," Rayburn turned to honor the laboring people in the capitol:

". . . I wish to say that they are the ones not so fortunate as we are, sent to the world to be hewers of wood, and haulers of water, but man's soul is not to be charged to the color of his skin. Though his skin be brown or black it is possible that it holds a soul as pure and spotless as any man's."

Those who knew Mr. Sam best fully understood why he was the spokesman for these porters. He came from a humble background and he had never become too busy to seek out these employees for an expression of gratitude or the offering of a word of encouragement. Anyone desiring to learn more about this side of Rayburn's life has only to talk with a member of the Capitol janitorial service in Washington, or to pull off into some side road in the Fourth District where there may be Negro field hands picking their own three or four bales of cotton. It is hardly an exaggeration to say that many of them, for years, did not know the difference between "Mr. Sam" and "Uncle Sam." Perhaps also there is no other congressman who has received more letters, written in lead pencil on narrow tablet paper. This was the kind of correspondence which indicated that Mr. Sam had a rapport with grass roots America. Earlier in his Congressional career he issued instructions to his secretarial and administrative staff to give priority to letters of this type. Most of them he answered himself because he believed that any person who wrote a letter in longhand had something on his mind. He likewise showed special favor in the matter of interviews to the people from this way of life. A Wall Street banker or industrialist was known to get an appointment delayed so that Mr. Sam could shake hands with people from America's small farms and tiny enterprises. These were his favorite constituents, and they all knew it. He made them feel important and restored their faith in themselves. Relaxed and friendly, he treated them all like next-door neighbors, and the more powerful he became the more solicitous he was of their friendly visits.

As one reads that portion of his tribute to the Negro workmen—"sent to the world to be hewers of wood and haulers of water"—he will recognize a concept which has been characterized as Southern. Mr. Sam always had compassion and sympathy for Negroes, though his active support of Civil Rights was slow in developing. Mr. Sam's position will have to be examined against the South's peculiar social system and what he thought were the ulterior motives of some congressmen. For years he feared Federal aid legislation because of the danger of amendments that would withhold funds where certain Civil Rights restrictions existed. Specifically, in 1948 he wrote to the author of these pages that he could not agree with his sentiments about Federal aid to education:

> I am very fearful that we would run into all kinds of segregation problems if we ever enact Federal Aid to Education. Our curriculum, I am sure, would be affected as I do not know of anything the Federal Government has gone into that it does not control. No one in the world could be more for education than I, but I do see these danger signals along the way. I am fearful that someone would offer an amendment pro-

> viding that no part of these funds should be used in any state where the races are segregated for school purposes. If it was offered, there are enough Republicans and Democrats in the North to adopt such an amendment, then we would be paying for something we would not get.

Nevertheless, he became steadily more liberal on this issue, evolving more rapidly than his section. The development of Mr. Sam in the broad area of Civil Rights is the most fascinating aspect of the Rayburn story.

The name of Sam Rayburn appeared more and more frequently in the House Journals of the Thirty-first Legislature and in the Austin papers. He was given still another assignment—the Committee on Common Carriers. John Nance Garner, in 1913, called attention to this fact in support of Sam's committee assignment when he was just breaking into the Washington scene. Particularly important as a proving ground was his appointment to the Free Conference Committee. This was a small group from both Houses which met to work out differences and conflicts over bills. In this area Mr. Sam has no rival. On several occasions, during the first and second called sessions, he even acted as Speaker when the presiding officer would step down to participate in debate upon legislation. The fact that Rayburn was mentioned by the newspapers as a possible replacement for Kennedy is indicative of his growing prestige; however, the selection went to John Marshall of Grayson County, which joins Fannin on the west. Rayburn made a speech seconding the nomination of Marshall.

The regular session of the Thirty-first Legislature and the first special session, called immediately by Governor Campbell to get some action on the appropriation bill, kept Sam Rayburn away from his parents' home for a longer period than he had ever known. Although he had little time to become bored or get homesick, his thoughts frequently went back to Flag Springs. Martha Rayburn (she signed her letters Matt Rayburn) furnished her son with many of the details about life on the farm and the members of the clan. Any reference by the papers to Sam's activities brought some comment from the mother. On February 4, 1909, she stated ". . . we notice your name and work in the papers and we are proud of the record you are making. Hope you will march onward and upward." On March 15 she replied to receiving the House publications: "And also glad to get the Records and that you are always present and on the side that we think is right. If you are as proud of yourself as we are of you you will always do right and we have the utmost confidence in you to believe you will." She added, "It was a feast to your Pa when you wrote that you remembered his last words ['Sam, be a man!']. We hope you will ever remember them and abide by them and we believe you will."

The news that the corn was planted and that the cotton land was ready always made him glad. He was pleased to learn that the "oats look well." Then he felt anxiety when she added, "The green bugs are on them some and of course that wearys [sic] your Pa." The following sentiments brought real concern, for he knew their full significance: "We often wish for you to be with us lonesome Sat. nights and Sundays to talk to us but we would rather wait a little longer than for you to accept free passes. We want you to come out free of the charge." Governor Campbell had assailed this practice during his campaign, and Rayburn agreed that too many people were getting "free rides," in more ways than one.

Paying his own expenses became almost a phobia with Sam. Some of the worst tongue-lashings ever given his aides have arisen over their careless acceptance for him of a night's lodging at a hotel, or of gifts only intended as a courtesy by a gracious host. Once he drove back to San Antonio to pay such an account. He refused to let anyone pay a bill when he was on official business. Almost fanatical on the subject, he always said, "I am not for sale." An honorarium for even a non-political speech, for example, a check of $200 for an address on Robert E. Lee to friends working with the restoration of the family mansion, was either returned or given to an appropriate charity or organization.

The mother's letter of March 17 contained this word of encouragement:

> Well it seems that you folks are having a time investigating. I feel so sorry for Kenedy [sic]. I am proud of the stand you took for him. We saw in the paper where some of them wanted you to take his place. Of course we all feel proud and think it quite an honor for you to be mentioned where there was so many that was so much older than you was [sic]. We see lots of things in the papers that makes [sic] us proud of you. Wish I could say that much for all of them.

In this early period Sam wrote few letters and his mother would frequently scold him gently for his failure to let them hear from him. A letter from Sam was always a big event, and with the many brothers and sisters and in-laws parading in and out of the home place, there was quite an exchange of his rare epistles—short though they were. But Sam Rayburn never wrote long letters; in fact, there are no more than two dozen pieces of official correspondence in his entire public career that exceed two pages. His sister Lou and brother Tom seemed almost provoked by his neglect, reported the mother, for they "both have been looking for a letter for sometime." Uncle Ab said, "he hardly ever heard from you," and she reported, "We told him we didn't think you wrote to anybody much." They had been reading about his activities and were really getting anxious for some word: "You have been taking trips and have such a hot time in the house looks like you would have lots to write if you have time. . . ." The representative from Fannin County was not taking pleasure trips, for he rarely went anywhere just to amuse himself. In later years after failing to correspond, he would frequently telephone instead of writing when he became lonesome and hungry for news.

The infrequency of Sam's letters home by no means reflected any cooling of affection for his family. Frequently his thoughts went back to that little homestead at Flag Springs. Once when his mother went for a whole month herself without writing, he felt a hunger for home when he read the salutation of her letter, postmarked April 25, "Dear Sam my precious boy:". The reference to their feeling of isolation on "this cloudy lonesome Sunday" sent a sharp pain through him. He was cheered by his father's request that he be told about the two good rains, the fine stand of cotton, the fair corn crop, and the little patch of oats. Interesting to Sam was the word that Tom's baseball team had won six of eight games since they went on the road. Tom pitched in the Texas-Oklahoma League. "Our little pasture," she wrote, "is good and you never saw such milk and butter. I sold 9 lbs. last week and I made 8 of it, made 1 lb. the week before."

When his mother began to write about butter, he immediately became fidgety to get home. This kind of talk made him think of her enormous biscuits and pones of yellow cornbread. Then came the fondest recollection about food—that of cotton bloom honey, about which he discoursed so much in later years. He had never been dissuaded from the belief that the best honey he had ever tasted came from his own locale. When his mother packed his "going away box" she never failed to include several jars of this "golden medicine."

From time to time legislative committees were asked to collect information or to act in liaison capacities. Even then Rayburn carried a law book along, for he was trying to quench an insatiable thirst for greater knowledge. He had always been a demon for work either intellectual or physical, and he drove himself so hard, even to the end, that his office staff and associates in Congress frequently expressed their concern.

Sam Rayburn, though, was not like most people or his fellow congressmen. His ability to relax, his sincerity and truthfulness, his sturdy body structure produced a harmony of both the emotional and physical in the microcosm; hence he did not respond to the storm and stress on Capitol Hill as might have been expected. Representative Clark W. Thompson, in a letter to the author (January 4, 1961), commented as follows about the Speaker:

> The Texas delegation had gathered in one of its regular weekly luncheons. Seated across from me was a comparatively young member. He said that he was very tired and that he sure had been working hard. About that time, the Speaker came in and sat down beside him. The young member turned to the Speaker and said: 'I was just telling the boys that I sure am tired. This is a pretty tough strain on all of us and I expect, Mr. Speaker, that you are pretty tired, too.' The Speaker replied, 'No, I am not tired.' He paused for a moment and then went on: 'If you *say* you're tired, you will *be* tired.'
>
> I have never forgotten it, and from that day to this, I swear I have never said that I was tired.

By 1909 the mark of dedication was clearly stamped upon his serious countenance. He went to Austin with his values straight and his mission cut out. The night life along Congress Avenue and the parties in the hotel rooms did not appeal to him, for they were expensive and debilitating. Instead, he preferred the quiet solitude of his own room to reflect on the activities of the day and prepare his homework for the next. And being a man who loved his nine hours' rest, he was apt to be sound asleep when some of his cronies were just having their first beer at the Bismarck saloon. R. B. Ridgeway, Sam's roommate while in Austin, insisted that Rayburn was not antisocial or unfriendly.

"He had no bad habits," said Ridgeway. He told this amusing story about how Sam once tried to stretch a nickel in being sociable:

"One night Sam came in and retired about 10:00 P.M., his accustomed time. He began to chuckle to himself and I inquired what the joke was.

"'I was down the street a while ago and started in the drugstore to buy me a drink,' he said. 'About that time along came Pharr [then a representative from Hopkins County] and I invited him in to drink with me. As we started through the door, I felt in my pocket and by grabs! I only had a nickel. So when we got to the counter I told Pharr I wasn't feeling so very well and I'd not take anything. He went on and got his drink and I paid for it. He didn't know I was broke, and I don't know what I'd have done if he'd ordered a dime drink.'"

Truly, these were formative years. He developed habits and attitudes that remained with him to the very end. He lived the kind of life which demanded no sleeping pills or alarm clock. The night before was never written on his face the next morning. "Everyone has to be his own doctor. If I eat something that does not agree with me, I don't eat it anymore." He and Benjamin Franklin would have enjoyed exchanging wise sayings and practical remedies. Rayburn was not a man with false pride, for he had been seen boarding the Texas and Pacific or Katy with a suitcase in one hand and a box lunch in the other. He was quiet and unpretentious, never calling attention to himself in public. His youthful smile, sincerity, personal magnitism, truthfulness, and logical mind, however, were qualities which would not allow their owner to remain for long out of the public eye and the stream of things.

☆ V ☆

Speaker of the Texas House

WITH the passing of the bar examination in 1908, the hanging out of his shingle to practice law in Bonham, and the completion of two successful terms in the Texas Legislature, Sam Rayburn ended his years of apprenticeship. Until now he had been earthbound. There came the urge to try his wings and gain greater heights. He craved greater responsibilities, the opportunity to serve and deal with some of the Texas problems.

He had given a good account of himself in the Thirtieth and Thirty-first sessions (1907–1910), and had made many friends. His roommate, Ridgeway, pointed out some of the reasons why people were drawn to him: "Sam was very modest. I never knew a man so loyal to his friends. Around legislative halls here he had a reputation for honesty and fair dealing. You could always swear by anything Sam told you."

When he returned to Bonham in the early summer of 1910 to think about his personal affairs, he found only distractions. His presence on the southwest corner of the square that summer day was no sooner known than four or five of his cronies hailed him.

In Fannin County there are two topics which will stir the people—politics and religion. In the summer before the primary (referred to by the charter members of the community as the "white" primary), only politics would bring the proprietors out of their stores onto the streets. In late August, following the tent meetings of the Methodists and Baptists, they might neglect their customers for a spell to reveal their ideas on the modes of baptism. However, they discussed this topic not so much for its importance to them personally, as for the opportunity it gave for friendly jesting and heckling.

This day, when Sam came home, was the beginning of the political season. The best authority, in their opinion, had arrived. If Sam Rayburn had a client waiting to seek his legal counsel, he was kept waiting, but Rayburn never built up a law practice. Sam was ready for one of those old-fashioned sidewalk confabs, surrounded by some of the town's most devoted pipe-smokers and consecrated tobacco-chewers.

The two most important issues of the decade—prohibition and Baileyism—had already muddied the political waters and confused even the best churchgoers as they tried to sort out the problems. Four candidates of about equal strength and reputation had announced for Governor. O. B. Colquitt, who in 1906 trailed the runner-up, Judge M. M. Brooks of Dallas, by only 1500 votes, was again seeking the top post in the State from his position as Railroad Commissioner. The other candidates were the capable Judge William Poindexter of Cleburne; Cone Johnson of Tyler, noted for his oratory and political shrewdness; and the popular Robert Vance Davidson of Galveston, Attorney-General. The latter had won the approval of small business with his successful prosecution of the cases against the Pierce Oil Company and other trusts, to add sufficient funds to the State treasury for a reduction in the tax rate.

No four candidates could have been found any better qualified to divide the populace into warring groups. Poindexter, a close friend to Bailey, counted on the Senator's support, but Colquitt's political chicanery appeared to be more effective in winning over the Bailey friends. Somehow Bailey managed to remain aloof and approve both without losing any friends from either camp. Johnson and Davidson were anti-Bailey; hence on this major issue the State actively split four ways.

Although the Rayburn family liked the Senator, Sam was already committed to prohibition and it was on this issue that he made his mark in the Thirty-second Legislature. By this time Bailey had reversed his earlier stand for prohibition and was now an "anti." The complicated issue of prohibition was that which catapulted the representative from Fannin County into the spotlight. He won his reputation not because he had nailed his colors to the mast on one side, but because he evolved as a trusted compromiser with the special knack for being able to work with opposing factions. To be sure, he had taken a stand and was numbered among those who had led prohibition rallies, along with two of the candidates—Poindexter and Johnson. In fact, he marched side by side with Dr. S. P. Brooks, President of Baylor University. Even so, Rayburn's position in this conflict bears analysis, because he took the type of stand that was moderate and not designed to open a fresh keg of beer nor marked to call out the Carrie Nation ax to destroy it. He was a "local option dry" always willing to accept the verdict of the majority. Poindexter wanted statewide prohibition by statute or by an amendment to the State Constitution, which would be instigated by submission of the issue to the people. Johnson was an ardent "dry" but had opposed prohibition in 1887; hence he was opposed to prohibition by constitutional amendment. Davidson favored submission as a good democratic procedure, but he was an anti-prohibitionist; hence his position became too complicated to win much confidence. Colquitt was widely known as an "anti," but he favored local self-government and local option as the best solution to the prohibition question.

In 1910 Colquitt's strategy was the soundest because, as an "anti," he gained support in counties that consistently opposed submission and, as a "local option" man, he added slightly to his strength in the conservative areas, which were split and confused by the position of their "dry" candidates—Johnson and Poindexter.

More than ten thousand people assembled at one meeting in North Texas to hear the virtues of prohibition. Although Sam Rayburn's section of the State gave a decisive vote for prohibition, the State as a whole defeated it. O. B. Colquitt, the "wet," was elected Governor. The anti-prohibitionists had elected a Governor who favored local option, a view which was identical with Rayburn's. Even in these early days Rayburn had a remarkable capacity for seeing the issues and making personal decisions that did not place him at odds with the stream of things.

So preoccupied were the people of Fannin County with the gubernatorial race and the prohibition question, that they forgot about their long established policy of not allowing their member of the House of Representatives to hold more than two terms.

The shattering of the precedent was predicted by such Bonham attorneys and political sages as Tom Steger and H. A. Cunningham as early as 1909. They were saying that the Fannin County man was galloping around the Austin arena like a thoroughbred. He also galloped around the political arena in Washington with the same vigor, shattering records all along the way.

By early December, 1910, the Governor-elect, O. B. Colquitt, was formulating his philosophy and settling privately on his choice for Speaker of the House, a post which the Chief Executive should control if he does not wish to see his legislative program go on the rocks. However, he has to be wise enough not to become too embroiled in a preliminary encounter, such as the selection of a Speaker, lest a wrong choice derail his program before the session opens. Four candidates had announced their ambitions: Sam T. Rayburn, Fannin County; Luther Nichols of Hill; C. E. Gilmore of Van Zandt; and Jeff Cox of Rockwall.

Colquitt had been elected by the anti-prohibitionists, and he was aware of the fact that, after the selection of a Speaker and the passage of the per diem and mileage bill, the Legislature would turn its attention to submission of the constitutional amendment providing for state-wide prohibition. Two-thirds of the members were already pledged for submission and the only controversy anticipated was over the date of the election, the "antis" favoring the earliest possible time of four months from the passage of the resolution, and the "pros" arguing for the next July. Although the issue was destined to be settled ultimately by the voters, Colquitt believed he could keep a stronger hold on the reins if a Speaker of his choice were elected.

He knew that representatives who had run the gauntlet of the summer primary would still be showing some of the bruises from the issues of Baileyism and prohibition. Regardless of the bill, he knew also that the disputants would be divided by these older issues rather than by the differences over new legislation. Representative W. O. Stamps from Upshur County, sensing this anxiety, released the following statement:

> "The same people who elected me representative, elected Colquitt Governor. While we disagree on the prohibition question we ought to try to get along well together. I am in favor of putting no obstacles in the way of the Administration. We ought to help the Governor along."

Rayburn could not have phrased the State picture or his own attitude any better.

The Governor made his first formal statement on January 7, regarding the Speakership race:

"Cox is my personal as well as my political friend, but it is up to the House to select its Speaker without suggestion from me, and all I am hoping for is that it will select a presiding officer as soon as possible in harmony with my views in order that the business in front of us may be disposed of in a manner that will bring about the most good to the people of Texas."

Since both Gilmore and Rayburn were prohibitionists, Colquitt indirectly endorsed Cox, a personal friend and fellow anti-prohibitionist. The real reason, however, for his endorsement of Cox was a fear of Senator Bailey's power. He wanted to make certain that he did not help Bailey build up his machine by selecting anyone friendly toward the Senator; in fact, Colquitt had ambitions of his own. Reid Williams of Dallas, one of Cox's most loyal supporters, assured Colquitt of his friend's thinking: "Bailey and Cox love each other just about as much as two strange bull-dogs." This apparently strained relationship between Bailey and Cox, however, did not deter many of the junior Senator's friends in the House from trying to throw a rope around the candidate and drag him into their sphere of influence. Speculation was that Colquitt might cool off on Cox, as would some anti-prohibition supporters who basically bore no love for Bailey.

Gilmore certainly had no affection for Bailey, but many of his supporters did. For some time Rayburn had been watched by the Senator with appreciative eyes, but without appearing to offer direct support. Gilmore had been given the unqualified backing of the Anti-saloon League, headed by J. H. Gambrell of Dallas.

The Speakership races in Texas usually begin during the late summer and gradually develop momentum by January 1. The month of December is the period of back slapping and "glad handing," but the real "horse trading" does not start until the air in the hotel lobbies becomes so stale from cigar smoke that the bleary eyed lawmakers have to retreat to the champions' headquarters on the mezzanine.

On the basis of the somewhat tenuous early returns and claims made by the three headquarters, C. E. Gilmore seemed to hold a slight edge. However, it appeared that Rayburn might have a slight advantage when the race reached the concluding phases, since he was a prohibitionist and had as his manager, A. M. Kennedy, whose superior organizing ability and skill in manipulating legislative caucuses was unquestioned. Kennedy, in a special telegram on December 5 to *The Express* (Marlin, Texas), had disassociated himself from the Speakership race to put his full support behind Rayburn. He concluded his statement with these words: "Rayburn was, and is my friend, and I shall not stand in the way of his laudable ambition. If he is elected, he will make one of the best if not the best Speaker who has ever held that honorable position." Kennedy held the unique position also of being a "pro" with a strong "anti" backing, the latter coming from the most dedicated of the Bailey organization, men who recalled the treatment Kennedy was given during the previous session.

Sixty-seven votes were needed to elect a Speaker and on the night of January 5, Representative Caves, Chairman of the Gilmore Campaign Committee, released a report with a claim of sixty-two:

> "Statements of strength in a political contest, to be of value to those directly interested, and such of the public that feel an interest in these matters, should be fair and candid. Believing that our friends and all concerned are entitled to such statements in reference to the Speakership contest, we are very much gratified to say that we have at this time sixty-two votes expressedly pledged to Mr. Gilmore for Speaker. This number, with even a portion of the unpledged members known to be inclined to Gilmore, make his election an absolute certainty. We know the situation and with the number of members known to be unpledged, it follows that Mr. Gilmore's pledged vote is more than that of any other candidate. This is a frank, candid statement of conditions as they actually exist."

An earlier statement by Rayburn was quite consistent with his usual calm and adroit handling of publicity: "I do not care to discuss my candidacy, but I will say that the outlook is satisfying and I think my prospects are bright." By nature he was a man of few words. He believed that he could not be blamed for something he had not said, an idea which, years later, he enjoyed hearing expressed by President Coolidge.

Although every member of the 136 in the lower House had been ardently courted by the three candidates remaining in the race, some were actually still unpledged. Committees were designated to meet every train into Austin to keep an eagle eye out for these much sought-after lawmakers.

On the morning of January 5, before the occupants of the sleeper even realized that their car had been pushed off on a side track, several top talent scouts for each organization waited around the station for the first sign of life in the pullman. After a quick coffee and breakfast, the uncommitted legislators were hurried to the lobby of the Avenue Hotel, where the three candidates had set up headquarters. After a round of hearty handshaking someone would then "buttonhole" each and draw him aside for the kind of *tête-à-tête* that only politicians can fully appreciate. Searching for any show of enthusiasm for a given candidate, campaign managers sometimes made mistakes in their interpretations of responses. The frequent release of totals and estimates in those days was quite often without meaning, with some names possibly appearing on more than one list. The early returns, however, did show that Gilmore and Rayburn were both strong and close.

The usual strategy under circumstances such as this was to begin a whispering campaign to confuse those whose minds might still be unsettled. The Rayburn people promptly denied the first accusations—that they planned to defer the prohibition elections until the primaries of 1912. They declared that no such thing had been discussed and that each legislator should follow his own judgment. The Bailey issue lay rather far out on the periphery, but as tension mounted the junior Senator's name passed some lips in connection with the young man from Fannin County.

The Cox leaders tried to be philosophical over the realization that their candidate would not show up well on the first ballot; deriving some comfort from the fact that their man was the second choice of practically all the supporters of the House. Feeling that no one would be elected on the first ballot, they entertained a lively hope that Mr. Cox would go in on the subsequent ballot when the forces of one or other of the prohibition candidates would begin to scatter. F. F. Hill, manager of the Cox campaign, declared on the night of January 6: "Cox is in it, unequivocally, until the last, and we are confident of the result. We are not losing any sleep, but are resting on our oars; we will be doing things at the right time."

While the Cox forces were waiting for "the right time," other forces were at work without their knowledge. The function of a State Legislature is to handle expeditiously the great volume of business in a very limited time; a deadlock in selecting a Speaker, or too much animosity, could throw the session off schedule by several days, postponing the announcement of committees. Retiring Governor Campbell expressed fears that important bills might not receive attention if time were lost during the opening days, unconscious of the damage his anxiety would have upon the position of his favorite—Gilmore, who was well entrenched. The Governor-elect, Colquitt, sensed that Cox had only a mathematical chance of victory. What happened between January 6 and 9 will perhaps never be completely understood, but those who have watched similar Speakership races can draw their own conclusions. There was some talk around Austin that Colquitt greeted Rayburn with a friendly "Hi, Sam!" as he passed him on Congress Avenue. Since Cox, who had refused to get out of the race, supposedly had the door locked and the key tucked away in his pocket in this deadlocked race, rumors were about that the Gilmore people had tried to make a deal if Cox would throw his strength in their direction. On January 9 he affirmed that he would remain in the race unless "something happens between now and tomorrow noon to change my mind. If I should decide to withdraw, the question of where my strength would go would depend entirely upon circumstances."

There was a prophetic note in Cox's statement; however, he was unaware that something actually was about to happen. The Bailey men were applying pressure in an indirect way to get Cox out in favor of Rayburn. On January 8 former Senator W. D. Hanger of Fort Worth, who had been under the care of a physician, made a special trip from North Texas. He stated emphatically that he had not come to Austin for his health, that he wanted to visit with some of his old friends—Jeff Cox and his manager, F. F. Hill, Jacob F. Wolters, and A. M. Kennedy. Cox reflected what was to be discussed by these remarks: "It will do him no good to even suggest such a thing to me." On January 6, figuratively speaking, he and his gear were already being packed for him, without his full knowledge, with the plans being formulated for an abandonment of his plane. The formality of bailing out and pulling the ripcord were not scheduled until the tenth.

The role of Kennedy cannot be separated from these strategic developments, for he had been in communication with Senator Bailey in Washington. The Senator apparently had taken a great deal more interest in the Speakership struggle than even his closest friends realized. There were fourteen Cox "last ditchers" about whom he was concerned because he believed that their support of Cox was both futile and unwise. He favored Rayburn and promptly passed the word down to his friends. "Get right" was the message from Washington which suddenly came by wire and United States mail to his closest associates among the fourteen.

Bailey's message, brief though it was, must have had a profound effect on Cox, because at midnight, before the opening session on January 10, he released the following statement, which seemed to indicate that he was beginning to get back in step with the Senator:

> "After a conference with my friends, in which the Speakership was gone over with absolute candor, I have concluded to withdraw, not because the situation was hopeless so far as I am concerned but because I am disinclined to involve my supporters in a controversy that will delay the peaceable organization of the Legislature and engender a lack of harmony that might prove embarrassing to the Administration of Governor Colquitt in its laudable hope of giving Texas a season of quietude from unreasonable and vexatious agitation."

Although Cox withdrew in no one's favor, Louis J. Wortham, who participated in the caucus, reported: "You may quote me as saying that Sam Rayburn will be next Speaker of the House."

Immediately the Gilmore headquarters released a somewhat lengthy analysis, showing how the withdrawal would favor their side. Rayburn thought awhile then responded with "No comment!" Orders had been given out from the Rayburn headquarters that only written statements would be released. Within his office an attaché remarked on January 8, "We had enough votes to secure an election yesterday, and today we are putting in a few rivets to hold them." The arrival in Austin of R. M. Johnson, editor of the Houston *Post,* and John A. Hulen, former Adjutant-General and prominent Colquitt supporter, to take an active interest in Rayburn's campaign may have been a favorable omen. As the time drew closer it appeared that the anti-prohibitionists would give Rayburn more support than they would Gilmore, because Gilmore was too much of a "pro" to suit them. Besides, by the middle of December they had realized that they did not have a ghost of a chance to elect one of their own persuasion; so they were willing to put their faith in one of the opposite belief, provided he possessed certain essential qualities requisite to a competent and able Speaker. They found in Rayburn the qualities they expected—"a disposition that would treat all questions arising with a just fairness and impartiality in the most expeditious and efficient manner."

The first day's activities in the Texas House reminded some of the opening day of school. In excellent humor the representatives, like pupils, took their seats, knowing there would be no hard work or lessons to recite on the day school was being organized, because there had been no assignments. The newcomers were a little shy and well behaved, but some of the holdovers were a bit boisterous. The teacher was all smiles and not strict with discipline, permitting even a few naughty and rowdy boys to enter the gallery with "real Texas shouts." This opening day on January 10, 1911, was no exception to the usual pattern.

At 12:05 P.M., W. B. Townsend, Secretary of State, called the House to order. There were two thousand crowded into the galleries. When the members saw he was using the top knob of a very heavy oak railing as a gavel, much laughter occurred. The noise of its blows upon the Speaker's table was thunderous, and a moment of dead silence followed. To a witness in the gallery, the administration of the oath was an impressive ceremony. There were venerable members, supported on heavy canes, whose raised hands shook slightly as they looked steadily at the Chief Clerk through or over their glasses and repeated the oath. There were young men serving their first term in the House, who, though appearing impressively dignified, betrayed their composure with chuckles as they repeated the section on not having fought a duel. Such archaic ritual did not affect old men. There were also those members whose hands were steady and footing secure—these men controlled the House, for they carried lists of names in their pockets to verify prior commitments.

The Secretary of State called the roll of members in alphabetical order; then the roll of members according to districts in numerical order and then certified that the correct list of names had been presented. He then announced that the next item of business in order was the election of the Speaker. W. W. Caves nominated C. E. Gilmore; Luther Nichols of Hill County nominated Sam T. Rayburn. Seconding speeches for Gilmore were made by C. C. Highsmith of Harris (an occurrence which brought R. M. Johnson of the Houston *Post* much sorrow),

Brown F. Lee of Tom Green, and R. D. Rowell of Marion. Seconding speeches for Rayburn were made by C. A. Martin of Lamar, Homer A. Dotson of Nacogdoches, and Ed. P. Mangum of Hunt. The following tellers were appointed to collect the ballots: J. B. Wood, G. E. Hamilton, W. T. Bagby, Z. Broughton, Luther Nichols, A. D. Rogers, J. J. Singleton, L. M. Teel. The ballots were counted by Maxwell, Maddox, Humphrey, McDaniel, Yarbrough, Haney, McDowra, and Dillard. After the results were announced, Gilmore asked to be recognized. He moved that the election of Sam Rayburn be made unanimous. Gilmore had followed the balloting rather closely, with no more than five votes ever separating them; and when the name of Rayburn was announced for the sixty-seventh time, he believed the race was concluded.

Gilmore had no sooner sat down, the response to his motion still thundering in his ears, than Hamilton of Childress, one of the tellers, came running from the crowd surrounding the ballot box. His obvious excitement caused every eye to follow him as he rushed to Gilmore's seat. A number of representatives crowded around him while the heated discussion was in progress. When Gilmore rose and withdrew the motion to make the vote unanimous, everyone knew that something was obviously wrong. This was one rare moment in Rayburn's career when he was confused. Townsend then announced the vote was seventy-one to sixty-five, but that there were three votes in excess of the 133 total membership in the House. Hence, he declared that there was no election.

This dramatic incident was followed by shouting and motions to clear the aisles. Hamilton moved that the gray hat be placed on a table in the center aisle, and that each man come forward as his name was called and deposit his ballot. This motion carried. Terrel of Bexar moved that the sergeant-at-arms summon back all legislators who might have left the floor after the first ballot. This necessitated the calling of the roll again to establish the presence of all representatives.

Bob Barker, the Chief Clerk, explained that he thought the mistake had been made by some of the legislators putting two slips in the box by oversight. Since the slips had been fastened together he believed that some had accidentally torn two off the pad instead of one. Another supposition, advanced by an onlooker from the gallery, was that there were three votes cast by people not eligible to vote, who were sitting on the House floor at the moment. The discrepancy was noted more quickly because everyone knew that the winning candidate would slip by with a very small majority.

The second ballot was a drawn-out ceremony, because as each representative's name was called he delivered his own ballot to the gray hat placed well within full view in the middle of the center aisle. The vote was promptly announced; hence the campaign managers could easily compare this performance with their own score cards. When Gilmore's name was called he walked to the hat and deposited a ballot for his opponent; when Rayburn's turn came he reciprocated. The suspense mounted as the magic number approached when Sam had the votes to win. The vote on the second ballot was seventy to sixty-three in favor of Rayburn. Lee Aston, one of his lieutenants and a legislator from the adjoining county, said, "Sam jumped up and gave a cotton patch yell and sat down real quick—like he was ashamed of hisself. That was the day Sam Rayburn got his start." Again Gilmore arose and received approval of his motion to make the selection of Speaker unanimous. Thus the Thirty-second Legislature elected the second youngest Speaker in history, one who had just turned twenty-nine on January 6.

The presiding officer appointed Maxwell and Kennedy of McLennon and Nichols of Hill to escort Rayburn to the rostrum. According to a witness in the gallery, one representative at this very moment clapped his hands together for a messenger. He scratched off two words on a blank form of a telegraph pad—"Sam won!" It was addressed to Martha Rayburn, Windom, Texas.

The three men walked forward with their victorious colleague. As he stepped lightly between the two gentlemen beside him, he bore a striking resemblance to the man of destiny—the right hand in his coat pocket, chin up, jaws set, and very serious. During those fifty steps there flashed through his mind the more dramatic moments of his childhood—the rainy evening in 1895 when he announced to his brothers and sisters that he would someday go into politics, the day in the cotton patch when he received his father's permission to go to college, the image of his mother at the gate holding a wrinkled apron in one hand as she waved "Goodby," and finally his father's words "Sam, be a man." He could show restraint and then again his emotions could overflow. On a day like this he was not ashamed to express his feelings.

As the party passed down the aisle, Mr. Gilmore was sitting

over at one side with one of the smaller candidates for page on his knee, his arms around the boy and talking to him with playful earnestness. Little did the boy comprehend that the man who was giving him so much attention had just lost a campaign which had been waged fervently for two weeks and had held the attention of the press for the past month. Nor did the page boy realize that another candidate was about to make his debut into the larger realm of politics.

After Townsend administered the oath to Mr. Rayburn, the new Speaker delivered the following brief address:

"The members of this House have just paid me a compliment I do not fail to appreciate. This office carries with it duties and responsibilities which I do not fail to appreciate. The loyalty of the friends who have stood by me in this campaign is such that a life of friendship is too short to repay them. I hope to preside over this House to its satisfaction and the glory of this great commonwealth. I would not be true to myself nor my friends if I did not thank this House on this occasion not only for myself but for every friend. But up there in Fannin County, there is an old man already passed his three-score, and there by his side sits an old woman at whose feet I would now delight to worship. For them I also thank you."

(The House Journal makes reference to a "huskiness in his voice" and the "touch of moisture in many eyes.")

"There is no feeling of bitterness by me for those who have opposed me in this campaign. The man who was pitted against me is a gentleman in every sense of the word.

"Again thanking you, I ask for the pleasure of the House."

Isaac M. Standifer of Houston, "personal counsel" for R. M. Johnson, moved to recess until 4:00 P.M. As he spoke he moved his hand over his stomach to indicate that he was hungry. The vote was unanimous, for everyone was in need of food and rest. The week had been an unusually strenuous one, because of the excessive emphasis given the Speakership race. Some of the more spirited of the legislators in the role of "varsity boys" then gave a yell, ending in "Rah, rah, rah for Rayburn." These were the friends of education. They had reason to be jubilant, for Rayburn was a graduate of East Texas Normal, had attended classes at the University, and was kindly disposed toward State support of education. Hundreds of people gathered around the Speaker's stand to extend congratulations and shake his hand.

On the opposite side of the wide hall sat the defeated candidate, who was by no means alone, for his more ardent supporters were gathered about him also. Disappointment was evident on Gilmore's face but no bitterness marred his countenance.

If the statistics of the Cox lieutenants are correct, then it was his withdrawal at the psychological moment which made the difference. Of the fourteen Cox men who had agreed to hold out until the end, eleven voted for Rayburn. Among these were some of Senator Bailey's closest friends, those who were the recipients of his telegrams or brief letters.

Though the prohibitionists had a large majority in the House and Senate, the "antis" controlled the organization of both. They held the balance of power in the Speakership race and used their influence for a man who opposed them ideologically but gave promise of impartiality in a post where impartiality was so greatly demanded. They knew he could be objective and expeditious in making decisions. They also viewed him as a practical man with common sense. Already he had acquired the reputation of never getting "rattled" and always acting in accordance with parliamentary usage and practice. They recognized that there were prohibitionists and prohibitionists, and they preferred Sam's type. These were some of the reasons for casting their lot with Sam Rayburn of Fannin County. From the political point of view it was also a victory for Senator Joseph Weldon Bailey and a rebuff to retiring Governor Thomas M. Campbell. Governor O. B. Colquitt likewise appeared well pleased with the verdict, despite the fact that he was a "Johnny-Come-Lately" as far as Rayburn was concerned.

Speaker Rayburn promptly assigned Cox and Gilmore choice seats in the House, as was the custom. The front seats when needed were given to members who were deaf or blind. He next appointed a legislative committee to draft a set of rules entitled "Duties and Rights of the Speaker." Being a very systematic presiding officer, Rayburn wanted a clear definition of his job. The following was approved. The Speaker was to take the chair at the time of day specified in House adjournment; was to preserve order, decorum, and control behavior in the galleries; was to regulate the House and conduct in the corridors and conference rooms; was responsible for the business to come before the House; was to enforce the rules as prescribed by the Constitution; was not to vote unless the vote seemed decisive; was to decide all questions of order; was to examine, correct, and approve the Journal; and was responsible for the appointment of all committees and chairmen. For the first time the Speaker's post became a powerful and dignified one, with the duties codified. Succeeding Speakers for the next half century felt the influence of this meticulous and orderly mind.

The most difficult work for the House under Rayburn's leadership was related to the redistricting of the State, after Congress passed a reapportionment bill. Two new congressional districts were to be carved out of already existing districts. Such changes as these always stimulate quite a bit of interest among the people, as well as the congressmen who are directly affected. There was also speculation that an effort would be made to set up a few more legislative districts, since the State was entitled to 150 representatives, with only 133 at the time.

Other legislation already being formulated was a new mining law to make it easier for prospectors to develop the mineral resources of the State. A constitutional amendment was being proposed to provide for the election of a penitentiary commission composed of six commissioners, one to be elected each two years to hold office for six years. A plan was also being formulated to establish a state sanitarium for tubercular patients with farms rather than expensive buildings, where greater use could be made of Texas sunshine. Besides bills aimed at prison reform and reducing the expense of assessing and collecting taxes, the most interesting one was a measure involving Federal aid. Its purpose was to secure the cooperation of the Federal Government in sharing half the expense of surveys, and other costs, in an investigation of the irrigation opportunities in Texas.

There was something in every piece of legislation which appealed to Mr. Rayburn. The development of natural resources, reform and sound business procedure, care for the handicapped, and Federal aid to increase farm production were measures he liked best.

Although he tried to show his impartiality as long as he was in the chair, he would on occasion reflect more enthusiasm for some issues and items than others. For example, on the twelfth day of the session he read a petition from seventy-six ladies of Lockhart asking the Legislature to so amend the law as to forbid Sunday games of all kinds where money was received for the game by the players or managers. Rayburn agreed with the intent of the ladies.

Although Rayburn's performance in the regular session demonstrated a certain calm and innate capacity for his job, he encountered some problems and had moments when the famous ire was aroused. But even at this early stage he revealed the poise and aggressiveness which characterized his more mature parliamentary career.

As early as 1911, in this Thirty-second Legislature, some recognized the Rayburn formula of procedure which started evolving at the very outset of his legal career and public life. Those who knew only the Squire of Bonham, and not the Speaker in Washington, could easily overlook a rather basic Rayburn concept and fail to see the logic of his actions. Rayburn cannot be understood by men who are guided in their own judgments primarily by the emotions rather than by a rational, legal reasoning. Whether or not he liked an issue was actually immaterial to the Speaker. He believed that his responsibility and first loyalty was to the Constitution, precedent, or the whole. As long as a law was on the statutes it was his duty to operate within its framework. Any objection to the law should be expressed in the courts or at the polls. In applying his formula he had on occasion found himself in conflict with his own colleagues, governors, and even presidents. He had sometimes found himself at odds with the mores or traditions of his own region. In still more unusual instances he had been at variance with the inner self—head with heart, Speaker with Squire. These inner clashes were caused by the human element, the compulsion to be fair and honest in a world of inequity and greed, the necessity to forget self and regional biases in favor of the whole. He never closed his eyes to human need or walked away from the call of duty; hence he withstood pressures that would have broken weaker men. With such a philosophy his lengthy career was not exactly destined to be marked by tranquility.

On February 23, 1911, B. B. Sturgeon of Lamar County introduced a bill in the Senate levying a $100 tax on billiard and pool tables. Speaker Rayburn promptly returned it to the Senate, ruling that since this was a revenue measure it should have originated in the House. Actually Rayburn was Sturgeon's constituent, from the third senatorial district. Sturgeon proceeded to rise to a question of personal privilege to "take the Rayburn hide into the tanyard." He made some remarks which he desired printed and others which he preferred omitted. For example, he said caustically, "Rayburn would not know the Constitution if he met it in the road."

This outburst between two rival prohibitionists set off controversies between House and Senate. Rayburn proceeded with his own "tanning of the Senator" and the placing of their differences in proper constitutional perspective, since the Senator had raised this issue. The San Antonio *Express* for February 25 analyzed the incident as the beginning of a feud:

> It is whispered about Austin that both Senator Sturgeon and Speaker Rayburn are casting wistful eyes on a seat in Congress. The chairs in the House of Representatives at Washington are spacious, but one is not big enough for both the gentleman from Fannin and the gentleman from Lamar. They are saying it was as well to have the first round over the poolroom bill as anything else, but perhaps, neither gentleman will relish this current talk.

Some members of the House could not refrain from a little fun as a result of the incident. Bagby and Buchanan, directing a stinging pleasantry at Senator Sturgeon, entered on February 27 the following resolution:

> "Whereas. The Legislature of Texas, by legislative enactment and otherwise, has given expression to its desire to protect and cultivate the game and fish industry in Texas; be it
>
> "Resolved, that the Legislature of Texas direct the attention of the Honorable W. G. Sterett to the fact that the Honorable Sam Rayburn, Speaker of the House of Representatives, has by the process of legal reasoning, transformed a Sturgeon into a Flounder, both in form and habits, and the said W. G. Sterett is requested to throw about this new creation the full protection of the law and see that it remains in waters which are conducive to its development, and will not interfere with the culture of those species which are useful and profitable to mankind."

After considerable merriment had resulted, Speaker Rayburn ruled the resolution out of order, and no action was taken on it.

He enjoyed a joke or prank, for he believed that levity cleared the atmosphere. He had a keen sense of humor, though his characteristic seriousness may have indicated otherwise. In these early years he was prone to become indignant and explode. He never suppressed this quality. Such an instance occurred during this same Thirty-second session when he believed that a group of obstructionists in the House and a group of lobbyists, for whom he acquired an early dislike, were trying to block legislation and prevent measures from coming up for consideration. He also believed that former Governor Tom Campbell was involved. In a speech to the House he said that it had gone forth to the people that there were insurgents who had banded themselves together; then he proceeded to reveal the Rayburn courage but not his more mature taste. In later years he refused to deal in personalities, but in 1911 Rayburn was only in the chrysalis stage of statesmanship. He did not evolve from his cocoon until the New Deal. Then he unfolded the broad wings of statecraft which marked him for immortality.

In 1911, in a speech, he affirmed:

> "Speaking only for myself, I want to say that I will not be a party to a fillibuster [applause]. But I expect to meet the issues squarely and to vote against all measures I believe to be vicious. It matters not to me whether Tom Campbell stands for a measure or against it. Tom Campbell, in my opinion, is the least thing to be considered in legislation. It is what is to the interest of this great State. I may be accused at times of being bald-headed, but no man can accuse me of being a sore-head. I expect to vote for platform demands if the measures are drawn as I believe the people of Texas want them. So far as binding myself with any man or set of men to slap any man or class of men by opposing measures which are in the interests of the people of this great State is concerned, you will not find me there.
>
> "So far as these newspaper reports go, taking the news back to my people that I am afraid to meet the issues squarely, it is not true. Sometimes men draw measures and call them platform demands which do not meet the platform, in my opinion. House bill No. 2 [the full rendition bill] in my opinion, is farfetched. As far as the bank guaranty bills are concerned, I believe they are in the interest of the people, and I will stand here day by day and vote for them. I am not here to represent any man nor any class of men, and it matters not to me what Mr. Campbell's views are, nor does it matter to me that certain bills may further the political ambitions of some men. Such things ought not to influence us in the discharge of our duty.
>
> "I expect to stand for the people of Texas and the people of Texas alone [applause]."

At the conclusion of the session, A. D. Rogers presented a resolution, acting for the people of the State, that

> ". . . we extend to the Honorable Sam Rayburn our sincere thanks for the uniform courtesy, fairness, and intelligent manner with which he has presided over the desk as Speaker of the House. And that we congratulate the people of Texas on having had the services of Mr. Rayburn in this exalted position, and we bear willing testimony to his zeal, energy, and fidelity in the discharge of every public duty."

As was the custom upon the closing of a regular session the Speaker was honored with appropriate gifts. A. M. Kennedy, representing the members of the House, presented him with a gold watch; Louis J. Wortham, for the officers, clerks, and stenographers, a set of diamond cuff buttons. E. A. McDaniel, acting for the porters, gave a traveling bag, and Marvin H. Brown on behalf of the pages presented Rayburn with a suitcase. There was something of the prophetic in the last two gifts, for the time was imminent, as some commented, when the Speaker would be traveling. Sam Rayburn had made some material gain over the student days when he rolled his clothes in a bundle and tied them with a piece of rope.

As Rayburn himself looked back upon the session, he saw progress in other directions. He was pleased with the great deal of legislation enacted, despite the many Party and partisan quarrels, which he thought were too frequently precipitated by Governor Colquitt. The "dry" factions in the two Houses did not hesitate to add fuel to the fires. The controversies between Colquitt and the Attorney-General, as well as a protracted dispute with the Land Commissioner, J. T. Robison, coupled with attacks on the prison system, kept legislative circles in an uproar.

Rayburn recalled the lack of judgment the Governor demonstrated in rewarding political friends with his appointive power and also his inability to work cooperatively with the Federal Government. He remembered also the Governor's efforts to defeat the prohibition amendment in the July election, an action which set off a storm of protests from both factions.

On the positive side the Speaker recalled pleasantly the legislation providing for shorter working hours for women in industry, the child labor laws, pure food laws, the appropriation of money for a Confederate women's home and a tuberculosis sanitarium.

Because the Legislature adjourned without acting on the appropriation bill, the Governor called a special session for July 31–August 29. Immediately the controversies of the regular session began anew. Public sentiment had built up for an investigation of alleged irregularities in the July prohibition amendment election. Certain "pros" went to Rayburn, a prohibition Speaker, and asked him if he would appoint all "pros" on the committee. He declined to do so, pointing out that he would pick nine of the best legal minds in the State, that their identification with the "pro" and "anti" issue was irrelevant. The "pros" then charged out of his office in a huff, declaring that they would elect an all prohibition committee over his protest, but they failed.

The Governor's veto of that portion of the appropriation bill marked for school improvement bothered Rayburn because the action hurt education and was a gross repudiation of campaign promises to the people. To Rayburn, a man's word was a contract. A governor's platform was entirely different from a Party platform in that it reflected his own personal commitments.

During Sam Rayburn's six years in the Texas House of Representatives he saw many bills become laws, and as Speaker he had a hand in guiding a number of controversial measures through the gauntlet of committees and on the floor. Some of the more significant laws of this session anticipate the Congressman's interests after 1913. For example, the banking bill, which provided for the deposit of State and county funds in depository banks, made possible a higher rate of interest. State Bank guarantee laws were passed. Several laws affecting the railroads were put on the statutes. There was the Robertson insurance law, the full rendition law, and laws for the establishment of the Confederate home. Rayburn had an interest in certain creative laws: the establishment of a state board of health, a department of agriculture, experimental farms and the teaching of agriculture in secondary schools. There were also a state textbook law and laws restricting gambling, horse-racing, and speculation in cotton futures. There were local option laws which placed many restrictions on the use and distribution of liquor, such as prohibiting drinking on railroads and bootlegging in dry counties. Some of these measures were also related to the later legislative interests of the Congressman. Rayburn liked to refer to this valuable experience as a sort of apprenticeship. He later commented upon his study of earlier state officials and their valuable lessons, specifically the economic reforms of the Hogg and Culberson Administration and the laws of the Sayers-Lanham era. In reminiscing about this early period, Rayburn always worked his way around to the "political phenomenon, Joseph Weldon Bailey," whose influence must have been considerable during these formidable years. Rayburn learned well the lessons of his tutors, as evidenced by his own success as a professor of practical politics.

☆VI☆

Flag Springs to Washington

ON THE wall of Sam Rayburn's home there hangs an artist's reproduction of the verse that closes the novel, *Eben Holden,* by Irving Bacheller. These are the lines which catch the eye of a visitor and set off a reflection on the similarity to the Rayburnesque:

I ain't afraid
'Shamed o' nuthin' I ever done.
Alwuss kep' my tugs tight,
Never swore 'less 'twas nec'sary,
Never ketched a fish bigger'n it was
Er lied 'n a hoss trade
Er shed a tear I didn't hev to.
Never cheated anybody but Eben Holden.
Goin' off somewhere, Bill—
dunno the way nuther—
Dunno 'f it's east er west er north er south,
Er road er trail;
But I ain't afraid.

Eben's manifestation of honesty, humility, and fearlessness was clearly portrayed in the long and eventful career of a man who had always looked forward.

That Rayburn was planning to make the race for Congress was discussed in Bonham as early as January, 1911, when he won the Speakership race. When Representative Marvin H. Brown, on behalf of the pages, presented the Speaker with the suitcase, he had expressed, as already indicated, the hope that Rayburn would use it in his travels to Washington. A. M. Kennedy in giving the watch made reference to the hope that it would "keep good time in Washington."

When Choice B. Randell vacated his Congressional seat to run for the Senate against the incumbent, Joseph Weldon Bailey, Rayburn declared his intentions. But at the time, he did not know what district Fannin would be in, since the final redistricting had not been completed. Prior to the announcement, William T. Bagby, representative from Hallettsville, had stated when it appeared redistricting might not go through, that he would like to see Sam T. Rayburn and Louis J. Wortham of Fort Worth elected congressmen-at-large. A retiring Speaker in those days was expected to seek the Attorney-General's post or run for Governor, but Sam had demonstrated such a flair for legislation that people were suggesting him for another political route. As a lawmaker he had revealed the qualities of a professional. He was before the eyes of all Texans as a result of his most recent success, and the State-wide publicity of Bagby's appraisal merely helped to crystallize the home folks' thinking. Bagby also spoke for many Texans when he proclaimed:

"I want to say that while Speaker Rayburn is a prohibitionist, he should be supported for the place of congressman-at-large, if he should run for it, by every anti-prohibitionist in Texas. He is a man of judicial temperament and of analytical mind who in his official position, and without prejudice, rendered his official judgment upon all questions without reference to the political affiliations of any man.

"He is honest, conscientious and just in his official adjudication and no man, either prohibitionist or anti-prohibitionist, has any right to question the honesty of his rulings."

As Senator B. B. Sturgeon bade adieu to a group of brother senators, he expressed the feeling that unless his plans were changed he also would make the race for Congress. Sturgeon added to the interest by affirming that one of his smallest worries was the ambition of this Speaker Rayburn. The two men had already been at one another's throat, politically speaking, for nearly two years, and the followers of both men awaited with interest the showdown of the grudge battle that appeared to be developing. Next to a good prize fight or an open-air revival meeting the people in Northeast Texas liked an old-fashioned political "horse race." The redistricting, however, left Lamar County out of the new Fourth District (originally the Fifth), and many of the populace felt disappointed that they had been deprived of a spirited Congressional race.

When Rayburn bought a Model-T Ford everyone knew that he was in business and ready to pay his filing fee. The press received his declaration on February 2, 1912. Appropriately, he opened his campaign where his life in Texas began—in Windom—on Saturday afternoon, February 3. His father and mother still lived on the old homeplace just three miles away. Though it was a community of scarcely three hundred people at the time, it seemed larger on this day as the merchants closed their dozen houses of business to commemorate the biggest occasion they had known. His announcement stirred the ambitions of seven others, who also paid their filing fees and launched their campaigns even before Congress had completed the apportionment of representatives on the census of 1910, or the Legislature had redistricted the Senate. These men included B. J. Jones, Judge of the 15th Judicial District; Tom Perkins, State Senator; J. B. Erwin, W. J. Gibson, Tom Wells, M. M. Morrison, and R. A. Lovelace.

Almost before Sam Rayburn set up campaign headquarters, he had a volunteer committee, frequently referred to as the "inner sanctum," to help formulate the strategy. They were Thomas P. Steger, H. A. Cunningham, R. T. Lipscomb, Lawyers; A. B. Scarborough, a banker; Charles Halsell, T. B. Williams, and C. A. Wheeler, businessmen.

At this time a pattern of organization was born which was in use for almost half a century. In the early days efficiency counted most, but when Mr. Sam became a national figure, detailed planning was less important. His vote appeal was always the difference. Fannin County became the focal point of the organization, with radii extending to each county seat and town in the District; and from each town other radii reached into the homes of the prominent men throughout the countryside. In every home they spread the information about the virtues of their candidate. The interrelationship of every part to the whole will remind one of a pocket watch. Each wheel turned another wheel once the winding began. The "Rayburn clock" never ran down nor did the parts become broken, for son replaced father. Mr. Sam merely kept the complicated machinery clean and well-oiled with a life of service that inspired confidence throughout the District. He kept the main spring wound tightly for a record number of years and saw three generations perform their respective functions. New faces appeared in his headquarters, but once he had placed his hand upon their shoulders, people did not leave Mr. Sam. Many passed away, but the ranks were quickly closed.

In 1912, the local committee called a public meeting in the Bonham Firemen's Club, a recreation hall on the northeast corner of the town square. The attendance revealed a cross-section of society in Fannin County. A. J. Moore presided, but Steger was appointed Chairman of the Fannin County Committee. After discussing subjects related to the campaign, Rayburn clubs were then set up in every precinct for the purpose of spreading information and getting the voters to the polls on election day. Similar groups were then perfected in other counties of his District—Grayson, Collin, Hunt, and Rains.

Automobile caravans were assembled to make trips to the larger towns. With "Vote for Rayburn" banners draped along the sides of touring cars, citizens of Bonham moved from one community to another. The personnel most active in this first campaign were W. A. Thomas, former county clerk; Sherwood Spotts, editor of the Bonham *Daily Favorite;* J. B. Gober, presiding elder of the Methodist Church; W. H. Evans, popular Sunday-school teacher in Texas; T. P. Steger; E. H. Prichett; L. K. Crawford; A. J. Moore; Sid Smith; E. S. McAlester; George Jones; Will Nevill; and Ed D. Steger, a member of the State Democratic Executive Committee. They entered every place of business, shaking hands and carrying the message of their first citizen.

To Bonhamites the month of July, 1912, was eventful. There was no concern about hydrogen bombs, slaughter on the highways over the holiday, or fear lest the children were ruining their eyes watching television. They were playing baseball and flying kites on the school ground. Bonham was usually a quiet place, but the Fourth of July brought some excitement. Simpson Park had just been opened with an impressive ceremony, highlighted by addresses from Mayor T. W. Ragsdale, the Reverend Richard Morgan, and Judge Rosser Thomas. The most exciting item in the *Daily Favorite* was an advertisement for the Maxwell "Special" car, fully equipped, including self-starter, with the listed delivery price at $1480. A testimonial by a Nebraska man reported that he drove his Maxwell 28,600 miles during eighteen months and had to spend only $6 for repairs. The Post Office Department announced that the firm of Moore and Payne of Joplin, Missouri, had been awarded the contract for construction of a new $50,000 structure in Bonham. The city council fixed the total tax levy, including schools, at $1.65 on the $100 valuation for 1912. A committee from Bailey Inglish Elementary School and the West Side Mother's Club had met with the School Board President, D. W. Sweeney, to discuss ways and means of getting sanitary drinking fountains at the high school.

This quiet little town went about its daily routine, recording its events on the back pages of its newspapers. Suddenly the front page reflected the tension of the national scene. The Republicans had just nominated William Howard Taft for President, as the Party frankly admitted it was "facing the greatest crisis in its history." The people of Bonham had already read that the Democrats were deadlocked in the historic convention in Baltimore, and on July 1 the thirty-fourth ballot had not produced a nominee. The *Favorite* headlines read "Wilson in the Lead! Many Fistfights!" The subheads said delegates were getting weary and were switching their votes to Woodrow Wilson. The July 2 paper carried the news of Wilson's victory on the forty-sixth ballot over Clark, Underwood, Harmon, Kern, and Foss.

Perhaps the most sober reading material in the *Favorite* at this time was W. Sherwood Spotts' editorial about the inadequacies of the convention system for nominating candidates, as he wrote:

> Amid all the uncertainties of the pre-convention campaigns of 1912, one certainly looms like a mighty cliff. The system of nomination by convention has enjoyed its most prosperous days. It will shrivel and decline—and in time may cease to be anything except a recollection.

It is interesting to note that Senator Mike Mansfield of Montana, following the Los Angeles Convention in 1960, expressed opposition to what he considered an outmoded system used in America to select nominees and presidents.

The announcement that Judge W. F. Ramsey would speak in behalf of his candidacy for Governor did not stir up any more excitement than the Best Theatre front-page ad that its night program would include *For His Necklace*, or the Rogers, Woodward and Roberts Hardware Company's advertisement that they were selling the Springfield—"the wagon with a reputation."

By the end of the first week in July the pulse of the *Favorite* began to beat more rapidly. It was beginning to get excited about Bonham's own Sam Rayburn, who was stirring up the District with his straightforward talk about the issues in the Congressional race. Then on July 15 he made his final speech in Bonham supporting his campaign. The farmers from every part of the county came at least an hour early. By two o'clock the District courtroom and the gallery were filled with gray beards and boyish looking faces. The presence of many ladies was the beginning of something relatively new in politics, certainly for Fannin County. While the crowd awaited the arrival of the speaker, the Bonham band, which only a few days earlier had thrilled the Fourth of July crowd at Simpson Park, played some exciting music.

At 2:15 P.M. Rayburn, accompanied by T. P. Steger and C. A. Wheeler, entered the chamber amidst enthusiastic applause. Before Rayburn was introduced, A. L. Springfield of Ector was called on to make some remarks. He was taken somewhat by surprise, for he was in his shirt sleeves just as he had come in from the cotton patch. However, he brushed aside the absence of a coat with a quick apology. He said he did not have a prepared speech but welcomed the opportunity as the Secretary of the Farmer's Union to comment on the generous reception their honored guest had given him and their bills in Austin.

After an introduction by Steger, Rayburn spoke for one hour, setting forth his philosophy of politics. This speech before the home folks might well be considered Sam Rayburn's manifesto, for he nailed his ideas firmly to the door of his political structure where they could be seen by present and future voters. He began his speech in 1912 with the simple statement: "I am a Democrat." One Sunday afternoon in 1961 he told an American television audience that he was still a Democrat "without prefix or suffix or apologies or handles." After forty-eight years of repetition and consecration his words had come to define a creed—a sort of religion. Mr. Sam uttered his creed so reverently that it sounded like "I am the way, the truth, and the life."

In 1912 he went on to explain his faith:

"I believe that the principles advocated and adhered to by the Party since its birth are the same fundamental principles upon which our Republic was founded: a government of the people, by the people and for the people, where every man, rich or poor, should stand equal before the law and Government with the exemplification of 'equal rights to all and special privileges to none.' This is the Democratic doctrine of the Party in its old illustrious days when she boasted of a Jefferson and a Jackson."

He expressed a hope that the Party of the fathers might return to power because the Republican Party, he said, had forfeited its right to command further respect from the people by trampling under foot all its campaign promises.

Then he proceeded to apply his philosophy by discussing his belief in tariffs "for revenue only" and not for protecting one special group. "I would like to see an era of absolute free trade both in the raw material and the finished product if such were possible under our theory of government." He assailed the policy of giving the manufacturer all his raw materials free of duty and allowing him to lay a heavy tribute to the consumer on the finished product. He touched on the grievances of Southern agriculture when he cited the undemocratic policy of penalizing the producer of raw materials and protecting the producer of manufactured items so desperately needed by the farmer. Thus he advocated free trade and began his chant which was to be heard again and again in the halls of Congress for almost half a century.

He had much to say about the income tax, which, though provided for, had not yet become a law. He believed that wealth, and not consumption, should bear the greater part of the burdens of taxation, that the rich instead of the poor should pay the greater share. Then he proceeded to make a plea for a Federal inheritance tax. "Taxes levied in this way will bring to the Government a great deal of revenue and will reach to a great extent the hidden fortunes of those who have profited most by the robber tariffs built up under Republican misrule." He predicted that revenue from this source would permit the lowering of tariffs. He pointed to his part in the Texas House in passing a law levying a tax on inherited riches.

Next, he argued for the election of United States Senators by a direct vote of the people instead of by the state legislatures; and the election of every official from constable to President and Vice-President by popular vote. In these early days, he believed that the Electoral College should be abolished, because the method of public approval would come nearer insuring the selection of the people's choice instead of the politicians'.

Then he proceeded to express his faith in that government which is closest to the people, reflecting their will, for "I further believe that the representative form is the best yet devised by men. When the people have the right of recall of every public official every two years, this government is indeed close to the people. . . ." Then he discussed the use of the initiative, referendum, and recall as being too new and untried to be adopted as national policy. It was a local and state matter.

In answer to the widespread belief that the legislatures contain evil men, he said, "I believe that bad men do get into office" but that enlightened people will weed these out and elect good men. He never lost faith in people and their ability to eliminate the culls. He promptly laid the foundation for his own belief, from which he never wavered, that an elected official should be a full-time employee of his constituents. He affirmed that there was no place in Congress for "the retained attorney." "I believe that a man when he is elected to Congress should, if he has such clients, sever his relations with them before entering on the duties of that position."

Since his speech was partly aimed at answering charges hurled at him by two of his opponents, he made specific reference to certain slanderous statements to the effect that he had been a paid railroad attorney.

> "Never in my life have I represented a public service corporation. When I became a member of the law firm of Steger, Thurmond and Rayburn, Messrs. Thurmond and Steger were representing the Santa Fe Railroad Company, receiving pay monthly. When the first check came after I entered the firm, Mr. Thurmond brought to my desk one-third of the amount of the check, explaining what it was for. I said to him that I was a member of the Legislature, representing the people of Fannin County, and that my experience had taught me that men who represent the people should be as far removed as possible from concerns whose interests he was liable to be called on to legislate concerning, and that on that ground I would not accept a dollar of the railroad's money, though I was legally entitled to it. I never did take a dollar of it. I have been guided by this principle in all my dealings."

Facts seem to substantiate that he never deviated from this early pronouncement. However, he went on to add that he saw no objection to a man's having supplementary employment when he was not in the Legislature if this work was unrelated to his duties and did not sway his decisions as a lawmaker.

Rayburn was on this day harsh in his condemnation of the speculator in the futures of farm products. "I hold that any species of gambling is a moral wrong as well as an economic wrong."

He reaffirmed his faith in the rural free delivery by pointing out that the "carrier many times going through rain, sleet and snow is the most welcome visitor at the farmhouse." He brought news from the outside world, particularly the daily paper, which helped the farm family to keep abreast of the times. Rayburn insisted that an enlightened citizenship would help perpetuate a free government.

On the matter of States' Rights, Rayburn showed very clearly his parental influence and took a position which he found quite defensible in this early period when government had not yet become complex. His views were quite compatible with those of his people:

> "I am unalterably opposed to the further encroachment of the Federal Government upon the rights of the States. The right of the State to adjudicate matters referring wholly to intrastate affairs should be held inviolate and any encroachment upon this right is usurpation of the right of the States in the grossest way. I believe in the doctrine of local self-government as between the State and National Government which is a time-honored tenet of democracy and one for which our fathers fought with the ballot for all the life of this Government and one for which they went to war from 1861 to 1865."

His views on labor at this time are also quite significant. That labor had a right to organize, he deemed elemental. That it must be protected by adequate legislation was likewise necessary. Capital also had its rights, he quickly added, and justice should be meted out when conflicts arose between the two.

He concluded his address by summarizing his achievement as a State representative and related some of the biographical data of his parental background and life on a Texas farm—facts which always made the people of the Fourth District feel that here was a man like them, in whom they could place their trust. His accurate prediction by counties about the outcome of the election almost leads one to believe that he was reading from a copy of the *Daily Favorite* for July 29; however, he was always famous for his prophecies. In making his final plea he said in all humility: "I will not deny that there are men in the District better qualified than I to go to Congress, but, gentlemen, these men are not in the race."

On July 27, 1912, the people of the Fourth Congressional District went to the polls and cast their votes. In the Rayburn Memorial Library there are many documents of historical significance in the life of this man who began his career from obscure surroundings, but there is none more provocative than that of July 27, written by the electorate. It is the official returns, certified by W. W. Clendenin, Chairman of the Democratic Executive Committee of the District. The eight candidates polled a total of 21,336 votes distributed as follows:

Sam T. Rayburn—4983
B. L. Jones—4365
R. A. Lovelace—290
M. M. Morrison—798
Tom Wells—1961
W. J. Gibson—3790
J. B. Erwin—656
Tom Perkins—4493

The returns from Fannin and Hunt provided the winning margin of 490. Since this was prior to the days of the second primary, the candidate with a plurality was declared the nominee of the Party and was assured victory in the General Election of November in the solid Democratic Fourth District.

Expressing in all the papers his appreciation to the Democrats of the Fourth, Rayburn wrote:

> I desire at this time to thank the democracy of this great District for the signal honor conferred upon me. It shall be my constant purpose and my main hope to conduct the affairs of the office that no man who supported me shall ever have cause to regret having done so.
>
> For the men who were opponents of mine in the race I have nothing but the very kindest feelings, and the only pang that comes to me in the hour of my triumph is that so many good men must suffer defeat. To those who supported my opponents I have no word of censure but shall strive to discharge the duties of the position that they will be led to believe that the people made no mistake in electing me.

Although Mr. Rayburn had no fears that the Republican Party would upset the Democrats by a write-in campaign, he did not settle down to the responsibility of planning for the new job until after the General Election in November, 1912. This he considered a courtesy to the Republicans in the District. However, there were only fourteen registered Republicans in Bonham at the time, and probably not more than two hundred in the District. At heart, there may have been more, but in the Fourth District people so afflicted were not prone to discuss this eccentricity. As a matter of fact, Rayburn gave more thought to his law practice and the notes at the bank than to plans for going to Washington. He somehow managed to pay these bills, but it was many years before he did not have to worry about notes at the bank, and other debts, as the folders about his personal business would seem to suggest.

According to the national press, the biggest events in 1913 were the introduction by Henry Ford of the assembly line in the production of the Model-T, and Woodrow Wilson's "New Freedom." The two phenomena were destined to influence American life and thought for a good many years. But according to the *Daily Favorite* and the Fourth District, Rayburn's election seemed more important. It did prove to be of more lasting significance. Sam Rayburn, though, had faith in both Ford and Wilson: he had traveled all over the District in one of the famous "Tin Lizzies" and had already declared for many of the planks which were to appear in Wilson's platform. Both men had a feeling for humanity, and the similarity of their beliefs came as no surprise to anyone.

Martha Rayburn applied herself to helping Sam get ready to go to Washington. She saw to it that he had the right clothes and accessories for a colder climate. Although he carried more belongings on this trip than he had on any previously, he left behind one big piece of luggage. He had carried around from birth the name Samuel Taliaferro Rayburn (the middle name pronounced "toll-i-ver"), and finally he decided that all of this was too big a mouthful for a man with his kind of politics, certainly for one who made no pretense at being the sort of person that Samuel Taliaferro implied. After all, he thought, he lived in Bonham not Boston. So he unofficially dropped it and became just plain Sam Rayburn. Years later when the American people became better acquainted with the man they reduced it to just Sam or Mr. Sam. Only strangers ventured to use the formal nomenclature, because his friends well knew that the shortened form suited his simple dignity much better. For almost half a century he signed his name in a heavy, sharp, angular script which handwriting experts say is indicative of authority, determination, and strength of will. Only in his declining years, when his eyes began to dim, did the signature waver and lose some of its earlier style. The inner force and power, however, never left him. It always connoted strength and inspired faith and confidence wherever it appeared.

☆ VII ☆

The New Freedom

SAM RAYBURN employed a secretary, Hal C. (Spec) Horton, and left early for Washington, February 27, so that he would be able to enjoy the color of the Presidential Inauguration on March 4, 1913. The two men boarded the train at Bells; and at Denison, Hatton W. Sumners, Congressman-elect from Dallas, and his secretary, Bradley Hogue of the Dallas *Times Herald,* joined them. Sleeping accommodations were provided in the same coach.

The trip was somewhat uneventful, except for one incident which is reported by Rayburn's secretary. Horton struck up an acquaintance with an attractive young lady in the diner. She was a talkative sort, reporting many facts about herself, including that she was a student at the National Park Seminary in Washington, D.C. She told Horton that the young ladies were permitted to have visitors on designated evenings. Horton had already succumbed and was making plans to see her again; but his hopes were suddenly dashed on the rocks. Horton's three other companions came into the coach and sat down. Horton made the appropriate introductions, and she immediately gave Sam the same routine. He took out a notebook and wrote down her name and address. It was a case of a congressman out-ranking a secretary.

Sumners was quite an authority on agricultural problems, having studied them abroad and written for farm periodicals.

The man from Fannin, something of an agrarian himself, kept Sumners busy expounding upon his ideas and plans for improving the farm program.

As soon as they arrived in Washington they rented rooms at the old Cochran Hotel, a famous hostelry on the site of the Tower Building, where John L. Lewis at one time had his CIO headquarters.

They became inseparable friends and Sumners provided Sam with just enough touch of home to prevent the kind of nostalgia which plagues a country boy in a big town. With the opening of the Sixty-third Congress not scheduled until Monday, April 7, the date he took the oath of office, the two got acquainted with the capital.

The Washington of 1913 was quite unlike the granite and marble city of today, just as it was far different from the dusty or muddy village of Franklin Pierce's era. Its tempo was more like that of Charleston in 1875. It was a drowsy, Southern city rather than a more energetic metropolis like Philadelphia. Instead of the impressive structures which now line Constitution Avenue, in 1913 only frame and shabby brick buildings dotted a marshy, wooded terrain. "The Avenue," with its huge ramshackle residences, many leased as apartments, and unsightly business houses, was a far cry from the Pennsylvania Avenue down which the inaugural procession of John F. Kennedy and Lyndon B. Johnson moved on January 20, 1961. Mr. Rayburn remembered the one streetcar in Bonham and the clanking contraptions in Austin, Texas; hence he became accustomed to Washington's clattering transportation. Streetcars provided the people with conveyance, but the many horse-drawn vehicles and the few automobiles were distracting to one who preferred the silence of a Texas homestead. By a stretch of the imagination Rayburn might have been able to see L'Enfant's blueprint of the orderly and well-planned Washington, but the architecture was unborn. The city of 1913 may have been unlike that of 1961 but the climate was the same—a humidity that made the cold winters intolerable and the summers debilitating. While Mr. Sam continued to be awed by the historical connotations of Washington, he always longed for that cool breeze rustling through his beloved hackberry trees, the cadence of the locusts, and the sweet smell of freshly-cut alfalfa.

The well-established families, whose mansions and estates antedated the Civil War, had little respect for a transient society whose faces changed with each administration. A freshman congressman did not attract much attention in a Potomac society. In December, 1960, Mr. Sam remarked, "I really did not amount to much in those days."

The Inauguration was the biggest spectacle Sumners and Rayburn had ever witnessed. On March 4, they were out early even before the overcast cleared. It was a raw, cold day but in reality a sunshiny one to the Democrats, for it had been many years since their Party had placed an Executive in the White House. Grover Cleveland in 1893 was the last Democrat to take the oath of office. The elements may have seemed cold to the people as they pushed against the barricades to hear the professor President explain with inspiring rhetoric his "New Freedom." When Wilson, from the platform on the east portico, saw the policemen struggling to keep the mass of humanity from overrunning the coveted reserved sections where the two congressmen were huddled together for protection from the cold, he spoke out in a clear and emphatic voice, "Remove the ropes and let the people in!" In a moment the great multitude pressed forward among the dignitaries to fill the empty spaces which separated them from this man who was heralded as their spokesman.

Not since Thomas Jefferson had there been such a student of government and intellect to stand on this platform. Only Jackson and Lincoln had faced their responsibilities with such enthusiasm and positive programs. Rayburn recalled with emotion the areas needing reform to which Wilson dedicated himself on this day: 1) tariff reform which would restore America to a place in world commerce and a realistic tax on incomes; 2) a banking and currency system; 3) an industrial system that would offer greater opportunities to labor and would not exploit natural resources; 4) greater agricultural activities; 5) development of waterways and reclamation of untended forest and waste land; 6) safeguarding the health of the nation through sanitation laws, pure food laws, and laws determining conditions of labor. Rayburn remembered also those concluding utterances, especially since he figuratively clasped hands with the new President and pledged a dedication to a legislative program which resembled his own:

> "This is not a day of triumph; it is a day of dedication. Here muster, not the forces of party, but the forces of humanity. Men's hearts wait upon us; men's lives hang in the balance; men's hopes call upon us to say what we will do. Who shall live up to the great trust: Who dares fail to try? I summon all honest men,

> all patriotic, all forward-looking men, to my side. God helping me, I will not fail them, if they will but counsel and sustain me!"

This was the beginning of Rayburn's admiration for Woodrow Wilson, in his judgment the best trained mind of the eight Presidents he knew. He was Rayburn's conception of the scholar President. On December 27, 1960, he spent an afternoon reminiscing about the Presidents with whom he had served, and he had a great deal to recall about this man Wilson. One thing that appealed to Rayburn was his indomitable will which would not submit to political bosses like Jim Smith. His vision and originality, too, made him a leader to be respected.

Since Sam was at home running for Congress he had not had the opportunity to attend the Democratic Convention of 1912, when Wilson was nominated. Yet the reports of that Convention continued to stir his imagination. Speaker Champ Clark had led on nineteen ballots and had a majority on nine ballots, but not the two-thirds required in those days. However, says Rayburn, if Mitchell Palmer, who later became the Attorney-General, had withdrawn Wilson's name, as Wilson's telegram instructed, Clark might have won. But he kept quiet and ignored the request; thus occurred one of the quirks in history which turned out for the best, observed Sam Rayburn.

But not until years later did Rayburn change his views about Wilson the man:

"I had always thought that Mr. Wilson was a very cold, frigid individual. William C. Adamson, Chairman of the Interstate and Foreign Commerce Committee, took me to meet him. He had heavy glasses and he looked at you through rather large gray eyes. Wilson had the longest face, from lock down to chin, that I have ever seen, what you would call a horse face. But, he was not an unhandsome man. And I thought he was just cold, a Presbyterian, you know. I think Wilson loved humanity in the mass, with a commoner's fervor to go out and do something for humanity. I always felt, though, that individuals bothered him."

At a dinner party one evening years after Wilson's death, Rayburn was sitting next to Wilson's daughter (William Gibbs McAdoo's widow), who gave an entirely different version. "You were never more misinformed in your life about a man," she said. "We had more fun together. When he would come home from his office we'd go to having fun. He and I used to get up on the floor and we'd dance and sing, and he said that when he got out of the Presidency he was going in for vaudeville. One day he came in reading an article in the newspaper on the Presidency, just giving him 'Hail, Columbia' and Mrs. Wilson said, 'Woodrow, I can't stand it; don't read anymore.' And he kept on reading down to the bottom of it and he remarked, 'That's what they said about Abraham Lincoln.' "

Thus Rayburn's earlier conception of the President, who was already something of his ideal, was enriched by an accidental seating arrangement that put him next to the late President's daughter. He might have found this interpretation in books but they could never have impressed him as did this personal touch. People's testimonies impressed Rayburn far more than scholarship.

Rayburn made friends readily. He had already met Martin Littleton, who had been a neighbor of his father in the Clinch River Valley. According to Joseph Alsop and Robert Kintner, Littleton, a successful advocate and Tammany congressman, was a son of the elder Rayburn's close friend. He showed the young Rayburn around the city and invited him to his hotel room to watch the inaugural parade, an invitation which Sam greatly appreciated, since he could now escape from the penetrating wind. A prolonged outing on a cold day, even then, gave him discomfort because of a sensitive skin and a slight baldness. His once wavy, dark brown hair was already vanishing.

Littleton wasted no time in his indoctrination; he gave Sam some good practical advice, urging him to seek a place on the House Committee on Interstate and Foreign Commerce. He talked to Judge Adamson, Chairman of the Committee, and John Nance Garner, who was on the Ways and Means Committee and had been around Congress for ten years. It was really John Nance Garner who was responsible for Rayburn's appointment. He made a strong case for his Texas colleague in pointing out that Rayburn came to Washington not as a green congressman but with the equivalent experience of a governor, citing his achievements in the Texas House as evidence. He became a member of this Committee on June 3, 1913, and later its Chairman. Judge Adamson recalled that Rayburn was very prompt and rarely missed a meeting, frequently staying over for hours to work. Rayburn reciprocated by recollecting that Adamson ran the Committee smoothly.

An interesting sidelight was the arrival of Alben W. Barkley (D., Ky.) on the Committee scene just a step ahead of Rayburn. Although they entered Congress at the same time, Barkley gained seniority on a sort of technicality by being elected to the Committee, instead of being appointed; and for years Barkley, Rayburn's close friend, always stood in his way. Sam joked that he stepped on Alben's heels for years. If Barkley had not moved over into the Senate, perhaps Rayburn would never have become Chairman at all. Hence he might never have moved up into the position of Speaker, because it was his leadership in the Interstate and Foreign Commerce Committee that gave him the opportunity to achieve his reputation for guiding some very significant legislation through Congress.

In these early days he began an orderly life, from which he did not deviate. He liked a rigid schedule and routine which made him the efficient legislator he was. Not until he became Majority Leader and Speaker did he deviate materially from his schedule. He always was an early riser, who took exercise before breakfast. Then, before going to his office he took a long walk, a practice he continued through the years. About this practice thirty-five years later he said:

"There is a nice big circle out there in front of the Library of Congress and Supreme Court Building—three times around is a good two miles. I used to walk on Washington streets but they got too crowded. I now prefer an early morning stroll in front of the Capitol before the tourists and congressmen begin arriving." Hence he came to work charged with energy.

In these early days his first office was in the old Malthy Building. A short time later Garner invited Rayburn to move to his office in the House Office Building, since Garner's wife (his secretary) did most of their work at home. Here Rayburn remained until an addition was made to the House Office Building. Sumners drew an office next to Sam's and he was frequently the victim of Rayburn's practical jokes. "Spec" Horton reported that there was a large closet in Garner's office in which he kept "refreshments":

"He had many bottles in it—some in glass and some in foreign designs like unto which I had never seen—some in little crock jars with funny little stoppers, some green liquids and some amber, etc. Mr. Garner would come to the office late in the afternoon with some of his many cronies and with much bantering and jesting, just like school boys, they would 'strike a blow for liberty.'"

He also reported that Garner would always "sweeten his refreshments" with "branch water." Horton added, facetiously, "I got to believe that Liberty was safe as long as there was anything in the closet—and it was never empty. Liberty evidently was an elusive thing and must constantly be guarded." It was here that the idea of the "Board of Education" was conceived. Some years later, under the Speakerships of Longworth, Garner, and Rayburn, it was referred to as a small conference room where problems were settled under friendly cirumstances. While reference is made to "liquid refreshments," the prevailing atmosphere was that of dignity and moderation.

At his office Rayburn spent his mornings answering mail, going on errands for constituents, and attending committee meetings. When he was ready to work on a bill he would say to Horton, "Get your pencil and make some notes." He would then stroll back and forth across the office dictating and redictating. Then would follow the typing of the notes and Rayburn's revisions. However, the secretary recalled that most of the typing on the Stock and Bond bill, for example, was done by a typist in the Committee on Interstate and Foreign Commerce.

In the afternoons he was on the House floor attentive to the business of legislation. In the evenings he retired to his abode, where, for example when he stayed at the Cochran Hotel, he frequented the lobby to play dominoes—never poker—or to strike up conversation with older associates. Here he profited much from the experiences of men like Cordell Hull, who in his *Memoirs* many years later referred to Rayburn's capacity, statesmanship, parliamentary skill, intense patriotism, and teamwork. Though Rayburn was an inveterate after-dinner conversationalist, he knew when to "hit the hay" as he frequently phrased it: "I don't want my ole mule to have to drag both the plow and me around the turn-row tomorrow." Nine hours in bed was always his need. Seven o'clock was the usual time for rising.

About a month after the Inauguration, Wilson appeared before a joint session of Congress, an unprecedented procedure. Not since 1796, before Thomas Jefferson in 1801, had a President so crossed over the line separating the White House and Capitol Hill. Years later Rayburn said that this was the college president coming out in Wilson in wanting to talk to his faculty on university problems. The address dealt with the tariff as he asked for free competitive enterprise, the reduction of duties from forty to twenty-six per cent to direct American energies toward the markets of the world. The fact that the Eisenhower Administration accepted this formula years later implies something of Wilson's foresight.

In response to the President's request, Oscar Underwood of

Alabama, Chairman of the Ways and Means Committee, fathered a bill which ultimately became the Underwood Tariff Act, that reduced the tariffs of the Payne-Aldrich legislation. The whole tariff question was bitterly debated and Rayburn maintained a difficult silence. He listened with great interest to a topic on which he had done both research and previous debating. It had been one of the planks in his platform. Finally on May 6, violating his own advice to freshmen congressmen that they should hold back awhile, he asked to be heard. Years later he explained that he had not actually broken one of his own principles because he was prepared, so the fact that he had been in Congress for only three months was not relevant. This maiden speech enlarges upon his July, 1912, utterances and lays the foundation upon which he built about a dozen significant pleas for trade agreements in the years ahead. This speech, though inspired primarily by his interest in the tax provision of the Underwood measure, anticipates Rayburn's connection with regulatory legislation:

> "Mr. Chairman, as a new Member of this great body I, of course, feel that I should have regard to some extent for the long-established custom of this House, which in a measure demands that discussion of questions shall be left in the main to the more mature members from the standpoint of service, but on the other hand, I feel that as a representative and commissioned spokesman of more than two hundred thousand citizens of the Fourth Congressional District of Texas I should be allowed to break, in a measure, whatever of this custom remains, and exercise my constitutional right to speak my sentiments on this floor and refuse to be relegated to that lockjawed ostracism to some extent typical of the dead past."

With this introduction he proceeded to discuss the business for which the President had called Congress into an "extraordinary session"—"to revise the tariff and to provide revenue for the support and maintenance of the Government." Again, as in his speeches during the Congressional campaign, Rayburn discussed inequities in levying taxes for protection rather than to provide revenue for the Government. He firmly established his Party's opposition to a "system of protective tariff built up under the Republican misrule" which had worked "to make the rich richer and the poor poorer." The Republican doctrine, which he believed was designed to protect American industries from foreign competition by establishing prohibitive tariff walls, had been censured by the electorate. The philosophy of Jefferson and Jackson had been called back to place the leadership "in the hands of the clean and matchless Woodrow Wilson." He praised the Baltimore Convention in its selection of Wilson and revealed his enduring faith in the Democratic Party's decisions. "Men who came from every walk of life, and who were fresh from the people, who knew their hopes and their aspirations, their wants, and their sufferings, they placed at the head of the Party and as spokesman for the Party a man whom they believed had the great heart and mind that could interpret the inarticulate longings of suffering humanity." He portrayed the Democratic Party as being on the side of these masses and the Republican Party as on the side of the classes who would oppress them.

After paying his respects to the new President, he referred to the "stainless, able, and peerless Oscar Underwood as Majority Leader and Chairman of the powerful Committee on Ways and Means," who was the guiding genius behind the tariff bill. Rayburn's praise of Underwood included a reference to him as Presidential timber.

This young Congressman sounded a warning to "the gentlemen on the other side of the chamber . . . who by reason of their broken pledges and unkept promises to the American people" had reduced themselves to an opposition party only.

> "A panic may come at any time, but it is my deliberate judgment" [he said] "that this bill [Underwood tariff] will be no more responsible for any panic that should come than it was the cause of the panic of 1907, which came not after a reduction of the tariff, but came amid the prosperous times of protection about which our Republican friends talk so much. The Republicans talk about the hard deal the producer is getting in this bill. I would call their attention to the fact that when they were in power they put hides of the producer on the free list, but they were too good to the rich manufacturer to put the shoes that he manufactures and sells on the free list. This Democratic tariff bill leaves hides on the free list and also puts shoes that the American consumer must buy to protect the feet of himself and his children on the free list. The Republican Party was willing, according to their argument, to do an injustice to the producer of

hides, but was not willing to make a corresponding reduction in the shoes for the consumer. This eternal Republican solicitation for the American manufacturer makes me tired, willing and anxious to take that small rich class under its protecting wing, but unwilling at all times to heed the great chorus of sad cries ever coming from the large yet poor class, the American consumer."

In his plea for the justness of the Underwood bill he paid his respects to the intelligence of the common people and their ability to see through Republican deceit and propaganda that would destroy the proposed legislation.

Sam Rayburn concluded his address by setting forth his concepts of a tariff and his own ideals as a lawmaker:

"Mr. Chairman, I am one of those Democrats who believe that the only reason for the levy of a tariff is to raise revenue to defray the expenses of the Government; and when the time comes that money to defray the expenses of the Government can be raised from the income tax and other legitimate sources, then free trade should come in its stead. And along this line I advocate a Federal inheritance tax. To me this is a just tax and easy to pay. When a man by inheritance comes into a large fortune out of no effort on his own part and only by accident of birth, accumulated by his ancestry under a Government which protected him in his property rights, I believe he should be willing to pay some of it as a tribute to the agency that protected his ancestry in the accumulation. . . .

"Mr. Chairman, I came to this body a few weeks ago with childlike enthusiam and confidence. It has always been my ambition since childhood to live such a life that one day my fellow citizens would call me to membership in this popular branch of the greatest lawmaking body in the world. Out of their confidence and partiality they have done this. It is now my sole purpose here to help enact such wise and just laws that our common country will by virtue of these laws be a happier and a more prosperous country. I have always dreamed of a country which I believe this should be and will be, and that is one in which the citizenship is an educated and patriotic people, not swayed by passion and prejudice, and a country that shall know no

East, no West, no North, no South, but inhabited by a people liberty loving, patriotic, happy, and prosperous, with its lawmakers having no other purpose than to write such just laws as shall in the years to come be of service to human kind yet unborn."

After hearing the favorable comments on the tariff speech, the Dallas *Times Herald* on May 10 was quite complimentary about the man from Bonham. He was depicted as "a comer." The *State Topics*, however, expanded the concept by adding:

> *Times Herald* is mistaken. Sam is not a comer, but a goer. He has already come. Yes, Samuel has arrived. But he's not a goer. That gives the suggestion Sam is on the toboggan. Sam is like the Reno cowboy who exclaimed after the Jeffries-Johnson fight: "You bet I can come back, for I ain't ever been away."

The Sherman *Sentinel* called attention to his praise for Wilson and Underwood. The paper noted with enthusiasm the manner in which he hauled the Republicans over the coals for having fooled the people into believing they were getting protection on their raw products, "stealing it back from them on the manufactured products." The editorial concluded with this word of encouragement:

> Go to it, Sammie, we're wid you. It seems to us that the Honorable Sam was tinctured just a little bit with stand-patism before going to Washington but never again can one accuse the Honorable Sam of pusilanimous inclinations along this line. Get you some more adjectives and stay with them.

Not every action of Sam Rayburn, however, met with approval in his home state. From the beginning to the end of his career he encountered both silent and open opposition because of his head-on collision with issues and straightforward way of expressing himself. This maiden address was considered by some as strictly political. For example, the reference to "the clean and matchless hands of Woodrow Wilson" provoked the following editorial comment from the *Texas Republic* of May 17:

> That speech should be good for two post offices placed at the bestowal of the Honorable Sam in the Fourth Congressional District, and Woody should see that he gets the two appointments. Parrot-like performances are worthy of some reward.

A few years later the Dallas *Morning News* picked up the chant of anti-Rayburn sympathizers and harangued him to the end of his career, with only a few "praises" here and there.

Sam's conscientiousness about his job and that characteristic serious expression might have led some of his older colleagues to consider him a drudge, with no soul for fun. The Farmersville *Times*, May 5, picked up a news item from the Sunday Houston *Post*, which will discount such beliefs and will shed some light on his extracurricular life:

> Representative Sam Rayburn and Representative Hatton Sumners, the two bachelor members of whom the Texas delegation is very proud, bachelor congressmen being at a right good premium, were among the guests at a box party given by Senator Ollie James and Mrs. James in honor of their house guest, Miss Nancy O'Donahough, of Philadelphia.

The box party was not a new experience to one from a rural section of Texas. He had done a great deal of talking about the weather and politics with his feminine constituents while enjoying a leg of fried chicken and a slab of his favorite dessert—fresh coconut cake.

Although he did not have a passion for vaudeville, as did Woodrow Wilson, he found this early nineteenth-century entertainment amusing; however, Sam Rayburn, according to Bernice Carleton, had no ear whatever for music. She had played the violin for him during his Congressional campaign and tried to open his soul to music appreciation, but frankly admitted that she failed. "I do not recall even hearing him whistle a tune," she said. Of course, Rayburn enjoyed attending the social functions in the Flag Springs church, also a community gathering place, and participated in the singing. He also went with the young people to the homes where there was an organ and sang, but he was attracted more by the opportunity to be with people than to show off any musical talents.

The Chautauqua appealed to Rayburn because of its educational value. One of W. M. Scott's daughters (the author's aunt), and a girl friend remembered very pleasantly an evening in 1914 when Sam escorted them to such a program at Ladonia, Texas. They observed that Rayburn liked Chautauquas for their emphasis upon public speaking.

It may come as a surprise to many that Sam continued to be quite a baseball player after leaving college. Though lacking the talent of his brother who pitched professionally, Sam could play the outfield with the speed and skill of a "bush leaguer." The Fort Worth *Record*, June, 1913, carried a story on the annual game between the Democrats and Republicans in the House. He was referred to as "a ball-tosser of renown." The game was played "for sweet charity's sake."

Even after his retirement from active participation in Congressional baseball, his passion for the game continued. The number of autographed baseballs on his desk told part of the story of his activities and interests at Griffith Stadium. His arm never got too stiff to toss out the opening ball to send the Senators off to a good start, nor his legs too stiff for him to stand hopefully during the seventh inning stretch. The old adage about Washington, D.C.,—"First in war, first in peace, but last in the American League"—never made him lose faith in his team or interest in the national pastime.

Only his love of fishing surpassed that of baseball, and this was the sport which became his specialty in later years after he decided he was too old for golf. Whether he sought the big ones off the Atlantic coast, or the catfish in Lake Texoma, this recreation satisfied his craving for solitude and relaxation.

Mention of Rayburn's extracurricular life will prove only one thing—he had some diversion. But he devoted most of his waking hours to the business of legislation and keeping abreast of the thinking in the White House. With the tariff problem temporarily behind, he awaited the President's next legislation—a tax bill.

After setting in motion legislation to provide for tariff reform, President Wilson turned to an old idea, the income tax, which was related to the total fiscal problem. During Grover Cleveland's second Administration, provision had been made for such a tax, but it had been declared unconstitutional by one vote. The Democrats had been unsuccessful during this long period in securing the necessary amendment to validate the provision for such a levy. On February 25, the Underwood-Simmons Act created the graduated income plan. Since Rayburn in his campaign for Congress had made a strong plea for this tax, he threw support behind the Underwood-Simmons measure.

Wilson next proposed revolutionary revisions of the currency and banking system, efforts which culminated in the creation of the Federal Reserve system. He initiated this legislation by appearing before a joint session of Congress on June 23, 1913. Mr. Rayburn remembered the Washington weather on this day more than the President's message—the heat and depressing humidity. He recalled in general that the Chief Executive was quite aggressive in pursuing each campaign pledge to the American people. He also approached the problems of the farmer to secure the Federal Farm Loan Act and asked for legislation to give labor an eight-hour day.

Rayburn's major interest during the spring and summer of 1913 was his Stock and Bond bill, which he revised many times after consultation with fellow committee members to remove the objectionable portions. Some of his trouble came from the White House. His secretary remembered a dinner at the home of Senator Joseph W. Bailey, to which he, Sam, and Congressman Buchanan of Texas were invited. After the meal, in the study, the Senator asked Sam if he would be able to get his bill through the current session. Sam reported the "static from the White House"; however he refrained from calling the President's name.

Woodrow Wilson was quite interested in the Stock and Bond bill. One time, reported Horton, the President's secretary, Joseph Tumulty, telephoned Rayburn's office to find out if the Congressman could have a meeting with him. When Tumulty learned that Rayburn was in Texas, he asked whether there was someone else who could discuss the bill. Horton stated that since he had typed and read it several times he could meet with the President. He reported that Wilson was satisfied with his explanation. The bill, however, was destined to wait for a period before there was any action on it.

In his campaign for Congress, Rayburn had declared against subsidies for shipping; hence he supported vigorously the President's view that the granting of exemptions to shipping companies using the Panama Canal was actually a subsidy. On March 4, 1914, the President made his appeal to Congress in person during the second session. Through the assistance of men like Rayburn, Wilson was able to live up to another pledge—the repealing of the law that gave American ships freedom from these tolls in the use of the canal. Like Wilson, Rayburn believed there should be no discrimination and that American prestige would be enhanced by fair play. As Chairman of the Subcommittee on Interstate and Foreign Relations Committee, which was scheduled to conduct hearings on Wilson's Trade Commission bill and the bill to regulate the issuance of railroad securities, Rayburn was in a position to discuss with a sense of authority the Panama question and other items relative to commerce. In a press conference April 10, 1914, he reported that he had joined the Democratic majority on the Interstate and Foreign Commerce Committee in ordering a favorable report on the bill removing the exemption of American shipping from tolls.

On January 21, 1914, the President appeared before the second session of the Sixty-third Congress asking for new antitrust legislation. Mr. Rayburn had been formulating such a bill for many months. Other bills were also promptly submitted and placed in the hopper.

Rayburn's real test, as far as his own measure was concerned, came on the evening of June 2, when he spoke for one hour in defense of his much discussed Stock and Bond bill. It was scheduled to be voted upon jointly with the Covington Trade Commission bill and Clayton Antitrust measure. His thesis was that no railroads doing business in interstate commerce should issue stocks and bonds, and place them on the market, without first securing the approval of the Interstate Commerce Commission. He was listened to attentively as he set forth three things necessary at the time for regulating railroads. 1) Greater publicity was needed in all financial transactions of railway corporations. 2) Railroad corporations should not issue stocks and bonds or other evidence of indebtedness except for certain specified purposes, and in all such instances the consent of the Interstate Commerce Commission should be secured. 3) No one should hold the position of director or officer in more than one railroad, or receive any remuneration or dividends resulting from the sale of stocks and bonds. Rayburn pointed out that he believed the railroads needed a "house cleaning" and that Congress had the constitutional right to invade the field of interstate commerce to break up the interlocking of the administration of large companies. Under the present undisciplined procedure, a director who had a controlling interest in one company could favor a company in which he had only a small stock, thus strengthening his investment. Two members of the Texas delegation—Garner and Buchanan, who cast the only negative votes—wisely recognized that Rayburn was merely re-enacting, at the national level, James Stephen Hogg's law of two decades earlier, when the Governor of Texas was denounced as a Socialist by his political opponents. Rayburn's bill passed 325 to 12, but not without Garner's pointing out that the Texas law would be abrogated. Garner perhaps also felt that there might be some basis for socialistic tendencies in this type of legislation. In anticipation of such assumptions Rayburn concluded his defense by reaffirming that the Democratic Party was not an enemy of capital or big business.

> "We know that there must be large aggregations of capital to carry on the great and growing business of the country; hence we would be more than foolish to do anything that would hinder or retard the growth of the country."

He expressed the desire for simple justice to business and for business to deal justly with the people. "No honest man," he said, "will ask more, and no man, be he honest or otherwise, may expect less."

This bill went to the Senate but was defeated. Six years later, in 1920, his measure was finally accepted almost without change, written into the Transportation Act of 1920 to become a Federal law. Rayburn attributed his success here to knowledge gained back in his home State under the tutelage of Senator Reagan, Governor Hogg, and Allison Mayfield of the Texas Railroad Commission.

Although the President could not count the Stock and Bond bill among the antitrust achievements of this second session, he did look with pride on the Clayton Antitrust Act and Federal Trade Commission Act. Nevertheless, recognizing that this freshman Congressman from Texas had distinguished himself and had rendered invaluable service to the Administration by his skillful handling of the bill in the House, he wrote the following letter, dated June 9:

> My Dear Mr. Rayburn—We have all looked on with admiration and genuine appreciation as your Stock and Bond bill has been put through the House. It seems to me you deserve a great deal of praise for your part in the matter, and I want to make my humble contribution to the congratulations which I am sure you must be receiving.
>
> Cordially and sincerely yours,
> Woodrow Wilson

His mother, on June 16, also wrote concerning the bill:

> I think it should go down in history as the greatest bill that was ever introduced by any man of your age and his first session in Congress. I feel so proud and thankful that I have raised a boy that can and will do

> things that will be an honor to his self [sic] and his people. You will never know the earnest prayers that I have sent up for your success and I feel like they are being answered. I don't think there is anything like trusting in our Savior and thanking Him for his blessing. I think the way your bill went through and the letter Wilson wrote you was the greatest boom [sic] that a man could have bestowed upon him. At least we feel that way about it.

While Rayburn was basking in the warmth of public and parental approval, trouble began on the home front. He learned very early in his career that the job of congressman was full-time. It meant not only fighting the Administration's battles in Washington, but also surviving political intrigue back home. Perhaps no other representative was ever expected to make so many campaigns for re-election. In these early years his friends were compelled to assume considerable responsibility, because his duties in Washington kept him away from his district until just before the July elections. The date of the Texas primary was often in conflict with both Congressional sessions and National Democratic Conventions. The second session of the Sixty-third did not adjourn until October 24, 1914.

Former Congressman C. B. Randell, who hoped four years hence to win the Senate post held by Morris Sheppard, had already begun sounding out public opinion as to his chances of knocking over "the young giant of Fannin County." Although he looked on the whole business as merely a warm-up "skirmish" for the battle with Sheppard, he apparently changed his mind when he sounded out the incumbent's strength.

However, Tom Perkins of Collin County, who had run a good second two years earlier, could not be dissuaded from making the man from Fannin County earn his full salary and spend a little money. Mathematically, he seemed to have a good chance since there were 11,850 votes from that first race to be divided between himself and Rayburn. But when asked by the Denison *Herald* to bring one charge against Rayburn's record and show reason for violating "the time-honored Democratic custom of rewarding a faithful public friend with a second term," he remained silent.

Realizing that Rayburn would be detained in Washington until early July, the friends of the Congressman held a meeting in Bonham to unfold the blueprint of the strategy used in the previous campaign. Similar meetings were set up in other towns to perfect the organization there before Sam's arrival.

The opposition resorted to a technique which would attract the disgruntled populace as well as those who were previously anti-Rayburn. After attacking the Administration, it distributed circulars in "dry" territories which tried to show that Rayburn had betrayed the prohibitionists. The absence of the Congressman made the whispering campaign more effective. The attack on Sam's labor record was answered by the publication of his votes in both Austin and Washington. The illness of his brother Abner, who died of typhoid fever later in the summer, prevented the Rayburn family from conducting a vigorous campaign. Rayburn made only a few speeches, but the results clearly showed that he had gained strength since his first campaign. The Chairman of the Democratic Executive Committee for the Fourth District certified his election to a second term on July 25, 1914, by 9146 votes. A report of the balloting by counties follows:

	Rayburn	*Perkins*
Collin	3625	2313
Hunt	4576	1743
Fannin	4629	1124
Grayson	3991	2703
Rains	509	301
	17330	8184

After his return to Washington for the completion of the session, he found himself overwhelmed with responsibilities of a personal and public nature. In October, 1914, he wrote his sister Kate about some of his trouble, apologizing for not corresponding:

> I hope you will forgive my long delay in writing but as I have no secretary now I am kept quite busy. I really have not had a secretary as I wanted to save that money. If you think for a moment that my campaign cost me between $1500 and $2000, and the improvements made out on the place [the new farm] over $2500, along with expenses incident to our sad bereavement last summer [Abner's death] which will necessarily fall on me, you will realize how long it takes to pay that out.

Secretaries were paid out of a gross allotment, which allowed him $125 per month. He later appointed O. L. Couch of Bonham to this position.

The Rayburn family had sold the home south of Windom and in July moved to the property one and one-half miles west of Bonham. The deed is dated July 8, 1914, when a tract of 120 acres was transferred by R. J. Abernathy to Tom Rayburn for $6000 ($3000 cash). Tom Rayburn then deeded a half interest to Sam. There are now 250 acres in the farm. On December 20, 1938, the property was deeded to Miss Lucinda Rayburn, and she willed it to Sam.

Wilson had not achieved his complete objective as far as antitrust reform was concerned, despite the fact that he had two pieces of major legislation to show for his efforts—the Clayton Antitrust Act and the Federal Trade Commission Act. Although Rayburn had successfully engineered his version of railroad reform through the House during the second session of the Sixty-third Congress, the Administration did not provide adequate guidance for it through the Senate; primarily because it was trying to muster up support for too much related legislation and there was a strong railroad lobby against it.

Though the President fell short of his objective, Rayburn remembered that he worked Congress overtime while he was in the White House. There were only six weeks between the second and third sessions of the Sixty-third, which convened December 7, 1914, and ran until March 4, 1915. On the last day of the session Rayburn recalled the great pressure as he helped push through the Cummins bill. The Federal Trade Commission, Mr. Rayburn said, was the culmination of this legislation. "I was a member of the subcommittee which drew up the bill establishing it." Since the railroads would freeze out the shipper when damages occurred, a commission was needed to make the initial carrier liable for any damage to a cargo in transit. The shipper was thus relieved of fixing responsibility. With this earlier enactment, he explained, related legislation followed.

The Cummins Act, Rayburn explained, prohibited an interstate carrier from limiting its liability in shipments of freight. Railroad exporters were incensed because the bill had been crammed through the legislative assembly line, imposing an additional burden of ten per cent upon shippers of the country. Rayburn had pointed out that the shipper gained through the legislation by being able to collect the full amount of the loss, if one occurred. It required the shipper to pay no more than he had been liable to all the time under the authorized tariffs, and the fact that he was not in all instances required to pay the full charge was due to the voluntary act of the carriers which sought to limit its liability. Rayburn felt that the Cummins bill was essential to shippers from Texas and Oklahoma because in the Southwest the limitation was considerable when figured in shipments of livestock. For example, if a man had a damage on a carload of steers worth $75 per head, he could previously collect only $10. His point was that a damaged animal was a complete loss, for it was dead, while a piece of damaged furniture was less perishable. This piece of legislation reflected the practical turn of his mind and his keen sense of responsibility to the needs of his constituents in an agrarian sector.

Sam was not a man to watch the clock or look at the calendar, but he always believed that Christmas should be spent in Bonham among those closest to him—his father and mother, brothers and sisters, and later, his nieces and nephews. But this December 25, 1914, was one he knew would not find him at his parents' fireside. He realized, that with Abner gone and his father ailing, he should be in Bonham, particularly since there were others who would have to miss the Christmas dinner. His mother's letter of January 14, 1915, reflected her disappointment:

> Well, Sam, Xmas came and went and a very sad one to me. When they began coming in I would miss Ab so much. I felt like that when you all got here and him absent knowing that he never could be here any more I felt it would almost be more than I could bear, but when Christmas Day came there were so many absent to what ever had been it didn't seem like Christmas to me and I believe I stood it better than I would if they had all been here. However, when the message came that you would not be here it nearly broke my heart. I felt then like it would add to my grief, but it seems like sometimes things work out for the best.

Matt Rayburn had a great inner strength, else one with her responsibility would have been twisted by the vicissitudes of a farmer's fortune. She snatched hope out of sorrow and passed it on to others. She believed Sam's homecoming in April would bring her greater joy than the visit at Christmas because, as she explained, she had the problem of Ab's absence, and this was one which only she alone could work out. She was delighted that

Sam planned to stop over in Tennessee to visit with "all of those old uncles and cousins." She asked him to bring Harriett Pickel home with him: "Tell her that I am still the same old Matt that I was in Tenn. living in a log house." She concluded with a homey touch in sending wishes to Mr. O. L. Couch, his secretary, ". . . tell him everytime I cook hogs feet I think of him and wish he had one."

The correspondence reveals that Sam's father and mother were both strong willed, and when they refused to heed his wishes that they not work so hard he recognized streaks of stubbornness. Once his father insisted on helping gather the corn in the heat and came down with a chill and a 104-degree temperature. A suit of clothes from Sam, a box of cigars from Jim, and $5 from Katie made him very proud, and he was soon well; but the Congressman knew his father was waiting for the next opportunity to try again to prove he was not an old man.

Sam felt alarmed when his seventy-one-year-old mother wrote about her own actions:

> . . . I can say one thing we have had the longest coldest winter and the deepest snow I've ever seen in Tex. but I went right on through all the blizzards and snow, never missed wading to the lot to milk and never had a particle of cold and was just as well as could be, but we had three or four hot days the last of Jan. that got me down. I just wilted like you had thrown hot water on a green weed but I took some medicine and quinine and was all right in a few days.

The depth of Sam's affection for his sister Lou, and the appreciation he bore her for assuming her position of responsibility and leadership in the family, is partly reflected in his letter to her February 7, 1915:

> My darling Lou,
>
> I hope you are fine and as happy as can be for you truly deserve everything that is good. You are such a dear sweet sister to us all.
>
> I am hoping that we will get through here by March 4 and I can come on home after a brief stay in Tennessee.
>
> I am sending you a little money for your little needs. When spring comes I want you to get all the nice clothes you want and will pay all your bills if I

am not at home at the time. I hope from now on to give you everything you desire and I want you to be absolutely free about things.

Your devoted brother
Sam

Later, after the mother's death and Sam's rise to prominence, Lou became his official hostess in Washington and remained so intermittently until her death in 1956. The high regard which the whole family had for her is partly revealed in their deeding the homeplace to her, because of the unselfish devotion to home and Sam's career. After William Marion Rayburn's death in 1916, she assumed an even larger role in the family. The mother did not die until 1927, but she was a source of concern to Lou with her self-reliance and frontier way of living. Her indomitable will, housed in a physical frame that could not persevere indefinitely, both baffled and irritated Lou and Sam.

During the first session of the Sixty-fourth Congress (December 6, 1915—September 8, 1916), Rayburn again submitted his bill for regulation of stock and bond issues in interstate railways. Feeling that the President would have the same enthusiasm for the bill as he did during the previous Congress, as manifested by the complimentary letter, Rayburn went to the White House to solicit support. Wilson expressed the same interest but explained that with World War I having begun on the Continent, the time was not right to push it. Picking up his hat, Rayburn spoke firmly, "Mr. President, I'm sorry, I can't go along with you," and left the White House quite abruptly.

He was by no means a "yes" man, for as he liked to say, "When two men agree on everything, one of them is doing all of the thinking." On any matter so close to his heart, he was not one to accept rebuffs or a negative answer. "I hate to take a lickin'," he remarked on many occasions. Though his victories outnumbered his defeats, he could not count his Stock and Bond bill on the credit side until 1920. The Rules Committee removed it from the calendar, together with a large number of other measures which had little opportunity for passage. However, he announced almost defiantly that he would be back at the beginning of the Sixty-fifth Congress with this very same measure, expressing the belief that it would be passed, since it provided the best means for correcting the transportation evils confronting the country.

When the appropriation for the Patent Office came up for debate on February 9, 1916, Mr. Rayburn made strenuous objection to what appeared to him an unnecessary increase. Economy in government was one of his concerns throughout his career; he was not indifferent toward the fabulous spending programs after World War II. Specifically, he could not see any justification for two new personnel at a cost of $7000 each. There was no evidence to support the need and he refused to vote for costing the Government this additional and unnecessary expense. His voting record in the Wilson years strongly indicated that he was tight-fisted in handling public funds.

Sam Rayburn frankly admitted that in these early days he was terribly inexperienced in foreign affairs because he had had little occasion to learn of the world outside his own State and section. Nevertheless, he learned quickly about America's perils in international relations. He granted that he had a natural preoccupation with setting straight the economy which had shaped the lives of those people in his own little world. He had dedicated himself especially to solving those problems plaguing the farmer and small businessman. Tariff reform, an income-tax law, a sound banking system, and conservative spending were to him logical steps toward the achievement of his goal. His admiration for the President, who shared the same views, led him to accept his Party's objectives.

Rayburn was always given to accepting on faith those whom he trusted. Since Wilson and William Jennings Bryan, the Secretary of State, were both fundamentally men of peace, he was blinded by their assurances. They preached a doctrine of pacifism, finding security in the geographical isolation of a country surrounded by two wide oceans, believing that America could be prevented from being swept into the maelstrom.

Europe had been at war since the latter part of July, 1914, and Wilson on August 4 finally issued a routine proclamation of neutrality, declaring that no citizen in this country would be permitted "to take part, directly or indirectly, in the said wars, but shall maintain a strict and impartial neutrality." The sinking of the *Lusitania* on May 7, 1915, had set off agitation for a more aggressive preparedness program, but the "Arabic" promise of August 19 by Germany temporarily appeased the President.

Rayburn's views on preparedness, however, reflected a compromise between the two prevalent positions: the idea of a large continental army against that of the largest navy in the world. In February of 1916, he explained that preparedness was one of degree:

"I think we should have a good supply of ammunition on hand. Our coast defenses should be strengthened, and the State militia increased. I know that if we are ever to need an army of any proportion that it will be a volunteer army."

At this time he could not reconcile universal military training with the American way of life. "I, therefore, favor an increase in the officers of the regular army that we may have them ready to drill and equip the volunteer force." Rayburn believed America needed an adequate navy but not the largest in the world, because he considered that the Germans had already demonstrated the superiority of the $500,000 submarine over the $20,000,000 super-dreadnought.

While he was getting orientated in strengthening America's defenses, a telegram from home brought the news that he would have to spend a part of his summer strengthening his own political fences back in the Fourth District. Andrew Randell of Sherman, the son of C. B. Randell, who had built quite a strong machine while in Congress, was attempting to drape his father's mantle about his shoulders. With Wilson still trying to put through his domestic program and the talk about preparedness, Rayburn doubted that he would be able to leave Washington for a campaign. Congress did not adjourn until September 8, 1916, six weeks after the Texas primary; however, friends back in the Fourth advised him to come home.

Randell had already campaigned for four months before the incumbent could leave Washington; and again Rayburn was forced to conduct one of his whirlwind tours of the District. Recognizing Rayburn's shortage of time, Randell promptly challenged him to a series of debates. John Marshall, also of Sherman and the ex-Speaker of the Texas House, who had succeeded A. M. Kennedy when he resigned and whom Rayburn helped nominate, tried to drag Rayburn into this type of campaign. Rayburn, noted for his shrewdness, saw through the Randell-Marshall strategy. He believed that Randell was only bluffing and was waiting for Sam to decline so that he could "proudly wave before the people his bold challenge to wordy combat and my refusal to meet him." Sam always gave the other person credit for having as much sense as he had, frankly admitting to some of his friends that Randell's strategy was good. Had he been so foolish as to rush into the debate, he would have been hopelessly tied up during the two weeks before the election, in communities where Randell had already worked rather thoroughly and he would not have had time to appear anywhere else. Thus he would have been prevented from making his own type of campaign—covering three or four towns per day accompanied by the citizens from his various headquarters.

Randell had so thoroughly "muddied the waters" that the faint of heart were predicting Rayburn might lose. He had accused Rayburn of being against child labor laws and an enemy of labor, of being an anti-prohibitionist in prohibitionist garb, of waving in his constituents' faces the "famous congratulatory letter of June 9, 1914, from the President," which, he mused, had already served its purpose in the previous campaign. Rayburn's use of the Presidential approval for his House victory on the Stock and Bond measure produced an embarrassing moment, for Randell, one of Wilson's former students at Princeton, wrote to the President of Rayburn's abuse of the correspondence. Wilson's declaration of neutrality follows:

July 11, 1916

My Dear Mr. Randell:

I learn that certain things I have from time to time said in praise of the work of Mr. Rayburn in the House have been interpreted to mean that I was opposed to your nomination. It is hardly necessary to assure that this is an *unjustifiable construction*. I do not feel at liberty to express a preference in *any Congressional fight and would certainly take no such position when a friend like yourself was involved.*

Cordially and sincerely yours,
Woodrow Wilson

Mr. Andrew L. Randell
Sherman, Texas

The question of Rayburn's stand on child labor laws had been the subject of much discussion in his correspondence since February. His defense followed this reasoning: Texas had a child labor law superior to that proposed by the Federal Government, and he deemed such controls the function of the State, a position consistent with that in other instances where State laws seemed in conflict with new Federal proposals:

"If these people expect me to vote to abrogate every law of my State and every right of my State to make laws on subjects entirely under the police regulations of my State in order to get their votes, I am very candid to say that I will not get their votes, as I have some principles of government firmly fixed in my make-up that I will not surrender in order to get anybody's vote or any office within the gift of the people. I am, and have always been, an earnest advocate of child labor legislation, but when forty-four States of the Union have child labor laws that are enforced by local authorities, I can see no reason for the Federal Government to force its hand into our local affairs." Governmental interference, he believed, would follow the pattern of Federal officers moving into the states to see that the laws were enforced, and States' Rights would be jeopardized.

He frankly states that there was, however, a very fundamental point in the Child Labor bill, as proposed, which he did not like. It provided that no article or product which any child sixteen years old or under had helped produce could be shipped across a state line. This provision seemed essential in large cities where the sickly children of the slums were exploited; but for Texas, where the families worked together in the clean out-of-doors gathering their crops for the financial and physical benefit of all, it was a liability. The bill as written put the burden on father and mother to pick their own cotton, for example, with hired help unavailable and prohibitive in cost. The boys, Rayburn feared, would be freed from such responsibilities as he deemed essential to prevent them from becoming tramps and completely worthless. He remembered his own past and was of the opinion that the farm work was beneficial.

Randell made a serious mistake when he brought up this whole question, for it gave Rayburn an opportunity to compare his own background of hard work with that of a man who knew only the sheltered life of Sherman, Washington, and Princeton.

Farmers in the Fourth enjoyed Rayburn's wit at the expense of the city boy: "Not an hour of toil ever soiled his silken palms, so that he doesn't know the necessity of labor, nor realize the good effects of keeping boys employed." Sam Rayburn, aware that the man in overalls had not yet developed an affection for Randell's type, told his own "Horatio Alger" story quite effectively.

Rayburn also made an impression in explaining his vote for the Eight-Hour Government Office Law. Randell had favored a shorter day. Again Rayburn talked the language of his constituents:

"I worked fourteen to sixteen hours a day in the hot sun on a Fannin County farm, and I voted to make these white-handed, bay-windowed gentry work at least eight hours a day under an electric fan, and sitting on easy cushioned seats."

Rayburn's affinity for work had already been widely publicized in the District. Farmers were kindly disposed toward a congressman who wore overalls and a jumper and consistently helped harvest the hay and gather the corn. To get a word with Rayburn when the corn was still in the field, many a constituent had to throw a few ears in the wagon himself while conversing. Only one accustomed to the heat could talk politics with Mr. Sam this time of the year.

Since the labor record was injected into the campaign, the National Legislative and Information Bureau released on June 29, 1916, a certified report on Rayburn's voting in the Sixty-third and Sixty-fourth Legislatures on every issue where labor was involved. The report gave the dates, bills, Rayburn's vote, and labor's attitude on each. The only essential disagreement between the two was on legislation relative to this child labor question. Rayburn then proceeded to examine the labor record of both C. B. and Andrew Randell to produce what he considered uncomplimentary results.

The prohibition question continued to be discussed because Rayburn, a "pro," had been elected Speaker of the Texas House by the "antis." He was again accused of having favored the anti-prohibitionists in his committee appointments. Although Randell and John Marshall seemed to be "whipping a dead horse," they raised the point that he had voted against submitting the prohibition issue to the Federal Government. Rayburn's thinking here, however, was consistent with that relative to child labor. The enforcement of the liquor traffic he considered a local and state problem; hence he did not want Federal policing when local authorities could handle their business. When Rayburn made much of the fact that C. B. Randell had been an ardent "anti," this issue also lost some of its glamor, because the voters had difficulty visioning Andrew Randell as a prohibitionist in view of the father's thinking.

As the rebuttals indicate, he was versatile at turning all issues to his own advantage. His amazing consistency and compatibility with the agrarian mind led to his construction of an impregnable fortress. They remembered that he too had once been an underdog and knew that he was on their side. Yet he did not lose his perspective and get carried away in a crusade. He did not, according to David Cohn, think that a man was a saint because he wore overalls and chewed Brown Mule, or was a devil because he was tailored by Savile Row and smoked Coronas. However, there were more voters in the Fourth District in 1916 who chewed Brown Mule than smoked Coronas, as Sam well knew. He won his third term by a plurality of 4500 votes.

After he had forwarded his "Thank you" letters to the papers, he promptly returned to Washington since the first session of the Sixty-fourth still had another six weeks of work ahead. Even after the September 8 adjournment, however, there was little relaxation for a dedicated Party man like Sam, with Wilson seeking re-election in November.

Despite the eminence of their leader, the Democrats had no assurance they would be returned to power. Wilson came into the White House as a minority President with only forty-two per cent of the popular vote, the balance having been divided between Teddy Roosevelt and William Howard Taft when they had their split. The Democrats controlled Congress for the first time in sixteen years, but unaccustomed to governing, they did not know how to pull together, the bitterness in the Baltimore Convention having been transplanted to Washington. Wilson and his followers' complacency about preparedness alarmed the American people, so the approaching election brought them to grips with the unrest on the home front. Wilson had a good record on domestic achievements, with defeat on only two major issues—Rayburn's Stock and Bond bill and the law forbidding children under fourteen from being employed, this latter statute having been declared unconstitutional by the Supreme Court. But it was the unfinished business of the international situation which was to affect the popular mind in the 1916 Election.

Charles Evans Hughes went to bed thinking he was to be the new President, but by the next morning the California vote had come in to give Wilson a slight lead of twenty-three electoral votes. He trailed in the popular vote by more than half a million.

Rayburn went back to Washington in early December for the opening of the second session of the Sixty-fourth, which ran until March 4, 1917. Though Sam was pleased with Wilson's victory, he saw an ominous sign in the loss of the popular vote. He had already expressed his concern over the war in Europe and had said, "The time is coming when a self-respecting country will have to fight."

For several months Speaker Champ Clark had been watching Sam Rayburn. About a week before the Christmas holidays, when there was a lull in activities, he asked Rayburn to come to see him. It was a case of an older man's giving some fatherly advice. Clark was quite blunt. He told Rayburn that he had a tremendous potential and if he stayed around long enough he might possibly achieve the highest rung in the House; but, Clark explained, he had come to Washington with definite weaknesses. The Speaker recognized Rayburn's native talents—shrewdness, dedication, friendliness, and energy—but told him frankly that he did not know enough. Clark advised Rayburn to do some reading. He recommended the biographies of the Presidents, including the Adamses, Washington, Jefferson, Polk, McKinley, and others. Clark recognized that Rayburn had an alert mind but needed some background. Years later Rayburn said, "This was some of the best advice anyone ever gave me."

On December 15, which Speaker Clark announced as unanimous-consent day, Mr. Rayburn, showing that dogged persistence for which he became famous, rose to argue for the consideration and passage of a bill relative to the issues of securities by common carriers. The bill was partially related to his own Stock and Bond bill, which had been stricken from the calendar for this Congress. He pointed out that the need for railroad legislation was so pressing that they could not wait any longer for the Newlands Committee to report. This Committee, Rayburn believed, was set on resisting needed changes, and on January 9, he accused the Committee of deliberately postponing their report to kill needed legislation. The whole concept of a Newlands Commission was shocking to his States' Rights views, for the individual states would be prevented from controlling their own transportation matters. In referring to the December debate he said, "They tried here the other day to lead in this Trojan horse in its worst form." In his judgment, it was only "chloroform" to put everyone to sleep while the individual states had their rights stolen.

During the latter part of February, Senator James R. Clarke of Arkansas died at the age of sixty-two. Clarke and Rayburn, residents of the Cochran Hotel and frequent companions at the dinner table, had been great friends. The loss to Rayburn was considerable, for the Senator had given the younger man some valuable lessons in practical politics. He taught him how to defend principles where the opposition was fierce. Clarke also gave Rayburn a rather fundamental conception of the public servant —that he should be a leader of his people and not a follower. Rayburn also acknowledged another indebtedness to Clarke: he taught the younger congressman that a man should express his love to his family and friends. Rayburn remembered this through the years and from time to time reminded his colleagues that a person who loved people would find no place in his heart for hate.

Some of Rayburn's most interesting reminiscences of the first four years in Congress were those about several key men during the Wilson Administration. For example, he thought Henry Cabot Lodge was a little jealous of Wilson because the former had been the scholar in politics before 1913, and now another scholar had come along. Rayburn regretted that Wilson did not take Lodge with him to Europe a few years later to help work out the League of Nations which he considered the only hope at the time for continued peace in the world, just as he thought the United Nations was the only hope in present times. This jealousy might have been suppressed, Rayburn thought, under different circumstances.

The Colonel House—Wilson friendship seemed rather strange to him:

"This shy little Texan [Ed House] had developed the reputation of being a setter-up and puller down of Texas governors, but he had no selfish purpose to serve, merely seeking to be of service to President Wilson. He got in trouble finally when he played the role of a prime minister in trying to reach some far-reaching agreements when Wilson returned to America."

About William Jennings Bryan, he stated:

"I visited in his office a time or two. I always doubted that Bryan was equipped to be Secretary of State. He had a massive brain and all that but whether he ever buckled down or went to the bottom of things I am not sure. Joseph Weldon Bailey, the biggest brain man I have ever known, said that Bryan was so anxious to speak that he started talking before he got to the bottom of a question."

Rayburn thought William Gibbs McAdoo, Secretary of the Treasury, was an able citizen, although ambitious, and perhaps too desirous of being President for his own personal happiness. Rayburn had a way of recognizing facts, and he saw no hope for the fulfillment of McAdoo's ambitions because of his closeness to Wilson.

The greatest personality of this era, to Rayburn, was, of course, the President himself. Had war not interrupted his creativity on domestic and social issues, he believed America might have moved forward more rapidly toward some of the ideals voiced by later Democratic Administrations.

☆ VIII ☆

War and Peace

THE first session of the Sixty-fifth Congress (April 2–October 6, 1917) was one Sam Rayburn remembered particularly well because of the war clouds hovering on the horizon. Wilson had delivered another epic-making Inaugural Address, a message charged not with the zeal of a reformist, but with the prayerfulness of a tired and mellow statesman who felt an impending tragedy: "I pray God I may be given the wisdom and the prudence to do my duty in the true spirit of this great people. . . ." A man with Wilson's background and charitable instincts could not easily make the emotional adjustment necessary to meet the impending crisis. Germany, feeling that she could win the war before America could mobilize her industrial might and put an army in Europe, had now become bolder in her submarine attacks.

At three o'clock in the morning of April 6, Rayburn remembered, he was called out of bed: "Wilson was the most serious-looking man I ever saw with the haunting appearance of death on his lined face." He spoke in pained eloquence, weighing each word and measuring every statement. Rayburn was tense also and could hear his own pulse, for he already pictured the agony in the homes of the Fourth District—the farm boys would turn their backs on their chores and the store clerks put aside the routine of their jobs. But he said, "It was the only decision that

America could make with a madman like the Kaiser on the loose."

The second session (December 3, 1917—November 21, 1918) was preoccupied with winning the war. The legislation in which Sam Rayburn played the largest role was that related to Federal control of railroads, war-risk insurance, and vocational rehabilitation. The bill debated February 22, relative to the railroads, had three important provisions: 1) compensation to the owners; 2) power to determine rates and the delegated authority to exercise this power; and 3) the time after the war at which the railroads should be returned to their owners. Rayburn clearly stated that the President should be granted every authority to expedite transportation, but he did not want to establish in wartime an economic policy that would prevail after hostilities had ceased. Economic policies, he affirmed, should be discussed in calm, when men were not under stress. It is only "fair to us who do not believe in Government ownership of railroads and other socialistic doctrines" that we should not be saddled with prolonged war policies when the country is trying to get back into a peacetime routine. He opposed the indefinite tenure policy of Government ownership because it established one contrary to the philosophy of free private enterprise. It also, he said, placed a dangerous power in the hands of a President, whoever he might be. He would have 1,700,000 railroad employees looking directly to him for leadership and he could, if he were of a mind to, direct their interests into political channels to perpetuate his Administration.

Mr. Rayburn was given credit for the authorship of the War Risk Insurance Act which provided servicemen of the First and Second World Wars with insurance up to $10,000. This was a new venture in soldier legislation because soldiers, their widows and orphans, received hospitalization and compensation. Though there were some later amendments to the law, the original legislation was sponsored by Rayburn. In later years, when the need arose, Rayburn was instrumental in the continuation of the concept to provide adequate hospital facilities for the care and treatment of veterans for non-service disabilities or diseases as well as for disabilities incurred in service; education or training of servicemen; loans for purchase or construction of homes, farms, and business property at a low rate of interest; compensation and pensions.

However, as in any piece of major legislation like this, there were others who shared in its final passage. Rayburn explained that legislating required team play and not grandstand antics. However, after the Republicans gained control of the House in the election of 1918, and held control until 1930, Mr. Rayburn said that no Republican dominated committee ever allowed a Democrat's name to appear on a bill, even though he introduced it. In his campaign speeches he told his constituents that he had his name replaced by that of a Republican's time after time. This was his answer to those opponents who accused him of not doing anything.

During the war, the Interstate Commerce and Foreign Affairs Committee had jurisdiction legislation relating to war risks, soldiers' compensation, and insurance for service men; thus Mr. Rayburn, because of his identification with the original bill and his membership on the Committee, was charged with the responsibility of handling such war measures on the floor. The Insurance bill, debated on May 18, 1918, was his most significant accomplishment of the year.

There was a bill up for debate on June 8 which provided for a Federal Board for Vocational Education. In the discussion Rayburn set forth his interpretation of rehabilitation:

> "My opinion of this legislation and the legislation in other countries upon this subject has been that it is to rehabilitate—to prepare a man mechanically, as near as we can, to what he was before—and not go into all kinds of professions, not try to teach a man to be a doctor or a lawyer or a preacher, something that will take three or four or more years out of his life, and probably will not be according to the idea we are trying to put into this legislation."

He was opposed to wasting vast sums of money and time trying to train people to be something which they could not become, simply because the money seemed available. He insisted that rehabilitation and re-education when related to a previous way of life would better insure the individual's adjustment and happiness.

In late July, 1918, Mr. Rayburn again had to defend his Congressional seat, against Robert Lovelace of Fannin County. The pressures in Washington and the necessity for remaining on the job prevented his making more than a token appearance back home. But even campaigns of this sort always cost him at least fifteen hundred dollars for publicity and the expenses of some who worked for him. In these early years most of the expenses were paid by Rayburn because he had not yet won national prominence. The vote in Fannin County was favorable to Rayburn by almost five to one (5802 to 1202), with the same ratio prevailing throughout the District. Thus he was awarded a fourth term.

The second session of the Sixty-fifth Congress ended on November 21, but Congress was back in harness on December 2, 1918, for a third session. The sudden termination of hostilities on November 11 created a shift in emphasis from war to peace. The third session, lasting until March 4, 1919, Rayburn remembered as one whose interests were devoted almost entirely to reconversion. As Rayburn looked back on this Congress, he marveled at the variety of legislation. He had to make many adjustments in his attitudes but saw his own as wholesome, believing that a good congressman could not afford "to get in a rut." While he was evaluating his development he also viewed the full sweep of his own tenure in Washington, with all the different moods and circumstances. He could not keep from being impressed by the tremendous variety of legislation that was demanded by the eras in which he had lived. He said he was slightly overwhelmed by what he had seen and learned since leaving Flag Springs back in 1913.

Rayburn was never a man to run from responsibility but at the same time felt great humility as he went about his daily work. His appreciation of Wilson's dedication was tremendous.

The President had already focused the world's attention on America's idealism in his "Peace without victory" speech (January, 1917), and his actual declaration of a state of war message three months later had also stated that the United States' objective was "To make the world safe for democracy." He had further tried to put at ease the fears of defeated nations when he delivered his "Fourteen Points Speech" before Congress on January 8, 1918. On February 11, he added "Four Principles," as additional assurance.

While the President was preparing the world for a peace conference, Congress was trying to get America back on a normal economy. Mr. Rayburn's first thoughts turned to the veterans' welfare and the organization for administering their programs. By a carefully conducted investigation to get at the source of the trouble, he found the Bureau of War Risk Insurance plagued by internal dissension and inefficiency. When reconversion measures were taken, he wanted his favorite pieces of legislation to be effectively administered. He promptly opposed the Pension Office's taking over soldiers' insurance, as some were advocating. The announcement that a new head of the Bureau had been appointed and that internal affairs were more peaceful gave Rayburn the added impetus to carry his ideas to fulfillment.

On another reconversion measure, January 30, 1919, Sam Rayburn spoke with inspiration against Government control of the railroads and general interference with business, as he declared that:

> "The civilized world has just passed the supreme crisis in its history. We should make it our highest hope and our first ambition to preserve for our service men when they return a representative Republic and not a conglomerate mass of socialism and all the other isms."

In arguing against continued Government controls and pointing out the dangers, he said:

> "I fear that the trend of the times is a sinister portent for the preservation of the Government that our soldiers fought to continue. Instead of the established way of curing evils that grow up in industry by legislating to correct those evils, from many quarters the only suggestion that comes is for the Government to take over, own, and operate the industry—and every time some sick and tottering makeshift of the industry gets into the deep waters of real affairs it comes running to the Government, crying 'Take me ere I perish.'"

The packing industry, for example, he observed, came crying for the Government to "operate the allied lines of the packing industry" instead of proposing a program that would help it solve its own problems. Then the telephones and telegraphs "started screaming." Rayburn put the full responsibility for all the "desperation begging" at the feet of the railroads. But he pointed out that they had been forced into it because of the war. The conflict was over and now he wanted to return the railroads to private management:

> "Government ownership has been the football of politics everywhere. . . . If we had Government ownership of railroads there would be more political

> log-rolling by members of Congress and influential organizations to get new roads built. . . ."

He warned that we would have the stench of "pork barrel" legislation such as we have never experienced. In defense of his bill he presented historical evidence to prove that a government is incapable of managing any private enterprise without a show of extravagance, inefficiency, and incompetence. But when the House defeated his bill the determined Rayburn came back with an amendment to a related measure to fix December 31, 1919, as the deadline for transfer of ownership, instead of the previously established period that had prolonged it by another year.

While Wilson's thoughts were directed toward a peace that would be strengthened by a permanent organization, the Republican leaders were busily mending their fences to regain the power lost as a result of their Party schism. Roosevelt and Taft had terminated their feud and had joined ranks under the leadership of a new National Chairman, Will H. Hays of Indiana. Urged by his own Party members in Congress, Wilson on October 24, 1919, asked the voters for an expression of confidence. But his appeal was so full of condemnation of the "pro-war" Republican opposition that the populace refused to respond to the President. Instead they gave control of both Houses to the Republicans in the November elections.

Thus Sam Rayburn entered a new era in his career as a public servant, finding himself for the first time affiliated with a minority group. There were new faces in the Sixty-sixth Congress which assembled under the gavel of Frederick H. Gillett, a Republican from Massachusetts. The reign of Speaker Champ Clark of Missouri, which began in 1911, had come to a sudden end, and with it the decline of a Party that was not destined to elect another Speaker until 1931, when John Nance Garner of Texas was to reign briefly for two years before becoming Vice-President. After Gillett was to come Nicholas Longworth (1925–1931).

Men with less vision might have been destroyed during this extended period, but Rayburn went to Washington with a program which promised assistance to the people—those who needed the most and had been passed over for want of a spokesman. His identity with the inarticulate masses of rural folk gave him an indestructible spirit. Had he been merely a demagogue and politician he could not have survived these lean years, but he had all the markings of a statesman who possessed a stoical poise and had his values straight from the start. It was his love of America that provided the strength for survival. Clark W. Thompson of Galveston pointed out this quality in a letter dated January 4, 1961:

> . . . sometimes some very ill-informed person suggests that Mr. Sam is first of all a Democrat. To this, I would say that no one but a fool would ever question Mr. Sam's patriotism or would say that he places anything or anyone ahead of his country, except his God. First, his God; then, his country; then, those of us fortunate enough to be his neighbors; and last, himself.

Somewhere between country and neighbors he necessarily placed the Democratic Party, which was actually symbolic of his way of life, or what he termed his "crowd." On December 28, 1960, he remarked, "I have always stayed with my crowd; can I be blamed for this?"

Rayburn watched with sadness the decline of Wilson's power and health; and in reminiscing about the man, he expressed the thought that:

"Wilson was ahead of his times and if the war had not come along there was no telling what he might have achieved with his New Freedom, for he was another Franklin Roosevelt. There would perhaps not have been the Second World War either, if Wilson had put across his peace program."

Illustrative of Rayburn's perseverance was his renewal of his fight on the railroad question. Early in the first session of the Sixty-sixth, he again made a valiant effort to achieve the termination of Federal control of the railroads, an issue still unsettled. The Interstate Commerce Committee had overruled its subcommittee, of which Rayburn was a member, and reported out a bill containing two flaws, as he saw it, the provision for rate control and restricting labor's rights:

> "I do not agree with the provision in the bill for a statutory rule of rate making. I am against guaranties to railroads. . . . It seems to me that it is fundamental that when you rob the railroads of this country of the incentive of competition and service, you have taken away from the railroads the greatest incentive to perform a great public service to the people. It would also be a mistake to pass a drastic strike provision which would take in and penalize every member of the railroad brotherhoods."

Later in the debates Rayburn recognized a dangerous development in the railroad controversy. Apparently some of his colleagues had been intimidated by Samuel Gompers, who wanted the railroads to remain in Government hands for another two years. Rayburn defied such pressure groups, as he asked, "Has it come to pass in this country that the free representatives of a free people can be scared by the threat of Mr. Gompers or anyone else who represents less than five per cent of the people of the land?" He served notice that this was only one of the many measures yet to be considered by Congress to repeal war powers and get the Government out of this "expensive and socialistic business."

In his concluding remarks he referred to the Americanization law, which was an aftermath of the war, and became involved in Congressional discussion about a return to peacetime conditions. "I believe in an America for Americans," he said. "This country is too small for any man or set of men who pay allegiance to any other government or any other flag. This is no place for the man who violates our law—be he high or low, rich or poor. The anarchist and the Bolshevist shall go." He was not only sounding sentiments in Washington but those permeating men's minds back home. Rayburn was already one of the best public opinion barometers in the country.

When an amendment to the War Risk Insurance Act was being debated on September 9, 1919, Rayburn held the center of the stage because his name had become identified with the measure from the previous Congress. He was proud of the legislation and wanted to prevent its being exploited, but the Republican dominated House did not always agree with his thinking and took away much of the personal glory that he might otherwise have achieved. He was trying to resist a liberalizing which would make this insurance free for two years; this was a wedge, he feared. Human nature being what it was, he saw some conceivably asking for five years or life exemption. He had no tears for those who did not convert their term insurance at the cheap rate:

> "I am not so crazy about the Government going into business anyhow, and I never would have agreed to this insurance and the Government going into the insurance business if it had not been that we raised a draft army and we were taking men from their homes and their loved ones whether they wanted to or not. . . ."

For this reason he was willing to make it liberal but not so liberal as to take in everyone, including those who had not been in the military or naval forces during the war. The fringe groups he would exclude, but he favored increases for bonafide combat soldiers.

The Bonus bill, which was on the calendar for the second session, brought forth an abundance of political clichés from the demagogues who, he thought, inevitably got into high places when the voters reacted emotionally rather than rationally during periods of great economic stress. He was well aware that he could damage his own political career if he appeared too critical, but nevertheless, he waded into it. Rayburn made an appeal to common sense in his objection to the way the bill was written. He felt that Congress wanted to take care of the disabled and the dependents of those who had died, but he did not want to join in the "greatest act of hypocrisy that the Congress of the United States has ever perpetrated." "You start with the payment of this money twenty-four months after the soldier has been discharged from the Army, and then you insult him by paying a paltry sum of 50 cents a day, and string it out over two years.'" He appealed to his Southern cohorts to think seriously on the effect that this would have on the able-bodied veterans: it would keep the cheap labor of the South—some colored labor—out of the fields, and it would make no friends among the uncrippled white soldiers who would be trying to get their crops out. He knew that there were thousands of day laborers, white and black, who for want of ambition, would not work until dire necessity stared them in the face.

History has a way of repeating itself, for a few years later he was compelled to examine a similar set of circumstances when some people found themselves content with the weekly subsistence from relief agencies during the Roosevelt Administration. However, he was friendly toward temporary relief because job opportunities did not exist.

In the debate over civil service retirement he sounded the same theme: he argued for the equality of all men before the law of the land, opposing the dividing of people into classes by setting up pensions for them simply because they fell into this class. Pensions, he explained, should be paid to soldiers and employees only where there existed a need stemming from misfortunes incurred in their country's service.

On June 5, 1920, Congress adjourned to go back to their respective constituents. They promptly learned that the Presidential Election would be conducted in an atmosphere of tension and anxiety. The people who had praised their professor President for his charity and altruism were now clamoring for a return to the normal conditions they knew before the war. They cared little for the League of Nations and Wilson's dream. They thought only of the "good old days."

With Theodore Roosevelt dead, the Republicans nominated Warren G. Harding and Calvin Coolidge. The Democrats cast their lot with James Cox and Franklin D. Roosevelt. William Gibbs McAdoo seemed the logical choice, but the fact that he was Wilson's son-in-law made him a bad risk in the judgment of those who believed the trend was away from the thinking of idealists and toward practical business views.

Rayburn hit the campaign trial through the Midwest and into Ohio, delivering some of the most eloquent addresses of his career. After the election he returned to Bonham. His homecoming was celebrated by a tremendous patriotic rally. Festivities began in the district courtroom, where Rayburn had made his first speech in the Congressional campaign of 1912, but so many people had come from all parts of the county that the meeting adjourned to the out-of-doors. Every person who owned a flag brought it along to cheer for Rayburn and America. He stood on the south steps of the courthouse overlooking an excited populace. His speech was an old-fashioned Armistice Day special for which he became so famous during the next few years. The *Daily Favorite* and closest associates of the Congressman remarked that it was the finest speech they had heard him make. His idea of deporting "certain European trash masquerading as citizens" set the crowd on fire. When he concluded, the band played patriotic marches and closed the ceremony with "The Star Spangled Banner." The people were in a holiday mood. The Democrats of the Fourth had lost Cox in the General Election, but they still had their congressman. With Mr. Rayburn as their spokesman they felt secure, even though both Houses of Congress had again gone Republican.

The next week Sam began making plans to get back to Washington for the opening of the December session. If he was discouraged with the results of the election, no one detected his pessimism. He knew his own people had faith in him, because he had just been to the mailbox and had read the editorial in the Denison *Herald:* "Sam Rayburn is one of the biggest men in Congress, and if there were more like him there would be less occasion for criticism of that body." He really did not believe he deserved this praise, but he resolved to use every ounce of his limited ability to be worthy of confidence and to help Americans everywhere to respect the body of which he was a member.

According to Rayburn's memory, when he returned to Washington, Marvin Jones, Hatton Sumners, and he rented an apartment where they could have more privacy and better meals. They employed a cook but sometimes they prepared their own food. Each man took turns, but Rayburn had the best reputation as chef. Later, Rayburn recalled, Silliman Evans, then a newspaper man, moved in with them for a while. These were Rayburn's quarters until he took the four-room unit in the Anchorage Apartments, where he lived for the rest of the time. Rayburn's secretary said that in later years his boss paid between $200 and $225 rent.

Before Rayburn could settle down to the business of legislation he had to clear the atmosphere around Capitol Hill. Smarting under attacks upon President Wilson's personal life and character, he asked Speaker Gillett for the privilege of making some appropriate remarks as follows:

> "In God's name, when will small men cease this campaign of slander and abuse upon the retiring Chief Executive of this country! The big men of the Republican Party have seldom engaged in this kind of business. They have differed with him upon great policies but they have not allowed those differences to make them hate the man or stoop to defame his character."

Although he was still young, he was beginning to speak with maturity. Men on both sides of the aisle heard him with a respectful silence; for many Congresses they continued to pay respect when "Mr. Sam was up," because they believed him wise and honest, and knew that when he opened his mouth he had something important to say.

☆ IX ☆

The Return to Normalcy

RAYBURN, who already had the reputation of being able to bring warring elements together, was selected by the Chairman of the National Democratic Executive Committee to campaign in Ohio, the home State of both candidates—Senator Harding and Governor Cox. Although he made some of his best speeches here, he felt at the time that he did not move the people; on the other hand he learned later that the Republican leaders also had been disturbed by the lethargy of the masses. It seemed as if their minds were not on the issues of the campaign at all. Instead they dreamed of getting back to normalcy. This same attitude prevailed throughout the country as was reflected in the popular vote, which was 16,000,000 for Harding and 9,000,000 for Cox. Harding represented the sixty-one per cent of the electorate who had spoken for a repudiation of Professor Wilson's political philosophy and a return to the "good old days" before the war.

The type of man they selected to carry out their mandate was also indicative of their mood, for he was the exact opposite of President Wilson, both intellectually and temperamentally. Senator Boies Penrose said, prior to the campaign:

> "Keep Warren at home. Don't let him make any speeches. If he goes on tour, somebody's sure to ask him questions, and Warren's just the sort of damn fool that'll try to answer them." [1]

Although Rayburn did not recall ever having seen President Harding around the White House, he remembered him from the Senate and his wordy speeches as recorded in the *Record.* His flamboyant style, lack of organization, and play on the emotions did not appeal to a man who resisted similar outbursts from House members when he became Speaker. Rayburn did not know too much about Harding's intellectual equipment to be President, but thought he was a shocking contrast to Wilson. Years later, Rayburn said, however, that he did not want to be unkind to Harding. Rayburn remembered Harding as a very handsome man and one who "looked like a President." He recalled that Harding had the reputation of being more friendly than his predecessor. Rayburn believed Harding was sincere, honest, and unaware of the intrigue that later clouded his Administration. About the Teapot Dome scandal he made this comment:

"I never thought Mr. Harding was a dishonest man. I believe he was trusting, and some people who were not honest took advantage of him. I don't believe there has ever been a President of the United States who was a dishonest man."

Rayburn's later denunciations were not of Harding personally but of the Party he headed.

Rayburn had vivid impressions of the temper of the Sixty-seventh Congress, which, with four sessions, had kept everyone busy. He believed, though, that its achievements were not tremendous, since its efforts seemed aimed at repudiating many of the Democratic gains made during the Wilson Administration. He felt that it was an angry Congress. The majority continued to support a philosophy that favored the wealthier groups at the expense of small businessmen, farmers, and the masses. For example, one of the first bills entered on the calendar, the one Rayburn remembered most vividly, was that designed to raise the tariff schedule above the levels provided for by the Underwood Tariff Act. The Republican majority wanted to restore the earlier protection which manufacturing concerns enjoyed, under the Payne-Aldrich measure, to the detriment of agriculturists of the South and small producers everywhere.

By the middle of July, 1921, the tariff debates gathered momentum, with each congressman trying to gain favor for the commodity of his locale or region. The drift was toward particulars and away from fundamental philosophies. Sam Rayburn watched and listened with his characteristic stoical calm until most of his antagonists, as he put it, had congregated in one end of the barnyard, "where the shelled corn had been spilled on ground." Then he loaded both barrels of his ten-gauge gun with heavy shot.

On July 20, he rose from his seat, pulled both hammers back, and fired point blank into the whole flock that would destroy the Underwood Act.

> "The two great Parties" [he said] "are again brought into conflict on the tariff question. The mode of the levy of duties at the custom house on imports is now and has been for many years a question of vital difference between the Democratic and the Republican Parties. This measure brought in at this time makes the issue keener than it has ever been before. The intentions of the two Parties in placing a tariff on imports differ as widely as two views could. The Democratic Party's historic position is and has been that the only reason for the levy and collection of a tariff tax at all is to raise revenue to help pay the expenses of Government, and if any benefit should come to any individual or any industry that benefit is only incidental. The Republican Party's theory is and has been that the reason for the levy of the duty is not to raise revenue but to protect American manufacturers and industries against competition from the outside, and that what revenue is raised is only an incident and not the reason for the tax. A Democratic tariff would help support the Government and encourage trade and commerce. A Republican tariff would raise little, if any, money for the Government and would stifle trade and commerce."

Thus this twentieth-century Jefferson echoed certain of his basic agrarian or physiocratic beliefs. He continued to be an advocate of States' Rights and *laissez-faire*, for he believed that the economic system was not so complicated that certain *a priori* rights need be violated. On the other side of the question one might visualize the historic Hamilton, with no adherency to *a priori* principles, with a belief in checks and balances to protect a minority who held a financial stake in society which they deemed essential to economic growth. Hence the Republicans believed the tariff tax a bounty to be passed to some favorite and the Democrats deemed it a burden.

In 1921, Rayburn said, there was never a time in the history of American agriculture and industry when an exchange of surplus commodities with the rest of the world was more necessary for stimulating markets both at home and abroad. He mentioned debtor nations and their inability even to pay interest on loans if barriers were set up to stifle free trade with them. America needed to stay in the forefront of commercial activity instead of retreating behind a protective barrier that would isolate the United States from those countries trying to make new alliances and new friends. He said America took pride in winning the war but could blindly destroy the possibilities of establishing a peace. He warned that Americans could make new enemies throughout the world by their own selfishness and sow the seeds from which would spring ultimate belligerencies. Rayburn added:

> "I cannot escape the conviction that many men, even in the Republican Party, honestly believe that this is not the time, if it will ever come, for committing this outrage."

He taunted the Republican leadership in Congress with their weakness and fear

> ". . . to resist the lash of their masters, who are the unconscionable beneficiaries of this, little less than a steal. A steal from every laborer and consumer and producer in the land and a plunderer of everybody."

He made reference to the emergency tariff bill, against which he protested, as a complete failure, "a deception, a delusion, and a snare."

In discussing the broader aspects of pending legislation, he noted that the emergency tariff did not improve the wheat and cotton market. A further tax on cotton would only promote a high protective tariff on cotton goods which would inevitably lead to increased prices on manufactured products to the consumer. He applied the same principle to crude oil, hides, and other raw materials. History told him that the industrial states got what they wanted in protection without any regard for those areas of the nation they exploited to realize their ends. He best defined his position here in 1937, in paying tribute to Cordell

Hull's reciprocal trade program, when he referred to himself as one of the few "reasonably low tariff" men left in Congress. His record on the whole issue revealed a position of moderation.

From 1816 to present times, Rayburn explained, the United States had tended toward a protectionist policy for domestic manufactures. Such a policy was designed to strengthen new industries. As long as Americans moved west of the Mississippi they continued to purchase enough of this country's manufactured products to prevent surpluses. Even when surpluses began to occur and foreign markets became necessary, no problems arose so long as the United States imported more than she exported; protective tariffs then did not hurt too greatly the foreign trade. There was no cause for alarm until this country's surpluses of manufactured products became excessive and recurrent. The tariffs had become so restrictive that foreign imports could not be exchanged for our manufactured products. Even the McKinley Tariff Law of 1890 did not cause the United States to abandon its protective trade policy. The Underwood Tariff Act passed shortly before World War I, Rayburn pointed out, reduced the protection.

Rayburn's efforts were in vain because the protectionist tariff was increased. He recalled that in the next session the Fordney-McCumber Act of 1922 added a further phase to protectionist tariffs. It established flexible tariff rates which the Commission recommended to the President on the basis of all market conditions. Not until 1934, with the setting up of the Reciprocal Trade Agreement Act under Cordell Hull's guidance, did Rayburn begin to feel any degree of satisfaction with American policies.

Although Sam Rayburn sensed that he represented a minority opinion on July 20, 1920, he did not speak with timidity. In evaluating the legislation, he stated, "It will endure until an outraged people have time to get to the ballot box and turn out of office the people who plundered them by passing it." He thought it was loosely written in darkness and not in the light of world events. The people had clamored for a change—the farmer for higher prices on his products, the laborer for lower costs, the manufacturer for better foreign markets, and everybody for reduced taxes. The drift seemed to him away from these hopes.

From time to time he reminded the Harding Administration of its promised peace—of the so-called peace resolution for a separate peace with Germany, of the Administration's inability to execute negotiations and get the American troops home. His condemnation of the Republicans was best contained in these words:

> "For eight years you have criticized, you have sneered, you have stood in the middle of the road trying to impede progress. You became a Party of obstruction, not construction. You have hungered for power and office. Now you have both. What will you do? Will you carry on the great matters of progress or will you halt and fail? Under your leadership I pity you. I am distressed for the country."

During this session he frequently warned against the encroachment of the Federal Government upon the rights of the states and against private ownership. On August 22, 1921, a bill was before the House which proposed to refund $500,000,000 to the railroads. Rayburn promptly pointed out that in the Esch-Cummins bill he had voted for the guaranty period of six months to enable the railroads to assemble their equipment which had been scattered by the war emergency. The cost to the Government was $600,000,000 plus a loan of half this amount. He itemized the staggering gifts previously made and the increasing intermeshing of Government and private investments. The proposed extension of the six-month period, with an additional gift to railroads, he thought, would only make the return to private management more difficult. The continued subsidizing seemed to him to be making management weaker and amounted to involving the Government more and more in an operation that might become permanent:

> "You are going to be eventually where you will have to take the railroads if they continue to be the pampered pet of this Government. What incentive is there for them to go out and take hold of business and try to do something for themselves, if every time they get into deep water they can come to the Government of the United States, and get the money nobody else can get?"

Here, and previously, he explained that individuals and companies will not learn to stand on their own feet if the Government continues to be a crutch, because the more these people receive the more they will expect.

He applied the same line of reasoning on August 30, 1922, during the second session, to a bill up for consideration, which was designed to declare a national emergency in the production, transportation, and distribution of coal and other fuel. Though almost four years had passed since the Armistice, there was an atmosphere of hysteria. Rayburn attributed it to the fact that the White House was asking for legislation to give it authority, with no warehouses, to take over coal mines and transportation for a second time. "I do not expect to be swept off my feet," he said, "and pushed into a mass of socialistic legislation which I believe will destroy this representative Government in the future." The numerous and prolonged strikes, plus labor's agitation for Federal control, had Congress quite disturbed, because it was an election year. Rayburn asked his colleagues not to become intimidated by those ten per cent who were organized, when the other ninety per cent were the ones who had the best interests of the country at heart. To organized labor he directed these remarks:

> "Unless that part of business that has some regard for public opinion comes forward and takes charge of that end of business and pushes from the stage the public-be-damned groups, and unless those men who are conservative and patriotic in labor come forward and push away the radicals that have taken charge of the labor organization of the country, we are never going to have peace in industry."

With respect to strike legislation he questioned Congress's ability to get the bill out of committee and the courage to vote for it even if successful. He urged Congress to resist pressure and not pass legislation that would come back and haunt them.

In 1922, the Rayburn who had predicted back at Flag Springs that he would go to Congress and be Speaker appeared only half a prophet. At this time his chances of reaching the top rung of the ladder, with the country reeking with Republican sentiment, seemed remote. Nevertheless, he continued to execute a sort of routine perfection and gave outward appearances of being a machine. But those who had felt his warmth were viewing him as a human machine, filled with compassion along with his meticulous precision in legislative business.

His only ambition in life was to be a congressman and eventually to achieve the exalted position which inspired his childhood fancies. To be sure, he wanted fame, because he was a human machine. On February 19, 1922, he wrote a brother-in-law about his own interpretation of fame:

> I would rather link my name indelibly with the living pulsing history of my country and not be forgotten entirely after a while than to have anything else on earth.

He explained that fame was sweet but also that it could never be achieved without the involvement of others. He did not want to be called a king or emperor to rule over an unhappy people, but he did want to be loved by humanity because of his share in helping provide a way of life where people by their own labors could live more abundantly.

There is something in human nature which seems to resist men in political life with a Messianic philosophy. People have been slow to accept those with altruistic motives. Even the humanitarians and prophets of old more frequently died at the stake or followed the conqueror's chariot through the streets in chains, than they rode at the head of the triumphal processions with garlands around their necks. Although the people of the Fourth District are "nearly all good folks," as their leader said so many times, there was an odd quirk in their nature. The more victories Sam scored for them, the more frequently they called upon him to justify his role and to campaign for re-election. America called him "Mr. Democrat," then "Mr. Congress," and then "Mr. Speaker," but they continued to say, "You had better run again!" Not until he became the international "Mr. Sam," did the Fourth District admit that he had earned his seat in Congress. But a man who hitches his wagon to the people's star and challenges all those who would humble them should be prepared to make a fight of it. There were those groups and interests outside the District who did not believe in his type of America. On the other hand, he bore no affection for their type either. These groups had money to spend and they spent it, because generally, there were men available who served their purposes and who had the same ambitions. So, as long as he lived, he knew he would have to resist some forces because he had no intention of compromising his ideas.

During this Sixty-seventh Congress in 1922 he began to wonder about the practicality of continuing to fight these little political skirmishes every two years because they were expensive and perilous. Friends from all over the State of Texas were urging him to make the race for the Senate. The array of senatorial talent in 1922 appeared to him either too old or too weak, and the many flattering letters seemed to make sense. However, he was dedicated to the House of Representatives and preferred to remain there, but he paused to take a look at his past and future.

He recognized that one of his problems was that he had been identified with Joseph Weldon Bailey; in fact, he was the last surviving man in public life whom the Senator had befriended. Bailey was dead politically and had become more of a liability than an asset, despite the fact that Sam and he differed ideologically. But a small faction in the Fourth District continued to drag out this "dead horse" and conjure up opposition just for old time's sake. Rayburn was growing hoarse from refuting their charges but this minority did not care to listen. The road to the Senate was one way around the irksome and recurring campaigns. But only for a few days in February did he even entertain the thought of abandoning the dream of the thirteen-year-old boy, and even then he did not appear too serious about it.

Never again did he listen to those who would see him make the race for the Senate. He recognized in later years that some of the "well-wishers" did not have his real interest at heart, being more desirous of pushing him out of the Fourth than into the Senate. Some of the so-called "well-wishers" finally turned their thoughts to redistricting and gerrymandering, but this did not work either. By this time Rayburn was well on his way to achieving his fame—a goal to which he rededicated himself back in 1922.

Reconciled to facing opposition almost every two years, Sam Rayburn told his friends to leave him alone to finish the job he loved. With opposition facing him again, he released on May 13, 1922, to his constituents the measures he had supported affecting farming and agricultural classes, as well as other things of interest to them:

1. Exemption of farmers' organizations from operation of the Sherman antitrust law so that no farmer organization would be held to a violation of the antitrust law.

2. The Lever Agricultural Act to extend educational facilities to farm boys and girls.

3. The income tax law requiring wealth to bear its proportion of taxation.

4. Federal Reserve Act to expand the volume of currency and to allow farmers to borrow money from banks on notes secured by staple agricultural products and on improved farm lands.

5. Standardization of cotton and grain in the interest of the producer.

6. Standardization and warehouses so that farmers could borrow money on their warehouse receipts.

7. Underwood Tariff Act, reducing tariffs on necessities and putting many articles that the farmer uses on the free list, including agricultural implements, barbed wire, bagging, and ties.

8. The Ship Purchase Act to provide ships to carry American products to all the markets of the world.

9. Cotton Futures Act to curb gambling in cotton and to regulate the transactions of the cotton exchanges.

10. Farm-Loan Act, which established the system of twelve farm-loan banks, with one in Houston, Texas. (The system affords farmers the opportunity to borrow money to be used in purchasing and improving homes at low interest rates and long terms of payment. As of the current date the Farm Loan Board had let out $500,000,000 of which $55,000,000 had come from the Houston office.)

11. War Finance Corporation, which enlarged and extended the facilities of the War Finance Corporation and enabled it to make advances to banks, cooperating organizations of farmers, and other financing institutions to assist in production of farm products and livestock in an orderly marketing ($300,000,000 had been distributed in loans as of May 13.)

12. Farm Organization bill (or Capper-Volstead bill), which made broad and liberal provisions for the organization of farmers (including planters, ranchmen, dairymen, nut or fruit growers) to organize and bargain collectively.

13. Farm-loan bonds, authorizing the Secretary of the Treasury to purchase farm-loan bonds, to establish farm-loan markets, and to encourage and assist farm-loan banks.

14. Good roads, providing Federal assistance in improvement of highways.

15. Federal Trade Commission (Rayburn was a member of the subcommittee of the Committee on Interstate and Foreign Commerce. The Commission was created to investigate and regulate the unfair practices of big business so that small business would be given a fair chance.)

16. Vocational Education Act, providing for practical education to cooperate with the states and to provide for training of teachers in vocational subjects.

17. Exempting labor organizations from prosecution under the Sherman Antitrust Law.

18. Clayton Antitrust Law, prohibiting interlocking directorates and defining and expanding the provisions of the Sherman Law to provide protection to legitimate business.

19. Readjustment of salaries of Post Office employees.

20. Laws extending Rural Route Service.

21. National prohibition and all laws to make its operation effective.

22. The Budget system, providing for one appropriating committee and rigid economy in Government expenditures, declaring that government should be on a business rather than a political basis.

23. The forcing of Federal Reserve Banks to give long-time credit on agricultural loans.

24. Immigration laws (Rayburn wanted to keep out of the country all dangerous alien elements).

25. Sheppard-Towner Maternity bill.

26. Soldier Bonus bill.

27. Against all bills that tended toward a military despotism or building a military caste in the United States.

28. Rayburn Stock and Bond bill, finally enacted as a part of the Esch-Cummins bill.

29. Cummins-Rayburn amendment to the Carmack amendment, providing for the shipper to recover full amount of damages.

30. Transportation Act, returning the railroads to private management and eventual reduction of rates.

31. Priorities Shipment bill, which gave the Government priorities to move equipment during wartime.

32. War-Risk Insurance (it became the law as part of the Sweet bill).

In July, 1922, with this record behind him, he returned to his District for a brief campaign of several days against Ed Westbrook of Hunt County. Mr. Rayburn had already been opposed by the same man in 1920, the year Joseph Weldon Bailey had made an unsuccessful race for Governor. Rayburn was prevented from conducting an active campaign this time because of duties in Washington, but his overwhelming victory in 1920, carrying his home County of Fannin 4113 to 1414, encouraged optimism within his organization.

This second bid by Westbrook, however, developed into a serious one, since the labor unions fought Rayburn vehemently for his defiance of their grip over the railroads and his blunt language condemning the strikes. One of the most remarkable things about this campaign was not the issues or even the outcome, but Mr. Rayburn's refusal to "fight fire with fire." He was invited by labor to enter into one of the old-fashioned mud-slinging orgies, but he refused to stoop to this level. He said that he would never deliberately hurt an opponent's feelings or jeopardize a reputation in order to win. Therefore he refused to follow the pattern which the campaign seemed to be taking. During his brief race he told the citizenship that the time had come for them to vote according to their consciences. He was almost defiant in his speeches. He firmly stated that he had made some big decisions, but he had done what was right. He admitted that he had made enemies in the Sixty-seventh Congress, and pointed the finger of scorn at the lobbyists. He flatly refused to make any promises and told the people that he would remain faithful to his inner self.

About ten o'clock election night, as the returns were coming in, Rayburn turned to a friend who was keeping the tally sheet and remarked, "I have lost this race." At this point he was losing boxes he thought were safe. However, he managed to carry every county, but his majorities had dwindled. He won his home County by fewer than a thousand votes, the results here being 4114 to 3196. His lead in the district was only 1254 votes, an indication that his aggressiveness and head-on collision with national crises had alienated many who had previously tolerated his outspokenness. Some political historians around Bonham believe that this campaign marked the beginning of Sam Rayburn's emergence from politician to statesman.

☆ X ☆

That Republican Prosperity—Calvin Coolidge

DURING a national campaign or Congressional debate Sam Rayburn had been known to follow the dictates of his spleen in his appraisal of the Republican Party. He had assailed without mercy the Administration of Warren G. Harding. In paying tribute to the high office of President, however, he became more compassionate. The ailing Chief Executive—the man himself—who in the summer of 1923 went West on his "voyage of understanding," had Rayburn's complete sympathy. He saw him as a kindly soul who wanted to be liked by his fellow Americans and to convince them that he had been "more sinned against than sinning." The Harding who died on August 3 was Mr. Rayburn's President; hence he mourned the loss. Rayburn's sympathy also followed the First Lady back to the White House; and the crowded railway depots along the route across the continent gave him comfort that, within Americans, was a deeply implanted love for a President and respect for the office itself.

Two trains converged on Washington. The one carried the

body of a dead President out of the West, across mountains, plains, and valleys. The other bore a solemn man down from the Green Mountains toward a Capitol where the scandal of the Teapot Dome was soon to set officialdom into a turmoil. Yet against such a cloudy horizon, the era of America's greatest prosperity was approaching. It was to be a business boom, when the rich grew richer and the poor became poorer. The latter had waited, Mr. Rayburn said, "a mighty long time for something good to happen to them," and he feared they had a still longer wait.

The world had already formulated its impression of Calvin Coolidge, the new President—a pure Yankee, who was serious, shy, shrewd, efficient, self-confident and internally humorous. According to William Allen White in his *A Puritan in Babylon*, the four lines of doggerel verse which hung over the fireplace of Coolidge's home during his earlier years of public life had become ingrained in a Yankee soul:

A wise old owl lived in an oak;
The more he saw the less he spoke.
The less he spoke the more he heard:
Why can't we be like that old bird? [1]

The more Mr. Rayburn studied this slight, unpretentious man in the White House, who was referred to as Cautious Cal, the more he was tempted to call him simply Yankee Cal.

About Coolidge he had this to say:

"He was a rather different type of man than lots of people thought he was. I had breakfast alongside him in his office a few times and twice at the White House. There was one time when I was filling in for a fellow who was sick and so I drew this place alongside the President. You see, everybody had to sit according to his importance, but I didn't amount to much then and happened to be filling in for this fellow who was important.

"I believe I had as gruesome a forty-five minutes of talk as I ever had in my life. There was a man named Ike Hoover, who was a kind of major-domo around the White House. He came and whispered something over Coolidge's shoulder and he turned around and asked, 'Did you hear what Hoover said to me?' and I said, 'No.'

"He said, 'Mr. So-in-so is sick; couldn't even get out of bed this morning.'

"Well, everybody in Washington then had some kind of

throat trouble. And I said, 'Yes, there is a lot of throat trouble going around.'

"He said, 'Yes, I have had a little of it. We had one of these receptions here last night and I had to stand there and say *Howdy-do, Howdy-do* two thousand times and it didn't do my throat a bit of good.'

"That tickled me, but the first thing that struck me as funny was this fellow Hoover, who was trying to get everyone in the right seat, was stirring around among us saying, 'Good morning, good morning.' And there seemed to be still a lot of confusion in the Red Room when the President arrived. He saw the complication and he blurted out, 'Sit down, gentlemen, the eating is just as good one place as it is another.'

"Well, that kind of got me. Then, to top that, he fed his dog at the table, a rather nice-looking dog. It was a good breakfast —flapjacks and everything, and I rather enjoyed it."

Perhaps, unaware at the time that anyone would later discover a similarity between himself and this almost unique political phenomenon sitting there at the breakfast table, Rayburn enjoyed what he termed "gruesome fun." Calvin Coolidge in 1924 was one of the last of his kind—an authentic mountain Yankee. Sam Rayburn in 1961 was about the last of his type—a statesman of the old-school with a flair for politics. The point of tangency is that each in his respective era belonged to the vanguard of a type almost extinct. If one labored the point other parallels could be drawn, such as temperament, taste, ethics, and attitudes, but from the standpoint of economics they had different loyalties. Coolidge appeared as an average American, a Party man who cast his lot with the conservative Republicans interested in economy of government and big business. Rayburn also prided himself as an average American, yet a Democrat who was interested in economy of government and agriculture.

Rayburn was a distinctly middle-of-the-road man with the conservatism and skepticism usually found in the rural mind. Thus Rayburn revealed in these early years a distrust of big business and big government. His views might be expressed by his own idiom:

". . . just as you do not break a horse's leg to keep it from straying on the plains, but tether it or hobble it for the night, so big business ought to be regulated but not destroyed; that the law should never be used as an instrument of revenge; that there is room in this country for free men and free enterprise; that the frontier is closed only to those who have closed minds."

With the adjournment of the Sixty-eighth Congress in March, 1925, Rayburn would have concluded six terms and had made six campaigns. A few years earlier he had remarked in one of his speeches that a legislator must serve a sort of apprenticeship:

> "It takes a while for a man to learn and get established and gain his full influence. He doesn't reach his full usefulness his first term or two, and the worst thing a district can do for itself, if it's got someone here doing his job, is to keep changing its congressman. A man makes a record here about the way he does in business, or the law, or anything else; it's hard work that makes the difference."

When his brothers wrote that M. M. Morrison of Grayson County had decided to oppose him for a seventh term, some of his colleagues must have remembered this remark and felt the irony of it all. Rayburn had served a reasonable apprenticeship and had reached a level of usefulness, but he could not avoid the perpetual opposition.

He remarked to some people very close to him that there were apparently some constituents whom he would never be able to please, but that he had just about made up his mind that this element, after all these years, were so much against his philosophy that he had grown accustomed to their differences. He said he certainly had no intentions of altering his views or softening his verbal attacks on obstructionists. If they did not like the kind of country he advocated, then he would not let these variant attitudes bother him, and there would be positively no alteration in his legislative program to soften the resistance. Of course, he was aware that some of the opposition was personal and cumulative, having arisen over patronage, such as his refusal to recommend certain small-town politicians to post office jobs for the sake of appeasement. He had his own notions, and sometimes he failed to recommend where opposition could have been silenced. Then again in the judgment of some, he had made appointments that hurt him.

Rayburn did not have the time for an active campaign against Morrison, and save for token appearances he virtually ignored him. In the July, 1924, primary the vote was 23,244 to 14,435. Two years later (1926), much to his astonishment, he had no opponents at all. It was the first respite since he had become a Congressman; however, the many races never made him quit repeating this favorite maxim: "I believe in people and the soundness of their judgment when they have the facts. I know that ninety-eight-and-one-half per cent of the people have more good than bad in them and can be trusted to do the right thing." This precept was so constantly on his lips that he must have uttered it to himself with the beginning of each new day.

A great many comments have been made about Sam Rayburn's favorite foods—fried chicken, coconut cake, watermelon, chili, string beans, turnip greens, turkey, and bermuda onions. Martha Rayburn and later, Bobbie Phillips, and his three sisters had their opportunity to see his face light up when these delicacies were put before him. He always liked the country accent in the seasoning of foods and serving of his meals. It was about this time (shortly before her death in 1927), that Martha Rayburn revealed one of his favorite eccentricities about dishes. While en route to Bonham he telephoned his mother that he would arrive shortly. She promptly asked what dish she could prepare, and he promptly replied, "Fix up a bowl of 'crummin' [cool sweet milk with corn bread crumbled in]. I've been longing for a big bowl of that for months."

Rayburn's recollections of the years following Harding's death and of the early years of the Coolidge Administration were not considerable. There were several pleas to ease the pressure on agriculture. Since both these Congresses had a substantial Republican majority, he recalled that the bills favoring agrarian peoples met with strong resistance. He considered that in Washington there was an almost inconceivable partiality to big business in all its variant forms.

Proposed legislation to revise railroad rates provoked an interesting Rayburnesque logic. He accused some of his own Democratic friends of being political in their fear to vote for rate adjustments which would benefit farmers, because the beneficiaries might feel so grateful to a Republican Congress that they would bolt the Party at the next election. He argued, on June 6, 1924, that

> "It is essential to the prosperity of the whole people that they pay the lowest possible lawful rates for that service. Freight rates are like tariff taxes in that rates may be set so high that traffic will not move and, therefore, less revenue will be collected than there would be on a lower rate. There is a medium somewhere that is fair to all parties and that rate should be found if possible."

Agricultural areas were in the throes of a depression, and one of the things the previous Congress should have done, he believed, was to repeal the Fordney Tariff law:

> "The streams of commerce are very sensitive, and a thing like a toll or tariff will change the whole course of our neighbors' patronage. Nations are like individuals. No merchant can hope that customers will come to his store and purchase his wares if he charges an entrance fee to his place of business."

The point was made that the Republican Party had long exacted a tribute from the farming classes and had slowly reduced them to a form of servitude. The promised relief never materialized, and the agricultural groups, Rayburn predicted, might have to generate their own relief through the building up of cooperative marketing systems to dispose of the products at home and abroad with agents replacing professional exporters in the role of middlemen.

He could see no permanent relief for any section if all of the so-called "blocs" were not eliminated:

> "With a Wall Street bloc, a railroad bloc, a labor bloc, a town bloc, a country bloc—all with special purposes to serve—the general interest could not be fostered. Let us, if possible, have done with strife and bickering that divide our people, and which can bring nothing but woe to any country whose people do not work together for the common good and the general welfare."

During the next four years he talked with farming groups throughout the Midwest and South, answering many letters that contained a note of despair and frustration. The despondence was motivated by the intermittent failures of the McNary–Haugen bills. The first in a series was introduced in January, 1924, but was defeated in the House on June 3, as was a second version in May, 1926. But a third attempt passed both Houses, only to be vetoed by President Coolidge. A fourth attempt failed because of a Presidental veto.

Rayburn's feelings were the best expressed in his remarks of May 29, 1928, when the McNary–Haugen bill was being sharply debated. Rayburn demonstrated a rather comprehensive grasp of the economics involved. Governmental activities in agriculture had been restricted to functions that would help farmers themselves perform a better job of producing and selling at the highest possible competitive prices. The system, however, had not worked and the agriculturalist found himself at a disadvantage because farm prices were much lower than industrial prices. Farmers complained that they could not benefit from protective tariffs as could industry. These inequities between industry and agriculture provoked some of his most sincere Jeffersonian and agrarian concepts—that when tillage begins the other arts follow. The farmers were to him the founders of civilization. He spoke about farming as a career with almost the same physiocratic devotion as did Hector St. John de Crèvecoeur in 1782. Rayburn stated:

> "The farmers have been the pioneers in all the advancement of our country. It was the farmer who went forth to clear away the forests and turn the sod of the prairie to make it a home for man that products may be brought forth to feed and clothe the world. He went into the tractless forest before the railroads went there or the factories or other businesses went there, and there never would have been railroads and factories or towns if the pioneer farmer had not blazed the way and settled the country and brought forth by his labor the things that the railroads, the factories, and all used to build towns. Every other industry in the land should want agriculture to be prosperous. If the farmers are not prosperous the revenue of the railroads shrinks and labor upon the railroads is idle. If agriculture is not prosperous the smoke will cease to lift from the factories and their business shall perish from the earth, and thousands upon thousands of men and women will be left unable to buy the output of the factories. So, with the merchants and the banks. We are all interdependent upon each other, and if the greatest and most basic of all industries is not prosperous, then every other industry fails to prosper."

He cited statistics to show how the wealth of the country in fifteen years had increased more than two hundred billion dollars while farm values had shrunk twenty billion during the same period and farm indebtedness had grown nearly ten billion. Of the 3785 bank failures during the Harding and Coolidge Administrations, 2800 were in the twelve leading agricultural States. The thousands of business houses which had been forced to close in the agricultural States also reflected the insolvency of the farming class that had lost its buying power owing to the inequities between prices of the products bought and sold.

Rayburn particularly assailed the indifference of President Coolidge to the whole farming problem because he stood for high tariffs, being a product of that part of America where industry was predominant. One provision of the McNary-Haugen bill was the establishment of a $400,000,000 fund to buy up crop surpluses to keep them off the market at certain seasons and feed them gradually back to the market. The manipulating of the markets, Rayburn believed, was becoming a national scandal, for prices would fluctuate from a lower level to a higher level after the products left the farmers' hands. The Interstate Commerce Commission, he pointed out, had a regulatory power over the whole railroad industry and the right to fix rates to protect all parties, but there was no equivalent to protect agriculture. Such a board would set prices in a domestic instead of a world market. This board would protect this fair exchange value from world price by a tariff fluctuating with it and with world price. Rayburn pointed out that during the two Republican Administrations the commodities farmers purchased had increased in price, but those products they sold had decreased to an all-time low at the season for marketing. On the other hand, he recalled that the Wilson Administration could look with pride at the Farm Loan Act, the Federal Reserve Act, the Smith-Lever Extension Act, and other measures aimed to help the farmer rather than to discriminate against him.

Rayburn's information about agricultural conditions and farming came from close range. At this time he was a director in the Fannin County Fair and was active in improving local conditions—by demonstration, better seed, better farming, terracing land, dairying and livestock raising, diversification, planting several money crops instead of one. He was involved in all of these but still could not make a living from his own farm. Other farmers in his District were having no better luck because they could not buy the necessities with their incomes. He considered the farm picture in 1928 as "the tragedy of the age and a black page on our history that this Congress should adjourn with nothing done for agriculture." One of his favorite rebuttals was to threaten to take his problems to the people:

"My hope and trust is that in the coming election the people will rise up in their might, in their power,

> and elect a President and a Congress that will do its duty and do justice to agriculture, the greatest of all our great industries."

His remarks were particularly aimed at the White House, since although Congress had passed this McNary–Haugen bill in 1927 and 1928, Coolidge had vetoed it, the farm bloc having been unable to muster the vote to override the Administration. Both political Parties, however, did manage to graft some of the measures of the bills into their respective platforms which led to the setting up of a Federal Farm Board in 1929 under the Hoover Administration.

On October 15, 1927, Sam Rayburn and Metze Jones of Valley View, Texas, were united in matrimony. They went on their honeymoon to Tennessee. The groom signed the guest book at the hotel as "Sam Rayburn and bride."

After the honeymoon the couple went on to Washington. On October 31, 1927, Sam Rayburn, on office stationery in pen and ink, wrote to Bernice Carleton (daughter of Dr. J. C. Carleton), who had sent him a clipping and picture from a newspaper in Gulf Port, Mississippi, of Sam Rayburn and his attractive bride-to-be. Bernice, one of Rayburn's very close friends from Bonham, was teaching at Gulf Port at the time. The letter follows:

> Your note came when I was in a great hurry to get married, and therefore not answered. In a hurry because I wanted to get it over before she changed her mind.
>
> We drove through from Memphis and reached here last Monday. We are located for the winter and hope it will be possible for you to come this way some time and visit us.
>
> All good wishes to you,
>
> Sincerely yours,
> Sam Rayburn

The couple lived together for only a short time. Two months and three weeks later they dissolved their marriage.

Metze Jones is the sister of Marvin Jones, who had been a Texas Congressman from Amarillo and became Chief Judge of the U.S. Court of Claims in Washington. The two men were staunch friends before the marriage and continued to be friends; indeed, their friendship may have encouraged the romance. Years later, Sam remarked, "It was so long ago, it doesn't seem as though I was ever married." He refused to discuss the incident, not out of anger, but real pain. Most people thought of him as a bachelor, although newspaper men report that no other Washington celebrity received more proposals of marriage by mail.

His continued silence and the absence of publicity in the Fourth District press at the time aggravated the whole incident. Tom Steger represented Rayburn, who was not present, and the case was tried in the District Clerk's office at Bonham. Rayburn filed and the divorce was granted to Mrs. Rayburn on a "cross action answer."

Out of respect for the couple the matter was never discussed around Bonham. She was twenty-seven and he forty-five. Sam Rayburn had already been wedded a long time to Congress and his constituents before he decided to share his affections with a wife. A friend of the bride who was familiar with the strenuous social activity in Washington observed that Metze did not feel up to this type of life. Another lady who knew the two remarked, "There is always a man's side and a woman's side to these things. This appeared to be a case of incompatibility of temperaments." Afterward Rayburn wrote a friend in Bonham that he had made a mistake. He never made further reference to the marriage and always avoided discussing it with journalists.

The failure of his only venture into matrimony was one of the major disappointments of his life. Since he did not have a family of his own, he gave his love and time to relatives, friends, and country. At children's birthday parties he was the center of attraction. Many a secretary poured out her problems to him. Many a congressman's wife came to him through the years for help in coping with a husband's eccentricities. His views were sound and were not tinctured with a personal bitterness.

He was thought of as a solitary figure. As early as June, 1913, articles appeared with reference to his single state, such as the Fort Worth *Record* on this date:

> Too bad he is a member of the Bachelors' Club recently organized at the national Capitol, with Honorable Hatton W. Sumners as its President and Lord Chesterfield.

Forty-seven years later Rayburn was still sought after for membership in such organizations. For example, on October 18, 1960, the Bachelor Club of Hickory, North Carolina, added his name to its roster.

Mr. Sam perhaps joked as much about his handsome looks and the many hearts he made flutter, as the press did about his bald head. Once he received through the mail several of his own photographs which friends had asked him to autograph. He looked at two of them and promptly tore them up, saying, "If I permit a thing like that to be hung up in an office, it will frighten off some old maid who might want to propose!" About his good looks he made this quip to a policeman, who in July, 1960, was on duty in the area of the House of Representatives. Rayburn had left the rostrum and was en route to the clockroom; just as he passed under the portrait of Speaker Samuel J. Randall, a distinguished looking man with well-groomed black hair, he ran his hand over the top of his own head, looking up at the former Speaker in passing, and chuckled, "There is the second most handsome Speaker in the history of the House."

A sampling of Rayburn's activities during the remaining years of the Coolidge Administration indicates that the Congressman was alert, though held down by the Republican majority. Yet he continued to speak out.

In settling labor disputes, for example, he favored moderation, and opposed legislation which was designed to punish rather than to correct an injustice. He wanted both management and labor to prosper, and when he advocated high wages he believed both interests would be served: "I believe in buying high and selling high. When the farmer and the agriculturalist receive high prices they can afford to pay high prices. Low prices mean stagnation in industry."

On many occasions during these lean years he stated that men should have an opportunity to rear their families, house them properly, clothe them properly, and feed them properly and be able to buy books so that the children could go to school. He argued that America should have a healthy, virile, educated, and cultured people. Prosperity should be passed around and not restricted to any one class or group.

His frequent laudatory references to the Interstate Commerce Commission would indicate that he kept a watchful eye on its activities and welfare. Back on January 19, 1927, when a Cyrus E. Woods, a Republican of Pennsylvania, was appointed to the Commission, he had raised strenuous objection because the gentleman held bonds in at least five of the country's major railroad lines. Rayburn reminded the House that a year previously he had opposed the appointment of a Democrat for identical reasons. Even though such men do divest themselves of their holdings, he believed that their long association with the railroads would destroy their impartiality and cause the American people to lose faith in a most important commission.

A bill authorizing additional employees for the Federal Power Commission and other purposes also drew his sharp criticism on March 20, 1928. He did not want to create and expand another bureau, for the civil-service employee in charge of the Commission would be under no restrictions. "We might as well face the proposition," he said, "that this is a bill to get the camel's nose under the tent." The bill would give the director more power, more men, and more tools with which to work when he appears before the Committee on appropriations. He chastised his colleagues who had pledged to resist expanding the bureaus but who seemed to be making an about-face to favor this measure.

The question of constructing the Nicaraguan Canal came up again in 1929. The original idea had been turned down June 28, 1902, in favor of the Panama Canal, the site which Theodore Roosevelt really preferred. Under the Taft Administration in 1909, a financial protectorate was established over Nicaragua, and at the end of the President's term a treaty was made which gave the United States some very profitable economic advantages, including the right to build an interoceanic canal across the territory. For this and other rights the United States paid the Nicaraguan Government $3,000,000. American dollar diplomacy continued to foment trouble. The Marines were withdrawn in 1925 but returned shortly afterward because of revolutions and counter-revolution staged in objection to violation of United States pledges. President Coolidge did not improve America's popularity in Nicaragua when he sent Henry L. Stimson down to find a solution. The operation, however, was carried out efficiently, with American troops supervising the election. But military intervention, it appeared to Rayburn, made no friends for the United States in the Western Hemisphere, despite the fact that the wisest Nicaraguans realized they were incapable of conducting fair elections and solving their own domestic problems. They did not want to operate under an American supervision which they believed was aimed primarily at protecting lucrative economic interests.

Rayburn had grown weary of all this talk about Nicaragua and was disgusted with the deterioration of our foreign policy under two Republican Presidents. He felt that the human element had gone out of our interests in Latin American countries, that we had become more interested in helping big business further their exploitation down there, than in raising the economic and social level of an underprivileged people. He was also particularly disturbed by the loss of life among the marines who were stationed in Nicaragua to supplement the national guard and to protect the lives of American businessmen.

Feeling as he did about the dollar diplomacy and the absence of a real foreign policy, he resisted the plan to reopen the investigation of the route for the Nicaraguan Canal. Rayburn had seen the Panama Canal shortly after its completion and had always felt that it was one of our greatest engineering feats. He simply did not believe that another canal was needed. The important thing to him was to make a study of the existing canal facilities and potentialities, for practical business consideration, in order to forestall involvement in another area which would immediately create diplomatic entanglements and lead to staggering financial commitments. Such was the pattern of Rayburn's thinking at a time when the hope of a broader and more optimistic approach to diplomacy was remote. He had little faith in the White House's foreign policy; however, at the time he kept quiet lest a public expression might detract from America's position and prestige abroad. An election year, though, was always an open season on Republican Administrations, for then he was without mercy or sympathy.

☆ XI ☆

Frustration and Calamity Under Hoover

SAM RAYBURN knew Herbert Hoover when he was Food Administrator in Belgium during World War I, while Wilson was President. Rayburn remembered him also as Secretary of Commerce under Harding:

"He appeared for eight years off and on before the Interstate and Foreign Commerce Committee, of which I was a member because they had some kind of little transportation division down in the tax department. My estimation of Mr. Hoover was that he was a good engineer. He was an efficiency man, always being on some kind of commission. And when he was nominated for President, I made it clear that I thought he was a good man on the team but not a good man to be captain. And it turned out like that. Herbert Hoover is a good, a patriotic man. But this 1929 thing—I don't know—it might have fallen on anybody as President.

"Yet the strangest thing about it was that he had Mr. Mellon to help him, a great banker and businessman. The country had been riding so high that they didn't think there was anything that could stop it. They kept saying, 'Let's be patient, prosperity is just around the corner.' It just went from bad to worse, and I think they just wrung their hands, hoped and trusted but had no vision about what we were getting into, but believe me the captain who followed him in the White House had ideas. He didn't wring his hands. He tried to stop it."

Thus Sam Rayburn, in December, 1960, looked back at the years which he described as an era of "frustration and calamity." Although Herbert Hoover did not become President until March 4, 1929, the stage had already been set for the debacle.

Of these tragic years Rayburn frequently spoke in a painful tone because the people of the Fourth were bowed down by the burden they carried. When he attacked the Coolidge and Hoover Administrations he hurled his most caustic barbs, "giving it to them with the bark on," as he liked to say.

In the spring of 1928, while the favorite sons of both Parties were casting longing eyes at the White House, the battle of the stock market continued. At the Republican Convention in Kansas City, Herbert Hoover was nominated on the first ballot, since Coolidge was out of the picture. "I do not choose to run," he had said. At the Democratic Convention in Houston, Governor Alfred E. Smith likewise was awarded the nomination on the first ballot.

Rayburn was pleased that this time the Party was able to settle on a candidate so quickly, recalling the previous convention in New York.

"The party," he said, "had in 1924 thrown Smith and McAdoo at each other for over a hundred ballots, and just about gave away any chance of electing anybody because the people were saying if the Democrats haven't got sense enough to nominate somebody, they certainly haven't sense enough to run the Government. So John W. Davis came in as a dark horse in 1924, but was defeated."

But by 1928 Smith had completed a fourth term as Governor of New York. He had convinced the political leaders of his State of his effectiveness as a campaigner and his competence as an administrator. The Southern hostility to his Catholicism and anti-prohibition views was somewhat pacified at the convention by the selection of Senator Joseph T. Robinson of Arkansas as his running mate. The platform itself was designed to stir no sectional wrath, being against sin and favoring virtue. The Party, hungry for victory, put complete faith in the New York Governor to appease both the farmers and industrialists. However, Rayburn said that the Party misjudged public sentiment, for in the Solid South and the rural sections of the North, Smith was destined to be mercilessly attacked by religious bigots and rabid prohibitionists.

Before Rayburn could lend his help to the Party he had to put out his own fires on the home front, since he had three opponents. His majority in the District turned out to be more than 5000 votes, and the vote in Fannin County showed a slight gain in popularity. However, as the results indicate he had the usual nucleus of opposition at home: Rayburn—4374, Wallace Hughston (Collin)—1163, John L. Andrew (Grayson)—461, and B. L. Sherley (Collin)—198. This 1928 campaign was his eighth, 1926 having been his only respite thus far.

Those who lived through the summer and fall of 1928 in Northeast Texas report a violent spirit in which the religious question was discussed. People who previously had little interest in the almost dead issue of prohibition were now easily stirred to wrath. The Fourth District was a hotbed of bigotry and strife. Warfare broke out when a predominantly Protestant and "dry" electorate found themselves trying to be jubilant over the Catholic and anti-prohibitionist Al Smith. The solid core of old-line Party men tried to reunite their forces and hold the people in line by creating an image of Hoover that was distasteful to a good Southerner. Rayburn held a responsible position in this Party organization and in generating enthusiasm for loyalist ideas. He was opposed in his own State by the "Hoover Democrats," led by former Governor Oscar B. Colquitt, Thomas B. Love, and Cato Sells.

The speech Sam Rayburn made at the First Baptist Church on a Sunday evening in September, 1928, was a saber-rattling spectacle. The author of these pages, an impressionable sixteen-year-old who sat in the balcony on that night, believed he saw the flames exude from Rayburn's nostrils. He watched the Congressman adorn "this ogre Herbert Hoover" with a devil's suit, including the tail pinned in the right place. When he assailed the Republican candidate for trying to abolish segregation and promote a "deal with Negroes" for convention votes, little did he anticipate that he himself, thirty-two years later, would speak in gentle terms about tolerance and racial equality. One of the so-called "dirt farmers" in Fannin County explained the change thus: "Mr. Sam was a politician in those days, but no demogogue, for he had the makings of a statesman. There was love, not hate in his heart. He arrived under Roosevelt."

This States'-Rights Democrat of 1928 rekindled smoldering fires when he shouted defiantly:

> "As long as I honor the memory of the Confederate dead, respect and revere the gallant devotion of my Confederate father to our Southland and wear his name, I will never vote for the electors of a Party which sent the carpetbagger and the scalawag to the prostrate South with saber and sword to crush the white civilization of the South to the earth."

The Rayburn who spoke on this night still wore his father's uniform of gray. The Negroes, however, who worked for him understood the mores and biases around Bonham, but they bore him no personal animosity. They did not discuss this great social issue. Each man played his part well and praised the other for his efficiency. They worked together through the years in a congenial fashion, from time to time complimenting one another on the skillful way he handled the tools of his profession—one the gavel and the other a hoe or ax. Their social difference had been created by forces beyond their immediate control. Change, however, did come. In 1928 the Congressman was "Mr. Rayburn," but by 1960 he had become the venerable "Mr. Sam." Life had bared its bones to him.

Rayburn's attack on the enemies of the Southland and leaders of the "Hoover Democrat" organization was personal. They were depicted as second-rate political "has-beens" who would ignore the Republican corruption of the Teapot Dome in order "to seek a shady place by that overfed and fattened sow, the Federal Treasury."

His most serious criticism of the Hoover followers was the way they were injecting the religious issue into the campaign and trying to destroy one of America's basic freedoms.

> "I understand" [he continued] "that tomorrow night a New York *dee-vine* is going to come here to attack Governor Smith in this auditorium. He is the man who made the attack on Governor Smith in his pulpit when he knew that Governor Smith could not go to the same place and answer him. Our leaders must learn, sooner or later, that free men will not contribute to a leadership which seeks to destroy religious freedom in this country. For nineteen years I was a Sunday school superintendent in a Baptist church and I hope our good Christian preachers will forsake politics and lift up the cross of Christ to a hungering world."

This is a sample of his message in 1928, the kind of gospel he preached to the home folks. As a rule he was sent on a speaking circuit remote from Texas, but the home picture was too critical for him to leave the State. The temper of his speeches indicated some of the areas of excitement and uncertainty, as well as his own anxiety.

The whole South became a battlegound when other Party leaders tried to use the same appeal and type of emotionalism. Religious Fundamentalists, especially in rural sections, and the Anti-Saloon League fought Smith for his Catholicism and ideas on the liquor question, although he conformed rather closely to the acceptable views of Woodrow Wilson, who had argued for enforcing laws so long as they were on the statute books.

The advocates of white supremacy did considerable damage to Al Smith and the Democrats by spreading the reports that he secretly favored giving liquor to the Negroes in exchange for patronage. Also the Pope of Rome was portrayed everywhere in the Southland as a foreign monarch just waiting to take over the Government when Al Smith moved into the White House. So bitter became all these discussions that families were often divided, with the wife usually standing against the threat of foreign "isms" and moral corruption, and the husband remaining loyal to the Party. These are generalizations based on the thinking of the Fourth District.

Rayburn was rarely wrong in his predictions, certainly not those made confidentially to his family. Though he fought gallantly and spoke with confidence, Tom and Will Rayburn knew of their brother's anxiety. They sensed his concern that even Texas would go Republican. To Rayburn this was humiliation in its rawest form. His fears were confirmed, for Virginia, Tennessee, North Carolina, Florida, and the Southern "border States" joined Texas in the revolt. The Republican victory in both Houses of Congress, however, was the real upset, because Rayburn had not suspected that the controversies would touch the Legislature.

Gathering the corn crop and picking over the cotton a second time provided some relief for Rayburn from his thoughts about the Party's problems. Internal strife complicates rebuilding and the seriousness of his disposition during the following week gave some indication of the complexity of the times. Sam Rayburn was not the best company immediately following a defeat like this. Deets Dorough, the long-time Chairman of the

Democratic Executive Committee in Fannin County described Mr. Sam's mood thus, "Mr. Rayburn reminds me of a biting sow in brooding season, after he has taken a licking like this."

Rayburn went back to Washington a few days before the "Lame Duck" session of the Seventieth Congress (December 3–March 4, 1929). He was on hand for Hoover's inaugural ceremonies.

The Seventy-first Congress convened April 15, 1929, to face some rather significant tariff legislation that had been under consideration for several months. While the President gave some thought to this also, he was more interested in the fluctuation of the stock market. Any alarm was arrested by an implicit faith that America was on the verge of "a new economic era." The best minds in the country confirmed his optimism, and his advisers assured the country that what goes up does not necessarily have to come down. Congress, busy with writing and debating bills, took no serious concern until October 23, when stocks suffered drops averaging eighteen points. The bottom fell out of the market on Tuesday, October 29, 1929. Prices reached even newer lows, a trend which continued through November.

Sam Rayburn had previously groaned about the Republican depression which gripped the farming section of Northeast Texas, but now, with the stage set for an authentic demonstration of economic adversity, he developed a monotonous moan. Secretary of the Treasury Mellon tried to offer assurance: "I see nothing in the situation which warrants pessimism." By nature not a man to trust Republican economists, Rayburn felt that the Secretary was wrong in his prediction and believed that the general economic picture would get much worse before it got better. His Democratic colleagues and constituents had already learned the source of his anxieties—a Republican President in the White House—so that they had grown accustomed to his pessimistic chants even though they were humming the tune along with him. However, they agreed that it had been a long time since Woodrow Wilson, and that Sam was justified in singing a sad song.

Economic collapse was not restricted to America. The whole world was affected by several malignancies. Basic to the condition was the loss of life and property from World War I, universal indebtedness, political upheavals and fear of aggression, rearmament costs, and the decline in value of exports. But

America had certain internal problems, aggravated by wild speculation, fluctuating prices, excessive buying on credit, low incomes, and the slow strangulation of agriculture.

Picking up the loose ends of projected tariff legislation from the preceding Congress, the Seventy-first began re-examining America's import-export ratio. As far as this problem was concerned, the new President inherited trouble from the progressives within the Party, but he suddenly acquired a more serious threat within the "Old Guard." Governor Fisher of Pennsylvania appointed Joseph W. Grundy, a rabid protectionist, to fill a Senate vacancy. The President and the Senator found themselves in sharp disagreement, the one being a moderate and the other a full protectionist. The President had already committed himself to flexible provisions and was so successful in amending the proposed legislation that the Senator openly stated that he would not vote for the new tariff bill, though it bore his name—at this stage called the "Grundy bill."

Rayburn, on June 14, 1930, also spoke against the bill, calling it "infamous, unconscionable, and unprecedented." Historical in his approach, he surveyed the evolvement of tariffs, making reference to the years 1833 and 1846 when realistic legislation was achieved and trade was stimulated to an unprecedented degree. He described that as the era of great growth and prosperity. But since 1861 the Republican Party had been in control, scrapping all of the gains made under the Democratic regime and steadily raising the rates without regard to how the policy would affect the country. "The methods of writing tariff laws by Republicans has, since the first, been characterized by log-rolling, trading and trafficking, and throwing to the winds every consideration of justice and fair dealing to sections of the country and groups of citizens." He cited the gains of 1913 under Wilson, when a Democratic Congress created a tariff commission to investigate all tariff schedules and recommend just rates. The commission, he said, functioned efficiently until 1921 when the country began losing confidence because the caliber of its leadership had drastically declined. They were men who were appointed to do the bidding of selfish interests seeking favors through Federal legislation.

He remembered that in 1922, when Congress enacted the flexible provision, he denounced it as a violation of Congressional authority. Since the taxing power should be vested in Congress, tax measures, he believed, should originate in the House of Representatives, because its personnel were elected each two years and came fresh from the people with an expression of their will on public matters. Rayburn objected to the flexible provision because the President, by a stroke of the pen, could place additional taxes on products, many of them being those things essential to the operation of farming enterprises. The Grundy bill placed higher tariffs on items the farmer buys than on things he sells. In explanation, Rayburn pointed out that some people simply do not understand the way a tariff works. Seventy-five to eighty per cent of the land planted in the United States raises crops that a tariff cannot reach. Only crops where there is exportable surplus can be helped by a tariff. He used cotton as an example. The United States exported from fifty-five to sixty per cent of the cotton raised, and no cotton in competition with the ordinary American cotton was shipped into this country. Hence a protective tariff here seemed to him irrelevant. The protective tariff was designed to make the country prosperous, but instead it had contributed toward bringing the American farmer and small businessman to the brink of bankruptcy. Broken campaign pledges, he believed, should be incentive enough for the electorate to vote the Republicans out of power and save the country from economic chaos.

The Hawley-Smoot bill, providing for revised, flexible rates, was passed and signed into law by President Hoover, but not without strenuous opposition from Sam Rayburn and Democratic leaders in Congress.

As one of the measures to alleviate the depression, the President, near the end of December, 1930, had begun negotiations with all the railways in that portion of the United States east of the Mississippi to consolidate the lines into four systems. The purpose was to achieve lower operating costs and greater economic stability. By December 31 he was prepared to announce the achievement of his objective.

Sam Rayburn promptly argued against Hoover's plan by declaring that it was not one which should be thrust into partisan politics. Since the Interstate Commerce Commission had been established to pass on such matters, Rayburn believed that the Executive Branch had no right to step out of its jurisdiction and appear to be ordering a legislative branch to approve such a measure. He pointed out that members of both Parties had some constituents who had invested all their wealth in properties situated on weak roads. The proposed consolidation would result in the closing of such roads and consequently in financial ruin to some in small towns dependent upon them.

The Transportation Act had been amended in 1920 under Wilson to preserve service on weak lines and to establish a more orderly grouping of properties in the larger systems. The Clayton Act, he stated, had to be invoked to force some of the greater interests to divest themselves of properties which had not been approved.

Since the consolidation of railroads had been proceeding in a systematic fashion for ten years, Rayburn, in elaborating further, saw no reason for the White House's stepping into partisan politics with the hope of getting credit for something already underway. As he pointed out, the grouping of railways had already been brought within the jurisdiction of the Interstate Commerce Commission. Since about one-fourth of the railway mileage of the country was owned by little companies which were in no position to compete with the more fortunate ones, Rayburn had in earlier legislation worked out a grouping so that the burden could be distributed in such a way that the revenues could support service for all and allow a credit. He was opposed to enriching a few and crippling many; hence he argued for gradual consolidation in preference to the accelerated plan offered by the Administration.

Transportation and taxation were, in his estimation, two of the most vital issues before Congress during this era. Though he had studied the former rather diligently for the years he had been a member of the Committee on Interstate and Foreign Commerce, he frankly admitted that he felt great humility every time he tried to discuss one of the intricate transportation problems. Yet as a member of the Committee he felt compelled to fight for the defeat of all legislation not in the public interest. On the other hand, he recognized his more positive function as a Representative to write necessary legislation that would be in the public interest. Though he was a member of the minority he always deemed it his responsibility to sustain the majority, where necessary, in support of essential legislation.

The country's economic plight had already begun to have an influence upon Congress. During the Seventy-first Congress the Republicans had controlled the House under the strong leadership of Speaker Nicholas Longworth, but a coalition of progressives and liberal Republicans weakened the Administration's position. Hostility toward the Administration had increased, both in Congress and in the country at large. After the November elections of 1930, conservative Republicans appeared to control the House, but several untimely deaths among the "Old Guard" gave the Democrats a majority of four. Hence they promptly reorganized the House and elected John Nance Garner of Texas as Speaker, the first Democrat to hold the position since Champ Clark.

Speaker Garner almost immediately made Rayburn one of his lieutenants. In so doing, he passed over Democrats with more seniority, also to bring such men as John McCormack (Mass.) and Fred Vinson (Ky.) to the forefront. It was at this time that Rayburn cultivated the friendship of Fiorello H. LaGuardia (R., N.Y.), who became helpful to the Democrats on many liberal issues, with his refusal to hew to his own Party line.

The rise of Sam Rayburn to a position of influence and power was the result not only of his own unique qualifications, but was also to be attributed to circumstances other than seniority. According to George Rothwell Brown in the Washington *Herald* for January 8, 1933, after the toppling of the Cannon regime (the most complete legislative dictatorship that Congress had known in modern times), a Jim Mann of Illinois became a potent force in the House of Representatives. Demonstrating both genius and finesse, this Republican Chairman of the Interstate and Foreign Commerce Committee immediately capitalized on the conditions prevailing as the Cannon dynasty lay in ruins. He brought within his domain the railroads, public health, the coast guard, the Panama Canal, navigation, lighthouses, the Federal Trade Commission, the Power Commission, aviation, and several other areas indirectly related to transportation. He welded the Committee into an efficient and powerful unit to function as a Republican dominated instrument: however, he was not without a public-spirited bent. Jim Mann, though as calculating as any human being could be, overlooked one flaw in his superstructure—his own mortality. That which separates a Vice-President from President, or a political czar from oblivion, is but a single heartbeat. Yesterday's greats cannot rule from the grave. Mann died very suddenly. With Garner's rise to the Speakership, Rayburn subsequently became Chairman of the Committee in 1931, falling heir to this rich Republican legacy.

During the Administrations of Harding, Coolidge, and the first two years under Hoover, Rayburn's torch almost lost its flame. But with the sudden turn of events his hopes came alive. He found himself with a Chairmanship that paved the way for the majority leadership and ultimately the Speakership.

On February 21, 1931, Rayburn and Representative John O'Connor (D., N.Y.) were debating a measure entitled "Welfare of Mothers and Infants," in which Federal aid was involved. Rayburn had expressed his objection to any sort of aid over a term of years where the State matched Federal funds, because he feared local authorities would ultimately have to "come crawling up and agree with every condition" to get their half of the money. He called this type of grant the "fifty-fifty bribe to states," insisting that the one hundred per cent grants were preferable to avoid humiliation and Federal domination.

He went further in his definition of aid to say that the Government will state that money is given "for the hog, the cow, the horse, corn, oats, and wheat. . . . But Congress does not appropriate money for cows or horses as such. Congress makes appropriations to stamp out diseases among horses in order that they may pull plows and till the soil."

Sam Rayburn was depicted as the silent type, but many people overlooked the fact that he was reflecting, even calculating, while his more loquacious colleagues were filling up the pages of the *Congressional Record*. For a long time he had been collecting data on flood control in the Red River Valley. When the time was right he planned to ask Congress to add one additional item to his series of "cows and horses," that is "a dam"—a dam across the Red River at Denison. The idea had been in his mind since the early Twenties, when he saw the ravages of a flood and watched the muddy Red River change its course, to leave a newly constructed bridge "high and dry." He had also pondered over the utility of water power.

During the third session of the Seventy-first Congress (December 1, 1930—March 4, 1931), he incorporated into the *Record* a Resolution of the Texas Legislature, as well as his own remarks relative to flood control in the Red River Valley. He reported that the people of the upper valley believed that the best way to control the flood waters of the Mississippi River was to control the waters of the upper reaches of the lower tributaries of the river. He reasoned, along with many engineers, that a dam built at Denison, Texas, would impound the waters of the upper Red River and keep them from rushing into the Mississippi at a time when it had already reached its flood stage. This was the official beginning of his Texoma project, only a dream at this stage and not destined to become a reality until June of 1938.

The Seventy-second Congress, while it was not remarkable for finding permanent solutions to the country's economic ills, was an historic one in its pioneering effort to deal with crises. President Hoover was the first Chief Executive to attempt Federal leadership in mobilizing the economic resources of the people and in appealing to the individual citizen to lend his assistance in meeting the problems posed by the depression. Though this type of executive leadership was new, it was conducted within the constitutional powers of the Federal Government. It was applied to both the foreign and domestic fronts in a search for solutions.

The idea came to the President a month before the convening of Congress when he observed hopeful signs of economic recovery. The price of wheat, for example, was up fifty per cent, cotton fifteen per cent and industrial stocks forty per cent. Bank deposits were mounting some $25,000,000 a week with the hoarding craze temporarily arrested. Banks were optimistic. Trade at home and abroad showed signs of improvement, and unemployment seemed on the decrease. The gains, though, proved only temporary, for the symptoms of recovery mentioned above were offset by sudden relapses, to be followed by brief intervals of hope.

As a safeguard, the President convinced banks that the National Credit Association should be organized, its primary function to rediscount bank assets not eligible in the Federal Reserve System. Banks were frequently threatened with runs and it had become necessary to make loans against the assets of closed banks for purposes of paying dividends to depositors.

In January, 1932, the President took more decisive action by asking Congress to approve the creation of the Reconstruction Finance Corporation (RFC). Under this new agency, banks, insurance companies, railroads, and industrial corporations were able to borrow from the Government sufficient sums to prevent disaster, or to make essential developments which would prevent what otherwise would have been inevitable collapse. Thus large businesses essential to the country's economic stability were able to remain solvent and eventually to move ahead under their own power.

While the Reconstruction Finance Corporation bill was being discussed, Rayburn came forth with two amendments that reflect the pattern of his thinking—fairness in distribution of funds and the elimination of graft or exploitation. His first amendment set a limit of $100,000,000 for a single borrower. His second would bar attorneys, bankers, or intermediaries from participating in any of the funds to be loaned. He knew that there were many ex-congressmen, ex-senators, ex-members of boards and commissions who had opened law offices in Washington, who were able to convince the companies needing money that they knew the right people and could get it. Sometimes these firms charged more than ten per cent for their services. He gave a specific example:

> "A member of one of these commissions told me the other day that a claimant for $100,000 before that commission, who would only have had to file his claim in writing and it would have been reached in the usual routine and he would have gotten every dollar of his $100,000, was convinced by some of these hangers-on around town here that the only way he could get his money was to hire this lawyer and pay him a commission. Papers were filed, and the claimant got the $100,000 but attached to it was a contract for an enormous fee."

The practice was shocking to his sense of justice. He believed that corporations in dire distress applying for a specific amount of money should be protected to the end that they would receive one hundred per cent of the money, and not be penalized in any way by the amount of fees, which in the long run affected the general welfare.

Coming from a rural section of Texas, Rayburn naturally kept his eyes open to the needs of his kind of people, but he was not blind to the interests of the metropolitan areas. He recognized that congressmen had to cooperate, else they would never accomplish anything by simply voting for their own sectional needs. He illustrated his point in a debate on a measure for emergency relief from a grasshopper pest.

Explaining that he had never been one to ask the Federal Government to go entirely out of its sphere to aid the states, and reminding his colleagues of previous precedents of assistance with respect to the boll weevil, the pink bollworm, and predatory animals, he cited the destructiveness of the current grasshopper plague in Texas. He called attention to two congressmen, one from Kansas and the other from North Dakota, both agricultural States. He reminded the House that they had voted against the distribution of flour by the American Red Cross, with the privilege to the Red Cross of exchanging that flour for food "for the poor starving families of New York City, Chicago, Boston, and the other large cities." Rayburn did not want to be identified with these two congressmen or any group that thought exclusively of its own interests: "I want you gentlemen to remember that I helped and when the time comes you help us." Rayburn was not given to subtleties. In broad letters he spelled out the facts of life lest he be misunderstood.

The rise of Garner not only quickened Rayburn's powers of debate in the House, but also steered his thoughts into political channels. On January 12, 1932, he wrote Lewis T. Carpenter, Dallas, Texas, concerning the general political situation back home as it related to the forthcoming Democratic National Convention. Franklin D. Roosevelt was forging into the forefront with his successful job as Governor of New York.

> It appears to me [wrote Rayburn] that Franklin Roosevelt is far and away in the lead of all probable Democratic nominees. There is quite a movement throughout the country, however, designated to be a "Stop-Roosevelt" campaign. Roosevelt with his position in New York has appealed to the popular imagination of the American people as no other man does at this particular time. However, within the next two months there will be developments that will show us all, I think, a clear road whether it leads to Roosevelt or another direction.

Little was left to Carpenter's imagination as to the meaning of "another direction." Rayburn went on to discuss the qualifications of John Nance Garner as the man who occupied "the highest position of any other Democrat in public life in America today" and who was "doing the job of Speaker and leading the Democrats in the House in a masterly way." Believing that the times created the need for a certain type of leadership, he predicted that the weakness of Hoover would bring into focus a two-fisted variety like Garner, with his type of intelligence, courage, and statesmanship. Garner clubs, Rayburn told other friends, were springing up all over the State, but he believed it was too early for similar enthusiasm to be manifested in other parts of the country.

To T. W. Davidson, on January 26, he reflected similar views about Roosevelt's probable nomination unless another candidate was found. "I can say, however, that there is a nation-wide movement having for its purpose the stopping of Roosevelt." Rayburn believed Roosevelt would win, unless someone appeared who had "the popular appeal to the imagination of the American people as John Garner would have." Rayburn made his position clear that he was not *against* Roosevelt, but was *for*

Garner as a favorite son. "In other words," he explained, "our attitude should be that we will not fight any candidate but if neither of those most prominently spoken of now is satisfactory to the Convention, then we offer a man that everybody can and should get together on."

The names of Ritchie, Smith, Young, and Baker had been mentioned, but Rayburn proceeded to show why they could not win. The first consideration to him was always whether a candidate could win. His strategy was to express his respect for the leading figure, discourage the opposition so as to narrow the field in preparation for his candidate or dark horse, should the two-thirds rule prevent the convention from nominating its candidate. Thus he would be in a position to maneuver in two directions by rallying support for his candidate and, if necessary, he would be prepared to release at the strategic moment his own delegations to break a deadlock. He also learned very early that if one cannot place his man first he could place him in the position where he could accept the Vice-Presidency.

By the early part of May, Texas was buzzing with Garner talk. Californians were also beginning to see that perhaps the recently-elected Speaker of the House might be just right for the Presidency. Sam Rayburn's friendship for, and similar background to the Speaker made him the logical choice to manage the Garner campaign. With the multitude of ideas that came from people all over Texas, Rayburn did not feel alone in his assignment. Garner clubs in the State offered suggestions as to the organization of the trip to the Chicago Convention and the selection of delegates.

One letter from a businessman, dated May 10, 1932, reflects the type of zeal that was in the air:

> One of the most spectacular of Convention publicity stunts would be the presence and playing of the famous Old Gray Mare Band—mare, pretty girl and all. The Old Gray Mare would have trademark qualities exceeding those of the houn'dog of Champ Clark. A hall demonstration led by this band would be calculated to provoke more than the usual enthusiasm from floor and galleries, and would go well over the radio. Possibly the band could do some street parading in two or three cities en route to the Convention and, also, of course, in Chicago itself. I believe the cost of bringing the band would prove a good investment.
>
> If the idea appeals to you, you may wish to shoot it along to Silliman Evans.

Rayburn's replies to such letters left no doubts as to his feelings about sensationalism. Texans, he thought, should leave their broad-brimmed hats and Tom Mix boots at home, as well as all the ballyhoo and music that would be distracting. He felt they should go the Convention in the most dignified manner.

The booster club attitude and behavior was always shocking to Rayburn. Somewhat shy and reserved by nature, he was repulsed by the whole idea "of going Texan." He knew, too, that Texans were at a geographical handicap anyway, and if "they acted like fools at the Convention the rest of the country might believe they were." He had a pair of fancy cowboy boots but he used them strictly on the ranch to discourage chiggers and snakes, not for parade purposes.

Sam Rayburn told the story of the rise of Roosevelt and the Chicago Convention many times. His account, supplemented by that of James A. Farley, throws a very interesting light on the creation of a new and revitalized Democratic Party.

Perhaps two weeks before the Convention was scheduled to begin, the Roosevelt forces counted noses and learned that the newspaper reports of a deadlock were not too far wrong. The solution seemed to rest in a compromise with Speaker Garner, to prevail upon him to accept the Vice-Presidential place in exchange for supporting Roosevelt. Rayburn, as the middleman, became increasingly valuable as the days passed. Senator Harry B. Hawes of Missouri was selected to communicate with both candidates, and Farley was designated as the one to handle Sam Rayburn, who was the "generalissimo" of the Garner-for-President movement. When Garner got wind of the plan, he gave Hawes an old-fashioned tongue lashing over the telephone, making it very clear that he was not running for Vice-President.

Rayburn had also heard of Farley's intentions and suddenly dropped out of circulation. Farley searched through hotel corridors for Rayburn and telephoned everyone who might have seen him. He did manage to reach Silliman Evans of Texas, who was close to both Garner and Rayburn. Evans seemed to know where Rayburn was and promised to bring him to Farley's Washington apartment in the Congress Hotel. Rayburn knew exactly the nature of Farley's interest in seeing him and was playing 'possum, waiting for his value and popularity to increase. He was also planning his own strategy. When Sam Rayburn "got the drop" on a man, he might just as well have thrown up his hands.

Farley hurried back to his hotel and was alone with Mrs. Farley when at 11:00 P.M. there was a knock at the door. He opened the door and there stood Sam and Silliman, both very solemn. It is regrettable that Rayburn had no flair for poker because nature gave him the face. They had managed to slip in without anyone seeing them.

> The three of us [Farley states] went into the bedroom to confer. . . . I used all the salesmanship at my command to convince them of the necessity for a combination of Roosevelt-Garner forces. I pointed out that the New York Governor would have a substantial majority over all his opponents combined on the first ballot and that by all the rules of the game he was entitled to the nomination without delay. A parallel situation had taken place at Houston in 1928 when Al Smith had a majority, and his opponents had graciously given way and permitted his nomination without further contest. I recalled that Governor Roosevelt and Speaker Garner were personal friends and had always thought highly of one another. I pointed out the obvious fact that the first delegation to see the light of reason would naturally be in a strategic position if it switched over to our side and assured the Governor's nomination. The Texas delegation with its forty-six votes was big enough to do the job even without California. And then came the big moment—I promised to do everything in my power to secure the Vice-Presidential nomination for Speaker Garner if Texas made the switch.[1]

During all of Farley's appeal Sam remained very attentive and silent, elbows on knees and fingers interlocked as he leaned slightly forward. He never shifted his penetrating eyes from Farley's. When his turn came to speak, he selected his words carefully, as though he were dictating a telegram.

> "We have come to Chicago to nominate Speaker Jack Garner for the Presidency if we can. We are not against any other candidate and we are not for any other candidate. Governor Roosevelt is the leading candidate and naturally he must be headed off if we are to win. But we don't intend to make it another Madison Square Garden." [2]

Rayburn referred to the Smith–McAdoo slugfest in 1924, as well as to the connotation of the Garden as the scene of America's biggest prize-fights. Sam then looked at Silliman Evans, who nodded his approval.

Farley was satisfied even though Rayburn had made no promise. He gave no indication that he was interested in securing the Vice-Presidential spot for Garner. Farley knew these men, ". . . both Rayburn and Evans had given me the impression that they were reliable, candid, and willing to listen to reason." They agreed not to reveal the fact of the conversation to anyone, except the Governor and Louie Howe, because the news of the meeting could hurt both sides. Farley and Rayburn knew that there were some real mavericks in the Texas delegation. They agreed to meet again.

Since Congress was still in session, Rayburn waited until the last minute before catching the train to Chicago. First, though, he went over every detail with Garner. There was no fancy talk, just plain Texas lingo, which the two understood. They agreed on several points: 1) that Garner's name would be kept before the Convention as long as there was a legitimate chance for his nomination; 2) that the Democratic Party's interests should come before the ambitions of any individual; 3) that only Rayburn would have a direct line of communication with Garner; 4) that Rayburn would call Garner if he detected a deadlock.

On his own, Louie Howe was trying to negotiate with Governor Harry Byrd of Virginia for his twenty-four votes, but Governor Roosevelt preferred the Texas-California combination if it could be had. Roosevelt had the secondary motive of an arrangement which would secure Rayburn's support.

The "Stop-Roosevelt" forces were just as alert as the Governor's in keeping up with the other's movements. Sam Rayburn later reported that his activities were watched with interest by both groups, despite his utmost caution to be secretive. At a time like this there is a certain element of distrust and a desire among lesser lights to shine. The Roosevelt forces unofficially assigned Swager Shirley, a former congressman from Kentucky, to spend as much time as possible with his friend from Texas. The frequent references to Roosevelt's ability and strength, Rayburn admitted, did have a certain conditioning effect upon his thinking.

Nine candidates were nominated and then the real fight for additional votes began, even before the seconding speeches started. Farley said he drifted over to the Garner headquarters for a "goodwill visit," but he really wanted to make a plea with

Sam to make the break on the first ballot. However, his move was more from desperation than common sense, because he should have known Rayburn better than this. Rayburn liked formality and enjoyed the dignified implications of the word "conference."

> I swapped good-natured banter with several Garner men who were at headquarters, and in the meantime Rayburn and Evans were arranging so that we could leave unnoticed and go into another room for a conference.[3]

At this stage the story is essentially Farley's:

> When we were alone, I recalled that at out last meeting I had promised to do everything in my power to secure the Vice-Presidential nomination for Mr. Garner if Texas would swing to Governor Roosevelt and had stated that in my opinion, he could be nominated. "Now this time I know positively that we can bring his nomination for second place on the ticket."[4]

Rayburn bluntly asked what it was Farley wanted him to do, to which he responded:

> "Have the Texas delegation record its vote for Garner on the first ballot and then before the result is announced switch to Roosevelt. I feel certain that some state will make the break after it becomes apparent that the Governor has a big majority, and Texas might as well be first."[5]

Rayburn then explained his position. This is essentially his own account twenty-eight years later:

"We had more than 180 delegates and as many alternates who for months had been thinking about this Convention. They came to Chicago to back Jack Garner. It would have been unfair to these folks for me to commit them to any such arrangement. Texas had already pledged to stay with the Speaker for two or three ballots, certainly until we could tell what his chances were. 'How many ballots can you go without beginning to break?' I asked Jim."

When Farley had replied, "Three ballots, four ballots, and maybe five," Sam Rayburn resembled a poker player glancing down at his hand which he held close to his chest.

"Well," Sam had said, "we must let the Convention go for a

while, even if we are interested in the Vice-Presidency and I'm not saying that we are."

There were three painful roll calls during the night, Roosevelt having moved up from 666½ to 682. The Convention adjourned at 9:15 A.M. to meet again at 9:00 P.M. The Governor's lieutenants had tried desperately to get a break, making overtures to the other big delegations.

Physical fatigue and emotional stress often cause the amateurs to wilt and even some ambitious veterans to get excited, but not Sam Rayburn. While many were rushing around wearing themselves down, he was conserving his energy and trying to get some rest. Not a very sensitive or high-strung person by nature, he was not upset by the confusion around him, for he knew the people and how they would respond. He went to Chicago with a role to play; he trusted his judgment of the other characters in the drama, and waited calmly for the plot to unfold.

Sam Rayburn liked to use a rather homely illustration, however, in his portrayal of the events and the timing of his personal intervention. He knew that a rambunctious calf was easier to brand and doctor after it had choked itself to exhaustion at the end of a tight rope. "Why should a fellow try to throw a big calf," he mused, "when he's still stomping and running? Wait until he is easy to throw." The Roosevelt forces he could see were getting nervous and frantic, for there was no more slack in the rope. The Garner delegates were also getting exhausted and discouraged, not knowing what to do.

Senator Pat Harrison of Mississippi, a close Party friend to Sam Rayburn, was asked by the Roosevelt people to find Sam Rayburn and arrange a meeting. Stating that he and Silliman would come to Pat's room, a neutral zone, in twenty minutes, Rayburn hung up the telephone.

When Rayburn and Evans arrived, Farley dispensed with formalities and came to the point. He reviewed the problems, made references to the two previous meetings and the strict secrecy, which they agreed had been maintained. It took him about five minutes to lay the ground work. After he had finished, Sam rose to leave and spoke only these words, "We'll see what can be done." No reference was made to the Vice-Presidency.

Only the top Roosevelt people knew what was going on because at the very moment Farley and his companions were meeting, others in their organization were, out of desperation, trying to barter the Vice-Presidency to at least a dozen different delegations. While Rayburn was trying to get his Texas delegation together for a caucus, Speaker Garner telephoned him from his office in Washington. Garner was brief:

"I think it is time to break that thing up. This man Roosevelt is the choice of that Convention. He has had a majority on three ballots. We don't want to be responsible for tying up this Convention and bringing on another Madison Square Garden that might defeat the Party in November."

Garner asked that the nomination be settled on the next ballot. Rayburn concurred and said, "that he would try to work it out." This was in the middle of the afternoon.

While the members of the Texas delegation were assembling in the Sherman Hotel around 6:00 P.M., Rayburn left the room to find a telephone to call Garner for an official release. The Speaker was expecting Rayburn's call. The conversation follows:

"Do you authorize me to release the Texas and California delegation from voting for you for the Presidential nomination?"

"Yes."

"Do you release the Texas and California delegation from voting for you for the Presidential nomination?"

"Yes."

Sam Rayburn said goodby, hung up the receiver, and went back to the Texas caucus armed with Garner's statement. Only 105 of the 180 delegates could be rounded up, but those awaiting Rayburn's arrival were pro-Garner, with strong Newton D. Baker leanings. The more articulate Roosevelt people had been carefully screened before the delegation was made up, because of moderate and conservative thinking in Texas. Rayburn knew he was up against a hard core that would prefer to go home rather than vote for Roosevelt. Many of them did not feel as Garner and Rayburn did about the Democratic Party. In fact, some of these very same people in 1952, 1956, and 1960 bolted the Party. Even Garner himself later leaned toward their conservatism but quietly remained in the Party fold. Like Rayburn he always put Party loyalty above personal views, suppressing objection to individual planks in a platform.

Rayburn entered the room and stated that he had a release from Garner. He told this story about the reaction to his announcement and his own actions:

"A good friend of ours then jumped up and said, 'I'm gonna make a speech,' and he began telling Garner had said this, that and the other. He kept on going around and around, saying we don't want to run out on Mr. Garner, and then some of the women around me began crying, and then I said, 'We're not running out on Mr. Garner. He's not a candidate any more.' We just argued and argued. I tried to tell them Garner was out of it. Finally, though, when they began to row, I had to squeeze down on them and we voted fifty-four to fifty-one to go for Roosevelt.

"Then I had to get word to McAdoo, the head of the California delegation. I found him in the hall and he said, 'Sam, we'll vote for Jack Garner until Hell freezes over, if you say so.' But I told him to release his delegation, and he rushed in to his group and had no trouble with his outfit. He convinced them to go for Roosevelt; then he jumped on his motorcycle and struck off for the Convention hall.

"Finally I told Silliman Evans to go to the Convention and find Jim Farley and say, 'John Garner is out and we're going for Roosevelt.' And one of Roosevelt's States was Mississippi and it was about to quit him. Pat Harrison was the leader of the gang and he was strong for Roosevelt, and he walked up about that time when I was talking to Silliman. He stuck his head in and asked, 'What is it?' And Silliman told him 'John Garner is out and Texas is going for Roosevelt.' When Pat heard this he started running. He got halfway down the hall and came back running, 'Are you sure about this?' Then he took off again to get back to his delegation. In fact, he was already about to lose some of his people."

The deadlock in the Convention was finally broken by Speaker Garner himself in the interest of Party harmony. Several tried to get a telephone call through to Garner earlier but he would not talk to them. Only Sam Rayburn was in direct communication with him. The reward of the Vice-Presidency was never involved in Garner's decision; in fact, the first reference to it was made by Rayburn in a second telephone call to Garner after his name had already been placed in nomination and the balloting was about to commence. Since many of Garner's friends knew his high regard for the House Speakership and his lack of enthusiasm for the Vice-President's duties, they were hesitant about going ahead with a scheme that might not meet with his approval. But when Garner was convinced that Roosevelt honestly believed the country and Party needed him, he acquiesced. Of course, he relied a great deal on Rayburn's judgment since he knew Sam would do what was best for everyone concerned, and was able to ascertain people's real wishes and motives. Then it was actually Rayburn who made the decision on the Vice-Presidential position, partly to please the new liberal element and partly to offer a token reward to his Texas delegation. Fundamentally, it was done in the interest of unity and strategy.

There are some things that men of common minds do not discuss, certainly not before an election when victory is the prime concern. The opposition to Roosevelt in the Texas delegation came from a conservative element, likewise found in other states resistant to the new liberalism. Rayburn knew that if any man could win the confidence of this substantial minority and hold the Party together it was Garner. Neither the Speaker nor Governor of New York needed this fact spelled out for them. Rayburn's skill as a diplomat, in holding his delegation together and preserving good will, was clearly revealed. Aware of the trouble in his delegation, Rayburn on the fourth roll call refused to accept California's and McAdoo's offer to yield to Texas because he did not want his own group to be responsible for starting the break. It would look better, thought Rayburn, for another state to start the bandwagon. The die, however, was cast before Texas answered the roll call.

Despite all of Sam Rayburn's efforts to soothe his delegation's wounds and remove the Convention scars with plastic surgery, a disgruntled nucleus went home to sow their seeds of discontent. Though they did not begin to germinate for several years, their fertility is manifested in some of the stormy state conventions which Sam Rayburn wanted to forget, particularly the one in 1944. The Texas Regular movement was one expression of the conservative opposition to the "swing to the left." Rayburn found himself between this opposition and the new liberalism. He was from this time forward the titular head of the Party in Texas and as such its principal "trouble shooter."

Roosevelt had won on the fourth ballot, and Garner was nominated on the first ballot. There were mixed feelings at Chicago. Al Smith left the following day for New York City in something of a huff because he had lost to the man he helped groom for national politics. The delegates prepared to welcome the nominee at the Convention. Roosevelt then made his historic and unprecedented flight to Chicago to accept in person the Party's nomination. Rayburn had arranged for Garner to "talk to the delegates over a voice-amplifying system connected with the telephone." Rayburn thought this would have a good effect on some of the embittered people in the Texas group and would also set the tone of unity and victory.

When Rayburn saw Franklin Delano Roosevelt enter the hall, wearing the broad smile which was to become the trademark of good will and public confidence, a whole chain of reminiscences was set in motion.

"The first time I ever saw Mr. Roosevelt was when he walked out on crutches and nominated Al Smith in 1924 at the Convention in New York at Madison Square Garden. He called Smith 'the Happy Warrior.' Roosevelt was good at phrases and names that people liked to grab up. Of course, I saw Roosevelt in Houston in 1928 when he again nominated Smith. I do not remember that I ever met Franklin Roosevelt while he was around Washington. I talked to him on the telephone one time about something. I called up the Navy Department, when Wilson was President, to speak with Josephus Daniels, and the operator told me he was out but that I could talk with the Assistant Secretary. Well, when I hung up the 'phone I said, 'That's the nicest man I have talked to in Washington since I have been here.' But I did not actually meet Franklin D. Roosevelt until that morning in 1932 in his hotel room after he was nominated for President."

Rayburn remembered vividly that night in the Chicago auditorium when the Democratic nominee declared war on the Republican Party, on the Eighteenth Amendment, and on economic depression. The delegates thundered their approval when he promised a "New Deal" for the masses. Thus he set the temper of the next two decades. Little did Rayburn realize at the time that this new dynamo of political magnetism—empirical, impressionistic, and pragmatic—would provide the impetus to launch his own political rocket into orbit. The two men complemented one another very well, as the right hand does the left.

An almost monotonous routine had been worked out for the Congressman of the Fourth District—a national convention, a campaign for re-election, a speaking tour for the national ticket, and the resumption of duties in Washington for the short session.

His own opposition for an eleventh term consisted of a somewhat ancient figure in Texas politics—Choice B. Randell of Sherman (Grayson), who had held the office prior to Rayburn, and Jess Morris, a journalist from Greenville (Hunt).

The news about having the two opponents had come as something of a disappointment, as he expressed his regrets to several of his friends: "It was my thought along with yours and thousands of other friends that I would escape opposition this time but it seems that that is not in the cards for me." He accepted the state of affairs philosophically: ". . . there is a feeling abroad to oust everybody in office and have a new deal." He could not believe, as he explained during the campaign, that the people would "want to change executives in all offices and especially legislative ones any more than they would want to change doctors, lawyers, tenants, school teachers or bankers." In this frame of mind, Rayburn opened his campaign officially on July 12, 1932, at Whitewright, where the annual American Legion picnic was in progress.

Morris conducted a vigorous and spirited campaign, but was unable to bring into focus any criticism of the incumbent which could be construed as damaging. Though personable and affable in small groups, the absence of the tongue-in-cheek technique found Morris tangled up in the "back lash" of his own "casts." He rarely went so far as to discuss economics or politics, sensing that the laughter indicated approval of his ridicule. He was doomed to failure because of his utter seriousness in discussing what some regarded as trivial. He made these points: 1) the Bonham man had drawn $200,000 from the people in twenty years and had been in office long enough; 2) the Congressman lived in a "mansion" (the reference was to the large family home west of Bonham); 3) he should have resigned his Congressional seat and gone to war with the rest of the servicemen; 4) Morris said he was going to clip Rayburn's wings and send him back to the farm; 5) Morris said Rayburn spent his off-season time with well-to-do people and not with the common folk; 6) Morris called attention to the fact that he himself was six feet tall and weighed 215 pounds and was able to take care of himself in any crowd anywhere. Most of Morris' speeches dealt with the more personal elements. While he did not conduct an impressive campaign, he did succeed in "muddying the waters."

During the three weeks before the primary, Rayburn said many times that he welcomed the opportunity to visit again "with all the people who had been good to him." He recognized that his principal opponent, Morris, was exploiting the depression conditions, realizing quite well that unemployed people would not be rational in their thinking. For this reason, Morris continued to depict the incumbent as one who lived in plenty among those who were in need, volunteering his services to right all the wrongs which, he tried to show, this Congressman had helped generate.

Rayburn discussed his own major legislative achievements rather fully, and reluctantly made reference to the slurring remarks. He knew the people were angry and "the times were out of joint," but expressed the hope that the people would not settle the Congressional race by merely using a tape measure, by having the competitors step on a pair of scales, or by asking the disputants to go out into the back alley. He believed that recent political history in Chicago would support the assumption that a short man could handle himself all right. As to the accusation that he was a "snob and ran around with the big shots," he simply said, "Ask the people."

Apparently many voters who were in doubt did "ask the people" and received a satisfactory answer. Mr. Rayburn received a majority of 503 votes over the two opponents, so a run-off primary was unnecessary. The vote certified by the Chairman of the Democratic Executive Committee was Rayburn, 17,895; Morris, 10,481; Randell, 6,911.

Sam Rayburn always received numerous letters and telegrams, of a congratulatory nature, from people in high places and low, from men, women, and children. The latter correspondents brought him the greatest joy. Among the many letters from the younger admirers the following pleased him particularly:

Caddo Mills Texas
October 18th 1932

Hon, Sam Rayburn
Washington D. C.
Dear Sir, I am the little girl, you ask to write you, the night you spoke in our little city, on your campain. I will say that Daddy, Mother, and I are very happy that you were relected. I am going to school now and love my Teacher and my books. I am eight years old and I am in the 3rd grade. We have a good school. I guess I will close this little letter. I am very sorry, I have waited so long to write you.

You Little Friend
Hester, Joyce, Foster
Caddo, Mills, Texas
R. F. D. #2

While he was looking after some of his affairs connected with the farm and conducting what had turned out to be an ugly campaign, he received, on July 12, the following telegram from James A. Farley, National Chairman of the Democratic Committee:

> We will appreciate it if you can arrange your affairs so that you can devote your time and efforts to the election of Franklin D. Roosevelt as President and John N. Garner as Vice-President. The Democratic Party now has its great opportunity and it is the occasion for every Democrat to get behind the ticket and help win the victory in November. We greatly need your counsel and help in the direction of the campaign and would appreciate your immediate assistance in the North and East.

The same day the *Daily Courier–Gazette* of McKinney reprinted a story from the Washington *Daily News* which discussed Sam Rayburn as one of the five most likely to succeed Garner as Speaker if the Democrats should win. With this statement, the District began humming with speculation about his possible rise to Congressional heights. Having delivered the keynote address at the State Convention and having been selected as head of the delegation to Chicago, he was viewed as the power behind the throne in Texas. As Chairman of the Interstate and Foreign Commerce Committee he was gaining in national stature. He was now receiving correspondence unrelated to the problems of his District. To A. Y. Creager, Sherman, Texas, he wrote (February 9, 1932), about the effect of the Chairmanship to which he had arisen:

> My time is so entirely engrossed as Chairman of the Committee on Interstate and Foreign Commerce that I do not have the time to read bills before other committees and only study them when they have been reported and come up in the House from the committees.

During the second session of the Seventy-second Congress (December 5–March 4, 1933), he handled considerable correspondence relative to reducing the cost of Government expenses. The country was in a bad condition and there was a general unrest and uneasiness. The Democratic victory in November had merely set the stage for a change, but no one knew what the future held in store. Sam Rayburn's replies relative to economy followed this pattern. He favored reducing Federal salaries by eleven per cent and consolidating the War and Navy Departments for an estimated savings of $200,000,000 as immediate economy measures to reduce the cost of government. Later, when the proposal for merger failed, he blamed President Hoover for throwing Administrative strength against it.

Rayburn's correspondence during these three months reflected an unusual amount of pessimism, but these were perhaps the grimmest days of the depression. Relieving the pressure on people who owed money and relaxing the rigidity of banks and the attitude of the Federal Reserve Board were some of the problems that concerned him most.

> I have always been an anti-inflationist but this time I have certainly turned around on that and believe that the only hope of the country is in making money easier and getting the people in shape so that they can do some business of some sort.

He was also bothered that the Senate had failed to push a bill which would have increased commodity prices. The necessity for providing food for hungry people was another of his concerns. A certain amount of money had been made available to the President for such a purpose where local organizations were unable to meet the emergency. Rayburn used the plight of Chicago as an example of the conditions in 1932:

> It is reported that the city of Chicago is now feeding 600,000 people, a great majority of whom are willing to work. Just how long a city that is already broke can carry this on I do not know. The prospect before us, if we have a hard winter, is a very ugly one throughout the country.

The element of frustration was apparent when he tried to explain that the Government would have difficulty doing anything directly for the people. A typical letter of this type went to a gentleman in Celeste, Texas, on June 17, in which he described the vicious circle created by the Republican Party and President Hoover with their high protectionist policy that had put thirty million people on the farms out of business.

> If the farmers could buy, the railroads would be hauling to and fro. If they could buy, the warehouses and the factories would be emptied and factories would start and put people to work so they could buy some of the surplus.

Not only did he blame discriminatory laws but frequently referred to the extravagance of government: Federal, state, county, and municipal.

His vote for the Soldiers' Bonus stirred up many critical letters, for his action seemed to be contradictory to the economy measures he supported. Aware of the belief that he had violated a surface consistency in such matters, he explained that Congress had made a contract with the veterans to pay at some future date this Adjusted Service Compensation. Also the money released, he explained, would partially alleviate the more immediate financial distress among a few and put money into circulation.

However, when one views the man's over-all voting record, an amazing amount of consistency, even including his emergency actions, is revealed. Yet he evolved with the times. Such newspapers as the Dallas *Morning News* were quick to detect any show of inconsistency or an action which might be described as political. Some journalists have tried to determine whether the District molded his attitudes or he the District's. Since there is such a remarkable compatibility between the two, one finds himself faced with the ancient dilemma of the "chicken or the egg." But the closest observers of this long relationship will recognize that Mr. Sam kept abreast of the national trend and was always in the driver's seat and not in the harness. He shaped public opinion in his District, despite the existence of some ultraconservatism and a reluctance to yield to the times.

Two problems fell in his lap in 1932, which gave him no little concern. Although history has revealed that Roosevelt and Rayburn were amazingly congenial, there was considerable adjusting to be done by both men. The Eighteenth Amendment was the first barrier which might have separated the first citizen of Hyde Park and the gentleman from Bonham. On December 21, 1932, a "Beer bill" was being debated. Rayburn pointed out that the Democratic platform adopted at Chicago contained a plank that proposed legislation which was unconstitutional: "Sale of beer and other beverages of such alcoholic content as is permissible under the Constitution." He stated firmly that the alcoholic content mentioned in the Volstead Act outlawed the sale of beverages containing enough alcohol to make them intoxicating, and that 3.2 beer contained alcohol sufficient to be intoxicating. Since the Eighteenth Amendment had not been modified and was still a part of the Constitution, he did not feel that Congress could entertain new legislation which obviously set up a conflict.

He said he could not support a bill that was unconstitutional but that he would favor resubmission of the whole question to the people to see if they would repeal or modify the Eighteenth

Amendment. On this point he was walking a very narrow and precarious line because his District was full of people who were so violently opposed to the liquor traffic that they were unwilling to discuss such things as constitutionality. Here was Rayburn's view: "The people of the United States did a radical and drastic thing when they adopted the Eighteenth Amendment." They did it because they were convinced that the local and state authorities could not adequately control a nationally organized liquor traffic. He referred to the open saloons and the belief that the brewers were responsible for them. He stated that the present "Beer bill" would bring back the offensive open saloon, which the Eighteenth Amendment had abolished. Though the Eighteenth Amendment was radical and drastic he chose to defend it, but preferred to submit it for reconsideration by the voters and not pass this subterfuge bill which was unconstitutional. Therefore, he voted with the House to resubmit the Amendment but stated that he would oppose its repeal. Many people, interpreting his vote on resubmission as a vote against prohibition, flooded him with letters to find out why he had shifted his earlier position—the one he held during his early campaigns.

It was on just such an issue as the foregoing that his colleagues recognized a rather fundamental assumption on the part of the man who was later to become one of the most celebrated leaders of the House of Representatives. Years later, Mr. Sam explained the nature of leadership thus: "You can't be a leader, and ask other people to follow you, unless you know how to follow, too." In the case of the prohibition issue he was following the strong command of the Constitution of the United States. Later, as Majority Leader and as Speaker, it might have been the majority opinion of the House, or as in the Tidelands case, the will of his section of America. Sam Rayburn was the type of leader who was aware of those people whom he led. Such a person could never have become a dictator.

If the problem of prohibition gave him some concern, that of redistricting caused even more. It is a topic which the agriculturists of the Fourth have thought about periodically, with the census figures from time to time being a reminder. The Dallas *Morning News* has also played the role of gadfly in this particular issue; however, Mr. Sam was never too appreciative of efforts that would destroy a balance between rural and metropolitan areas. The Fourth District in 1932 was short by 60,000. The State Legislature in 1931 had played with the issue, but the

House and Senate in Austin could not agree. Rayburn wanted Lamar and Rockwall Counties in the Fourth because these had an economy similar to that in his District. The Senate version of the bill was not congenial to Rayburn's plan, but he hoped the new bill in 1933 would follow his thinking. He and the people of the Fourth did not want to be swallowed up by a redistricting that would place a slice of Dallas County in their District.

The people of the Fourth have always rejoiced in a quiet pastoral atmosphere and the setting of their rolling countryside, and have never had a yearning to be contaminated by the views of a neighboring "Yankee city," to voice the 1932 thinking of some in Fannin County. Its citizens preferred the editorial policies of papers like the Bonham *Daily Favorite,* Sherman *Democrat*, and Denison *Herald* to those of the Dallas *Morning News*. They believed that the people should shape the philosophies of their press, and not the press the philosophy for its citizens. They held some rather old-fashioned concepts about politics and economics, and they looked to Sam Rayburn to help them preserve these beliefs. He never shirked this mandate.

☆ XII ☆

The New Deal

IN THE late summer of 1932 two "country squires," as their opponents might critically refer to them, met at Warm Springs, Georgia, to get acquainted and discuss their mutual concern—the November election. Both at the age of fifty appeared at the peak of health and prepared to face the physical stress that the approaching challenge would demand of them. Though one was from Hyde Park and the other from Bonham, with different economic and social backgrounds, they were united in a single purpose—to help the "forgotten man," an expression Roosevelt used frequently during the campaign. The one saw the "forgotten man" as a person who lived in the crowded tenement sections of our larger American cities, without a job or opportunity for employment. The other envisioned him as the agriculturalist who had lost his purchasing power. Much of the liberal social legislation for the next decade can be attributed to the cooperative efforts of these two Democrats, and others like them who possessed social consciousness. With at least two things in common—a loyalty to Party and a love of fellowman—they united their efforts to give America a New Deal.

Rayburn came back to Bonham from Warm Springs with the firm conviction that FDR would win the election and make a good President. In his tour of the campaign circuit, Rayburn spread a new optimism and renewed faith, pledging that Roosevelt would do something about America's plight. The promise of liberation from a twelve-year bondage under a philosophy which had stifled his Jeffersonian instincts now sharpened Rayburn's tongue. Roosevelt and Rayburn spoke as prophets and emancipators.

The people believed them, for Roosevelt received 472 electoral votes to Hoover's 59; but the popular response showed only 57.4 per cent for Roosevelt, that is 22,821,513 to Hoover's 15,761,787. Perhaps more significant were the million votes for the Socialists and Communists, which seemed to be an expression of the general unrest and loss of faith during the "sterile years."

The Roosevelt triumph gave Mr. Rayburn perhaps his biggest thrill over a Democratic victory. He enjoyed reminiscing about his Party's triumph; and, if one wanted to set him off on his favorite theme, it was only necessary to ask: "What were the conditions under Hoover? Don't you believe Roosevelt would have done something had he been President at the time?"

Here is a portion of his reply to these questions:
"Well, he did. It was bad when we came in in 1933 with fourteen million people unemployed. People just don't think about how bad that was. If the breadwinner in the family had a wife and one child, that would be forty-two million who had no buying power at all. And, at that time there were thirty-three million people on the farms of the country. They were selling the products of their toil at a price so far below cost of production that their buying power had vanished. We add those two classes together and that is seventy-five per cent of our one hundred thirty-three million people. No wonder our factories and 5,770 banks and trust companies closed. And Mr. Hoover just didn't meet the condition, but when Mr. Roosevelt came in, he had a program and we went into action."

Rayburn's speeches for the next eight or ten years were flavored with this material. There is one statement he repeated countless times: "In 1932 your cotton sold for 4½ cents per pound, oats 9 cents a bushel, corn 15 cents a bushel, wheat 28 cents a bushel, a canner cow 1½ cents a pound and a good steer 3½ cents a pound." Some of his constituents quietly observed that his speeches along this theme were like recordings because of their exact repetition; yet most of them admitted that they could not refute the statistics. This 1932 political oratory never wore thin or became obsolescent in the Fourth. One of his closest advisers once asked him why he did not change this speech. His reply was, "It must be all right, for it continues to get the votes." He used it for the twenty-year period of Democratic rule without any ill effects. He believed, too, that over a long stretch of time like this, there were many young folks coming along who needed to know just what a depression was like, to understand what their parents endured, and above all, who should be aware that the seeds for it were planted under Republican leadership in the White House and Congress. As he added, "I want the children in the Fourth to be properly educated about history."

Franklin Roosevelt from the outset was fascinated by the phenomenon of Sam Rayburn. He had already received a brief exposure to "Cactus Jack" Garner, and now he discovered another out of the same mold. The thing about these two men which charmed him most was their independence of mind, individualism, uninhibited appraisals of people and problems, their sincerity, trustworthiness, and basic honesty. Roosevelt remarked many times to Rayburn's friends that he had to accustom himself to the man's sincerity and frankness. In New York society, for example, Roosevelt had been used to saying that "Mrs. So-and-so looked lovely" or he had "a delightful time at a function" when actually he felt the opposite. Then came the refreshing experience of Sam Rayburn. This man from Texas refused to indulge in small talk. He was not a sorehead or a cynic, but he refused to speak an untruth about anything just to make pleasing conversation. Instead he would find a more appropriate evaluation of a social function or a celebrity, which would not offend but be closer to the truth, or he would make no comment. Roosevelt admitted that politicians in New York generally said just the opposite of what they really believed. Rayburn and Garner, on the other hand, spoke with uninhibited simplicity.

What Roosevelt was trying to say can be illustrated by an incident much later, during the 1960 campaign. Rayburn and Truman were attending a reception on the Baylor University campus following a political rally, and by some strange coincidence Truman found himself at the piano giving everyone his routine. There were "ooh's" and "ah's" from the weaker sex, and it appeared that Mr. Sam was not too pleased with the frivolity. He had his mind on the "shivaree" the Baptists were organizing throughtout Texas to give the Catholic Presidential candidate. One of the older women standing next to Mr. Sam remarked, "Oh Mr. Speaker, isn't it a shame Mr. Truman didn't go in for music instead of politics?"

Without batting an eye Rayburn remarked, "I am certainly

damned glad he didn't, for it would have been a hellava loss to the country." The lady apparently did not hear a word he said, but the roar from the gentlemen was evidence that the Speaker made his point.

Roosevelt once asked Rayburn why he did not bring along a secretary when he made sweeping commitments or pledges, to which he replied, "I always tell the truth the first time and do not need a good memory to remember that." Herein rests the reason for the silence in committee, or on the floor of the House, when Rayburn took his position to speak. People enjoyed hearing his brand of the truth.

Roosevelt was also once heard to say, "I like the way those two Texans perform." About Mr. Sam he added, "The man's word is as binding as a legal contract." Thus with a mutual respect for one another the two men began their labors to pull the country out of the depression and disillusionment which had virtually broken the spirit of business and crushed the hopes of younger America.

By March 4, 1933, when the new President took the oath, the business and banking enterprises were at a standstill. A frightened people began drawing their savings from the banks and created near disaster because the Federal Reserve branches were dangerously stretched. A great deal of the business in areas like Rayburn's part of the world was even conducted by means of bartering; for example, a medium fryer on foot was worth several spools of thread and some buttons.

During the short session of the Seventy-second Congress (December 5, 1932—March 4, 1933), Rayburn watched many futile efforts to win the race with disaster. He made a courageous stand on the Farm Loan Relief bill, January 12, 1933. Here he covered familiar ground in his story of the depression and its effect upon the farmer. Being a farmer himself and quite approachable by those with his interests, he received correspondence, like the following, with unrestrained emotion about the effects of economic adversity:

> There is one thing I think ought to be done at once and that is stop all land foreclosure. it isent right to foreclose on property at a time like this. it is breeding trouble. A many a man has been crushed that if he had been given a chance would have made good. you cant pay anything with present prices of farm products. neither can a man unemployed. I believe the loan co should be protected I believe they

> should be given a lien on one-third and one-fourth of crops. but this foreclosure must stop or else it will cause trouble most of loan banks are fair. but there are a few who are not. they should be made stop.

The letter, written in pencil on narrow tablet paper, is a good example of a type Mr. Rayburn received on farm problems. This gentleman was selected as the community spokesman by a committee to write because he considered himself Mr. Sam's "second best friend" in the County. Rayburn valued the man's loyalty and gave this communication his personal attention, as he always did sincere expressions and particularly those so written.

Sam Rayburn was not a man to show undue emotion, but he did feel deeply about the people's problems. About such a letter as the above he had been known to say, "Now, these are the folks I enjoy helping." He knew people had faith in him, for their delegations had called on him frequently at his Bonham home. Many times they had been heard to remark, after wrestling with a problem, "Let's go talk to Sam." Just as a son takes his troubles to his father, so the people of the Fourth took theirs to "Mr. Sam." He knew they were coming and expected action. He considered them his personal responsibility and never ceased to fight their battles.

To another constituent at Trenton, Texas, on the verge of losing his farm, he wrote that he had already moved to get the Farm Loan Bank at Houston to make loans in Fannin County. He added, "To me the most tragic thing in our economic set-up is to see a man who has spent a lifetime trying to pay for his home and has paid it all except for a small amount and then see it get away from him." He also argued for home ownerships and said he would solicit every bit of American statesmanship to do something for agriculture. In closing, he assured his dedication to the cause.

The Democratic victory and the festivities associated with ushering in a new President brought some satisfaction to Rayburn, but an ominous overcast of national pessimism gave him a sense of uneasiness. Specifically, he feared those "forgotten men" who walked the streets in grim silence, like phantoms waiting to strike down the living. Economic necessity had divided America into two groups—"the have's" and "have-not's." Although it had been sixteen years since Rayburn had last sat at an Inauguration in the box seat of victors, his joy was colored by anxiety. He wondered if the people had waited too late to change Administrations. The activity surrounding the opening of Congress on March 5, and his own increased prestige as Chairman of the Interstate and Foreign Commerce Committee, brought some comfort. He derived benefit, too, from repeating over and over again in his mind the thoughts of the new President, whose words inspired courage and renewed faith:

> "This great Nation will endure as it has endured, will revive and will prosper. So, first of all, let me assert my firm belief that the only thing we have to fear is fear itself—nameless, unreasoning, unjustified terror which paralyses needed efforts to convert retreat into advance."

The Fourth District was now beginning to appreciate more fully the potentialities of their Congressman. Some believed that he should have succeeded Garner as Speaker when he went to the opposite end of the Capitol. Twenty-six years as a lawmaker, however, had taught Sam Rayburn to have a great deal of patience, and no one on Capitol Hill knew any better than he that "they also serve who only stand and wait." Texas held six important chairmanships of committees; hence Garner and he saw the futility of pressing their cause at this time, since commitments had already been made to promote Henry Rainey of Illinois. Though not yet a contender for Speaker, this five-foot, six-inch Texan was already one of the tall men in Congress. His Stock and Bond bill, transportation and War Risk legislation, the bill for the return of railroads to private ownership with the rate-making power vested in the Interstate Commerce Commission, were only a few of his interests that proved he had a program which was respected, and which had kept him in the forefront of discussion by the gentlemen on both sides of the aisle.

His practical turn many times dissuaded him from indulging in the rhetorical and emotional flourishes with which men like the silver-tongued Daniel Webster had stamped their imprint on American political oratory; yet Rayburn's innate feeling for the word and compassion for humanity on occasion exploded into simple but refined utterance.

Early in the Seventy-third Congress, he sounded the keynote of representative responsibility during the so-called One Hundred Days. Pointing out that he had served with five Presidents and had never failed to uphold the emergency recommendation of any of these, he appealed to everyone to support the leader in his effort to help "our unhappy country":

"My program, your program, is not here, but the program of the man to whom the people of the United States are and must be looking today is before the Congress, and what are we going to do with it?"

The eyes of America, he said, were focused upon the Capitol, looking to this man for leadership. "Are we going to defy the electorate that has already spoken so emphatically and tell them that we have refused to give him the instrumentalities with which he can meet the emergency with which we are faced?" His plea was phrased in such a manner that no one could misunderstand. As his rural constituents liked to describe Mr. Sam's oratory, "he pitched the fodder where even the smallest heifer could reach it." "During my service here," said Rayburn, "I have found that those members who submerge their own wills to those of the leaders of the nation are the ones who survive." Despite the fact that Democratic leaders failed by fourteen votes in their caucus to support President Roosevelt's economy program, Rayburn's message to the House had its influence, as the vote of 266 to 138 indicated.

However, Rayburn was not always this successful. He had tasted defeat many times during the long twelve years of opposition rule, but he refused to admit that he had been beaten. One of his more rustic constituents observed that Sam Rayburn was like the scarred and veteran bronc rider of the rodeo. The only way he could be stopped was to cut off his head and hide it where he could not find it. Famous for his dogged persistence, he would reopen issues on which he had been beaten many times.

His Federal Securities Act, approved by the House in 1914 but defeated in the Senate, is an example of a measure he brought out of mothballs in 1933. This bill, an outgrowth of the Stock and Bond bill, was designed to regulate credit in security transactions, to limit speculation; in security markets to prevent unfair practices; in securities publicly traded in, to make public adequate information and to discourage the unfair use by insiders of information which was not made public.

The life of a congressman like Rayburn was filled with variety. The more influential he became the greater was his sphere of activity and service. He was, first of all, the servant of the Fourth, but his radius was beginning to reach across Texas and even into other states. By 1933, his correspondence indicated that he was a political oracle, a devotee of historical shrines, as well as a specialist on anything relative to agriculture. Somehow, he found the time to give of his knowledge about these problems even though the requests did not come from his own district.

For example, a young man wanting to run for Congress wrote and asked if Rayburn would analyze the situation in a given district and advise if he thought there was a chance of his victory and if he considered the career worthwhile. Rayburn stated that he could not make the decision for someone else, but he would subject the young man to the following inquisition. What is your personal strength? What are your limitations? How well are you acquainted with the district and how well are you currently known? How much money do you have? How much free help can you get from devoted friends? Can you carry your home county solidly? Can you run reasonably well in all parts of the district? Do you have sufficient media for publicity to offset the incumbent's use of the Congressional frank and publicity from Washington? How many candidates will there be? Then Rayburn proceeded to comment on the problem of staying in Congress after being elected and the expense of maintaining an office in Washington and back home. He suggested that this person talk to friends who would tell him the truth about his chances, for they would be committing themselves to his cause. He did not neglect to point out, however, the great opportunity for public service.

Rayburn's love of or interest in American history is revealed in both his speeches and concern for public shrines. In 1933, he became interested in the restoration of Stratford, the home of the original Lees in Virginia—Thomas Lee, Richard Henry Lee, Francis Lightfoot Lee and Lighthorse Harry Lee, who was the father of Rayburn's hero. Mrs. Harry B. Hawes, wife of a former Senator, and a group of ladies, knowing of the Congressman's affection for Robert E. Lee, had little trouble convincing him that the old mansion should be reclaimed. Mr. Rayburn then made an appeal to some of his Texas friends who shared his appreciation of history. Some time later he visited the mansion to see what progress had been made.

A product of the farm, with at least a quarter of a century of his own experimentation in crop rotation, conservation, planting, animal husbandry, and the like, he had been rather widely known in progressive agricultural circles. But, perhaps it was not until about 1933 that most people around Bonham became conscious of the man's full capacities and insight as an agriculturalist. Valton J. Young, the newly appointed County Agent, who in 1955 collected his reminiscences of these early years, was the first to discover the depth and breadth of the man's knowledge, and will probably remain for years the best source of information about Mr. Sam's rural economics.

Young recalls vividly that hot afternoon in 1933 when he made his first County Agent visit on "the Congressman." The sun was so hot on Rayburn's bald head that beads of sweat stood out all over it. Ordinarily he wore a hat to protect his sensitive skin from heat and cold and the obnoxious mosquitoes. An extra handkerchief for mopping the scalp was a necessity from June to September.

Rayburn had an instinct about people. He could recognize character by the shape of the jaw and the feeling in the eyes. He could be as quick in his judgment about a member of the human race as the cattle buyer at his auction. Valton Young sensed that he had passed the examination, but such approval did not mean that the two men would become immediately confidential. Rayburn had a knack for recognizing integrity and honesty; he could also make a man feel that his arm was around his shoulder and that he was doing something important. But there would be no slap on the back or future greeting of a "good time Charlie." Many congressmen observed this quality and paid tribute to the reserved and sincere type of friendship that they enjoyed.

Majority Leader John McCormack of Massachusetts phrased it this way:

> "The man with a heart of gold. That is my estimate of Sam Rayburn. His friendships are based upon loyalty. He is a man who fights for his friends no matter who they are, no matter from what section of the country they come, or what their political affiliation may be; a man whose nobility of character has impressed itself upon everyone who ever served with him during his long, honorable, and trustworthy service in this body. My association with him, no matter how long I live, will be always one of my treasured memories."

The amazing thing to Valton Young was the absence of conversation during these moments of judgment. Rayburn had briefly pointed out the great opportunities for an agricultural agent who really "meant business." Both men made passing remarks, not of a complimentary nature, about the previous Administration and the lingering effects of the "Hoover Depression" upon the economy of Fannin County. Young was made to feel that he had been placed in a position of importance in troublesome times to do something for the people.

He had heard Minnie Eldridge, his co-worker and County Home Agent, refer to the Congressman's brothers and sisters; and when they left the living room and went out into the backyard they found Tom and Miss Lou sitting under one of the hackberry trees, where Mr. Sam did a great deal of talking about cattle, farming, fishing, government, and politics.[1]

On this day Young saw the man in action and discovered the brevity with which he could satisfactorily dispense a piece of business. While Young was talking with Miss Lou in the backyard, Sam Rayburn went into the living-room for a meeting with a group of his constituents, but not more than ten minutes was required for him to whip out a solution and decision. He did not delay or hang around waiting for people to make up their minds to leave. Though kind in his manner, he left no doubt in a visitor's mind that he had finished the specific business. He expected a constituent to come with a problem clearly in focus, for he would not thrash around with a man who had not done some thinking beforehand. The issue had to be sharp, like a bill which had gone through a committee. Rayburn was not necessarily a man to help someone clarify his thinking. Instead, he viewed his job as that of finding solutions. His constituents said he could find them almost as quickly as a bolt of lightning could split a cottonwood tree. When the conference was over he instinctively made a move toward the door, smiling, and shaking every hand before he had taken scarcely three steps.

Young heard the front door slam, looked up, and almost instantly saw this man of strong physique and medium height coming out the back door and down the steps to the place where they had stood only a few minutes before. He had a lighted cigarette clutched between his tight lips and wore a soiled narrow-brimmed Panama hat pulled far down on his head.

Rayburn showed a change of pace, despite his great amount of energy. He liked to show land but there came a time when he could slow down and be a connoisseur. Young remembers his remarks:

> "Mr. County Agent, how about my showing you some blackland farming? Let's go by the windmill for

a cool drink of free country water. It's going to be mighty hot out there in the sun where we are going today, but this kind of weather is just what it takes to make cotton grow. With plenty of underground moisture such as we have now, I never worry about the heat. Especially if the wind continues from the south. A north wind here in the summer burns our crops up in no time, because it has no moisture in it."[2]

As they neared the dairy barn and granary at the entrance to the pastures noted for their clovers, Rayburn continued:

> "You see, Agent, our main cash crop on the one-hundred-and-sixty-acre farm is milk. But in my opinion a cash crop is only secondary to a successful farm family. The first function of a farm is to make the owner's family a good living. This includes a good family food supply grown right on the farm. If a family goes on a farm or ranch to make a livelihood, they usually do that—plus making some money. If they go on a farm just to make money, they nearly always end up doing neither."[3]

As they toured the sanitary dairy barn, they met "Old Henry," as Mr. Sam affectionately referred to him.

> "Henry is responsible for this clean-smelling barn. These half-dozen milking stanchions are cleaned twice daily. Our milking time starts at five in the afternoon and at five in the morning, rain or shine. If we have a special cow on a butterfat test to make an official record of high merit, she is milked three times daily instead of twice, but that is not usual."[4]

The harvesting of the oat crop had just been completed and a young neighbor boy was trying to back a heavily loaded wagon, pulled by a nervous team of black horses, against the granary door. Seeing the problem, the Congressman stepped in front of the team. Clutching the inside bridle bits, he aimed the wagon perfectly, with the same authority and precision he used in Washington and as Permanent Chairman of the Democratic National Conventions.

As they entered the breeding pen to examine the prize Jersey bull, Rayburn's caution became obvious. He knew the dangers involved and was always careful to insure the maximum safety for herdsmen and admirers of this celebrated animal.

> "This rugged monarch, White Sox" [he said] "has a name very becoming to him. Do you notice the peculiar white markings on all four of his legs and along the sides of his massive body? You will observe, as we look over my entire herd, that he transmits some of these flashy white spots to all of his daughters. At least half of my twenty registered cows are his offspring. You see, Agent, some sires have the hereditary ability to produce outstanding qualities in their daughters and not in their sons. White Sox is that kind of bull. All of his daughters are show animals in type, conformation, and temperament. Although he is not a great show animal himself because he is too rough and completely void of many fine points in Jersey type, White Sox does give all the better qualities of the Jersey breed to his female progeny. This potent sire is not unlike some ugly men who have very beautiful daughters." [5]

This pilgrimage through the Rayburn farm and others, known to those who are less familiar with animal husbandry than the two gentlemen on this special tour, often set in motion a stream of generalizations because to Rayburn his bull, each of his cows, even the hogs had qualities that were different. He knew their weaknesses and strengths, as well as their behavior patterns. One who had made both this inspection trip, and the tour of the legislative halls with Mr. Sam, would recognize the same master, with a knowledge and understanding of the many people and their individual differences.

While Young and Rayburn were making a quick swing down a narrow lane east of the dairy lot to the horse barn, poultry yard, garden, and orchard, the colored maid named Bobbie brought word that a delegation of farmers had arrived. Returning to the house they inspected the rich soil of the cornfield and looked across the field of cotton in full bloom.

Mr. Rayburn asked the Agent to remain for the interview because the problems of the farmer would be discussed. The more outspoken of the six men had been president of a national farm organization and had fought Rayburn politically. This fact was revealed to the Agent before the two reached the house, but Rayburn's comment was, "I simply haven't room in my heart to hold hatred. I am never opposed to farm organizations unless they have some leaders trying 'to farm' the farmers." [6]

During these depression years the constituents all told the

same story whether they came alone or in delegations. They expressed their woes while the Congressman listened in pained silence. Financial ruin to farm and city, ministerial prayers for God's guidance to relieve adversity, low prices for all farm products, no markets for some things, hogs and cattle selling for prices lower than production costs, and no credit—this was the thread out of which the farmers spun the fabric of their depression woes.

Knowing that their way of life was a part of him and that they were the backbone of America, he tried to offer some encouragement to these six men and others like them. The message followed a line of reasoning which some heard many times in his speeches:

> "You gentlemen know, as all my friends should know, I never listen to or get excited over the whims and the caprices of the selfish and the cynical. I consider politics as the intricate science of government. I know that without vision nations perish. I love friends and I try to be a friend, but if I had listened to all that even my best friends told me, I would have been out of politics a long time ago.
>
> "As you know, agriculture has some very great needs. These needs must be met in order to help bring back the whole country to better standards of living. The good people will go along with such a program, I believe. You know, in order to get along, a person sometimes has to go along. That does not imply that anybody ever has to become a rubber stamp, because when two minds always agree, one of them is doing all the thinking. But where there is an umpire in the game and a ruling is made, I learned in baseball that it is a poor player who becomes angry, throws his bat at the umpire, and quits the game like a spoiled child.
>
> "Our long-range program for agriculture must not discriminate against any segment of the national economy. It must be beneficial to all the people, and I predict that it will.
>
> "The greatest domestic problem facing our nation is saving our soil and water. If the next few American generations continue to be careless and wasteful with our soil and water as have the last few generations, our great problem will not be one of burdensome sur-

pluses such as we have today, but the crisis will be one of a more serious nature—one of thirst, hunger, and malnutrition. Our soil belongs to more than its present owners and occupants. It also belongs to unborn generations. Society has a public duty to help protect it. In every community of this nation there should be and there will be a soil conservation program that will reach into every neighborhood, and out into every farm and ranch.

"The agricultural scientists say, and with very good proof, that it is not the well-balanced farms that are creating our surpluses—that in most sections a diversified agriculture would be much more profitable.

"Excessively low and unstable prices, inadequate credit, poor conveniences, and the high percentage of tenants on the farms and ranches are so serious that it would be fatal to keep ignoring them. There will be something done in the near future about each one of them, too. It is going to take money, patience, vision, and time.

"Many more of our good people should own the farms and ranches on which they live, and many more of them will when given adequate opportunity. A few will not do well by this opportunity, but very few things in life attain perfection.

"At the time farmers plant their crops, especially the basic crops, they are entitled to know something about the price those crops will bring at harvest time. A more orderly marketing plan that calls for more stable prices for agricultural crops of a basic nature is on the way now. This will mean a more stable income and a more stable economy for all in the end. It is good insurance, and it is just good common sense.

"Another thing, too, many worthy people who live on the soil do not have any dependable source of credit, local or otherwise. Our present local lending agencies cannot be justly blamed for this condition. They need protection, too, and they are already getting it. You have already heard about the Federal Deposit Insurance Corporation. I do hope their memories will not be too short, and they will remember that their protection came first. Once these good people are on their feet, they will be an asset.

"The rural homes must have an opportunity to become more attractive and have more conveniences.

> Drudgery, darkness, and muddy roads are not conducive to anything that is good. They are not profitable in a democracy. Conveniences will eliminate the feeling of drudgery in the necessary rural tasks that must be done each day. We have enough low-cost power now going to waste in our muddy streams, our best engineers say, to light all the rural homes in America I simply hate to think of the social, the economic, and the moral loss to about one-third of the people of my State who live on roads that will not permit travel so much of the time to market, to school, to church, and to obtain a doctor for the sick. All-weather roads and rural electricity will drive mud and darkness away in more ways than one."[7]

The six farmers sat in silence while Sam Rayburn spoke slowly and distinctly. Leaning forward in his chair, he would tap his knee repeatedly six or seven times to emphasize a point. These impromptu remarks contained the rich ore out of which he smelted his liberal legislation of the New Deal. These utterances in the summer of 1933 were prophetic in nature. His speeches in Congress, major addresses over radio and at commemoration banquets, rephrased these ideas, perhaps more fully but not as intimately as Valton Young remembered them. The several campaign speeches during the summer of 1934 reflected these same ideas, later to find their way into legislation.

Although Sam Rayburn was carving out for himself a rather flattering record in Washington he seemed unable to avoid an almost permanent barrier—opposition in the July primaries. Had Grayson County not turned out in strength he might have been defeated by Jess Morris, the journalist from Hunt County, who had made the race in 1932. The vote by counties, as certified by the Chairman of the Executive Committee follows:

County	*Morris*	*Rayburn*
Collin	3,626	4,482
Fannin	2,863	5,411
Grayson	3,268	8,052
Hunt	3,704	3,658
Kaufman	2,857	2,811
Rains	866	631
Rockwall	632	941
Totals	17,816	25,986

The people were stirred up by the economic ills—angry with anyone who appeared to have a good job. Rayburn was just one of their irritations. He had little time in which to conduct his campaign and suffered as a result, as his loss of three counties would indicate.

Some men find their inspiration in travel abroad, others in books, but Mr. Rayburn of the Fourth, got his stimulation from talking with his people about their needs and from looking into their faces to discover their deepest emotions. He was their congressman and to serve them best he believed he should know them, and to know them he had to be in residence as much as possible. They gave him the desire to dedicate a life to helping others. His words were not empty. The Farm-to-Market Roads, Soil Conservation, Rural Electrification, Production Credit, Tenant Purchasing, Production Marketing, and Commodity Credit were titles of legislation expedited during the Roosevelt years which clearly evidenced that Rayburn's words were translatable into action.

Rayburn recognized the farm problem, but he was constantly reminding his people that there must be two approaches—the short range and the long range. While he recognized the immediate needs, he emphasized the importance of viewing the entire economic life of the agriculturist. The farmers who visited with him during the month of July, while he was conducting his campaign for re-election, were still suffering from the shock of getting accustomed to the Agricultural Adjustment Act (AAA), which had become a law on May 12, 1933. Rayburn spent a great deal of time trying to assure farmers that the concept was a good one and that it would probably be expanded in time.

The Act was only the first in a series designed to reestablish something of an equality between agriculture and industry by improving farm prices and lightening the credit and mortgage burden. Henry A. Wallace, the Secretary of Agriculture, was authorized to enter into agreements individually with producers in return for Government subsidies. The costs of the payments were to be secured from taxes on the processing of the particular products. The original version of the Act was designed to reduce the volume of cotton, corn, rice, tobacco, wheat, hogs, and milk; later the Act was amended to include barley, flax, grain sorghums, peanuts, sugar, and beef cattle. The idea was that the individual farmer would rent to the Government land taken out of cultivation or accept certain benefit payments on restricted allotments grown. The purpose of such a pragmatic scheme was to turn loose cash payments and raise price levels. The immediate result was a three-fourths cooperation and a one-third reduction in acreage. The price of cotton, for example, increased from 5½ cents to 9½ cents a pound. The Bankhead Cotton Control Act of April, 1934, was instituted to suppress the total production to 10,000,000 bales. It assured a price of 10 cents and continued benefit payments.

For the first year the contracts between farmer and Government were voluntary. It was the second year of the AAA which gave Rayburn the most trouble, as evidenced by his correspondence. In 1934, Congress modified the Act to limit cotton and tobacco production to that which could be grown on an allotted acreage at average yields. Excesses offered for sale were subject to a special tax, which proved to be the "Achilles heel." Most of the farmers were temporarily satisfied, but many of the "old-timers" around Bonham were horrified by the waste involved in the slaughter of cattle and hogs. An elderly gentleman was very bitter after he saw his cows herded into the pit for destruction, "This is wrong, morally wrong, to destroy food that cannot be satisfactorily consumed, with people here and abroad hungry. God will someday punish America for this act. I voted for Roosevelt in 1932, but I will never do it again, regardless of what Mr. Rayburn says." Some of the meat was salvaged, given to men who stood around with their long skinning knives waiting to charge upon the carcasses in order to fill their burlap sacks. Those inexperienced with economics and world markets, like this gentleman, saw something ominous in the experience. The symbolism also disturbed the rustic mind. Many had heard the radio address of Will Rogers during the dark days of Hoover's Administration in which he made an appeal for help. Rogers' reference to feeding the hungry with the surplus made a profound impression upon those who had little interest in or knowledge of economics.

Generally, the farmers did not resist a law that was having visible effects on prices, but the payers of processing taxes objected to the extent that one case (*Hoosac Mills–U.S.* v. *Butler*) reached the Supreme Court. The first AAA was, on January 6, 1936, declared unconstitutional on the grounds that the regulation and control of agricultural production, which is a purely local purpose, is a power to be retained by the states under the Tenth Amendment.

Looking back, in 1960, Rayburn made the following comment about the preceding:

"I thought the AAA was about the best farm program that

was ever passed. It was working and then the Supreme Court came along and said it was unconstitutional and threw it out. I don't think we have had as good a farm program since. That was the Roosevelt-Wallace program, as well as Congress's."

As for the Bankhead bill, he considered it strictly temporary. On September 28, 1934, he wrote, "I spoke for the amendment limiting it to two years when the bill was in the House, and was glad to see it adopted, limiting it to one year when it was finally signed by the President." He saw a definite flaw in the legislation. Texas had suffered a drought, but the Southern States that had produced bumper crops would be called upon to pay the tax while his own section would be protected by the price stabilization. He advised his constituents that they should be broadminded and consider the welfare of all the people over a long period of time.

The critics of Mr. Rayburn at this point have examined his position on Government controls with a great deal of interest, searching for evidence of inconsistency. If he had been completely free to settle all issues satisfactorily, he would have favored state and local controls rather than Federal. But he recognized the wealth was unevenly distributed among the states and that some Federal regulation was inevitable. The cotton problem, for instance, was too big for Texas to settle alone. The very nature of the issue, and the absence of a state machinery to work with it logically, threw the cotton problems into the lap of the Federal Government.

On the other hand, the oil problems, Mr. Rayburn believed, had to be approached differently, despite the fact that here also surpluses were involved. This was before sources outside the United States became available in quantity. In 1933 and 1934 there was an oversupply of crude oil resulting from the discovery of the East Texas Field, forty miles long and three to five miles wide, with reserve estimates of five billion barrels. At the time there were no proration laws or regulations, the oil belonging to the discoverers. Some wells produced as many as 10,000 barrels per day; hence the market became glutted and the price dropped to 10 cents per barrel. As in the case of cotton, the market was saturated and the price low. The oil operators were panicked and some of them completely irrational as it seemed to Mr. Rayburn.

Most of the oil operators and oil and gas associations asked President Roosevelt and Secretary of Interior Harold L. Ickes to appoint a czar of oil. This was to be Federal control sponsored by the Independent Petroleum Association of America, the American Petroleum Institute, the Texas Oil and Gas Conservation Association, and many other associations throughout the country. Vice-President Garner and Rayburn, Chairman of the Interstate and Foreign Commerce Committee, were however, ideologically opposed to the principle of Federal control, arguing for state control.

However, Secretary Ickes was acting under the advice of most oil and gas people in favoring legislation to transfer the controls from state to Federal Government. He seemed destined to become the so-called czar. Several bills were submitted, but the final piece of legislation was called the "Ickes Bill," which was prepared by counsel associated with the oil industry under the Interstate Commerce Clause of the Constitution. Ickes secured quick approval by the Mines and Mining Committee of the Senate, but Rayburn caught on to the strategy and insisted that since the bill was written under the Commerce clause, it was in the wrong committee. He succeeded in convincing the Speaker of the House and received custody of the bill himself in the Interstate and Foreign Commerce Committee. He immediately began holding hearings which lasted for thirteen weeks. Patiently, explains J. R. Parten of Houston, he listened to all groups and citizens affected. Roosevelt wrote two letters urging that the bill be reported favorably out of the committee. Mr. Rayburn resisted all pressure and insisted that the matter was too important for a hurried decision.

During the final week of the hearings, the President in a letter to Congress recommended the divorcement of oil pipelines from their parent companies. The issue now became so complicated that the Ickes bill died in the confusion.

The interesting thing about the whole problem was that Rayburn and Garner virtually stood alone in resisting the pressure for Federal control. Only very few oil men in Texas supported Rayburn—Ernest O. Thompson, Chairman of the Texas Railroad Commission, and James V. Allred, Attorney-General, counseled with him. Some of the Houstonians who talked with Rayburn about the problem were James S. Abercrombie, Jack Blalock, Dan Harrison, Mike Hogg, J. R. Parten, Jim West, Sr., and a few others. Most of these seemed to see the merit of Rayburn's approach, in part or in full.

As a result of Rayburn's hearing, the Railroad Commission of Texas continued to exercise the responsibility for Texas and the equivalent commissions of other states continued to exercise a similar jurisdiction. Rayburn realized that the public interest was involved since there was a serious waste of a natural resource, but he saw no reason why the Texas Legislature could not enact legislation to establish quotas for the individual producers. There were two problems: 1) that of correlating the policies of the various states to prevent one state from profiting at the expense of another's conservation measures, and 2) the curbing of traffic in hot-oil (the oil produced in excess of state-imposed quotas). However, agreements were reached among the states to resolve the matter of quotas, and then came the Connally Act of 1935 which dealt with contraband oil.

Mr. Rayburn firmly believed that his action in this particular case and in the support of the 27.5-per cent depletion allowance, in which he had played a consistent role, identified him as one of the oil industry's best friends. If there was one topic that would almost make him "cry in his beer," it was this one. Rayburn was a man who believed in loyalty and would never desert any one or a group that had befriended him, and he expected a little reciprocity. In discussing the matter he used some rather strong language, but he never failed to pay tribute to certain people for their professional attitudes and loyalty. As for others he was unable to comprehend this lack of appreciation of the Democratic Party: "The one quirk in human nature I can't understand is that the people who were the worst broke when we came into power were the ones who recovered the fastest and got the richest and they are the ones who hate us the worst."

In 1960, after reminiscing for awhile about this 1933–1934 era, he suddenly drifted off on the topic of depletion:

"These same men are scared of the Democrats. Depletion has been in effect for thirty-four years and the Democrats have been in control of Congress twenty-eight of those. Do you suppose if we'd wanted to do something about depletion that we wouldn't have done it by that time? But, they just hate. I went to one place . . . this place . . . in the State and spoke in a big oil center. And, those fellows had gotten out and told their employees that if the Democrats were elected they would lose their jobs. Now, of course, they wanted to meet with me at the Petroleum Club and thank me for what I had done, but what they were trying to do then was to destroy me. Destroy Lyndon Johnson. Destroy me. If you can't carry Texas, why, you can't lead anyone. Your own State pulls you down. It's just . . . to me . . . oh, I just . . . I don't like to think about it and don't like to talk about it." At this point he was close to tears as he covered his face with his hands, and the interview had to be delayed until he could regain his composure.

Rayburn's sensitivity to the public interest was manifested in the previous Seventy-second Congress with his Holding Company bill which was designed to prevent the railroads from consolidating the properties of two or more carriers into a single system through the device of the holding company. However, to prevent unfair practice to the companies, he had authored the Coordinator bill which directed a study of all the railroad problems so that better ways might be devised for better controls and regulation. He had based his thinking upon the findings in a 1742-page report, which had cost $40,000 and involved months of research.

His Federal Securities Act in the spring of 1933 has been cited as an example of his concern for the individual, or small group. As he explained, over a ten-year period twenty-five billion dollars of worthless securities had been pawned off on the public. His bill required proof of the corporation's status—assets and liabilities.

Pursuing the same interest in protecting the people's investments, he authored the Securities Exchange Act of 1934 during the second session of the Seventy-third Congress. This bill had two major provisions. First, it provided for effective registration statements as a prerequisite to the public offering of securities by means of the mail or by other means of interstate commerce. Second, it stated that no sale or solicitation of offers to buy could be made prior to the registration statement, except that underwriting arrangements be made between the issuer and the underwriter to be concluded prior to the effective date.

Congressional action is a good barometer, or index, of the times. The Federal Securities Act of March, 1933, and the Securities Exchange Act of 1934 were indicative of public demand for protection against exploitation of their investments. The third bill in this particular series (The Public Utility Holding Company Act) was not a new type of thing; in fact, Committee attention had been focused on holding companies since the Seventy-first Congress. Between February 20, 1931, and June 19, 1934, the following related bills were considered: Railroad Holding Companies (President's signature, June 16, 1933); Oil Pipe Lines; Power and Gas Companies; and Communication Companies (Communication Act, June 19, 1934).

During the first session of the Seventy-fourth Congress (January 3–August 26, 1935), Rayburn moved to complete his own chain of legislation and carry forward the legislative trend. His Public Utility Holding Company Act, after five months of Committee consideration, reached the floor for debate and held the attention of Congress from June 27 through August 1. In the judgment of some, this was the most far-reaching piece of legislation during the session. President Roosevelt had called him to the White House several times about it. Rayburn had discussed it with Dr. Splawn, the Federal Trade Commission, the Attorney-General's office, and the Securities Commission. Hence, he was well prepared for his defense.

In the explanation of the bill he defined holding companies, pointed out the technicalities and loopholes in the law which brought them into existence, and then discussed their practice of buying and selling to themselves at their own prices, which consumers paid.

"In one system," he pointed out, "the pyramiding goes so far as to pile one company on top of another until there are ten corporations in the pyramiding, or the local operating company is nine companies removed from the corporation at the top which controls it, along with hundreds of others. In this particular set-up an investment of $1 at the top enables the managers of the top to control over $30,000 of book value of the operating companies, or with less than $50,000 to control over a billion dollars of book value."

The concentration of management was "staggering to the imagination." The example was a paper holding company in an office building in New York City, which with a very small investment and risk of capital, controlled hundreds of operating companies throughout the country in "what they shall buy, from whom they shall buy, at what price, and with whom they shall exchange services and contract for supplies." In another instance, he found that one man was secretary or officer in more than two hundred corporations. These paper companies at the top of the pyramid very often operated nothing, claiming that they were beyond the control of any state authority since they were not selling transportation or any type of public service. By holding themselves out as investment companies, they had attempted to place themselves beyond the reach of Government.

Briefly, the bill had two main objectives: 1) to protect investors and consumers by supplementing state regulation of utility companies with a Federal regulation of interstate holding companies and their subsidiaries; 2) to break up monopolies by turning back control of the operating utility business to the local communities which create the business, and by opening up to independent local concerns the supply, designing, and construction of plants which heretofore were controlled by Wall Street for their own profit.

His attack on the reprehensible practices of such holding companies was indeed bold and straightforward. Here are samples of the arguments he used against them:

1. They have been used in paper transactions to defeat assessments of income taxes to the Government, and were successful in circumventing the technical requirements of the Bureau of Internal Revenue.
2. The officers are able to pay annual salaries of sometimes $300,000 in addition to allowing bonuses which come out of profits—transactions enveloped in secrecy.
3. Huge paper transactions have been effected by only entries on books without any transfer of money or credit.
4. The companies have inflated their income by taking on their books the earnings and donated surpluses of subsidiaries without ever receiving the amounts. Hence dividends were paid out of capital instead of earnings.
5. Manipulations of system securities by the top holding company have been instigated to support the market with the result of reflecting fictitious market values.

Rayburn elaborated in a more specific way on the organization of this type of business. The operating companies were controlled by the holding companies and the holding companies by banking houses. For example, one big banking house on Wall Street, through a concern called United Corporation, had an arrangement which held eight or ten of these big holding companies under its thumb, so that one-fourth of the electric-light companies in America were subject to this particular banking influence. Whenever an operating company, for example in Fannin County, wanted to put in a new dynamo it had to be approved from the top and often not without someone's paying a price which did not have a dollar sign in front of it. Rayburn compared these companies to the practice of piracy on the high seas or banditry along our frontiers. The only difference to Rayburn was that the companies had "high-class white-gloved desperadoes," with a delicate touch, while the more classic highwaymen were only "hardened thugs."

Already he had won the reputation of being the champion

of small business, but he did not want to be regarded as the enemy of big business.

"I am not," he said "an enemy of business—clean business. I state now that what I am trying to do in this holding company thing is what I hope we did in the Security Act. I told the President of the New York Stock Exchange at my office during the consideration of that bill: 'I am not an enemy of your business. I think the sale of stocks and bonds is as honorable a business as a man can be engaged in. What I want to do is to take the desperadoes out of your field who have been disgracing what otherwise would have been a clean and honest business in the minds of the people.' What I want to do here is to take from this field the desperadoes in the utility business who in the past by their actions and by their deeds have brought the whole utility business into disrepute. I know there is a great deal of it that is in disrepute. It should not be held in disrepute, but I want to take the Insulls and the Hopsons and the Dohertys out of this business who are controlling this giant business, so it will stand before the American people as it deserves to stand—clean, honest, with the people having full faith and confidence in it."

In trying to draw a line between right and wrong at this level of American economy, he knew that he would be unable to win complete approval among the top echelon of business. The opportunities for amassing fortunes had distorted some men's objectivity and made them callous to the general welfare. Being one who followed a simple code of ethics gleaned from the Scriptures, he had little difficulty making value judgments whether the issue involved the sale of a Jersey bull or a million dollars in stocks.

The Public Utility Holding Company Act of 1935 was the third in this network of legislation designed to place a limit on bank credit for speculative purposes. Dixon Wecter observed that this legislation set up safeguards against manipulation of stocks, decreed full information from the buyer of securities, created the Securities and Exchange Commission as an overseer, "passed a death sentence against all utility holding companies after the end of 1937," except those composing a "geographically and economically integrated system." [8]

These pieces of legislation assured greater security for all depositors and small investors. While they were favorably received by the masses, they gained for men like Mr. Sam the permanent opposition of some rather powerful forces in American business. While they could not provoke him with their diatribes, they became from this day forward a formidable foe in Congress.

In a radio address on August 30, 1935, over NBC he reflected something of their resistance and the bitter struggle that took place in getting the bill through Congress. "It was a battle against the biggest and boldest, the richest and the most ruthless lobby Congress has ever known. That lobby was a professional, mercenary army, long trained in what it was paid to do." With the signing into law of the bill by the President, he expressed the hope that the powerful lobby which had haunted state legislatures and Congress for many years was now destroyed. But being the prime assassin of these sophisticated gangsters, Rayburn knew that in the years ahead he would have to show a certain frontier caution. Figuratively speaking, he knew that he would always have to sit with his back to the wall and never walk into a hall or onto the street without first looking and fingering his side arms. This constant vigil was the price he had to pay for looking after the welfare of his kind of people, but he recognized that he was fortunate in having a sanctuary like the Fourth to which he could go. There were districts, even in the Lone Star State, which he knew would not have provided the same approving atmosphere for one with his aggressive and liberal program. Rayburn, though, was not to be intimidated. He defied the holding companies to seek legal recourse, threatening that if the Supreme Court should deny the power of Congress, it would "tax the holding company out of existence." He reminded them that if anyone thought he was joking, he had only to make a close scrutiny of the tax on intercorporate dividends in the new tax bill. This he said should be an "example and warning enough to those who rashly think they can persuade the Supreme Court that the American people must be gouged, and bullied, and lobbied forever."

Although such legislation is referred to as liberal, Mr. Sam refused to accept the label himself. They were conservative measures, he thought, because they were essential to the preservation of our system of private property. The system of individual enterprise and private property needed these restrictions to insure fair play and protection from the "predatory rich men" and "selfish demagogues." When he went to Washington in 1913 he observed that the Government tended to steer a middle course by refusing to yield to pressures from either the right or the left, and hoping that the extreme forces would counteract each other. On February 21, 1935, he recognized that the Government was having difficulty holding to the middle course because the extremists to the right and left held similar philosophies—both wanting "to run everybody."

"I find little difference," he says, "between the state Socialists on the one hand, who would subject us to the tyrannies of a superstate, and those whom my friend, Ray Moley, so aptly called 'private Socialists'—the greedy, power-mad managers of other people's property—who would subject us to the tyrannies of supermanagement and superindustry. Twenty years ago the conservative middle-of-the-roaders could afford to remain calm and be content to resist compulsive action. Today the true conservative must fight and fight vigorously to maintain the principle of fair play for individual enterprise against competing tyrannies."

The most significant interests of Mr. Rayburn during the second session of the Seventy-fourth Congress (January 3–June 20, 1936), were in rural electrification. Again he was treading on dangerous ground, according to some business interests. The New Deal had already ventured into the domain of public housing and now it was encroaching upon the power industry. On May 11, 1935, President Roosevelt had issued an Executive order, by virtue of the authority vested in him under the Emergency Relief Appropriation Act of 1935, which established the Rural Electrification Administration. He allotted $100,000,000 to be loaned by the Reconstruction Finance Corporation to cooperatives and to corporations for the purpose of implementing the order. With less than one-tenth of the amount actually having been made available, Congress passed the Rural Electrification Act in 1936. As co-author of the bill, Rayburn made his defense on April 9. The most serious resistance came from the metropolitan areas that tried unsuccessfully to require the farmers to put up fifteen per cent of the cost.

The utilities companies resisted this legislation just as strenuously as those who fought the Holding Companies bill. Everywhere was heard the cry of "Socialism." In rebuttal, Rayburn cited utilities' failure in his own District where only 621 farm homes of the 30,490 had been electrified under existing procedure: 83 of 6069 in Collin, 94 of 5894 in Fannin, 101 of 5169 in Grayson, 219 of 5905 in Hunt, 88 of 5131 in Kaufman, 4 of 1691 in Rains, and 32 of 1031 in Rockwall.

Getting the farmer out of the mud with hard-surfaced roads and lighting his semi-dark home with electricity were two of Rayburn's dreams, and the two achievements which brought him the greatest satisfaction. With strong support from the White House he moved ahead with greater speed. Both men agreed that the farmer, his wife, and children had too long been among America's forgotten people. Since they constituted the backbone of the economy, Roosevelt and Rayburn believed they deserved to live more efficient and attractive lives. Before REA, school children and parents would hover around smoking kerosene lamps, sometimes almost in the shadows, trying to glean some knowledge from their textbooks or the daily newspaper. Rayburn remembered his mother in the rocking chair with the Bible held toward the light as she strained to make out the unsteady print. He recalled also her flushed face as she worked over a hot woodstove in canning season to preserve vegetables and meats essential to a well-rounded farm economy. Years later he dwelled on the thoughts that refrigeration, home-freezers, electrical appliances, and the like could have liberated this farm wife from much of her daily toil. The farmer's labor likewise could be greatly simplified by the advantages of electricity.

Prior to the REA, in 1934, only one rural home in ten could have electricity, even at an expensive rate. Eighteen years later, after additional pieces of legislation to improve and expand the facilities, he was glad to report that only one out of ten homes was without electricity. As late as 1960, he said he could still smell the odorous coal oil lamp, the musty family storm cellar for refrigerating food and storage of home-canned commodities, and feel the wobbly, wooden well bucket for drawing all the family water supply—not altogether unpleasant childhood sensations—and he was happy that a new era had arrived:

> "I experienced such handicaps during my childhood, and during my mature years, I observed their drawbacks from the great dairy farms of the East to the scattered cowboy bunkhouses of the lonely Southwest, and from the fertile farmlands of the Middle West to the often dismal tenant houses of what was formerly known as the Old South." [9]

The power companies hurled their charges of "Socialism" Government interference, and extravagant spending. Valton Young recalled some of his replies to their criticism, but Rayburn's "Extension of Remarks" show his mind on the subject:

> "This country's unwilling servants of the washtub and water pump or bucket need more and want

more than electric lights. They deserve electric power in order that they may turn a faucet or push a button to get the same results as their city brothers and sisters.

"However, there is this difference, remember. Aids from electricity for the rural family are many times more numerous than they are for city residents. All thoughtful citizens can see that natural condition too. The average city housewife can choose between washing and ironing electrically in her own convenient home and simply sending the family wash to the washateria or laundry. Her family is contented to use electricity for lighting, cleaning, refrigeration, radio, and making the morning toast and coffee. If she has an electric range, food mixer, sewing machine, and a few more precious electrical appliances, she feels fortunate. In short, when the list of household appliances is exhausted, the saturation point is usually reached with the city folk.

"But in the country, the case is ordinarily very different. More than a hundred ways in which electrical devices can help the farm and ranch have already been developed. Such development is quite natural, and will be continued, because farms and ranches afford ways of earning a living as well as places for living. Therefore, rural electricity is fast becoming the most versatile of all aids offered by modern science to country life. It can pump water and thereby make modern plumbing possible in all rural homes for the first time in history. Its power can operate hay loaders, feed grinders, milking machines, and numerous other machines. It will make our noble country friends, from whom most Americans are now removed in lineage, have lighter and more comfortable work.

"Electrified farms and ranches will tend to head off the swift movement from farm to city by banishing drudgery, making country work more efficient, and by changing the outside as well as the inside of the home, because electricity is the cheapest and most tireless hired hand that a rural family can have.

"Throughout the length and breadth of our land, a new rural community life has sprung up, bespeaking the wonders that electrical service has wrought since its inception only a few years ago. I am proud to have had a part in this movement that made life brighter

> for church, school, and playground. And increasingly, new rural cooperatives appear along the country's electric power lines—a mushroom growth from the hybrid seed-corn drying plants fed by the fertile fields of Iowa to the cold-storage locker plants dotting the pine-covered hills of deep east Texas, and from the isolated lumber camps of the vigorous Northwest to the village waterworks in the peaceful valleys of Pennsylvania."[10]

Believing that cleanliness is next to godliness, he was thrilled with a sort of religious emotion when he looked upon the transformation wrought by electrification. The attractive interior of a rural dwelling gave him an inner satisfaction that there was both prosperity and contentment in the housewife's immaculate home. "I am happy," he said, "for everyone of these rural mothers who can now have clean homes and fitting environment in which they can rear a God-fearing family." If this be "Socialism," then it must also be a new definition of American strength and prosperity.

Through low-interest loans of two per cent from the REA, farmers were able to establish cooperatives which would set up transmission lines and supply electricity to homes not serviced by private companies. Where private industry was already in operation, farmers' associations were encouraged to purchase electricity rather than to set up their own generating facilities. The threat from cooperatives, however, led to the private corporations going into rural electrification also. The effect of competition was wholesome. Not only did the two sources of supply accelerate the REA program, but it helped remove some of the general criticism that Roosevelt's New Deal was socialistic. Rayburn continued to state that the name-calling had its origin among political groups without any basis in economic fact. Sam Rayburn's first bid for political immortality was made during the New Deal, when he was both a priest and communicant.

☆ XII ☆

The Second Phase of the New Deal

ON MAY 26, 1936, Sam Rayburn was in San Antonio, Texas, as temporary Chairman of the Democratic State Convention. He gave an address about "a proud, militant, and victorious Democracy." Interrupted frequently by noisy applause, he surveyed the accomplishments of the Roosevelt-Garner Administration and paved the way for the Convention's endorsement of the ticket for a second term.

Sam Rayburn continued to be mentioned as majority leader or speakership material, because many Democrats had been uneasy since Garner's moving over into the Vice-Presidency, with the instability and uncertainty that prevailed. Henry T. Rainey's death in 1935, Joseph W. Byrns' in 1936, and the unpredictable health of William Bankhead gave reason for alarm. The Party recognized in Rayburn a leader with political insight and the necessary physical stamina. The Speaker was expected to assume a certain type of leadership to give the legislative branch its rightful recognition in the eyes of the public. Consequently, some thought was given to grooming Rayburn for greater responsibility, which resulted in his becoming head of the National Speaker's Bureau to conduct Roosevelt's campaign for a second term. This assignment required both sound judgment and knowledge of the Party's speaking talent and suitability for some areas and unsuitability for others. Rayburn seemed the desirable co-ordinator because he knew all the danger spots, and above all, he knew men.

The Congressman, however, had little time to bask in the sunshine of all the praise and projected plans for him in the National organization because it was again July in the Fourth District. The opposition this time was Will A. Harris of Rains, and again Jess Morris from Hunt. On July 18, Rayburn seized upon the opportunity to launch his campaign before the vast audience assembled at the fifty-seventh annual picnic at Leonard. "I shall always be grateful for your constant and steadfast friendship throughout all these years," he said, "and now I am asking that you return me to Congress to finish the work of the New Deal which I have had a large part in inaugurating." He asked the people whether they wanted to trade horses when they had one that would not balk. "As long as I am right, I am asking you to uphold my hands: when I am wrong, vote against me." Though a bit out of character for him, Rayburn concluded by referring to the scurrilous charges of the opposition in these terms: "Any man who will deceive you during a political campaign will deceive you after he is elected."

Jess Morris received little encouragement on July 23 from an audience of 150 assembled on the courthouse lawn in Bonham. The people were unresponsive to either the music of the Greenville band or the guest. Their silence undoubtedly reflected approval of the New Deal and their Congressman, as the results indicate:

RAYBURN	30,907
MORRIS	12,768
HARRIS	3,633

Shortly after this 1936 campaign and prior to his departure for New York, where he spent two and a half months arranging the speaking schedules for the Party, he and Valton Young attended a dairy show in Dallas. Some Jersey cattle very similar to his were being shown. According to the County Agent, Rayburn had a habit of always picking his own winners before the judges' decision, and this day he had settled on a Jersey cow named Lavender Lady. Worried by the way the herdsman was leading her around the arena, he whispered to his friend: "Lavender Lady will win if her herdsman will only let her do her own natural posing for the judge to see all her beauty and style.

The herdsman's lead rein is too tight. She knows more about showing her natural beauty than the man leading her does." [1] Finally he became so impatient that he got up and went to the attendant with some advice that was followed; later the judges reached exactly the verdict Rayburn had predicted, and Lavender Lady was declared the Grand Champion.

Sam Rayburn's influence upon the dairy industry during the Thirties in Fannin County was considerable. He gave away more advice and bull calves than anyone, primarily because he wanted to upgrade the herds in his area. Young reports that if the Reeds of Trenton, the Bates brothers of Honey Grove, the Scotts and Kerbows of Ladonia, A. P. Grider of Leonard, and Doss and Wise of Bonham had brought together their best animals, they could have put on a superior show of their own. The Rayburn farm became well known as the replacement center for foundation stock of the registered Jersey variety. Later, however, for financial reasons, he began to shift his emphasis to beef cattle, but he really never abandoned his regard for fine Jersey cows.

Though he liked good cows his basic love was for the land itself, and he prided himself in recognizing quality here also. In the summer of 1936 he became really serious about a conservation program. He could be almost philosophical about the good earth as he walked across it. For example, he said,

> "The one thing besides people that I claim to know is land. There is no feeling in the world like the satisfaction of owning the good earth over which you are treading. Just think, there is no limit to its depth or its possibilities! We must not forget the rock from which we were hewn!" [2]

As Young reports, as early as 1933 Rayburn was using the Bostrum level for surveying terrace lines and the Martin Ditcher for constructing the terraces. Saving soil and conserving moisture in a single process brought forth one of the Congressman's more profound utterances: "I like to make running water walk." Although Rayburn set a good example, credit goes to the persevering efforts of the County Agent, who daily resisted the rural prejudices. Farmers continued to remark, "Our long and straight rows let us work our land so much easier." Rayburn helped Young here by replying, "Yes, keep running your straight rows up and down the hill and your harvest will be much lighter and easier, too." Young and Rayburn also tried to import the practice of plowing under the stalks instead of raking and burning them after the harvest, but progress was slow here because the farmers would grumble: "We can't stand to work foul land." [3] During the summer of 1936, Rayburn began formulating his ideas about the type of legislation which would encourage the intelligent treatment of soil, such as that pertaining to the "re-establishment of the land" by enriching it, through soil-and-water conservation methods and through soil-building crops.

After completing his duties for the National Speaking Bureau, he went to Washington, where he spent November and December before the opening of the Seventy-fifth Congress. His recent election to a thirteenth term and the talk about his being a contender for the Majority Leader's position inspired him with confidence.

While Rayburn dwelled upon the pleasant sensation of being promoted, he came back to reality with the thought of the present and past bickerings in the Democratic Party. He was both saddened and vexed by the behavior of Alfred E. Smith, a one-time venerable man among Democrats. In a pre-election festivity the "Happy Warrior" virtually destroyed his influence among Party loyalists when, at the banquet hall in Washington filled with wealthy Liberty Leaguers assembled to assail New Deal socialism, he gave comfort to anti-Roosevelt sentiment. The upsurge of Southern conservatives under the leadership of Eugene Talmadge of Georgia had been an annoyance to Rayburn, but not a matter of serious concern at this time. He had viewed Huey Long at the outset with amusement but later with increasing alarm. The death of the "Kingfish" in 1935, however, brought an end to the talk of a coalition with Father Coughlin and Dr. Townsend into a Union Party. The decisiveness of the Roosevelt-Garner triumph over the Landon-Cox ticket removed some of Rayburn's fears, but did not make the cautious strategist throw discretion to the wind. Harmony among Democrats, he realized, had to be cultivated.

Rayburn recognized that one step toward unity had been achieved in the 1936 Convention by the substitution of the majority-rule for the 104-year-old, two-thirds rule in selecting Presidential candidates. Factionalism could no longer block a popular choice. The rule had been a major weapon for the South in making its influence felt in the Party, but now Rayburn was glad to abandon this weapon of sectionalism in the interest of unity.

He also saw in the Democratic platform several planks

which he thought could be translated into a legislative program which should appeal to the majority. That portion for which he was partly responsible read thus:

> "We hold this truth to be self-evident that government in a modern civilization has certain inescapable obligations to its citizens, among which are (1) protection of the family and the home; (2) establishment of a democracy of opportunity for all people; (3) aid to those overtaken by disaster."

Certain sentences from the President's acceptance speech at the Philadelphia Convention also flashed through his mind:

> "This generation of Americans has a rendezvous with destiny. . . . We are fighting to save a great and precious form of government for ourselves and for the world. . . . I am enlisted for the duration of the war."

While the reference was to the war against want and greed, it had a twofold prophetic tone, with the rise of Hitler in Germany and the determination of Roosevelt to remain on the job until the country's ills were cured.

One of Rayburn's pleasantest memories of this period was the sound of old familiar voices expressing their wishes and support to make him Majority Leader, a position which he believed would put him in line for the Speakership. Congress operates very much like service institutions and fraternal organizations in selecting their officers. At the time, there was only one other serious contender—Tammany's John Joseph O'Connor of Manhattan, brother of Franklin D. Roosevelt's former law partner. O'Connor, an honor graduate from Brown University and a graduate of the Harvard Law School, had been a member of Congress for thirteen years and was the current Chairman of the extremely important Rules Committee. He had already filled in briefly as Majority Leader during the Seventy-fourth Congress, after Bankhead moved up to replace Speaker Byrns, who had died on June 4, 1936, during the last few days of the second session. O'Connor appeared to have an initial advantage, since Rayburn until rather recently had been a more obscure figure than O'Connor. Rayburn, however, had a better legislative record, was ten years older, had almost twice the years of service, but he had dwelled too long in Garner's shadow to loom as a front runner. Rayburn had an excellent knack for promoting someone else in the Party, but neglecting his own interests in the process.

Yet Rayburn's prestige had risen very rapidly. When Speaker Rainey died, Garner from the far end of the Capitol in December, 1934, tried to secure the Speakership for his fellow Texan. Senator Joseph F. Guffey, the boss in Pennsylvania, after canvassing his delegation, announced at the time that he would support Joe Byrns. With Pennsylvania holding the balance of power, Rayburn politely withdrew from the race with this statement: "I am no longer a candidate for Speaker. There are no alibis. Under the circumstances I cannot be elected." Actually Rayburn was not too sure of his strength, for he and Garner had failed to elect John McDuffie (Ala.) over Rainey, though they failed by only a few votes. By January, 1937, however, the several years experience as Chairman of the Interstate and Foreign Commerce Committee, his continued liberal legislative measures, and the success of the Speakers' Bureau during the 1936 campaign had attracted the attention of Roosevelt.

The President was in South America and could not take a hand, but Vice-President Garner and his wife turned up ahead of schedule at their apartment in the Hotel Washington. By strange coincidence Rayburn was on hand to greet them, at which time the Vice-President announced that he would support his friend 200 per cent. Roosevelt outwardly was assuming a position of safe neutrality, but privately it may have been another story. Garner undoubtedly had talked to the "Chief." What passed through Roosevelt's mind is unknown, but Rayburn's loyalty to the New Deal and the later purge of O'Connor would seem to imply that Roosevelt distrusted the O'Connor brand of New Dealism from Tammany. Rayburn had already demonstrated adroitness in mirroring Administrative principles in Congress, and with only a few exceptions he did do so without reservation. The Party had its brand on Sam Rayburn and he emanated its concepts. Although he was repulsed by labels, his program lay somewhere between the conservative and progressive. Roosevelt knew he could trust Rayburn, and he liked especially his country style of bare-knuckle fighting, always to the finish with no judge's decision. A trip through Texas with Mr. Rayburn on the "Presidential Special" served as a get-acquainted mission, probably in anticipation of an ultimate promotion.

The President was fearful that this internal contest for the floor leadership could split the Party, yet there was too much at stake for him to be completely indifferent to the outcome. Garner's personal loyalty to Rayburn and devotion to the Party's platform gave him a good excuse to promote his friend. Garner may have recalled previous conflicts, recalling where some of O'Connor's strength rested—among the Wall Street bankers who had given the Wheeler-Rayburn Public Utility Holding Company bill its greatest opposition. He suspected too, but without proof, that the Tammany supported candidate had been behind the 1935 protection of the utility lobbyists and efforts to embarrass the Administration for its own lobbying activities.

Again the figure of Senator Guffey appeared as a decisive force. He had been responsible for Rayburn's previous withdrawal in favor of Joe Byrns for Speaker. He felt now that he should do something to square himself with Garner; yet he was also under obligation to O'Connor, as Chairman of the Rules Committee, for his assistance in the previous session with the Guffey Coal bill. The Chairman of this Committee always carries around a pocketful of political I.O.U.'s. On December 3, Guffey gave a luncheon in the Hotel Mayflower for the Pennsylvania caucus at which they voted eighteen to six on a secret ballot to support Rayburn. He stated that, "We should settle this contest before the President and Mr. Farley return to save them embarrassment." Reporters, knowing that the meeting was one of import, seized each person as he came out of the small dining-room to get the news. Representative J. Burrwood Daly of Philadelphia, irritated by senatorial interference in the affairs of the House, replied to a reporter for *Time* as to what happened: "Ask Senator Guffey about it. He is the big cheese." Bound by the unit rule the caucus decided reluctantly to make the vote unanimous.

According to Joseph Alsop, Jr., Rayburn, who was dressed in a chocolate-brown suit and tie, had carefully selected a cigar to match his ensemble in shade. He made these remarks to reporters about Pennsylvania's decision: "I am more than gratified at the action of the Pennsylvania delegation. It will mean a lot in the final wind-up of this thing. I've been sitting pretty tight for the last few hours."

Fred Vinson (Ky.) and Carl Vinson (Ga.) managed the campaign very skillfully. The first break in the race, which seemed to be deadlocked, appeared to start a rush for the Rayburn bandwagon. Governor Richard Leche of Louisiana promptly wired Rayburn as follows: "The entire eight votes of the Louisiana delegation will be cast for you." Then came support from Mayor Kelley of Chicago, Mayor Frank Hague of New Jersey, Boss Ed Crump of Memphis, and Postmaster General James A. Farley. Representative Sam McReynolds, a close friend of the late Speaker Joe Byrns of Tennessee, also openly endorsed his fellow colleague whom he praised as "a former Tennessean"; so did John McCormack and others in the House. Thomas Cullen, the titular leader of the New York Tammany delegation, much to O'Connor's disgust, expressed the desire to second the nomination of Rayburn. Quite logically, Hatton Sumners of Dallas, Chairman of the Judiciary Committee, was selected to place his friend's name in nomination. The caucus, scheduled for 3:00 P.M. January 4, went off according to plan with the Fannin County man winning 184 to 127; though two days early, this was regarded by Sam Rayburn as a birthday present.

Although the vote would seem to imply that it was an easy victory, there were objections to Rayburn. He came from a section of the country already well rewarded by important assignments—the Vice-Presidency, Chairmanship of the RFC (Jesse Jones), and the Chairmanships of the Appropriations, Judiciary, Agriculture, Interstate and Foreign Commerce, River and Harbors, and the Public Buildings and Grounds Committees of the House. This objection was removed, however, when the observation was made that New York alone had the Presidency, three cabinet posts—Treasury, Labor, and Post Office Departments—and several House chairmanships. Anticipating that Rayburn could likely rise to the Speakership, someone from O'Connor's camp observed that Texas might eventually have both the presiding officers in the House and Senate. History always has a way of providing the rebuttals, for a man friendly to Rayburn noted that at one time Coolidge was Vice-President when Gillett was Speaker, both Massachusetts men.

While Senator Guffey's luncheon was in progress Rayburn was seen in the hotel lobby talking with reporters. They were eager to learn the whereabouts of John Garner, inquiring of Rayburn as to whether he was attending the function. The answer set the newspapermen to wondering. "Not in body, but in spirit!" The man from Uvalde had a great capacity for his indirect type of leadership. Actually Garner was probably in his apartment resting, just waiting for the telephone to ring. He had already done his work. He was a man of few words, but a nod of the head or a wink of the eye brought many a caucus under his control.

Sam Rayburn had been trained in the "Garner School of Politics," and this victory in the campaign for majority leadership amounted to his commencement exercises. He was graduated *summa cum laude*. He later outdistanced his mentor, for he developed a technique far more effective than the "wink of the eye" or political chicanery; he perfected the art of quiet persuasion. During these sessions men came to know each other better and to respect one another's honest differences. Here Rayburn learned more about his own limitations and realized that the only way he could overcome them was by hard work, not trickery, since he believed that deceit destroyed the foundation for future relations. Blessed with common sense, better than average intelligence, a strong body, a pair of legs that were not lazy, and a generous spirit, he became more effective than his proud mentor. Like Garner, he held firm views about loyalty to Party, but above all, loyalty to friends and country.

After the victory, Rayburn's celebrations were brief, for he was awed and sobered by the realization that he now walked in the footsteps of giants. Oscar Underwood of Alabama and Champ Clark of Missouri were early predecessors who set the ideal—the one was suave, diplomatic, commanding; and the other, leonine, brilliant in debate, statesmanlike, loved and feared. Rayburn knew he was one of Champ Clark's "boys" and had his blessing, recalling the private briefing on the day when the Speaker gave him a list of books to read. This silent approval from the past supplied the impetus that he needed to swing into the job like a veteran. The overwhelming majority of 332 out of 435 made the job more complicated, because the types of legislation facing the Seventy-fifth Congress could easily split the Democrats in factions, as was the case.

Even in those days some of his most boisterous partisan enemies were Rayburn's closest personal friends; for example, Bert Snell, the Minority Leader. Visitors who watch one of the legislative dog fights might become disillusioned and fear that there is a basic discord in the House, when in reality there is a fundamental good feeling. The fights, though not "fixed" like some of those in the prize ring, do make the spectator suspicious. There is a great deal of word exchange in the clinches, while some combatants watch the gallery out of the corner of their eyes. Rayburn was on his way toward becoming a referee, so he had to practice the technique of making the fighters break cleanly, keep their blows up, and give the people an honest show. He was, however, unaware that there was a gallery.

After the Speaker William Bankhead held his conference with the President, Rayburn was made aware of the priority legislation for the Seventy-fifth. In the judgment of the President, the Party's forces behind the leadership of Bankhead and Rayburn lined up to support the following:

1. A deficiency appropriation measure to supply relief funds to enable the WPA and other agencies to function through the remainder of the current fiscal year.

2. The continuation of the Presidential powers to vary the gold content of the dollar and to maintain the $2,000,000,000 exchange stabilization fund.

3. Extending the lending powers of the Reconstruction Finance Corporation.

4. Extending the President's power to negotiate reciprocal trade agreements with foreign nations.

5. Changes in the social security statutes.

6. An experimental program of crop insurance and a bill under which farm tenants would be given an opportunity to operate and purchase farms of their own.

Out of the meeting with Bankhead developed a set of circumstances where Rayburn probably won his reputation as a good Majority Leader. Though they did not reach a culmination until May 27, the issues were discussed the moment the President introduced his deficiency appropriation measure. Rayburn's victory helped to redeem him in the House for his part in the court bill and executive reorganization measure which preceded it on the calendar.

The President's deficiency appropriation measure set off violent conflicts within Party ranks, because the "pork-hungry" Democrats had earmarked one-third of the $1,500,000,000 for home projects and had cut WPA Administrator Harry L. Hopkins' salary $2000 annually. On Thursday, May 27, 1937, the White House became desperate and called on Sam Rayburn to save the bill. Rayburn left the telephone and stepped into the well of the chamber in an effort to check the rout of Roosevelt's legislation. The bedlam which had characterized the day's session quieted immediately when the leader slightly lifted his left hand. He knew that he could not muster the votes for adjournment, so he resorted to quiet persuasion. He spoke in a soft, conversational tone. He did not shout, storm around, or threaten anyone. Instead he talked as a man would around the dinner table. Silence prevailed as he said:

> "I appeal to the cooler judgment of my colleagues, I appeal to what I know is their fairness. I appeal to their better judgment. I pledge you, for and against

> the amendments that have been adopted allotting this money, that between now and the time this bill is taken up for consideration again everything that is humanly possible to be done to bring about an adjustment to every man, to every section, and to every project in this country will be done by me."

Following the applause came the roll call for adjournment. His personality and popularity had won the first round.

During the five-day recess Rayburn revealed another of his qualities. Few men were as willing to work with such perseverance. Conferences began with Hopkins, with the leader of each faction of the House—Joe Starnes of Alabama, Alfred Beiter of New York, and Wilburn Cartwright of Oklahoma—and with the Administration. When the House resumed its business, he took the floor and reported that he had carried out their wishes and had received promises from Hopkins and the President that adjustments and concessions could be made. Mr. Rayburn eliminated the objectionable concept of the blank check notion by showing that the money was specifically earmarked. When the bill passed, it was essentially the measure which the Administration wanted, without the amendments aimed to build political strength back home.

Perhaps his success here may have been the result of the confidence which both sides of the aisle had in his way of making haste slowly. If a bill was ready for consideration, he could crack the whip, but he also knew when to let the team take a slow gait.

In his assignment as Party leader, Rayburn was compelled to play a new role. He led his Party in debate and brought forward their programs and policies, and in advocating or opposing proposed legislation, he reflected their preferences. Though he had from the first day on Capitol Hill acted like a good Democrat, he was never blind to the nation's needs. But it was easy for Sam Rayburn to be the mouthpiece for his group. Winning complete Democratic confidence, however, came only with experience and maturity.

On an ordinary day a spectator in the gallery might have been puzzled by the kind of disorganized activity on the floor of the House. There may have been thirty or forty men moving about from one group of two or three, to another of about the same size. The Speaker on the rostrum frequently appeared asleep, with his eyes closed, but he was merely resting. The person to watch, though, was the stocky bald-headed gentleman with a fringe of gray hair. This was the Majority Leader. He was often draped across the brassrail at the back with his elbows supporting his stout frame. If he leaned forward over the rail he sometimes rested his chin in the palms of his hands and still he looked toward the rostrum. Unless one watched this solitary figure for a while he would never have given him a second look. The spectator would notice eventually that men from the Democratic side of the House kept walking up to this person and seemed to whisper in his ear. He either nodded, gesticulated with one hand, or made a brief remark. They seemed to be carrying out his plan or strategy. He gave one the impression of a football coach on the sidelines, but was calm and casual about it all. However, he left no doubt that he had his mind on the game in progress. This was Sam Rayburn, the Majority Leader, during the Seventy-fifth Congress.

The title of "Mr. Democrat" was forthcoming, for the name "Sam Rayburn," which until now denoted the congressman from the Fourth District, had taken on the connotative qualities of a Democrat from the North, East, South, and West. He amalgamated sectional differences into a singleness of purpose. Some of his own sectional individualism was disappearing to be replaced by concepts of governmental regulation and paternalism in the public interest, with a special concern for the underprivileged. "Mr. Democrat" was evolving. The seeds of this philosophy had been within his being from the start, but only the emergence of a new America through the leadership of FDR, and the challenge of responsibility enabled him to shape epithets into ideas and ideas into a school of political thought. Thus Mr. Rayburn eventually became "Mr. Democrat," because he reflected quite clearly the majority of opinion in his Party and commanded the full cooperation of the White House.

He became "Mr. Democrat," as well as the President's legislative general. Roosevelt in his second Inaugural declared that "we have just begun to fight." While his New Deal had proposed legislation on farm tenancy, housing, wages and hours for labor, taxation, hydroelectric development, and far-reaching administrative reorganization, the Republicans were hopelessly outnumbered in Congress, though they held one fortress which had become impregnable through three Administrations—the Supreme Court.

Alphabetical agencies became popular. The farmers had their AAA and business their NRA; the latter Rayburn thought was good in principle as an emergency measure but did not turn out well. But these two, along with certain other New Deal programs, were given the *coup de grace* by the elderly gentlemen in the halls of justice. Roosevelt derived no comfort from the realization that Jefferson, Jackson, Lincoln, and Theodore Roosevelt had also deplored the fact that the old men who sit on these benches are occasionally out of step with the times. He found even less satisfaction from the awareness that several restraints had been unsuccessfully attempted, such as impeachment, withdrawal of jurisdiction, requiring more than a majority vote for nullification of legislative acts, and so forth.

Roosevelt determined to break this Republican stop-gap and the stranglehold that their seven members had over the nine-man body. Six of these were over seventy years of age. Therefore, he called "Mr. Democrat" into his White House office and submitted his Court bill, designed to enlarge the body to bring in "younger blood." The court was to be enlarged by the appointment of one new judge, but not more than six for every justice who, having passed the age of seventy and served for ten years, failed to retire. Although the provisions of the bill were in line with civil service regulations, the practices among the services, and previous precedents for changing the number, they frightened some congressmen on both sides of the aisle. The new Majority Leader had always prided himself in being a marvelous sleeper, but he tossed about considerably on the night of February 5, 1937. Congress was dictator-conscious and he was aware that some congressmen misjudged Roosevelt's intentions. Rayburn, recognizing the President's love of people, was not disturbed by the White House's motive. He had misgivings, though, about the technique prescribed for the achievement of the goals. He left the White House in silence, believing that Roosevelt had made an error in judgment, but he was prepared to support the decision since the meeting in the White House had produced a majority vote for "packing." This moment may have marked the beginning of the decline in the Rayburn-Sumners friendship; since the latter, as Chairman of the Judiciary Committee did not appreciate the Majority Leader's "knuckling under." Sumners was the logical one to introduce the bill, but he refused. Maury Maverick was finally called upon to do the chores, but with O'Connor sitting on the Rules Committee, the bill had little chance for consideration by the full House.

In looking at the matter in 1960, Rayburn stated emphatically: "I thought the two things that Roosevelt made his great mistake on were advocating what he did about the Supreme

Court and his effort to purge people. I regret this about the Roosevelt Administration more than anything else. It was the way in which he tried to change the Court. By the time he left the Presidency, he'd appointed a majority of the members anyway, and he appointed pretty good men."

Rayburn believed Party harmony was at stake and might have proceeded differently had he known the widespread hostility to the measure.

Rayburn knew that he would have real difficulty rallying enough Democratic strength to pass the bill, for the whole concept of "packing" the Court, a supposedly non-political body, was an heretical idea. He recognized that Roosevelt had failed to prepare the people and Congress, by showing the pattern of rulings coming down and their effects upon the public welfare. Instead, impatient for action, Roosevelt emphasized that he wanted six new people regardless of whether the elderly incumbents chose to serve or retire. The "packing" concept was the unpalatable portion, not the retirement of old men which already had its precedent in the services.

After Justice Roberts' shift on minimum-wage legislation, several decisions that were pro-New Deal, and the retirement of Van Devanter under a new Supreme Court Retirement Act, Mr. Rayburn and several other Democratic leaders tried unsuccessfully to get Roosevelt to withdraw his bill. When men like Senator Connally took a firm stand against it, the President then believed Rayburn's advice was sound. Garner was called on to work out a solution in the Senate. After compromises and debate a measure was finally passed which revamped procedural reforms in the lower courts but not in the Supreme Court. By the end of 1941, however, there were only two justices (Roberts and Stone) left who belonged to the pre-New Deal era; so actually seven new judges were eventually named to fill vacancies caused by death and retirement.

On January 12, 1937, Roosevelt sent to the House his carefully prepared plan for the reorganization of the Executive branch of the Government. This type of reorganization appealed to the Majority Leader to the extent that he made it the subject of a radio address over CBS on February 9. He described it as one of the most important and urgent questions facing Congress. For 150 years the country had been growing and changing, he said, without any consideration having been given to revamping or modernizing the Executive structure. "It is now as out of date, as unsuited for modern use, as the stagecoach or pony express."

There were five broad recommendations, designed to make a savings and improve service to society: 1) expansion of the White House staff to provide assistants to help the President keep abreast of Administrative affairs; 2) strengthening those managerial agencies working with budget, research, personnel, and planning; 3) extension of the merit system and reorganization of civil service; 4) overhauling the numerous agencies and commissions to place them under the proper executive department; 5) reform of the auditing methods throughout the Government.

Though Rayburn gave this bill his support, he was handicapped in the first session by the internal Party feuds which the Supreme Court fight had stirred up. Rayburn had warned the President about the dangers to Party harmony, but Roosevelt was strong-willed. The Majority Leader was discussing the problem and the Supreme Court legislation one day with the President and became irritated when he noticed that Roosevelt was not listening. "Looky here, Mr. President, by God, I'm talking to you. You had better listen." In a flash the President recognized that he was not talking to a "yes" man on this legislation, and the incident seemed to clear the atmosphere.

Shortly afterward Rayburn discussed the issues over radio. His address was mainly designed to divorce this executive reform measure from the court bill with the hope of improving Party feeling and understanding. The techniques which were employed against the Court bill had been leveled against executive reform. Some of the same opponents, like John O'Connor, later had a major part in defeating it. At this time perhaps, was conceived Roosevelt's scheme to "purge" certain legislators who were, in his judgment, considered obstructionists.

During the next Congress, however, a Rayburn-inspired group of New Deal Democrats did salvage the heart of the whole Executive reorganization plan to secure passage of a bill to allow for six administrative assistants to the President, the provision to permit the elimination of superfluous government agencies, and the regrouping or consolidating of assignments for economy and efficiency.

Considering himself the friend of both management and labor, Rayburn tried to understand their mutual problems. The fact, though, that he had a better "labor record" than "management record" caused some to question his objectivity on legislation related to these segments. It is not debatable that he had sympathy for those who toil and were the economic underdogs.

He admitted his respect for labor unions, but he promptly deplored that reckless, radical element that would go too far and use violence to achieve its end.

This feeling is best revealed by his reaction to the sit-down strikes in January and February, 1937. For a period of six weeks strikers tied up the principal General Motors plants defying all sense of authority. In exchange for tear gas and buckshot they gave "pop" bottles, pipes, nuts and bolts, automobile accessories, and water from firehoses. The strikers were quite destructive and were delaying the armament program. Governor Frank Murphy, determined to avoid bloodshed and the property damage that would result from routing the strikers from the plants, restrained the National Guardsmen while efforts were being made to reach a settlement.

To all of this uncivil behavior on the part of the radical element, Rayburn reacted as follows in this portion of a letter (March 22, 1937) to his Sister Lou:

> I am distressed at these sit-down strikes. They are the most terrible things I can think of. When people can come on another's property and stay, it approaches anarchy. If Governor Murphy would throw them off he would be the hero of the hour. I hope he does. I certainly would.

On the other hand, Rayburn was also bothered by management's sit-down against the National Labor Relations Act, which pre-empted the violent recourse of labor. He objected to irrationality among any segment of society that would use force to resist an established order.

Related to the victories of the CIO and AFL was the pressure for wage and hour legislation. Rayburn at this time took a conservative position because he recognized that high industrial wages would magnify the problems of both agriculture and small business. His policy here and later was to scale down Administrative recommendations and to exclude the groups related to agriculture. Wages, he believed, should be in line with the income of producers.

An exponent of benefit payments and parity payments to farmers, Rayburn consistently worked for improving the economic life of agriculture. Beginning with the AAA, he held a continuous vigil and shepherded succeeding legislation that would achieve the goals of those friendly to his way of life.

With his rise to the majority leadership Rayburn came to

be more and more in demand as a public speaker. For example, on February 27, 1937, he went up to Cambridge, Massachusetts, to address the Harvard Law School on the subject "How a Bill Passes Congress." As the veteran Congressman tried to explain to the students some of the practical aspects of the trade—those things not found in their books—one might have been reminded of Babe Ruth's trying to lecture a group of Little Leaguers on how he hit one of his home runs, when the secret was in the "snap of his wrists." The best way for neophytes to learn from champions like Ruth and Rayburn is to see them play because there is so much in actual performance which cannot be defined. With Rayburn, especially, much of his technique lay in the "snap of the wrists," so to speak.

At the Semi-centennial exercises of the Interstate Commerce Commission, Washington, D.C., April 1, 1937, he gave one of his speeches on improving standards of living as related to improved service by the railroads and control of utilities companies. Here, as on so many occasions, the press became frantic in their effort to follow the text before them. Rayburn deplored the use of a ghostwriter, and instead he scribbled out the texts of his addresses in pencil, had them typed, then mimeographed for the benefit of the press. When he got up to speak, he rarely referred to the manuscript; hence newspapermen who did not know his technique became quite fidgety and confused in trying to reconcile the extemporary remarks with the text before them. Once, when questioned about this method, he simply said, "if a fellow has to read a speech, he's not prepared. I get all of my facts together in my head and then just talk. I'll say it all before I am through." In later years, when he put on his pince-nez glasses, a rare occurrence indeed, he did follow a prepared text for a television appearance, where time was a factor.

On April 25, 1937, the Majority Leader had an experience rather unusual for him—to leave Washington on business while Congress was still in session. He was called to Shreveport, Louisiana, to speak to the Red River Valley Improvement Association. Explaining that he had not been away from Congress for more than an hour since January 5, he stated that he arranged the calendar to permit this brief escape. His mission was to discuss the plans for developing navigation, stopping soil erosion, bringing about irrigation and flood control, and developing power. The Denison Dam project, which had been in his mind for years, was now before a Congressional committee. Because of the magnitude of the measure he did not expect action until the next year's session. Although he had his attention focused on a specific program at the moment, he expressed an interest in all of the problems of Oklahoma, Arkansas, and Louisiana. His concern for this whole region, he explained, extended over a twenty-year period in which he had "watched the fertility of soil become depleted" and the "soil drift into rivers." Along with soil conservation he saw the problem of producing hydroelectric current. The opposition from Oklahoma led him to state in defense of the Denison Dam, "I have been a member of Congress for twenty-four years and have never introduced a bill to spend a dollar of Federal money in the District I represent."

In discussing the logic behind the Denison Dam and similar flood control measures, he pointed out that damage from one disastrous flood, for example that in 1927 on the Mississippi, amounted to seventy per cent of what the total flood control program would have cost. With industry moving out of the East into the South and Southwest, the necessity for additional electrical power was also a consideration in building these much needed dams.

On Sunday, June 6, 1937, he delivered the principal address at the Confederate Memorial Day Services at Arlington Cemetery on the Potomac. He was very clear in his belief that the War between the States was finished and that he did not want to perpetuate prejudices, but he did want to emphasize the value to be derived from "one day in the year taking down the gray uniforms, putting them on, and marching for a moment." He justified the reliving of the past for just a brief instant by using this illustration:

"It has never seemed to me that the mother who had lost a child was untrue or lacking in love to those living if she went to the closet some day and took out the baby's shoes and fondled them and remembered the child of her bosom that wore them." He then spoke of the lessons of history and the inspiration to be derived from remembering soldiers like Robert E. Lee and Ulysses S. Grant. He paid his respects to Southerners such as Stonewall Jackson, George H. Thomas, and Phil Sheridan, and called attention to "the matchless leader" Abraham Lincoln, and the "great statesman" Jefferson Davis. The scene of Appomattox was relived also and then the tragedy of Lincoln's death:

"If the great Lincoln had lived, he would have retained and maintained the leadership of the country, and the Southland, in my humble opinion, would not have been ground under the heel of the carpetbagger that kept our people so distraught for many, many years. If Lincoln, the great emancipator of the colored race, had lived, he would have emancipated the great white population of the South and taken the dastardly heel off their necks and they would have been back under the flag many years before they came." On occasions like this Rayburn never passed up the chance to praise men like Woodrow Wilson and Franklin D. Roosevelt, "under whose leadership, sunshine and happiness were returning to American homes."

In his job as Majority Leader, Rayburn was in a position to report to the nation on the achievements of his Administration. On the other hand, the minority party, whether Democratic or Republican, at adjournment generally tries to attach the label of "Do-Nothing Congress," for such is the way a two-party system operates. Hence it is the responsibility of the titular leader to examine the evidence and refute charges. Rayburn shared this responsibility with Speaker Bankhead.

On August 25, 1937, Sam Rayburn, over NBC, made a report to the nation relative to the achievements of the first session of the Seventy-fifth. He prefaced his remarks by affirming that "this had been one of the working Congresses in which I have served and that when anybody says that this has been a sit-down Congress, that it has not worked, and has not enacted a great program of legislation, they are ignorant of the facts or they want to distort them."

He was quick in refutation of criticism that Congress did too much for recovery while subservient to the President. In featuring the achievements of the Seventy-fifth Congress he emphasized those things favorable to agriculture—that legislation closest to his own heart and the Fourth District because he had his eyes on the next campaign for re-election:

1. Extending the operation of the Soil Conservation Act to 1942.
2. Agricultural Marketing Agreement Act.
3. Farm Tenant Act.
4. Reduction of interest on Land Bank Loans.
5. Perishable Agricultural Commodities Act.
6. Great Plains Drought Act.
7. Farm Credit Act of 1937.
8. Crop Loans for 1937.
9. Cotton Classification.
10. Extension of Commodity Credit Corporation.

Then he proceeded to list and discuss legislation concerning the RFC, reorganization of the Executive departments, pensions for railway employees, sugar, rivers, and harbors, court reorganization, neutrality, coal, slum clearance, tax loopholes, public building programs, retirement of Supreme Court justices, public works—Grand Coulee Dam, and numerous others.

He assured everyone that there was no split between the President and Congress and that good humor prevailed between the executive and legislative branches. He expressed the hope that his colleagues would have happy vacations at their homes and would soon "feel the pulse of the people," an experience which would reassure them all that the overwhelming majority of the American people looked to Franklin D. Roosevelt for leadership because he had done more for the farmer, laborer, and legitimate industry than anyone else during a four-and-a-half-year period.

Whether he was campaigning, relaxing on the farm, or performing his duties in Washington, he always found plenty to occupy his mind. Regardless of his responsibilities, he lived fully one day at a time. Hence the past never haunted him and the future offered no fears. "As to my volume of work," he said, "it never worries me because I do what is to be done each day. If I did not budget my time, I would not get anywhere." He always planned ahead and after he became Speaker he knew exactly when the various Congresses would adjourn. Since few could ever predict when Congress would finish its business, some more canny members of the press got in the habit of checking at the railroad terminal to learn the day of his ticket reservation for Bonham, because he timed activities accurately and was prompt in his departure:

"I never fail to start home the day the Congress adjourns, and I always get back to Washington by the time it convenes. The people elect me to look after their business there. I never considered that a few days abroad would enable me to speak with any degree of authority on foreign affairs, and working with my own land gives me more pleasure."

He wasted no time in getting home because he had already begun plans for his ranch and had contemplated giving up his emphasis upon Jersey cows.

During the summer of 1937, Rayburn purchased several abandoned and worn-out farms at the headwaters of Coffee Mill Creek, in all about nine hundred acres of land, badly in need of attention. Valton Young reports the occasion when he first learned of the venture. He was sitting next to Rayburn at a dairy meeting at Simpson Park on Pig Branch in Bonham when the topic was mentioned:

> "I recently bought the old Steger Ranch and three small adjoining tracts out here fifteen miles north on Coffee Mill. After doing some necessary fencing, pool digging, and barn building, I plan to stock the place lightly with young registered beef animals of a popular breed, and then grow into the business as I am able, and as the grazing capacity of my land will stand. Possibly other parts of the State with higher altitude and more minerals in their soils grow bigger beef cattle than my land will, but we have good rainfall and an abundance of home-grown feeds around here. My soil is well adapted to improve grasses and clovers, both of which provide the things that my land and cattle will need in abundance. Eventually, I should produce beef as cheaply, if not cheaper, than most places. We no longer have the time, labor, and management available to keep our well-developed dairy herd."[4]

This change of emphasis was destined to upset the routine in the Rayburn family, for at the time he had thirty head of registered Jerseys, animals of all ages. According to some statistics he made available to the Dairy Association, he was doing rather well with some of his cows. Four of them were in the Register of Merit, with an excellent production record. For example, Sybil's Raleigh's Lady Jane, on twice-a-day milking, has made a yearly record of 10,564 pounds of milking, containing 519.94 pounds of butterfat. According to the Dairy Herd Improvement Associations the yearly average record is 319 pounds of butter fat; so Lady Jane was sixty-three per cent above the average. With the dairy cows of the DHIA test producing approximately twice as much per cow as the average dairy cows of the United States, Rayburn's animal was setting a very good example. His Beuveland Jilt, on twice-a-day milking, had a yearly production record of 8,863 pounds of milk, containing 460.27 pounds of butterfat; Sybil's Beauty produced a record of 9,913 pounds of milk, containing 468.16 pounds of butterfat. In compiling these results, Rayburn said he did not feed his cows beyond the point of economical production. They were on pasture, legumes, and grain.

He was trying to prove that high performance was achieved by feeding cows that were well-bred. When he showed his herd, he never failed to remark that some of the cows were imported from the Island of Jersey. Some came from the Meridale herd in New York State and his first herd bull, Sybil's King Carter, was a gift from his old friend and colleague, Senator Carter Glass of Virginia, who was well known in the Old Dominion as a breeder of Jersey cattle.

The principal market for the Rayburn milk was a cheese factory in Bonham. Selling at low wholesale prices, he had to make his profit from the high production per cow. He pointed out that he fed roughages consisting of millet, alfalfa, and wild hay. His concentrates consisted largely of oats and cottonseed meal. Rayburn leaned considerably on the heavy oats his farm produced.

Since he had a large acreage of hay crops and pasture, the cropping system lent itself to the best methods of soil conservation. He did not grow a great deal of Indian corn or have a silo. Although silage was an excellent roughage for dairy cows, he was convinced that it was not necessary for an economical production of milk and butterfat. Legumes he considered more valuable than silage.

Once in an interview, S. R. Winters asked him why he chose the Jersey breed, and he answered: "Because of the high butterfat test of the milk; because this is the Jersey district; and because I like Jerseys."

Many Jersey people locally and regionally puzzled over his decision to shift his emphasis to beef cattle. Recognizing that he could not provide the time, labor, and management to continue the qualitative and quantitative dairy program, he moved into another area of cattle husbandry which promised to be more lucrative with less effort. Raising beef cattle, though not strictly a gentleman's business, would permit a more leisurely pace than the regimented life of milking large numbers of pedigree cows.

At a meeting of the Milk Dealers Association, in Dallas, shortly after the beginning of the new venture, Rayburn commented on his busy life and thought of trying to find some leisure: "I bought myself a little ranch. I thought I was going to get out in the woods and stay there for a month or more, but as yet I haven't been able to get there."

Rayburn's reference to his lack of leisure can be explained by the fact that the Seventy-fifth Congress had three sessions. There were only forty days between the first and second, and his trip to Bonham was delayed. Then he had many interruptions once at home. Since his mind was on his own recent purchase of land and decision to raise beef cattle, Rayburn talked about some of his own problems.

He mentioned the shifting economy in Fannin County, with the Rayburn brothers' activities as an example. They had been trying to diversify, quit raising so much cotton and grow grain to feed livestock. Having lost money producing milk, they had decided to cut down on milk production. This shift from dairying to cattle production, however, did not really become significant in Fannin County until the war, but Rayburn was always a little ahead of the trend. Soil depletion and shortage of young manpower forced many of the older cotton and dairy farmers into ranching. However, he reminded the dairymen in Dallas County that they had continued to find the business profitable because they were near a good market and had a land less susceptible to erosion.

Sam Rayburn, more active in planning Party strategy than in debate during the third session of the Seventy-fifth Congress (January 3–June 16, 1938), did break his silence on such issues as reciprocal trade, rising costs of Government, the reorganization of the Executive branch, military preparedness, and the Denison Dam. Privately he expressed concern over the Roosevelt efforts to purge dissenting Democrats.

As to reciprocal trade he enjoyed repeating his much expressed belief that America could not hope to continue to sell where she did not buy. As to Democratic blindness to rising costs of Government operation he was irritated and expressed assurance that he was going "to take each opportunity . . . to call to the attention of this House again and again the condition of the Government's finances." He explained that he would not oppose appropriations for expanding and developing natural resources but he would resist such things as the construction of new post offices all over the country in smaller communities that already had vacant buildings for rental.

"Some of these days," he predicted, "whether we want to or not, we have got to do what the sane individual would do, what the sane, sound management of a corporation would do if it is to continue to operate; that is, at some time this Government must balance its outgo with its income."

When the Reorganization bill was under fire, Rayburn's greatest contribution was not so much the weight he threw on the Administration's side but his calm analysis of public sentiment. Telegrams came in by the bushel against the bill, but Rayburn assured the House that they were meaningless. Congressman Rogers (Mass.) took sharp issue with Rayburn's indifference to this reflection of public sentiment. Rayburn was very polite, almost courtly, in his reply. He stated that on previous occasions he had rebuked himself for constantly taking issue with this lady for her fears. He said that he was compelled to remind her again that her imagination was running away with her, that she did not understand the hard, cruel techniques of lobbyists. He illustrated her state of mind with this somewhat sly anecdote:

"There was a man in our State one time who claimed to have been a great soldier. A story went the rounds that during a battle the mule he was riding ran away with him, ran away from the enemy. An orator was making a speech in our State and said that his opponent was a peculiar man, that his imagination ran away with him in time of peace and his mule in time of war. I think the imagination of the gentlewoman from Massachusetts is in flight." Already a type of maturity was developing which placed Rayburn in his inevitable position of leadership. His faith and understanding of people, his wholesome attitude of mind and sparkling wit, coupled with a bountiful share of common sense, were being fused into a composite called "political wisdom."

Sam Rayburn had already begun watching the developments in Europe with some anxiety. Admitting his own inexperience, or even short-sightedness, back in 1914, when the war clouds were hovering over Europe, Rayburn determined never again to be guilty of gambling with America's security and freedom. The Naval Authorization bill, debated on March 17, received his full support. The legislation proposed the increase in American tonnages—capital ships, aircraft carriers, cruisers, destroyers, and submarines. The broad and friendly oceans were not enough to give him comfort in a "distraught and unhappy world." He declared, "I want this country and expect to help make it so strong with a navy and defenses that these two great friends [Atlantic and Pacific oceans] will remain our friends." Hitler, he affirmed repeatedly, would not have taken Austria; Mussolini, Ethiopia; Japan, the heart of China, if these countries had been prepared. Expressing a desire to keep America out of war, he urged that the way for a democracy to do so in an age of dictators was to make them afraid to infringe upon our territory and freedom. Isolation was to him a thing of the past, and for the sake of protecting American interests and security, the United States needed to be strong if it was to exercise its influence in world affairs and insure peace.

Rayburn's arguments for his "pet project," that of the Denison Dam, were diffused through twenty years—among the home folks, in cloakrooms, in committee, and on the House floor. His approach was both direct and indirect. In June, 1938, Congress approved the fifty-four million dollar project, without appropriation at this session. Such men as Leon C. "Red" Phillips, Governor of Oklahoma, had tried to block it by lining up his delegation and his own State Legislature. He tried to withhold the necessary land on the Oklahoma side, so as to push through his idea of smaller dams, without the hydroelectric feature, because he was trying, for one thing, to protect the rich farming areas that would be flooded. During the controversy Oklahoma came close to losing all of its other flood control projects. Rayburn won his fight, for by August, 1938, engineers were drilling test holes.

Sam Rayburn also won another fight in connection with the dam. By July 1, the citizenship of the Fourth District was soliciting Congressional support to call the project "Rayburn Dam." He refused bluntly because the name proposed had no geographical connotation and would not inspire friendliness between Texas and Oklahoma as would something like "Texoma" or "Denison Dam." He raised exactly the same objection later when the question arose about naming the Boulder Canyon project "Hoover Dam." While his wishes were granted as far as the Fourth District project was concerned, he lost on the latter.

During the summer of 1938, when Sam Rayburn talked with the people around Bonham he already seemed to be developing a sort of paternalistic feeling toward the House and to sense more keenly a personal obligation toward the national welfare. He also mentioned such things as the importance of competence among lawmakers, the need for experts and not amateurs, "performers and not promisers." He commented on the many complaints from constituents that had come across his desk during the Seventy-fifth Congress about the expense of the so-called "priming of the pump" to sustain America's buying power. And then he mused that when the President and Congress finally decided to terminate what had been described as "socialistic" and "reckless spending," the name callers "let out a howl" that the country was not yet ready to abandon the artificial stimulation of buying power.

Rayburn also recalled the factionalism in the Legislature

which complicated his job as Majority Leader. Congressional differences over such legislation as the Supreme Court bill and the Reorganization measure more and more drove one-time congenial Democrats into liberal-conservative, New Deal and anti-New Deal camps. Determined and unrelenting, inspired and self-confident, Roosevelt was not to be restricted in his patrician role. On behalf of the public welfare he felt justified in removing opposition, whether it was white-haired judges or recalcitrant Democrats.

During the summer of 1938, Roosevelt entered the Democratic primaries and tried to defeat men like Walter George, Cotton Smith, Millard Tidings, and John O'Connor. Rayburn looked with disfavor upon these efforts because these men had reflected both personal views and those of their constituents. In 1960, reminiscing about the decorum involved, Rayburn said:

"I thought it was a mistake, for instance, to get up in the presence of Walter George on a platform in Georgia and tell the people, those crackers, not to elect him. For George merely said, 'Mr. President, I accept the challenge' and that was enough to put him over with those people. Walter George was an outstanding man. He had no right to be purged. He was a great man and a great Chairman of the Committee on Foreign Affairs. This purging was one of Roosevelt's mistakes, and I regret it very much." Except in the case of O'Connor, Roosevelt's efforts failed.

Economy, dignity, and morality—these were some of the other ideas which came to Rayburn's mind as he surveyed the mass of legislative material which began crossing his desk during the first session of the Seventy-sixth Congress (January 3–August 5, 1939). He began on the theme of holding "the expenditures of the Government to the lowest point consistent with taking care of the needs of the people." He hoped that his Party would some day have a balanced budget and that the economists on the other side of the aisle would talk less about his abstract ideal and vote in a manner consistent with their theory. The spending of money to expand the programs of the Works Progress Administration was in his judgment an example of a thoughtful and progressive building of America's human and natural resources. He also had much to say about rivers and harbors and flood control because his own Denison Dam was under construction, although the Texoma project was not completed until 1945.

The proposed extension of the Reciprocal Trade Agreements Act threatened a division in Democratic ranks. Rayburn feared that a defeat for Roosevelt and Secretary of State Cordell Hull on this bill could hurt the Party's chances in 1940. Rayburn knew the President's request for two billion dollars for defense appropriations would stir up interest, as would the attempts to cut down Federal spending in the relief and emergency agencies. These were several of the major hurdles faced by the Administration, but in actuality, Rayburn's hurdles.

A bill which proposed a reasonable annual appropriation for the Franklin D. Roosevelt Library brought the Majority Leader into a violent debate over the importance of preserving a President's papers in one central place. Already approaching a position of seniority, he took advantage of the chance to comment on his own high regard for the office of the Presidency. Wilson, Harding, Coolidge, and Hoover were to him all men who should have been honored in a similar way—as Presidents. Although he did not believe these men equal in ability, he considered them all honest men. The office they held merited respect and tribute; hence he thought Congress should forget politics long enough to think clearly about the importance of the Presidency and the value of history. He said he was particularly annoyed by all the Republican hatred for men like Wilson and Roosevelt, and that dignified people did not behave this way.

Sam Rayburn, in his discussion of neutrality and the Arms Embargo, showed growing concern that America, as before World War I, could find herself in a vacuum and become a nonparticipant in world affairs. An isolation bloc was trying to freeze American shipment of munitions on the grounds of morality, to which he replied:

"We talk about immorality in connection with the exportation of arms. Is it immoral to ship a gun to China so that a Chinaman may protect his sacred fireside from invasion, or from the murder or ravage that may be committed upon his wife and upon his children? When great governments, with ambitious men who have a desire to control the earth, attempt to stamp out liberty and democracy, is there any immorality in supplying arms to a little weak country so that it may let the dictators and autocracies of the earth know that it can . . . get arms to protect its liberty?"

Then he asked all of the isolationists the question:

"Is it immoral to stand up in this great democracy and say that we believe in freedom, that we believe in self-determination of people, or that we want in a world conflict the democracies of the earth to survive that conflict?"

Regardless of the storm and stress of a session, the bitterness or personal conflicts which could well characterize the Seventy-sixth Congress, Sam Rayburn attempted to portray the positive side of the great American game of politics. At a session's end he knew how to bury the hatchet in an instant, pay a friendly farewell, and walk out of the House with a former Republican adversary hooked on his right arm and a recalcitrant Democrat on the left. He was realistic about this game, expecting some disappointments along the way, but he refused to let these defeats shake his perspective or change his attitude toward his fellow men. He explained it this way:

"I have had my disappointments, but I have had no heartaches. Men on that side of the aisle on controversial questions I expected to vote against the position I took when Party matters were involved. My heart has not ached, but I have been disappointed many times when some members on my side of the aisle did not see things exactly as I saw them; but I know that when they did not see things as I saw them, when in good conscience and believing that they represented the views of their constituents they cast a vote differently than I cast mine, they had no pleasure out of it, and that it really hurt them more than it hurt me."

Knowing that men of both Parties derived their inspiration from the people, he trusted their ability to lay aside all differences in a crisis to defend, maintain, and perpetuate the "beloved Republic" against all enemies, foreign and domestic. Though congressmen might have their political differences, he trusted in the human element to make them all appreciative of the common welfare.

The benevolent tone of his parting remarks upon the 1939 adjournment clearly revealed that he already had his train reservation in his pocket and his thoughts were in Texas. He was always eager to get back to his "own blood for a while and with the friends of a lifetime." In his imagination he had already fenced and cross-fenced his new ranch, had seeded it with grass, and stocked it with a foundation herd.

After his address on August 5 over NBC for the National Radio Forum on "The Work of Congress," he was prepared to take the night train. There would be a day of relaxation, another night of good rest, then one of his brothers would be waiting for him at Denison, and then home—"under the roof where my father and mother lived." Tom was now manager of the homeplace while Sister Lou ran the domestic end. She was a symbol of strength and Mr. Sam knew it. Her presence became more indispensable with the years. Here he became refreshed with enough vim and vigor, he said, to carry him through the seven long months of the next session.

Will and Jim Rayburn, Valton Young reports, had already begun the work of fencing the nine hundred acres. They used strong posts and six heavy strands of barbed wire. Then they divided the acreage into six pastures with a deep pool in each. About his two brothers he made this observation:

> "There was never another fence-builder like Will Rayburn. Never will you find the slightest crook or bend in a fence that he has lined up with nothing but his naked eye. You can examine any fence on this place and it is as straight as a gun barrel, if Will had anything to do with its construction. And Jim Rayburn knew these rural folk and their habits around here as a housewife knows her kitchen. He knew how to be a good neighbor, and they still reciprocate his favors. All these neighbors around this ranch would get up at the dead hour of midnight to help us if they thought that we were in trouble. That is the way that I try to be with them, too." [5]

The dairy herd had been sold. White Sox was dethroned and Old Joe, a Polled Hereford from a registered herd at Jacksboro, Texas, now reigned in his stead over heifers from the Johnson brothers' ranch. Bringing in good foundation stock was a slow but skilled business in which the owner was well versed.

There was the job of cutting away the underbrush and the postoaks which smothered the grass. The Majority Leader knew how to swing a double-bitted axe and lay a big tree flat against the earth with minimum ease. He could split a three-foot log of twelve-inch diameter in three strokes. His steel bit into the wood, not with the thought of chopping away Republican opposition or freeing himself of tensions, but with the positive idea of rescuing the undeveloped sandy soil from half a century of sleepy decay. He was at heart a builder and conservationist, setting a good example for his neighbors to follow with a type of rural economics which he visioned someday would grip his community. His partner at the other end of the cross-cut saw needed stamina to stay on his feet with the Congressman. This was a game for two, one Mr. Sam knew how to play.

He had worked to get approval of the Executive Reorganization bill, which was designed to remove outmoded procedures. Now he was faced with a more immediate reorganization of his own. The scars of the past dotted the landscape, such as rusty barbed wire, unsightly barns half-demolished by weathering, discarded household effects, and rubbish. To Valton Young, Rayburn philosophized upon the parallel between the decay of the homestead and the citizenship:

> "Back in my wooded area were signs where fairly recent moonshiners had left excavations by removing their white lightning stills—and just ahead of the sheriff, no doubt. Rumors, not too ancient, floated around of a little cow-stealing in this vicinity when I bought this place.
>
> "But I like to see the good in things and in people. These oldest settlers tell me that this neighborhood of Ivanhoe won first prize at the Chicago World's Fair with its commercial apples. At one time their cotton gins hummed day and night all season long. Their hogs and cattle in the good old days passed the winters on the open range in fine condition from the mast and native grasses respectively, without any assistance whatever. Trading was good with the sulky Choctaws from the Indian Territory around the crowded community saloon, and their prosperous country doctor hardly had time to attend his closest friend's funeral." [6]

The thud of the axe and the lowing of the cattle against a background of locust music produced a symphony of progress to men like Erwin E. Smith and the Congressman. Separated by only a mile, these two bachelors were now brought together with their mutual interest in beef cattle. Though from opposite economic backgrounds, the one indifferent to profits and the other compelled to watch the budget, they recognized the eternal wealth stored up in the soil of the Southwest. Their pride and confidence stemmed from the belief that, long after the earth had been squeezed of its black gold, it could retain its fertility and produce the best legumes and grasses known to modern agriculture. Talk about the Southwest cattle lore and the qualities of Polled Hereford stock with which Rayburn began his foundation herd, filled up many hours when these two exponents of the cattle business came together.

Rayburn translated words into action. "Miss Lou" matched her pace to his. A five-thirty breakfast of fried chicken, hot biscuits, jam, jellies, honey, fruit and coffee—this is only a sample of the man's breakfast when he was on rural vacation. He went to the ranch to work.

Such industry was rewarding, for by 1945 he had built up his grass to carry seventy registered Polled Hereford breeding cows and three sires. His barns were never wanting for baled hay from his meadows and the cottonseed cake, accessible at the local oil mill. With these he supplemented the rations.

His improvements kept pace with his production. Good barns and a small ranchhouse evidenced prosperity. His cabin, near the entrance, was a three-room frame structure with a large fireplace, running water, electrical appliances, bunks for a small party, appropriate furniture and pictures. The twelve-foot table at round-up time frequently groaned with food Rayburn prepared himself. Once he cooked a nineteen-pound fish—cleaned it, cut it in pieces, seasoned and fried it in deep boiling hot fat, preferably hog lard. The hands left only the bones as a token of their appreciation. His cornbread made them reach across the table for more.

If a person wanted some advice about raising good stock, he could find no better source. The best time of the day for him to arrive was twelve noon, because Mr. Sam always expected someone but rarely knew who.

According to accounts by Young, Lee Simmons, H. G. Dulaney, and others, at the appointed hour he would say:

> "Well, let's see how Miss Lou's food is going to taste today. She usually puts enough in this grub basket when I leave for the ranch in the mornings to feed an extra hand or two. So, pull your chair up to the table while I pour the coffee. You know, I like to sit on this bench better than on a chair. Reminds me of my childhood meals out there at Flag Springs, I guess. And my little mother, who, in my mind, was the smartest woman who ever lived, cooked food like this for her family of eleven children. I always eat some of this pure honey once a day—to which I attribute part of my extra-fine health." [7]

He made these remarks so many times to friends that one wonders if he had not memorized his reminiscences.

After his initial round of talk, which would bring even the high and mighty back to earth again to find the lowest common denominator in human relations, the visitor had to speak his piece, if he came on business, because with one cigarette Rayburn would disappear into the woods as quickly as he emerged. A dynamo of energy like this could never be contained for more than an hour. He was not geared to the siesta type of living. His motor churned to a full stop at 10:00 P.M. and resumed its motion the next morning with complete efficiency. The friend could stay as long as he liked, even ride one of Rayburn's saddle horses, but his own work had to go forward. This was the avocation which toned his muscles and sharpened his mind for the next season's work when the gavel called the political combatants together again.

Lee Simmons, who had been at the ranch many times, recalled these early days when the ranch was just beginning to take shape:

"I have snacked with him at his little box house, where he ate on a plank table and had nail kegs for seats. I have helped him get his winter wood where he and I would do the chopping and sawing and old Henry [the colored man] would do the loading, and when we would build a fire and boil the coffee and eat a fine lunch prepared by Miss Lou."

There was no telephone, radio, or television to steal his thoughts away from his Walden, but Mr. Sam did not retreat to his sanctuary to escape the world's problems. His isolation was brief and his abode was merely a field office where he applied the theory he knew to a practical solution for specific rural problems. And like the Concord Sage he was not writing an "ode to dejection" but "to wake my neighbors up"—to show them by example what America's worn-out soil can do when treated with a little intelligence and kindness.

A political seismograph like Rayburn could not be insensitive to the tremors in men's hearts, though he was briefly off the thoroughfare of life. His communicative manner opened the door to humanity, whether people were of high or low degree. He needed no interpreter. His idiom was intelligible to all and his sympathy warmed every man with an honest face who came to his door.

This late summer and fall of 1939 was a fruitful one—not a period of hibernation, but rather a moment of hesitation when he could view the New Deal and its author with a sort of perspective. A realist or pragmatic liberal himself, he recognized the need for social reform and was aware that America would never return to the political philosophy which prevailed prior to 1932. Like Roosevelt, he saw two phases of the New Deal; first the recovery and next the reform. Rayburn's problem had been selling Congress on legislation which might be merely experimental. His silent judgments told him that his Chief was no economist in the academic sense, and relied on personal magnetism and luck to guide his overwhelming zeal. Rayburn was convinced that Roosevelt was the only occupant of the White House he had known who was able to weave together completely incompatible ideas and come out with a message that would ignite the populace and inspire their confidence. Rayburn was not bothered by Roosevelt's trial-and-error approach because he saw no ready-made solutions to America's domestic ills. America had gone too long under a Republican leadership to find an easy route back to prosperity.

Rayburn followed Roosevelt's leadership because he recognized a sincere social outlook which aligned him to the underprivileged. There were millions of people who needed a spokesman at a time when men were losing faith in what they had believed about America. They had been neglected too long, but Rayburn believed they were beginning to smile again. He could see the sunshine on the streets of Bonham, in Savoy, in Ladonia —everywhere he went that summer. Evidence of the optimism was further apparent on August 22, when a crowd of ten thousand assembled at Denison for the Chamber of Commerce Rayburn Day home-coming celebrations. Hailed as the 1940 Democratic nominee for President, he was honored as the Party's standard-bearer and the driving force behind the Denison Dam.

Even before the first session of the Seventy-sixth Congress adjourned, he had been acclaimed by an editorial in the St. Louis *Post Dispatch* as a dark horse, being one of the very few men who might unite the conflicting factions which had occurred after Roosevelt's Supreme Court bill, Reorganization bill, the effort to purge conservatives, and the sweeping social legislation. Cordell Hull, though sixty-seven at the time, was also mentioned, along with Bennett Clark of Missouri (for his handling of the Pendergast case) and John Garner, with his adroit approach to public affairs. But late in August, Rayburn quieted all rumors about his personal ambitions when he issued this statement to the press: "I am for that outstanding Texan and liberal Democrat, John N. Garner for the Presidential nomination in 1940, believing that if elected he will make the country a great President." Rayburn's position cleared the way for the older statesman from Uvalde to make another bid for the nomination.

When the reporters questioned "Cactus Jack" about the steady stream of visitors to his office in the Senate Building, including his friend Mayor La Guardia, all of whom had discussed everything from national defense to the spending program, he merely put on his best poker face and replied, "No comment." Mopping his shaggy, white eyebrows, he stated: "I am just a Christian gentleman, who has been out in the country for six months living my own way, and these gentlemen around here are just calling to visit with me."

Rayburn's speeches, however, all confirmed his faith in the New Deal and his loyalty to the Party, and there was no disloyalty involved on Rayburn's part, because at this time Roosevelt was not a candidate. Yet rumors began flying that a rift had developed between the Majority Leader and the White House and that steps would be taken to unseat him as Party leader. However, Roosevelt understood the circumstances and he had also learned a few lessons during the attempted purges, not to push his luck too far.

John L. Lewis, CIO leader, had helped put Garner into the national focus by leveling a savage personal attack on him; and every Texas congressman who might have been up for re-election, with an ounce of common sense, knew which side of the feud his shooting irons should support. The Texas delegation had already been polled and they were with Garner.

The attention which was focused on the Vice-President did irritate the White House. Roosevelt's statement about conservative or "straddlebug" Democrats was made to stop the Garner boom, and Rayburn's use of "Liberal Democrat" in reference to his friend was designed to neutralize the effect of this attack. Rayburn and Garner were friends before Roosevelt moved into national politics, but their devotion to Party was too sincere for them to jeopardize their chances of victory in 1940 for the sake of pressing their personal ambitions or interests. They had played this poker hand before and knew when to "raise" and when to "pass."

With a big State Convention, National Convention, and a Texas primary ahead of him, Rayburn had to anticipate the future. He knew his people back in the Fourth expected him to be true to his own nature and support a friend like Garner. Even the militant pro-Roosevelt sentiment of the National Convention of Young Democratic Clubs did not make him delay his decision on Garner. A moderate or conservative by nature, he was philosophically at odds with the Young Democrats; however, the two somehow managed to work together, but not without a little grumbling on the part of the younger generation.

While the people on the home front were engaged in Presidential talk, there was something ominous about the dark cloud which hung over Europe. Adolf Hitler, in the spring of 1938, had denounced the Treaty of Versailles and scrapped the Locarno Pact of 1925. On March 11, 1938, he moved into Austria in violation of a pledge to honor neighboring territories. The occupation of the Sudetenland followed the Munich pledge; then came the conquest of Czechoslovakia. Roosevelt all the while had been trying to play the role of peacemaker, with messages to the principals in Europe. Congress had finally taken a more realistic view of Hitler's activities by approving a rearmament program. On September 1, 1939, Hitler invaded Poland, and two days later Britain and France entered the war in a struggle to stop the aggressor. World War II had erupted. These were the events which helped shape the direction of the Democratic National Convention and created the circumstances which helped make Mr. Sam indispensable.

☆ XIV ☆

An Ambition Fulfilled

ON JANUARY 6, 1940, three days after the opening of the third session of the Seventy-sixth Congress, "Mr. Democrat," as he was popularly referred to, addressed a group of loyal Party members in the Lord Baltimore Hotel. The occasion was the Jackson Day Dinner of the Concord Club on the 125th anniversary of Old Hickory's victory at New Orleans. More and more Rayburn had become the spokesman for his Party at Jefferson-Jackson Day celebrations. The poor health of Speaker Bankhead had forced Rayburn to the front on Party functions. The name of "Mr. Democrat" had virtually become synonymous with that of Sam Rayburn whether he spoke in Maryland, New York, California, Illinois, Texas, or anywhere. In the role of "Mr. Democrat" his message remained the same—the achievements of Democratic Administrations and the failure of the Republican philosophy. The essayist Ralph Waldo Emerson unknowingly defined one facet of this "Mr. Democrat" in his *Self-Reliance*, when he wrote a hundred years earlier:

> "If I know your sect I anticipate your argument? . . . Do I not know that he is pledged to himself not to look but at one side, the permitted side, not as a man, but as a parish minister? He is a retained attorney. . . ."

In a public relations capacity at a state or national convention, on the streets, or on the campaign circuit he was a "retained attorney."

But in committee, on the House floor, later on the Speaker's rostrum, and in the quiet sanctuary of his home he was Mr. Sam. Had he been otherwise, men like Joe Martin and later Charles Halleck could not have trusted him. They understood his partisan views, respected his own consistent program, but they were convinced that his first concern was America. The Democratic philosophy was merely his approach to what to him seemed best. Joe Martin's philosophy, Rayburn granted, was another way, though in his judgment, not the best. However, he remarked many times after friendly conversation with Joe Martin that he could have been a Republican had he lived in another section of America. Once when asked to enter Massachusetts and make some speeches against the Republicans and Joe Martin, he exclaimed emphatically, "Hell, if I lived up there, I would work for him." Their differences were honest ones on domestic issues. They were gracious in their manner of disputation. They were convinced that one was just as good an American as the other, for they had stood together too many times on foreign policy not to know the depth of the other's patriotism. They felt that the more vigorously they represented their respective views in the House, the stronger would be the two-Party system and the more secure the American way of life. But only gentlemen and men of goodwill could play such roles. They were aware that they set the example for all Americans who must live together with their differences.

Perhaps the case could be proved better by moving forward eighteen years and substituting the name of Charlie Halleck for Joe Martin. The older gentlemen were too much alike in attitude, habit, and ideas to arouse violent disputation, and with the passage of time they became even more similar. Halleck, on the other hand, competitive and ambitious, made Mr. Sam work harder to achieve harmony. The man from Indiana was on the way up, and he was quick to seize the advantage. Mr. Sam had to be more alert in dealing with this gentleman, for he belonged to the "new school" of Republicans, not the "old." He was commissioned to recover some of the faded glory and prestige his Party had once enjoyed. Although Mr. Sam got along with Halleck, the younger man forced him at times to follow John Garner's advice back in 1931, when Rayburn appeared too soft.

He said, "Sam, you've got to get your knuckles bloody once in a while."

It seemed appropriate on this January 6, 1940, in Baltimore for "Mr. Democrat" to review some of the accomplishments of the Administration of Franklin D. Roosevelt, who in spirit, purpose, and achievement represented what Old Hickory symbolized more than a century earlier. Rayburn spoke first of neutrality and national defense:

> "The Administration's neutrality legislation has changed the public attitude from one of fatalism to one of hopefulness. This act prohibits the two things that got us into the last war. It forbids American ships to go into dangerous waters and American citizens to travel on the ships of the belligerents. Since the enactment of the Administration's neutrality program not an American life has been lost and not an American ship has been sunk."

He emphasized, also, that the armament program was proceeding according to the plan for making America strong. He then referred to the Foreign Trade Agreements, under the Tariff Act of 1930, as amended.

On the domestic front he cited the effects of the social-security and old-age pension program, the Civilian Conservation Corps, the Public Works and Work Relief Agencies, the Federal Deposit Insurance Corporations, the Securities and Exchange Act, the Federal Housing Administration, the Home Owners' Loan Corporation, and the Reconstruction Finance Corporation. He answered the criticism of "reckless spending" by showing that the expanding economy would eventually absorb the additional expense. To the criticism of mistakes he replied that when action is substituted for inaction errors are inevitable. Rayburn affirmed:

> "Our program has been based on that sound old Democratic principle of doing the greatest good to the greatest number and, all in all, the program of the last seven years has been unmatched in the history of our Republic for the amount of good that has been done for all the people."

Then he concluded his Jefferson-Jackson remarks with his favorite theme that the Republicans had only the failures of the dead past to offer, and that the American people preferred the philosophy which would bring prosperity and hope for the future. Since this was an election year, audiences about the country were destined to hear these remarks many times.

During the Roosevelt years, Rayburn became identified as a liberal, but he never liked the designation. He preferred to be called a conservative, an outlook which best suited the District he represented and gave a happy balance to the philosophy of the New Deal. In its broad sense he found the word "progressive" acceptable. He frequently tempered the pragmatism or opportunism of Roosevelt with an old-fashioned "hoss" sense, which in the last analysis was fundamentally just plain instinct. Rayburn's type of sense was difficult to outwit and out-argue. It rarely made blunders, and was just as good in the Sixty-third Congress as in the Eighty-seventh. As early as 1940, some conceived of him as a sort of political genius because of his knowledge of the ten thousand House rules, and legislation like that regulating holding companies, rural electrification, flood controls; but his modesty discouraged any such association with intellectual greatness. He said his meager success came from a basic love for and faith in people, with a zeal to do what was right by the standards of that "Man from Galilee." He listened well and had a good memory. His long experience had taught him the difference between good ideas and poor ones, and his grasp of the human equation made him invaluable in executing a program. But if he had no faith in a measure the Administration liked, he would register his objection calmly. He could "go along to get along," but he knew when to let a measure die a natural death instead of killing it before the public eye. Some of this kind of sense his parents gave him or nurtured around the fireside and in the cotton fields at Flag Springs. Not much of it came from books at East Texas or at the University. Association with men of his kind in the Texas Legislature may have helped some to sharpen his instinct to a fine edge, which never became dull with the passing of time. Many of the gains of the Roosevelt Administration were probably the result of this old-fashioned Rayburn "hoss" sense, of a country style.

Illustrative of his type of common sense was his attitude toward the committee's report on the general Post Office appropriations. When it recommended a $415,000 cut he accepted the reduction but objected to one phase of the so-called "economy effort." He believed that many members of the House were unfamiliar with the "small post-office business." He thought it was a penny wise and pound foolish policy which would starve the employees of the little third-class post offices, who were terribly underpaid already. This attitude is illustrative of his general way of looking at the country's needs, particularly the interests of the folks at America's grass roots. These people were to him the ones who deserved recognition, because they received less economically and gave more of themselves, without reward, during international crises. He used the question of the Post Office appropriation as a point of departure to express his consideration for these Americans at the headwaters of Democracy. Rayburn's position here was consistent with that on other measures concerning them. They gave him life and encouraged his dreams. His roots were never torn from the friendly earth and people of his District.

The people on his staff, colleagues on both sides of the aisles, the hundreds of recipients of letters or telegrams in hours of adversity point up another quality in Sam Rayburn which was quite unusual—a sincere, personal interest in those whose lives had touched his at one time or another. An incident, though it occurred several years later, illustrates the point. It was originally told by *Life* magazine and reported in the Sherman *Democrat* of December 29, 1959, in the following manner: A young newspaper reporter who had been to Mr. Sam's press conferences several times had lost his teen-age daughter. Mr. Sam early on the morning after the child's death went to the family's apartment and knocked on the door. The father opened the door and was surprised to see the Speaker standing there.

"I just came by to see what I could do to help," he said.

A bit flustered, the father replied, "I don't think there's anything you can do. We're making all the arrangements."

"Well, have you all had your coffee this morning?" Mr. Sam asked.

"No, we haven't had time."

"Well," he replied promptly, "I can at least make the coffee this morning."

And while Mr. Sam was puttering about in the kitchen, the reporter said, "Mr. Speaker, I thought you were supposed to be having breakfast at the White House this morning."

"Well, I was, but I called the President and told him I had a friend who was in trouble, and I couldn't come."

As a result of such an outlook people who knew Rayburn searched for opportunities to pay their respects. Many used birthdays as just such an occasion. Friends across the nation sent their congratulations, and Washington associates gathered to pay homage. January 6 was encircled on many calendars to remind that it was "Mr. Sam's day."

The *Congressional Record* contains numerous "Extension of Remarks" by Rayburn concerning people who had died. For example, he had this comment to make about Carl Mapes, who was a member of the Committee on Interstate and Foreign Commerce:

> "I take this moment to refer to a man who is absent from that Committee now, but who was for many years the ranking minority member of the Committee during the years that I was Chairman of it. Mr. Chairman, I have served with probably eighteen hundred men since I first entered this hall, but I say to you that I never served with a better man, and in my opinion there was never a finer gentleman, a finer Congressman, or abler statesman in this House than my lamented colleague Carl Mapes. He was gentle; he was fine; he was able. As I say, I have taken this moment not only to congratulate this great Committee upon its fine work, but to say this word in tribute to a great man who has passed on."

The war in Europe quite naturally motivated considerable thought about foreign policy. The isolationists in 1940 had a great deal of support because America's geographical position and traditional self-sufficiency created a feeling of aloofness. The country was busily arming, but at this time few in Congress believed America would embark upon another great crusade. Although their optimism was suddenly shattered by the aggressive policies of Germany and Japan, men like Rayburn hoped the United States could remain neutral by being strong militarily. Yet he was not an isolationist. For example, in explaining the President's National program he remarked:

> "I think I speak the heart of America when I say this; the heart of America, from the head of government down, intends that not one dollar of this money shall ever be used to equip an army of aggression, because we covet not one foot of soil over which the flag of any other nation flies today. And may I say further that as far as I am concerned, and I still feel that I speak the heart of America from the head of the government down, that not one dollar of this money shall ever be used to equip and send American boys to fight on European soil."

The turn of events, however, led him to reverse this way of thinking and admit he was wrong.

Rayburn had become concerned about Republican slogans to fix the Democrats in the public mind as the war Party and themselves as the peace Party. Realizing that this was election year, he did not want to be misunderstood; so he clearly stated the President's policy thus:

> "The Democratic Party at this time is not the war Party, it will not be the war Party, but it intends to be, wishes to be, and it will be the Party for the defense of America and its great institutions."

Public sentiment in America at this time was becoming increasingly anti-German and anti-Russian, in the latter instance because of the conquest of Finland, to whom the United States had advanced a loan of ten million dollars for the purchase of agricultural surpluses. Rayburn said that he had little regard for the Russian Government and their leadership, but he hesitated to see America sever her diplomatic relations with Russia primarily because of a dislike for a particular form of government. If the embassy were closed, he feared America would lose its source of information about developments in that country. He did not deem it wise for America to set out on a campaign to change the governments of the earth which were objectionable to her.

Democrats were also becoming increasingly concerned over the health of Speaker William Bankhead. When Bankhead was hospitalized April 1 with complications from a severe attack of influenza, the House on the following day promptly elevated the Majority Leader to Speaker pro tempore. Rayburn's responsibilities were now doubled, but he had the physique to bear the strain. He carried his 176 pounds well. The Democrats had confidence in his physical and mental strength. There was continued talk about running him for President.

Despite his own previous endorsement of Vice-President Garner for the Presidency, his name now came to be mentioned, along with that of Jesse H. Jones, Director of RFC. On the other hand, the Young Democrats and other liberal groups continued to discuss a third term for Roosevelt. Rayburn, however, kept the bills moving and quietly conferred with members of the Texas delegation and visitors from back home. The latter brought reports that the State Convention promised to be a free-for-all if the Roosevelt faction tried to force a third term. Such information made this loyal New Dealer feel a bit uncomfortable, but as late as April Roosevelt had not committed himself to a draft.

Since Congress remained in session continuously, recessing only for the conventions, Rayburn was compelled to ignore the problems in Texas politics, including the opposition in his own District from Dr. Biven R. Galbraith of Fannin County. In the primary his opponent received only 1205 of the 10,068 votes cast in the County, and only 5457 of the 37,912 in the whole District. The fall of France and Hitler's continued success was of far greater interest than a Sam Rayburn Congressional race.

Additional responsibilities in Washington had also compelled him to miss the State Convention in Waco. On May 21, he wrote H. A. Cunningham and Travis Lipscomb of Bonham, on several occasions his traveling companions to these state meetings: "The Convention coming on Tuesday, I would be away from Washington a whole week as I do not fly and would have to go and come on the train." He expressed the hope that they would "help look after matters at the Convention." Rayburn's letters were rather vague sometimes, but Henry and "Trav" knew exactly what he meant. A few lines later he added, "Of course, we hope that no one will be put on the delegation from our District who is not friendly to us." Similar overtures urging Party harmony had been expressed to others in the State.

The name of Garner had already been agreed upon by some of the leaders in the Party, but despite all Rayburn's early planning, intra-Party conflicts seemed to be the order of the day at this State Convention and almost all succeeding ones. Several of these fracases took an even greater toll of Rayburn's energy and spirits than did the national conventions themselves. The issues became rather personal, and too frequently he found himself fighting people he thought should have been cooperative. In later years, perhaps more from despair and disgust than anything else, he suggested that a strong Republican Party was the answer, but he never gave a great deal of thought as to how he could help the opposition Party.

In the State Conventions there were smoke-filled rooms, to be sure, where problems were settled and Mr. Sam was still the master; but when someone, so to speak, turned out the lights and the fight started with "flip knives," he frankly admitted that he was not as versatile as some he knew. He was schooled in fighting in the daylight against opponents who fronted him face to face, but even so, sometimes in one of Rayburn's smoke-filled caucus rooms the visibility could be rather poor. Unity was his goal, and occasionally he had to use a "big stick" to achieve it.

He regretted that he could not get down to keynote the Waco Convention, because he had performed this function since 1932. However, he agreed to accept the Chairmanship of the Texas delegation and expressed the hope that Myron G. Blalock would be elected National Committeeman. As to the temporary chairman and permanent chairman, he frankly admitted he could not express an opinion without being on the ground. To people who did not know the workings of his mind he wrote more specifically thus:

> A clear-cut endorsement of the policies and accomplishments of the Roosevelt Administration and an unequivocal instruction to the delegates to vote for Mr. Garner for the Democratic nomination for President is what we want.

The Republicans held their Convention in Philadelphia on June 24. Wendell L. Willkie emerged as the popular choice, with Charles L. McNary of Oregon as his running mate. The others considered were Thomas E. Dewey, who had been propelled into the public eye by his successful prosecution of racketeers in New York; Senator Robert A. Taft, "Mr. Republican"; and Senator Arthur H. Vandenberg. Rayburn had a very high regard for the two Senators, but while he favored a foreign policy of neutrality, he did not agree with their isolationism or semi-isolationism.

The Democrats assembled in Chicago the second week of July. When Senator Alben Barkley completed his keynote address, he read Roosevelt's statement that he did not seek the nomination and was releasing his delegates to vote for whomever they wished. Believing, though, that the President would respond to a draft, the delegates the next day promptly placed his name in nomination along with Garner's. It then became a New Deal Convention, but there was enough opposition to suggest a revolt. Rayburn was gravely concerned because he headed a delegation already pledged to Garner, though divided; however, he held the delegates together through the roll call. With Garner receiving only sixty-one votes, he quickly stepped to the Speaker's platform to move that the nomination of Roosevelt be made unanimous. There was no time for Rayburn to quibble or pout over a "rigged convention" or to worry about what his fellow Texans would say. He made one of the quick decisions for which he was famous. The turn of events left the Chicago Stadium in an uproar, for many resented the way Roosevelt circumvented the third term issue by never making a statement relative to it and by making his nomination appear as thrust upon him. The Roosevelt offensive was well executed, but the Rayburn retreat was not without some finesse itself. By means of radio Roosevelt accepted, making reference to the perilous times and his conscience calling him to duty.

Behind-the-scenes developments show that this was a strenuous Convention, though brief. One of Garner's close friends, Richard W. Norton, a delegate-at-large and oil man from San Antonio, went back to his room in the Sherman Hotel and died of a heart attack. Several brawls were reported involving members of the Texas delegation. Sid Richardson, another delegate, reported that he was robbed in the hotel elevator; however, this incident was not necessarily Convention inspired. Nor was this an episode for which "Mr. Democrat" would blame the Republicans.

After Roosevelt's nomination, Texans began talking Garner, Rayburn, and Jesse Jones for Vice-President. Secretary of State Cordell Hull, Postmaster James A. Farley, Senator James F. Byrnes, Speaker William Bankhead, and Secretary of Agriculture Henry Wallace were also mentioned by other delegations.

Garner's behavior implied a strong desire to get back to Uvalde to begin catching up on his hunting and fishing, because he had been opposed to a third term, as were many others. He refused to be associated with the ticket himself, but later quietly assured Rayburn he "would stay hitched." The Texas delegation caucused, with Representative Lyndon Johnson as Chairman.

Vann Kennedy of Austin made a motion to split its vote fifty-fifty between Rayburn and Jones. Wright Morrow of Houston suggested that they wait to hear from the President. Jones promptly thanked everyone thus:

"I appreciate the friendship that prompts you to think of me for the honor of Vice-President. When I learned May 23 that Mayor Oscar Holcombe of Houston had suggested the State Convention at Waco endorse me for the office, I immediately wrote W. P. Hobby and told him I preferred that my name not be presented. These were my sentiments then and they are my sentiments today. I would consider the nomination only if it came as a suggestion of President Roosevelt. I also will be glad to join in any tribute to Sam Rayburn."

Frank Roberts of Breckenridge made this plea:

"Let us suggest to the President that the Democrats of

Texas are behind Rayburn. Let's not have a divided house. I offer an amendment to the motion that we pledge our support to Congressman Rayburn."

After a hubbub, Vann Kennedy withdrew his motion; then Maury Hughes of Dallas seconded Roberts' motion. Claude Birkhead of San Antonio urged that the delegation think of the Party rather than of personalities. "Beating the Republicans in November is not going to be any cinch," he said. "Willkie has great strength in business and financial circles and we need a man to meet him on equal terms. I love Sam Rayburn, but we must select an outstanding candidate for this job. Jesse Jones has the confidence of the business world and would make an outstanding candidate, but I suggest that we not tie ourselves. Let's wait until we hear from the President."

Then there were short speeches in Rayburn's behalf. Lyndon Johnson ruled that the motion to back Rayburn was before the caucus, refusing to recognize Birkhead, who was jumping and shouting to be heard. The vote was eighty-eight to seven, and at this point Jesse Jones announced that he had just received word that the President preferred Henry Wallace.

Rayburn then asked everyone to calm down and spoke firmly: "If that information is correct and I will check it immediately, I ask the delegation not to submit my name but to support the choice of the President." When he received confirmation of Roosevelt's wishes, he asked that his name not be placed in nomination: "Let me say that if I consulted my loyalty, my love, I would probably second the nomination of another. But under the circumstance, I cannot do otherwise than follow the wishes of my leader." He added that he would second the nomination of Henry A. Wallace, the farmers' friend. The Texas delegation, however, did not follow Rayburn, but supported Bankhead.

Myron G. Blalock of Marshall, the State Chairman, then hurried to the platform and stated: "Only one man has been voted on by this caucus. No one has been repudiated. Let us all remain friends and go home to work in harmony for the election of our ticket in November."

What emotions Sam Rayburn felt during the period March–July perhaps no one ever knew. Certainly he was not the type to dwell upon disappointments. He knew the shape of things to come too well, however, not to recognize the facts. Rayburn undoubtedly believed the President would seek a third term; in fact, he remarked in 1960, "If Roosevelt had not died and had remained in good health, he would have asked for a fifth term and might have been elected. He was the type of man who did not want to quit." Therefore, Rayburn was aware that in supporting Garner he was attempting to curtail Roosevelt's ambitions and was also going against a liberal stream. His was a value judgment, not a political one. He had never deserted a friend or violated his own beliefs, so he cast his lot with an old friend, even though he probably realized Garner could not win. He recognized that eventually he would be called upon to hold the Party together, to play the familiar role of peacemaker. Hence he did what was ethically sound and this he knew he could live with in the years to come. He derived some comfort in the realization that Roosevelt needed him, needed his leadership in the more conservative sections of the nation and certainly in the House. In this dilemma the Congressman moved with dignity and poise, and Roosevelt, reading Rayburn's mind, telephoned him early on the Friday morning, following the turbulent session of the night before, to thank him for his unselfishness and invaluable help.

Rayburn appreciated this expression from the President, because he actually had been torn between two loyalties and he was pleased to receive an acknowledgment of his dilemma. He had manifested courage and honesty and he was glad that Roosevelt recognized it. He had also demonstrated skill in holding the huge, seething Texas delegation together for Garner until he had fulfilled every obligation to the Vice-President and his followers. Then, he quickly loaded them all onto the Roosevelt band wagon by asking that the Convention make the nomination unanimous.

In the selection of the Vice-President he revealed a characteristic unselfishness by stepping aside in favor of Wallace, who was Roosevelt's choice. This was the real soul-searching moment, since he already knew that Roosevelt had narrowed the field to Wallace and himself. He could have created a stalemate by remaining as a contender and could then have broken it by supporting Bankhead, for whom he had enough votes to beat Wallace. Then his great ambition of the Speakership would have been his. Yet Rayburn did not even lift a hand to oppose Wallace. Roosevelt had telephoned Rayburn asking him to nominate Wallace, and he agreed to do so. He preferred Roosevelt's pre-established harmony to that type of harmony which would have to be achieved later. There were some from this Texas delegation who still believed in 1961 that Rayburn made a mistake in not staying in the race. They thought he could have beaten Wallace. Rayburn, though, told them that he had only one ambition —to remain in the House and some day become Speaker.

How many items of correspondence Rayburn wanted to throw away one will never know, but if he had been given to such impulses he passed up many good opportunities, for not every correspondent approved of his actions. Rayburn's support of Roosevelt at the Convention brought some response from Texas, to which he courteously replied in a few lines thanking the individuals for expressing their "views on matters of public interest."

One gentleman in the Fourth District sent "Mr. Democrat" a 457-word telegram, into which he poured all the criticism of the Roosevelt Administration he could muster. About his Congressman he said:

> Based on the stand you took at the Chicago Convention I am wondering if your sense of obligation to him and to his organized minority of professional political patronage dispensers is not greater than your sense of obligation to those who elected you to the office you hold. . . . I challenge you to meet with me and discuss these other questions of vital interest before the people of North Texas.

Rayburn answered briefly and courteously, in his usual manner, merely thanking the gentleman for his "views on matters of public interest" and assuring the constituent of his own dedication to foreign and domestic legislation. Angered by Rayburn's irrelevant form letters and refusal to stop everything and "fight a duel," he sent an eight-page single-spaced manuscript cogently and thoughtfully written, which enlarged upon the telegram. "Mr. Democrat" replied in even briefer terms this time, for he recognized that this constituent was sitting in the saddle backwards facing the wrong end of the horse.

Republicans did not bother Mr. Democrat so much as did the "Willkie-Democrats," who paraded as one thing in the primaries and another thing during the general elections. Consistent honesty he could respect, but not chameleon-like Democrats. Until his last days he always mused about this "mugwump" attitude among some of the Texas Democrats. They could sit squarely on the fence with portions of the human anatomy on either side.

Following the Chicago Convention, Rayburn returned to Washington to divide his time between heavy legislative responsibilities and public relations work within the Party. He knew in advance, though, that the third-term issue would cost the New Deal some of their stalwarts. Men like Raymond Moley, Budget Director Lewis Douglas, and Hugh Johnson did join the Willkie camp. Alfred Smith and Jim Farley became lukewarm toward Roosevelt, although Farley always remained a Democrat. The attempted purge and Supreme Court reform had already forced many loyal Party men to sit on their hands. Some continued to call themselves Democrats but voted Republican for the next twenty years in national elections. John L. Lewis made a futile attempt to turn CIO support to Willkie. Roosevelt, however, had set in motion a trend which perhaps attracted more liberal Republicans than it alienated Democrats. The world crises had fixed in the minds of the electorate the dangers of "swapping horses in midstream,"—Rayburn's argument when he discussed foreign affairs.

About two months before the election, the Majority Leader found himself more and more in the nation's eye. The press liked to make references to Rayburn's relation to the "Board of Education." It has also been called the "Bureau of Education"; a misnomer, Mr. Sam thought, but he liked to say with a chuckle, "I guess some fellows have been educated down there." He merely referred to it as the room "downstairs," but it came to be known as the "Rayburn Bureau of Education."

Actually the Bureau was only a conference room, or hideaway, in the Capitol, where in the old days men like "Nick" Longworth and Jack Garner met to discuss their problems. Membership in this "club" was by invitation only. Here men of both Parties could gather for relaxation and serious talk. One afternoon many years back, when a Republican held the gavel and Rayburn was still a fledgling, he made the prophetic remark about the speakership:

> "I'll tell you what I think—I think someday a man will be elected who'll bring the speakership into respectability again. He will be the real leader of the House. He will be the master around here, and everyone will know it. My guess is that one of you [referring to Longworth and Garner] will be the man." [1]

He was correct, because Longworth followed Gillett in 1925 and Garner succeeded him in 1931. Little did Rayburn realize at the time that he was also destined to be identified with this Bureau and would eventually take over the gavel himself.

These two men unconsciously taught him many things which later proved invaluable. He observed them as they gave practical demonstrations on resolving conflicts. Here he saw men learn how to work together, not by sacrificing principles but by learning to understand one another. There may have been "deals," but "compromises" described the transactions a little better, as Rayburn resolved legislative differences. Rayburn considered pressure and trickery as unbecoming, but demagogues and lesser men may have been outmaneuvered. If a congressman felt later he had been cheated, it was really his own fault for not having had the integrity or brains to survive under challenging conditions. Rayburn confessed that weak men always get pushed around in any walk of life. "The people learn to keep congressmen like these at home," he stated, "because they cannot learn how to work with people."

Later, when asked what qualities a Speaker should have, Rayburn thought about Longworth and Garner, and replied: "A Speaker should command respect and affection, have a long legislative experience, show persistence, have a good business head, possess a determined ambition plus shrewdness." A good leader, he added, must understand the "human relationships, fears and ambitions which permeate politics and make it an art —a feeling for the situation." Sam Rayburn was too modest to realize that he was actually looking in a mirror and not at the picture of his two predecessors, though they also qualified by these broad categories but not as completely as he did.

Garner's effect upon Rayburn during these formative years can be exaggerated. But down in the Fourth the people suggest all sorts of influences. Some believe Cactus Jack persuaded Sam to give up cigarettes in favor of his brand of cigars, but the habit was not to endure. Some saw the Garner influence in the brand of bourbon, but of course, he would substitute scotch. A few believe the Uvalde sage taught him how to cuss, when the occasion prompted, but Sam had certain aptitudes here before he met Garner. No doubt the older man encouraged Sam Rayburn's abhorrence of embassy teas and cocktail parties; yet Sam never had a real flair for dressing out in tails. The moths perhaps did more damage to his formals than actual wear. The truth of the matter about Garner and Rayburn is that they were cast from the same Texas material, but the Majority Leader had more refinements and was a shade gentler.

Speaker William B. Bankhead died rather suddenly on Sunday, September 15, 1940. Earlier, a blood vessel in his abdomen had ruptured and Dr. George W. Calver, Capitol physician, had urged him not to attend a function. Another hemorrhage occurred at 5:00 P.M., September 14, and he passed away early the next day.

The White House promptly announced that the President would leave for Jasper, Alabama, aboard his special train, immediately after the state funeral for the Speaker which was to be held in the House chamber on Monday.

Under the rules of the House, the death of the Speaker leaves that body without organization, and a Speaker must be elected before any regular business can be transacted. The Clerk of the House called the body to order at noon on Monday. He solemnly announced with emotion that Speaker William B. Bankhead had died on Sunday morning and that the election of a Speaker was in order.

Representative John W. McCormack of Massachusetts, Chairman of the Democratic caucus, introduced a resolution for the election of Rayburn as Speaker, and that the President and the President of the Senate be formally notified. The clerk read the resolution and put the motion for its adoption, which was unanimous by voice vote.

The clerk then appointed a committee consisting of Representative Hatton W. Sumners, still Chairman of the Judiciary Committee, Minority Leader Joseph W. Martin of Massachusetts, and John McCormack to escort the new Speaker to the stand. Representative A. J. Sabath of Illinois, Chairman of the Rules Committee, administered the oath to the new Speaker. He stood in the well of the House near the casket as Mr. Rayburn was on the Speaker's dais.

Thus, Sam Rayburn became Speaker on September 16, 1940.

After the oath Rayburn moved slowly to the rostrum. The gavel, the symbol of authority that was to be his for years to come, lay only inches away from his right hand. Appearing a bit uneasy in his formal dress, he stood quietly for a few moments, eyes moist and bald head shining dully in the soft illumination from the skylight. A lifetime ambition had been realized, but as he looked into the pale face of his friend below he could feel no pleasant sensations. As he later reminisced, the greatest joys in political life really come about from anticipation; their fulfillment too frequently follows in the wake of painful adversity to someone you love.

There was no acceptance speech. Rayburn's first action was

to outline the arrangements for the funeral. He appointed the committee in charge of inviting the President, members of the Cabinet, justices of the Supreme Court, members of the diplomatic corps, and members of the Senate to attend the services in the House. He also appointed a committee of sixty-three members to accompany the body to Jasper for the ceremony there at 2:30 P.M. on Tuesday. He announced that the burial would be in the family plot where the late Speaker's father, Senator J. Bankhead, was also buried.

Long before the appointed hour the Capitol was surrounded by a heavy police guard. The galleries were packed, admission to which was by special card. One of the Speaker's secretaries recalled seeing the President arrive and be assisted to his chair, which someone had failed to place at the proper angle for him to ease into. When he almost fell she caught the expression on his face—one of intense anger which turned into a sort of helpless despair, after he had secured himself with his strong hands. Throughout the service the secretary observed that he solemnly watched the gray casket. Near him was Mrs. Bankhead, heavily veiled. Next was State Senator Bankhead and Colonel Henry M. Bankhead, brothers; then actress daughter Tallulah and Mrs. Eugene Hoyt. There were also members of the Cabinet and diplomatic corps, then James C. McReynolds of the Supreme Court.

When Rayburn tried to speak, he faltered, cleared his throat, then uttered these words:

> "For twenty-five years or more I was given a rich friendship which I will remember to my last days. It was given to me by a great statesman, by a great man with a great soul. The House has lost a great man. Will Bankhead was a human being. He loved people *en masse*. His was a great soul."

Martin noted that Bankhead was a strong partisan but was fair in his dealings with the Republican minority: "A fine life is ended. A great American has passed on to his reward that comes for a life of service."

The Reverend James Shera Montgomery, Chaplain of the House, read the *103rd Psalm* and prayed:

> "O Blessed Lord God, the memory of this scholarly Christian gentleman we will not knowingly allow to die out of our aching hearts. He loved the good, the

> beautiful and the true and saluted a greater future for his brother man."

After singing by a double male quartet from St. Margaret's Episcopal Church, the Rev. William S. Abernathy, a substitute Chaplain of the Senate, pronounced the benediction.

The President, the Cabinet, the family, the diplomatic corps, and the Senate filed out of the chamber. The House and all committees recessed until Thursday, the Senate until Wednesday.

Speaker Rayburn left Washington at 4:30 P.M. on the train carrying the body and members of the funeral cortege to Alabama. The President's special train was the second section. This was the third time President Roosevelt had traveled from Washington to pay his respects to a Speaker—to Henry T. Rainey of Illinois in 1934 and Joseph W. Byrns of Tennessee in 1936.

Sam Rayburn remembered several things about the following afternoon: the dusty roads of Walker County, the hot Alabama sun, the Jasper First Methodist Church roped off with binder twine from a telephone pole to a soapbox, to a fireplug and to another telephone pole. The men in overalls and blue denim shirts reminded him of his good friends from the Fourth. He sensed their grief. Fans and umbrellas gave the ladies some relief from the heat. When the prayer came over the loudspeaker, the men removed their sweat-stained hats. Because of the solemnity of the occasion, the people acknowledged Roosevelt's presence with only subdued applause and a nod of the head. A reporter heard a farmer remark, "'Tain't no time for cheering." An almost identical sign of silent approval was given John F. Kennedy on November 18, 1961, as he left the First Baptist Church by the side entrance after the ceremony for Mr. Sam.

Following the interment, the funeral train left for Washington. Rayburn brought his colleagues' thoughts back to the affairs of the living by reminding them that there was a Majority Leader to be selected. With only two candidates in contention—John McCormack and Clifton Woodrum of Virginia—Rayburn began reflecting on qualifications. The Massachusetts man was already popular for permitting debate to exceed the allotted time of five minutes. The other frequently had opposed much of the New Deal spending which would not benefit his own section. Though Rayburn followed discretion by staying out of Party mat-

Mr. Sam revisiting his birthplace, the log cabin built by his father in 1868 near Lenoir, Tennessee, in the Clinch Valley. "My parents, especially in the early years," said the Speaker, "were faced with all the real hardships of farm laborers . . . opportunity was limited in the Clinch Creek district of Tennessee, ravaged by the Civil War." (*The Sam Rayburn Library*)

Mayo College (East Texas State Teachers' College) at Commerce, as it looked about 1900 when Mr. Sam was a student. He swept floors and rang the school bell to support himself. (*The Sam Rayburn Library*)

The 1903 graduation class of Mayo College. Sam Rayburn stands in the last row, on far right. (*The Sam Rayburn Library*)

The Rayburn family about 1905 in front of their Flag Springs, Texas, hor
Standing, left to right: Dr. Frank Rayburn, Sam, Dick, Tom and Jim R
burn. Seated, left to right: Will, Abner, William Marion (the father, w
rode with Nathan Bedford Forrest in the Civil War), Martha Waller, Lucin
("Miss Lou"), Katy Rayburn Thomas, and Meddie Rayburn Bartley.
Sam was the eighth of eleven children. (*The Sam Rayburn Library*)

In 1906, age twenty-four, Mr. Sam first ran for political office. Before paying his filing fee, he said to a friend: "I'm going to get myself elected to the State Legislature. I am going to spend about three terms there and then I want to be elected Speaker. After that I am going to run for Congress and be elected." (Photo by the Elliotts, with permission of Dorothy Hallman, Chief Clerk, House of Representatives, Austin, Texas.)

On May 17, 1934, Congressional conferees sought an agreement between the House and Senate views of what eventually became the Securities Exchange Act of 1934, authored by Mr. Rayburn, then chairman of the House Interstate and Foreign Commerce Committee. Seated, left to right: Rep. Huddleston (Ala.), Senator Couzens (Mich.), Rep. Rayburn, Senators Fletcher (Fla.), Barkley (Ky.), Byrnes (S.C.), and Goldsborough (Md.). Standing, left to right: Rep. Cooper (Ohio), Rep. Lea (Calif.), and Rep. Mapes (Mich.). (*Wide World Photos*)

Mr. Sam talking to reporters the day after a Democratic caucus elected hi Majority Leader of the House (Jan. 4, 1937). Although he won by a wid margin over his chief competitor, Rep. John O'Connor of New York, ther was some objection because his section of the country was already we rewarded with the Vice-Presidency and seven major committee chairma ships. Someone observed, however, that New York alone held the Presidenc three cabinet posts, and several House chairmanships, including O'Connor House Rules Committee. (*Wide World Photos*)

Rep. Fred Vinson (Ky.) on the left and Majority Leader Rayburn on the right listen carefully to Speaker William Bankhead as he discusses forthcoming legislative procedure in the second session of the 75th Congress (1937). In his new role as Majority Leader, Sam Rayburn was beginning to evolve into that position of leadership which caused most people to refer to him as "Mr. Democrat," the first of many names epitomizing his growth into a national statesman. (*Wide World Photos*)

The Congressional leaders of the second phase of the New Deal are shown leaving the White House December 20, 1937, after discussing with President Roosevelt problems relating to a special session of Congress. Left to right: Speaker Bankhead, Vice-President Garner, Senator Barkley (Majority Leader), and House Majority Leader Rayburn. (*Wide World Photos*)

In 1938 two of Mr. Sam's brothers paid their first visit to Washington, where the Majority Leader had been a Representative for almost a quarter of a century. When asked by reporters why they took so long to pay a visit, they replied they had been too busy before. Left to right: Tom, Dick, and Sam. (*Wide World Photos*)

Speaker Rayburn is shown signing on December 9, 1941, the Joint Resolution of Congress declaring war. Four months previous Mr. Sam faced the biggest test of his career thus far, the question of extending the Selective Service Act. Against strong isolationist and emotional opposition, the extension was passed by one vote on August 12. The Speaker had stood behind the clerk as the votes were being counted; immediately after the last name had been called, the Speaker announced: "On this vote 203 members have voted 'Aye,' 202 members have voted 'No,' and the bill is passed." The speed with which he exercised his knowledge of parliamentary procedure caused some time to pass before the House members realized that no one can change his vote after it has been announced. (*Wide World Photos*)

By 1943 Speaker Rayburn had already earned the title of the second most powerful man in the government. He is shown here with Vice-President Wallace and Majority Leader McCormack discussing domestic issues with President Roosevelt the morning he returned from the Cairo and Teheran conferences. (*Wide World Photos*)

When the Democrats lost control of Congress in the 1946 elections, Rayburn stated: "I will not be the Minority Leader." He is shown here talking to reporters after being "drafted" as Minority Leader. Even the Republicans wanted him because during the elections Mr. Sam refused advice to make speeches attacking specific Republicans for transgressions. The realization that defeat had brought unity to the Party caused Mr. Sam to accept the position. Joseph Martin of Massachusetts, one of Mr. Sam's closest friends, became the Speaker. (*Wide World Photos*)

Mr. Sam and Valton J. Young sitting on the entrance gate of his ranch north of Bonham (1949). The Speaker bought the ranch, consisting of several abandoned and wornout farms, in 1937 because he wanted to raise beef cattle, a less time-consuming occupation than raising dairy herds although he had been a successful dairyman. Mr. Sam had recognized the shifting economy in Fannin County—he knew that soil depletion and shortage of young manpower forced many cotton and dairy farmers into ranching. The shift did not really become significant until after the war, but he was always a little ahead of his time. (Photo by Erwin Smith, from *The Sam Rayburn Library*)

On January 30, 1951, Mr. Sam surpassed Henry Clay's record for tenure of the Speaker's chair (3056½ days). In honor of the occasion, President Truman presented him with a gavel fashioned from timber from the part of the White House erected in 1817. Between the President and the Speaker are Senator Johnson and Mr. Rayburn's sister Lucinda. (*Wide World Photos*)

The 1952 Democratic National Convention was marked by intense bickering and it was to Chairman Rayburn's credit that he managed to salvage order out of the confusion. Samuel Neff, Pennsylvania (Ellwood City) delegate with paper in hand (at right center) is shown arguing that fellow delegate James Finnegan (second from left) could not vote for any candidate except Estes Kefauver because Finnegan had pledged to support the "popular choice" in his Philadelphia district. Mr. Sam settled the argument by ruling that a delegate's vote is a matter between him and his constituents. Finnegan voted for Adlai Stevenson. (*Wide World Photos*)

The complicated tidelands oil issue had done great damage to Democratic Party unity, causing some to bolt. Mr. Sam said, "I, with many other Democratic colleagues from various states, have worked for years trying to settle this tidelands issue by quit claim to the states or by compromise, giving to the states more than their historic boundaries." On May 22, 1953, President Eisenhower signed the off-shore oil lands bill. He looked over a group of senators and congressmen and asked, "Where's Texas?" Mr. Sam stepped forward. (*Wide World Photos*)

In 1954, at age seventy-three, Mr. Sam is shown at his ranch demonstrating one of the ways he kept in trim between Congressional sessions. (*Wide World Photos*)

Miss Lucinda Rayburn, the beloved sister and Washington hostess of Mr. Sam, is shown leaving with her brother for President Eisenhower's State dinner for the Speaker in 1955. (*The Washington Post*)

Mr. Sam with President Truman and Adlai Stevenson at the Sam Rayburn testimonial dinner, April 16, 1955. The affair was in lieu of the traditional Jefferson-Jackson Day dinner and was the first time in its history that a living man was honored. (*Wide World Photos*)

Mr. Sam is shown in front of demonstrators the moment he took over as Chairman of the 1956 Democratic National Convention. Remembering the chaos of the 1952 Convention, Rayburn made some changes in the parliamentary rules to lend more order to the proceedings. He was noted for his ability to cut corners: "Those in favor say aye . . . there are no noes . . . it is unanimous." When the more agitated delegates shouted for recognition and charged into the aisles, he sometimes failed to see them, and rapped for order with, "Clear the Aisles." In a convention, Mr. Sam was a thoroughgoing Democrat who insisted on order and Party unity, especially with the vast American TV audience looking on. (*Wide World Photos*)

President Eisenhower is shown persuading Mr. Sam to move in closer for a group picture with Sir Winston Churchill and Vice-President Nixon. The photograph was taken at a British Embassy dinner party given by Churchill in 1959. There were times when Churchill sought Mr. Sam's advice on a point of parliamentary procedure. (*Wide World Photos*)

At the 1960 Democratic National Convention Mr. Sam, after having presided as Chairman for the three preceding Conventions, chose to attend as a delegate on the floor. Florida Governor Leroy Collins became his successor and was carefully coached by Mr. Sam and Clarence Cannon, the well-known parliamentarian who wrote the Convention rules. Governor Collins was ideal for the position, thought Rayburn, because he was free of Congressional pressures and was a moderate from a cosmopolitan state on the periphery of the South who would appeal to Northerners and retain the confidence of the South. Mr. Sam liked men who were on dead center for parliamentary posts. Mr. Sam is shown under the Texas standard flanked by national committeeman Byron Skelton on the left and Texas Governor Price Daniels on the right. (*Wide World Photos*)

After the election, President-elect Kennedy interrupted his Palm Springs vacation to pay a visit to Vice-President-elect Johnson and Speaker Rayburn at Johnson's ranch to discuss plans for the new administration. Mr. Sam is shown talking to the President-elect just before his return to Florida. Rayburn was pleased with the prospects under Kennedy's leadership. When asked how he could be so enthusiastic about a man who was Senator Johnson's adversary at the Los Angeles Convention, he replied curtly: "That boy grows on you! People everywhere seem to like him." (*Wide World Photos*)

In December, 1960, Mr. Sam visited President-elect Kennedy at Palm Springs along with Vice-President-elect Johnson and Senator Mike Mansfield to discuss the legislative picture facing the new Congress. During a lull in one of the sessions, Mr. Sam's eyes kept roaming out the window at the water. Mrs. Kennedy, reading his mind, followed behind after he went out to do a little fishing and snapped this picture. The picture was autographed by his hosts: "The fish haven't got a chance! Affectionately, Jacqueline Kennedy. And neither has the House of Representatives, John Kennedy." (Courtesy of Mrs. John F. Kennedy.)

Standing before his proud mentor, Vice-President Johnson is sworn in by Mr. Sam. At the end of the brief ceremony Rayburn's solemn expression changed to a joyful smile. He clasped the Vice-President's hand and said, "God bless you." (*Wide World Photos*)

At a dinner in honor of the President's forty-fourth birthday, Mr. Sam leans over the back of the chair to have a word with the President, seated next to former President Truman, two of the eight Presidents Mr. Sam served. (*Wide World Photos*)

The Speaker's chair where Mr. Sam presided longer than any other man. (*Wide World Photos*)

ters of this sort, he was not disappointed when his Irish friend was elected by the caucus on Thursday, September 19. The White House reaction was similar to Rayburn's.

Minority Leader Martin watched Rayburn's activities with sly amusement and expressed the hope that the Democrats would enjoy themselves while they could, since he expected to be called upon to reorganize the House himself when the next Congress met in January.

On September 21, in the first exclusive interview with the press, Rayburn said, "I still can't realize I'm Speaker." He mentioned at this time his much celebrated policies on speech-making. The word, however, had already made the rounds from Cal Tinney's report while Rayburn was in charge of Jim Farley's Speakers' Bureau back in 1936. At this time he advised his speakers to "lay off the five-cylinder words." He had urged his fellow orators to face the issues squarely and if a Republican called Mr. Roosevelt a Communist, this "may be mean, vicious propaganda" but "the people will never know it if you call it that. Instead tell them that it's a hell-born lie." This he believed was their kind of talk. His advice to congressmen was just as direct. They were told to make short speeches and avoid all the "multi-syllable and tongue-twisting words." One syllable words he explained would come nearer getting a point across and it would be remembered. "The steam that blows the whistle will never turn a wheel," he admonished them.

The news that their Congressman had at last achieved his ambition came as no surprise back home. The story of the thirteen-year-old boy who set his sights on the Speakership after hearing Joseph Weldon Bailey had been related so many times that the people believed a man with Sam's determination and ability would eventually get his wish. There was, nevertheless, much rejoicing and the Rayburn kin stayed quite busy for a week talking to the people who telephoned or dropped in to extend congratulations. Every newspaper in the District carried full accounts of this success story—from his humble beginning, through all the steps and achievements on the way to the top.

By the end of October plans were rather well formulated for a big homecoming celebration, just as soon as Rayburn could slip away from Congress to receive their plaudits. The committee in charge of arrangements were from groups to which Sam belonged—the Fannin County Fair, the Lions Club, the Rotary Club, and the Masonic Lodge. Around Bonham there would be an inevitable sprinkling of Baptists among the workers; however, as of this time he had not formally affiliated himself with their denomination.

A few days before his departure for Bonham, Rayburn telephoned George Stimpson about going with him on Sunday, October 18 to visit Stratford, the ancestral home of the Lees. He hoped Stimpson would write an article about the "Plantation Day" celebration, where the Speaker had been asked to say a few words. As the two men drove through the picturesque and historic countryside they commented on what they saw along the beautiful Mt. Vernon highway near the Potomac River—the Washington home and, eighty miles further along, the Lee mansion, built in 1727, but recently restored, thanks to Rayburn's influence and that of others who admired Robert E. Lee. When they passed the fine herd of white-faced Herefords, the Speaker remarked that he had furnished the original breeding stock here. He also told the story of the flock of black-nose Hampshire sheep, which he had contributed, that were destroyed by predatory dogs that drove them over a high bluff. Then he began listing the numerous women who were on the board of directors and had helped raise some of the needed funds. His information about these people and their activities on the project was considerable.

The Fourth District was now beholden to Rayburn for a number of recent accomplishments. There was the $54,000,000 Red River dam near Denison, under construction, which would create one of the largest man-made lakes in the world. In the confines of Fannin County alone there were also three other lakes and diversion spots—Lake Fannin, Lake Crockett, and Lake Coffee Mill—all created as a part of the Northeast Texas Land Utilization Project. They were built primarily for soil conservation, wildlife restoration, and reforestation, but recreational facilities were abundant in the nature of cabins, bathhouses, docks, and playground equipment. His latest project for Bonham was a $100,000 County Fair plant, cinched by a $20,000 revenue bond issue.

Before his arrival in Bonham, there was much conversation about the kind of man Sam was. There were feature articles which referred to his hobbies and habits, such as his love of fishing and golfing. The latter sport he was slowly abandoning, though, because it did not give him the kind of exercise he wanted. His Washington apartment was two miles from his office, and he tried to walk half this distance each day, in addition to his ritual of taking a few turns in front of the Capitol. His reading habits, some observed, were geared toward books of a lighter nature—western and detective stories. Collecting watches, someone mentioned, was still a favorite activity. The high school graduation gift and that from the Texas Legislature were the two he appreciated most. He continued to carry the timepiece which A. M. Kennedy had presented to him back in 1912. One of his most intense pleasures was straddling a fine quarter horse to inspect his Hereford stock down on the ranch; in fact he had already written that a horse should be in the corral when he reached home.

Bonham is not a large town, relatively speaking, but it was a big one when Sam came home for the celebration. He led a mile-long parade in which were floats, soldiers, and eleven bands. A brilliant red airplane hovered overhead. That morning Colonel W. T. Knight had collected $2,000 from people in Wichita Falls for the National Democratic War Chest, and he had come to present the money in person. Fifteen thousand people were parked around the walls of the public square. Mayor Joe B. Hrdlicka had invited county and city officials from every subdivision in the District and many from surrounding districts. Long lines of automobiles had blocked the highways since early morning. When Rayburn stepped up on the platform he was presented with a gavel on which carpenter Nat Lovelace had worked all night, carving it from a piece of bois d'arc wood. The mayor had gathered three tubs of prize roses from his thousand bushes.

At a reception in the high school auditorium a long receiving line greeted the people who filed through the building. Besides Sam, there were his four brothers and three sisters, Senator Tom Connally, Representatives Lyndon B. Johnson, Hatton Sumners, and Wright Patman. That evening there was another assembly in the football stadium.

By coincidence the date for this homecoming was that of the hundredth anniversary of his father's birth. In commemoration of this Mr. Sam had begun the day by spending some time in the cemetery by his parents' graves.

Although he went to Honey Grove the next morning to dedicate a $110,999 high school building, Rayburn did manage to find enough time to inspect his cows and have a good visit with his brothers and sisters. He asked Miss Lou to cook him a big "mess" of fresh turnip greens.

Then he took half a day's drive over the back country roads

to look at the land and see how the people were getting along. In a reminiscent mood he told how in the early days he had hauled cotton to the gin at Honey Grove and taught country school. He said he could call by first name most of his students and thousands of his constituents, and they greeted him in the same manner when he walked around the square at Bonham or stopped at the country stores.

Talking rather freely, he confessed that he appreciated the confidence the people had demonstrated in the mammoth homecoming by applauding the references to him as Presidential timber for 1944. But he confessed that there were only two things in the world he had ever coveted—a good load of hay and a load of lumber. A stack of fine, green alfalfa hay set his mind to thinking about the pounds of beef or gallons of milk it would make; the load of lumber stood for progress—new barns and stock pens. He was a farmer at heart, but with an ambition to help his own kind.

Well-preserved farm dwellings inspired him with confidence, but those that were in a state of decay left him depressed. When he pointed out to reporter Dave Cheavens one large house, bare and unpainted, in a patch of cotton blighted with root-rot, he remarked: "The man who once owned that house came here about the same time my father did. He was a day laborer, then a tenant farmer, then a landowner. He got together hundreds of acres of good cotton land all in one block, but when he died the children split the place up and sold it piecemeal. Now look what's left." He spoke of the virtues of farm ownership and of the potential of the soil. He took pride in believing his North Texas neighbors came rather close to being typical Americans, with a "reasonable prosperity." The thing which pleased him most on this tour was the discovery that many farmers had broken away from the one-crop idea and were branching out into dairying and stock raising.

He firmly believed that the farmer should stay with the soil and accept better ideas of management to avoid loading it with debt. "It's pretty hard for a farm to carry a big debt and make a living for the man who works it."

Rayburn's journeys through the back country were not joyrides. They were business trips in which he checked to see what effects the farm program were having upon rural economy. He had played a significant role in implementing the Administration's agricultural ideas, some of them coming right out of his own past. For example, after the war on a similar trip, as he passed a black-topped paved road leading into a main east-west highway, he remarked, "I've hauled cotton down the road when mud was so deep it came to the wagon hubs. That," pointing to the hard-surfaced road, "is better."

These hard-surfaced roads were the fruits of Rayburn's labor during the second session of the Seventy-eighth Congress. Wright Patman remembered the instant in Rayburn's office in 1944 when they were conceived. Bill Robinson, of Utah, Chairman of the House Committee on Roads and Highways, came into Rayburn's office to find out whether he could take up the highway bill. Rayburn asked, "What have they got in there for country roads?"

Robinson replied, "We don't have anything that's designated but we expect to have part of the authorized funds spent on secondary roads."

Rayburn answered, "Have your Committee agree to an amendment that will earmark thirty per cent of the funds for farm-to-market roads. We will then take it up and pass it."

Robinson's Committee agreed and Rayburn got the bill through Congress as he prophesied. This was how hard-surfaced roads became a general thing in rural America.

Running parallel to the black-topped roads were rural electrification power lines to which he liked to make reference whenever he drove through this land of his childhood. He was also pleased to see the telephone lines reaching into the farmhouses because he counted this service as a part of his farm program. He could see the advances made since the day he stood in one of the fields at Flag Springs, but what gave him the greatest thrill was the realization that the farmers had made more gains during the Roosevelt years than during the rest of the period combined.

The following day Rayburn went to Dallas, where a similar welcome was staged, with Rayburn heading a 200-car caravan through the crowded city. The Young Democrats had taken care of the arrangements, since this celebration was designed to give the Roosevelt-Wallace campaign impetus. With the election only a few days away, Rayburn proceeded on through four Southwestern states where he expressed optimism about the Party's chances.

The results confirmed his faith, because the Democrats won the election with 27,243,466 votes to 22,304,755. The

Electoral College cast 449 votes for the President and 82 for Willkie. Rayburn then returned to Washington for the continuation of the third session of the Seventy-sixth Congress.

On December 10, the Speaker was back in Dallas for an appreciation banquet at the Adolphus Hotel. Fifteen hundred distinguished citizens from Texas, Oklahoma, Missouri, Arkansas, and Louisiana assembled to hear such men as Congressman Lyndon B. Johnson laud their Speaker.

Lyndon B. Johnson had been around Washington for about ten years, and after he was elected to the House he developed a strong attachment for Rayburn. Lyndon became ill shortly after his arrival in the capital, and he reported that Sam Rayburn literally sat by his bedside until he was well and that he had looked after him ever since as a father would a son. A very firm bond was established which became even stronger with time. The young Congressman was always glowing in his praise of Mr. Sam, as he was on this night in the Adolphus.

Rayburn's remarks were on the theme of democracy and free enterprise, with reference to the kind of government which makes these possible. The city of Dallas seemed to him a notable monument to the blending of the two.

During this third session of the Seventy-sixth Congress, considerable thought had been given to reports by the Special Committee on Administrative Law, and the result was a recommendation aimed at obtaining uniformity in the procedures employed by all the independent commissions. The Walter-Logan bill had been passed by a big majority. It was an attempt to set up a system that would provide judicial review of cases acted upon by administrative tribunals. Surprisingly, Roosevelt vetoed the bill, apparently upon the advice of some who believed that it would place too many restrictions upon the administrative tribunals and weaken their authority.

When Congress was unsuccessful in overriding the veto, the President, on December 23, wrote a very warm, personal letter to the Speaker, in which he cited those Rayburn qualities that had been dominant factors in the victory: "Courage—just sheer courage—brought that about" [the failure to override the veto]. He went on to say that he did not "want the advice of 'yes-men.'" He did "want the advice of fighting leadership, with the adjective *fighting* underscored." The President predicted that the approaching Seventy-seventh Congress would be a difficult one for him, Rayburn, and McCormack, and he frankly stated that they could not afford to meet with a series of defeats. He expressed confidence in Rayburn's ability to guide the Administration's program through the Congressional maze. For the sake of the Party, but more important for the nation, Roosevelt wanted Sam and John to work day and night, fighting every step of the way:

> What I want to get across to both of you before the new session begins is that good fellowship for the sake of good fellowship alone, an easy life to avoid criticism, an acceptance of defeat before an issue has been joined, make, all of them, less for Party success and for national safety than a few drag-down and knock-out fights and an unwillingness to accept defeat without a fight.

Roosevelt recognized in Rayburn a fighter after his own heart, a man who could get up after being knocked down and go ahead to win. Indifferent to public criticism and alert to his opponent's weaknesses, Rayburn had, in the President's eyes, the instinct of a champion. No prima donna, he never sulked and walked away if the press did not recognize him. His philosophy was one of victory, success for the masses. His battles were for the many rather than for the few. For this reason Roosevelt felt sure that in the Speaker he had superior leadership.

The admiration and respect of Republican Joe Martin for Sam Rayburn is well known. On the last day of the Seventy-sixth Congress, January 2, 1941, the Minority Leader asked to offer a resolution:

> ". . . Because it signifies my honest appraisal of a warm personal friend and one who has endeared himself to every member of this House. . . ."
>
> "As Majority Leader the gentleman from Texas acquitted himself as a great American and as an able leader of a great Party. He won the affection and respect of everyone, and we were all happy to see him elevated to the high position of Speaker. In the performance of the duties of the great office of Speaker he has given evidence of what we expected. He was able, impartial, and just, fully measuring up to the many brilliant Speakers who have preceded him. I am happy to pay through this resolution this tribute to a great American and a great parliamentarian."

The Democrats met in caucus on January 2, and went through the formality of nominating Rayburn to a full term as

Speaker of the House, and on the following day at the opening of the Seventy-seventh Congress, the solid majority re-elected him over Joseph W. Martin. At the outset he reaffirmed his policy on curtailing the flow of oratory to restrain the more talkative members, who in the past had used more than their share of space in the *Congressional Record.*

Congress remained in almost continuous session because of the dangerous international problems. Japanese expansion in Eastern Asia motivated the President's request for appropriations to improve the harbors at Guam and several Pacific bases, but the isolationists voted down the measure. Even Cordell Hull's report to the House Foreign Relations Committee on January 15, 1941, was insufficient to alert the opponents of the Administration's preparedness program in Congress. Rayburn, however, was solidly behind Roosevelt's efforts.

The President's Lend-Lease bill also encountered some isolationist resistance, but the Administration was not to be denied. Roosevelt had been known to reveal a domineering attitude toward members of Congress; yet he had sufficient insight to know when to seek counsel. He called Congressional leaders to the White House for a fireside, after-dinner conference on the controversial amendments that had been proposed. Rayburn had already canvassed the House and knew what Congress would do. The Speaker had also briefed the President and brought him around to a more conciliatory position. He found that there were four types of changes needed: 1) a two-year time limit; 2) a specific anti-convoy provision; 3) a provision calling on the President to make trimonthly reports to Congress on his use of the powers granted in the bill; 4) a provision requiring Army and Navy participation in all decisions to release war materials to other powers.

Rayburn had already made a speech in which he expressed a major objection to certain phrasing; however, he favored the bill but cautioned against letting emergencies stampede Congress into an irrationality. For example, one amendment to the seven billion dollar Lend-Lease bill, he said, gave the appearance of handing the President a blank check for this vast sum. Rayburn insisted that this money should be set up as an "appropriation" rather than as an "authorization" so that Congress could retain power over it; otherwise critics of Congress, he feared, would have ample basis for believing that they had surrendered their function of controlling all appropriations. His reasoning did not reflect a lack of faith in the executive branch but an insistence upon preserving Congressional prerogatives. The President respected the Speaker's convictions and loyalty to the House of Representatives.

Through Lend-Lease Rayburn saw a possible way of keeping America out of war and, at the same time, giving assistance to those nations who were fighting to preserve the ideals for which this nation stood. The passage of the act, in his judgment, marked the end of the isolationist policy which had plagued the United States since the close of World War I. He felt America could follow no other course than to commit herself to the aid of those peoples resisting the totalitarian powers. He liked the legislation because it gave the United States the chance to say what should stay at home and what should be shipped abroad. This country could now control the distribution of munitions among the democracies.

However, in his radio address of February 9 over the National Broadcasting Company, Blue Network, he was not quite this plain-spoken. His speech was more of a report to the nation in which he pointed out that the House of Representatives gave only one month to clearing this unprecedented legislation. He assured the people that Congress did not want war, but the two political Parties had joined to make effective the expressed will of the American people:

> ". . . To give the fullest material aid short of military participation to those nations resisting the Nazi aggression which threatens the peace, liberty, and well-being of the whole world. . . . Let us awake. Let us defend America now. Let us give Britain the support necessary to hold Hitler at bay and to keep war from America."

He defined the relationship which should exist between Congress and the executive branch. The legislative branch should determine policies and direct the President, who should be free to carry them out.

The people of the Southwest had read so many articles and editorials in their newspapers about this powerful Congressman from the Fourth that they had begun to lose all sense of discretion about their requests to him. When a town suffered a catastrophy from a flood, tornado, or other act of God, they would say, "Write Sam to help us." He was the cure-all for everything which disturbed the peace and harmony of his section. He almost was expected to perform miracles, and even to help people with personal problems that lay beyond a legislator's domain. The frequent requests required a great deal of his energy.

One of the most interesting cases at this time came from Oklahoma. The Madill *Record* and Oklahoma City *Times* published editorials about the impassable and dangerous U.S. Highway No. 70, which ran parallel to the Red River from Broken Bow to Waurika and beyond. On March 13, 1941, an editorial asked the question: "What would Sam Rayburn do?" The final sentence read, "If Sam Rayburn were Chairman of the Roads Committee in Congress and represented this district in Washington, southern Oklahoma would have a passable highway."

The Representative of this district, Wilburn Cartwright, also Chairman of the Committee, promptly wrote to the Madill paper and thanked them for inferentially comparing or contrasting him with the Speaker, and stated that if Sam would move to southeastern Oklahoma and represent the district, he would retire or resign. Cartwright agreed that Rayburn was more experienced and abler than he or anyone else in the district.

> But Sam, honest and forthright as he is, would be the first to tell you and others in our district that no congressman—not even the Speaker of the House of Representatives—can control the expenditure of state and Federal-aid highway-improvement funds in his state or district.

The Federal Government, Rayburn explained in support of Cartwright, had no right or authority to invest in state highways without the voluntary cooperation and participation of the state.

Some people in his own District came to lean on him, to ask for endorsements, and to use his name as a reference. Many believed Sam Rayburn's name on a "To Whom it May Concern" would unlock the closed doors of opportunity; and in reality, after he gained stature in Congress, the worn letters of introduction did have remarkable influence. His kindness was exploited by a few too weak to stand alone. His only comment was, "Ninety-eight-and-a-half per cent of our people are good folks, and I like to help when I can." He looked for the best in every person and expected people to be just as unselfish and fair minded as he tried to be. Sam Rayburn refused to be a cynic. He would not discuss personalities, except to make a positive comment that someone was a "good man." He continued to extend the right hand of fellowship and lend assistance to those who seemed deserving. He liked to believe history would never condemn a man for kindness.

In a speech before the Bond Club of New York on March 6, 1941, he declared that the billions being spent for defense—even up to the immense amount of thirty-five billion dollars—should be paid for by the taxpayers of this generation. He stated that he would add to the estimated income of two billion dollars from the present defense taxes a billion and a half additional annually in order to make the defense debt self-liquidating in ten years. Stressing the point that the tax burden should not be passed on to later generations, he emphasized that the economists should do some sound thinking. "I would like to see my generation pay for the defense program," he stated. He knew that selfish and jealous men had destroyed a dream back in 1918, when Wilson drew the blueprint of the League of Nations, only to see it blocked by political intrigue in the Senate. Rayburn had read his Bible enough to know that it was written there that the iniquity of the fathers would be visited upon the children unto the third and fourth generation, and he wanted to spare, as much as possible, these unborn taxpayers a debt which they had not helped accumulate.

He frequently expressed complete faith that the youth of his day and those of the tomorrow would be "willing to accept the challenge of citizenship." This was the theme of his speech on May 18 over CBS. It was entitled *Citizenship Recognition Day.* He elaborated upon "I am an American." One of the things he urged every citizen to do as an American was

> "Vote for the men and women who are best prepared by learning and by patriotic love of country to carry on the great business of preserving, protecting, defending and perpetuating the institutions of this Republic. Every American—whether native-born or naturalized—should stand for this Government without reservation and regardless of any other government in the world."

No people, he reminded the radio audience, can remain free who are not willing to make the sacrifices the times demand:

> "Vigilance is the price of liberty today as it has always been. The youth of the land will accept this challenge and under proper leadership will be prepared in the years that are theirs to be the kind of citizens

> that will carry on and fulfill the hopes of those who labored here in the years gone by to see that that great work does not come to naught."

His thoughts were on those postwar years when Americans sloughed off their responsibilities in the world community by not supporting the initial peace program.

On August 10, 1941, the Speaker returned to Roane County, Tennessee, the place of his birth, where he attended with his kinsmen and their neighbors an old-fashioned country picnic. Mrs. Mose Waller, Sr., remembered that Sam Rayburn cherished this old country and its customs. One of the first things he asked for when he entered her house, she said, was "an old wash pan and an old sack towel like I used to use." While he stood on the back porch and washed his hands, she could tell by the way he looked toward the hills that his thoughts were wandering back half a century.

Several hundred people from the Waller community had gathered at Kingston, the county seat. They brought baskets of country food such as fried chicken, stuffed eggs, white bermuda onions, sour pickles, potato salad, fried pies, fresh coconut cake —the sort of fare which brought back memories to Mr. Sam of that famous mother whose culinary arts were learned here and transplanted to Flag Springs.

It was only on the day before that Rayburn and Representative John I. Jennings found they would be free to make the trip; so a delegation was quickly formed to greet the guests. Heading the group was M. L. Waller, a second cousin and stock farmer and banker, who met the 6:30 A.M. train at Lenoir City. They went on a tour of the Fort Loudoun dam project in connection with TVA. Next he saw the old log house where he was born, then went to the farm his grandfather had owned. As Rayburn talked with his relatives he reminded them that the Waller community was settled by a Revolutionary War veteran, William Waller of Virginia, who was given a large tract of land along the Clinch River for his services in Washington's continental army. He added that over fifty years earlier William Marion Rayburn helped build the Macedonia Primitive Baptist Church where they had assembled for the reunion. "Father was not only a carpenter but a moving spirit for this church."

Waller reported that the Speaker inquired about the individual members on both sides of the house, about the new families that had come into the neighborhood, that he expressed great interest in the people but had not made one reference to himself or to national and international affairs. This visit was the fifth he had made to the Waller community since he left Tennessee with his parents back in 1887.

One of the most remarkable things about Rayburn was his ability to leave his own problems in his office and not take them along to a friend's home in the evening or on a trip. It was significant that his cousin had commented on the Speaker's making no reference at all to his job, because Rayburn all the while knew that just two days hence he would face the biggest test of his career thus far—the question of extending the Selective Service. A great many parents had sent their sons off to army camps in the belief or hope that the period of training was to be of one year's duration. Some people had looked on the experience more as a wholesome vacation at the Government's expense.

The President had been advised by the Army's Chief of Staff and by people in the diplomatic services that tension was mounting between the United States and the totalitarian powers. The isolationists were well organized, and pressures from back home were causing the more impressionable lawmakers to yield. Rayburn believed that the action taken by the House on August 12, 1941, could well shape the course of history. He even reflected that our freedom was hanging in the balance.

He, John McCormack, and Pat Boland, the Democratic whip from Pennsylvania, made some desperate last-minute attempts to line up colleagues who were already yielding to pressures from home. Ordinarily Rayburn would not risk a vote on something when he was not sure of the outcome one way or the other, but consideration of this measure was necessary with Selective Service soon to expire. An extension was imperative. He planned to win and felt confident, but he was afraid of those people who were shifting around. On the day of the roll call there were soldiers in the galleries and "pathetic-looking mothers carrying American flags." [2] Capitol Hill had felt the impact of emotionalism and sentimentality. The opponents of extension had done a thorough piece of lobbying, some congressmen having broken under the strain.

The Speaker sat in stoical silence as the clerk began to call the roll. Then he took a stand immediately behind the clerk to keep a check on the count. By the time the last name of the 435 had been called, only the tally clerk had the outcome. Immediately the Speaker picked up the vote and announced: "On this vote 203 members have voted 'Aye,' 202 members have voted

'No,' and the bill is passed." According to the House rules no one can change his vote after it is announced. It is frozen.

However, a recapitulation of a vote is permissible when it is so close. Representative Short of Missouri demanded the review and the Speaker ordered it. He knew the original tally was correct, but it was his duty to be fair. After the roll was called the Speaker stated: "No correction in the vote, the vote stands, and the bill is passed and without objection a motion to reconsider is laid on the table." His action was so decisive and rapid that there was no immediate objection to the motion. Rayburn hit hard and fast. It was over before the opposition realized that the gavel had sounded their death knell.

When it dawned on the House what had happened a clamor arose. Representative Short made an effort to recover and asked for reconsideration of the vote. The Speaker promptly announced that it was too late because he had already announced that "without objection a motion to reconsider is laid on the table." Few men in the House could approach Rayburn's knowledge of parliamentary procedure and still fewer had his reflexes. A second's jump on the opposition is more than sufficient to spell victory in the House, governed as it is by strict and numerous rules.

Representative H. Carl Andersen of Minnesota, after Short's failure, rose to protest: "I beg to differ with the Speaker. The Speaker did not announce that a motion to reconsider had been tabled."

Rayburn promptly replied, "The Chair has twice stated that he did make that statement."

Again Andersen said, "I beg to differ with you—"

But the Speaker cut him off with a reply that contained no thread of conciliation: "The Chair does not intend to have his word questioned by the gentleman from Minnesota or anybody else."

History proved Rayburn's action to have had tremendous implications because within a few months Pearl Harbor was bombed and America was at war. But now she had an Army of 1,600,000 instead of a token force of 400,000.

Rayburn's triumph on this day may be attributed to his friendly persuasion. Just a few minutes before he took his place on the rostrum he prevailed on four men to change their stand, to take his word that America was in real danger. This was not necessarily a partisan question, for these men had many times voted against the Administration. They made the switch because they trusted "Sam"; they saw the truth in his eyes. However, Rayburn confessed that he had several men on the floor who would have changed their vote. In the area of foreign affairs many believed that this may well have been Mr. Sam's greatest stroke for freedom, since on December 7 his judgment was proved sound.

A few days later, Rayburn started receiving letters from relatives and friends back home with reports that the people were beginning to act strangely and make insane remarks. They were torn up emotionally by his apparently dictatorial move. The newspapers seemed to be fanning the flames with editorials about a Communistic infiltration of labor, strikes in war industries, lagging production, substandard maintenance for the soldiers, many of whom had volunteered prior to the enactment of the Conscription bill (September 16, 1940). Roosevelt was getting the brunt of the attacks, with some of the most vicious coming out of Texas. David Cohn relates Mr. Sam's reaction to a letter signed by "Mother." She wrote that her son had been in the army for sixteen months and had not been issued a rifle. The implications were that the President was unable to administer the war program and that labor was getting fat while the underpaid soldiers suffered. After a violent Rayburn explosion which involved some rather fancy cussing, he announced that he was going back to Texas to tell those mothers a thing or two. "Not even the United States," he remarked, "can fight a civil war and a foreign war at the same time."

In his first speech, reports Cohn, he replied to "Mother" by informing her that the son in question had been issued his rifle, that he had learned how to use it, and had been transferred to the Quartermaster Corps, where he had for a long time been getting some combat experience by attacking with a dolly well-entrenched bodies of canned corn.[3]

At Plano on September 8, the Speaker was almost bitter in his condemnation of the isolationists who were parading round the country in what Rayburn considered an effort to disunite the American people, although he defended their right to speak their minds. "We must not destroy the very thing we are preparing to defend. The guarantee of free speech is in the Constitution." Rayburn, however, stated that the people were under no obligation to give them an audience.

He defended Roosevelt's armament program and efforts to prevent direct intervention by America. In answer to these many letters from mothers he affirmed that the men in our army were not drilling with broomsticks instead of rifles, and that the nation already had on hand enough Enfield, Springfield, and Garand rifles to arm three million soldiers. He predicted that by 1942 this country would break all records in mass production of planes, with perhaps as many as twenty-five hundred a month. He made reference to Charles Lindbergh and the comfort he was giving the isolationists and the enemy with his criticism. While Rayburn respected Lindbergh as a flier, he considered him something of a child in the field of statesmanship.

September 16 marked the first anniversary of Rayburn's promotion, and on each succeeding anniversary he was to have many encomiums in the *Record* relative to his qualities and achievements. Representative Cochran of Missouri set the tone of the future commemorations as he described the Speaker's importance as next to that of the President. The wisdom of the present choice, he said, had already been confirmed. "I say without fear that a more fearless and fair Speaker has never occupied the chair." He made reference to his prior experience and the confidence everyone had in his ability to handle the position.

Cochran's reference to fairness might be documented with the Speaker's own words in connection with debate on the Neutrality Act on November 13, at which time he stepped down from the rostrum to praise the high plane upon which the debate had been conducted. With reference to his friend Mr. Richards of South Carolina, to all of whose arguments he objected, he said, "I was glad to see the ovation given him as a man and as a patriot."

On November 12, Rayburn and McCormack wrote the President to learn his wishes on the Neutrality Act, to which he replied with a request for the repeal of only three sections—the bans on arming merchantmen, on entrance in combat areas, and on entering belligerent ports. The sinking of American ships had caused men like Senator Kenneth McKellar of Tennessee, who until then had supported the 1939 measure, to speak out for total repeal. The loss of the destroyer *Reuben James* on convoy duty to Iceland, with the loss of nearly 120 men, furnished the final incentive needed to promote the President's recommendation and the position supported by the Speaker. It was not an easy victory, though, because Congress knew that the passage of these three amendments would be the last step toward a shooting war. The Speaker in his presentation expressed the belief that America's course was clear if she was to preserve her way of life: "Let me appeal to you, whether you love one man or hate another, to stand up today for civilization as it is typified by the United States of America." The closeness of the vote—212 for, 194 against, 22 not voting—indicated that many were not prepared to take this last step.

Rayburn's letter of November 12 to the President dealt strictly with foreign affairs, but the President's reply contained this reference to one phase of the labor problem that had been harassing the New Deal, and was now also wearing the Speaker's patience thin, not to mention the people's:

> I am holding a conference tomorrow in the hope that certain essential coal mines can remain in continuous operation. . . . It is obvious that this coal must be mined in order to keep the steel mills at work. The Government of the United States has the backing of the overwhelming majority of the people of the United States, including the workers.

Defense labor legislation had already been approved by the Rules Committee. It was on the calendar, but Rayburn did not want to call up the measure until the National Defense Mediation Board had exhausted all efforts to prevent the slowdown. But when the coal miners went on strike and the CIO members walked out on the Mediation Board, Rayburn on November 22 spoke with finality. He pledged that the House would get a chance to vote on a "fair" labor bill, one which would hold up in the courts. In defense of making haste slowly, he repeated one of his own epigrams: "Legislation should never be designed to punish anyone. It must be fair. Fair!" Troubles with labor and the threat of war were now his most immediate concerns. He faced both during the next four years with his usual courage.

☆ XV ☆

The War Years

WAR came with a destructive suddenness when the Japanese, while engaging in conferences aimed at conciliation, attacked American bases at Pearl Harbor on December 7, 1941. "Why our folks weren't alerted at Pearl Harbor I don't know," remarked Speaker Rayburn. "On a Monday morning sometime before this day, President Roosevelt called us to the White House for a conference. He said, 'Hitler has the Japanese warlords in Berlin today and he's trying to convince them he's won the war and if they'll come in, they would be in on the big cut, and if he does convince them, Japan will attack us.'"

Rayburn knew the President was getting some kind of information from sources in Germany. At the time the extension of the Selective Service Act was being discussed, rumors were going the rounds but many members of Congress kept saying, "Nobody is going to fight us." "They thought," added Rayburn, "we had two oceans to wrap around us, but when submarines and things like that came, the oceans were our biggest hazard."

Continuing to discuss Pearl Harbor, he said: "Why we weren't more alert, I don't know. We had fifteen battleships at that time, eight of them in the Pacific and nearly all of these in Pearl Harbor. Why they ever stacked them in there with any danger at all, I don't know. They could have found the carriers from which these bombers came, since they didn't come from Japan. Another thing that bothers me is that several hours after that happened, in the Philippines, we had two or three hundred sitting on the ground and they just bombed and smashed them up. Now, why wouldn't MacArthur have been alerted that we were going to be attacked anywhere they could?"

Thus Rayburn reminisced about these tragic events. He also made some references to General Short and Admiral Kimmel, but he did not like to discuss matters where he had no authoritative information or where he felt that damage could be done to our prestige or morale. Also, Rayburn deplored the practice of congressmen posing as specialists on foreign affairs and military strategy, when they knew only what they had read in the papers, observed on week-end trips abroad, or had been told by someone not well informed. He said he was basically opposed to hearing people talk when the only result was a noise.

The attack on Pearl Harbor came on Sunday, 1:20 P.M. EST, and Rayburn remembered the President's call for a joint session of Congress on Monday, December 8, around noon. The Speaker knew the routine, the same as that followed by Wilson. The President would acknowledge a state of war, since we had been attacked. The speech was brief. He recalled the intonation of Roosevelt's voice and his opening words: "Yesterday, December 7, 1941—a date which will live in infamy—the United States of America was suddenly and deliberately attacked by naval and air forces of the Empire of Japan."

Reference was also made to the peace talks with Japanese officials, the Japanese attacks on Guam, Wake, Midway Islands, the Philippines, Malaya, and Hongkong.

After the President's acknowledgment of a state of war, it took Congress only four hours to give him authorization to prosecute the war. The vote in the House was 388 to 1 and in the Senate 82 to 0.

When, three days later, Germany declared war against the United States, the President immediately sent another war message to Congress in which he affirmed, "Never before has there been a greater challenge to life, liberty, and civilization." Congress responded without a dissenting vote with an acknowledgment of a state of war between this country and Germany and Italy.

The Speaker commended Roosevelt's fireside chat to the nation on December 9 for its tone and declaration of higher aims. The following section appealed to him:

> "We are now in the midst of a war, not for conquest, not for vengeance, but for a world in which

> this nation, and all that this nation represents, will be safe for our children. . . ."

Rayburn made another observation that while the bombings of our bases damaged our war efforts and prestige, they had a certain solidifying effect. The shock of the attack and the threat of impending invasion caused the "Isolationists to shut up." "It also made Christians out of a lot of fellows in Congress who were always trying to argue about things just to argue and get their words into the *Record*." The Democrats and Republicans now closed ranks. Management and labor improved their relations. The American people were quickly united in their belief that totalitarian powers around the world had to be checked. The change-over from peace to war, Rayburn said, affected his pace as Speaker, for he became more of a "trouble shooter" along with "cracking the whip" on Capitol Hill.

In looking back on the war years, he marveled at this country's achievements. On December 7, 1941, the country had only 1,600,000 men in the army, with most of these ineligible for overseas service under the Burke-Wadsworth Act, and far too many unprepared for modern warfare. By August 15, 1945, the army had 8,300,000 well-equipped and trained personnel.

"It is remarkable that we got ready to fight on the land and sea as fast as we did. It just shows the ingenuity of these Americans, what they can do when they put their brains and brawn to it."

The first session of the Seventy-seventh Congress adjourned on January 2, 1942, and the second session opened three days later, remaining on duty until shortly before the Christmas holidays. During this period, the Speaker's correspondence almost tripled and along with it his duties.

Such letters as that from John Garner, dated January 3, gave him brief moments of amusement and relief from the pressures: "I have been in the woods most of the time since November 15 when the hunting season for deer, quail, javelins, ducks, etc., opened." This brought a chuckle from Sam because he knew Garner's habits and love for the open spaces and hunting. He was also aware of Garner's displeasure at the Roosevelt Administration and his decision to take himself out of the public eye. References to his wife and children in their preparations for Christmas made Rayburn remember this family group and the pleasant times he had had in their home. The last two paragraphs assured Rayburn that Garner was now thinking in more positive terms concerning Roosevelt:

> You can tell the Boss that I am at his service—Tully has already tendered his service as a soldier.
>
> I hope the Boss will not draft me since there are many who can do any job better than I can. I am selfish enough to want to stay in Uvalde and enjoy health and all that goes with it, but I repeat, I am subject to the call of the Commander-in-Chief.

Although the declaration of war had a temporarily sobering effect upon both industry and labor, the increase in production and the upward trend of living costs brought the two economic groups into a greater number of bargaining situations. On January 12, 1942, the President established the National War Labor Board, which consisted of representatives from employers, workers, and the general public. This body acted on disputes which could not be settled through the regular channels of collective bargaining and mediation on the part of the Labor Department. Strikes continued to occur but were settled rather promptly with the twofold machinery. The public grew more and more hostile to work stoppages, and men like Rayburn were continuously harassed by constituents who reminded congressmen of the sacrifices being made by the men in service and people back home.

Rayburn continued to be attentive to all such correspondence. For example, in reply to a postal card from a gentleman at Forney, Texas, he gave the essence of his thinking on all of the current topics. He pointed out that he had become quite concerned about the labor problems near the end of the previous session. He made reference to the Smith Anti-strike bill which passed the House on December 3, 1941, and had not been acted upon by the Senate. This bill, he thought, had "teeth in it." "The so-called Smith amendment voted on week before last [about March 1] was nothing like as strong . . . ," he said.

The thing which irked the home folks was the time-and-a-half pay for work above the forty-hour week. Farmers, cattlemen, and soldiers worked for more than forty hours at no additional remuneration. Rayburn was sympathetic toward these grievances, but pointed out that even the Smith measure would not stop time-and-a-half for overtime because "practically every man who is a member of a labor union has a contract with his employer for time-and-a-half for overtime." At the outset, the people around Bonham, for example, who trusted Sam's sincerity were patient, but they steadily grew more irritable. Throughout the State a spirit of hostility developed, and 1942 came to be a hard year on many incumbents, like Mr. Sam, regardless of records or political beliefs. The problems of pay and strikes, though only two bones of contention, gave congressmen from rural sections no little trouble. As Speaker, Rayburn felt the brunt of complaints. For years he had held the dubious title of the second most powerful man in the Government, and the people now wanted him to use some of this power in removing the inequities.

Another problem which plagued Rayburn was the charges of waste in food and materials around military installations. For example, citizens called his attention to the following at an airbase in his District: surplus paper and good lumber were burned; food, such as lard, fried chicken, roasted turkeys, beans, whole loaves of bread, was thrown away in large quantities. One truckload of good food was hauled away each day to feed hogs, according to reports. The constituents were angry because they recognized the absence of supervision, and they were still angrier when the Government continued to ask for additional money with which to buy more materials to waste in similar ways. This was the theme of much of Rayburn's fan mail in 1942.

He also received complaints about money being spent on the Denison Dam, AAA, PWA, WPA. Many people believed that these projects should be suspended for the duration.

Finally the vexations became so numerous that congressmen began asking Rayburn for advice and assistance. The people back home were making all sorts of demands which kept them from doing their work. They were kept busy running errands, collecting data, investigating, and responding to the accelerated volume of mail. Some congressmen had become intimidated, and at this stage Rayburn acted. As a rule he was slow to anger, but when he saw that home-front criticism was crystallizing into a repudiation of Congress, he boiled over into caustic rebuke. On March 11, he called an unusual press conference to answer at one time every congressman's constituent in the country. He heatedly declared that "Labor stoppages have been reduced to about zero" and he was quite indignant over the unjust criticism of Congress.

"From every section of the country come letters and telegrams, many of them very insulting. They charge that Congress is playing politics . . . that the people are divided. If this is true, Hitler, Mussolini, and the Emperor of Japan would have paid a lot of money for what they are getting free.

"On March 17—Tuesday—there were between 7,000,000 and 7,500,000 men engaged in war industries. These figures are from the War Production Board. Of these there were one hundred on strike. It appears that stoppages in production have been reduced to about zero, regardless of what is said by some writers and speakers.

"On last Sunday it came over the radio that in one state some war industries were running only forty per cent capacity, clear inference being that it was on account of labor disputes. At that time there was not a man on strike in a war industry in that state. It was a shortage of material and not a shortage of management or labor. I hope every paper in the United States carried Donald Nelson's statement over the radio.

"I quote from Mr. Nelson: 'Beware of the man who instills doubt in your mind. He may not be Hitler's agent, he is doing that agent's work. Let me repeat once more, groundless fears of a few people could bog down the whole war effort.'

"The enemy is clever at this sort of thing. He has done it successfully before. He knows that this is a critical time. Unless he can divide this country now—unless he can set one group against another—unless he can lead us into the same pitfalls he prepared for the people of France and Norway—unless he can do these things to our people, then he is licked."

Rayburn referred to the mass meetings that were being held in both Democratic and Republican areas which were called to criticize and pass resolutions about the President, Congress, management and labor. These meetings, he believed, too frequently became indignation gatherings and produced publicity that gave comfort to the enemies in their newspapers. "Congress," he said, "has given the President every law and every dollar he has asked for for defense purposes." He concluded by asking the people who specialized in creating division, discord, and discontent to direct their attention from the forces of wrath and apply themselves to helping win the war.

Most of the mass meetings to which the Speaker referred were called, however, to ask for resolutions that would challenge the forty-hour week, because they favored forty-eight. The Administration, though, was trying to have its cake and eat it by retaining the social gains made for the working man and by maintaining production through overtime. Rayburn's position was a difficult one, because he personally favored the forty-eight-hour week for periods of emergency; and he was posing as a referee for Congress, the Administration, the working man, industry, and the people. His skill as a compromiser was taxed during these years. In an atmosphere of emotionalism and turmoil he could not act immediately, but he did set Congressional wheels in motion. While the committees were at work he became a buffer between the people and the legislative body.

First, he appealed to those people he knew best—the farmers. The tone of his message to them was quite calm in contrast to that at the press conference. The agriculturalists were beginning to plant their crops, so he urged them to do specific things, such as produce more long staple cotton needed in combat planes, balloons, flotation gear, machine-gun belts, and uniforms. Cotton farmers were asked to plant the full national allotment of 27.4 million acres in medium and longer staple varieties. This would mean an increase of seventeen per cent in acreage for the nation as a whole. Particular attention, he thought, should be given to seed selection, seed treatment, planting, cultivating, and harvesting for increasing staple length. Something of an authority on fertilizers, Rayburn urged mixing them because there would be an inevitable shortage of nitrogen, with so much going into explosives. Insecticides, he advised, should be applied at the right time.

Since the war in the Pacific had cut off the supply of soybeans, castor beans, peanuts, and flaxseed for oil, he explained that these would have to be produced in greater quantity; dairy products, eggs, hogs, cattle, lard, small grains, potatoes, and sugar crops were also mentioned. Home vegetable gardens would likewise be valuable to the war effort.

The Speaker recognized that the farmer was the backbone of the nation and that his patriotism was unquestioned. Rayburn understood the rural people perhaps better than any other public official. He knew their patience, endurance, and reputation for unselfishness, and the realization that their reward would not be proportionate to their efforts and would be out of line with that received by the peoples in industry was a source of constant pain. This was something he could not discuss without damaging their morale. When his friends wrote that they sold their cotton for seventeen cents before the war and paid ninety-eight cents for a pair of overalls, and were now trying to buy the same product at a dollar more with only a three-cent increase in cotton, he recognized their predicament. Food prices had likewise increased far beyond their ability to purchase. Their tastes were the same as those of other Americans, but they had no bargaining boards to plead their case. But when in trouble they always came to him, "Mr. Sam, you are the only mediator we have; we are on a seventy-two, not a forty-hour week, and we get no overtime." He had spent many years on this kind of shift himself and he did not call them cynics or cranks, or believe them unpatriotic. He knew the realities of a profession where a man's work was around him every hour in the day and every day in the week.

The Speaker was also very much in demand as an ambassador of goodwill during these war years. He seized upon every occasion, as with the farmers, to show what individuals and groups could do. He tried to respond to as many engagements in the Washington area as was practicable, without jeopardizing the flow of legislation. A trip in excess of one hundred miles was almost out of the question. On February 18, President Roosevelt had written to Sam Rayburn to cancel his date at the George Washington Dinner in Fort Worth with the request that he not leave town. There were some vital war measures which he was not willing to trust to anyone else, so he frankly stated, "I feel it my duty to ask you to stay here with me at least until the House has disposed of the much needed legislation."

When Rayburn became Speaker he set up a regular schedule for seeing reporters. These sessions came to be important occasions, particularly during the war years, and gained for him the reputation of being a straightforward administrator. At 11:55 A.M. each weekday a small group of press representatives, sometimes as few as six, assembled in the office of the Speaker to receive a briefing on the day's proceedings in the House. Rayburn may have told the press about a breakfast or conference at the White House or pending messages from the President. His relaxed manner and abrupt frankness made these brief sessions a reporter's joy. The value of his news depended a great deal upon the nature of the forthcoming business. Also Mr. Sam's mood had something to do with the atmosphere. If the Democrats were working together as a team, he would be penetrating and affable in his treatment of the news. On the other hand, if they were behaving like mavericks, he would appear more restless, non-committal, and general in his utterances. If the Republicans were the source of his annoyance, he gave the newsmen their money's worth. On such occasions his extemporaneous remarks were earthy in their simplicity and packed full of homespun philosophy and anecdotes. He threw bolts which every level of society and intellect could comprehend. His tongue was never in his cheek and he looked the reporters in the eye as he gave them his frank version of the things to come. He preferred to look ahead, not backward. Newsmen enjoyed these few minutes more than any other assignment on their daily beat because here they could get unsheathed information from a man with courage and sincerity. He also inspired them with a faith in the Congressional system by his grasp of the job.

His conferences broke up as quickly as they began. Like an automaton, the secretary opened the door at 11:59 A.M. and announced, "Time to go, Mr. Speaker." As the secretary escorted him across the hall to the rostrum of the House he would likely say, "Mr. Speaker, you're late." Of course, Rayburn was never late. When the gavel banged, the representatives could set their watches at 12:00 noon.

Keeping the public informed without alerting the enemy has always been a problem during wartime in a democratic society, where the people have a right to know what is essential. Rayburn, however, knew how to pass out information. When he appeared at Sulphur Springs, Texas, during the Easter holidays in 1942, he demonstrated his method for bolstering morale, alarming the enemy, and freeing the Administration of the blame for concealing facts which people should have. Rayburn dropped the information that the United States had hit a production level of 3300 planes a month—a figure well over fifty per cent above the pre-Pearl Harbor level. He said that tank production was also ahead of schedule, "with one company alone turning out an entire trainload daily." The achievements of management and labor were placed in a very favorable light. The effectiveness of the assembly line community was already bringing home to the German leaders that American industry understood war, a generalization German economists had made themselves.

Rayburn betrayed no confidence and divulged no secrets of Donald M. Nelson, Director of the War Production Board. He knew that the time was ripe for some statement through official channels before individual congressmen began blurting out statistics that might be conflicting and damaging.

One of the highlights of Rayburn's visit to Sulphur Springs, reported Dave Cheavens, was the renewal of his old friendship with Hopkins County stew, a dish he had not tasted since he taught his first term of country school at Greenwood, in the eastern part of the County. He was the honored guest at a luncheon which featured the celebrated dish. For this occasion the chef used a twenty-five-gallon cast-iron pot, and under Rayburn's advice and supervision followed these directions: When the hot coals brought the lard to a boil, several chickens and chunks of fresh pork were dumped into the pot, together with strips of bacon and fat. Rayburn remembered that squirrel was tasty also, if chicken was not available. While the meat was browning, onions, tomatoes, turnips, potatoes, and fresh corn were prepared. He forgot to say that water was needed, but the chef remembered something about adding cornmeal or flour to thicken the mixture. It had to be stirred constantly. After seven hours the bones would fall to the bottom and only the kernels of corn would retain their identity. He failed also to mention the seasoning, but he did not forget to remind the chef that plenty of saltine crackers should be within reach when the stew was ready for serving. A reverie of the old days, he said, begins with the first taste.

While Rayburn was in his District during this Easter recess, he decided to investigate some of those complaints about waste at military bases, beginning with the case which earlier had been placed on his desk. After returning to Washington, he prepared a very thoughtful analysis which discussed each accusation. The inspection perhaps had a good effect, although some of the irregularities were explainable or had been resolved before he made his report to the constituents and proper authorities.

The observance of Polish Independence Day, May 3, 1942, gave the Speaker an opportunity to pay tribute to heroes like Kosciusko and Pulaski, who served America during the Revolution. He made reference to the thousands of Poles fighting in the armies of the allies and the millions in slavery:

> "Poland's battle today is our battle, and our battle is Poland's. In the days of the past, Americans and Poles have stood shoulder to shoulder in the battle for human liberty. Today they are again brothers in arms in the greatest struggle in history, in which human liberty is on trial and the fate of civilization itself is at stake."

Paying tribute to those who have made America strong came to be one of the Speaker's special pleasures. He enjoyed the inspirational stimulus a man in his position could give. When Rayburn delivered the principal address at the Muhlenberg Bicentennial Celebration at Allentown, Pennsylvania, on May 30, he found himself performing just such a duty. Frederick Augustus Muhlenberg, the first Speaker of the House of Representatives, had distinguished himself as a Lutheran minister, educator, and statesman. Since the first Congress after the Constitution was ratified, there had been forty-six speakers and thirty-one Presidents over the 153-year period. Rayburn observed that from the very outset, men like Muhlenberg, who were doing the world's great work, were attacked by those who seemed anxious to destroy the faith and confidence of the American people in their elected representatives. Rayburn undoubtedly took comfort in knowing such statesmen must be prepared for combat and public criticism. He may also have derived personal satisfaction from knowing that he had followed in the footsteps of one so courageous and devoted to God and country. It was at this celebration that Sam Rayburn received the honorary Doctor of Law degree, the first of eight such honors.

Rayburn had paid his respects to this first Speaker of the House of Representatives. The President of the United States on September 16 offered homage in a letter to the forty-sixth Speaker:

> "Congratulations on the completion of two years of faithful and efficient service in the great office of Speaker. An important post always, the Speakership has assumed a special importance because of the gravity of the issues with which you have continually had to deal. Keep up the good work. The country has need of you."

Roosevelt was referring to the many important conferences that had gone on behind the scenes where this Texan had won support for Administration measures to prepare the country for what proved to be an inevitable conflict and for the prosecution of the war. Lend-Lease, the repeal of the Neutrality Act, arming of merchant ships, granting war powers to the President, the enormous war appropriations, the Selective Service Act, price control bills—these were the particular achievements which Roosevelt had in mind. The success of these measures was largely due to Rayburn's legislative skill and adept handling of the gavel.

On October 16, Rayburn told Congress that there would be no "dilly-dallying over important war legislation." Although the proposed cutting of the draft age to take the eighteen and nineteen-year-olds into the service brought forth stacks of correspondence from ministers, mothers, and people everywhere, he was unmoved. He surrendered his own objections to calling up the younger men and moved quickly to direct the President's appeal through channels. Five days after the President's request for such legislation, Rayburn had steered this highly controversial measure through the House. The Speaker had been advised by many congressmen to wait until after the election to tackle this item. Instead he made a quick poll of the membership and discovered that he had the strength in the right places to proceed. Rayburn telephoned the White House to send Secretary of War Stimson and General George Marshall, Chief of Staff, to the Capitol. Congress was briefed by these men on a Tuesday, and on Saturday the bill passed—to the complete surprise of the President, who never dreamed the Speaker had the House so well in hand.

Rayburn proceeded posthaste because he was motivated by the urgency of war and the continued criticism of Congress. With the election only a few days away, he wanted to show America that the Democratic majority could act. However, he did make a good many fathers and mothers angry in his own District, as reflected by the opposition. After the House passed the bill, Rayburn made a report to the people in order to reassure them that our democracy as embodied in Congress was capable of responding to any emergency. The only really partisan portion of his comments was the request that they return the seasoned members of Congress:

> "In my many years as a representative in Congress it is my observation that the district that is best represented is the district that is wise enough to select a man of energy, intelligence, and integrity and to re-elect him year after year. A man of this type serves more efficiently and effectively the longer he is returned by the people."

Although the electorate returned a Democratic majority, they did not heed the Speaker's advice in every instance. The people felt they had cause to be angry and they were just as ruthless about replacing some congressmen as the military through the years had been in recalling generals in the field.

George Balch, a Baptist preacher from Commerce, furnished the Speaker with his opposition in 1942, but Rayburn was unable to conduct a campaign for his sixteenth term. The press had this to say about his opponent's efforts:

> Balch waged a vigorous campaign of slander, and if he were to remain on his knees for the next hundred years it is doubtful that he would get forgiveness for the reflections he cast and direct untruths he uttered against Rayburn, who stands second to President Roosevelt not only in politics but in the hearts of the people of the country.

Something of the spirit of the times was reflected in the type of campaign Balch conducted.

Although the results of the election are of little value, they may reveal one thing—the more powerful a man becomes and the more he achieves, the more public resistance there will be. By counties the vote was as follows:

	Rayburn	*Balch*
Hunt	5,692	2,151
Fannin (2 boxes out)	6,509	2,060
Rains	1,053	545
Collins	5,257	1,907
Grayson	11,049	1,793
Kaufman	4,229	1,111
Rockwall	1,437	500
Totals	35,226	10,087

The Texas home front continued to seethe during the summer and fall of 1942. From the quantity and quality of the mail one might assume that Mr. Sam was the cause of the country's miseries. Some of the grievances were the increasing number and power of Government bureaus, gasoline rationing, the rubber shortage, and foreign trade.

The delegation of authority by the President and Congress without a follow up to curb it or prevent the assumption of unwarranted powers was portrayed as liable to weaken the republican concepts of checks and balances. The example most frequently called to Rayburn's attention in these years was that of Leon Henderson and the OPA. Shakespeare expressed the public thought quite well in his *Measure for Measure,* an irritated constituent affirmed, when he wrote, "It is great to have a giant's strength, but to use it like a giant is tyrannous."

The oil industry in cities like Houston informed Mr. Rayburn that the whole concept of gasoline rationing was calculated to destroy the industry. It would restrict the making and delivering of high octane gasoline necessary in the war effort and would ultimately eliminate business dependent upon gasoline. Some maintained that rationing gasoline in Texas, where it was "almost as plentiful as the waters of the sea," was foolish. And it seemed to many "the most asinine, jittery proposal any serious-minded and honest government ever made." While Rayburn was receiving communications like these from the Southwest, he was being reminded by other sections of the country, where gasoline had to be shipped in, that they might not get their share and be able to maintain their way of life with the demands of the war machine requiring so much fuel. For six months he had been successful in forestalling the rationing of gasoline but when the issue became linked with the saving of rubber, he admitted he could not hold out much longer. He tried to reason with his own people that the national welfare had to be considered.

Closely related to gasoline rationing was that of rubber for automobile tires. The general public kept writing that vast amounts of old rubber were being stockpiled over the country and were not being put to use. The secondhand car lots were reported to be loaded down with automobiles, which the owners could not sell, on which were vast quantities of tires. There were accusations that for more than six months Washington had talked about synthetic rubber industries but had taken no action.

Free trade was another topic of interest to Mr. Sam's constituents. Vice-President Wallace and Sumner Welles had been giving thought to the subject and were in conference with people about the country who were experts in the area. A few years later, during the Truman Administration, Rayburn profited from the wisdom of William L. Clayton, Under Secretary of State, whom he considered the foremost authority in the field next to Cordell Hull. Rayburn frankly admitted that he did not have time to read up on all these economic problems so he relied on the people whose judgment he trusted when he wanted help on trade. He said he called, for example, Will Clayton in Houston. If it was oil, he knew he could trust men like J. R. Parten and James S. Abercrombie, also of Houston. Much of this advice, he reported, was given by telephone or in person.

However in 1942, Rayburn received some unsolicited advice from other sources. Some of this displeased him because it seemed to stem from emotionalism. This is in essence what his correspondence contained:

> We are expected to let down the bars and have free trade and so doing make the Japs, the Germans, the Gandhi Indians, and all other foreigners our equals in trade, civilization, and citizenship. . . . cut out all the damn-fool ideologies, the Bureau Bickering and Back Biting and 'social gains,' including the forty-hour week, the closed shop, and over-time pay, and win this war before we get licked.

There had been certain political developments in the Lone Star State which a prognosticator like Mr. Sam could view with real alarm. However, before one can comment intelligently on the picture in 1942 he must look briefly at the backgrounds, beginning with the 1938 gubernatorial race. The outcome of this election was instrumental in setting the stage for some of the intra-party conflicts that had helped accentuate the differences in Texas between conservatives and liberals. The seeds of discord had already been planted, and the wartime economy, with all of its superimposed controls, gave the dissenting groups ammunition for their diatribes against the "power mad" bureaucrats and socialistic school in Washington.

Mr. Sam always liked to believe that the people of Texas were capable of electing their own governors, and the results would show a Democrat in Austin. He and these officials, he thought, would then have enough in common to work together quite satisfactorily when their paths crossed at state conventions. Hence Rayburn had no ambitions to be a political boss. He preferred to trust the people's judgment and take what they sent to Austin. His only aspirations were to have delegations to national conventions that could work together harmoniously, and he firmly believed that good Democrats should be able to find sufficient basis for agreement within their own Party ideals.

To make a long story short, a certain gentleman by the name of Wilbert Lee O'Daniel, with a Republican background and no poll tax receipt, created a mild revolution in 1938 Party circles. With his "Light Crust Doughboys" orchestra and personal flair for Texas history and ecclesiastical jazz, he lulled the electorate to sleep with platitudes and sentiment in one of the most masterful pieces of mass salesmanship and showmanship Texas or the nation itself has ever seen. It was a shocking spectacle and a dangerous trend, in Mr. Sam's judgment, but he kept quiet, knowing that giants could be rolled under, because the people were not happy. Many years later, though, he made one cogent remark about this experience: "God, that O'Daniel!"

"Pass-the-Biscuits Pappy" was perfectly correct when he announced late in June, 1938, that there "ain't gonna be no runoff." The more such candidates like William McCraw ridiculed O'Daniel's antics, and Ernest O. Thompson tried to talk intelligently about Texas' problems, the more popular "Pappy" became. One of his thirteen opponents, George W. Winningham, Editor of the *Harper Herald*, on July 15, 1938, perhaps made the most prophetic remark, besides "Pappy's" own ungrammatical utterance: "No candidate who talks sense and acts like a human being has a chance to beat this political freak." [1] Despite the fact that O'Daniel received a majority of the votes, Rayburn was puzzled when he found relatively few people who confessed they had supported him.

In his 1940 race O'Daniel conducted a less sensational campaign, but he turned his attention more on the bureaucrats, oligarchies, and professional politicians. Sam Rayburn was one of his targets. O'Daniel was consumed with anger because the famous "56 Club" in the Texas House had blocked a combination sales tax and natural resources tax, which he considered essential to paying the much discussed old-age pensions and to balancing the budget. He castigated all public officials who might have been hostile to his program. The electorate again agreed with O'Daniel and favored him over five opponents, giving him 54.3 per cent of the total vote, Thompson again being one of his victims.

During the first campaign O'Daniel passed tin cups and small flour barrels through the crowd to collect nickles, dimes, and quarters. Some who had no money brought fryers and sacks of eggs. But during the second venture he had attracted the attention of some more prosperous donors, some of whom had oil interests and were able to donate large sums of cash and even a sound truck valued at about $16,000. It was this second campaign which really opened Mr. Sam's eyes to the danger, for it focused the attention of the State upon the "professional" politicians and a united, rather affluent, conservative group in Texas. Some of the oil interests that had prospered during the prewar years under the Democrats began to drift away at this time from their mooring, observed Mr. Sam. Their prosperity had turned their heads and hardened their hearts to the Party that had given them a new birth.

Rayburn had already demonstrated, in the 1940 State and National Convention, the ability to work with all groups, even those who had been stirred up by the O'Daniel crusade. The

Roosevelt Administrations, however, had planted many concepts in the minds of some Texans which were unpalatable. The drift toward socialism was a theme O'Daniel exploited during the remainder of his time as Governor.

With the death of United States Senator Morris Sheppard, O'Daniel appointed the eighty-seven-year-old son of Sam Houston—Andrew Jackson Houston, who died after answering only three roll calls in the Senate.

The race for the Senate in the special election, set for June 28, 1941, attracted a field of sixteen candidates at the outset, including Congressman Lyndon B. Johnson, Rayburn's and Roosevelt's close friend; Gerald C. Mann, Attorney-General; Martin Dies, Jr.; and Governor O'Daniel himself. The Governor in the Democratic primary led the ticket by only 111 votes, coming from behind during the final tallying to nose out Johnson, who had already been declared the victor by most experts. Only a simple majority was required. As would be expected in a contest where the vote was so close there came rumors of irregularities, and there was some delay and oratory before the Senator was finally seated.

O'Daniel had a stormy two years before facing the electorate again in 1942 for a full six-year term, to begin in January, 1943. Although he had already been critical of Congress and the President before he entered the Senate, his anti-labor thinking, opposition to extending the Selective Service Act, opposition to overtime pay for labor, and other controversial items about which Sam Rayburn was being harassed from back home, brought forth brief cheers from the masses and some rather influential people in Texas.

However, O'Daniel's tactless haste and dedicated opposition to the Administration diminished his effectiveness and alienated some original well-wishers. Although his star had declined somewhat in July, 1942, he led James V. Allred and Dan Moody, both former governors and able lawyers. He was forced into a run-off by Allred.

There was no question as to Rayburn's and the Administration's loyalties and preference in this campaign. Walter Winchell brought the duel between Roosevelt and O'Daniel into focus when he reported that the White House had accepted O'Daniel's challenge. The Texas papers reported that Lyndon Johnson, Rayburn, and other Administration faithfuls were coming back to Texas while Congress was in recess, the implication being that they were going to do some work for Judge Allred.

Then Mr. Sam began receiving some "vicious" correspondence. One of the more printable remarks came from a lawyer at Greenville:

> I understand that you have cotton crops and other crops on your Fannin County farms. You have cattle and sheep and no jackasses, and you have chickens and other poultry, and there is pure air in the atmosphere all about there and nature is there in its greatness and purity. Stay on this farm during your vacationing, commune with nature there, breathe in the unadulterated air, visit the farm often and the crops, and the denizens of the pasture, pens and yards. You will then be refreshed and strengthened, a wiser one, and will make no mistakes, and you do not want to make any more.

The years of combat had given Mr. Sam a rawhide skin, and this type of communication did not stir him up quite as much as the correspondence from preachers who continued to argue for pacifism and accused the Administration of employing some of Adolf Hitler's "Divide and Conquer" techniques. When Mr. Sam read the accusations that he was a rubber stamp and was interfering with the democratic processes in Texas, he jumped like a mustang with a cockleburr under its saddle:

> I do not know of anyone who is trying to take away anyone's privilege of having a free ballot. I have certainly never tried to do this and never intend to. I want those who write things in papers to understand that I do not like to have them question my actions because I come home every chance I get when there is a short recess in Congress.

Rayburn tried to be discreet, though everyone knew where his sympathies lay in the run-off. He had known Judge Allred for years, had worked with him during and after the "hot oil" era, and found him a reliable Party man. He recognized that O'Daniel was not an unpopular candidate in his own District, despite the fact that Allred had relatives and many friends there, as evidenced by the vote he polled when elected Attorney-General and Governor. The rural vote, including the older people, was the thing that caused Rayburn to see that O'Daniel was a potent contender, and a man to be feared. He had already derailed or retired several of Texas' "professional politicians" and threatened to get on the radio to call names in order to take care of a few others. He seemed to thrive on the affected martyrdom of his past two years by calling attention to his senatorial failures. He indicated that he had been alone in the people's fight.

O'Daniel announced no platform but pledged to support the war effort. At the same time he criticized Roosevelt's legislative program and his conduct of the war. The bureaus and their "crackpot" ideas, such as gasoline rationing, were assailed. Interference with small business, regimentation, higher taxes, and increased cost of living provided the incumbent with all the ammunition he needed. The rural people liked to hear him attack the communistic labor-leader racketeers and their strikes in war industries. The old folks, anti-Roosevelt, and anti-labor union groups united in the absence of the younger voters, who were at war, to provide the Senator with the necessary margin in the August primary of 1942.

Sam Rayburn's troubles had further sources. When O'Daniel went to Washington the first time, in 1941, he was succeeded by the Lieutenant-Governor, Coke R. Stevenson, one of those who had profited from O'Daniel's endorsement. Both the Senator and the new Governor were associated with a conservative and anti-New Deal group in the Democratic Party called the Texas Regulars—a movement that actually had its origin back in the depression. The group met as Constitutional Democrats in Detroit on August 7, 1936. They later were referred to as "The National Jeffersonian Democrats." The history of these dissenting Democrats was a long and confusing one to Rayburn. He noted that some rather distinguished and affluent personages were associated with them at one time or another. He remarked many times that some of these fellows would have been better off in the Republican Party, and certainly, he believed, the Democrats would not have missed them. But they hoped to stay in the Party and reform it by driving out the radicals. Mr. Sam, a conservative himself, was caught between the Regulars and the more liberal Young Democrats. How he survived to maintain even a semblance of unity among the Democrats was either a credit to his genius or to the fundamental loyalty of Texans to their Party.

O'Daniel's function, in Rayburn's estimation, was the muddying of the waters, for he had no real roots in the economic conflicts between the old and new order. When translated into quotable language, Rayburn's opinion of O'Daniel was, briefly, that he was something of an opportunist who happened to appear on the political scene when frictions were fomenting. The Regulars simply tried to use him for what his temporary worth might be to their cause. Their main basis for agreement was simply the anti-Roosevelt feeling. The role of Stevenson was another matter, for he was no opportunist and was sincerely dedicated to a States' Rights philosophy.

Sam Rayburn returned to Washington in January, 1943, with some rather unpleasant memories of a disagreeable summer, politically speaking. The Seventy-eighth Congress opened on January 6, 1943, with Mr. Sam being elected Speaker for the third time. By coincidence his election fell upon his sixty-first birthday. The narrow margin of 217 to 206 indicated the close division in the House, but even so, he was pleased with his birthday gift.

As was the custom, the Minority Leader (Joseph Martin) introduced the Speaker after his election. Following a prolonged ovation, which was a tribute to his thirty years of service and recognition from both sides of the aisle for his ability as a presiding officer, Rayburn delivered an appropriate address to set off a new Congress in a world at war. He averred his unwavering determination to protect and defend the rights, the prerogatives and the power of the House of Representatives. He stressed the importance of teamwork between the executive and legislative branches of the Government, which he deemed essential to making this the "Victory Congress."

During the first two months of the session there was some evidence of intra-party strife, and as a result the Democrats suffered a number of repeated defeats on the floor. The Party leaders came to Mr. Sam early in March and asked him to lay down the law to these rambunctious souls and also to do something about the Southern Democrats who were absent at the roll calls. He asked the delegation to accept his judgment as he gave an emphatic "NO" to their requests. "There won't be any serious trouble," he said, "if we just give these fellows time enough to let off steam." The Speaker understood men in public life and explained that the recalcitrant Party members had not recovered from the strain of the Congressional election. They were all full of ideas and wanted to continue talking. So he advised his own special tonic of "time and patience—plus a little quiet persuasion." He added, "The Democrats in this House are closer together than they ever were. There will be division on domestic issues, of course. There always is division on domestic issues." His faith in their ability to agree on war measures or basic legislative mechanics and to respond to his "quiet persuasion" had been confirmed about ten days earlier, when the House turned down by 114 votes a resolution to create a separate standing committee on aviation, despite its ardent support by Republican leader Joe Martin and its sponsorship by the popular Jack Nichols of Oklahoma.

Rayburn took advantage of this conference to teach them a few things they had not observed: "One thing our fellows have got to do is to unlearn some of the habits they acquired in the days when we had big majorities. It didn't make much difference then whether a man stayed in his office and answered his mail or picked up his hat and walked over to the floor. It makes a lot of difference now."

As a conservative, he had not been in sympathy with some of the legislation proposed by the New Dealers. He was neither to the left nor to the right. Perhaps it was his moderate views that enabled him to ride out these Congressional storms and hold the reins of leadership in his own State organization. More important in 1943 was friendship. For example, the leader of the Southern bloc, Gene Cox of Georgia, was Rayburn's friend, and on the other aisle was Joe Martin. On really important issues where America's security was involved, he knew he could talk to his friends and they would understand. Rayburn had been able to keep his friends because he did not demand one hundred per cent loyalty to him personally. He said he was aware that their problems were not exactly like his and their obligations were not always the same. This attitude is best illustrated by an incident which occurred many years ago when he was campaigning for a seat in the Texas Legislature against a strong opponent. A close friend came to him with a problem. "Sam," he said, "I'd like to work for you; but I'm going to be a candidate for prosecuting attorney and I will need this other man's support. What would you advise me to do?"

"Go ahead and vote for him," was the reply. "I'm going to lick him anyway."

This calm level-headedness and unselfishness cost him one vote but gained a life-long friend. Time and time again Mr. Sam re-enacted this little drama in Congress. He was honest with his colleagues and continued to remind them that their first loyalty was to their constituents and personal problems, and he gladly released them. They reciprocated in a like manner. But if the country's future was at stake or there was something where his word had to be taken on faith, he would resort to his quiet persuasion—one man at a time. One congressman admitted that under these circumstances: "Mr. Sam is terribly convincing.

There he stands, his left hand on your right shoulder, holding your coat button, looking at you out of honest eyes that reflect the sincerest emotions. He's so damned sincere and dedicated to a cause and he knows his country and job inside out so well that I would feel pretty dirty to turn him down and not trust him, knowing that he would crawl to my assistance if I needed him. And there are a great many people who feel the same way about him."

It was conceivable that a moderate could hold the House in line but it was puzzling to some that he could continue to maintain White House confidence, since his honeymoon with the more liberal ideas had ceased. The President even jested about his Speaker's sober views and habits. At a White House party early in March, Rayburn chaperoned the new members of Congress, and he was careful to give each a chance to talk with the President. He was also considerate of the President's energy, for he herded his boys together to take them home early. Roosevelt saw through the Speaker's strategy and teased him with the remark, "Father Sam, you want to send the boys to bed too early." Rayburn thought the boys had enjoyed themselves enough for one evening and it was time for him to take them home.

A good illustration of the Rayburn method is revealed in the debates leading to the passage of the measure providing for the Federal Communications Commission, which owes its existence to legislation carrying his name. During this period, when Congress was recovering some of the power it lost during the early days of the New Deal, the FCC was receiving rough treatment by the Dies Committee and the Cox Committee. Rayburn wanted to protect competitive rights in the radio field and to shelter the independent radio stations while they were being so penetratingly examined. On February 17, 1943, an amendment was offered which would have taken away all funds. A majority in the House was prepared to kill the Commission. Suddenly, a short, bald-headed gentleman was seen to appear in the Committee room. These were some of the remarks which resulted in another Rayburn victory:

> "Mr. Chairman, I think I have a right to speak on the amendment because I happen to be the chairman of the committee that reported the bill to set up the Communications Commission and was the author of the bill. Before that time there was chaos in communications throughout the length and breadth of the land.

> The telegraph and telephone business had hardly been touched by the agency that was supposed to handle them, the Interstate Commerce Commission. The old Radio Commission was devoting a little time to broadcasting and to broadcasting only. It was thought at that time that all communications should come under one commission of the Government. This was done back in 1934.
>
> "Now, Mr. Chairman, if the amendment offered by the gentleman from South Dakota should be brushed aside as sheer demagogy, that would be one thing. If the begging of the question by the gentleman from New York, that is if the investigating committee's report between now and the first of July were convincing, that would be another thing. I do not appeal to your prejudice or to your passions, and I do not respect people of demagogy, but I do want to counsel with your reason. I repeat with all the earnestness I can command. A great war is on, the world is aflame and the air is full of propaganda from every conceivable portion of the earth. There is only one agency in the United States of America, let me say to you, that has any control whatsoever over the air of the United States. Do you by your vote at this time wish to strike down that only agency?"[2]

It was the "Rayburn touch" that brought about the defeat of the amendment. The majority was against him, but for a brief moment they listened and accepted his appraisal. They had always found him steady, practical, and progressive in his thinking.

On March 16, the Speaker received the news that his brother Will had suffered a heart attack at their home in Bonham. He died about an hour before Mr. Sam could get the House business in order and catch a flight from Washington.

On April 27, the Speaker returned to Texas on political business. When he arrived at the Capitol Building in Austin he went directly to the Governor's reception room. Here Stevenson greeted him with "Ha-Ya, Sam," and the Speaker replied with "Hello, Coke." The friendship between the two went back thirty-two years when Stevenson, then at Junction, used his influence to help get Rayburn elected to the Speakership in Austin. Mr. Sam had already publicly acknowledged his appreciation to the Governor.

Mr. Sam was quick to express his appreciation to people who had befriended him, and he often repeated his ancient belief that friendship was the best gift one man could give to another. He worked diligently trying to hold up his end of the relationship, but when the other person did not respond, Sam Rayburn could effect a prolonged silence.

Shortly before the Governor introduced Mr. Rayburn at a joint session of the Texas Legislature in the House chamber, Representative Choice Moore of Bonham presented a portrait of the Speaker which currently hangs in the rear of the room. It is an oil painting by Douglas Chandor, a Weatherford artist, to commemorate Rayburn's Speakership of the Thirty-second Legislature.

Rayburn made this comment about the President: "A greater Commander-in-Chief could not have been found if we had conducted a country-wide search for one, and as long as he is Commander-in-Chief and as long as he wants it he shall have my uncomplaining support." This statement was directed at a few critics of the third term and was a subtle suggestion that, with America at war, they could expect a fourth term. War emergency problems, personal sacrifices, and a defense of Congress against unjust criticism were other themes on the Speaker's mind.

Among those who joined in the round of handshaking afterward were Congressman Lyndon Johnson and some of the former Speakers of the Texas House—Lee Satterwhite, Emmet Morse, Homer Leonard, and Stevenson, besides Rayburn and the present Speaker Price Daniel, who was later Attorney-General, Senator, and Governor.

Although the audience was courteous and responsive, there were those who did not approve. Lieutenant-Governor John Lee Smith made his presence conspicuous by listening from an inconspicuous corner. Even before news stories of the Rayburn speech were printed he had released his own lengthy statement, in which he was caustically critical of the "squat, bald Sam Rayburn, wielder of the world's most potent legislative gavel." Smith observed that Rayburn must be running for Vice-President. Attention was also called to Stevenson's apparently feeling "the knife twist in his own hide as Rayburn minimized the sacrifices of the complainers" because Stevenson made no reference to the Capitol's guest at his press conference on the following day. Smith's "tub-thumping" was instigated by his dislike of the Administration's labor policies and the "plague of bureaucracies."

As long as Rayburn sang Roosevelt's Alma Mater, Austinites said, he could expect a small minority to "throw off their Sunday manners and give him the hot foot."

At a $50-a-plate Jefferson dinner on June 21 in the Hotel Commodore, Washington, Sam Rayburn delivered essentially the same type of speech as that in Austin. Although there was no discussion of a fourth term, he gave "unswerving and uncomplaining support" to the President. Since Rayburn had already been mentioned as a possible running mate, every ear awaited some reference to the President's plans. Wallace was regarded by the experts as out of the picture because of his ultra liberal views and the accumulated animosities. The real blow to Wallace came in July, 1943, when his Board of Economic Warfare was abolished by the President, after a dispute between the Vice-President and Secretary of Commerce, Jesse Jones, over the Reconstruction Finance Corporation's policy on advancing funds for several imports essential to the war effort. After this bad publicity there was some casting about for a conservative to strengthen the Party's ticket.

The Texas Legislature had already unveiled a portrait of Mr. Sam on April 27, and on the morning of August 6 it was his Alma Mater's chance to do the same. A barbecue and reception were also on the program. He had returned to his home State to receive the honorary degree of Doctor of Law from East Texas State Teachers College at Commerce. A Douglas Chandor portrait, which cost $7500, was unveiled and presented to the school as a gift of the class of 1940. Following speeches by Congressman Wright Patman of Texarkana and Fritz Lanham of Fort Worth, President Sam W. Whitley introduced Mr. Rayburn, whose address was carried over the national broadcasting system. Rayburn appraised the nation's war effort and tried to silence the "symphony of sour notes on the noisy, squabble-ridden home front." In his report he added a new word to the vocabulary when he called the "saboteurs of the spirit," "grumlins," in allusion to the sprites referred to as gremlins, who made life miserable for the pilots of our planes. The gremlins haunted the airways while the "grumlins" did even greater damage by destroying faith and confidence in the nation's leadership and the prosecution of the war. "The main feature of the 'grumlin,' " Rayburn explained, "is a fellow with a big mouth who at breakfast drinks orange juice and coffee, eats cereal, two eggs and toast, then feels sorry for himself as he grumbles at his wife because she has used up her red stamps and was unable to give him bacon." Rayburn's more sober talk dealt with the caliber of the United States Army of 2,000,000 overseas, the Navy with its 200 war ships, the air force with its 64,000 new planes, the fight on U-boats, the transport service and air umbrella, increased production of food, regulation of the cost of living, and the physical fitness of our fighting men. This was ETSTC's biggest celebration, for they were honoring their most famous graduate, whom the students cited in November, 1961, as their "most beloved and distinguished alumnus." President Roosevelt, in sending his regrets at being unable to attend the ceremony, reflected the regional and national feeling: "I share your pride in Sam Rayburn. It is fortunate in these difficult days that the nation has the benefit of the judgment and wisdom and ripe experience which he brings to the high office of Speaker."

Rayburn was quite active during the period before returning to Washington. He went to Houston to dedicate a Liberty ship named after his father. On August 11 he dedicated the Army's Ashburn General Hospital at McKinney, Texas, where he advocated a postwar rehabilitation program to fit members of the armed services for useful citizenship. In anticipation of the war's end, he called for even greater aid to the returning soldiers than did the President in his most recent fireside chat. "No matter how much money it costs," Rayburn asserted, "every returning soldier who wants a farm must be given a start toward owning one." For those who would be unable to pick up where they left off, he declared, "we must spend the money and take the time to re-educate them so that they again may be useful citizens."

He also gave some attention to the prevention of wars in his remarks about the disarmament of aggressor nations. Of the softness of some Americans, he declared:

> "Within sixty days after the end of the war, sob sisters and sob brothers will start crying that the common people of Germany, Italy, and Japan had nothing to do with this war. This is rot. If it had not been for the common people of Germany, Italy, and Japan there would have been no Hitler, Mussolini or Hirohito.

At Terrell, he continued the theme of grumbling:

> "When I hear complaints about the shortages in civilian goods, my thoughts turn to the South Pacific where the boys are fighting in sunshine, wind and rain to preserve our liberty. And when I hear complaints

> such as these, I think of the fathers and mothers who have given from one to seven sons to the country's service, and I would despise myself if I complained of any minor inconveniences."

Most of the complaining, he said, was being done by people who had contributed little to the overall war effort.

In all of his analyses of America's debt to the servicemen his thinking followed a practical pattern. The problem of employment for the returning soldiers and sailors was one for industry to solve rather than for the Government. Hospitalization for the sick and wounded, financial aid to those disabled in the defense of country, but no doles or humiliating jobs like raking leaves or picking up paper with a spear—these were some of his ideas. Free private enterprise should provide the opportunity for men to earn an honest living for themselves and their families that they might resume their pursuit of happiness. He predicted that the President's recent fireside chat would set the imagination of Congress in motion, and that the September session would bring a flood of bills to the hoppers with proposals to give the servicemen every conceivable kind of benefit and gift, some perhaps "including the moon with a pink ribbon around it." Rayburn advised that the able-bodied veterans did not want anything more than an opportunity and warned that the veterans' postwar aid could degenerate into a political football like that of old-age pensions.

Before the Speaker returned to Washington he had an opportunity to preside over a somewhat unique ceremony at the Lone Star Steel Plant on September 4, 1943, where he laid the last brick in one of the huge ovens. He saw the Dangerfield enterprise as a deviation from the sort of economy which characterized this part of Texas. This new Texas industry had taken an unprecedented stand to reflect both the ingenuity of the Lone Star State, and the courage of the people in providing the necessary capital. As he spoke from the top of one of the ovens, he reflected upon the wealth of Texas in cattle, oil, cotton, forests, and other natural resources:

> "We lacked just one thing—an iron and steel industry. Millions of tons of rich ore deposits have lain here dormant for years, and now through the courage and combined efforts of a group of great Texans we are at last to realize the dream that has tantalized east Texans for generations."

When Sam Rayburn returned to Washington, he began reading what the papers back home were saying about him. They were building him up for the Vice-Presidency or Presidency. As a student of Congressional history he paused briefly to reflect on former Speakers who had attracted attention for the country's top position. He was aware that only one Speaker had ever won the Presidency, although several had been more capable men than the one in the White House. Clay and Reed were such men, the former being unsuccessful three times and the latter losing the nomination to McKinley in 1896. The only Speaker ever to become President was Polk, who was an accidental nominee for reason of his obscurity at the time. Champ Clark and John Garner had made their unsuccessful bids for the nominations. Blaine was successful in 1884 in getting the nomination, but was defeated by Cleveland. Two Speakers, Colfax and Garner, had used the top position in the House of Representatives as a stepping stone to the Vice-Presidency. Mr. Sam was also aware of one thing—that most of the forty-four men who had held the Speakership were already in oblivion, perhaps because they had their eyes on something else and did not seek their immortality through the job at hand. But he had already found in his present position an opportunity to play a role which could well set him apart from his predecessors and cause historians to remember him as the most powerful political figure of his era. He had already earned the title of the second most powerful man in the country, and he could also foresee the possibility that of all the men behind the scenes, he was making his mark. For one who measured power in terms of the opportunity to serve his country he had already achieved his goal and certainly his childhood ambitions. Yet Rayburn did not seek fame; it was thrust upon him.

The world was always too much with Rayburn for him to contemplate long upon his own fortunes, personal problems, or dilemmas. His apparent melancholy and chronic seriousness offered no relief from the feeling of responsibility. Yet at the most unexpected moments that irrepressible sense of humor would break through the enveloping cloud of solemnity. Plagued by Party squabbles in Texas and Washington, by concern for the country's welfare, he once came forth with this story for the amusement of a visitor who had just unburdened his troubles.

"I have just received a cheerful letter from a fellow whose problems remind me of yours. He said that one of his young baldfaced heifers had broken her back and died; 'some hunters had set fire to his oatfield stubble, burning down a fence; a tornado had blown down his windmill; some storms had killed all his chickens; the rain soaked his oats so they couldn't be stored. Hoping you are the same, I am, truly yours!' "

It was his sense of humor which kept him on an even keel during the fall of 1943. The two months of escape from the Washington humidity and heat had made some lawmakers less irritable and sounder in their judgment, for which Mr. Sam was grateful. Association with the people back home had a salutary effect in reminding them that there was a real war on and not just a tug of war between the executive and legislative branches.

On December 9, the fears which had been accumulating deep within Mr. Sam exploded like a bomb. There were some dangerous trends which seemed to him to be threatening American unity. The loose talk which had been going the rounds convinced him that this country was not psychologically prepared for a long and total war. He complained about the references to likely discord with our allies, the criticism of our military leadership, and the fears that this country would not be able to maintain its standard of living for the duration of the war, and the years to follow. He made a plea for unity and maturity of thought. He gave an honest appraisal of home-front problems and urged Congress to quit protecting certain portions of our population that needed the experience of risk and sacrifice. He wanted every segment of society to feel the pinch of the emergency for the sake of moral discipline and unity of effort. These were his thoughts when he went home for the holidays on December 21, 1943.

When the time came to return to Washington, he caught a northbound train at Denison, driving from Bonham through one of those sleetstorms which bring cheer to the hearts of children and the more adventuresome, but misery to the line crews of Southwestern Bell and Texas Power and Light. He carried under his arm one of Miss Lou's box lunches, including such leftovers as the choice pieces of an extra fried chicken and some sweets. The Speaker, however, had already eaten a noonday meal of fried chicken, spareribs, hot biscuits, turnip greens, and such country delicacies as his three sisters could put together to pamper their brother. Each tried to outdo the others in preparing the foods he liked.

The Seventy-eighth Congress began its second session on January 10, 1944. A few days later the Speaker opened the political season at a Jackson Day Dinner by adding two Democratic names to the Hall of Fame—Franklin D. Roosevelt and Cordell Hull. "We still have among us," he asserted, "that small minority who were afflicted with jaundice of the spine in 1940 and enlargement of the spleen in 1943." After riding the hecklers out of town on a verbal rail, he proceeded to view the achievements at home and abroad which would make good Americans love this country and her enemies fear her. He promised that the Democratic Party would nominate a particular type of man who could do a special kind of job. Anyone knowing Rayburn would have been blind and deaf not to recognize his choice from the description of the Presidential image.

Two months later Rayburn still had no word from the White House, no way of knowing whether the convention would be "open." An editorial in the St. Louis *Post Dispatch* suggested that the "open" convention would be a good way for the President to ease Wallace out of office, if the desire existed, and remove the basic objection to his own leadership. As the Vice-President, Wallace had been more than a figurehead. He had written a best-seller entitled *The Century of the Common Man,* which argued that the only way to secure a lasting peace was to raise the standard of living throughout the world. In 1942 he delivered his "Free World" address which expressed a desire for an industrial democracy: "The new democracy, the democracy of the common man includes not only the Bill of Rights but also economic democracy." Although philosophically inaccurate in their judgments, many of Mr. Sam's constituents referred to this as the American version of Marxism. Mr. Sam became increasingly silent on the subject, but he did watch the White House with growing concern, perhaps fearful that the President might attempt to salvage Wallace.

Rayburn seemed to many a logical replacement for Wallace and was given a good chance in an uncontrolled convention. At a White House press conference Roosevelt mentioned only one name in connection with New Deal legislation and the defense of his program, and that was Sam Rayburn's. Mrs. Roosevelt had been quite impressed by one of Rayburn's speeches about the war effort, seeing it as the most statesmanlike speech made in Congress since the beginning of the war. As a result of her comments, the President read it before preparing his Christmas Eve address to the nation. However, Rayburn was already much in the President's eye.

Barkley and Truman were also mentioned as possibilities,

if the President wanted to placate the Democratic Senators who threatened "to run off the reservation." The former, however, had recently experienced a showdown with the President and had resigned as the "Roosevelt" leader. In exchange for his courage the Democratic caucus conferred upon him the title of new Majority Leader, restoring him to his former position, an act which enhanced his prestige nationally. Truman had also achieved national recognition by virtue of his courage as Chairman of the Committee to Investigate National Defense. Many conservatives were talking James F. Byrnes, if Rayburn was not acceptable. By January 25, 1944, Southern members of Congress had started a campaign to put one from their section in the second place, for they had practically conceded the top position to Roosevelt. Rayburn was the favorite with eighteen votes. According to Senator Maybank of South Carolina, "We all want to see a Southerner nominated but we can't agree on the man."

The early prognosticators, however, favored Rayburn over all the rest because he was "regular." He was an organization man who could work with a President, who was neither to the left nor the right, since he was on dead "center." This meant that he possessed the desire to progress with the times, not two jumps ahead or behind. His philosophy was one of remodeling rather than rebuilding. It was an outgrowth of the persuader school of leadership, where compromises and understandings replaced strong-arm tactics. Though he had studied under Garner, he soon recognized that there were several ways to deal with men. Kindness and consideration of the other fellow's rights and his constituents' thinking were good prerequisites to understanding and achievement. These attitudes enhanced his popularity.

Mr. Sam began his activities in the spring with a speech at Los Angeles, California, on March 28, but he was so awed by geography that he could not follow strict Party lines. His new inspiration came from leaving the crowded metropolises of the East and going West. For the first time he was made aware of the bigness of the great, sprawling democracy that was peopled by peace-loving folk, who had faith in the ideals of a free government. A practical man had discovered, at the age of sixty-two, that his soul could be kindled to poetic flights of the imagination. The factories, assembly lines, fields of newly-planted grains, ranches with thousands of beef cattle, and the shipyards gave him an enthusiasm for the Western civilization that was being born. The Congressman who had confined his travel essentially to that part of the country between Washington and Bonham, who had hugged the earth and watched America go by from his parlor car, now dared to say that "after this war, America will do it again, will make the crystal-gazers look like pikers." He had always been earthbound, but as he looked across an expansive America, he confessed that some day he too would be compelled to fly. The awareness that a new day was approaching made him young at heart and a prophet for his country: "Air transportation will change our lives, will make our vast land smaller and smaller, geographically speaking. It will put that grapefruit you grow out here on the table in New York City the morning after it is picked. It will widen the distribution of everything you produce. There will no longer be any need to mark things 'rush' to prevent spoiling before they reach a market. What is 'rush' to us today will be the slow motion of tomorrow."

A Texas statesman-farmer had been reborn! He had served notice on those who were insensitive to progress. A practical man confessed that he had become an "impractical dreamer."

Then his thoughts turned to the country's leaders in civil and military affairs. His praise for President Roosevelt's insight in selecting leaders like Marshall, Eisenhower, MacArthur, King, Nimitz, and Halsey was irrepressible. His tribute to Cordell Hull's job in diplomacy was equally glowing. The highest tribute went to the American mothers who had given the men who were now winning the war. He saw himself only as "an average American citizen, no better I know, no worse I hope, than the average." The second most powerful man in the country was brought face to face with himself in complete humility: "I have no son to give to this war nor the reconstruction of a stricken world after it is over, and I am wondering what real sacrifice I have made, and I cannot think of a single one that hurts."

Mr. Sam tried to talk politics, but he was too carried away to put on his glasses and follow his manuscript. Instead he spoke from his heart the thoughts that had come home to him about the greatness of America—". . . the men of all walks of life, men of all political views, but with one faith that brings them together to see their country through crisis, a faith above personal interest, above personal politics."

Two days later at a Jackson Day dinner in San Francisco he tried to be partisan again but found that he was still under the spell of his trip West. He told the Party faithfuls that for every nine hundred miles he traveled west he set his watch back an hour. By the time he had reached the Pacific, he confessed, he had "to set his mind ahead a generation." He had succumbed to the challenge of the West: ". . . out here where tomorrow is always more important than yesterday; where the traveler, if he has eyes that see and ears that hear and a soul that responds to his fellowman, always catches the contagion of looking ahead, always has a feeling that he has reached the gateway to a new world."

To be sure, he discussed the effectiveness of the war machine and gave thought to the end of hostilities and peacetime economy, but this was an American rather than just a Democrat who spoke at the fund-raising dinner. Even his references to our blunders in the distant past after World War I, perhaps intended to bring shame to the Republican Party, were actually aimed at all America to chastize a country that considered itself superior, invincible, and secure. He hoped for a national wisdom to cope with the future, a wisdom that involved a frank admission of past stupidities and follies with the resolve to profit from mistakes. At this moment he anticipated the transcendental thinking of the "Mr. Everything" of 1961.

The first week in June of 1944 was famous for the shattering of two myths—the invincibility of Hitler's defenses and the impregnability of the Rules Committee in the House. The world knows how the former gained a reputation but not many citizens understand the source of the latter's strength; that is the power of the group to select bills, pass "gag" rules that limit debate, to mark any legislation for the death sentence, censor representatives who defy the Committee's recommendation, and ultimately to withhold campaign funds. Finally under the generalship of the Speaker, the House voted overwhelmingly against the Rules Committee's handling of certain urgent matters, such as price controls.

According to *The Progressive,* a LaFollette magazine (July 17), there were two Souths—that of Martin Dies, "Goober" Cox, "The Man" Bilbo, "Pass the Biscuits Pappy" O'Daniel, and their kind, and that of Lister Hill, Claude Pepper, and Sam Rayburn. The first were referred to as Tories and the name of Howard Smith of Virginia for the first time came to be associated with the conservatives of this ilk. Smith became the key figure in the 1961 fight between Rayburn and the Rules Committee. As early as 1944 some of the South's strength was vested in its influence upon this Committee, and when Mr. Sam defied his own section's claim to power he naturally expected to face the consequences. However, he kept reminding himself that a Speaker in his administrative function must transcend a district or section and act for the whole.

For months he knew that he would have opposition in the Fourth District because he had made some decisions which Texans and Southerners did not like, but he simply had to hope that they would forgive him for acting in the interest of all Americans. He knew the source of his strongest opposition and was aware that this opposition would supply unlimited funds, for he had already been identified as one of the moving spirits behind legislation to regulate Wall Street and its subsidiaries. He recognized that he would have to give an accounting to some for Rural Electrification, TVA, the Wagner Act, and the Wage Hour law, which were approved under his leadership. Rumors spread rapidly that some of the oil men and big business interests in Texas were prepared to help defeat Sam Rayburn. His liberal legislation under FDR was the principal basis for complaint, but all the while he insisted he was a conservative.

Some politicians in the State believed Rayburn had a good chance at the Vice-Presidency. According to Dallas Blankenship, who had been all over the State in his bid for the Speakership of the Texas House, Speaker Rayburn was the choice of the voters. He had also observed that "most people are either for Franklin D. Roosevelt or believe that he'll be the candidate anyway." Blankenship said the thing that surprised him was that he encountered avowed Republicans and New Deal opponents who maintained they would feel better about a fourth term if a "solid man like Rayburn was riding in the sidecar," but his information had come from the predominantly rural sections of the State.

The State Convention, which met in Austin on May 23, however, did not reflect agreement on Rayburn. Since the Texas Regulars controlled the Party organization through the influence of Governor Coke Stevenson and others of his persuasion, the Roosevelt sympathizers moved from the Senate chamber into the House of Representatives, where they held a rump convention. They elected Sam Rayburn and Senator Tom Connally delegates-at-large, but the Regulars paid no tribute to the Speaker.

Earlier in 1944, Rayburn was nationally prominent as Texas' favorite son for the Vice-Presidency and had the commitments from numerous other states at the national convention, but not from Texas, because there were these two warring delegations. The Texas Regulars, though now disbanded as such, later argued that they were not opposed to Sam Rayburn and really preferred him to Harry Truman, but they did not want Wallace and disliked Roosevelt. According to Congressman Ed Gossett, as reported by the Wichita Falls *Daily Times*, the machinations of the delegation, dominated by the Texas Regular element, prevented action on Rayburn's name when it was presented, after Wallace had been eliminated. Some thought Truman was too close to Roosevelt, and even suggested Marvin Jones, but took no action on him either. The truth of the matter about Rayburn was that some in this delegation had already committed themselves to the program planned for his liquidation in the Fourth District. He had become too big and powerful, they thought.

Their bitterness, hatred, and negativism caused them to put on a demonstration, since affirmed as having brought discredit to the whole State and destroyed the best opportunity Texas perhaps will ever have to put a man in the White House. Rayburn's friends years later maintained that a mere handful of sentimental, impressionable, hate-mongering, self-righteous, self-appointed custodians of Americanism entered into a brief orgy of political spasms to commit an unforgivable sin against those people who had proudly worked for the welfare of the State. It was not a value judgment, and it is just such behavior as this, they added, which makes sane and sober folk take a dim view of Texas politics, come convention time. The ironical thing about this so-called emotional debauchery is that there are few survivors of the plot. No single person in 1962 will admit any blame. It appears as an instance of collective blundering.

Sam Rayburn survived the humiliation and intrigue but the Texas Regulars as a party died. Perhaps, as someone has suggested, the words of Oliver Goldsmith best serve to commemorate the occasion and reflect the appropriate epitaph for the Regulars:

> The man recovered of the bite;
> The dog it was that died.

The fruits of the delegation's labors are known, but a bare outline of the events is pertinent. Texas, a stronghold of both pro- and anti-New Deal sentiment, sent two delegations to Chicago. Getting moral support from several Southern states, the Regulars braced themselves for trouble.

On July 17, the delegates from the Texas Regular movement, who had held their separate convention, were seated. Colonel Myron G. Blalock, Democratic National Committeeman, had been told that the pro-Roosevelt delegation from Texas would be seated, then National Chairman Frank Walker and his successor-to-be, Robert E. Hannegan, ruled in favor of the official but anti-Roosevelt group. When Blalock tried to carry out their wishes he was left stranded, and after the roll call both delegations were seated in a peculiar compromise that split the State's convention vote and made no one happy. Blalock, so the story goes, then sent a note to both Walker and Hannegan with the suggestion "to please go to hell." The pro-Roosevelt delegation took seats immediately behind the conservatives, some of whom walked out.

After the overwhelming victory of Roosevelt, the two factions in Texas decided to fight over the Vice-Presidency. Briefly, Wallace appeared to have a chance at the renomination. Allen Duckworth of the Dallas *News* reported that Ed Pauley asked Blalock, "Can't you do something with your Texas delegation?

"Look here, Ed," Blalock burst forth, "don't make me madder. It's Walker's and Hannegan's delegation—not mine."

Pauley then suggested: "Try to get Texas to pass on the first ballot. If Wallace isn't nominated on the first ballot, we can beat him."

Blalock and Tom Miller, of the liberal delegation, reached an understanding, and Texas passed on the first ballot, probably having a part in preventing the nomination of Wallace.

Had the Texas delegation advanced the name of Rayburn, some believe he would have been selected by the convention. The Texans, however, finally agreed on Truman, though he was not especially acceptable at the time. Harry Truman saw the direction that the Vice-Presidential race was taking, so he promptly called Sam Rayburn at his home in Bonham to confirm a rumor that Rayburn was not available. It was a case of two men each supporting the other. Before the conversation was terminated Rayburn's will prevailed, and he pledged his support to Truman.

Long after the convention the conflict between the two factions continued. It became a legal struggle over the electors. This phase of the Regular—New Deal battle perhaps attracted more attention back in Texas than did the Roosevelt-Dewey campaign itself.

For years to come Mr. Sam's closest friends in the Fourth will talk about this Chicago meeting and the coincidence of the July primary falling on the fourth day of the National Convention, when the Vice-President is usually nominated. Many Texans and California Democrats had tried to get the date changed because it was in conflict with their Party primaries. The California primary was set for July 20 and the Texas primary for July 22. Governor Coke Stevenson rather early in the year foresaw the possibility that he might not be able to attend the convention if he found it necessary to make a race for renomination. National Democratic Chairman, Hannegan had already expressed the thought that perhaps something could be done about the matter. Some believe Mr. Sam might have won after all if he had been in Chicago to look after his interests; but he had too many problems in the Fourth District because he was fighting for survival. Some at the time were disappointed over Roosevelt's proposing Harry S Truman or Supreme Court Justice William O. Douglas, when Wallace proved unacceptable. The truth was that the President thought he needed Rayburn more as Speaker, for Rayburn could get his legislation through Congress. Roosevelt had no use for Rayburn as a mere understudy in the Senate.

A month before the Chicago Convention, when Rayburn returned to Bonham after the recess of Congress, he found that his major opponent, State Senator G. C. Morris of Greenville, had already stumped the District and had shaken hands with nearly thirty thousand people. His campaign literature had been rather thoroughly distributed throughout the District. George Balch, who had received 10,265 votes in 1942, was also well advanced in his campaign.

Morris, however, was the man Rayburn had to beat, for he had traveled hundreds of miles up and down the highways, on to the side roads, denouncing the incumbent. He had told the people that Mr. Rayburn was a "yes-man" for the Administration; that he had ceased to be a representative of the Fourth, being a Washingtonian instead of a Bonhamite; that he and his colleagues had allowed a vicious bureaucracy to arise even before the war started, and that the war was only an excuse for entrenching and expanding this bureaucracy. There had been a note of alarm in the correspondence as early as April and the atmosphere was one of pessimism by the time Mr. Sam reached home. Morris' pledges to return the Government to the people, to put an end to so-called emergency controls, and to call a halt to Congressional submission on the home-front matters to White House directives, were well received by a populace harassed by wartime restrictions.

Balch also made a strong anti-Rayburn campaign in which he assailed the incumbent for his support of creeping socialism.

He carried a large sign throughout the seven counties reading: "No Seventeenth Term."

Perhaps the most damaging blow to Rayburn was struck through the whispering campaign. The FEPC (Fair Employment Practices Committee) was voted a half-million-dollar appropriation, and he was blamed for not speaking out and blocking it. There was considerable talk about his having deserted the Southern people; they thought he could have spoken for his section and asked that the South be permitted to deal with this complex social problem themselves.

Radio commentators over NBC and CBS made rather suggestive references to certain opposition to the Speaker, their headquarters in Wall Street and two of Texas' great metropolitan centers. Afterward, when all the estimates were in, Mr. Sam said, "I have it from reliable sources that upwards of $200,000 was spent to beat me."

The closeness of the vote reflected the seriousness of the opposition and Rayburn's lack of interest in the Vice-Presidency: Rayburn 22,052, Morris 16,705, Balch 816.

October 12, 1944, found Mr. Sam in Abilene, speaking for the Democratic ticket.

On October 19, he was in Wichita Falls, where he received the kind of publicity which his friends considered long overdue. *The Record* saluted him thus:

> "It has been quite some time, too long in fact, since Sam Rayburn has been in Wichita Falls. We remark on this because this city and its important industry, the oil-producing business, owes to Speaker Rayburn a life-long debt of gratitude. . . . his efforts in behalf of the oil industry are not restricted alone to Wichita Falls and North Texas. But occupying the powerful position which he does, Mr. Rayburn has been effective in retaining for the industry something vital to its welfare—the twenty-seven and one-half per cent depletion rule."

The effect of this rule allowed producers tax deductions for the exhaustion of capital—the oil man's reserves. The depletion allowance, Rayburn believed, made it possible for the independents to remain in business, for without it they would have been taken over by a few. Hence the wealth would not be properly distributed.

In a conversation about the problem he stated: "It looks like the majors are taking over all of the independents and that pretty soon they will have everything they want in their laps. They are paying ridiculous prices for oil wells, but they are not drilling new ones."

He had a great deal more to say on this subject, however, in the later campaigns. For some ten years he had been in close touch about this problem with several Houston oil men whose judgment he respected.

When the results of the November 7 election were all in, Mr. Sam temporarily ceased to feel the pain from the summer upheavals. There was a record-breaking vote, with the absentee soldier ballots. The President was given a vote of confidence—25,610,946 to 22,018,177. The Electoral College cast 432 for Roosevelt and 99 for Dewey. The Party gained 21 seats in the House and held a 57 to 38 control over Senate.

After a victory of such magnitude one would expect the Speaker to have a long vacation in some quiet resort, but not Mr. Sam. A few days with his brothers and sisters, some quiet hours in his rural hideaway and he was ready to return to Washington. Leaving his Bonham home, he drove to Denison in his tan Pontiac. As his brother double-parked at the station, where he was to catch the Katy's *Bluebonnet,* some of the storekeepers and pedestrians came out to shake hands or to wave goodby. When he boarded the train, they chimed out: "Good luck, Mr. Sam."

Back in Washington, the press wanted to know how he felt. They could see he was in good health. Talking about physical fitness in general, he referred to the fact that he had never ceased to marvel at the President's inexhaustible stamina and recuperative powers:

"He has that rare capacity of being able to carry the most crushing burdens of this nation's history and go to bed without a worry on his mind. I have seen him completely exhausted at the end of a busy week. He just goes off for some peace, puts the worries out of his mind, and comes back looking as fit and healthy as when he first took office. He is undoubtedly the most remarkable specimen of manhood who ever sat in the White House."

Rayburn affirmed that he had adopted some of the same tactics:

"After ten years, I have learned to go to bed and go to sleep without worrying; I figure that if I can't do my job standing up, there's no sense in stretching out and worrying about it all night."

Friends knew where to locate Mr. Sam if he was not seated in his chair on the rostrum of the House. They would go to the "back office" where he conducted most of the private business, and if he was not there he would be in the more pretentious "front office" where he liked to look after official affairs. In whichever office he was to be found, he liked to take off his spectacles, lean back, smoke a cigarette, and talk quite frankly and cogently about legislation. People continued to be surprised at his directness and simplicity, but his grasp and authoritative manner left no doubt about his qualifications. Mr. Sam was regarded as one of the top men in Washington. Anyone, from porter to the man in the White House, agreed that his reputation was secure.

Cecil B. Dickson tells about the breakfast he had with Speaker Sam on December 15, when he was trying to get a story about what might happen in the Seventy-ninth Congress. He went to the Speaker's bachelor apartment at the Anchorage on Connecticut and Que, where he had lived since 1927. Another purpose of the breakfast was to introduce Bob Dillon, editorial writer from Frank Garrett's Binghamton Press, to the Speaker. Dillon, however, was unable to make it because of a New York engagement. But Mr. Sam went on and ordered two breakfasts—orange juice, two poached eggs, bacon, toast, and coffee—from Pierre's restaurant across the street. Mr. Sam's apartment was kitchenless. Andre, the houseman who was a native of Switzerland, served the meal on a bridge table.

Dickson said he had a very informative and interesting conversation about the approaching session, jotting down such notes as the following as the Speaker was talking:

"It looks like that 'cradle to the grave' Social Security program is coming. It's coming sooner or later. I'm convinced that for the health of the nation we need more medical attention for our people. I read a statement that came from Selective Service that rejections of country boys from the services were greater than from the cities and towns. It couldn't apply to Texas, but those figures indicate that in the rural sections, where our birth rate should be larger in proportion to those of cities, they do not have enough medical attention.

"Our children should come from the great middle class. So many people of this class limit their number of children according to their income, while in crowded sections of cities you see nine or ten children living in back rooms of stores and eating things their parents can't sell.

"In many towns and villages throughout the country, there are no doctors. Many people in them can't afford to get sick because they can't pay the doctor in the next town a dollar a mile to come see them. There are counties of several thousands of persons with a single hospital of only forty beds.

"I'm not so strong for this socialized medicine, but some improvement in medical aid must be made. There is one thing that must be revived and I'm going to talk to the President about it. Once he suggested, as a starter, Congress appropriate $150,000,000 to be matched by local governments for construction of hospitals in areas that need them. I'm going to suggest that he revive this proposal."

Dickson, before leaving the apartment, had a good look at a twenty-five-pound roasted turkey which was to be served at a buffet dinner. This was a gift from the Georgetown restaurant owner, Jack Martin.

From time to time Rayburn would serve his friends in the apartment, having most of the food brought in from nearby restaurants. He liked to eat at Martin's, a place on Wisconsin Avenue where his favorite booth was one near the kitchen door because here he thought he would get better service.

Since it was the Christmas season, Dickson reported that there were gifts of all kinds, such as grapefruit, nuts, dates, sandwich spreads, cans of chili and tamales. Rayburn instructed George, his chauffeur, to distribute the Christmas foods to some of his less fortunate friends whom he named.

Rayburn and Dickson then rode to the Capitol in the old limousine which belonged to the late William B. Bankhead. Mr. Sam gave every evidence that his thoughts were turned toward Bonham and the holidays.

☆ XVI ☆

New Deal to Fair Deal

WITH the opening of the Seventy-ninth Congress (January 3, 1945–December 21; January 14, 1946–August 2), and his election to a fourth term as Speaker, Mr. Sam renewed his pledge "to preserve, protect, and defend the rights, the privileges, and the honor and the power of the House of Representatives." He also reaffirmed his affections:

> "I love this life. It has been my life for nearly thirty-two years. Next to home and family and friends, it is my love. If any action of mine at any time should lower the standards of those who have served her [the House] or reflect in any fashion upon this great institution, I would to my dying day hang my head in shame."

As he looked toward the cessation of hostilities and a world organization that would prevent the recurrence of another such holocaust, he drifted into a somewhat reminiscent mood. He warned of indifference and reminded his colleagues of a former President's dream twenty-five years earlier which could have spared civilization this present tragedy if it had been heeded:

> "In my opinion, Woodrow Wilson had a dream of world cooperation, world concord, and world peace, unsurpassed by any man who has walked this earth since the lowly Galilean walked the shores twenty centuries ago preaching peace on earth, good will to men."

Going into a fourth term as Speaker, he was mentioned as a man who was destined to break many records for years of service. Only four others in the history of the country had been elected four times to his office.

There is the frequent complaint that positions of influence in Congress are selected on the basis of seniority, without regard for merit and ability. The filling of committee chairmanships does depend a great deal upon length of service, but Mr. Rayburn considered experience an indispensable qualification in Congress. He affirmed repeatedly in defense of the policies on Capitol Hill that a brilliant man without knowledge of "the ropes," so to speak, could be very ineffective, and that devising a yardstick to measure abstract qualities that could be administered, without prejudice, was no little task. In measuring a man's worth, he believed the ability to maintain the confidence of the people back home year after year was a point which should not be overlooked.

As far as the Speaker's position is concerned, the choice is not necessarily the senior member of the majority Party. The post usually goes to a man who has served as Party leader. This assignment presupposes that the individual is the best qualified and his selection as Speaker is merely a symbol of strength and ability to hold the Party together. Once a person achieves this exalted position, his influence and power increase rapidly with each session of Congress.

There are two considerations—the man and the job. The only authority greater than a person like Mr. Sam is the Speakership itself. A recognition of this duality is essential to a proper evaluation. He becomes, in a sense, a captive servant, subject first of all to the needs of America, and secondly to the will of a given political party. Only the statesmen Speakers have recognized this twofold nature of the self and have achieved a harmony of the two. Mr. Sam was one of those rare individuals who had the capacity to live at peace with his responsibility. This process of fusion had begun in him before his promotion. When he reached an identity with his Party to become "Mr. Democrat," he was already moving in the direction of a mystical union with the symbolism of the Speakership.

In such a role he was motivated to think, not as Mr. Rayburn, but as Mr. Speaker who listened to the cosmic soul of America. Not embittered by his rejection at Chicago in 1944, he looked with optimism toward the future. For example, he spoke not as an unreconstructed rebel but with the pride of the great new South, "the South of industrial expansion, of diversified agriculture, of flowering resources, of booming cities and teeming harbors, of modern airports and green golf courses."

This South was in search of a new destiny as an integral and spiritual part of America. During the past two decades the nation had been in the process of discovering the new South, and, as he liked to believe, the South was discovering itself. Millions of new capital had set in motion the wheels of industry. As he beheld the extension of the vast mineral frontiers; the expansion of railroad lines, air-transport routes, waterways, hard-surfaced highways; the development of water power to electrify homes and turn the wheels of industry, he visioned a new wealth, a new health, and a more progressive section. The tangible evidence of progress made him feel keenly his own role in the shaping of a country without sectional barriers.

On Friday evening, January 19, 1945, Mr. Sam staged his first large party in Washington in his thirty-three years. The gala affair was held from 5:30 to 7:30 P.M. in the Carleton Hotel for several hundred notables, honoring the Presidential electors from Texas, Miss Lou, and other Texans who had come to attend the inaugural ceremony the following day. For the first time the name of Miss Lou appeared in conjunction with her brother's. She was soon to play a prominent role in Washington circles as the Speaker's hostess. In the receiving line, besides the Speaker and his sister, were Myron Blalock (the National Committeeman from Texas), Mrs. Blalock, Mrs. Oscar Lowry of Dallas and Mrs. Robert Bartley of Washington (two nieces of the Speaker), Mrs. H. H. Weinert (National Committeewoman), Harry Seay (State Chairman), William Kittrell (Secretary of the State Committee). The guests included the President, Vice-President, Henry Wallace, Jesse Jones (Secretary of Commerce), Will Clayton (new Assistant Secretary of State), and their wives and nearly every notable in the capital. Miss Alla Clary, who had been Mr. Rayburn's secretary since October 1, 1919, was a popular figure because she was probably the only person besides Rayburn who knew everyone at the Party. "The Speaker," she said, "knows everybody; that's why everybody is here."

At the meeting of the National Press Club on January 27, Rayburn administered the presidential oath to Edward Jamieson, member of the Washington Bureau of the *Star-Telegram*. Comedian Jack Benny was the master of ceremonies. Accompanied by Vice-President Truman on the piano, he played his famous violin, which, jested Bascom Timmons, "murdered" his favorite songs—"Love in Bloom" and "The Flight of the Bumblebee." After being introduced by Jesse Jones, publisher of the Houston *Chronicle,* Sam Rayburn made a plea for a world free press. He considered freedom of information on a global basis essential to freedom at home and the establishment of a lasting peace and an ordered world.

Members of his staff, like Miss Alla Clary and others who had been around the office for some time, would verify that Mr. Sam derived a great deal of pleasure and benefit from the correspondence with his family. His nieces and nephews gave him great delight, and their letters could very quickly make him homesick. The postscript on Morris Lightfoot's February 6, 1945, communication was just what he needed to stir up thoughts of home: "Sure hope you get to come home soon." Another postscript reflects the Speaker's previous admonitions to his young relatives about being studious and careful with their writing: "I made three A's and two B's this six weeks, but I still can't spell. Also please pardon the pencil." "Uncle Sam's" reply included an expression of his pride in Morris and the promise that he would send him an autographed gavel used on an important occasion.

There were other letters at this time which turned his mind toward Bonham, and some of the people involved were very often in the "know" about such things as the time for Congressional adjournments and recesses. Sometimes the workers on Mr. Sam's ranch even knew of these dates before the congressmen themselves or the press. Albert Huff, a seasonal hand on the Ivanhoe ranch was told on March 22, 1945, to prepare for his home-coming:

> Confidentially . . . we will probably have a little recess around Easter and I calculate now to reach Texas about March 31 and spend a few days at which time we can look over and separate some cattle and get some back in the big pasture. Another very important thing, I would like to have a good many minnows where we could get our hands on them to do a little fishing two or three afternoons.

The reference to fishing is no surprise, for as the Speaker grew older he became a more and more dedicated angler.

Following the Easter recess there were several events which brought Vice-President Truman and the Speaker together for serious conversation. In all of Washington there were few friendships as deep and as genuine as the one between these two.

"We were great friends" said Rayburn "for ten or eleven years before he became President. He was so much in love with his job as Senator from Missouri that he hated to give it up for the Vice-Presidency. And after he was elected he dreaded the responsibility that would be his if anything should happen to the President. Truman once told me about a dream, rather a nightmare, he had during the 1944 campaign. He said he awoke in a cold sweat, for he had dreamed that the President had died and he was called into service."

From time to time there were rumors floating about the Capitol concerning the health of Roosevelt. Once on February 20, 1945, the word was circulated that the President had expired, but it was Major General Edwin M. Watson, the appointment secretary, who had died. Then in his March 1 speech before the two Houses of Congress the President was compelled to sit in his wheelchair while he spoke. Afterward Roosevelt announced that he was planning a trip to Warm Springs for a rest. His departure was set for March 30. It was during these weeks that Rayburn and Truman made comments about how weary the President looked after the Yalta experience.

The Speaker reported that he had been hearing so much talk about Roosevelt's failing health that he had a premonition of tragedy in the White House. It was a day or two, he said, before the events were unfolded. At a dinner with friends, Rayburn remarked: "This country is in for a great tragedy, and I feel it's coming very soon. I don't think the President will be with us much longer." Naturally everyone was stunned and waited for Rayburn to continue. "Roosevelt's not a well man."

Mr. Sam then went into a deep, reflective silence and stared across the room, away from the people at the table. Then he finally said, "I think I'll have a talk with Harry tomorrow. He's got to be prepared to carry a tremendous burden. He's got to get himself ready for this."

It was the next afternoon at 3:00 P.M. that Rayburn telephoned over to Truman's office and asked if he could see him that afternoon when the Senate recessed. The following is Rayburn's account, as recalled in 1960:

"On April 12 I phoned him. I said, 'Harry, why don't we have a little meeting?' Well, there were three or four or five fellows in the office. Lew Deschler, the parliamentarian of the

House was there, and I think Bill White of the New York *Times* was there, and one or two more. And he [Truman] says, 'All right, I'll come over.' And I went to the office which they used to call the Bureau of Education. It isn't like that now, but a great many people have been educated down there.

"I have had meetings of the whole committees. I mean the Democratic end. They had problems that they wanted to discuss with me and they wanted me to make a decision on what I thought should be done, or we would just have a general discussion and plan a program.

"And I went down there and in just a few minutes, why the telephone rang, and they said, 'Is the Vice-President there?' And they said, 'Tell him to call the White House, Mr. Early at the White House, as quickly as possible.'

"Well, Truman came in, and I said, 'Harry, they said for you to call the White House.'

"Well, he said he didn't know what it was about. Roosevelt was at Warm Springs. He thought he might have come back suddenly and wanted to see him, or something like that.

"And he picked up the telephone and he said, 'This is the VP, and Mr. Early wants to talk to me.' And he [Early] talked. He [Truman] is kind of a pale fellow anyhow and he got a little paler, and he hung up the telephone, and he said, 'Steve Early has asked me to come to the White House as quickly as possible and as quietly as possible.'

"And he left. I think he went out and caught a taxi and went to the White House, as well as I remember. [Mr. Truman states that Tom Harty, his chauffeur, drove him to the Pennsylvania Avenue entrance without the Secret Service guard, whom they had eluded. The time was 5:25 P.M.]

"In a few minutes we got a flash that the President was dead. And then in a little while we had a call to come down to the White House, which I knew was to see Truman sworn in."

William S. White picks up the story at this point and describes Rayburn as he sat there briefly before going to the White House.

> "His heavy and very immobile face was still in the shadows and the only movements upon it were the small and barely visible traces of tears. He swept them away roughly. For a long time no one said anything at all. Then Mr. Rayburn hunched his shoulders and, looking out unseeingly into the dusk, he spoke slowly in short, hard phrases as though talking to himself

> . . . an oath . . . that Sam Rayburn—Southern Democrat and all—had followed Franklin Roosevelt in life, and that Sam Rayburn would follow Franklin Roosevelt in death. . . ."[1]

When Mr. Sam had regained his composure he called George, his chauffeur, and drove to the White House. His story continues:

"Well, all the Cabinet were there, and of course, they were bubbling and sad and some of them were in tears about Roosevelt's passing away. But Truman was a very much composed man when we got there. I have a picture somewhere with all the people who were there from Congress.

"Truman walked over to us and I said, 'Mr. President-to-be, why we're gonna stand by you.'

"And Truman said when he went into the White House, Mrs. Roosevelt walked up and put both hands on his shoulders and said, 'The President is dead.'

"And he said, 'Well, what can we do for you?'

"She said, 'You can't do anything for us; what can we do for you?' knowing the load that was on him.

"But it took them an hour to find the Chief Justice, Harlan Stone at that time. And Mrs. Truman and Margaret were out of pocket. It took quite a while to find them. So they finally came and he was sworn in."

(Truman does not report these complications, affirming that he talked to Stone and he was present within twenty minutes. He also telephoned Mrs. Truman and Margaret, but they did not arrive for an hour since they went to see Mrs. Roosevelt first.)

During the one-minute ceremony Speaker Rayburn and several members of Congress stood behind Chief Justice Stone facing the President-to-be.

So Franklin Delano Roosevelt passed quietly into history at 4:35 P.M. (EST) April 12, 1945, at Warm Springs, Georgia. Two hours and thirty-four minutes later, at 7:09 P.M., the nation had a new President.

Mr. Rayburn remembered that Truman's first official act, right there on the spot, was to tell Secretary of State Edward R. Stettinius to go ahead with the plans that were in progress for the San Francisco Conference. The Speaker also recalled Truman's saying that he would carry on as he thought the President would have done. At an emergency meeting Truman asked the President's Cabinet to remain in service; he met the following day with the military leaders and immediately pledged to the nation a prosecution of the war "with all the vigor we possess, to a successful conclusion."

The Speaker reported that President Truman then came up to the Capitol to see certain Congressional leaders in Les Biffle's office, where he arranged for a joint meeting of Congress on April 16. Afterward Rayburn said the President had lunch with him and other Congressional leaders.

During the quiet hours when men in public life were paying their respects to their fallen warrior, Mr. Sam sat down at a typewriter in an alcove near his main office and tried to type out with one finger his feelings of the moment. A friend took his place at the machine and typed the following remarks as Sam Rayburn dictated:

> A towering figure in world affairs has passed. President Roosevelt lived in a time when big things were happening. He took a leading part in them and in a big way. He did grand things grandly. Throughout the length and breadth of the earth today good people who love and cherish freedom feel that they have lost a great advocate and a great friend. They felt that he was their friend and helper. He was truly one of the outstanding figures of all time. Under President Truman we will move forward in trying to carry out Roosevelt's policies and the achievement of his hopes and ambitions for a better and safer world.
>
> We know not how to interpret God in the way He performs. The world has lost one of the great men of all time. President Roosevelt's passing will shock and sadden good people everywhere. The American Nation has been well led in every crisis. In Harry Truman we have a leader in whom I have complete confidence.
>
> The deep personal sense of loss that everyone of us feels throughout our nation is the surest evidence of the eternal greatness of Franklin Roosevelt. He was our close friend even more than he was our great leader. We each are better and stronger because of him. We are better and stronger that we are able to bear the news of this casualty.
>
> Roosevelt knew people. He loved people. Therefore, he understood people. Out of this knowledge and his love and this understanding came his greatest contribution to our age: His unshakable belief in the dignity of the individual—a belief that he held in a

time when that philosophy was being blacked out in large areas of the world.

Members of Congress who were closest to Mr. Sam at the time, expressed the belief that of all those in the House who mourned the President's death, it was the Speaker's whose grief was the most penetrating. Such deep emotions were the result of unselfish loyalty and friendship to a man who was a symbol of Party and country, to which he had so completely dedicated himself.

President Truman had expressed his humility and feeling of inadequacy at having to take hold of the job without any forewarning; hence he sought the immediate counsel of men like Sam Rayburn. Mr. Sam, three days after Truman took over, went to the White House. In an interview with Martin Agronsky, Mr. Sam reported this first visit. Rayburn had been worrying about the new President.

"I wanted to help the fellow," stated Mr. Sam. "So I went down there and said to him: 'You don't have anything in the world that I want . . . . I have come down here to talk about you. I have been watching this White House for many years. I know some of the hazards here and I want to tell you what your biggest hazard is in this White House. You have a lot of people around you here. Some of them are going to be men of outstanding ability and character, and some of them are not going to have too much ability. That is natural when you have a big group around you. And some of them are not going to be able to stand up and battle it out with men of more ability than they've got, and they are going to try to do to you what they have tried to do to every President since I have been here. They are going to try to build a fence around you and in building that fence around you they will be keeping the very people away from seeing you that you should see. That is my first bit of advice.' "

Mr. Sam then went on to add: " 'The next one is the special interest fellow and the sycophant. If some old boy from Missouri comes out here, he transacts his business and he has a ticket on that 6:30 B & O going back to Missouri, and he telephones down here and says he wants to pay his respects to the President. They will say, "Why you can't see him for two or three days." He gets on the train and goes on back. But the special interest fellow will come like the king of old. He would stand in the snow a week because the king had to see the Pope before he could navigate, and I said that fellow will stay around here for a month and will come in here sliding on his vest and, sycophantic, will say that you are the greatest man that ever lived in order to make time with you; and you know and I know that it just ain't so.' "

President Truman promptly stated, "Well, I know I am not." [2]

As the Speaker was leaving, he said: "Mr. President, I will want to see you about two or three little things once in a while. And I can't afford to walk through those newspapermen out there and say we didn't talk about anything."

Truman replied, "Just any afternoon after five o'clock, come in the East entrance of the White House, over by the Treasury, and walk through there and come up to my study. I'll be in there."

April 16 was a cloudless day. The President stepped out of the elevator and went directly to Speaker Rayburn's big office. While in the Speaker's office Truman conferred for thirty minutes with Rayburn, President pro tempore McKellar of the Senate, and others invited for the special ceremony. At 1:00 P.M. the delegation escorted the new President to the House floor and up to the rostrum. In the excitement Truman forgot the protocol. The standing ovation and newness of the situation caused him to begin to speak before he was introduced. But Rayburn quickly whispered to his friend and said, "Just a moment—let me present you, Harry, will you." Truman backed up; Speaker Rayburn, as if nothing unusual had happened, announced: "The President of the United States." This was the simple formula which the Speaker used to introduce all dignitaries.

Three days later, Speaker Rayburn, Senator McKellar, Senate Majority Leader Barkley, and House Majority Leader McCormack—the Big Four of the Legislature—were called to the White House to receive the latest information relative to the war and diplomatic problems. They also discussed the revisions in the Federal budget that would be necessary when the European war was over.

As Sam Rayburn on April 20 sat at the long table in his private "room" across from the House Café in the Capitol Building, he talked about all the sound and fury out at the San Francisco Conference where the blueprint for world peace was being drawn. He spoke in the idiom of a Bois d' arc creek bottom farmer as he expressed faith in the outcome. "We beat up a lot of underbrush but we usually find the big tree."

Mr. Rayburn had been over this ground before. He remembered how Woodrow Wilson's dream of the League of Nations was crumpled because the Chairman of the Foreign Relations Committee in the Senate was not above partisan politics. However, he had done considerable thinking during the intervening years about the problems of peace, and the adjustments a nation and people themselves have to make in a cooperative venture of such magnitude. He somehow doubted that the American people were emotionally ready after the first war, because there was too much isolationism and aloofness from the world scene. Much as he hated to admit it, he believed there had been a lack of maturity and awareness which he thought could come only from sacrifice. In 1945, though, he thought the nation was ready to take over the position of world leadership which it had rejected after World War I. While he was in Bonham during the Easter recess he had observed the thinking of his constituents.

"My people are ready. I've been home and talked with them. They want peace. As I said in a press statement some days ago, they want a tough peace." He believed the people in his District were ready to pay whatever was the price of peace. Rayburn was glad that the peace talk had begun before the shooting stopped so that partisan politics would be less likely to enter in. "While I wasn't in an isolationist territory," he affirmed, he believed that Americans generally did not want "their son's children to go through the same Golgotha that they themselves experienced in 1917–18 and that their sons have experienced in this second world war."

The war in Europe came to an end on May 8, 1945. Mr. Sam promptly sent the following telegram to the Fourth District:

> This is the day we have fought for. To every man and woman in the armed services we owe our grateful thanks. To every man, woman, and child in civilian life, who has contributed one mite, we owe thanks. Instead of this being a day of celebration alone it should also be one of dedication and consecration to bring about victory over Japan and peace in that quarter of the world. We must not forget the thousands of our blood who are in the Pacific and the Far East. We must sustain them until victory is won there and they can be brought back home.

To the nation he released a similar statement which began in these terms:

"With all Americans and good people everywhere, I rejoice

in the signal victory achieved by the American and other Allied armies over the hordes of Hitler. It is my fervent wish that this may shorten the war all over the world."

Although the ratification of the United Nations World Charter was the sole responsibility of the Senate, the Speaker voiced his support of the President's endorsement of the plan:

"The other nations of the world would be convinced that President Truman has the forceful backing of Congress and the American people if he should be able to go to the Big Three Conference [Potsdam, July, 1945] armed with Senate ratification of the World Charter, the Bretton Woods program enacted into law, and the Reciprocal Trade Agreements Extension bill approved with authority to reduce tariffs."

In a letter to Speaker Rayburn, dated June 4, President Truman tried to clarify the policy on Lend-Lease. This communication necessitated one of the Speaker's visits to the White House. The two men spoke the same language, seeing eye to eye on the problem. Congress had consistently put a time limit on every Lend-Lease appropriation instead of authorizing it for the duration of hostilities. Hence each time the bills came up the hearings and debates all had to be repeated. Also, there was always some amendment that changed the administration of the program. Rayburn told the President that he had some fellows in the House who wanted publicity back home so desperately that they were willing to jeopardize the national welfare to secure it. He also pointed out that the home folks sometimes did not understand the issues sufficiently well to know what their congressmen were trying to do. The compatibility of the two minds, plus their combined knowledge of the congressmen in the two Houses, was partly instrumental in their achieving a type of Lend-Lease which had some practical value. However, the two men never got the kind of program they really wanted.

It was conferences like these which convinced Truman of the Speaker's potential worth to the nation. White House confidence in Rayburn was clearly revealed in the Chief Executive's proposal to Congress on June 19 that the line of succession to the Presidency be changed. Under the existing procedure Mr. Truman would be replaced by the Secretary of State, Edward R. Stettinius, Jr., should he be unable to complete his term. Truman explained that a member of the Cabinet is appointed by the President, whereas, the Speaker would be a congressman elected by a certain group of people. The fact that he held the Speakership would indicate that he had the sanction of a broad majority of the people in our democracy.

Truman's ideas, voiced in a special message to both Houses of Congress, were prompted by the realization that his duties would compel him to make several long and perhaps risky journeys across the ocean, not to mention the flights within the country. Also, there would be no elected Vice-President for nearly four years.

The bill to carry out the Presidential succession proposals of President Truman was introduced in the House on June 24 by Hatton W. Sumners of Dallas for the House Judiciary Committee, of which he was the Chairman. The Sumners bill provided that, if by reason of death, resignation, removal from office, inability to qualify, there be neither President nor Vice-President, the Speaker should, upon his resignation as Speaker and as a representative in Congress act as President until the disability be removed or a President elected. The next in line would be the President pro tempore of the Senate, then the Secretary of State, in the order prescribed by the existing law. The bill passed the House July 5 with a noisy voice vote.

The last phase of the war in the Pacific came to a rather speedy conclusion following two catastrophic occurrences on the Japanese mainland. When Japan disregarded the July 26 warning, which called for unconditional surrender or annihilation, an atomic bomb was dropped on Hiroshima (August 5) and another on Nagasaki (August 8) with devastating results to military installations, industry, and human life. The signing of the articles of surrender on September 1 preceded VJ Day.

Mr. Sam had an interesting story to tell about the atomic bomb—one that illustrates the confidence which the military and Congress had in the Speaker. However, not until the following January did Rayburn divulge to any of his constituents the circumstances leading up to the creation of the bomb.

Rayburn said he had sat on this top war secret for fifteen months before the bomb was dropped. "I received a call from Secretary of War Henry L. Stimson. He told me that he, General George C. Marshall, and Dr. Vannevar Bush wanted to come to my office on a vital matter." Rayburn called in the Congressional leaders and the Chairman of the Appropriation Committee.

"They told me they had to have quite a bit of money, [$800,000,000] that somebody on the Hill has got to know what we're doing and we can't go before a committee with it."

Rayburn told the gentlemen he was aware that the Army was spreading a great deal of money in eastern Tennessee at Oak Ridge and elsewhere, but he had no particulars on the projects. Rayburn reported that at a later date when additional money was needed he was invited to go take a look, but he declined because he felt rather sure he would see only some buckets, barrels, jars, and rubber hose, and if someone tried to explain how all this paraphernalia was being used he wouldn't understand anyway. "I didn't want to know," the Speaker said, "because I knew if I didn't know a secret, I couldn't let one leak out."

The Speaker received Committee and then House approval with only the minimum discussion. He told them in confidence that it would mean saving the lives of thousands of American soldiers and would shorten the war. He explained that this was something of great secrecy which he was not prepared to discuss, that Congress would simply have to take the whole thing on faith. He asked for immediate action. This was perhaps one of the biggest blank checks Congress ever approved.

During the month of August, 1945, Mr. Sam had an opportunity to spend some time at his home in Bonham. However, there was little escape from his job, for the automobiles of constituents lined his driveway. Farmers, returning veterans, friends, politicians, and businessmen came to seek help and advice, or hear his plans for reconversion legislation. The principal topic was the proposal to have the Government guarantee full employment. "It's a pretty tough deal to guarantee full employment for everyone," he stated, "but I do not look for any depression after this war. With all the billions of dollars people have saved and are now ready to spend, they will be able to buy all that factories can make for five or ten years."

In answer to questions relative to probable legislation he predicted that social security laws would be adjusted to provide for a liberalization of unemployment compensation. This revamping would be necessary during the brief reconversion period while industry made the adjustment to a peacetime economy. Rayburn referred to laws that would be designed to insure veterans their former jobs, with fair provisions to allow promotions and seniority rights. Existing laws contained flaws that required correction. One of the big problems would be the disposition of war surplus properties, which might not bring more than ten per cent recovery for the original Government outlay. Although he believed some tax reductions were in the offing, he predicted high taxes for many years. The consolidation of bureaus in the Executive department for the sake of economy and efficiency was one thing he knew Truman would undertake immediately.

The Speaker spent more time indoors than usual during

this visit because of an unfortunate accident that confined him to his home west of Bonham, and made him more available to the public. He was forced to sit still and take care of a badly fractured arm which he rested on a padded chair. Though somewhat amusing to him after a week's convalescence, it was no laughing matter at the time.

It was the third week in August that the Speaker and Valton Young were together down on the ranch working some cattle on one of the hottest days of the year. Mr. Sam was walking through high grass herding twenty-five or thirty yearling heifers from the corral to his north pasture. He suddenly left Young and hurried around the herd to open the gate several hundred yards ahead. The County Agent states that he saw the Speaker collapse and disappear in the high weeds. The County Agent's first thought was that he had been bitten by one of the numerous copperhead snakes which plague the ranches north of Bonham. The Speaker called to his friend, who ran quickly to the scene. There Young found him sitting on the ground holding his left arm. By his side, almost hidden in the tall grass, lay some rusted bed springs that had no doubt been there unnoticed for many years.

Although the injury was a very painful one, Rayburn did not lose his composure. Lighting a cigarette with his good hand, he asked Young to drive him in to the Allen Memorial Hospital, which was fifteen miles from the ranch. When the two men reached the hospital, Dr. A. B. Kennedy and a nurse sat Mr. Sam down on a bench and went to work.

They had no sooner finished setting the arm and putting it in a cast when the local radio station let the news out. Before Rayburn had time to get home and take off his dirty shirt, the telephone rang. It was the President of the United States calling to say that he was sending his private plane to Jones Field in Bonham and that the Speaker was to be flown to the Naval hospital at Betheseda, Maryland, for an X-ray.[3] Mr. Sam protested, saying that the best doctor in the country had already set his arm. The President did not want to take any chances with the health of his most valuable friend.

A week later Mr. Sam was able to joke about the incident, but he actually regarded it as a humiliating experience to be pitched upon the ground by some bed springs. "I wish I could have been thrown by one of those good quarter horses, then I wouldn't feel so bad about this busted up elbow," he said.

During the fall months, the Speaker wrote and talked much

about such topics as Selective Service and universal military training. The drafting of the young eighteen-year-old boys, he thought, should now stop, and Selective Service was also something which he thought should be discontinued at an early date. However, very shortly the events in the Far East made him change his mind on this matter.

Related to these problems was that of demobilization. The parents, brothers, sisters, wives, sweethearts, and friends of the enlisted personnel overseas expected the men to return home immediately following VE and VJ day, and when they did not arrive as promptly as they hoped, they called on Mr. Sam to do something. As in other matters of this sort he prepared a statement which would cover the requests and inquiries. He stated the terms of Selective Service, referred to the pending ratification of treaties of peace, assured deliberate speed, told about his talk with the War and Navy Departments and the President concerning his objection to drafting eighteen-to-twenty-year-olds, outlined the point system that would be used in demobilization, referred to a bill to stimulate volunteer enlistments, and expressed his sympathy to all families concerned.

Across the bottom of one of these letters an irate constituent scribbled this note and returned it to the Speaker: "Parents are not asking for your sympathy; they want you to get action and that now. We will have our turn at the bat next summer." The Speaker understood the meaning of such irrationality, but he never let these things worry him. He knew that the world was full of all types of people. His lengthy term of office and long life proved his wearing qualities and insulation against unwarranted criticism.

He received letters about the unpopular OPA but he promptly explained that it was essential for a while longer to control prices and prevent inflation. Without price controls during the war, many people, he believed, would not have had sufficient funds to buy the bare necessities such as food and clothing, and with inflation they would soon be stripped of their purchasing power during peacetime. The business of rationing, however, he deemed no longer essential.

On the controversial Federal Employment Practices Commission, the Speaker's attitude was perhaps best reflected in the following cogent remark: "The FEPC in all likelihood will be allowed to suffer a painless death before long."

His thinking on the War Production Board was logical, hostilities having virtually ceased. Since it was rapidly releasing all materials no longer needed for the war he thought the Board should be discontinued at the earliest moment.

With respect to foreign trade, he followed the position he had stated on previous occasions: "We have got to trade with foreign countries. If we should insist upon selling them everything we produce and taking nothing from them, it would not add anything to the good neighbor policy."

In relating his remarks to the problem of importing foreign oil, he added, "I note that oil men want a reduction of the allowable."

The Speaker was pressed perseveringly for some word on taxes, but he did not appear optimistic about any drastic reductions, with the big war debt to be paid. "I do think the excess profits tax will be removed," he said, "which will afford some relief." But he predicted that the income tax for individuals and corporations would "continue high for a long time to come."

The plain-spoken Speaker had much to say about the way the Republican politicians and their followers tried to discredit the late President Roosevelt. He thought their techniques were nefarious and hypocritical because they were preparing the public for the elections of 1946 and 1948. Especially did he resent the efforts to link him with the Pearl Harbor disaster and their refusal to assume any responsibility for having resisted the preparedness program. He was caustic when he reminded the opposition Party of its resistance to Lend-Lease, fortifying the Pacific bases, and building a large navy.

The Christmas holidays brought a welcome relief from all of these irritations and controversies. He had received more than his share of critical correspondence. The atmosphere in the big white house on U. S. Highway 82 showed no signs of the bitterness of partisan politics. The streams of people who milled through his home and around the yard were a friendly sort, emanating their gratefulness appropriate at this season of the year. A large Christmas tree, which Mr. Sam and Sister Lou decorated, touched the ceiling in the large living room. The burning embers in the fireplace added to the festiveness. The telephone continued to ring, but these were calls to convey season's greetings, not to talk politics or to ask for something. Two men from Sherman dropped in to invite the Speaker to a stag party. A veteran just released from service came with his wife and young son so that the youngster could have an opportunity to sit on the Speaker's lap. This ceremony was repeated many times because of the esteem in which Mr. Sam was held. It gave the children of the Fourth, who had been so blessed, an inner strength which they could recall in later years.

But whenever there was a quiet moment from seeing guests he slipped off by himself and worked on speeches. He was to give one on January 4 to the Democratic Women of Dallas County and another on the 5th to the Dallas Clearing House Association. Hampered by a bad cold he had difficulty in getting his ideas together on such relatively recent topics as the loan to Britain, the atomic bomb, the labor problems, and the military picture.

This was to be a special holiday season, for Secretary of the Treasury Fred Vinson and his wife were due to arrive on Thursday. The Speaker was to meet the Katy at Denison. When the train pulled into the station, Mr. Sam, Miss Lou, and Tom were waiting. R. J. Morfa, Chairman of the Board of the Katy railroad, was the first to hop off the private car to escort the reception committee in to greet the honored guests. Mrs. Vinson had already spotted the three Rayburns and exclaimed to her husband, "There's Miss Lou!" When a thick fog settled over the town, the Secretary remarked to Allen Duckworth, staff correspondent of the Dallas *News,* "I've been disillusioned; Sam told me the weather here was bracing, invigorating."

The quiet of the peaceful county seat of Bonham was disturbed on the afternoon of January 3. Only those born and bred in this quiet little city can imagine the effect of a Sam Rayburn open house upon community life. When Mr. Sam announced an open house he meant that the latch string was within reach of all, and they believed him. Bonham is relatively free of snobbery and class-consciousness. His many years of practicing the ideals of a democracy had shaped an image. Some of his simple dignity had rubbed off on the people themselves.

Long before the hour of 4:00 P.M. the automobiles began piling up along Highway 82. The people, two thousand in all, started filing through the big house to shake hands with Mr. Sam and his guests. The remarkable thing about the host was his ability to remember the people's first names. The Congressman also knew their family histories and the most obscure events in their lives. He could even look into their faces and recognize the dissenters.

For two hours the receiving line stayed on duty. Secretary Vinson said he had not shaken so many hands in years, that Texans were just as hospitable as Kentuckians but came in greater numbers. The crowds lingered in the yard for some time because there were some of Rayburn's out-of-town guests milling around—Myron G. Blalock of Marshall, Grover Sellers of Austin, Jim Abercrombie of Houston, Ed Clark of Austin, Harry L. Seay of Dallas, and so forth.

Before the Rayburns and the Vinsons departed for Dallas, Mr. Sam took his friend out to his hideaway at Ivanhoe. As they stood in front of the ranch house listening to the lowing of the Herefords, the Speaker remarked, "This is the breath of life. There's nothing like standing on land like this and being able to say, 'This is my own.' "

Mr. Sam enjoyed having house guests like the Vinsons because they appreciated what they heard and saw. By this time the Rayburn home was becoming a store place for treasures—pictures, chairs, chests, tapestries—valuable for their historical significance. The Vinsons admired the treasures and listened to his accounts about them. By 1960, three-fourths of the furnishings had sufficient interest to make the remodeled homeplace a virtual museum. Probably the most frequently discussed piece of furniture was a chair which was made of thirty-four pieces. Mr. Sam liked to tell about how his father brought it from Tennessee and how he had, in his own mind, countless times taken it apart and put it back together again. He said he liked to do this as a substitute for reading, when he was trying to solve a problem. It kept his subconscious mind occupied.

The Texans who had come to Dallas to see the New Year's football classic in the Cotton Bowl had gone home. The shouting and excitement over the University's 40–27 victory over Missouri had returned to Austin. By the evening of January 3, 1946, another classic was in the making. Democrats from across the nation were arriving at the Adolphus and Baker Hotels. They were assembling, not to pick a hero, but to honor one. It was homecoming for the Democrats. The bitterness and discord of 1944 which had divided Texans had temporarily subsided. The New Deal had blended into a Fair Deal, and no other American deserved greater credit for this marriage of ideals than the gentleman who was to be feted. It was to be Mr. Sam's moment.

Officials of the Texas form of Democracy met with the State Democratic Executive Committee in a business session before the two major events planned by the Dallas women, that is, a reception and a banquet. Colonel Myron G. Blalock set the tone of the meeting with this tribute: "As long as we can go down the line this year under the leadership of men like Sam Rayburn, our Party and our future will be safe."

Chairman Harry L. Seay expressed these sentiments:

"Speaker Rayburn has done as much, and more, for Texas than any man this State ever sent to Washington. He has made a good record as Speaker. He has tied the record for length of service in that office. Let's help to elect him for another two years so that he can break all records for length of service as Speaker of the National House of Representatives."

Remarks were also made by four potential gubernatorial candidates: R. W. (Bob) Calvert of Hillsboro, Dr. Homer Price Rainey, Congressman Lyndon B. Johnson, and former Governor James V. Allred.

The resolution about Party loyalty was handled gently as if it were dynamite. An effort was made to bar bolters from every Party precinct, county and state convention, but not from primaries. The Committee, however, was able to agree on the spirit of Chairman Seay's remarks that the Committee should not attempt to support one Democratic candidate against another one, but should support a candidate whose record as a Democrat was good against one whose record was not. Mr. Sam agreed that a race between two good Democrats in a primary should be wide open, as far as the Committee was concerned, but he affirmed that he would never endorse one of those Democrats who "sat on the fence" and talked like a Republican.

Preceding the banquet, the Democratic women honored Miss Lou and Mrs. Vinson at a reception in the Baker Hotel at 4:00 P.M. Although the Speaker and Secretary stood in the receiving line to shake hands with fifteen hundred guests, the ladies were the center of attraction. At a Democratic gathering in Texas one could expect to see mink and lamb rubbing elbows with coney, for this was the Party in which sables and mail-order tweeds could find a meeting of the minds. The little people from the precincts and grass roots crowded the mezzanine to shake hands with the big wheels of their Party.

One thousand Democrats had registered for the "love feast" on January 4 at 7:00 P.M. in the grand ballroom of the Adolphus. The radio technicians stood by for the hour of 8:30 when Rayburn's voice was to be heard by the nation.

President Truman, General of the Armies and Chief of Staff Dwight D. Eisenhower, Chief of Naval Operations Chester Nimitz, and Mrs. Eleanor Roosevelt sent congratulatory messages. The President's telegram contained this statement:

> Mr. Rayburn is a statesman of whom the Lone Star State may well be proud . . . three cheers for Sam Rayburn and the State that sends him to Congress.

General Eisenhower, wrote:

> I can claim birth in his District . . . I want to pay tribute to a great Texan and a great American whose support contributed immeasurably to victory.

The engraved program booklet contained these thoughts which set the tone of the evening:

> "His ability, his integrity, his great heart and his willingness to efface self for the good of a common cause have made him loved and respected throughout Texas and the nation . . . his great prestige, his poise, his wholesome common sense, his utter fairness to all, and his unselfish patriotism during a stormy and uncertain period contributed substantially to the preservation of democratic and legislative government in America."

Secretary Vinson and Attorney-General Tom Clark placed Mr. Sam among the all-time lawmakers in Washington and the immortals in Texas history. The former said, "The true significance of his service is not in its length, but in its quality."

This was a season of peace and thanksgiving. Americans had beaten their swords into plowshares and their spears into pruning hooks. Mr. Sam came to Dallas with a head full of wisdom and a heart filled with gratitude "to every human being who contributed to their great victory." Except for one reference to the lingering Republican Pearl Harbor investigation, this was a non-partisan address: "We should with our all consecrate ourselves to the preservation and the continuation of this mighty Republic, and that for which it stands—in our own country and all humanity we should seek to serve." America should be determined to keep open the door of freedom in such a way that no man would dare to shut it. As he referred to the atomic age and its potentialities, he made a plea for a "Resurrection and the love and cooperation that come with the old time Religion." If civilization is to endure "we must be brave; we must be wise; we must be determined; yea, we must be tough if need be." Before he made his last statement, he remembered something his mother had said many times: "There must be a light in this sad and sickened world that can come only when the Spirit of God moves upon the face of the waters."

On Saturday, Secretary Vinson was the honored guest. Before the Clearing House Association Mr. Sam discussed the

British loan as vital to the United States as a whole, to farmers, laborers, and businessmen. Since the British were our relations by both blood and language, he felt that the two countries should be brought closer together. About the Russians he said:

"Some people say that we must and will fight Russia. What for? If we should win a war with Russia, what would it profit us? Nothing! What would we lose if we fought Russia and lost? Probably everything! I oppose for us the kind of government Russia has, but the kind Russia has is more its business than mine. I think I know one thing, and that is the present government of Russia is better for the common man under the leadership of Stalin than under the Czars. The Czars had only to have an impressed army and a state church—these were the two classes they heeded and served. I am utterly opposed to both."

After the luncheon the Speaker saw Fred Vinson and wife off on the train for Washington. Sunday he was back on the farm. Monday he celebrated his sixty-fourth birthday, ordinarily a day which found him in the nation's Capitol. On Tuesday, January 7, he was feted again, this time by the civic and luncheon clubs of Sherman. Five hundred responsive citizens heard the Speaker discuss some of the economic problems of reconversion. Repeating many of the ideas in his speeches of the past six months, he praised the American people for their achievements during the war. One new thought, however, was added—that there be a study of profits so that reconversion might proceed more intelligently.

On Saturday, January 11, the Speaker left by train from Denison to return to the capital, where Congress resumed its session January 14 following a long Christmas holiday recess.

Legislative matters did not occupy all of his thoughts, for there are many letters in his files about personal items interspersed with those relative to Congress. His communication with Roy Gauntz of Ivanhoe, Texas, February 7, 1946, is a good example, since it refers to a picture of Secretary Vinson, the Speaker, and Gauntz, made out on the ranch. It had been autographed by the two men and was being sent to him. Rayburn also commented on some mesquite grass he purchased to be planted east of the house. The seed were not of the "curly West Texas" variety but a "velvet grass" type. His specific instructions show that he was no amateur:

> I believe the best way to do would be to sow it broadcast and then take your disc harrow and set the knives almost straight and cut the ground just a little.

> These seeds are very small and look pretty weak and I am afraid if covered to any depth they would never come up.

The Speaker was also curious as to how the "cake was holding out" for the cows. The cattle, he said, were "in mighty fine shape when I was at home."

More and more Mr. Sam demonstrated that he was the real boss on the Democratic side of the aisle and a power to be reckoned with in the House. Twice in one day he went into action to head off trouble. It was during the first week in February when the anti-strike legislation was being considered. Representative Randolph (D., W. Va.) was about to ask the House for permission to limit the debate on the Case anti-strike bill so that a final vote could be taken. Just as he began talking, the Speaker left the rostrum and walked toward him. Randolph stopped and a quick conference in the Rayburn fashion began. Mr. Sam shifted his left hand from Randolph's shoulder to his own coat pocket and swayed a little forward and backward on the balls of his feet, speaking in a very low voice. When the session was over Mr. Sam, like Yogi Berra after one of his conferences at the mound with a rookie pitcher, turned and strode back to his position to resume the game. Randolph seemed a bit confused at first and then asked to withdraw his request. There was a round of laughter, for everyone knew exactly what had happened—Mr. Sam had reversed the signals. Randolph responded to the jollying by remarking, "As a legislative son I am always willing to follow the advice of my legislative elders."

Within thirty minutes a similar thing happened. Representative May (D., Ky.) had become irritated by something Representative Green (D., Pa.) had said. He raised serious objection and asked that Green's words be stricken from the *Record,* and if May's motion had been accepted Green would have been prevented from speaking for the remainder of the day. As before, the Speaker began his walk toward his teammate, who this time had started a rhubarb. After a brief conference, Rayburn returned to the rostrum and May asked to withdraw his request. The Speaker knew the consequences of an intra-party squabble and he stopped it.

The behavior of the Speaker here has led some of his older friends in the Senate to compare Rayburn to one of those old-fashioned fathers with a house full of boys who sometimes "feel their oats." "If there was any fighting or cussing to be done," one remarked, "Sam would do it himself because he wanted things to be quiet and orderly." Mr. Sam applied an early nineteenth-century type of discipline to his boys in the House because he thought he had a better perspective of the total picture than anyone else. He knew what was best for them. He saw legislation in terms of an entire session or many sessions rather than in terms of just one bill or a particular day's proceedings. He was almost fanatical on the subject of harmony. As Speaker he was in the dual capacity of umpire of the game and manager of his own team. He played both roles very skillfully and conscientiously.

The Speaker was by no means antisocial, for his apartment was frequented at least one evening a week by his cronies. He tried to limit his evenings out to not more than three. Occasionally he would entertain on a grand scale. The following invitation went out to some two hundred dignitaries and personal friends in Washington:

> Miss Lou and I are giving a little party at the Carleton Room, Carleton Hotel, on Wednesday March 20th from 5:30 to 7:00. We will be pleased if you can come.

Newspapermen, generals, Supreme Court justices, Cabinet members, congressmen and senators came and enjoyed Rayburn hospitality. Mr. Sam did not "request their presence"; he merely sent them a Fannin County invitation. Dignitaries like Lord and Lady Halifax were particularly impressed by the atmosphere. The guests could see that the Speaker was trying to impress no one and that his sole motive was to bring his friends together under relaxed and friendly circumstances.

The announcement by the Speaker that on the afternoon of April 20 he and General Dwight D. Eisenhower would fly to the General's birthplace in Denison made many people in the Fourth District wonder whether their Congressman had slipped a cog or two. Mr. Sam swore off traveling by air, after his first eventful flight to Texas in 1936 and that one in 1943. The Speaker escorted the General to his old home and then Miss Jennie Jackson, eighty-five years of age and the only living person in Denison who had held the famous baby on her knees, guided the group to the room where he was born. Then they went into the small dining-room, where they had a brunch of ham, scrambled eggs, homemade biscuits, strawberries and cream, and coffee. While the General was having a second helping of biscuits, the bright floodlights of the newsreel cameras and the flash of the photographers' bulbs reminded them that they were not alone.

Following these ceremonies there was a giant parade out to Forest Park, where a number of orators paid tribute to both guests, before Rayburn had a chance to introduce the General. References were made in these preliminary speeches to his leadership during the war and to Rayburn's responsibility for the Denison Dam project. Lyndon Johnson's comments had a special significance: "Speaker Rayburn had been like a father to me, guiding me in my early days in Congress, and now he is guiding the entire House of Representatives in these crucial times."

After a Texas barbecue of beef, baked beans, potato chips, pickles, and onions, Eisenhower remarked to Mr. Sam, "I've had two meals in two hours and I'm tired." So he slipped away to a suite of rooms in the Denison Hotel to rest for twenty minutes before his press conference.

Mr. Rayburn told some of his closest friends that he would have to excuse himself and get back to Washington because there were several important measures pending which needed his personal attention, the REA being one of them. His concern for this bill was quite justified for during the two-hour debate the Speaker surrendered the gavel once to introduce one amendment raising the appropriation from $3,328,000 to $7,500,000, against the Committee's recommendation. The larger sum, he explained, would enable the Southwestern Power Administration to connect by transmission lines the Government-owned and operated Denison Dam, the Norfolk Dam in Arkansas, and the Grand River Dam in Oklahoma, soon to be returned to the State but whose power at the time was controlled by the Federal Government. The opposition was based upon a prevalent belief that building lines paralleling privately-owned systems would lead to socialization of the power industry and ultimately to putting private companies out of business. The House, however, voted 125 to 76 to accept Rayburn's amendment.

When Sam Rayburn said that he had worked *with,* not *under* eight Presidents, he meant to imply that he had shown a reasonable amount of cooperation but had never been a rubber stamp. Illustrative of this Rayburn independence of mind was the subtle and indirect method he used on President Truman's bill for the reorganization of the executive branch. Rayburn could effect a remarkable change of pace, so to speak. He could drive a bill through, let it sit around until it was watered down with amendments, or put it in his bottom drawer.

On June 10, 1946, the Senate passed a bill which was generally acceptable to Truman but it lay on the House table until July 25. During this period many congressmen had a chance to read it critically with the result that quite a number of amendments were proposed. The Speaker himself found several flaws in the streamlined proposal. He objected to the creation of majority and minority policy committees to replace steering committees. He also disliked the setting up of a new joint Senate-House legislative-executive committee to meet with the President and his cabinet for the purpose of shaping Administrative policy. The effect of such a reform would have been the creation of more Party responsibility and the insurance that legislative leadership did not circumvent Party platforms. While Rayburn was a firm believer in the separation of powers, he also wanted to perpetuate the existing system in which the Speaker and the Majority Leader of the House, together with the President and the Majority Leader of the Senate, met as they had always done every Monday morning while Congress was in session to plan the week's legislative program. Sam Rayburn was a practical man, not an idealist. He did not want to abandon this time-worn procedure because he could lose his personal grip on the House. Mr. Sam was a firm believer that a man in charge should be the master and not the servant if he expected to get anything accomplished, and as long as he was the Speaker he planned to see to it that the majority prevailed. This was Mr. Sam's understanding of democracy.

Another source of opposition came from the House Committee on Appropriations, whose Chairman, Clarence Cannon of Missouri, was instrumental in securing certain amendments which would eliminate the "Legislative Budget." This would have been established in joint meetings of Senate and House committees on taxation and appropriations. The objective of the "Legislative Budget" procedure was to require a balanced budget at all times. It seems that the Speaker and Cannon believed the provision unrealistic. They were supported, however, in their assumptions by the advocates of the Free Employment Act. The latter believed that a balanced budget would cripple their economic report and economic planning.

The House also succeeded in eliminating one other reform in the Senate bill—that of providing an $8000-a-year executive assistant for each member of Congress. While some argued against the provision in the interest of economy, there may have been the fear in the Lower House that these highly-paid and competent assistants could be put in a position where they might develop certain ambitions of their own and build themselves up politically. As a result, congressmen preferred for the time being to be satisfied and continue overworked.

The House of Representatives would be an unwieldy body if there were no rules, committees, and agreements among members. When Speaker Rayburn remarked that "we get together and decide how we are going to do things" he referred specifically to the gentlemen's agreements. Without them, there would be chaos.

It was reported that the Speaker had such an agreement with Congressmen Monroney and Dirksen for them not to reintroduce these reforms, which had been cut out in committee, as amendments from the floor of the House. The Reorganization bill which finally passed the House actually contained more than the Senate expected to get, but it still bore the mark of Sam Rayburn. It was illustrative of his technique as a compromiser, his ability to get men to work together congenially.

With the feel of politics in the air, the House completed its work at 3:19 P.M. on August 2, 1946. Some of the members indulged in the usual rounds of oratory before the Speaker's farewell and prophetic remark:

> "It is going to be said that many things were left undone by Congress that should have been done. In a few instances this may be true, but on many occasions it is better to leave things undone than to rush them through in too much of a hurry. There is always a new session ahead to take care of such matters."

In many parts of the country the Democrats were being reminded of this unfinished business. In October the White House suddenly became panicky and sent out an SOS to Rayburn. There was trouble, Truman thought, for the Democrats, particularly in the Midwest, where some of the President's closest cronies were being harassed. The most serious threat was in Missouri itself, where the Republicans were parading the resurrected ghost of Boss Tom Pendergast of the old Kansas City political machine. Truman had ridden to power when it was in existence but had been rather successful in disassociating himself from factionalism.

The seriousness of the Democratic position was reflected in the fact that both the Speaker and the President were scheduled to work in Missouri. Rayburn made one appearance on October 11 at Columbus and returned to Independence with Truman on October 31, in a bomb-proof special railroad car—a luxurious contraption the American Association of Railroads had sold the Government for $10. This type of protection, however, was not needed from the Republicans, for they promised to seek their vengeance with ballots, not bullets.

With his prestige at stake, the President traveled toward his home state in grand style. The train was flagged down at Lee's Summit, Missouri, thirteen miles east of Independence, to let Margaret get aboard. Some eight hundred of the older citizenry were waiting at Independence to greet the two Democratic notables. "Looks like all the city dads are here," snapped the President, "but where are the Republicans? Here, Sam, meet Mayor Sermon. And this is my brother Vivian." For the Speaker this was the beginning of many friendships and pleasant associations with people in Independence.

"No more calamitous thing could befall this nation in the next two years," said Rayburn, "with peace and prosperity in balance, than to repeat 1918, and divide the Executive and Legislative branches of the American Government, like Solomon's child, between the Democrats and Republicans." With a vigor reminiscent of his younger years he cited the plenitude of jobs, good wages, high farm incomes, and general evidence of prosperity. The snap in the October air made him remember the season of the year as he exclaimed, "Don't let the Republicans scare you out of your appreciation of the solid facts of prosperity with any Hallowe'en jack-o'-lantern of Communism." He expressed faith that President Truman and Secretary Byrnes would meet their challenge.

As an additional insurance measure, fifty-nine Congressional districts, where there was some chance of a Republican victory, received a carefully prepared recording of a message which defined the calamity that would befall the country should the people withdraw their support from the President. Then Rayburn left for Bonham on November 1 to cast his vote and await the people's decision.

The people, though, had been drifting away from the liberalism of the New Deal since the outbreak of war. The late President Roosevelt had warned against "fear of fear." The war and recovery had brought about many inconveniences and had produced a new set of economic theories. A crisis in the meat industry and the threatened coal strikes prior to the 1946 elections were symptoms of unrest before change. The electorate was not yet prepared to move still farther from the known past toward the unknown future.

When the results of the November 5 election were all in, the Democrats had lost control of both Houses of Congress. In the House the score shifted from 241 to 188 for the Democrats to 192 to 242 for the Republicans; in the Senate the shift was from 56 to 45 for the Democrats to 39 to 51 for the Republicans. Governor Dewey, the potential standard bearer of his Party, also gained in prestige with his victory in New York.

While President Truman was nursing his wounds, the Fourth District was awakening to the results of the new mandate from the people. They had lost their Speaker. Mr. Sam would now become just an ordinary congressman. He had one rather painful thought, also, which was a natural reaction for a man in modest circumstances. His salary would drop from $20,000 back to $12,500, exclusive of $2500 expenses under the new scale, effective January 1, 1947. He would also lose his limousine and chauffeur, two of his office suites, and the clerical help accompanying his more exalted post. The big office, with elegant red rugs and the large cut glass chandelier, would now change hands. He would have no use for a "Board of Education" room, except perhaps as a storeroom for his accumulation of *Congressional Records* and other Government documents. So after thirty-four years of service he considered briefly and privately the possibility of retirement from public life with an annual salary of $7000, as provided by his social security arrangement.

By midnight on November 5, he released this statement to the press: "I will not be the Minority Leader." When his friends came by the big house in Bonham to express their regrets, he was quite composed and philosophical. He persisted in his original decision, thinking the time had come for him to have a vacation from Party responsibilities, striking the initial blow against the inevitable advocates of his becoming Minority Leader. The thought of taking a rest appealed to him.

For a man who had considerable faith in people, this Republican victory was upsetting. He wondered whether they had forgotten the mistakes after 1918. What the people appeared to want, as reflected by their vote—the immediate abandonment of wartime restrictions—seemed to him dangerous to the security and the economy generally. He believed the scrapping of controls on prices and wages would set off a spiral of inflation. However, he recognized as early as April 26, when he spoke on a conference report relative to price and rent controls, that the time was fearfully close when there would be no restraints. Food prices would soar and tenants would be turned out in the streets because of a basic greed that would have no discipline.

By November 7, the Texas delegation had set in motion a movement to draft Rayburn. They did not want to lose his active services in the belief that his leadership was needed more in defeat than in victory. By November 11, John J. Sparkman, Senator-elect from Alabama and Majority Whip of the House, joined the House members who had already started the agitation. Southern Democrats did not look with favor upon replacing Rayburn with John W. McCormack of Massachusetts, Majority Leader; and Northern Democrats and Administration followers stood guard against any New Deal critics like Graham A. Borden of North Carolina and E. E. Cox of Georgia. Republicans, too, were not silent, for they remembered that during the campaign just completed, Mr. Sam was advised in Washington to make speeches attacking specific Republicans in Congress for their transgressions and that the Speaker had flatly refused: "I'm not going to say mean things about my colleagues, some of whom are fast friends, even if they are Republicans."

The President had nothing to do with the draft because there were rumors that he might have a Cabinet post for the Speaker; however, he naturally thought it a good idea to keep him in a position of legislative leadership.

On January 1, the Texas delegation braved sleet and snow to discuss their problem and Rayburn's continued rejection of the job. They reached no decision but agreed to meet again one hour before the Democratic caucus. Mr. Sam discreetly stayed away. He had arrived in Washington only the day before. McCormack, reports Leslie Carpenter, promptly came to see him to press the matter of his taking the minority post. Rayburn replied, "But you know that I telegraphed you in November that I was going to support you for the leadership."

"Yes," McCormack said, "but I think it would be best for the Party if you changed your mind and accepted it."

"Come to see me in the morning," was the answer. This was the first encouragement he had given anyone. Then twenty minutes before the Democratic caucus, McCormack was back again. "I am going to nominate you for Minority Leader," McCormack said.

"If you do, I will be forced to accept, although I don't want to."

At the caucus McCormack did nominate his friend from Bonham, and E. E. Cox of Georgia and John Rankin of Mississippi made seconding speeches. When Sam saw these champions, from areas that were philosophically miles apart, ask for his leadership, he could not hold out any longer. In a flash he recognized a type of harmony which had not previously existed. Defeat had brought the Party temporarily together. Mr. Sam discovered a fact of which he was too modest to be aware—he had become, during his thirty-four years, a symbol of leadership for his Party in Congress, and as long as he was a member of the House of Representatives, as he was soon to learn, he could not walk away from responsibility. A man in his position had to obey the will of his Party, because he had lived so long in identity with the Party that the will of the individual necessarily became submerged in that of the group.

In his press conference afterward, Rayburn told newspapermen that the President had had nothing to do with his consenting to the draft:

"I did talk to him yesterday over the telephone but it was about a budgetary matter. It just got to where I couldn't help it. McCormack came to me and others said they were going to elect me in spite of myself. I didn't want the job and I had said I wouldn't take it. When I was voted for unanimously I yielded like I figured a good soldier should do. We Democrats will make our voice heard by sticking together."

☆ XVII ☆

From Speaker to Minority Leader

WHAT transpired in the House on January 3, 1947, could happen only in a republic like America. When the Eightieth Congress was barely fifty minutes old, Representative Aime J. Forand (D., R.I.) nominated Sam Rayburn for Speaker in full knowledge that Joseph W. Martin of Massachusetts would win. The roll call required a mere twenty-three minutes, with Rayburn leading for the first five minutes. The final vote, however, was 244 to 182.

The ceremony which followed could be performed only by men of goodwill and dedication. Before a packed gallery and responsive congressmen, Mr. Sam took his friend Joe by the arm and marched him to the rostrum. He grabbed the gavel and banged it, much to the delight of both sides of the aisle, everyone applauding and laughing. Speaking with his usual cogency, he thanked his colleagues for their respect and cooperation and expressed his view about the House: "This House has deserved and has had the respect of thinking men and women in America." About the new Speaker, he said:

> "I predict for him a career such that history will record him as one of the great presiding officers. And I have the high privilege and great personal pleasure

> —if it has come to that—of presenting the forty-fifth Speaker of the House of Representatives."

There was laughter after his aside. As he left the rostrum to take his seat on the fourth row left, the ovation made everyone aware that Sam Rayburn was popular in this body, whether he sat up front or among his colleagues.

When the boisterous approval had run its natural course, the new Speaker set off another round of applause with his reference to Rayburn:

> "It is a great honor to follow the honorable, able and distinguished gentleman from Texas. He has been loved and respected by all and he has made a record in this House of which he can be justly proud."

Rayburn and Martin knew how to exchange the gavel in such a way that the great game of American politics appeared to have no losers.

Three days later the new Minority Leader celebrated his sixty-fifth birthday. There were the usual parties, his fresh coconut cake, telegrams from friends, and all the fanfare he had been accustomed to since January 6 was added to the Capitol Hill social calendar. Perhaps the most significant expression came from Charles Halleck of Indiana, the new Majority Leader, about his new adversary on the House floor:

> "We are happy that it is Sam Rayburn. He served illustriously and well as Speaker of this great body. He was always fair and square in his dealings with all of us. He was considerate and helpful; yes, helpful to the newest member as well as the oldest; always honorable, and possessed of a balanced, good judgment; an able speaker, and a man of complete integrity whose work was always good. . . . In committee, on the floor, in the chair of the Speaker, he has been studious, faithful in his defense of the Constitution, gentle of manner and ever cordial and genial in his relations with all of his colleagues, regardless of party, and unmindful of differences of opinions expressed in legislative debate. In that respect he has been not only a servant but a living symbol of the one best hope of mankind—the conviction that a society of free people is equipped by Providence to govern itself through representative bodies such as the Congress of the United States. . . . As a member who was only a boy of

> twelve years when the gentleman from Texas, Sam Rayburn, began his notable career in Congress, I count it a high privilege indeed to stand before this great body to pay tribute to a man who thus has served so nobly to protect, defend, and preserve the Republic. May he be with us on many future birthday anniversaries, and may his lot among us reflect always the high place he has won in regard, esteem, and affection of us all."

The full realization that he was no longer Speaker of the House of Representatives came to him very suddenly when George, the chauffeur, was not sitting in the 1944 Cadillac limousine outside his apartment. Instead it was parked in front of Speaker Joe Martin's quarters. Rayburn was now just an ordinary congressman dependent upon taxi service. Some of his closest friends began discussing the way their Mr. Sam had been de-mechanized by the Republican victory. Several of them who were sufficiently affluent to do something about it approached the ex-Speaker on the subject and asked if they could buy him an automobile. He expressed his appreciation of their thoughtfulness but said he would not consider receiving such a gift. Later he recognized their deep interest, and conceded: "O.K., boys, on one condition, that it be a gift from the Democrats in the House and that no one contribute more than $25."

Representative Frank Boykin of Alabama, chairman of the committee, passed the word quickly through Democratic channels of Mr. Sam's surrender to their pressure. A few days later he commented to the press: "The Republicans had our Sam walking and we Democrats couldn't stand that. The checks just blew in like leaves falling in a breeze." Within a few days the money was all in Boykin's hands, enough to buy a brand-new 1947 Cadillac limousine, listed at $3602. Many unsolicited checks outside Congress were returned and those from the Republican side were also graciously sent back, since the terms of Mr. Sam's agreement on the amount of money and donors was not to be violated.

The limousine was purchased and Democratic whip, McCormack, was selected to turn over the keys in the presentation ceremony on January 24. Southerner Boykin said, "We let John do it even though he's a Yankee, but he's a damn good Yankee."

The ceremony took place just a few feet away from where Martin had just left the 1944 model limousine. Rayburn chuckled about the turn of events and mused that Speaker Joe Martin now had to drive "my old 1944 model." Thus Mr. Sam was put back on wheels again, but with one drawback—a chauffeur did not come with the transaction. Since he was strictly a Fannin County driver, having won his license herding a pick-up truck over the back country roads, he did not feel qualified to fight the Washington traffic. So he reached down in his pocket each month for $200, the going rate for such jobs.

The demotion by no means diminished Mr. Sam's prestige or demand as spokesman for his Party, because he was still the top man among those of his political persuasion. He had lost the title "Mr. Speaker" but he retained that of "Mr. Democrat" and he was still, of course, the President's right arm.

In anticipation of a busy social season, he wrote Miss Lou to come to Washington. She rearranged her life so that she would reach the capital in time for two important occasions during the last week of January. The first was a ceremony, on January 30, in which Rayburn and other Democrats paid tribute to their late President.

The following night Mr. Sam was the honored celebrity at the biggest event of the year for Texans in Washington. The Texas State Society entertained in the Statler Hotel ballroom with a dinner honoring their Democratic leader. Attorney-General Tom Clark acted as master of ceremonies and comedian Bob Hope went through his routine. The newly appointed Chief Justice, Fred Vinson, made the only address. Besides nearly fifteen hundred members of the Society, there were one thousand others in attendance, including the President, some members of his cabinet, members of the Supreme Court, and people from both Houses.

The President's appearance was somewhat unexpected since the doctor had confined him to the White House because he was running a temperature and had laryngitis; but suddenly without any warning to the program committee the unpredictable Truman entered the dining room, surrounded by Secret Service men, while the alert Marine Corps band played "Hail to the Chief." President Truman said he wanted to come to the dinner just to affirm "how much I love you," as he addressed his remarks to his friend. Then he went on to speak for ten minutes without reference to notes.

During the Eightieth Congress, Mr. Sam's voice on legislation was heard more frequently than when he sat on the rostrum. It was more convenient for a congressman on the floor to enter into debate than for the Speaker; hence the House got a taste of Rayburnesque. His March 27 remarks on Republican politics in relation to Federal fiscal policies was a notable example. The new Republican Congress was attempting to reduce the President's $37,500,000,000 budget, which Truman later vigorously defended in his April 5, $100-a-plate Jefferson dinner speech. Rayburn in resisting the Republican demands scored them as sheer politics. He expressed the fear that the United States could not afford to pay on its national debt at the time without depleting the money in the Treasury and ultimately reducing the worth of the dollar. He concurred with Truman in scoring the false Republican economics which could invite disaster for this country at a time when it was faced with assuming a new world responsibility.

The Republican majority next tackled the problem of labor. Representative Fred Hartley, Jr. (N.J.), Chairman of the House Labor Committee, introduced a bill which Rayburn believed to be designed to punish labor for the transgressions of a few. He warned, however, that if some of these leaders in the labor movement were not a little more watchful they could bring down wrath upon the heads of many people who did not deserve it. Hartley's strike-curb bill seemed to be just the kind of legislation he feared would result. In his argument against the bill, he declared that it would abolish the National Labor Relations Board and substitute a Labor-Management Relations Board; would make strikes in industry illegal. It would forbid the closed shop, jurisdictional and sympathy strikes, mass picketing, all strikes by government workers; deprive violating unions of their bargaining for one year; prevent unlawful strikers from getting their jobs back; make unions subject to suit; require unions to make financial reports; and empower the President to obtain injunctions against strikes in interstate transportation, communications, or public utilities.

Senator Robert A. Taft had started a similar bill through channels at the other end of the Capitol. The two measures finally became fused into a single document, after joint committee action. Then on April 17, Rayburn led his unsuccessful fight against what he called a "punitive labor bill." The final Taft-Hartley Act which went to the President for his signature was a greatly modified measure. After the President's veto was overruled, the Administration reported to the nation a step-by-step approach to the whole labor problem, a program very similar to that advocated by the Minority Leader.

Sam Rayburn in his reminiscences about the Truman years

cited this action as a good example of the President's courage. He mentioned another on which he thought the President showed even more decisiveness—the $400,000,000 Greece-Turkey Aid bill.

On May 7, Rayburn, supported by Representative Lyndon Johnson, gave the closing speech in which he expressed the hope that "this thing called isolationism may not again crawl out of the shadows and defeat the hopes of men and again break the heart of the world." In an effort to block the spread of Communism in Turkey, Greece, the Middle East, the Mediterranean area, North Africa, Italy, and perhaps France, he tried to block Lawrence H. Smith's amendment which did not favor immediate aid.

> "Greece and Turkey need help now, not sixty or ninety days or a year from now, when it might be too late. Leadership has been offered us. People who love liberty and who cry for a fair chance want us to take that leadership in this challenging hour."

The economy-minded Republican Congress had also made drastic reductions in the appropriation for the Department of Agriculture, and on May 28, Mr. Sam was compelled to defend some of his favorite programs—soil conservation, rural electrification, farm-to-market roads, farm-ownership, and school-lunches. It was an attentive Congress that heard America's foremost conservationist speak on his favorite topic:

> "When I drive along the road or look out of the train window and see the fertile soil of the country washed down to rock bottom and gutted with ditches, it hurts me almost like the stick of a knife. . . . We plowed up the prairies, we did nothing to conserve them. They started to wash. Then in many instances we went down into the valleys, the rich valleys, and cut the trees away. We left nothing to hold the ground, nothing to stop the dirt that flowed down from the slopes. The water that flowed down from the slopes filled up the channels that the creeks did have before the slopes and valleys were cleared up. That soil has filled the creeks or the streams that used to exist and now when it rains on the slopes the water has no place to run except to spread all over the fertile valley and destroy it. Today millions of acres of ground, millions of acres of that fertile soil are in Johnson grass,

> in elms and in willows and have passed out of cultivation."

With a warning note he made predictions:

> "If we are the same kind of vandals for the next twenty-five years, even, that we have been in the past fifty years in the destruction of the fertility of our soil, we will not have any amount of surpluses to sell abroad, but we will be using every acre of this worn and torn land to raise the things that we have got to consume inside the United States of America."

In his argument for restoring the $20,000,000 cut in rural electrification he demonstrated with statistics the popularity of this improvement in country life. "I do not know of a single farm home," he said, "that has had the opportunity to take rural electrification that has not paid its bills or has had the lights taken out." He could not cite anyone who was willing to return to the coal-oil lamp.

The farmers and their families had been called upon time and again to produce more, and had been asked to offer their sons and daughters to the service of their country. These were the people he accused the Eightieth Congress of rejecting.

As Congress neared its recess the former Speaker, in an angry mood, prepared to make his report to the supreme judges in a republic—the people. He declared that this was the worst Congress in his thirty-five years of memory, for there were only broken pledges and promises to show for seven months of deliberation. He attributed the failures primarily to the Republican Party's basic distrust and lack of faith in the people, and to sheer inexperience. He observed that there was also manifested a "lack of desire to face up to the problems of the people." Specifically, he pointed out that the Republicans failed, among many things, to pass minimum wage legislation; to attack the housing problem; to live up to soil conservation commitments; to do anything to curb the inflationary spiral of prices; to provide for the training of our youth to defend the nation; to do anything to improve medical care for all the people. He also scored the GOP heavily for their tax bill which increased, by only 56 cents more per week, the take-home pay of the married man, with two dependents, in the $2500-a-year bracket, while the $1,000,000 income people received an increase of $103,000.

The Republican type of surgery on the President's balanced budget reminded him of a "man with a meat axe in a dark room."

Republican inexperience and bewilderment in such matters, and in legislation like the Taft-Hartley measure, resembled the scene from *Alice in Wonderland* where confusion reigned. He congratulated the President on keeping a clear head amid the indecision, by exercising his power of veto whenever "these Republican monstrosities" were sent to the White House for signature.

With a new 1947 Cadillac, Rayburn decided to drive back home this time and enjoy some of the scenic views in the Smoky Mountains. The beauty of Tennessee was, in Mr. Sam's judgment, surpassed only by the environs of his house near Highway 82. Here he thought he could escape from the furor he left behind as a result of his recent partisan utterances. However, he was mistaken.

In America there are at least two sides to any political debate, and Mr. Sam's tranquility was promptly disturbed by the announcement from junior Senator W. Lee O'Daniel that he was coming home to do a little talking, perhaps also to try out his new hillbilly band. Mr. Sam's remarks over the National Broadcasting System had stirred Pappy's ire. O'Daniel declared that his targets would be Communism and further loans to Great Britain. He warned those members of Congress who "run around the world trying to attend to everybody else's business while the Communists and Communistic spies are infesting this Government." O'Daniel singled out particularly five "Communistic laws" that he planned to tear to shreds: 1) Rural Electrification, which he laid at the doorstep of the Minority Leader from Bonham; 2) the Veterans' Housing bill, sponsored by Representative Wright Patman of Texarkana; 3) the Tennessee Valley Authority; 4) the OPA, and 5) Wagner Labor Relations Act.

Sam Rayburn, in sanctioning these so-called "Communistic measures," became a target for O'Daniel's opprobrious darts. The relations between the two men were none too cordial. Rayburn was not pleased with the Senator's behavior and record on Capitol Hill. O'Daniel had indulged in so much castigation of both national Parties for "skullduggery, deceit and deception" that he really had no deep Party ties. He was the closest thing, perhaps, to a Republican, excluding his predecessor Andrew Jackson Houston, that Texas thus far had sent to the Senate. O'Daniel had actually achieved an independent status, since he found the leaders of both Parties just "like two peas in a pod." He had also become something of a prima donna rather than a team man.

Although Mr. Sam tried to refrain from comment on the personality of the rambunctious Senator, his friends knew his mind. They heard him make sly comparisons between the newcomer and the late Morris Sheppard.

About the time when the leaves are turning yellow in East Texas, and the crops are gathered, the natives are in an advanced stage of talking politics. A visitor like the Minority Leader only accelerates the discussion. Rayburn was making a tour of this section of Texas and spent the night of October 19 with committeeman Myron Blalock at his new farm home near Marshall. Rayburn was returning Blalock's visit earlier in the summer.

The next day Sam Rayburn gave the Young Democrats food for thought at Longview when he assailed Republican ineffectiveness. The people, he said, had asked for a change in 1920 and got it with a vengeance. He explained that the Republicans had not had good Presidential material in 1920 and he saw no evidence of it in 1947. "This year they trotted out all their horses and they are now taking them all back in the stable because they feel that their best cannot hold a candle to the way President Truman is going to run."

It was at this time that Rayburn quieted all rumors about his future plans, for he stated that in "no remotest sense" was he a candidate for the Vice-Presidential nomination. Rayburn's emphatic statement was inspired by his recent experience in Congress as an ex-Speaker and Minority leader. He had discovered that his value to the President and his Party in such a position had increased; in fact, better informed people around the Capitol were saying that Truman and Mr. Sam were the top men in the Government, even though the Republicans held a numerical superiority in Congress. Rayburn believed that the 188 Democratic minority in the House was a more closely knit unit than ever before, and, of course, he counted on his many Republican friends to make up the difference where support for the Administration was really needed.

During the Christmas holidays (December 27), Rayburn took part in the groundbreaking ceremonies for the Lavon Dam on the banks of the Trinity's East Fork. With his Denison Dam completed, he had turned his attention to a companion project which would protect for the future the thousands of acres of fertile land in Collin, Kaufman, and Rockwall Counties.

Rayburn used such occasions as an excuse to discuss the most pressing legislative problems. Fresh from the fall session of

Congress he was in none too pleasant a mood. There was even a note of alarm in his utterances as he referred to the unfinished business connected with the Marshall Plan, and the unrest throughout the world from the aftermath of war. The Iron Curtain he feared posed real threats to peace. "I do not believe we stand in the face of a war this year or probably even next year," Rayburn said; "but I do not know and no one else knows when some incident will set off the holocaust of a third world war."

Mr. Sam's best Christmas present arrived several days late. The copies of the first contracts negotiated by the Southwestern Power Administration for delivery of dam power to REA cooperatives were presented to him in a ceremony at his home by Lee Simmons, manager of the Denison office. The occasion marked a new milestone in Rayburn's crusade to bring cheap power to rural homes. The transaction seemed to be partial proof that public power developments could work with existing private utilities for mutual benefit. As an expression of appreciation to Mr. Sam, the first power was to be delivered to the REA cooperatives in Grayson, Fannin, and Hunt Counties, since he was the original champion of this legislation and had continued to shepherd its progress. Keeping the projects alive was no easy chore; in fact four months later he was compelled to make a desperate stand for the First Deficiency Appropriation bill which involved $175,000,000 to sustain the program until July 1, 1948.

The second session of the Eightieth Congress began January 6 on a pleasant note with the celebration of the sixty-sixth birthday of the Minority Leader. When Mr. Sam was Speaker he would avoid convening Congress on his birthday, but now his friend Joe Martin had the say, and Joe always went out of his way to honor Sam. Majority Leader Halleck never failed to do his part either. He made reference to Sam's "fine comradeship, sportsmanship, and fair play." "Instead of his getting older," Halleck said, "he seems to me to be getting younger. I don't want him to get too vigorous. I have enough trouble with him without that."

Following the round of speeches, a birthday luncheon was given by Jack Cowart, Dallas Agriculture Department official, for a small group in one of the private dining-rooms. The President liked to slip into these functions unannounced. This time he stayed for an hour to visit with his Texas friends.

In 1948, Mr. Sam came face to face with the problem of the President's Civil Rights program. Rayburn knew that the South was not ready, certainly not the Fourth District, to eliminate their segregation laws. On the other hand, he could see little evidence that progress was being made in this area, and he was saddened that the South was willing to permit a second-class citizenship. When he drove through colored sections of his own community he always went away depressed. To Valton Young he once said:

> "I always feel a little blue when I see some of the dilapidated houses and dire circumstances in which too many of our colored folk have to live. Poverty is not only a sad thing to me, but I think it is very dangerous. Extreme destitution can defile any society. It can offer an excellent breeding ground for the worst things in life, and don't you forget it."[1]

He knew he could not bring his own people along any faster than they were willing to move of their own volition, but he decided to do one thing for the needy—to support public housing. Some of society's inequities, he thought, could be cured without stirring up conflict among races and classes.

Aware of the attitudes of his own section and the political dangers in Civil Rights, he called the Texas congressmen together late in April and declared a moratorium on all Civil Rights talk. Back home in the Fourth District, Mr. Sam's action was mistakenly interpreted as approval of the President's program, as his correspondence from constituents indicates.

Texas was aflame over the issues. G. C. Morris had already announced again for Congress and was trying to hang Mr. Sam on the President's program. A friend in Sherman wrote Rayburn on March 3:

> I have had friends listening and giving me information that they get and some of your friends who have stood by you and contributed money to the campaign have stated that the way things are they have 'voted for Sam Rayburn the last time.' "

The following report reflects the thinking of campaign headquarters in Grayson County:

> They are willing to get in the harness and do all they can to assist you, and they even say that it is going to be a hard job this time for you to be reelected, but that with a definite statement of your position they believe it can be done. They think if you in any manner undertake to defend the President's position that it will be hazardous for you.

He was forthright in his correspondence, stating that he was against the Federal repeal of the poll tax law, the so-called Federal anti-lynching law, the Fair Employment Practice Commission, any bill that would cripple segregation or interfere with local rights. Believing that the South was not ready for the type of legislation in the President's bill, he resorted to the best Rayburn strategy—to forestall action until the controversial elements could be eliminated. He knew that Truman did not fully sense all the hidden liabilities in the program, but refused to let his differences with the President affect their personal relationship.

Despite effort by the political opposition in the Fourth District to link Rayburn with the President's program, Mr. Sam's stand on Civil Rights was rather generally known elsewhere. At the University of Texas, in a joint meeting of the YMCA and YWCA cabinets on March 8, the Minority Leader's views were discussed, and students appealed to him as a "Christian and a Congressional Leader" to reverse his stand. They circulated a petition which contained this sentence: "Believing that all men are brothers created equal in the sight of God, we see in the points of the President, a step toward the fulfillment of these Christian ideals."

Rayburn was not a man to be crowded or stampeded into a decision. He frankly stated that he had spent twice as much time making up his mind on these issues as most of these students had lived. Therefore he scribbled in pencil across the left-hand corner of both documents these words: "Let lie around a while." Had he responded immediately he might have quoted the Scottish proverb: "Gie your tongue mair holidays than your head." Mr. Sam, though, had patience with youth and was not prone to cut it down in its prime, because he remembered his own restless enthusiasm for justice when a student in the Mayo Normal.

The people who chastised him sharply for his unwillingness to force Civil Rights were unaware of his own private feelings—the human side of the picture. The following incident seems to be helpful here. Once Frank McNaughton and Sam, according to Edward Boyd, had spent a whole day fishing from a small boat, for which they had employed a Negro man to do the rowing. Sam's luck was not at all good, but late in the afternoon he hooked a big one. The Negro rower jumped to Mr. Sam's assistance to help him in the struggle to get the fish into the boat. In the process he knocked the fish off the hook, but Rayburn made no comment. McNaughton noted the sadness in Mr. Sam's face and wondered about the man's silence. Later, McNaughton brought up the incident and the Speaker explained his behavior thus:

> "I naturally felt disappointed, but then I realized that, but for the grace of God, I'd have been pulling those oars myself today, not he." [2]

Rayburn formally opened his campaign for re-election on June 23, at a barbecue on the Fannin County Fair Grounds. At this time he released a somewhat lengthy statement about Civil Rights to all of the papers of his District. After declaring his opposition to the FEPC, he stated frankly:

> "I voted against everything that looked like an attack on our segregation laws. We have been able to hold down any vote on this measure this year because we feared the Republicans unanimously and many northern Democrats would support it."

He also affirmed his consistent opposition to the anti-lynching bill in the Sixty-seventh, Seventy-fifth, and Seventy-sixth Congresses.

Aware that Civil Rights would be a major issue in forthcoming events, the National Democratic Executive Committee during the first week of May had selected Sam Rayburn as the Permanent Chairman of the Convention and picked Senator Barkley as its temporary keynoter. The selection, however, was subject to approval by the total body scheduled to convene in Philadelphia at 2:00 P.M., on July 12, 1948.

At Philadelphia he performed well with the gavel and as spokesman for the Party he brought into sharp focus the achievements of the Democrats. He shared honors with the other so-called wheel horse, Alben Barkley, who assisted in giving the Convention a semblance of unity. Some show of professionalism was needed because the delegates on the floor, Party leaders in the committee rooms and even on the rostrum, performed like amateurs, as the Democrats broke into factions.

In his opening words Rayburn promised not to make a long speech. He said he would need less time for praising and defending eight Democratic Congresses than his good friend Speaker Joe Martin took in June just apologizing for that one Eightieth Republican Congress. When he began reminiscing about the failures of the Republican administrations and the accomplishments of FDR and Truman, he unconsciously broke his pledge of brevity. He had more to say than he wrote into the script. Speaking extemporaneously, he criticized the Republicans for nominating Dewey and Warren, men who did not reflect the Party's philosophy at all. He forgave Henry Wallace for his mistakes of the heart, but rebuked him severely for errors of mind—for, that is, his opposition to the Marshall Plan.

Rayburn's technique clearly demonstrated that politics is an art and that he got his diploma in the school of practical experience. After enumerating each achievement he asked a question, for example: "Who brought the farmer out of his bankruptcy courts in 1933 into his prosperity of 1948?" Then he answered with the refrain "The Democrats," which the delegates on the floor began to pick up, after eight or ten questions. Then he concluded by establishing a course along which he thought victory could be won, that is, the "middle way, our Democratic tradition of the 'American dream,' which has been featured in the people's hearts and minds by Thomas Jefferson and Andrew Jackson, by Woodrow Wilson and by Franklin Roosevelt—and by Harry Truman."

Rayburn tried to inject a sort of evangelism into the delegates who were teeming with discord and were threatening to turn the Convention into an uproar. Though Mr. Sam tried to aim for a unity of ideals amid dissension over the Party platform, he was not altogether successful. Not even the selection of Alben Barkley as Truman's running mate was enough to appease a fractious South. The Convention broke up with a note of discord when delegates from Alabama and Mississippi withdrew.

Two days later, on July 17, the Southerners assembled at Birmingham, Alabama, to hold a States' Rights Convention, where the name "Dixiecrat" was coined. Old and young alike brought their Confederate flags and sectional indignity. One elderly gentleman sitting in the gallery remarked to the author of these pages, who attended the Convention and the Texas caucus, "Them Damned Yankees—may have whupped us once, but just as shore as hell they've got another fight on their hands." Amid affected emotionalism and chauvinism a new party struggled to be born. The splinter group nominated their own ticket of Governor J. Strom Thurmond of South Carolina and Governor Fielding Wright of Mississippi.

About a week later another splinter group called the Progressives was formed, nominating Henry A. Wallace and Senator Glenn H. Taylor. Two extremes in American politics began to pull away from a center, which was itself tilting slightly to the left.

Mr. Sam was not excessively alarmed over the appeal of either extreme but was more determined in his "middle way" concepts. These he carried back to the Fourth District where he waged a strenuous ten-day campaign against two opponents, G. C. Morris and David H. Brown. His performance at Philadelphia helped pave the way for victory, although, while Rayburn was in Philadelphia, his two opponents in the Fourth gave him no respite. Morris' home-town paper, the Greenville *Evening Banner* (July 16), came to Rayburn's defense with an editorial which pointed out that State Senator Morris had worked "hand-in-glove" with big business interests at Austin; had imported a "high-powered, high-salaried" publicity agent and campaign manager; and had helped engineer through the Legislature an insurance measure "which is costly to the holders of windstorm and hail insurance policies." The results of the primary showed that the incumbent had gained in strength since his last campaign in 1944: Rayburn—31,559; Morris (Hunt)—12,377; Brown (Grayson)—5,681.

At midnight, when the results were known, Mr. Sam made one of his familiar speeches to the voters of the District over station KFYN. A huge throng of people had assembled on the courthouse lawn in Bonham to hear their Congressman make his victory comments. "Truth and righteousness won today," he said. "The people are fair. They want the truth and they know it when they hear it." He announced that within two days he would leave for Washington for the special session of Congress.

During September and October, Rayburn made many fiery addresses in an effort to stem the tide of the Southern revolt. He also concentrated on holding Texas in the Party fold. On the eve of the State Convention of September 13, he thundered a warning to fifteen thousand Party loyalists that they faced certain depression and possible war if they did not return the Democratic Party to power in November. In the Dixiecrat revolt he saw an effort to throw the election of the President into the House of Representatives, where each state would have one vote. Such an eventuality he warned would result in a GOP victory for Governor Thomas E. Dewey.

When President Truman made up his itinerary he placed Rayburn's home town on the schedule for Monday, September 27. The seven thousand citizens of Bonham began preparing days in advance for the biggest event in their history. President

Truman, the first lady, and daughter Margaret were to be Mr. Sam's and Miss Lou's house guests. A crowd of between thirty-five and fifty thousand was anticipated, but a public address system was set up to carry the President's and Mr. Sam's message to one hundred thousand.

Presidents had been in this area before, but never to Bonham. President Grant came shortly after the Civil War; Theodore Roosevelt was in Denison on April 5, 1905; Franklin Roosevelt twice—in June 13, 1936, and later during the war. Bonham is off the beaten path because the citizenry voted many years ago to keep the railroads away; hence the franchises went to Denison. They believed that railroad yards attracted undesirable elements to a city, but they finally condescended to allow one line, the Texas and Pacific, to invade the city's privacy. This was the route over which the President was to travel.

Mr. Sam came along too late as a congressman to have any influence on the community's basic attitudes. The pattern of living and thinking had been established even by the time he went to the Texas House of Representatives. The people had really never missed the conveniences of the railroads or the growth that accompanies such development. Their town was big enough to suit them and had preserved a certain pristine quality of which they were proud. Once it was voted the cleanest town in the State and later it won the distinction of having the second best school system in the State. The handful of surviving members of that graduating class continue to feel that they got off to a better start in life, for having arrived upon the scene when they did.

Bonham may have been a small town, but it was big and proud on September 27. As the President's train backed into the station a few minutes after 8:00 P.M., few saw the three-star General, Bedell Smith, Ambassador to Russia, slip away to enter a special car which was to take him to Sherman to board a plane for his trip back to Russia. Smith had boarded the Presidential train at Dallas for a conference on the critical world situation. What transpired between Dallas and Bonham perhaps had a greater impact on history than did the speeches during the next two hours.

Floodlights had been set up from the station to the football stadium, and the thirteen side streets were roped off. When the President appeared on the rear platform of his drawing-room car, after the train backed into the station, the Sherman High School band played "Hail to the Chief." Boy Scouts, Cub Scouts,

Camp Fire Girls, reception committees with flowers for the ladies, waited for the official party to disembark. Mr. Sam, who escorted Miss Lou, was the first to step down from the car and walk toward the line of shiny new convertibles. Then came the President and his family. Johnson was there too. He had descended upon the train by helicopter and got aboard before it reached Bonham. No one ever knew how many people were in Bonham that night, but there were certainly more than twenty-five thousand lining Main Street. The crowd was too dense in places for the people to move with the procession.

Mr. Sam had helped make the big turn-out possible, for he had pleaded a few days before, "I would like for every community in Fannin County to organize and come over in large caravans. Let's show Mr. Truman a real Texas welcome." The people always complied when Mr. Sam asked them for something. There were so many dignitaries in the stadium and on the gridiron that identities were lost. One lady turned to the gentleman standing next to her in the crowd and asked him to point out Senatorial candidate Lyndon B. Johnson. The man was Beauford Jester, Governor of Texas. The inquiry was unnecessary, however, for Mr. Rayburn a few minutes later gave Johnson a friendly recognition. President Truman later went so far as to endorse his candidacy, saying "If you Democrats send Senators like Bob Kerr and Lyndon Johnson to Washington we'll certainly make the Republicans dance."

The legal contest over the Duval vote came to an end the following day and Johnson was declared the victor by eighty-seven votes. Stevenson, his opponent, was officially retired from public life at this moment, and Johnson began his climb to the top.

Mr. Rayburn introduced the President as a "dear, personal friend of mine who has wanted to come to Bonham for a long time." "The first citizen of all the world is in Bonham tonight," he added, before the President's thirty-minute address over Mutual and Dixie Network radio stations. Western Union had established an office in the depot with sixteen operators to send out reporters' copy. Uniformed messenger boys, looking and acting quite officious, pedaled their bicycles back and forth between the depot and stadium with special bulletins during festivities. A hundred newspaper people with typewriters, cameras, movie cameras, and a sound camera were set up at tables below the speaker's platform.

Following this last address by the President on his whistle-stop tour of Texas, the Democratic committeemen and committeewomen went to the Rayburn home for a reception to meet Truman and his party. People stood in line to go through the house to shake hands with the President. It reminded several younger spectators of the scene at the box office at Yankee Stadium when the bleacher seats went on sale before the opening game of a World Series. To the Secret Service it began as a frightening experience, for after about forty people had gone through the receiving line and they saw several thousand lining up along the highway, they stated bluntly that this had to stop. Mr. Sam said, "You can't do this. These are my friends. I'll stand here and call them by name and thus you will know they are safe." This was the way Mr. Sam's constituents were allowed to shake hands with President and Mrs. Truman and Margaret.

Rayburn's knack for remembering names has been compared with that of James Farley's. The following incident which occurred in the law offices of Cunningham-Lipscomb, slightly earlier, would be difficult for Farley to match. Mr. Sam had climbed the steep steps leading up to the lawyers' suite, which adjoined that of Deets Dorough's, where the one reporting the anecdote was listening. A man by the name of Louis Wilkins was sitting outside Dorough's reception room when he heard the familiar voice of Sam Rayburn next door. Wilkins promptly got up and rushed into the private office and exclaimed, "Put it there, Sam!" Mr. Rayburn was reported as looking a bit stunned, when the gentleman asked, "What's my name?"

The Congressman looked out the window for a moment, frankly admitting to himself that the only name he could recall was "Rogers, Woodward, and Roberts"—a sign he could see in the distance. Then suddenly Rayburn was heard to say "Wilkins."

"Hell, I want you to tell me my first name" was the response.

Then after about a minute Rayburn exclaimed, "Louis."

"I am not through with you. When did you meet me?" There was a brief pause followed by a laugh.

"On November 11, 1918, at a show in Washington" was the reply. "Louis," he added, "that was one of the best shows I have ever seen."

The Secret Servicemen, who chaperoned President Truman on the night of September 27, were no more overwhelmed by this iron memory than was Louis Wilkins, when Mr. Sam reached back into the past thirty years to recall a man he had seen only once before.

Tuesday morning the crowds were on hand again as the Presidential train pulled out of the station. Mr. Sam rode with Truman as far as Gainesville and then returned to Bonham to participate in the opening of the Fannin County Fair. This was Bonham's red-letter day and Mr. Sam's triumph. The critics of the Administration, some observed, had crawled far back into their holes by the time the Congressman returned that afternoon. "What did you boys talk about on the train?" was the question everyone kept asking.

"Politics," he replied.

"What did you say about politics?" they asked.

"We discussed how the Democrats were going to whip the Republicans" was the answer. Then he changed the subject.

As a charter member of the Fannin County Fair, Sam Rayburn always had an active part in planning and exhibiting. While he tolerated such peripheral features as a carnival and rodeo, just to please some of the more pleasure-minded members of the executive board and the masses, his heart was in the more traditional and educational features of the enterprise, as they were first conceived in America. Valton Young quotes Mr. Sam as he talked about the merits of these activities:

> "What soul is so backward, what individual so mighty as not to profit from the bringing together of finely formed cattle, sheep with such magnificent fleeces, hogs so big that their legs can hardly hold up their thick bodies, and poultry with carefully groomed plumage to show what can be done by expert breeders in the way of improving the products of the soil on which mankind is totally dependent? The long, numerous, and handsomely decorated shelves of home-canned fruits and vegetables, as well as every variety of choice, fresh products from orchard, garden, and field; the daintily fashioned butter and cheese showing rural women's kitchen skill; the elegant embroideries and other fancywork denoting what trained hands can accomplish with a needle; and the separated sections for displaying the rural boys' and girls' products from their year's practical work in agriculture and home economics are true masterpieces in developing God's good earth.
>
> "Many people, and more especially our farm and ranch families, look forward to the Fannin County Fair as their big annual vacation. In fact, one of its noblest

services is in offering an occasion for the convening of people from all sections of the county so they may become better acquainted, exchange ideas, and relax from a year's steady work." [3]

These ideals which Mr. Sam injected into this local institution had a moving influence upon the five-day (Tuesday–Saturday) exposition. The fruits of the best thinking in agriculture and home economics were unveiled. People learned from others how to improve upon their way of doing things and accepted the challenge to be winners themselves.

The fair grew from one barnlike structure to several buildings on a sixty-acre tract. Much of the credit for its rapid development is due Mr. Sam because he provided an aggressive leadership and gave the people a faith in the value of their undertaking.

After enjoying his friends at the Fair and showing a few of his best cattle, he gave thought to his farm and ranch. Then he made preparations for his invasion of Dixiecrat territory during the last week in October.

Though personally acceptable to the South, he represented a Party that had some planks in its platform which were unacceptable in Dixie. He went first to Easton, Pennsylvania, and then to Columbia, South Carolina, armed with a message which he thought would bring his people "back into the fold." He told Southern Democrats in eight states why they should stay in the Party. He recited his personal opposition to phases of the President's Civil Rights program but pointed out that he was going to stick with the Party so that he could fight for his views within the ranks.

On Monday, November 1, the day before the election, he spoke over the Bonham station in support of Lyndon B. Johnson, Democratic candidate for Senator and for the entire Democratic Party. Rayburn opened old wounds. He recalled the days of the Texas Regulars when Coke Stevenson helped stir up the Democrats and reminded the voters that the Republican leaders were looking with sympathy on the former Democratic Governor.

By midnight of November 2, the Republicans had learned the evils of overconfidence. It was a personal victory for Truman. His "give-em hell" type of speeches at America's grass roots and whistle stops convinced the people that the Eightieth Congress, with its poor performance during the special session (July 26–August 7), had earned the title of "do-nothing." The

President also swept the Democrats back into control of both Houses of Congress (262–171, plus 1 American Labor in the House, and 53 to 43 in the Senate).

Rayburn's reaction to this new found Party prosperity is best contained in a remark by the Chairman of the Democratic Executive Committee in Fannin County: "Mr. Rayburn is just about the happiest fellow I have ever seen. It's a joy to talk to him."

☆ XVIII ☆

The "Indian Giver"— Speaker Again

FLORIDA has become a popular rendezvous for Presidents-elect to confer with their legislative chieftains. On November 20, 1948, President Truman called his leaders together for a conference. Afterward Rayburn gave his reactions to the negativism in the public mind, mentioning the Republican warnings of a depression. He expressed the belief that there were some people in the United States who seemed to enjoy being scared. With the buying power at its highest and the people able to purchase everything manufactured or grown at a reasonable profit to the manufacturer or grower, he saw no cause for fear. On the very complex international situation he was less confident: ". . . there can be no certainty, for nobody can look into the mind or heart of a dictator or a government that is a dictatorship." America, he added, must not withdraw but go ahead as a member of a world society.

Rayburn expressed pleasure in announcing that during the Eightieth Congress the Democratic side of the aisle had learned to work together sympathetically and that this spirit of comraderie would be carried over into the Eighty-first. Further optimism was contained in his belief that there was nothing approaching an effective coalition between Republicans and the so-called reactionary Southerners.

On more specific matters he stated that during the Eightieth Congress, Washington had been "loaded down" and "seething" under utility lobby pressure; for six months a desperate effort had been made to kill the Southwestern Power Administration bill he was sponsoring. In looking toward the future, he defiantly hurled a challenge, "If they are spoiling for another fight with me, they can get it." This was familiar territory, for he had beaten the same type of lobbies in fights over the Wheeler-Rayburn Holding Company Act, Rural Electrification, the Social Securities Acts of 1933 and 1934, Emergency Railroad Transportation Act of 1933, and the Federal Communications Commission. For a man who was now beginning to count the years, he seemed to have plenty of fight still left in him. The privately-owned public utilities would have agreed to this fact, for when they were trying to block the expansion of public power facilities in 1946, they remembered how he left the Speaker's rostrum, with flashing eyes and flushed face, to take a hand in crushing them.

With the Democrats back in power again, Rayburn's friends were confident that he again would become Speaker and be the second man in a hundred years to hold the position twice. Thomas B. Reed of Maine served split terms as such in the 1880's and 1890's. Rayburn had now been around long enough for his colleagues to regard him as a sort of phenomenon. As far as seniority in the House was concerned only Representatives Adolph Sabath (D., Ill.) and Robert L. Doughton (D., N.C.) were ahead of him in point of service.

There were predictions that the threatened Southern revolt would have its effects upon the spirit of the Eighty-first Congress. With a modesty, laced with self-confidence, the Speaker expressed the belief that he could handle any threatened coalition, because he had never been an extremist himself and possessed a basic kinship with many of the leaders of his section. Much of his own legislative record showed a liberal strain but there were such exceptions as Civil Rights. He admitted that he valued Party loyalty, but honestly believed that while he was "in the New Deal, he was not of it," that he was still Sam Rayburn. During the last session his votes to sustain vetoes on the Taft-Hartley, tax-reduction, and social security limitation bills, and his stand on rent control and public housing, all satisfied the New Dealers and Fair Dealers. But his thinking on Civil Rights and the administration of displaced persons was by no means in line with the liberal tradition. He also referred to FEPC, anti-lynching laws, and so forth as evidence of his contrary views. As to these problems he explained, there were some things which only time and human understanding, not laws or force, could work out.

Rayburn thought he was compatible with any intelligent group of men who had America's interests at heart. He wanted it clearly understood that he had never belonged to anyone and that he was not for sale. He had always been frank with his constituents and planned to continue his policy of making up his own mind, free from pressure. "I'll not hesitate to take a stand on any solid issue," he declared. He cited the Marshall Plan as an example of a measure he endorsed before he or anyone else could find out what the grass roots sentiments were. He said it was natural to drift with public opinion, but somehow he believed that in the Fourth he had shared in motivating group thinking.

In December, 1948, as Mr. Sam talked to friends and the press prior to the opening of Congress, he seemed more philosophical than usual, and had words of wit and wisdom. When interviewed on the prerequisites for success in Congress, he frankly stated that a brilliant, uninformed orator could be beaten in a House debate by a poor speaker who knew his subject matter. He believed that genius was ninety per cent hard work anyway. About people, he said: "There's really not much difference between people. When a man has common sense, he's got all the sense there is. The important thing is what he does with it. Some men ripen earlier than others and burn out early. Powder will flash but it won't last long."

About his own progress and age he smilingly commented: "Come January I hope to be the best $30,000-a-year cotton picker in Congress. Each of us hates to see the years slip away, but there is something kind in nature. It makes you feel that the age you are living in is the best for you. I know that after fifty was the best for me."

As he discussed the problems of the Eighty-first he lighted a cigarette and leaned back in his chair, putting his feet in a desk drawer, and remarked "I am optimistic for the future."

The election of Rayburn as Speaker on January 3, 1949, was a brief formality. Retiring Speaker Martin added some levity to the occasion when he recalled the ceremony back in 1947; "You know, at that time, Sam, I really thought you meant it. I did not think you were giving an 'Indian gift' to be recalled within two years."

Mr. Sam may have appeared an "Indian giver" but he was actually a good prognosticator of elections. In January, 1947, when he lost the Speakership, he sent his gavel to a friend, Roy A. Riales, then Speaker of the Arkansas Legislature, with the statement it was merely being loaned and that he would be needing it back after the November election in 1948. So while Martin graciously handed his successor the symbolic gavel, the other was being returned from Tulare, California, where Riales had recently gone to open a soft drink business.

Sam Rayburn, however, responded to Martin's tribute with an expression that was equally genuine in sentiment:

> "One of the beautiful things about service in the House is that personal relationships and personal friendships are not divided by the center aisle. Some of the nearest and dearest friends I have ever had in the House of Representatives were on the left of the Speaker's stand. I hope it may always be so."

On the afternoon of January 3, the President turned up at a surprise meeting in Mr. Sam's Board of Education room. Rayburn's victory over the Rules Committee and the desire to make a social call prompted the White House visitation. Shortly afterward Attorney-General Tom Clark and Secretary Stuart Symington of the Air Force also joined the group. Tom Clark made some reference to the "Board Room" and the early days when Speaker Jack Garner used to take friends there for "education" and also to "strike a blow for liberty"—another name for downing a dram of bourbon. History does not record whether Mr. Sam's patriots made either a "stand at Concord Bridge or charged up Bunker Hill." History does record, though, that Senator Johnson happened to look up sheepishly at the wall at the portrait of the late Senator Morris Sheppard, the ardent prohibitionist. The next day the picture was moved to one of Mr. Sam's other offices where the atmosphere was more appropriate for the venerable Senator.

As time passed, Mr. Sam's pleasure with January 6 increased. On this particular January 6 he did not get a single bite of his own birthday luncheon, at which President Truman was a guest. For shortly after the President arrived at the ornate Speaker's dining room in the House wing of the Capitol, Mr. Sam excused himself, explaining that there was a meeting upstairs. "I'm sorry, Mr. President, but I have to go up and see them elect a president." Truman laughed because he knew the routine of certifying an administration.

As had been the custom for thirty years, Rayburn had eaten his birthday dinner with Mr. and Mrs. J. L. Aston. Mrs. Aston, nearing eighty years of age, prepared the meal, as she had been accustomed to doing. Before the dinner Mrs. Lyndon B. Johnson, wife of the new junior Senator from Texas, held a reception in Rayburn's honor. Lady Bird, as she came to be familiarly known, had already won the reputation of being one of Washington's most gracious hostesses. Tom Connally, the senior Senator, observed that he would find Johnson a more congenial teammate than the predecessor, W. Lee O'Daniel.

About the receptions and dinners Representative Clark W. Thompson and wife gave for the Speaker they had many pleasant memories. He seemed to add something to the occasion which made the Rayburn affairs different, they said. Thompson wrote:

> I have noticed one thing in particular. Anybody who got an invitation showed up—ambassadors, cabinet members, and such as that. Invariably they loved to gather in comparatively small groups to partake of the Speaker's unique personality and to listen to the gems of wisdom which he always dropped.

When the deficiency appropriation bill was being sharply debated on February 15, Mr. Sam expressed strong views about remodeling the House chamber. He favored the expenditure of $2,274,500 for putting a strong steel structure in the ceiling and replacing the outmoded seats. This was only the beginning of the face-lifting and protracted discussions which culminated in the more extensive remodeling of the Capitol. The quite controversial subject was to be thrashed out in 1960, when both Rayburn and Johnson were denounced by many for extravagance in the remodeling enterprises.

After hearing the President at two victory dinners express his intention of making a tour of the country in order to define his legislative program, Mr. Sam decided to do some public relations work of his own. The Jackson-Jefferson Day dinner, February 24, at Nashville, Tennessee, was both a homecoming for him and a political rally. Twelve hundred loyal Democrats from every section of the State came to the dinner, but four hundred Party faithfuls who had purchased tickets had to be content to go hungry. However they stayed to hear the address by loudspeaker. He told a responsive audience that he could talk for two hours about what the Party had done for "the ordinary plain American citizen" during more than sixteen years, but would be compelled to curtail his enthusiasm.

At a similar dinner in Austin, Texas, on March 20, he invited the "strays" who had supported Henry Wallace and J. Strom Thurmond to come back to their home. The performance was repeated at Raleigh, North Carolina, on April 3. Here he added that the best way to prevent Federal interference in States' Rights was for the states to discharge the responsibilities that accompany those rights, because the Federal Government steps in only when the state has failed to exercise its duty. He made two other strong points which were relative to the public mood of 1949: 1) the indiscriminate practice of pinning the Communist label on innocent persons is both irresponsible and dangerous (his reference was to Joe McCarthy); 2) a strong America is an America which must maintain leadership in world affairs through the Marshall Plan and other foreign-aid programs. Thus he put little stock in label-fixing and name-calling and showed no patience with the isolationist clamor to turn the clock back.

With his return to the Speakership came more and more social functions which brought Mr. Sam into the public eye. He turned down many invitations but not that of May 1. The members of Congress and their wives turned out *en masse* at the Congressional Club to honor him and Miss Lou.

On Thursday evening, May 5, he and Senator Arthur H. Vandenberg (R., Mich.) were informed that they had won the *Collier's* magazine awards of $10,000 each for distinguished service in 1948 to their respective Parties. Rayburn promptly announced: "I'm going to use this money as the nucleus to establish a library. I want to do something for the citizens of Bonham and Fannin County who have been so fine to me all these years."

The plaque and $10,000 gift were presented to the Speaker by the President in a White House ceremony on Saturday, May 7. The luncheon which was held afterwards was attended by government officials, judges, and *Collier's* officials. The basis for the decision, stated Eric Johnston, chairman of the committee, was Rayburn's performance as Minority Leader, when he yielded to a Party draft instead of returning to a more comfortable role of just plain congressman. *Collier's* recognized particularly that he was a courageous leader, never hesitating to take a stand on major issues.

The Speaker gave further details about his ideas for a library: "I'm going to set up a Sam Rayburn library fund for Fannin County, and as the years go on, I'm going to add to it as I am able. I'll build a library building to house my books, papers, and documents for future generations. The building will also have space for Bonham and Fannin County to have a library." Thus an early dream now began to take shape.

While basking in the warm sunshine of public approval he was confronted with the task of finding a solution to the Taft-Hartley Act that would be acceptable to both a recalcitrant electorate and an indignant labor bloc. He sought one of his famous compromises, for he well knew that his Party's platform for 1948 promised more than a Democratic Congress could deliver. After several conferences at the White House he declared his intentions of seeking a compromise repeal bill—one which would keep the provision for Presidential injunctions to prevent strikes against the national welfare. Although labor leaders hated this injunction, Rayburn thought that only John L. Lewis of the United Mine Workers would be incensed. Rayburn added one new provision—the establishment of a joint Congressional committee to study labor relations. Rayburn felt that his proposal would pacify both the President and labor leaders because such a committee would seek some method other than the injunction.

Had Rayburn and Truman not been such close friends, with implicit faith in one another, there could have developed some moments of vexation over the publicity which was given the Speaker's activities. A misquotation in the press of a letter from Truman to A. F. Whitney, of the Brotherhood of Railroad Trainmen, left the impression that Rayburn had been rebuked for seeking this compromise instead of dealing directly with the Act. Both the Speaker and the President, however, were indignant over the implication left by the typographical error. The relations between the two Democratic leaders remained unaffected by the bad publicity. They were in communication and understood one another's position on this issue, as on others where they could have been drawn apart by personal or sectional differences. Rayburn had believed all along that Taft-Hartley was unfair, but common sense made him see that repeal was out of the question at the time.

Politics is often an offensive thing to the layman, like unto a field hospital behind battle lines. Only a realist like Rayburn had a stomach for some of its unsavory business. The Speaker's role was to find a middle ground that would be acceptable to both labor and the rest of the American people, and at the same time would live up to the Party platform. Rayburn was not attempting to feign nobility. He was searching for a solution which would not come back and haunt the Democratic Party.

The Speaker, on June 22, again found himself in the position of a compromiser, this time on the Tidelands question. During the two-year controversy he had withheld a commitment until the issue had crystallized. However, he had taken an unrelenting stand on Texas' rights within the ten-and-one-half-mile limit. The Supreme Court had given the Federal Government paramount rights along California's coast, including rights to the oil-bearing tidelands. It appeared that Texas and Louisiana were about to be given the same treatment. There was a bill pending in Congress which would give the States outright ownership of the tidelands. On the other hand, the Administration had a bill which would give the ownership to the Federal Government. Rayburn was in an impossible position. He was rebuked by his own section for keeping the States' bill off the House floor, but he knew that, should the measure pass, it would be vetoed by the President. He also was castigated by the rest of the country since the other bill was faring no better. Again Rayburn was seeking an acceptable compromise, since he believed "half a loaf was better than no loaf at all."

Since Price Daniel, Texas' Attorney-General, had a more partisan clientele than the Speaker of the National Congress, he could not reasonably accept such a proposal. Rayburn's action may have caused the Administration to agree to a new bill, one that proposed the following: 1) The Federal Government would quitclaim to the states the bed of inland waters; 2) it would hold paramount rights over tidelands for navigation, defense, and international affairs; 3) the states would control development and production of oil and exercise taxing and police powers; 4) the states would give the Federal Government thirty-seven and one-half per cent of oil revenues from the tidelands and get the same percentage from the Federally owned outer shelf. Mr. Sam was walking a rather narrow line in these peace-making efforts for he was attempting to retain state control of the oil lands, as well as most of the revenues, and at the same time serve the interests of the Administration and the country as a whole. He had a dual function of serving both State and Federal Government. His basic apprehension that Texas could lose the case, if it were adjudicated, led some to think that he had forsaken his original position. But one who has the insight to anticipate defeat is likely to be called a traitor or coward by the unthinking masses, when in reality he is a wise man or a prophet.

Eleven years later the Federal Government sold oil and gas leases on 400,000 acres outside the ten-and-one-half-mile limit off the coast of Texas—the so-called tidelands beyond the area claimed by Texas to which Federal title was conceded by State officials who fought for the tidelands through the years. The Federal Government got $35,732,031 for the leases off the Texas coast, and $285,180,648 for leases on 1,500,000 acres off the Louisiana coast. Geologists had advised Rayburn that this wealth was here; hence he effected a compromise, which he did not actually like to consider as a compromise.

Since Governor Allan Shivers' name later became linked with this controversy it should be mentioned that he too favored Rayburn's compromise (he was Lieutenant-Governor at the time). On June 8, 1949, according to Fagan Dickson's article, "The Segregation Cases," Shivers issued the following statement to the Capitol press, explaining his willingness to compromise Texas Special Tidelands claim to the ten-and-one-half-mile zone by exchanging a percentage of the revenue realized in the ten-and-one-half-mile zone for an equal percentage of the revenue obtained outside that zone:

"I resent as much as any other Texan the fact that the Federal Government, through a decision of the Supreme Court of the United States, is taking the so-called tidelands, a ten-mile zone off the shore of Texas, from the State of Texas; but the fact remains that it is being taken. I was reared to respect authority, and living under the system of government which I do, I recognize that historically the Supreme Court of the United States is the final arbitrator in disputes over legal rights."

Under the terms of Rayburn's bill, Texas would have received sixty-two-and-one-half per cent of the oil and other mineral rights inside the ten-and-one-half-mile limit, and one-half from the remainder of the continental shelf which in places extends up to 140 miles off the Texas coast line. Rayburn's bill would have granted Texas the ownership of the land out to the ten-and-one-half-mile point, the very issue which is still before the Supreme Court despite the 1953 quitclaim bill. Under Rayburn's bill Texas would have received more income than under the 1953 law which now exists.

The leadership in the State Government—Attorney-General Price Daniel, Governor Beauford Jester, Lieutenant-Governor Allan Shivers, and Land Commissioner Bascom Giles—decided not to accept Rayburn's compromise and went against him. Then Rayburn had to proceed to get a bill through that was congenial with the Texas sentiment. This one was vetoed. He tried again and succeeded. Sam Rayburn was trying to follow a leadership which he felt had made a mistake, but as the servant of his people he followed their wishes. His modesty forbade comment on the outcome, but in 1961 he could not keep from feeling that his judgment was sound, considering how it all turned out.

His compromise was a daring one because he was playing a hunch and going contrary to popular opinion, but he believed the State in the long run stood to profit. The salt domes beyond the ten-and-one-half-mile limit, he believed, might prove to be rich in oil; hence Texas could share these revenues. This is Mr. Sam's side of the story.

The Eighty-first Congress concluded its first session on August 19, and Mr. Sam went home for a much needed rest. Members of the press, as in the past, saw Rayburn's behavior during this Eighty-first Congress as resembling that of a poker player, and described him as playing several hands with the White House and his own section with his cards against his chest. Civil Rights, Taft-Hartley, and Tidelands—these were the issues which made the stakes high and the session strenuous.

This was one of Mr. Sam's most trying terms as Speaker, because he was faced with a strong coalition of Republican and conservative Democrats, who showed more strength on some domestic issues than the Administration could muster to offset them. The revolt in Dixie had also caused trouble within Administrative ranks, because the cry went up almost immediately, when the session opened, for Mr. Sam to purge from committees those Southern members who had deserted the Party. It took a great deal of diplomacy and talking in the washroom for him to cleanse people's minds of their vindictive ideas.

Sam Rayburn, however, was not always successful when it came to "pouring oil on the troubled waters" down in Dixie. One evening in June of 1949, Mr. Sam was in Lexington, Virginia, at a function on the campus of Washington and Lee. A group had assembled in the home of the president, Francis Pendleton Gaines, Sr.; the mansion had historic interest to Rayburn since Robert E. Lee lived and died there. James F. Byrnes, Secretary of State under Truman until 1947, was there, and asked to speak privately with Mr. Sam about a very important matter. Francis Pendleton ("Penny") Gaines, Jr., saw them ease off into the Green Room, where they had a bottle of Jack Daniels (sour mash)—"green label," as he recalled. "Penny" was being the perfect host and did not hear too much of the conversation; however, Byrnes said, "Sam, I have decided to break with President Truman. It's official as of this moment." Rayburn, knowing that his friend could cause the Party considerable trouble if he teamed up with the Southern revolt, put on a masterful demonstration of "quiet persuasion" but failed dismally, according to Gaines. The two, however, parted in the very best of spirits; that is, their relations did not seem impaired.

The two months of semi-freedom during the summer of 1949 were perhaps the most welcome Sam Rayburn ever knew. He had an opportunity to commune with nature and indulge in one of his most favorite recreations under the weeping willows around Lake Texoma. He also found relaxation in manual labor at his rural hideaway.

Where there were cows Mr. Sam knew work was involved. He belonged to the old school of ranchers who were not content merely to visit their cows in the cool of the afternoon to stroke their ears and reward them with pellets of cake. He worked with them himself.

Proof of this fact is an account by Joe B. Johnson, who owns a ranch adjoining Mr. Sam's. One afternoon he heard a terrific commotion in Rayburn's corral and went over to investigate. There he found the Speaker surrounded by about twenty-five rambunctious Herefords. He was cutting out several to put in his north pasture and was not using his "gentle persuasion" method. Some of the cows were as cantankerous as Dixiecrats in the Rules Committee. "Mr. Sam," said Joe B., "was cussin' and running against them with a vengeance." Joe B., seeing the danger, spoke abruptly to his friend, saying, "Mr. Sam, you are crazy. The country has too much money invested in you for you to be out there acting like this. Get up on that fence and let me cut out those cows. If they kill me it won't hurt so much." Reluctantly the Speaker crawled up on the fence in something of a huff and watched, all the while hankering to crawl down and kick one or two of them that had tried to run over him.

Mr. Sam rarely told a hired hand "to go ahead"; instead he said, "come on, let's do it." During the Forties this boundless energy caused others, besides Joe B. Johnson, to express concern. On another occasion a friend who had some business to transact with the Speaker found him one very hot day in the corn crib, hardly recognizable in his overalls, behind a mask of dirt.

"Sam," he said, "if you don't quit this foolishness, one of us fellows will find you some day flat on your face, and we'll have to telephone Joe Denton [the undertaker] to come get you."

The Speaker worked because he loved work for its own sake, whether it was in Washington, Bonham, or Ivanhoe. He would reassure his attentive friends that men died of their frustrations, not physical activity. He believed that manual labor gave him a reserve of strength to do his job in Washington. He thought his activities during the fall of 1949 were good for his spirit.

Among his other fall activities was a November 18 and 19 meeting in Houston with the Democratic leaders who had prepared a "feast of reconciliation," as W. A. Combs of Dallas described it. The Tidelands controversy, which stirred more immediate dissension than Civil Rights, was the issue that brought the "feast" to Houston, with Mr. Sam as the principal speaker at the Fourth Annual Convention of the Texas Association of Democratic County Chairmen. It was planned especially for the Speaker to show the Party nationally, and the voters of Texas, that old disagreements were healed and that their hangover of rancor was gone.

Democrats, Dixiecrats, Shivercrats, and neo-Republicans turned out in force at a luncheon in Glenn McCarthy's new Shamrock Hotel. The host sounded the keynote of the meeting, after his word of welcome: "There have been many differences among Party leaders during the past several years. Now is the time for complete unity in the Democratic Party." When former Governor W. P. Hobby introduced Mr. Rayburn he said, "It's only a hair's breadth from Speaker to President; and it might be that Sam will lose a hair by 1952." Rayburn had heard Texans' kind prophesies before and knew all the witticisms about men with exfoliated scalps. At this moment Mr. Sam looked up at Hobby with a twinkle in his eyes and stroked the back of his bald head. Perhaps he remembered the admiring matron's remark at a Washington party to a mutual friend: "What a nice head of hide he has."

After a brief address the Speaker retired to the presidential suite to discuss plans for the evening rally at Sam Houston Coliseum. During the late afternoon, he and Senator Johnson made a quick call to the campus of the University of Houston, where they had several mutual friends. E. E. Oberholtzer, one-time superintendent of schools and then president of the University, asked Johnson if he had returned to reactivate the leave of absence he had with the Houston Independent School District. Johnson had taught in the Houston system. Oberholtzer also told Johnson that he needed a debate coach, if that was the job he had come to apply for. Rayburn whispered slyly to his friend, "Go ahead and take it!" Riding back to the hotel, Rayburn expressed his fascination with the University, commenting on its development, "That school illustrates what these Americans can do when they have a dream and do something about it."

In the Coliseum that night only four thousand loyal Democrats showed up to rattle around in their spacious quarters. The speech, Rayburn's first of a political nature in Houston, was the kind Houstonians liked to hear, with references to progress, prosperity, industry, oil, Americanism. Those present were glad the Speaker "horsewhipped the Republican Party into nothingness." The Party was brought into a semblance of unity which could have been dissolved very quickly had such issues as Civil Rights and Tidelands been mentioned. Then the old anti-Roosevelt, anti-Henry Wallace, and anti-Truman Party feuds of 1936, 1940, 1944, and 1948 would have begun all over again. This career Democrat since the age of twenty-four looked upon Houston as a political enigma. He could not grasp the ephemeral quality among some Democrats—with *this* affiliation in the Party primaries and *that* affiliation in November; one thing in 1946, another in 1948, and still something else, he feared, in 1952. "Those Democrats down there should either get on the horse or get off," he said afterward.

When Mr. Sam returned to Bonham from Houston he found a letter in his mail box that was entirely non-political in nature:

Main Building 2108
The University of Texas
Austin, Texas
November 16, 1949

The Honorable Sam Rayburn,
Bonham, Texas
Dear Mr. Rayburn:

It gives me great pleasure to inform you that you have been elected honorary member of the Alpha of Texas Chapter of Phi Beta Kappa.

Very truly yours,
Lois Ware
Secretary

The citation, signed by W. J. Battle, Mrs. Anne Irving, and Minnie Lee Barrett Shepard, contained this statement as a part of supporting evidence of his qualification:

> As Speaker, Mr. Rayburn has used his great powers sparingly to gain his ends, employing instead a persuasion that by its brilliance has earned him the name of "the greatest compromiser since Henry Clay." His integrity, marked by humility, simplicity, and tolerance, has won the respect of his colleagues and of the world, and his native ruggedness has brought him widespread appeal.
>
> As statesman and lawmaker, Mr. Rayburn has written some of the most important laws on our statute books, and guided them to enactment by masterly parliamentary procedure, contending against some of the most brilliant specialists of the nation in law and finance.

Thus Mr. Sam became a Phi Beta Kappa and an "egg head," to borrow the phrasing of those who are not "egg heads."

The President of the United States paid Rayburn the supreme compliment at a luncheon January 6, 1950, given for the Speaker by Senator Johnson and Representative Wright Patman. As he presented him with a hat for his birthday, he said: "Sam is the only man I know who could stay in Washington over forty years and still wear the same size hat he wore when he came here. I don't know what kind of hat this is, but I'll show you how to fix it." Then he revealed some of his former skill as a haberdasher, flipping the hat into shape and planting it squarely on Rayburn's head. The crowd let out a roar when Mr. Sam pulled it down over his ears. After the guests quieted down, the President made a few appropriate remarks for a birthday celebration. He quoted Vice-President Barkley as saying that when he was a kid he used to listen to Sam on the lecture platform. "But, in view of Barkley's known age, I'll be damned if I can understand how Sam can be just sixty-eight." He introduced Rayburn at this bipartisan birthday luncheon as a man who has "made his friends proud and his critics ashamed."

As the Eighty-first Congress reached its halfway mark the Truman Fair Deal program was in real difficulties. The coalition of Southern Democrats and Northern Republicans threatened to shoot the major legislation full of holes. Foreign spending, further controls, additional revenue—these were the areas where the President depended most heavily on the Speaker because of his friendship with conservatives and his past reputation as a liberal. With his newly acquired power after the "teeth of the Rules Committee had been pulled," the Administration was more than ever beholden to the man who sat in the big chair on the rostrum. From long experience he was able to predict what most congressmen would do. Where he was not quite sure, he was capable of watching out of the corners of half-shut eyes the dying efforts of members attempting to attract attention, but he knew what these persons wanted. Their grievances had already been discussed by the appropriate committees.

Rayburn knew when to vote on measures. He always estimated the votes on important legislation beforehand. He would not permit bills containing controversial elements to come up until he was sure the controversial sections had been thrashed out in committee. He saw it as sheer extravagance to bring the House together for the purpose of editing a bill. This was the argument he gave, particularly for such a measure as the FEPC bill. Sometimes pressure from the White House did lead him against his judgment to permit something prematurely to reach the floor. When it was torn to pieces by amendments, the President quickly learned to yield to Rayburn's judgment in the future.

Mr. Sam went home for a brief visit during the last week of May to participate in two ceremonies from which he derived tremendous pleasure. First, there was the formal opening of the Denison public library, which gave him occasion to talk about his own plans for a similar project in Bonham. It was just seven months later that his own dream began to take on practical proportions, when the Rayburn Foundation received $50,000 from the close friends of Colonel Myron G. Blalock of Marshall, who had died rather suddenly before he could complete the final arrangements for a contribution which was intended to be anonymous. Second, on May 23, 1950, Mr. Sam was awarded an honorary degree of Doctor of Humanities from Austin College at its Centennial celebration. This occasion was especially significant since all the previous awards had been the Doctor of Law degree. Thus he reasoned that he was able now to dedicate his remaining years specifically "to humanity."

During the fall of 1950 he devoted much of his time while Congress was in recess to justifying the President's foreign policy as reflected by the performances of Secretary of State Dean Acheson. America was now involved in the United Nations policing of Korea. At Princeton and McKinney, Texas, on September 4 and 5, he directed his remarks to what he called the "knock and smear boys of political partisanship." At Electra, Texas on November 21, he concentrated on the short-memoried "sob-brothers" who cried "government bankruptcy" and "socialistic regime."

Before the Electra festivities were terminated, the Chamber of Commerce presented him with a Palomino quarter horse named "Whistle Stop," which he promptly mounted before the WBAP-TV cameramen had given the signal. He then walked around his new possession several times admiringly. To some of the men standing beside the horse he remarked that he had a quarter horse from the Matador Ranch called "Pansy," that was twenty-one years old, but that it was still the best mount in the business. "When a cow darts quickly to one side, you'd better start grabbing leather because Pansy is going to stay with that cow." "With one-hundred-fifty head of whiteface cattle to work," he said, "foreman Roy Gauntz could use another good horse like Whistle Stop!"

Back in 1913 the editor of the Texas, *Monitor* (Mineola), made a daring prophecy when Sam Rayburn climbed aboard the train for Washington:

> Sam Rayburn has served three terms in the Texas Legislature and his promotions have come with marked rapidity. In the national Congress he will build up in the same way and soon be numbered among the leaders of the distinguished body.

On January 3, 1951, when the new Eighty-second Congress elected Mr. Sam Speaker for the sixth time, relatives of the "prophet" from Mineola pulled out the clipping for display. Some who read it recognized that many years had elapsed since Sam's famous "cotton patch" yell in the Texas House of Representatives, when he won the speakership race down there. They realized that he had now become a serious type who would be repelled by such youthful expressions of joy. He always preferred a simple way of life. He agreed to go home one evening with Lyndon Johnson on the understanding that he would not "turn on the blamed television set." At one time he had resisted the airplane, but he surrendered to it and was destined to yield to TV before many more years. Although Sam Rayburn was slow to accept the luxuries of his day, in his political views he tried to be in advance of the times, when the mores would permit.

When Sam Rayburn mounted the rostrum on January 30, 1951, he surpassed Henry Clay's record of 3056½ days as Speaker. Clay's period of service was November 4, 1811 to January 19, 1814; December 4, 1815 to October 28, 1820; and December 1 to March 3, 1825. The President staged a surprise ceremony at the White House at which he presented the Speaker with a gavel made of the wood that was used to reconstruct the White House in 1817, when repairs were done on that part which was burned by the British.

It was on January 31 that the House had its special "Sam Rayburn Day" to commemorate the event. The death of Representative John B. Sullivan had caused a postponement. Rayburn took a seat in the back row while his colleagues, Democrats and Republicans alike, jockeyed to get a chance to make their remarks. The tributes did not overlook any facet of his ability and personality. Representative Stefan referred to him as a Christian, stating that his example had helped bring the philosophy of the Sermon on the Mount into the Halls of Congress:

> "I have gone with him when we fished together. I have heard him pray before partaking of God's food. I have watched him ask for God's guidance, on his knees, before going to bed at night."

Representative Robert L. Doughton (N.C.) made one comment which was different and brought forth a round of laughter. He had described Rayburn as a successful citizen, statesman, parliamentarian, and Speaker. Then he added:

> "I cannot say so much for him as a father but he's still young, handsome and popular. We still have hope for him in that respect. The same is equally true of our distinguished and beloved ex-Speaker, the Honorable Joseph Martin of Massachusetts."

Rayburn joined in the laughter.

The Texas delegation postponed their celebration of the event until April 18 when they could have a luncheon and present Rayburn with a plaque bearing the engraved seal of the United States. The Texas Legislature responded on February 3 with a House Current Resolution commemorating his "unparalleled record of unselfish and devoted public service."

The breaking of a record which had stood for 125 years gave Rayburn some occasion for philosophizing about his job and attitudes. During his long tenure he had observed many men, big and small, and he believed that the real test of a man was the way he carried success. A person who became conceited and arrogant when promoted to a big job was not big enough for that job. One thing he expected of a man was that he look him squarely in the eyes when they talked and tell him what he would or would not do. Rayburn looked his man in the eyes and when he gave his word he stuck with it. Of this quality Garner said, "Sam stayed hitched."

"I have found," Rayburn said, "that people respect you if you tell them where you stand. If you 'shilly-shally' and are afraid to say 'no' you'll get into trouble, and there's no reason for any man to get 'uppity' in a government job." The only exception he felt was the Presidency because any man would undergo changes as a result of the responsibilities of the White House.

As far as he himself was concerned, he felt that there was no reason to change his outlook and habits, although as he grew older he naturally curtailed some things. When he was a younger man he played baseball, but when he got a little older he found himself a good seat in the shade near the watercooler. He had put his golf clubs aside, but, as he phrased it: "I walk at least two miles every day. I stay in bed as long as I can. Although I don't sleep nine hours a night, I know that when I am stretched out in bed, all my insides are relaxed. Also, I don't worry. When I leave Capitol Hill, I leave my work there."

Rayburn frankly admitted one day: "I never did go in for all those social doings. I'd much rather be down home with my Herefords on my farm. Some days I get about three or four invitations, and I just have to turn most of them down. If it's an invitation from a friend to go on a quiet fishing party, that's different."

He preferred small parties to large ones, but admitted that the big ones sometimes had to be pulled off! "I don't like the mammoth affair where one is invited for official reasons, rather than out of friendship. I remember my first big cocktail party, one given by a celebrated Washington hostess right after I arrived here in the Capitol, a long time ago. No one knew I was there, or cared."

He enjoyed going to a friend's home, particularly when he was able to cook the meal or prepare one of his favorite dishes. Chili, which he could eat at any time except breakfast, was one of these. Once when someone asked for Rayburn's recipe, his secretary, Alla Clary wrote that she did not recall that he had one. She said she had seen him prepare one of his Mexican dinners but that he opened cans.

There is always a tendency to surround national figures with legends. One of these in Rayburn's case was his affiliation with the so-called "bourbon and branch water" school. Of course, Rayburn would take a little scotch as a substitute. He was referred to by his companions as a six o'clock drinker, and then only when invited out for dinner and on special occasions; he never drank after a meal. He had a reputation for moderation. About drinking in public, he told Raymond P. Brandt: "Since I was Majority Leader I have not been in a cocktail lounge. It's not that I have any prejudice. It's just because I don't think a public official should be seen in such places. I remember going to cocktail parties during the war and seeing some high ranking generals there who had arrived before I did. I wondered then why they weren't using the time to fight the war. Some people might have some such idea if they saw me in a cocktail lounge."

About one of his social affairs he recalled a rather embarrassing situation. He had gone down to the dock area of Washington to have a seafood dinner with his old fishing friend and writer, Frank McNaughton. When they were returning to the Speaker's apartment, they just happened to take the route by the Carleton Hotel. They noticed the people, the men and wives, going in, all dressed up in formal attire. McNaughton asked Sam what the occasion was that had brought so many people together. Rayburn stared at the crowd for a moment; then his mouth fell open. "Hey!" he yelled. "That party's for me!" [1] He said he could not forget that moment, his panicky feeling, and the mad dash to the apartment. Putting on a tuxedo under such circumstances, he recalled, was somewhat strenuous.

Since Clay was also reputed to be a great compromiser, Rayburn was asked in 1951 if he would venture a comparison between himself and Clay. "I am not a compromiser," he barked back. "I'd rather be known as a 'persuader.' I try to compromise by getting people to think my way. Of course, there are times when you haven't got the votes; then you have to make concessions. I have been in on White House meetings with the President, where the President, the Majority Leader of the House, the Minority Leader, and the Majority Leader of the Senate were against me on a proposition. I have told them that I thought they were wrong and had been ill advised, but that I would go along and let the rest of the fellows in the House thrash it out. But when the votes were about even in one of these meetings, I stuck by my guns."

Mr. Sam had the reputation for being determined and confident, not easy to dissuade from a course wherein he thought he was right.

While the Speaker was generalizing, he pointed out that he had been given some credit for things wherein he had received some able assistance. He mentioned the Railroad Holding Company Act, the Securities and Exchange Act, the Rural Electrification Administration Act, the Public Utility Holding Company Act, and the Communications Act as examples. Here he was quick to give credit to Thomas G. Corcoran and Benjamin V. Cohen, two brilliant legislative consultants, who worked out of the White House. About them Rayburn said:

"Taken together these two fellows made the brightest man I ever saw. They never insisted on their own views. When I told them what I wanted, they started to work to put it into the legislation, and they wrote it in such a way as to make it stick. I know that a lot of people say that Tommy Corcoran has made a lot of money. But he is a real Democrat and we could use some young fellows like him now."

Raymond P. Brandt, chief Washington correspondent of the St. Louis *Post-Dispatch,* asked Mr. Rayburn in 1951 whom he considered the ablest man he had known in the House. Rayburn replied with the same answer Speaker Champ Clark had given him many years ago—Joseph Weldon Bailey. He reported that another man whose intellect he greatly admired was Socialist Meyer London of New York City. Mr. Sam said that the question was really unanswerable because there were various kinds of ability; for example, John Garner was a man of rare intelligence and industry; Oscar W. Underwood was capable enough to have been President but came from the wrong section of the country; La Guardia of New York was unusual; Marcantonio had an incisive mind; and Fred Vinson had the ability to get things done, as did Finis J. Garrett.

"Our representatives today are better educated," he added, "better informed on issues and work harder and longer than in the old days. When I first came here I sometimes got as many as ten letters a day. Now a congressman's daily mail runs into the hundreds and thousands of letters and telegrams. Generally speaking, I think the intelligence in the House is higher than I have ever known it before."

As to qualifications in the Senate, he responded: "A member

of the House shouldn't comment on the other chamber. It is something of an index, however, that Senator Taft is the spokesman for the majority of the Republicans over there."

Along with the general upgrading of personnel in the House, he thought the responsibilities and prestige of the Speaker had also increased. The Norris "Lame Duck" amendment had done a great deal to raise standards by doing away with the short session from December to March 4. It was during those short sessions, he said, that the Republicans "pulled off some of their most important legislation."

In 1951, Rayburn admitted that back in 1946 he had given some thought to withdrawing from politics, because he sensed that the Democrats would lose control of the House and he did not want to step down from the Speaker's rostrum to take over the strenuous Minority Leader's job on the floor:

"I did want to go back to the farm and take it easy for a while, but I was afraid that my action would have been a public confession that I thought the Democrats would lose the Congress, and I feared also that this would have been interpreted to mean that I believed Truman would be defeated. If I should open this issue with myself in 1952, it would also have a bad effect. I have just reached the point where I have to consider the welfare of others and forget about the ranch and farm. A good soldier does not question. There is so much yet to be done in these troubled times. Love and duty take the matter entirely out of my hands."

By 1951 Mr. Sam had learned to jest about those who did not like his program. He could be sarcastic at the mention of some editorial in the Dallas *Morning News*. For example, he talked about the *News'* present to him on Easter Sunday—a front page spread, beginning at the top of the first two columns. He recalled that the previous Easter Sunday this space was filled with an article by Felix McKnight called "The Risen Christ." However, he feared that the *News* had gone sour since 1950. In 1951 there was an open letter addressed to "Honorable Sam Rayburn, Member of the House of Representatives," which lampooned him as the helpless prisoner of the Dixiecrats and Republicans and the enemy of Texans, with an indirect reference to the Civil Rights legislation, and direct reference to his compromise stand on the Tidelands.

Since there had been an earlier editorial attacking him for favoring Grayson County as the site of an Air Academy instead of some more densely populated area, which Rayburn took to be a subtle reference to "Big D," he was prepared for the "Easter Greetings." While he was in this reminiscent mood, he recalled the *News'* derogatory comments about the Denison Dam, back in 1944 when he was beginning "that hard campaign against G. C. Morris."

Mr. Sam, however disassociated the *News* from the people in Dallas, although he did fear that some could have their minds colored by the constant bombardment. But, he mused, "many read the *Times Herald,*" recalling the March 2 story and others about him.

Twice during the third week in April, following White House conferences, Mr. Sam told reporters, "We are in terrible danger." His critics charged him with playing politics to get the Universal Military Training bill through Congress. Since June 27, 1950, however, the United States had been involved in the Korean War. He had sounded this same alarm even before the President brought American forces into the conflict under UN sanction.

On April 11, President Truman had relieved General Douglas MacArthur of his command, bringing praise from United Nations headquarters but sharp condemnation from many Americans on the home front. In looking at this incident ten years later, Rayburn reflected thus:

"Truman went out to one of the islands and took MacArthur off to speak to him and treated him with every courtesy. I thoroughly endorse his recalling of MacArthur. Sometimes people just get too big. Douglas MacArthur always felt like he was a man of destiny, I think. And he just about was, to tell you the truth. Everybody that served with him told me he was a fine general."

Mr. Sam received many scathing letters about this whole incident, including a lengthy epistle from a Baptist minister. It made reference to the Tidelands, MacArthur, and other issues gleaned from hostile press releases. Rayburn was accused of not looking after the people's interests. The minister made one statement which undoubtedly brought a crimson glow to the Congressman's head:

> If the people of the Sherman, Dennison [sic], Bonham area ever elect you to office again, they will be blind, deaf, dumb, and ignorant. . . . the Bible is an intensely interesting book. It says that Judas Iscariot, the betrayer, went out and hanged himself. It also says "go thou and do likewise."

After three weeks the Speaker replied as follows:

> I have your letter of April 24. In days when charity should be practiced and good will spread among our people your letter is disappointing to say nothing about being highly insulting.
>
> Being a believer in God and His Word and the teaching of His Son which was, "And on earth peace, good-will toward men," I fear that your conduct will not be conducive to carrying out these things. In other words, I fear that God and His Son traveling with you would be in poor company. Your addressing me as "Dishonorable Sam Rayburn" would be an answer to anything you might say anywhere at any time.
>
> This will close my correspondence with you.

In answer to a telegram from one of the leading citizens of Bonham, who had suggested that Congress impeach Mr. Truman, branding him and Mrs. Truman as traitors, Rayburn was also quite direct. He stated that he was amazed at this person's intemperance and violation of his usual good judgment. The action on MacArthur, needless to say, inflamed many of Mr. Sam's constituents. From the point of view of good administration, he did not waste any words in defending the decision.

On June 2, Rayburn devoted much of his commencement address to the graduating class at the University of Texas to a defense of America's foreign policy. It was a speech which suggested an understanding of the subject without penetrating to the depths of it. He portrayed the United States as a comparatively new nation in the stream of history, but one that had competence and a humane civilization. He introduced the term "containment" as a technique for dealing with Communism. The doctrine implied patience, meeting and countering the enemy at various points, frustrating him, throwing him off balance, and generally impeding him. He defined a long-term program designed to avoid a catastrophic war. He cautioned against too much talk and "low breeds of journalism." In reference to the MacArthur incident, he affirmed that "there can be only one head of our Government and he must not only be executor of the laws but commander-in-chief as well."

After a ten-day visit back home, interspersed with speeches and a much publicized panel discussion at Austin College, Sherman, he returned to Washington on June 13 to make a report on what he found:

"Everybody down my way says Washington is talking too much. They're tired of this investigation and that investigation. They want to know why we don't quit stalling and get down to making the country safe." What Rayburn meant was that more statesmanship and less political showmanship was needed.

Certain members of the House were the first to feed his irritation. Having difficulty keeping the bills moving, and annoyed by the lack of promptness among some, he burst forth one day:

> "It is growing and growing and growing that when two roll calls are had, members knowing that they can come into the well and answer, delay in their offices. The Chair does not think there is any member of the House whose office is so far from the floor of the House that he cannot get here when his name is called the second time."

Rayburn warned that someday, if he had a quorum, he was going to cut these laggards off and not give them fifteen minutes after this second roll call because there was no time to waste.

The basic source of his irritation was the change that had been made with respect to the Rules Committee. In 1948, Truman had won much support for removal of the blockade and the Speaker had been vested with a power that sent up a cry of "czarism" and "cannonism." At the opening of the Eighty-seventh Congress in 1951, however, a coalition of Southern and Northern Democrats promptly rescinded the action of the previous Congress, to restore the power of the Rules Committee. The anti-Civil Rights group and anti-public housing congressmen feared Trumanism. While Rayburn had some mixed feeling about phases of the program he did not want to have his hands tied.

Some of the same bluntness and irritation was worked off on the Southern governors who assembled at Hot Springs on November 12. Governor Theodore R. McKeldin of Maryland walked out, branding the address as "more than an outrage," and Governor Allan Shivers, a critic of both Truman and Rayburn, declared: "Some fellow once wrote, 'methinks thou protests thy virtue too loudly.' "

Rayburn called on the Dixiecrats "to get in line" or face annihilation in 1952 at the hands of the Republicans when patronage and committee assignments were to be handed out. He defended the New Deal and Fair Deal, with reference to Federal spending. He warned that the South "must give the Negroes a better break if they want to prevent passage of Federal Civil Rights legislation such as FEPC." "You can't filibuster forever," he told them. Fearing that Rayburn was trying to start a Truman draft, men like Herman Talmadge, Sr., and James F. Byrnes set the wheels of resistance in motion.

The States' Righters responded by electing Allan Shivers to the conference chairmanship and set the stage for the 1952 revolt. In accepting the post, Shivers spoke highly of General Eisenhower, Senators Byrd and Russell, stating that he did not believe Texas would split its Democratic Party in a showdown between States' Righters and the national Party: "I myself have always supported the Democratic candidate and I hope I always can." Herein is reflected some of the tension between the Speaker and the Governor, which perhaps had its origin a bit earlier in the Tidelands controversy and Trumanism.

Back in his District after ten months of strenuous work in Washington, Rayburn began making as many as two and three speeches a day, reporting on the state of the union. The Eighty-first Congress, he explained, had committed the United States to world leadership in the Korean struggle, and the Eighty-second Congress was in the process of implementing America's position by marshalling the nation's men and resources. This concerted effort, said Rayburn, "had put a chill into the men of the Kremlin and had fired with renewed faith the hearts of free men the world over. We have armed the free world—with spiritual force, economic vitality, and with military strength. . . . Both the Congress and the country have responded with confidence to the challenge of a shrunken world in a jet-propelled, atomic era." He explained that much legislation of merit had to be put aside temporarily while the lawmakers were shaping the answer to world stability.

His 1951 fall and winter speeches carried him into the many facets of contemporary affairs—foreign and domestic. The Mutual Security Act of 1951, he explained, was the outstanding accomplishment in the field of international affairs. A two-year extension of reciprocal trade, which denied benefits of concessions to the products of the United Soviet Socialist Republics and satellites, was also a major achievement in the House. The flow of war materials into countries behind the Iron Curtain was shut off. The much needed aid to India was begun through a $190,000,000 emergency loan. The joint resolution was signed officially terminating a state of war with Germany. Senate Concurrent Resolution 11 reaffirmed the friendship of the American people for all the people of the world, including the inhabitants of the Soviet Union. Rayburn hailed the Defense Production Act as the main instrument in our economic and industrial mobilization. A new tax bill which increased personal and corporate income taxes was essential to provide needed revenues, but these additional levies, he explained, were offset by the nation's new prosperity. Further benefits to veterans and housing in certain critical areas seemed to have priority status.

For the first time in years, Mr. Sam was able to celebrate his birthday with family and friends. This seventieth anniversary was quiet, as compared with previous Washington January 6's when there were luncheons, receptions and dinners. Only Miss Lou, Mrs. W. A. Thomas, Dick, and Tom, and their families were present for the 1952 Sunday birthday dinner. Mrs. Carl Nall of Sherman sent a cake baked in the form of an open book. On one of the pages was a bouquet of pink roses in the icing and on the other side were the greetings "Happy Birthday Sam—1–6–82, 1–6–52." Through the opened book was a bookmark.

All during the day friends were dropping in or telephoning to extend their greetings. Western Union and the post office were conscious of the date because of the increased volume of mail. About the middle of the morning a delegation of twenty-two close Bonham friends called on the Speaker to present him with a Browning over and under double-barreled shotgun. "It's beautiful," he exclaimed. "I never expected to own a gun like this one," he added as he gingerly handled it, feeling the weight, and bringing it up to his left shoulder in a shooting position.

Congress convened on January 8, 1952, for its second session. Since this was an election year the Speaker's duties increased. He thought the flow of legislation should keep pace with the nation's needs and the Party should be on its good behavior. The Speaker carried the brunt of both responsibilities.

While paying tribute, on February 19, to Constantino Brumidi at the unveiling of a bronze grave marker, Mr. Sam took the opportunity to honor one who had left his imprint upon Capitol architecture. Rayburn felt a keen sense of obligation to those people who had participated in this phase of America's cultural development. As Speaker he was the proprietor of his end of the Capitol Building, its improvement and its environs.

On February 25, he demonstrated that he was truly the proprietor of the House's activities. At this time he placed a ban on TV and radio reporting of House committee meetings. The incident which prompted his action and started a prolonged controversy was the unauthorized broadcast of an un-American Activities Committee investigation of Communistic influences in Michigan. He deemed it best not to make a show of such personal and serious business as this, because it meant that individual privacy was being invaded for the sake of public entertainment and political exploitation. In his own defense he cited a report of the American Bar Association and elaborated on the importance of decorum. Only a change in the House rules, he said, would make him act differently about this or any other reproduction of committee hearings.

Something of a patriarch in his feeling for Congress, Rayburn resented any criticism of the body but he reserved the privilege of telling Congress about any of its own shortcomings. On March 4 he reminded the House of its dereliction. He explained that the House should remember always that Americans were members of the human race and that they should share in the responsibility of protecting the world against forces and ideas which would destroy freedom and nobility of thought. Man's technological development, he observed, was surpassing moral and spiritual growth. Congress, he said, must forget partisan politics and take a broad view of the future to be aware of what was happening to men's values.

On May 3, when two amendments were about to be added to the soil conservation bill which would have cut off $75,000,000, he went into action. The word was passed quickly through the cloakrooms and offices that "Mr. Sam was up." Seats on the floor and in the galleries filled rather quickly. The speech was a deviation from his usual pattern of brevity, since it was on a subject upon which he was a reported specialist. He directed his remarks to city congressmen and warned them that their factories would be closed and their constituents walking the streets in hunger if they denied the farmers the right to conserve and rebuild the soil. Both Republicans and Democrats applauded and shouted resounding "Noes" to defeat the amendments. When the voting began, Mr. Rayburn walked among his colleagues and observed their activities, for he was taking no chances. This was a clear-cut Rayburn victory, because the full $250,000,000 was approved, as he wanted it.

Anticipating that he would have to make the same vigorous defense when the military appropriation bill was debated, he prepared some notes and carried them in his pocket for two days. On May 23, he again walked to the well of the House. As he began, he warned that his remarks would not be cheerful, "because I am not happy about our situation in the world, nor in the United States of America, nor in the House of Representatives." Again his personal influence was felt as far as the House's response to the bill was concerned.

Before the second session of the Eighty-second Congress was three days old, Mr. Sam began receiving letters urging him to run for President; however, the Democratic Convention was still six months away. To all the letters which came during the first four months he replied in the following terms:

> A great many friends have been generous enough to speak to me about the Presidential contest in 1952, but frankly I think I am one man in public life who does not aspire to be President. I have told my friends that I hoped they would not make a move in that direction as I doubted that an effort along that line could be fruitful on account of matters that would take too long to go into.

After six weeks of being put off, one Rayburnite decided to do something constructive. J. W. Cummings, a retired mail carrier and ex-legislator at Ivanhoe, just a short distance from Mr. Sam's ranch, signed up eighty charter members of the first Rayburn-for-President Club. "I could have signed up two or three hundred, but I thought we had enough to get things started," Cummings stated. He continued: "Sam and I were boyhood friends when we both lived south of Windom. He's the best man for the job and wouldn't have a bit of trouble carrying the solid South."

The friends of Rayburn, Barkley, Russell, Kefauver and Stevenson could make no specific statement to their followers without knowing the secret locked up in Harry Truman's mind. The President had, however, according to his own account in his *Memoirs*, already made the decision on the day of his Inauguration in 1949, written it down on April 16, 1950, and secured it where no eyes could explore its contents.[2] In March, 1951, he read to his White House staff his decision to withdraw, and they agreed, some in tears, that the proper time for its publication had not arrived. The President held conferences with likely replacements, first with Chief Justice Vinson and then with Governor Adlai Stevenson. He was searching for a candidate who would continue the Fair Deal, Point IV, Fair Employment, parity for farmers, and a consumers protective policy. On

March 29, at the annual Jefferson-Jackson Day Dinner in the National Guard Armory in Washington, President Truman made public his decision. But at this point both Vinson and Stevenson had said "no"; however, Barkley was quietly willing.

Senator Mike Monroney of Oklahoma was among the first in Washington to begin beating the Rayburn drums and he expressed discontent over not hearing any sound on the Texas side of the Red River. Governor Allan Shivers, who was expected to control the Texas delegation at the national convention, a cautious man, was not making a noise for the Speaker. At a press conference he was asked what he thought of Rayburn as a candidate, and he replied: "I would like to find out what his views are." A Texas Congressman and friend to Rayburn snapped: "Sam Rayburn's views were well known before the Governor was born."

Rayburn's friends from other states were too familiar with 1944 not to understand some of the silence in Texas. At that time there had been open warfare between two factions of the Democratic Party that had led to the breakoff by the Texas Regulars, who were assisted by Governor Coke Stevenson's executive committee which grabbed the May Convention; thus the national convention votes were divided in half, between the Loyalists and Regulars. It was highly unlikely that these factions at that time could have agreed on anyone. The picture in 1952 promised the same lack of harmony, with some of the same faces but under different labels. The confusion in Texas, however, did not dissuade Rayburn's friends in other states. They concurred in the belief that Rayburn should not have delegates pledged to him at the outset, but that he should remain aloof, as Alan L. Otten explained, from the throat-cutting which would be going on among the followers of Kefauver, Kerr, Russell, Harriman and the other avowed candidates. The strategy was to wait until the active candidates had spent themselves and the convention had become deadlocked; then Speaker Rayburn would be advanced as the man upon whom all factions could agree.

"Ours is a tenth ballot proposition, not a first ballot one," stated Monroney; "for when a few ballots have gone by, and it becomes obvious that none of the candidates is going to get past first base, the delegates will be ready to switch to someone who can hit a home run."

Some expressed the thought that, as the Permanent Convention Chairman, Rayburn would be ever in the delegates' eyes and a natural to promote if the strategy unfolded as planned.

"He'll be standing there with the klieg lights bouncing off that bald dome looking as solid and substantial and trustworthy as the rock of ages," one Senator affirmed.

After four months of pounding from friends everywhere, Mr. Sam took time off from his Washington duties over a weekend for a two-day visit to Bonham. Thereafter his correspondence took the following turn:

> I am not going to be an active candidate for the Democratic nomination for President. I feel this is the proper course for me to pursue under all the circumstances. Many people have come to me and said they thought I could come nearer bringing the Party together—North, South, East, and West—than anyone else. This may or may not be true. Not being a candidate, if such a thing should occur at the Convention in Chicago after a deadlock, they turn to me and ask me to take the nomination, I would, of course, be a good soldier.

Rayburn, however, was not the only Texan who had been mentioned for the ticket. There was talk of Governor Allan Shivers for the Vice-Presidency. Personally attractive, intelligent, articulate, socially acceptable, and politically astute, he seemed to many to have the superficial prerequisites. But as Cab Calloway, the jazz king once explained to neophytes, "it don't mean a thing unless you've got the swing." Mr. Sam suggested, after the 1952 bolt, that the Governor could "shiver but could not dance to the music of the Democratic hoe-downs nor could he keep step to the soothing refrains of Republican waltzes." However, Rayburn would have admitted that he could have been a favorite at either function had he decided which party he wanted to attend and come to stay until the refrain of "Good night, Ladies." That is, "he wouldn't stay hitched," as Rayburn explained.

Having completed a year as Chairman of the Interstate Oil Compact Commission, Chairman of the Southern Governor's Conference, a member of the executive committee of the National Governor's Conference, Shivers succeeded in bringing the meeting to Texas on the eve of the two national political conventions. Governor Shivers' control of the State Convention looked a certainty, and he favored an uninstructed delegation to Chicago.

The name and picture of House Speaker Sam Rayburn

brought forth a tumultuous ovation on Monday night, May 26, 1952, from loyal Democrats assembled for the State Convention in San Antonio. They gathered in "La Villita," a WPA reconstruction of the original San Antonio village, to prepare for Tuesday's rump convention. Loyalists like Maury Maverick, Sr., Harry Seay, Fagan Dickson, and Walter G. Hall stirred the old-line Democrats. Denunciation of Governor Shivers and praise for New Deal and Fair Deal achievements brought almost unending cheers. It was Seay, former State Chairman, who lampooned Shivers the most. "Shivers," he said, "has been away from his Austin office so much he doesn't know what's going on. He has attended more previews than any actress; he's been to more rodeos than any cowboy, more hunts than Daniel Boone, more football games than Doak Walker, more parades than Hopalong Cassidy, and cut more ribbons than a bridegroom." The loyal Democrats, who wore lapel tags with the Democratic donkey insignia and the lettering underneath, "No Phony," whistled and yelled themselves hoarse.

Stephen Mitchell, Chairman of the Democratic National Committee, took one long look at the Texas picture and said: "We should use the term 'real' rather than any other prefix for purposes of clarifying the breed of Democrat we are trying to work with. We'd like to see Texans who are 'real' Democrats get back down to solid earth of political reality. We're tired of 'regular' Democrats, Dixiecrats, Ike-crats, Shiver-crats, and such off-color designations." He looked to a time when an end could be put to the practice of people's voting Republican while accepting shelter under the Democratic tent in order to garner votes to be elected. He thought Texas had a leader in Mr. Sam who knew the factions well enough to sort out public officials and give them their proper labels.

While some of the leading Congressional figures in Washington were trying to stir up some Rayburn enthusiasm nationally and goad Texans into an endorsement of his candidacy, the Fourth District was again considering his qualifications for Congress, not the White House. The Houston *Chronicle*, however, endorsed him on Sunday, July 20.

Reagan Brown of Kaufman was trying to unseat Rayburn. Socialism, graft, high taxes, "five percenters," mink coats—these were the clichès he used in defining the administration Mr. Sam endorsed. Brown talked about the rationing of ammunition in Korea and the twenty thousand American boys who had been butchered in the last two years. He attacked the "Tidelands steal" and "the pink thinking." "Rayburn," he said, "is seventy years old, makes $30,000 a year, has been in Washington forty years. Let's give a young man a chance and have a change."

Mr. Brown had little time for watching the TV show in Chicago and was not discouraged by his opponent's success at the Convention, where he was given top billing and number one rating. A poll of the television audience revealed that forty-six per cent thought Mr. Sam handled himself well at the Convention, four per cent disagreed, and thirty per cent had no opinion. While all of this was transpiring, Mr. Sam back in the Fourth District was also handling himself well in absentia, for he defeated his opponent 23,942 to 12,471. The Fourth District had decided by this time that there were three certainties—"death, taxes, and Sam Rayburn's re-election to Congress."

Rayburn, at the fourth session of the National Convention on July 22, provided a sort of balance to Senator Alben Barkley's inspirational address when he reminded the delegates of Party achievements. It was the routine, orthodox utterance of a leader repeating the routine, orthodox Party formulas. It was also a sort of sermon, as he spoke of compassion, duty, mercy. He made reference to the spirit, its torment and its peace. These sentiments were well received because they came from wisdom, a well-ordered life, and a well-disciplined mind.

Critics described this as another Democratic convention which even the best Democrats should try to forget, but most everyone recalled the patience, versatility, decisiveness, and strength of the man from Bonham who guided the more than twelve hundred delegates through their intense bickering. Whether he failed to see Claud Gilmer of the Texas delegation waving his banner for recognition to protest the Civil Rights plank, some will continue to debate, but Mr. Sam said he did not see him. Rayburn thought the South should leave well enough alone at this point, outnumbered as they were. The platform had some things in it that were unacceptable to him, but he felt these were issues for the Eighty-third Congress to legislate on after the mandate from the people. "There's a time to fish and a time to mend nets," he believed. Great issues like the Tidelands and Civil Rights would not be settled by a few isolated fist fights between distraught and weary delegates suffering from hangover, when the problems had been in the making for longer than the belligerents had lived.

Rayburn remained consistently in good form for this Convention. It is reported that one delegate tried to cook his meal over a campfire in the aisle. There was much shouting and dashing around. Walter Kiernan recalls that someone grabbed the mike and shouted, "Fire!" A man in New York who had fallen asleep with his television set on, leaped so high out of his bed that his shadow is still printed on the ceiling. The alarmist who almost started a riot ran out yelling, "There's a big fire in Chicago."

The policeman on the corner said, "We know. . . . We're sending three companies airmail special."

Mr. Sam quietly stepped to the microphone and restored order by asking Mrs. O'Leary to "please leave and take her cow with her." There were other instances, too, where Rayburn moved quietly and effectively.

James Roosevelt, for example, challenged Mr. Sam on one occasion. He jumped to his feet and cited a whole paragraph from the rules book to emphasize the point that a motion to adjourn cannot be tabled. The radio and television audience waited for Mr. Sam to crawl under the lectern. In a low voice, Sam remarked to his assistant, "He didn't read far enough." Then Rayburn calmly announced, "The Chairman is not attempting to table a motion to adjourn but a motion to adjourn to a specific time."

The Chair knew what it was doing but credit should also be given to Representative Clarence Cannon of Elsberry, Missouri, two years Mr. Sam's senior, who wrote the rule book for the conventions. Cannon is the character who sat behind and to the chairman's left. To the TV audience he gave the impression of having just eaten a sack of green persimmons, but when he wore this expression one knew that Mr. Sam was "on top of the game," with such able assistance.

A bit later, after fourteen hours of flaring tempers and the bonfire, Rayburn restored tranquility with an invocation to Divine Guidance, by calling for the singing of the Lord's Prayer. Thus he was able to bring about peace. The adjournment which had been vehemently resisted now was allowed.

Senator Kefauver was no doubt a bit irritated and flustered when Mr. Sam would not interrupt a roll call for him to make a statement. The Senator was trying to share some of the credit for electing Governor Stevenson on the third ballot, but Mr. Sam's action prevented him from even getting one foot on the bandwagon.

It is unlikely, though, that Kefauver suffered, for he waited too late to make the mad dash. Preferences on Vice Presidents are frequently settled in smoke-filled rooms, not on the convention floor. President Truman, Mr. Sam, Adlai Stevenson, and several others "had a little meeting about 1:00 A.M. on Saturday," Rayburn reported. Mr. Sam presided, and during the discussion of candidates, without expressing a sympathy one way or the other, he reminded the gentlemen that "Estes could run like a scared wolf." The President's comment indicated that he was not impressed. Then Rayburn asked, "Adlai, who do you want?" The Governor replied, "I like the man from Alabama [John Sparkman]."

The President responded, "So it shall be." Then the meeting broke up, but Senator Kefauver lived to fight another day—in 1956.

Returning from Chicago to Bonham, Rayburn promptly announced that he would soon take to the road in support of the Democratic ticket. He was critical of both Governor Shivers and Attorney-General Price Daniel, the nominee for the United States Senate who was replacing the retiring Tom Connally, for their refusal to support the ticket. Former Attorney-General William McCraw joined Rayburn in denouncing plans in the State for two slates of electors—one for Stevenson-Sparkman and another for Eisenhower-Nixon.

The new Senator, having fought the surrender of the tidelands, was unwilling to support a party with a platform that favored stripping Texas of this potential wealth. The Governor concurred in Daniel's thinking. Rayburn agreed with them that Texas should keep the tidelands, but their approaches were different, their goals the same. The political picture in Texas puzzled Adlai Stevenson so much that on August 11 he wrote Mr. Rayburn as follows:

> Some time I hope we can talk by telephone about the situation in Texas, which mortifies me. I am beset by pressure on the Tidelands oil issue and alternatively assured that Texas is safe, etc., etc. Moreover, I have little information as to what will happen at the State Convention in September.

This Convention was scheduled for September 9 at Amarillo. On September 4, Rayburn attempted to discuss some of the major issues over a State-wide network. He made an appeal to the people's reasoning rather than their prejudices and hates. Since the Tidelands issue had done so much damage to Party unity, he concentrated on this issue, pointing out that Stevenson wanted to sit down and try to work out something agreeable to both Texas and the Federal Government. This agreement could be put into a law which would give the State a chance to recover the lost ground after the Supreme Court's majority decision against Texas. Rayburn tried to show that Eisenhower had no clear-cut thinking on the Tidelands and that there was nothing for Texas here. "I, with many other Democratic colleagues from various states, have worked for years," he said, "trying to settle this Tidelands issue by quitclaim to the states or by compromise, giving to the states more than their historic boundaries." In arguing that bolting the Party would solve nothing, when he came to discuss the other issues, he quoted Senator Lyndon Johnson, ". . . . granting that Stevenson is wrong on this question does that make Eisenhower and the reactionary-isolationist Republicans right on every great issue?"

He asked those people in Texas who were crying out for a change whether they wanted every Texas congressman he had placed on a key committee to be replaced. Four-fifths of all the important chairmanships in the House and Senate were held by Southern Democrats. These were the questions he asked. Did they want to lose their power in Washington? Were they tired of prosperity? Were they unhappy with having a leadership that was friendly to their special needs? Were they dissatisfied with an administration that wanted to keep America strong at home and abroad? Did they want to trust their country to the leadership of one who had spent his whole life in the military and was inexperienced for the job?

Sam Rayburn warned Texans that they should think twice before they turned a country like America, with its potential, over to a group of "penny pinchers, reactionaries and isolationists." He concluded with this plea and hope:

"Please think these things over and I trust that you will heed the counsel of an old friend who for forty years has worked with no other purpose than to serve to make your path a little smoother and your burden a little lighter."

Rayburn abandoned his vacation plans in order to fight the upsurge of the "Democrats for Eisenhower" movement. Headed by Governor Shivers and a group of young Democrats, the movement was making inroads into the State organization, primarily because the Governor was the titular head of the organization. Mr. Sam pointed out in a press conference that the Governor's group had more money than did his. "How are you fixed for dough?" the Speaker was asked.

"Well, it's coming rather hard, but it's coming," he responded. "We're getting it mostly in small contributions—$1 to $5—as a result of some radio and newspaper appeals."

"How is the opposition fixed for money?" was the next question.

"They're lousy with it, lousy. And they're getting it from fat cats, fellows who got rich under Democratic administration of government. But do you know what? They've got hundreds of expensive billboards on every highway in the State, and not one of them says 'Vote Democratic.' They all say 'Vote for Ike.' Now, we've got a few billboards, too, and ours say 'Vote Democratic, for Stevenson, Sparkman, and continued prosperity.'"

During the month of October Mr. Rayburn played the dominant role in trying to fit together the broken pieces of a Democratic Party organization, and he was ably assisted by Senator Lyndon Johnson. With a knowledge of the State, dogged energy, and sheer "guts," Mr. Sam went about his task in a methodical fashion. However, the unpopularity of the Truman Administration in some quarters, and the appeal of Eisenhower, made this task quite difficult. People who timidly wore their small Dewey buttons under their coat lapels in 1948, proudly displayed large, gilded "Me for Ike" insignia in 1952. The press, oil men, bankers, industrialists, large ranchers, and large real estate developers joined ranks under the leadership of Governor Shivers and Senator Daniel to form an oligarchy, which, according to some of Rayburn's advisors, spent between three and six million dollars to promote the General's cause. Junior executives "on the way up" fell under the spell of their superiors' enthusiasm and began a sort of evangelical chant for a new and vibrant Republican Party. This, however, was a chant of restless youth, not altogether pleasing to some in the oligarchy because they knew only the old and familiar tunes of Senator Taft and his school of thought. But no one in the new crusade bothered to quibble over such differences of opinion at this stage.

It was wealth and influence, Rayburn thought, which breached the once powerful, old-line Party and paved the way for the Republicans to carry Texas. Mr. Sam believed it was an Eisenhower victory and not a Republican one, as this much-used sentence from his November post mortems indicates: "It took about two hundred and fifty thousand Republicans joined by bolters, so-called Democrats, to overcome us."

But Rayburn was not a man to moan over his misfortunes

and he turned his thoughts to constructive channels, as he instructed his friends throughout the State thus:

> Our work for the next two years should be to try to nominate real Democrats for State offices and not those who would violate their pledge or their promises. I think if we work together we can accomplish this end.

He meant just this. Deposed again as Speaker, by the Republican victory in the House, he would again be faced with the decision of becoming Minority Leader or retiring to the role of congressman. Replying in a telegram to John McCormack that he was available if wanted and that the Democratic Party would be rejuvenated, he stated:

> . . . that our opposition in the Eighty-third Congress will be constructive and not back-biting in nature and critical for criticism only. We should and will receive the recommendations of the incoming Republican Administration in a friendly fashion and go along with those recommendations when, in our opinion, they are to the interest of our country and look forward to a peaceful and ordered world.

Thus ended an Administration which Rayburn perhaps enjoyed most of all. He saw a President reluctantly take over the biggest job in the world and bit by bit grow in stature. Mr. Sam had a part in this evolvement. In the early months, for example, he shut off stifling amendments to such legislation as the hotly contested manpower bill which was designed to freeze civilian workers in their war jobs. He spent many hours, all told, in those 5:00 P.M. meetings advising with his chief.

After fifteen years Rayburn was asked to give his impressions of the man who to him "hung the moon." These are Mr. Sam's reminiscences:

"I have often thought of him, of the tremendous thing that was dropped on his shoulders. . . . Well, he kids me now and says he was for me for Vice-President in '44 when he got it. He said, 'If you had got that thing, then I'd still have been employed. I'd still be in the Senate.' I said, 'where'd I be? They'd have probably beaten me in '48; you got elected.' . . .

"But he went along with splendid courage and splendid composure. Now, I always kid him about shooting from the hip, you know. Somebody would ask him a question and without too much consideration, he'd shoot. He shot from the hip too quick. Of course, little things are not going to be remembered by the historians in writing up Harry Truman, who must go down as one of our great Presidents. He made some of the greatest decisions that any President ever made and he made them with courage and stood by them, because Harry Truman is physically and morally a brave man. There isn't any question about that right now. Harry Truman is an honest man. He wouldn't deceive you about anything. He never sought to deceive anybody while he was President of the United States. He always spoke right out. I look upon him in many ways as kind of an Andrew Jackson. . . .

"Truman worked hard at his job. One evening I slipped into his study there in the White House to talk to him quietly about some of these things on my mind, without being seen by some folks, and he had four or five or six, maybe seven, big envelopes with the official emblem stuck up there.

" 'You see that there,' Truman said, 'I've got to sign those things and I'm not going to sign them unless it's after I read them, and I've got to read everything before I go to bed.' "

Rayburn thought about this and could see that it would have been easy for him to have said, "Well, I'm sure these folks have got this thing fixed all right. I'll just sign it."

The Speaker added, "Well, that shows he was a working President. There's no question about that."

In almost every interview with Mr. Sam when the name of Truman was mentioned, he used the expression "Harry always shot from the hip," but he promptly admitted that Truman's aim got to be rather good. The last time that the author of these pages heard Mr. Sam laugh came as a result of reminding him of an anecdote inspired by one of the President's "hip shots." Too weak to sit in his favorite rocking chair, Rayburn was lying on his couch at the moment and listening intently, as he was reminded of the past.

Speaker Rayburn was in his big office one day when a visitor entered and promptly asked a very abrupt question. "Mr. Speaker, did you read that letter President Truman wrote a certain gentleman who made some uncomplimentary remarks about Margaret's musical performance?"

"No," he replied. "I have no idea what you are talking about. Tell me."

Then the visitor brought the Speaker up to date on the latest news. Mr. Sam's jaw dropped, then he raised both hands above his head, brought them down over the top of his bald cranium in a gesture of despair as if trying to pull out some hair. He said, "My God, why doesn't someone down there in the White House hide all the lead pencils from Harry so he can't find them?"

Realizing that the incident was being told by one writing a biography about him, he first responded with a groan. Mr. Sam was of the opinion that his behavior on this particular day was buried in the past. Then suddenly he started laughing. "See, I told you. Harry shot from the hip!"

When asked if he thought this incident should get into the book, he replied with a chuckle, "Oh sure, Harry knows how I feel about him."

☆ XIX ☆

Minority Leader Under Ike

THE clerk of the Eighty-third Congress on January 3, 1953, had just announced the results of the voting on the Speaker—Joseph Martin 220, Sam Rayburn 201. "I had a slight suspicion the vote would go the way it did," Rayburn said a few moments later amid laughter. The nine Democrats who were absent could have done little to repair the damage to the Party's prestige or pride. Too many Democrats had drowned in the backwash stirred up by the Eisenhower speed boat in the November race. At the other end of Capitol Hill, Senator Lyndon B. Johnson was experiencing the same emotions as his political godfather.

Although something of a student of the Scriptures, Mr. Sam searched his memory for some phrase of comfort, but he could only recall sadly that when the waters of the Red Sea came together again they enveloped all of Pharaoh's hosts. But then he found a parallel from which he could philosophize. The children of twenty years of bondage were now free—but free, Mr. Sam mused, to wander in the wilderness. Their "benighted leader," he prophesied, would learn in his own political lifetime that another of a different political party would be called upon to lead all the children into the promised land. Yet for his past achievements he would be granted a sepulcher on the mountain-top. Thus Mr. Sam characterized the next few years of American history.

As in the Eightieth Congress, the former Speaker showed his gallantry when he escorted the victor to the rostrum for a ceremony which was almost a replica of that in 1947. "Today," Mr. Sam mused, "I come back to present that same great American to be Speaker of the House—again temporarily." Amid applause and laughter, he suddenly restored a serious atmosphere as he pledged, "I am going to stand by the new Speaker on procedures because I know he is going to make the proper and fair rulings." With 434 people besides the Speaker in the House, it would be a little dangerous, politically and physically, not to be fair, he warned.

The recent death of Adolph Sabath and the retirement of Robert L. Doughton now left Mr. Sam with the deanship of the 435-member body. Only Senator Hayden at the other end of the Capitol had been around longer. A man who was entering upon his forty-first year of service and had attained seniority status could speak frankly and warn all recalcitrant Democrats that he was not going to tolerate any foolishness.

He also gave some advice to the new members who had any ambition to stay in the House for a long time. He told them that they had two constituencies: "You must please the people of your district, and if you want to be in a position which will enable you to help and please these people, you must also please your colleagues in the House." He pointed out that a congressman can make friends without violating his own legislative program, which should be consistent with the temper of the district. "When you go home, make yourselves available to the people so that you will know their wishes and they will regard you as their servant and leader." He said that he, as Minority Leader, would never ask a man to do something which would get him in trouble back home, if the congressman was acting in a consistent, honest, and ethical manner. "You must learn how to get along with people," he added, "and also command our respect." Then he took his seat behind the microphone assigned to the minority spokesman.

President Dwight D. Eisenhower, for the first five months, was either not reading the newspapers or had other ideas about how to work with Congress, for he virtually ignored the minority leadership in the two Houses, until shortly after June 5. George Rothwell Brown of the San Antonio *Light* wrote in effect that the General could be spinning his wheels and might do well to invite Mr. Sam over to the White House some morning for "a stack of flapjacks and molasses." The President, however, had not been a solitary diner, for Senator Bob Taft and Speaker Joe Martin had frequently enjoyed this early morning repast and hospitality. Rayburn remembered his breakfast with Calvin Coolidge too vividly not to feel that Democrats and Republicans could enjoy "flapjacks" together.

Sam Rayburn and Lyndon Johnson discussed their fall from grace and musingly expressed a curiosity about the new decorations in the White House. They also grumbled about the way Truman had been ignored during the period of transition. The elder statesman, with a biting wit, reflected some curiosity to take a peep into the so-called "officers' club" of Pennsylvania Avenue.

Rothwell Brown also observed that if Rayburn were less patriotic than he was, or if he had decided to put Party advantage above the best interests of the country, scarcely a day had passed since the Eighty-third Congress had been organized, that the elderly gentleman could not have tied the Republican Party into parliamentary knots. But the White House suddenly realized that it had been neglecting an old friend from the Fourth District, the district in which the President first saw the light of day. So to rectify matters, the President had Mr. Sam in for lunch twice in ten days, just the two of them. The second time they merely gossiped, and visited like two old friends. What was discussed is not known, because Mr. Sam was tight-lipped and kept confidences.

A few days before the invitations, Sam Rayburn had shown slight irritation. He was quoted in Texas papers as saying, "The Republicans haven't done much—I feel sorry for them, actually." Perhaps the White House detected something ominous in this remarkable silence and feared that the cogent comment could be a reconnaissance mission before a major assault. In all probability the White House had heard about some critical comments Rayburn made to the delegations from Alabama and Tennessee. Four months earlier, however, at one of the several birthday functions Rayburn had stated that his Party would not play the role of obstructionists and that he hoped the Republicans would learn the difference between obstruction and construction. "Any jackass," he said, "can kick a barn down but it takes a carpenter to build it. I hope General Eisenhower will learn fast and that he will get some good advice."

Mr. Sam learned many years ago that a successful congressman should give the other fellow credit for having some sense. Rayburn never prided himself on his brilliance, but rather on his common horse sense. On Capitol Hill he had the reputation of being a master at strategy and parliamentary procedures. Yet from time to time he found himself in the position of wondering what his political adversaries were contemplating. Particularly did he ponder over one measure before the Texas Legislature—that of redistricting. His correspondence of February, 1953, indicates that there was a movement afoot in the Texas Legislature to draft a redistricting bill which would add a portion of the silk-stocking section of Dallas to the Fourth. He gave the authors of this idea credit for a certain intelligence because efforts to unseat him had failed many times. "There's more than one way to skin a cat," he assumed they were thinking.

Quite naturally he advised his Texas friends that he really preferred to leave his District as it was, preferring a congressman-at-large for the State. The population of the Fourth added to that from Dallas he believed would be enough for two representatives anyway; so he argued for leaving these two districts alone. Although he had always wanted Lamar, he was not in favor of taking it away from Wright Patman. "If I had to take either Denton or Cooke, I would certainly prefer Denton, as Cooke is a Republican County or near so," he wrote on February 6. This effort to reshape Mr. Sam's District by combining it with a part of Dallas failed, as did all succeeding ones. Yet the issue continued to be raised after each census.

The Minority Leader knew his duties, but he had not worked in such an assignment before under a Republican Administration in the White House. Though he was at a sort of twofold disadvantage, he nevertheless enjoyed prestige both in Congress and throughout the nation. Illustrative of this appreciation was the honor paid him on February 11 when President Eisenhower delivered his State of the Union address. Mr. Sam was selected to escort the Republican President to the rostrum. The television announcer was carried away with the idea as he described the two men walking side by side—"President Dwight D. Eisenhower and Sam Rayburn of Texas."

On March 3, Representative Wright Patman addressed the House for fifteen minutes on the phenomenon of Sam Rayburn—elected to twenty-one terms, dean of the House, Speaker longer than anyone else, enviable legislative record, and a life-acquaintance with more than three thousand members of the House of Representatives.

Slow to realize that he had become a legend in his own time, Rayburn resisted invitations to get him to appear on television programs. He had established two policies: he would not perform on any sponsored programs, always explaining that he would not sell himself to those who advertised beer, soap, and the like. He consented, however, to participate with Speaker Martin on Edward R. Murrow's "See It Now" program on Sunday, April 19, 1953. His correspondence relative to this incident contains the reason for changing his former policy:

> I am not much on going on television, but when Mr. Murrow explained that he thought this would be historical and of great benefit to the people of the United States in seeing the House of Representatives and knowing some of the history of it, I agreed to go on.

In the correspondence for 1953 there are many inquiries about the Bricker Amendment. On April 18, to a gentleman in Houston, Rayburn made his own position clear in a framework which was used in reply to all letters on this subject:

> I am of the opinion that this is such a far departure from our policy for 160 years that it would be dangerous in that I fear it would be taking power away from the President of the United States that he has always exercised and that I think he should exercise in the future. In this sentiment, at the present time, I have the backing of both the President of the United States, Mr. Eisenhower, and the Secretary of the State, Mr. Dulles, who have both expressed strong opposition to the Bricker Amendment.

Senator John Bricker of Ohio, a conservative, who had been Dewey's running mate in 1944, responded to a national trend toward restricting the treaty power by amending the Constitution. His amendment was designed to resist the encroachments on the rights of the states or the people. In effect it gave Congress the power to regulate executive and other international agreements. Though Mr. Sam was jealous of the prerogatives of Congress, he was not one to tamper with sacred and time-worn procedures. He had no interest in building an empire to exalt his own ego.

On April 21, the Minority Leader was hanging on the rail of the House chamber listening to some talk on foreign policy, when suddenly his blood pressure went up. After hearing the remarks about how the people had become so discontented with the Democrats that they elected a Republican Congress and President, he stepped forward. Rayburn told the Republicans that they were skating on thin ice with their small majority and that they had better quit their partisan attitude, "because there comes a time when partisanship can be practiced on both sides of the House." He added:

> "I know how to cause trouble if I want to, for I know something about the rules of the House and the rights of the minority, and I want to see this Administration one of these days spread its wings and get off the ground, let us know where they are going, what they stand for, and when they are going to do something about what they do stand for."

He reminded them that the election was an Eisenhower victory, not a Republican one, and as such, the picture could change drastically in Congress in 1954, when the people settled down to facts. He did not want the majority to forget, either, that legislation depended a great deal on regulating the minority—"the pistol-totin minority," as he liked to put it.

Though slow to anger, he could be a terror when he went on a spree. The Health Insurance bill was up for consideration shortly after this incident. An Administration-proposed measure which he had agreed to support was being discussed on the floor by a Republican who gave his Party full credit for this humanitarian effort. He stated that the Democrats were not interested in such things as the nation's health. Rayburn proceeded to behave in a way unlike him, for in a state of anger he called off all Democratic support and left the Republican congressman with a dead bill on his hands; however, he made up for lost ground in later Congresses.

The utility lobbies at this session were set to make another attempt to strip the Southwestern Power Administration, but on April 28, Rayburn fought back with all of his logic and plain oratory in support of the rural way of life and its dependence upon electricity. "Oh yes," he explained to the House, "the utilities say they will expand and take power to the farmers and keep their rates low to the REA Coops. Well, I can only judge the future by the past." When the count was completed, Mr. Sam had lost by forty votes. This was the first time he had been denied on the issue since he began these annual battles to secure Federal funds. About his defeat he remarked on July 27: "I am sure the utilities in that neighborhood [Southwest] are laughing because when I took a licking on this one, they said, 'We did not do much but we did a job on the so-and-so Rayburn.'"

His devotion to this measure was only one reflection of his continued interest in farm problems. He had always been faithful to the farmers and always tried to remain close to them even during his campaigns, because he believed they had more to offer him than did the politicians. During the summer of 1952, while supervising the Stevenson headquarters in Dallas, he became angry when he learned that many of these rural folk were being denied the opportunity to see him. "Now, get this straight," he admonished the office staff, "I want to talk to anyone who comes in here to talk to me. I can learn more from these folks about how the campaign is going than I can from the fat cats."

On May 20 he stood in defense of another of his favorite measures—soil conservation—and again he called upon his knowledge of agricultural economics, and faith in the value of soil to the future of American growth. He had said these things so many times before that he wondered if some people ever listened or learned anything. He argued that if one large segment of the population is penalized the whole of America would suffer.

When the measure on Reciprocal Trade renewal was reported out for debate, Rayburn again assumed a militant position as he exploded in condemnation of the Republicans for their perennial support of high protective tariffs for the manufacturing interests:

> "This eternal Republican solicitation for the American manufacturer makes me tired. They are willing and anxious to take that small, rich class under a protective wing, but unwilling at all times to heed the great chorus of sad cries ever coming from the large, yet poor class, the American consumers."

The debate on the Mutual Security Act of 1951, on June 19, 1953, brought two old political warriors together in a battle against the isolation spirit that had risen. After Rayburn had presented his opposition to the cut of $2,602,000,000 off Eisenhower's revised budget, and had related his knowledge of wars known to America, Speaker Martin left the rostrum to stand by his friend's side. Martin made an impassioned appeal to those concerned with American security to support Rayburn's views. When the question of the country's prestige or welfare was at stake these two gentlemen, as they had done so many times before, worked hand-in-glove. They were Americans, not just Democrats or Republicans.

Six weeks later on Monday, August 3, filled with the venom of a diamondback rattler, the Minority Leader asked to pay his respects to the Congress before adjournment of its first session. Before Mr. Sam began his remarks he looked toward the Republican side of the House. Some felt like defendants before the bar of justice.

He began thus:

> "Mr. Speaker, it is with great constraint that I say this Congress is unhappy as it heads home. It is without restraint that I say my Republican colleagues have my full sympathy, because they return to face their constituents knowing that they have failed to keep their 1952 campaign pledges."

Then like the old farmer who had caught his 'possum hounds in the act of sucking eggs, he glowered at the culprits before he led them down into the creek bottom to give them a charge of buckshot. The voters, however, he implied, would perform this ceremony in 1954. Wherein this "egg sucking" Congress had failed, Rayburn reported the following derelictions: 1) no balanced budget; 2) no reduction in taxes; 3) no stabilized national economy; 4) no reduction in the national debt; 5) no new foreign policy; 6) no new farm policy; 7) no new tax program. Besides the returning of the tidelands to the states, Rayburn found only two achievements for which the Republicans could be commended: an uneasy truce in Korea and hard money—"They made money harder to get by increasing the interest rates." About the truce in Korea, he said Truman and Acheson could have secured this kind eighteen months ago.

As to the behavior of his own Party, Rayburn stated that the Democrats had supported President Eisenhower's program on national defense and American foreign policy, as they had done in the past. And on domestic issues they had been neither for nor against Eisenhower. "The American voters demanded a change in last November's election," he added in conclusion, and "they are getting it—with a vengeance." With these morsels to chew on for the summer, they were extended wishes for a pleasant vacation.

Mr. Sam's own vacation was not even a day old when the people began driving up in front of the big white house. The first to arrive was his ranch foreman, Buck Henson. The two men sat in the living room and went over the affairs of the Ivanhoe place since Easter. These were some of the questions the boss asked. How many head did you sell? To whom? What did they bring? How's that little scrawny bull we got? How had the rain affected the cotton? How much water was in the pools? Should we disc the lower field? Has the vetch been planted? Then their conversation drifted away from the ranch momentarily and they told some amusing incidents which had occurred since their last meeting. By this time Buck had picked up his hat from a table by his chair and was curling the brim in front. This was the signal that he was prepared to move along. As Mr. Sam walked with him out to the pick-up, he said, "I'll get over there this afternoon and take a look at the lower field." Miss Lou had already invited a half dozen men into the living room, just as the Congressman yelled that "he'd be right with them."

Mr. Rayburn found it difficult to take a real vacation and get away from his job because visitors like these had quite an affinity for political talk. His presence in the District stirred up much of it, and they sought him out to discuss their favorite topic. If they did not find him, then he would seek them out because these people, he affirmed, gave him strength and information. To him they were the pulse of America and he wanted to feel it beat. His conversations were charged with sentences that exploded like bombs. A few of the people may have cringed but they enjoyed the Rayburn fireworks display. These are some of the excerpts from his living-room remarks: "I am sorry for President Eisenhower," he said, shaking his head, but the farmers detected no profound grief; still they were all ears. "He didn't have much Republican support in Congress last time, and he's going to have even less next session." Someone asked about the strength of his Cabinet. "If there ever was a man, since General Grant, who needed help, it's my friend, General Eisenhower. He has the least helpful Cabinet of any President I have ever known. There are no men in the Cabinet who have had political experience except a little fellow named McKay [Secretary of Interior] who was Governor of Oregon a little while."

After a brief rest Rayburn began making speeches over the State in a tour designed to pull the Democrats back together, because the past November election had mangled the Party organization. Democrats who supported Party nominees were urged to go to the precinct and county conventions. Though he called no names, only the most naïve would fail to recognize the references to Governor Shivers.

At a luncheon gathering of local and State Democrats in the Menger Hotel (San Antonio) on October 15, Mr. Rayburn had a great deal to say about duplicity within Party ranks. He urged the Republicans to nominate somebody for all offices the next year and to take a clear-cut stand. In effect, he was trying to clean house by rounding up all the Trojan horses that had caused the trouble within the Democratic Party during the last election. "I want everybody who is not a Democrat to vote in the Republican primary. . . . I don't resent having a two-Party State. . . . Of course, the door is always open for prodigals to return."

Rayburn observed everywhere that President Eisenhower's program would be better off in the hands of a Democratic Congress, since the Administration was incompatible with the hard core in its own Party. He implied also that the President was not suited to handle this particular type of job.

The matter of Eisenhower's suitability for this kind of administration had been on Rayburn's mind since the cessation of hostilities in Europe. Rayburn's comments both public and private reflected his reservations. Rayburn had been approached on the subject of drafting Eisenhower for the Democratic post back in 1948, but he had rejected the whole idea in a laconic way—"Good man but wrong job!" This ended it.

In 1960, Mr. Sam was asked to elaborate further upon this remark and in essence this is the way he did it. He gave Eisenhower credit for being an able military man, but thought he was fortunate in having people like Omar Bradley, George Patton, Bedell Smith, and Bill Simpson around to help him.

"The Democratic Presidents took him as a major and made him a great general. . . . Eisenhower had been in the Army forty-four years. . . . I had been in Congress forty years, and I still didn't know all the answers on domestic and foreign problems, but even if I did know all the answers, that wouldn't qualify me to lead an army.

"I do know a great deal about men, and maybe I could have handled that job in Europe about as well as he could have handled the one in the White House. He's no better qualified to do that job than I was to do his. But you know how folks feel about fellows who come back from war with medals and ribbons. They go wild about uniforms. This was a big problem right after the war, with a lot of those fellows sorta out of work, I mean, the old ones. Some of them ended up in odd places. You know what? I have heard tell that even colleges began grabbing up these boys. But I am not surprised, because I have had some dealings with boards of trustees and I can't understand them. But back to the people. I was bothered by this thing that happened in 1952. The people were all stirred up, but they'll settle down. I have faith in people."

His travel around over the State was designed to restore the people's faith in the political Party which previously had their unquestioned support from the cradle to the grave. He also corresponded with the leaders in the Party.

In a letter to John Nance Garner of September 22, 1953, he first discussed a sad episode, before he gave his thoughts to politics:

> I left here and flew to Washington and then to Charleston, West Virginia, and drove ninety miles to help bury our old friend, Fred Vinson. I do not know how I am going to get along without him as he was my best friend in Washington.

Sam Rayburn's roots in Washington were interlocked with Fred Vinson's. The two gentlemen spent one evening out of every two weeks alone together, and during periods of stress it was a weekly arrangement. Vinson was the sort of man of whom Rayburn could never tire. Mr. Sam defined it this way: he had "the most unfailing judgment of any man I have ever known." While Mr. Sam was well possessed of wisdom himself, he liked to try out some of his plans on Vinson first, since he too knew the people in the House of Representatives. Rayburn and Vinson shared an enthusiasm for major league baseball and knew a great deal about the individual players and their performance from year to year. Vinson's death on September 8 cast a long shadow over Mr. Sam's mind for months.

What originally had set Rayburn off on the remarks about Fred Vinson was a letter from John Garner, written in lead pencil, dated September 15. Garner wanted to find out about the Democratic Executive Committee meeting in Chicago where some of the Texas people tried to cause some trouble. Garner wrote:

> That Chicago liquor must have a bad effect on Texans. Was this taken early in the mornings or late in the evening? You must have had a successful meeting. At least I hope so. Never in my time has the Party been in such a disorganized condition. I pray that it may get better. What about Texas in 1954? How

> many Congressmen will fight for *National* Democratic Party? How many will fail to show their colors?

Rayburn's reply (September 22) of several pages revealed his usual optimism: "I have never seen that big a group of Democrats get together where all were in such good humor with each other as they were there, and all left that way." He assured Garner that there was no cause for alarm, that all of these fine people would come through for the Party. He did not encourage Garner's belief that the "Chicago liquor" had caused ill effects.

To a lady in Center, Texas, on November 11, 1953, he affirmed the kind of faith his friends wanted to hear:

> The ball is rolling for the Democratic Party, not only in Texas but throughout the country. These people just can't sit on their pants and do nothing, and carry out none of their campaign pledges to people who are as smart as the American people.

To Booth Mooney, out of Senator Johnson's Washington office, he also wrote on November 11 about the scare the Republicans will be getting from the California election, and something of the shape of things to come. He expressed the belief that in the next session they would be "looking out after their own skins and have found out they just can't get elected by saying they are supporting Eisenhower, as this has not proven effective." Then Rayburn outlined the Democratic strategy thus:

> I think we can sit awhile and watch them try to do something, because we will have plenty of opportunity to criticize. They do not know where they are going on anything. I think they are going to have one of the worst split parties that we have ever seen in Congress.

By mid-December Rayburn had completed his tour of the $10-a-plate Democratic dinners, designed to put money into empty Party coffers. After this duty was performed, he traveled around over Fannin County. What he found provoked some very uncomplimentary remarks about the country's economic condition. Once, when he was hiking across his ranch with a visitor, he pointed out some of his better cows in the herd of one hundred Herefords. He said dejectedly that he had sold some calves for $50 each, a price which was one-third what they would have brought in 1951. "There is a mild recession and I'm afraid it's going to increase. I don't know what's going to happen," he added. To the many visitors to his Bonham home he conveyed the information that the Democratic Party was in good shape but the economic outlook was bad.

As he prepared to leave for Washington, he talked freely about the President in relation to the Congressional picture:

"I like President Eisenhower; I've often pointed out to him he's a constituent of mine. He was born over here in Denison, in this Congressional District. And I have been told," he chuckled, "that he was a good baby." Rayburn went on and qualified his concern for the President: Eisenhower had a Republican Congress that did not believe in his program, and he would be dependent upon the Democrats to put through some of the much needed legislation. All of this Rayburn recognized was galling to the White House and awkward for the leader of the minority Party. Rayburn said he would be criticized by the Republicans as being partisan and un-American if he dared question the President's program. However, he felt strongly that the people would straighten out the Congressional situation in 1954.

Also recognizing the complexity of the Congressional picture and Rayburn's position with respect to the White House, John Nance Garner wrote Mr. Sam on January 4, 1954, with lead pencil, as follows:

> Dear Sam:
>
> I just want to write you this word of encouragement for the year 54, I pray that you may have health and success in your service to your country for you have the *hardist* [sic] *task* and the greatest opportunity of any minority leader in this country. May the Lord give you *wisdom* and *courage*.
>
> Your Friend
> Jno. N. Garner
>
> P.S. Ben [sic] in bed for past 4 days with *bad* feet—will be O. K. in few days.
>
> G.

On January 6, 1954, the Second session of the Eighty-third Congress opened and Mr. Sam had another birthday—his seventy-second—which was made pleasant with a personal message from the President, signed "Dwight." He thus began the year thinking positively.

Rayburn in these years had mixed feelings about the White House. There was no basic quarrel between Ike and Sam personally, but the Party barrier separated them professionally. At times, when Rayburn thought he saw the outline of a general rather than the anatomy of Ike or Mr. President, he was not pleased. Because of his own compulsion for Party loyalty, however, he never hesitated to chide the Republicans for their failure to support their leader. There was a disaffection within Republican ranks, which he observed was caused by powerful individuals and groups working at cross purposes with the President. This condition made him more keenly aware that the Democrats would be compelled to give a good account of themselves, by a high-level performance. Rayburn's goal was to carry Congress in the fall elections, and he hoped to do so by showing the American people an efficient and successful legislative program. Of course, he realized that the White House would receive a great deal of credit for achievements that were Democratically inspired and engineered, but he reasoned that America would be the recipient of the dividends.

Rayburn guarded his Party's reputation more closely than ever before. The session was less than a week old when he had reason to serve notice on Republicans that he was tired of "it being open season on Democrats." Hence insinuations that ex-President Truman had been "soft on Communism" and that Democrats were "red sympathizers" were to him intolerable remarks. Democrats, he said, have been critical of an Administration, but "there is no one on this side going to attack the integrity of the President of the United States, because we have too much respect for that great office and too much respect for the man that is in it."

The name-calling became worse. Following the Lincoln Day orations, Rayburn and Johnson worried together about the unbridled partisanship. Senator McCarthy's speech which referred to the Roosevelt-Truman Administrations as "twenty years of treason" was the culminating incident which got Mr. Sam's bristles up and caused him to send a warning to the White House. "Some of our backs are getting mighty sore," Rayburn warned. Rayburn repeated this remark publicly at least a dozen times during the session.

Disturbed by Rayburn's words, the President promptly told reporters in a news conference that the times were too serious for anyone to indulge in political partisanship to an extreme, and he expressed the hope that the sensationalists in his own ranks would soften their activities in face of a crystallizing opposition to his program. Although Mr. Sam's appeal brought a "rebuke" to the more flamboyant GOP critics, it set off a series of speeches in the House against "rot sewer politics," Republican "blabbermouths," and political "immorality," to quote some of the more expressive phrases used by the Democrats.

Dirksen's faith in Rayburn's patience and bipartisanship is characterized thus: "I don't think the Democrats are going to vote against the President's program just because of the statements that have been made." While Rayburn and the minority searched for virtues in Administration-sponsored measures, they deliberated much longer than before, and at times the aisle seemed rather wide.

The first rattle of arms over legislation came during the second week in February, 1954, when the tax bill was brought into full view. Mr. Sam, however, would have called his forces into battle on this measure regardless of circumstances because he had consistently resisted any tax bill that gave "too many favors to the big taxpayer and followed the 'trickle down' system used in Andy Mellon's day of granting benefits at the top on the theory they would trickle down to the bottom." Rayburn pointed out five loopholes in the Administration's bill—dividend credits, accelerated depreciation, reduced taxes on foreign income, charitable trusts, and pension inequities. Rayburn's hostility affected Senate attitudes. The conflict developed such proportions that the President finally used it as a basis for a major address on March 15.

On the following day, in a speech, Mr. Sam gave his side of the story, reiterating his concern for the great majority of Americans in the small income bracket, and for the economy as a whole. He reasoned that the Democratic position was close to the basic philosophy of Abraham Lincoln, who preached liberty and justice to all, and that the Republican position was a strictly Hamiltonian concept of special benefits for the few. Six families out of every thousand would get $814,000,000 in tax relief while all the other families combined would not get anything like this amount. To correct the inequity Rayburn stated that his Party would insist on an increase in personal exemptions and would eliminate the "trickle down" dividend provision that gave special benefits to only the six families in every thousand.

Following this duel between the champions of the major Parties, the expressions from back home began to pour in to Washington. Mr. Sam received two types of correspondence. Those who liked Rayburn's stand wrote postal cards and letters; some who opposed his views responded by telegram. With Mr.

Sam, though, the people behind the one or two-cent postal card or the hand-written letter wielded the power in American politics. He listened because he understood their need. The House, however, passed the tax bill over his protest with most of the features he had found objectionable.

This type of defeat had the effect of putting him in a bad frame of mind, and his correspondence and speeches began to reflect his pessimism. He reminded the American people that the "mild recession" was only a forerunner of the kind of depression which had started prior to the era of the New Deal. For the remainder of the session he issued statements of a foreboding nature.

Rayburn's letter, with his check for his filing fee to the Chairman of the Democratic Executive Committee in Fannin County, implied that he had no intentions of letting this defeat on the tax bill put him out of business. There had been some talk around the District that Sam might quit in 1954, but those who were well informed in Bonham knew he would never pull out of politics with the Party in such a state of confusion. As Minority Leader he had mastered the technique of generalship. When a leader has learned the art of walking backward down an aisle to the cloakroom, without losing sight of the Speaker and the movements of colleagues during heated debate or voting, it is unlikely that he would be permitted to quit. Although he could see out of the back of his bald head, he learned better than to turn his back on a tense situation. There was no one else who had the feel of the job well enough to replace him, the opposition being what it was.

One week after mailing in his filing fee, he wrote H. A. Cunningham, chairman of the Sam Rayburn Foundation, giving clearance to the plans for the long projected library. Rayburn authorized that bids would be received until 10 A.M., March 11, 1956, at the office of Roscoe P. DeWitt, Dallas, Texas. The Foundation at the time had $200,000 in cash and a block of land where the old Duncan Elementary School had stood. Although Mr. Sam saw the need for $1,000,000 above building costs, to establish his permanent endowment, he had received enough encouragement from friends throughout the country to go ahead with the letting of a contract on the building, which was estimated to cost between $450,000 and $490,000.

He had become increasingly impatient to get his library started. He wanted to see his dream—a research center where school children could learn more about their country's politics and history—fulfilled in his own lifetime. Many times he had demonstrated his feeling for the importance of studying history and politics by saying that he wished he could go around the public schools of the land as a visiting lecturer just to reveal the splendid qualities in the American system.

At a March 4 luncheon honoring Representative Wright Patman for twenty-five years of service, Rayburn commented on other virtues, those of knowing about our Congressional operations. He referred to the recently published Patman pocket-size edition of *Our American Government—Answers to 1001 Questions as to How It Works,* which he hoped would find a place on the shelves of every public school and library in the Fourth District and reach the hands of every member of the Chamber of Commerce.

Mr. Rayburn's sacred domain of rural electrification was under fire during April and May, 1954. The appropriation for the Southwestern Power Administration seemed destined to be cut, and a reorganization plan on the desk of McKay, Secretary of the Interior Department, was designed to destroy many of Rayburn's contributions in this whole area. At the outset he had his back to the wall, but he fought so vigorously that he was successful in getting a $350,000 appropriation restored in the House bill. Of his victory he remarked, "I kept the boys over there from giving the SPA the 'meat ax.' "

Efforts to amend the 1933 Securities Act also brought forth his determined resistance. It would appear that the Republican Congress was trying to erase some of the measures he had piloted through the New Deal. At the time the bill was originally written, the amount which a corporation could float without being cleared by the Securities and Exchange Commission was $100,000. Years later Rayburn agreed to an amendment to double the amount, but opposed its going above $300,000. The 1954 amendment asked for half a million, and Rayburn predicted that the door would be opened and the whole intent of the original act destroyed. He argued that the dollar was worth only half what it was when the bill was written, but he said:

"I would rather have a 50-cent dollar and have some of them than a 100-cent dollar and not have any, and that is exactly what the situation was in many cases in years gone by when we had a so-called 100-cent dollar. . . . The people would rather have more 50-cent dollars and be able to buy something than to hold a lot of securities bought with 100-cent dollars as they did twenty years ago when this Act was passed in 1933, only to find they had nothing."

These repeated assaults upon his own legislation, though not entirely destructive, intensified Rayburn's irritations with the White House. By early May of 1954, Rayburn was openly critical of the Eisenhower Administration for its failure to Act—"to get off dead center." The so-called mess in Washington which had been widely publicized in 1952, the incidents of the mink coats and deep freezers, seemed to Mr. Sam to have turned into another type of mess. He referred to the exploits of Senator McCarthy and his attacks on American citizens. Rayburn thought abuse and wiretapping was an invasion of a citizen's privacy and that many innocent people could be hurt in rounding up a few strays. There were, he assured, procedures already set up to seek out subversives without smearing decent and loyal American citizens. He referred to the McCarthy-Army affair as "very damaging here and abroad to us and a very disgusting performance." Rayburn objected to the techniques, for he gave support to the Communist Control bill so that this whole issue could be taken out of politics.

As Rayburn was scanning the measures relative to the Eisenhower program for health, social security, and housing, he could not withhold caustic comment. He said he did not recall hearing the Republicans condemn these as "too New Dealish," "too Fair Dealish," and "Socialistic," though they bore striking similarity to Democratic measures in the areas mentioned. Mr. Sam said he planned to support the measures, but he wanted to remind "the boys across the aisle" that they were getting rather "socialistic."

Rayburn's heckling did not stop here. He called attention to the many broken campaign promises such as the talk about balancing the budget, the promises to the American farmer, housewife, workman, businessman, and neglect of the unemployed laborer. Then he gave his reflections on the popularity of the Administration. "Many reliable sources over the country report," he affirmed, "that the full bloom of Eisenhower's 1952 popularity is fading, and fading fast; that the stem is wilting, and the roots are curling." The loss of esteem, he thought, was due to the Eighty-third Congress's failure, after five months of the second session, to break up the open revolt over tax revision, farm measures, foreign trade, statehood, Taft-Hartley, housing, immigration, social security, and health.

But where foreign policy was involved, he pledged that he would ignore the insults from certain members of the Republican Party and the Vice-President and support the Mutual Security Act. The American people, he felt, should not have their freedom jeopardized because certain elected officials were tactless. The Democratic Party had set the pace under the Marshall Plan and it would continue to support a bipartisan foreign policy; however, he deemed a reappraisal to be quite in order. On July 10, he wrote:

> I feel the Republicans who cursed out the Truman-Acheson foreign policy so vehemently in the campaign in 1952 have not changed it as they threatened to do, but have simply administered it in a sorrier fashion and I think in such a way that we have fewer friends in the world than we did on January 20, 1953.

A Mr. K. T. Whitescarver, Magister of the International Legal Fraternity of Phi Delta Phi, wrote on March 29 inviting Sam Rayburn to honorary membership in the chapter at George Washington University. The banquet and formal initiation took place at the John Marshall Inn, George Washington University, on May 7, 1954. This recognition was bestowed upon the longtime Congressman and leader for his contribution to the growth and development of the law of the land. In the ceremony, he was cited for the passage of progressive legislation. His response at the banquet was of an inspirational sort to the young lawyers from an elder statesman who possessed an optimistic faith in the destiny of America.

Mr. Sam was unable to return to Texas to conduct a campaign because Congress was in session through the period of the Texas primary; however, he prevailed upon Halleck, the Majority Leader, to postpone a vote until a following Monday so that six members of the Texas delegation could put in an appearance back home. These men were in trouble and needed to do work. Rayburn's plea, "I have never made an unreasonable request of anybody in my life," was sympathetically heard by Halleck.

Rayburn's opponent, A. G. McRae of Fannin County, had been an agent for the Texas Power and Light prior to the campaign. He made a feeble effort to terminate Rayburn's political career, because the incumbent carried all counties handily, with a vote of 6102 to 1094 in their own home county. This appeared to be the last effort to derail the elder statesman, for no opposition materialized in 1956, 1958, or 1960. However a Jack Finney announced early in 1961 that he would make the race in 1962.

Though Mr. Sam had not been pressed by his own personal political problems, he received reports that Texas was having a grueling gubernatorial campaign. Ralph Yarborough was trying to unseat Allan Shivers. It was a liberal against a conservative, and before the contest was over much venom had been poured out. The candidates tried to define themselves. In the attempt to explain the nature of his liberalism, Yarborough used the expression "Sam Rayburn Democrat." Although the Congressman did not cast his lot publicly with Yarborough at this stage in his career, he was sympathetic toward his campaign, if for no other reason than for his opposition to Shivers. Rayburn was promptly attacked, only because his name was used by Yarborough.

The Shivers victory in Texas set off considerable anti-Democratic sentiment and revived the cult of "Eisencrats." Several county conventions on July 31 were thrown into a turmoil with the show of Shivers' strength. For instance, there was much hooting and booing at the Dallas meeting when a resolution was recommended praising Rayburn, Johnson, Stevenson, Roosevelt, and Truman. On the other hand, in the predominantly rural and traditionally Democratic areas, these resolutions were applauded.

Mr. Sam showed concern over all of this intra-Party strife, because it looked like a continuation of the old trouble with the Texas Regulars but under a different guise. He expressed the hope that the anti-Democratic feeling would finally crystallize into a sort of permanent exodus by the troublemakers from Democratic ranks.

As the Eighty-third Congress approached adjournment, Mr. Sam began searching in his vocabulary for a single word that could characterize it, and he finally settled on "inept." And in reply to Republican claims that their legislative program was "dynamic" and "forward-looking," he stated that it was just about as "'dynamic' as the dodo bird, as 'forward-looking' as yesterday." On domestic issues the Eisenhower Administration, he proclaimed, exhibited an ineptness in considering what was best for all the people, "an ineptness magnified by its desire and programs to benefit selected groups; groups that ignore the increased power of the masses of working men and women and the millions of farmers, who provide the food and fiber which create the basic wealth of this nation." Such was the theme of about half a dozen major speeches over radio or TV, and utterances to the press or to friends as he wielded the battle-ax during the fall Congressional campaigns.

After adjournment of Congress, Rayburn started back to Texas accompanied by his grand-nephew, Buck Bartley. In public appearances en route he aimed attacks specifically at a Republican Congress that did not support its President. Eisenhower, he maintained, was compelled to depend on Democratic leadership to beat down opposition within his own Party. Rayburn listed only five pieces of positive legislation—the anti-Communist bill, emergency refugee bills, revision of the tax structure, the St. Lawrence Seaway, and the restoring of the tidelands to the states. Speeches of this type were designed to encourage the return of a Democratic majority.

To his original epithet of "ineptness" he later added that of "vacillation," when he began the circuit during the fall congressional campaigns. For example, he noted, "One week defense spending was to decline, the next it was to rise; the Air Force was to have fewer fighting wings, then suddenly more fighting wings; universal military training was out one day and back in the next." This was the pattern of an Administration that could get no consistent support from its own ranks even after it finally decided what it wanted. Since the country had an Administration which the Republicans would not support, he advised the electorate to send a Democratic majority to Washington as a protection against the negativism of the Republican philosophy. Mr. Sam expressed the belief that he could salvage much of the President's program even with a Democratic minority but that the times were too troublesome to run this risk.

The effectiveness of Mr. Sam's logic and the drift of the times led Republican leadership, in a sort of desperation, to appeal to Eisenhower for help. On September 10, he was approached to portray a more harmonious relationship between himself and his Party in Congress than that implied by the Minority Leader. Of this plight in which Republican leadership found themselves Rayburn commented:

"So desperate have the Republicans become, that they forced the President, Mr. Eisenhower, to step out of character and make a very partisan speech, a speech forecasting a cold war between his Administration and a Democratic Congress." Rayburn and Johnson promptly sent a telegram to Eisenhower at his Denver vacation resort saying, "It takes two to make a war." They pledged that there would be no cold war unless it was initiated by the executive branch and that they would consider every issue on the basis of its impact upon America.

According to Mr. Sam, the electorate sensed the practicality of his logic, for six weeks later they gave the Democrats a substantial majority in the House and a slight edge in the Senate. The President's theme during the closing days of the campaign widened the gap between the warring factions in Congress. To Mr. Sam, who had helped salvage much of the President's program, this was an unpleasant memory that he would be compelled to carry with him to the Speaker's rostrum.

Rayburn announced almost immediately that the charges of "treason" would stop; then later in November, Johnson and Rayburn issued an 800-word statement assuring the President, Republicans, and citizens, that they would support a bipartisan foreign policy but would judge domestic issues on their individual merits. As proof of his personal loyalty to the Administration, Rayburn showed that "out of 164 votes in which his views prevailed during the past Congress, the President needed and received his margin of victory from Democrats on 121 votes." The two leaders also informed the President that the Democrats would conduct themselves in the future as in the past, examining each issue in the light of what they believed to be best for the country. They joined in a pledge that the Democrats would support the President when they believed him right and oppose him when they believed him wrong, but "always zealously helping the President husband and safeguard the legitimate rights and dignity of his office against the encroachments of the Republican old guard."

There was much speculation as to how the President and the Speaker would get along in the Eighty-fourth Congress since the Congressional campaigns had undermined their relations. The press thrives on conflicts and it probed for evidence of dissension. Yet there was a fundamental basis for understanding. They were both conservative, the one leading his Party slightly to the left and the other pulling a bit to the right. They were both basically friendly with reputations for seeking harmony. But there were certain fundamental differences which could well breed trouble. Mr. Sam was annoyed by the superimposing of military attitudes and behavior upon White House administration. Strained dignity was incompatible with his unrehearsed manners. Rayburn possessed an almost Platonic respect for the profession of politics. On the other hand he detected in the President a certain lack of respect for the machinery of civilian government. Then there was Mr. Sam's over conscientiousness which made him observe quietly that "a fellow can spend too much time on the golf course when he's needed to mind the store."

To celebrate Mr. Sam's return to power the people of the Fourth District staged several dinners and parties during the Christmas holidays. The affair at Greenville on December 22, 1954, was perhaps the most interesting to Democrats. Following a parade, Mr. Sam was presented with a little, fuzzy Mexican burro that had been flown from Mexico City to Dallas and brought by automobile to Greenville. In accepting the animal, Mr. Rayburn quipped, "For pep, for virility, for strength of character, he beats any elephant that ever walked the face of the earth." The photographers tried unsuccessfully to get Mr. Sam to kneel beside the burro, but he willingly squatted down with him. They resembled two old Texas political cronies, as he whispered in the big floppy, fuzzy ears "Beat 'em again, beat 'em again." The two continued their political conniving about 1956 as the TV crews performed their duties.

While all of the visible drama and plotting of future strategy went on before the cameramen, some sensed an invisible dress rehearsal of the Eighty-fourth, the details of which were known only to Mr. Sam. However, homespun philosophers around Bonham translated the act by depicting him as a man trying to ride two horses running in opposite directions, or as a man trying to jump over a fence while standing on a tight wire. During the Harding, Coolidge and Hoover years he had tasted wormwood and for the past two he had held a cup in his hand. As the leader of the majority Party he no longer had to drink a bitter draught. Now he could have a little sweet wine. But as an American during those dark days he felt a compulsion for conviviality in the interest of the general welfare. When it came to wrapping up a legislature measure a Speaker with his "delicate touch" was prepared for almost any set of circumstances. A commentator for a Lubbock paper said he was so proficient in such matters that he could tap dance on eggs carrying water on both shoulders and give the appearance of being all things to all men.

With a whispered conversation here, personal counsel there, or a soft-spoken speech at the right moment when the most good could be done, he was the inconspicuous star. There was no rancor or jealousy among the supporting cast. He saw to it that everyone was rewarded. His custom of permitting members to speak for one minute on any subject before the House got down to its regular business gave everyone who desired a chance to blow off excess steam. Rayburn considered that the practice of extending their remarks in the *Congressional Record* was an essential reward, for, he said, "A politician has to have publicity to live."

When this cross between a Houdini and a Sphinx went to Washington in January, 1955, he had achieved the status of the Congressman's Congressman, a symbol of perfection in American statecraft. He was a model for the neophyte and an institution among veteran lawmakers. Most of the older giants like Senator Taft (Mr. Republican) and Senator Vandenberg were gone. At a time when strong men could make their influence felt, Mr. Sam, save for Alben Barkley, stood almost alone among his generation. He was to be the tallest man in the Eighty-fourth Congress.

Under the two-Party system a President can check legislation with his veto if his opponents do not have the necessary two-thirds majority to override it. On the other hand, Congress can restrain a President by keeping a tight grip on the purse strings. Therefore, Sam Rayburn, with his eyes on 1956, held considerable power since appropriation bills originated at his end of Capitol Hill. With his protégé, Johnson, destined to be in charge of the Senate, Rayburn spoke with authority as he left for Washington. All factions sooner or later were compelled to feel his influence before getting a bill on the Statute books. His power was to be immeasurable.

Sam Rayburn, however, carried his power with dignity and modesty, never losing sight of the practical and human element. Before the Party caucuses and the formality of getting down to business, Mr. Sam chanced to meet retiring Speaker Joe Martin in the corridor one day in December, and promptly brought up the problem of office space, with specific reference to their own relationship. In the game of musical chairs, Martin and Rayburn had exchanged offices in 1947, 1949, and 1953, and now, with Mr. Sam destined to be the new Speaker, another move was imminent. Fully aware that the office in which Speaker Martin resided was more spacious and attractive than that he had occupied while Minority Leader, he approached him forthrightly.

"Joe," he said, looking quite serious, "Ah'm tired of all this shiften' around. What do you say, we keep the same room we got now?"

"You're the Speaker, Sam," Martin replied with a friendly smile. "Whatever you say."

And this was the way two rival friends made the transition, according to Robert Coughlan for *Life* magazine (February 14, 1955). It was by no means protocol or parliamentary, but for the two it seemed reasonable. Thus the House could settle down quickly to the things of importance which needed to be done "with the homespun comfort of a fat man slipping into a pair of old shoes." [1] Mr. Sam never asked for the larger office back, not even when Charles Halleck became the Republican Minority Leader. Sam had made a trade.

☆ XX ☆

The Game of Musical Chairs—Speaker Again

BY A vote of 226 to 198 Mr. Sam, on January 6, 1955, was returned to his favorite seat in the House of Representatives. As retiring Speaker Martin left it, he gave a "wee note of caution": "Don't get too attached to this chair. After all 1957 is just around the corner."

Before taking the oath of office for his sixth full term as Speaker and twenty-second term as congressman, he asked to make some remarks. "There are no degrees in truthfulness," he said. "There are no degrees in honesty. You are one hundred per cent or you are not." About the dangerous times that faced the Republic he affirmed:

> "We are all in this thing together whether we be Republican, Democrat, or what not. This Republic is going to live; if we do our duty, if we do the things that will preserve, protect, defend, and perpetuate these great institutions, we will be a free people."

He reviewed his pledge and stated that his Party would not indulge in personalities, and to both segments he stated:

> "We are going to do this business in good humor, not angry with anybody, but trying to work with the

instruments that we have to keep our country great, keep it prosperous and bring happiness to the American people."

The next important item of business was President Eisenhower's State of the Union address. Before the President began his formal remarks, he graciously acknowledged Rayburn's seventy-third birthday and offered best wishes for his health and happiness.

Rayburn's state of the union speech outlined the Democratic program—to follow the President's leadership in foreign affairs so long as it was bipartisan, to scrutinize American defenses very closely, to work with the President in liberalizing reciprocal trade agreements, and to support him in continuing corporation and excise taxes. He stated that the Democrats would make an effort to restore the rigid ninety per cent parity price supports for major farm products. However, he granted that with farmers divided as they were, many would favor retaining the Eisenhower-Benson flexible price supports. Rayburn expressed the hope that some revision would be made in the Taft-Hartley labor law.

If there had been a Republican or anyone but Rayburn on the rostrum on February 17, President Eisenhower would have lost his Reciprocal Trade program in the House. Through astute manipulation the Speaker pulled it out of the fire, but he had to resort to three roll calls to do it. On the first roll call the vote was 207 to 178 against the Administration. The question was whether the House would consider the trade act bill under a rule barring amendments from the floor, a procedure which had been followed consistently for such complicated legislation. The Texas delegation was divided 13 to 8 against the open rule and Rayburn, because the congressmen from oil-producing areas wanted a chance to limit oil imports through an amendment.

The Speaker, caught off guard by the initial defeat, surrendered the gavel to make one of his "back-to-the-wall" speeches in an appeal for the Eisenhower–Cordell Hull program. His argument contained three major points. First, he tried to show why there should be no prejudice against the "gag rule." Then, he appealed to the House not to lose sight of the national welfare in an age when international commerce was vital to defense. Finally, he asked his colleagues not to be blinded by local conditions, such as unemployment. About local interests in home districts he stated:

> "Everybody wants labor employed at good hours, at reasonable wages; but suppose we do not trade with the rest of the world. . . . We are no longer a debtor nation; we are the great creditor nation of the world. We are no longer a small producing nation; we are the greatest surplus-producing nation upon the face of the earth, and we have got to have it so that we can trade freely with the rest of the world or our factories will close and more thousands upon thousands of laboring men will be turned out of their jobs just because we refuse to trade goods for goods with them."

For years the struggle for a more liberal foreign trade had revolved around the tariff question and continuance of the Reciprocal Trade Act which allowed the United States to make tariff concessions. This program had been an established policy of the Government since 1934, but at each renewal period bitter controversies resulted before renewals could be effected. In 1948 renewal was granted for only one year with greater limitations. Both Eisenhower and Rayburn were seeking a three-year renewal, instead of one, and retention of reasonable discretionary powers for the President to make concessions. These were some of the economic and historical facts upon which the debates were founded.

On the next roll call the House switched its stand 193 to 191. This was a vote on a substitute motion by Clarence J. Brown. Then on the final roll call of the day, on taking up the bill with closed-rule-barring amendments, the Speaker carried the field by a one-vote margin, 193 to 192.

The morning before the final ballot, Mr. Sam called in twenty freshmen Democrats to have breakfast with him. When the voting began, these neophytes did not stutter in their "yea" votes. They stayed with "Mr. Sam." Joe Martin had also pulled his part of the load. He read an appeal from the President "for this act which underlies most of America's military effort abroad" and then added his own plea. The bill as approved by the House was a manifestation of a bipartisan vote of confidence in the Administration to establish a policy of "trade, not aid."

In trying to be bipartisan and strengthen the Administration's hand Rayburn ran into trouble within his own Party. During the first week in March dissension developed within Democratic ranks over the Speaker's support of Eisenhower on the Formosan resolution, which gave the President unlimited power without any debate. A delegation came to Majority Leader Mc-

Cormack first, but when he failed to quiet the people, they called on the Speaker, against McCormack's wishes, to question him sharply about his assistance to the White House. The conversation went something like this:

"I agree he [Eisenhower] doesn't need the resolution. He already has the power. But I want to show the world that we have a united country."

"This is just a method of sucking the Democrats in on whatever trouble he gets us into around Formosa," the group replied.

"Maybe so," Mr. Sam retorted, "but the country comes first. We're not going to play politics. I remember how the Republicans patted Truman on the back when he first went into Korea then kicked him in the pants afterward. We're not going to do that."

"O. K.," one member stated, "we'll pass the resolution but only after a couple of days of debate. Let the country know the facts."

"No," Rayburn replied, "we're not going to debate. I don't want one word said against this resolution when it gets to the floor of the House."

When the resolution reached the floor, it was passed on Mr. Sam's terms, with only one Democrat voting against it.

Mr. Sam had pledged to support the President where the general welfare was concerned—on Reciprocal Trade and the Formosan resolution. However, he did not agree to go along on everything, to withhold legislation of his own which he considered of value to the country; but the White House apparently thought the Democratic leadership was willing to be completely subservient to its wishes. Sam Rayburn quietly observed that this was a good illustration of a military man's "blind spots." Mr. Sam had caught the Administration unawares on the $20 tax reduction bill and crammed it through the House; however, the Senate, under the leadership of Byrd and George condemned it as unsound and dropped the measure dead in its tracks. Rayburn had moved quickly to get the Democrats on record as supporting a tax cut to prevent the Administration from using the issue prior to the 1956 election. Eisenhower was annoyed and referred to Rayburn's behavior as "irresponsible" in submitting such a measure as a separate bill.

President Eisenhower, according to an eye witness, revealed his irritation with Rayburn in the ballroom of the Statler Hotel, where the Speaker was a guest of honor at the White House correspondents dinner. Rayburn sat only three seats from the President, who had been the recent recipient of Democratic support on his two major issues. The dinner was a gay occasion, but the President refrained from talking with Rayburn, yet talked to those around him. The rebuke became conspicuous to newsmen like Drew Pearson, who reported that finally Rayburn left the table and went home. What Mr. Sam thought about this behavior, in the light of what he had done for the President, perhaps could not be expressed in either formal or colloquial English.

Texas oilman Sid Richardson, friendly toward both Rayburn and Eisenhower, telephoned the Speaker. Rayburn asked: "What does Eisenhower mean by saying I am 'irresponsible.' When I put through the Reciprocal Trade Treaty they thought differently down at the White House. When I passed that Formosan resolution for him it saved Ike's neck. But when I push a $20 tax reduction to give the little fellow a break, I am 'irresponsible.'

"The trouble with Eisenhower," stated Richardson, "is he probably didn't even know you passed the Reciprocal Trade Treaty for him. The boys around him forgot to tell him. Don't forget Ike never reads the newspapers." [1]

Richardson's explanation of the President's behavior was hardly enough to satisfy the Speaker. He might have forgiven him for not seeing the headlines of the Washington papers, but not for his blindness to a robust human anatomy sitting only seven feet away, particularly one that had "saved his neck." On March 26, Mr. Sam's irritations were reflected further in a speech before the Independent Bankers Association in Dallas. He charged that the Eisenhower Administration had "condoned and even encouraged the increased concentration of economic power." He went further to state that the first two years of the GOP had "witnessed the complete triumph of the big banker–big business combine." Continuing, he said:

"This of course is not the first time that the forces of monopoly have marched forward to victory under the protective cover of a friendly administration in Washington. . . . The history of the past sixty years has seen the development of monopoly, from trusts, to holding companies, to corporate mergers, and back to holding companies, with an ever-increasing concentration of financial control in the background. . . . We seem to be in the throes of a third great forward surge of monopoly in the history of our country. The last two such movements ended in catastrophe for the nation, accompanied by serious loss of our national wealth and grave waste of our human resources, consequences that are not lightly to be dismissed."

Rayburn's remarks were in support of a pending House bill designed to check bank holding companies. The legislation was aimed at confining "banks to the business of banking and giving some measure of power, authority and management over their local financial resources." Rayburn was applying his earlier thinking on holding companies to the banking business and was giving the Eisenhower Administration credit for encouraging the ills which again needed correction.

Then two days later, after a bipartisan meeting with the President on foreign affairs, Rayburn revealed his dissatisfaction and fears in an understatement: "I don't feel any better." He found no comfort in what Eisenhower reported about the Quemoy-Matsu controversy. Dulles had nothing to say in the meeting, and Mr. Sam was distressed by the absence of fact and conviction.

The April 16, 1955, $100-a-plate testimonial dinner in the National Guard Armory was regarded by many as the most elaborate and significant event on the year's political calendar for Democrats. It was set in lieu of the Jefferson-Jackson Day dinner, and was the first time in the history of the annual Democratic Party affair in the nation's capital that a living man was honored. The Texas Legislature marked its approval of the event by adopting a resolution of tribute to Rayburn with the entire membership signing their names to the document. The great number of conservative Democrats who turned out from both Texas and across the nation seemed to imply that at least a brief moment of tranquility had returned to the Party; however, as evidence that harmony was not quite complete there was a competing dinner to honor former Governor Jimmie Byrnes of South Carolina, who had teamed up with Governor Shivers and Southern leaders in 1952 against loyal Democrats.

The larger and more enthusiastic crowd, however, came to honor Rayburn: 3702 people—400 from Texas and 200 from Oklahoma—were seated at the banquet table. According to Paul M. Butler, National Chairman, the affair netted about $300,000 to resuscitate a depleted Party treasury.

There were a number of Texas officials present, including Attorney-General John Ben Shepperd, Agriculture Commissioner John White, Land Commissioner Earl Rudder, Speaker Jim

Lindsay of the Texas House, and President pro tempore Crawford Martin of the Texas Senate. Senator Ray Roberts and Representative James Turman (Fannin) of the Fourth District were also there. Governor Allan Shivers, however, passed up the meeting because he had to be in Washington on May 6 for the Governor's Conference. Senator Price Daniel was making a speech at the East Texas Chamber of Commerce, but Mrs. Daniel and her mother represented him. Majority Leader Johnson was one of the featured speakers. Notables recognized were former President and Mrs. Truman, Adlai Stevenson, Mrs. Eleanor Roosevelt, and Mrs. Woodrow Wilson. Rayburn's brothers and sisters were also introduced, along with other relatives.

For one night at least, loyalists, Shivercrats, Eisencrats, Maury Maverick Democrats, and just plain Democrats were all on speaking terms as long as they stayed on the subject of Sam Rayburn. They cited his "integrity" and honesty in public life. Many of these people, the press suggested, had recently come from the foul atmosphere of the veteran land scandals and insurance frauds in Texas; hence they were invigorated by the freshness of the clean air around the Speaker.

The mighty among the Party leaders gave their finest speeches, sometimes searching for words and new adjectives to pay the respect they thought due their leader. Mr. Sam sat quietly, removing his nose glasses and smiling briefly when his name was mentioned. Attention was focused upon two photographs of former Democratic Presidents, Jefferson and Jackson, with an even bigger picture of Rayburn in the foreground shunting them aside. Smiling, the two immortals seemed to be enjoying the occasion with the caption underneath reading, "Well, we couldn't have been replaced by a nicer guy." As the tinsel and glitter kept falling on his bald head, Mr. Sam tried to brush it away with his napkin and bare hands.

Finally, when his moment came, he stood amid incessant applause. He held himself under rather firm control until the band struck up "The Eyes of Texas" and that did it. Tears welled up in his eyes. Grinning and wiping his face with the back of his hands, he waved to the crowd that had come to pay him tribute at one of the most successful $100-a-plate dinners in the history of these affairs.

His address extolled the Democratic tradition of Jefferson, Jackson, Roosevelt, and Truman, with its humanitarian spirit. He portrayed a party which responded to changing times and new ideas. He discussed the war years and the depression and the sobering effects upon the Democratic Party and its leaders:

> "In the fullness of time and service to the nation, the Democratic Party has come to be more than a political party. It has become an Idea; an essential part of the American Idea. Political parties have their victories and defeats but great ideas go on forever. Hence we Democrats may look with equal serenity to 1956 or to 1976."

Then he became more serious as he made some personal observations:

> "But now we have come upon times whose like is not in the annals of mankind. For today it is possible to enshroud all men in a seamless, cloud-borne garment of poison, and make our planet as lifeless as the moon. I would, therefore, beseech Democrats and Republicans alike to conduct themselves with a becoming restraint in all those things that pertain to war and peace, since they pertain also to the life and death of all men. Let us guide our debates with wisdom and inform our hearts with righteousness, lest we fall into shame and so into oblivion."

After commenting upon our experiment in government and the masterful way our country dealt with foreign and domestic crises, he concluded in these words:

> "Today darkness broods over the face of the earth. Evil stalks the hills. No man knows what devouring monsters tomorrow may bring. May I say, then, to my countrymen—let us in this desperate hour nobly conceive and nobly act in the greatness that is our heritage and our light and our life. So doing, within the eye of God, we shall triumph over evil as did the founders of this great Republic."

Thus came to an end a celebration marking the climax of his career. As Speaker, Party leader, or American, he was never again to climb so high. He had dethroned temporarily two great Democratic Presidents—Jefferson and Jackson. He had taken a bow before Party leaders everywhere, and at that moment a unity prevailed which was not to be seen again. He had begun a partisan speech with his eyes on 1956, but concluded in the role of the great compromiser who would bring the factions and opposing parties together for the glory of the Republic and the salvation of the world. A narrow partisan view could not contain this cosmic soul that could vision the self only in relation to the mass of humanity. He took his seat amid thundering applause, and half an hour later, with Miss Lou, drove away into the darkness to their modest Washington apartment.

The attention and affection which were showered upon him might have been attributed to his power in the Party, but this was only one aspect of the picture. His love of people had drawn to him every hue and caste. Throughout the years in Washington he continued his acquaintance and friendship with kings, queens, presidents, generals, prime ministers, taxi drivers, secretaries, policemen, janitors, and newsboys. Among the latter, for example, Mr. Sam was something special. One day Edward Boyd heard one newsboy comment on the Speaker's baldness to another newsboy. The latter picked up the remark and snapped, "If you used your head as much as he does, you wouldn't have any hair either."

The story of Sam Rayburn cannot be told without alluding to the numerous receptions, dinners, and functions at which he preached the doctrine of the Democratic Party. The father of REA legislation went to Atlanta, Georgia, on May 10, to deliver an address before 1250 representatives of the enterprise on the eve of the twentieth anniversary of Rural Electrification. In 1938 President Roosevelt had stated at Barnesville how the whole idea came to him at Warm Springs. Rayburn, however, had really conceived of the idea much earlier, while sitting around a coal-oil lamp in his father's living room back at Flag Springs. Prior to 1938 he had pointed out the problem to Roosevelt, who with his patrician background really was not as close to the rural need as was Mr. Sam. Yet his sensitivity to the people's need made him quick to respond. Without the teamwork of these two humanitarians, and the support of strong Democratic majorities in Congress, the farm homes might have remained in semi-darkness for another fifteen or twenty years.

A few days later, Mr. Sam, in describing the miracle of the transposition of the Aladdin lamp, gave credit to the creators and organizers of rural cooperatives:

> "To you who have labored along the dusty roads, in the rich farmlands, and on the steep hillsides to sign up members by the light of a wood fire or a kerosene lamp goes the everlasting credit. . . ."

When he began the crusade to rescue the farmer from his backward condition, he found inspiration, he said, in the words of Thomas Jefferson, "I have sworn on the altar of God everlasting hostility to every form of tyranny over the mind of man." Rayburn recognized those economic forces at home and abroad which would keep man in bondage. The farmer must emerge from the physical darkness of economic tyranny, he believed, to pierce, "the dark shroud of cultural and spiritual darkness." With an evangelical faith, Rayburn went about the task of subduing the forces that had little interest in men's personal comfort or intellectual growth. Rayburn's struggle was never ending, for with almost each session of Congress he collided with the powerful utilities that stalked the struggling cooperatives with merciless ardor through economic pressure and propaganda.

After Mr. Sam had received the last handshake and congratulation at Atlanta, he left for Statesboro in his plane, together with Representative Prinie Preston and Governor Griffin. The barbecue at Statesboro was to his liking but he was quick to sneak off to the Canoochee and Altamaha rivers with his rod and reel which he had deliberately brought along for the purpose. The cares of the world always disappeared the moment his lure hit the water. To even the score between himself and the unsuspecting bass he sometimes used a bait on which he had filed away the barbs. This type of sportsmanship was compatible with his "live and let live philosophy of life."

After guiding a high and rigid farm support bill through the House, and a modified social security program to increase benefits to women, widows, and disabled persons, Rayburn had a brief period for relaxation. On May 23 he went south again, this time to Greenville, Tennessee, where he read the dim wording, chiseled on a marker commemorating the site of Davy Crockett's birth on August 17, 1786. Rayburn made remarks which were appropriate to launching a drive for a projected memorial. Each time he participated in one of these historical ceremonies he felt that he was revitalizing the national energy, his idea of insulating the public mind against degrading *isms*.

His commencement address on May 30 to the graduating class of the University of West Virginia also vibrated with the deeper values in the American system. In appearing before this college group he showed his great versatility. Within the past three months he had spoken to Party leaders, farmers, businessmen, bankers and historians—and now to alert young intellectuals. He always faced the challenge of young minds because he knew how to win their respect with the first volley of plain talk. To the West Virginians he admitted:

> "I have lived quite awhile but I know that I shall be old only when some day I find myself sitting around with others bewailing the younger generation and talking about how much better we did things in our day."

Then he reported how the young men by their achievements in Europe proved that the "professional croakers" prior to World Wars I and II were completely fooled. He declared that there was no weakness in American youth any time in history. Without reference to Party he traced American achievements since 1918 in foreign and domestic affairs, and concluded upon the theme that the price of freedom could not come too high. The American way of life should be defended without complaint, he declared. The climax of this college activity was the conferring upon the honored guest the Doctor of Law degree.

Much has been said about Mr. Sam's relation to oil and gas interests. His first real commitment to their needs was back during the New Deal. However, in 1926, when the twenty-seven-and-one-half-per-cent depletion allowance was conceived, he recognized its values. The industry has been able to expand and maintain its stake in American economy because of three tax rules which have been established in internal revenue policies. Participants in the perilous game of oil may deduct the twenty-seven-and-one-half per cent of its gross income as a depletion allowance, if this amount is not more than half of the net income. An operator who drills a dry hole may deduct all of the expenses from the gross income. An operator who brings in a well may deduct all the intangible expenses (equipment, labor, fuel, geological information, and the like, which add up to about sixty per cent of total costs) from the gross income. Oil men who are in the ninety-per-cent bracket can profit greatly from these three rules.

In fact, Rayburn argued that without these rules the independents could not stay in business and the wealth would become concentrated in the hands of a few major companies to the destruction of free private enterprise. Mr. Sam hastened to add, though, that producers of platinum, sulphur, lead, uranium, along with thirty-two other metals and minerals had allowances also from five per cent up, the amount depending upon the relative production risk.

His basic conviction was that independent oil and gas producers should be exempt from Federal controls, because they were the pioneers and experimentalists who gave the industry vitality and kept the big companies on their toes, preventing the consumer from paying monopolistic prices. The American public, however, had, he grieved, generally been unaware of the basic issues. People cannot understand, he said, that the twenty-seven-and-one-half-per-cent depletion is actually a subsidy to protect the consumer from a minimum increase of 4 cents per gallon on his gasoline. He recognized that since he was a product of the Southwest, rich in these natural resources, he was vulnerable to criticism, but he insisted that he was acting in the interest of the common welfare, as he had always done on other issues.

In the Eighty-fourth Congress there were proposed amendments to the Natural Gas Act of 1938 to clarify the jurisdiction of the Federal Power Commission over independent producers and gatherers of natural gas. The Committee on Interstate and Foreign Commerce had reported the Harris bill, which would exempt this group from Federal regulation as a utility and protect the consumers from unreasonable prices of natural gas, by providing control by the Federal Power Commission over prices which could be received by the producers.

Rayburn's position was clear and consistent. He had supported the bill President Truman vetoed and he supported the bill reported out of committee:

> "I think that if the Phillips decision stands unchanged, we would have less and less gas, which in my opinion might bring about an increase in the price of gas to the consumer. The passage of the Harris bill, I think, means the production of more gas and also if you have more and more of anything the price is more likely to go down than up."

He argued that the great cost in getting the gas to the consumer was not in getting the gas to the neighborhood of the consumer, but in distributing it to individuals after it was once delivered in bulk. There were some cities where it cost less than 70 cents to get the gas out of the ground and transported, but in these cities the consumer was paying at his home more than $3 for this 70-cent gas. He stated categorically that he would oppose the bill if he believed it would result in an increase of cost to the consumer, but he thought otherwise.

A Presidential committee and the FPC had recommended

such a bill, but the White House had become silent when opposition to Rayburn's theory developed among mayors of the large cities in the East. They predicted that prices would skyrocket if natural gas producers were removed from Federal control. Assuming all along that he had White House support, Mr. Sam asked for Eisenhower's endorsement on June 23, but it did not come, despite the original Presidential committee's report.

The division of opinion in Congress was reflected by the sixteen to fifteen favorable vote, and even with Rayburn's strong backing the bill had only a fifty-fifty chance as long as the White House withheld its support.

More encouraging, Senator Johnson, who also shared Rayburn's views, stated that he could get a favorable vote on a bill similar to that reported by the House committee, if the House approved the measure. Johnson hesitated, though, to attempt any such legislation during the current session, if the House rejected the Harris bill. The Majority Leader knew that Democratic members from the North and East, while susceptible to persuasion in 1955, an off-election year, would not go along with anything so political in nature in 1956, since the mayors of these cities had accentuated the sectional angle.

Only legislative action could void the Supreme Court's decision in the Phillips Petroleum Company case, which led to the FPC regulation of natural gas prices at the well-head. Rayburn and Harris had cited the 1954 survey which showed that the well-head cost of gas was only about ten per cent of the price paid by the consumer. Hence they were determined to break the stranglehold; however, the Supreme Court had consistently held for Federal jurisdiction over gas wells and offshore oil deposits. The first effort to free controls was the Moore-Rizley bill of 1947. Next there was Oklahoma Senator Bob Kerr's gas bill in 1948, shortly after his entry upon the Washington scene. Then there was the period when Mr. Sam played hide-and-seek with Truman and they worked out their compromise. Then came the Harris bill.

Mr. Sam received telephone calls from Houston oil men about the Harris bill, but his standard reply was, "Boys, you know how I stand. Why don't you call Eisenhower since some of you have done so much for him?" Whether they talked with Ike, Mr. Sam never learned. Some of them, he was told, were on good terms with Eisenhower, having worn their "Me for Ike" buttons in 1952 and had them shined up for use again in 1956. But as he mused a while longer, he remembered that there were still those who had not forgotten how to write checks for Democratic campaign funds. The behavior of some people he concluded, would not deter him from supporting legislation for the common welfare. He went ahead and whipped the natural gas bill through the House on July 28, 1955, by a vote of 209 to 203.

Also quite complicated, but not quite as protracted as the oil and natural gas case, was that of Wright Morrow, Democratic National Committeeman from Texas. The contention began in 1948. Morrow supposedly voted for Eisenhower in 1952 and offered to resign. He was barred from serving on the committee. His formal resignation was rejected by the State committee but accepted by Stephen Mitchell, National Chairman. Paul Butler, who replaced Mitchell in December 1954, was looking for someone of Morrow's caliber to take his place, but readily discovered that one man would not be enough. It would have to be a team like the Siamese twins, for in Butler's language, it should be someone who worked for Adlai Stevenson and someone who would be approved by Governor Shivers, Speaker Rayburn, and Lyndon Johnson.

While Paul Butler was trying to straighten out the political scene in Texas arising from the Morrow incident, the Speaker was looking toward an August adjournment of Congress. There were about a dozen "desirable" measures marked for clearance—foreign aid appropriations, military reserve, highways, minimum wage, anti-polio vaccine, defense production, customs simplification, and contract re-negotiation legislation. There was some hope of clearing the way for public housing, sugar quota, Colorado River development bills, and the atomic-powered ship proposal. Programs destined to be left stranded, he thought, were school construction, broader Social Security coverage, veterans' dependents legislation, revisions in the Refugee Admissions Act. These were only predictions from Mr. Sam's press conference of July 17.

Though Rayburn put the highway bill on a priority basis, he had reservations about it, especially if the President insisted upon General Lucius Clay's proposals. Rayburn was at this time against the President's bond plan. "I am utterly opposed to it," he declared. "I don't think that is the way we should finance our spending. It should be done the way the committee voted, paying for it now and not passing it on." Later he blamed the Republicans for rejection of the bill. "We Democrats gave Congress an opportunity to vote on the President's highway program."

On August 2, 1955, Rayburn reported that the first session had been a success. The President had received approval on about sixty of his proposals, an achievement which Rayburn attributed to Democratic cooperation. The failure of some measures was due to the Republican opposition to its own Administration.

The Speaker's vacation after adjournment scarcely materialized, for he had a full calendar during the late summer and fall. On September 24 he was at Sudan, Texas (Lamb County), for a fall festival, his principal theme being the United Nations as the way to peace. The speech was designed to carry out the motif of the year's theme of the festival.

On October 13 the big three in the Democratic Party—Rayburn, Stevenson, and Johnson—met at the latter's ranch east of Stonewall for a two-day powwow. Although a social visit, this type of political brass could not evade the public eye, much as they tried. By daybreak on the second day reporters, photographers, newsreel and television cameras were ready for business on the Senator's lawn. It would have been futile for the three to have said that they came several thousand miles to admire a new swimming pool which was being built on the ranch. Stevenson did express, though, the desire to return to the Johnson ranch when the pool was finished.

The Speaker went to Fort Worth on October 27 to attend a "Sam Rayburn Day" celebration there. Despite his seventy-three years, the Fort Worth people were talking of him for President. They recalled that Speaker Joseph Cannon retired at age eighty-six, that John Quincy Adams served in the House until he was eighty, that Robert L. Doughton was eighty-nine, and that Henry Clay was older than Rayburn when he was in the Senate. Mr. Sam had heard all of this talk before and was prepared to give a negative answer.

At a dinner for five thousand in the appliance building on the State Fair grounds in Dallas, he told cheering Democrats that the Republican Party had not changed since the days of Alexander Hamilton. It was still the Party of big business. He also warned against the smiles of Russian leaders since Communism was on the march in the world. And in at least a dozen other places he expressed the need for money to bolster national defense and increase foreign aid.

While Mr. Sam was touring the country raising funds for the Democratic Party, the people of Bonham and Fannin County began making plans for an appreciation movement to raise funds over a two-weeks' period for the Memorial Library. There was $350,000 already in the bank, but $100,000 was needed before construction could begin. Since most of the money had thus far come from outside sources, the home folks were beginning to feel guilty that they had done so little. Although the local drive was officially terminated early in November, money continued to come in long afterward. Local contributions ranged from pennies to five thousand dollars, but the amount of each donation was withheld from public eyes. Mr. Sam requested that a school child's name should occupy just as prominent a position on the roll of honor as that, for example, of an investment banker or oil man.

The ground-breaking ceremonies were held early in December and construction was promptly begun. His seventy-fourth birthday, he reiterated, was the happiest that he had experienced because the excavation for his library was well along.

Mr. Sam's January 17 address at the Jefferson-Jackson Day dinner in Baltimore was sufficient to alert the electorate to the fact that it was 1956. Only the day before in a press conference he accused Secretary of State Dulles of a "pitiful performance." "The Secretary," he said, "had endangered the United States' alliances by a statement in an interview in *Life* magazine that the Administration's diplomatic skill had saved the peace after the nation had walked 'to the brink of war.' "

This was the first time that a person in a top position had joined the rank-and-file criticism over the "brink of war statement." Four years later, however, he said, "Dulles was an able man and made a rather good Secretary of State."

After due consideration, which included competent judgment on the state of Senator Johnson's health after his heart attack, Rayburn early in March announced that his Texas friend was qualified and ready for action in 1956. His forthright statement placed the Senator in nomination to be the State's favorite son and chairman of the Texas delegation to the Democratic Convention in Chicago. Under his leadership, he believed that Texas would have a real voice in the proceedings of the Convention and would work for the nominees of the Democratic Party. "Under his leadership, we can begin now to put our house in order." He added, "Lyndon Johnson is no extremist. Rather, he is a happy warrior who has the tact and ability and understanding to unite in confident comradeship all fellow Texans. He is the man best equipped to restore order and prevent a repetition of chaos."

When Governor Shivers had fully digested Rayburn's endorsement of Johnson he made the following statement on a "Meet the Press" program:

> "I would not deny to him [Johnson] for an instant, the honor of representing Texas as the chairman of its delegation to Chicago or its 'favorite son.' I suggested him as possible Presidential timber long before any of the Johnny-come-lately DAC [Democratic Advisory Council] boys decided they liked him so much. I simply believe that Lyndon Johnson, Allan Shivers or anyone else who seeks either or both of those honors should be on record so far as his views on certain vital issues are concerned. I don't see how anyone could object to it."

The issues on which Shivers had asked for a statement were such things as States' Rights and Federal aid to education. Senator Johnson had told the Governor, "I am not and never have been the creature of the ADA, the DAC, the PAC, the NAACP, the CID; nor have I been the errand boy of the reactionary big business or the Republican Party." Shivers, a conservative, was unwilling to give a blanket endorsement of a program that was not spelled out; certainly he declined to support a liberal-loyalist campaign.

Shivers' March 28 speech in Houston referred to Rayburn's proposal as "cynical and calculated." This statement, issued by the Governor in Austin on April 1, and reported by Allen Duckworth of the Dallas *Morning News*, caused Mr. Sam to get "hotter than a ninety-eight cent toaster": "Rayburn still insists, as he has always insisted throughout his career, on being a Democrat first and an American second." Shivers also referred to him as a "brass collar" Democrat. Duckworth observed that Rayburn had challenged Shivers to a battle for control of the May 22 State Democratic Convention. When Mr. Sam arrived at Love Field, he raised his right hand and gave a V-for-Victory sign. In his interview with newsmen he described Shivers' statement as "cruel and untrue and Allan Shivers knows it."

There was no thought in Mr. Sam's mind of declaring an Easter moratorium on hurling political barbs. Later he told reporters that he thought he saw in the Governor's original statement about Johnson a faint hope of reconciliation:

"What has happened in the past few days to make him change his mind, I don't know. Perhaps some of the things he said haunted him and he became frightened at the prospects he envisioned—defeat. He appears to realize that he is on a leaking boat which may go down at any time. It appears that he didn't want to endorse anything that Byron Skelton [chairman of the Democratic Advisory Council] or that terrible Sam Rayburn stand for, but Byron Skelton and I still favor Lyndon Johnson." Then he continued, with reference to the remark which questioned his loyalty: "If I was as alarmed and cruel as Shivers," he declared,"I might say Shivers likes Shivers better than anything else, but I wouldn't say that about any man." The Speaker added that during his long public career, Shivers was the second man in the nation to make such a statement, but he declined to name the other person. Duckworth quoted a Dallas friend of Rayburn's as saying he believed the other person the Speaker had in mind was Dallas' Republican Congressman, Bruce Alger.

Rayburn continued the interview with these remarks:

"There are no skeletons in my closet or ghosts under my bed. I have lived a life of political integrity. I don't have to be a Democrat; I could be a Republican if my conscience allowed me to be. I do not have to go into Democratic primaries, but when I do I feel morally bound to support the nominees of the primaries."

He added that he also felt obligated to support the nominee of a convention, if he had gone into such a convention in an official capacity. What he was implying was that Governor Shivers had participated in the 1952 Democratic National Convention, but had refused support to Adlai Stevenson, the nominee of the Party. He recognized by the Governor's remarks that the same pattern would be followed in 1956. Rayburn concluded with the hope that the campaign would be kept on a high plane, free of personal attacks.

With Mr. Sam the issue was clearly one of Party loyalty. But with Shivers it was the implications of loyalty—acceptance of ideas "within the twilight of socialism." There was a clash of personalities and a struggle for the control of Texas. The Speaker concurred on about fifty per cent of Shivers' States' Rights views, as his legislative record indicates. At this time Rayburn was opposed to Federal aid to education (except for public school construction in depressed areas), socialized medicine, immediate desegregation, and such things, but he preferred to fight his battles in Congress. He believed that the Democratic Party had the philosophy which would help America move forward and meet these problems. The Republican philosophy, he believed, refused to examine them. Since we live in a world of change Rayburn wanted to direct the inevitable course of history rather than throw up a hopeless roadblock and let mankind be engulfed.

Hence, for Mr. Sam, the ten-day Easter recess obviously was not devoted entirely to thoughts relative to the season. A remark by Sherman Adams, President Eisenhower's top assistant, to the effect that the Democratic Congress had been disappointing and negligent of Administrative recommendations, stirred Rayburn's ire again. Johnson promptly pointed out, in rebuttal, that a good record in the Senate had been marred by Mr. Eisenhower's veto of the natural gas exemption bill, and the Senate's refusal to change the Electoral College vote counting system. Rayburn's colleagues likewise were having a distracting Easter season for most of them were back home mending political fences which had been broken by the explosive issues facing Congress.

After the Easter recess Speaker Rayburn on April 9 was awarded the order of Sikatuna, the highest honor the Philippines confer on a national of another country. The citation remarks were made by Ambassador Carlos P. Romulo in which he referred to Rayburn's piloting legislation leading to independence of the Islands. The reasons for the award were set forth in these words: ". . . in recognition of his services to the free world and as a far-seeing statesman whose vision has been unerring, in his uncompromising stand against the enemies of freedom." In accordance with the policy of the Government a citation could not be officially accepted until Congress gave approval; hence Mr. Sam deposited the document with the State Department until approval was received. Rayburn's speech of tentative acceptance reviewed the heroic struggles of the Islands' people for freedom, particularly at Bataan and Corregidor.

The selection of Mr. Sam on April 20 to be Permanent Chairman of the Democratic National Convention in August was just about as unexpected as spring's following winter. He had been the Chairman in 1948 and 1952 already, and some prophets could even see the familiar face on the rostrum in 1960.

A week later he made a plea to all precincts in Texas to send Lyndon Johnson to the Chicago Convention as favorite son and chairman of the delegation. He urged that Shivers not be selected as chairman because the choice would be equivalent to "the kiss of death to any hope of making Senator Johnson the Democratic nominee." Shivers and Rayburn again exchanged volleys. A story about Mr. Sam might leave the impression that he was always the victor in these verbal duels, but the Governor also had his skill with the language. He turned Johnson's phrase "from Sam Houston to Sam Rayburn" to "from Santa Anna to Sam Rayburn" and Mr. Sam replied thus: "This is an all-time low; it is rat alley politics." The May 5 Convention came none too soon for many Democrats who were becoming weary with the Speaker-Governor feud.

A five-piece cowboy band struck up "The Eyes of Texas" as one thousand Texans waved banners and cheered Rayburn and Johnson when they stepped from their plane at the Washington Airport on May 9. The red carpet generally used only for foreign dignitaries was stretched out to commemorate the occasion—a victory back home in the precinct and county conventions for the loyal Democrats. Rayburn spoke briefly, "We've put Texas where it belongs, a Democratic State in a Democratic column." Johnson was more exuberant as he hailed it as a "victory of moderation over the rash extremists and hot-heads of passion." Then he added, "Next time we'll knock down the extreme left wing; we won't allow either the right or the left to carry our buggy off the road." They agreed modestly that it was not a personal victory for either one but a triumph for moderation.

The victory should be attributed to the appeal the two men made to the thousands of rural and small-town Democrats who were neither extremely liberal nor extremely conservative. On the other hand the Shivers' defeat did not mean that Texas had repudiated the doctrine of States' Rights, for the man on the streets and some people in big business were, as a rule, opposed to Federal controls, centralization of government, and loss of state sovereignty. The Democrats of the rural areas and conservative elements in the big cities had joined ranks only temporarily behind Rayburn's leadership.

His campaign to put Lyndon Johnson in the favorite son position was further evidence of his sectionalism. In a national convention he recognized the trading value of having a favorite son. In 1932 he had maneuvered, though not deliberately, John Garner into the Vice-Presidency by breaking the deadlock for Roosevelt. The 1956 Convention he foresaw could turn into another 1940 affair where harmony would be needed; hence Rayburn wanted to be in a favorable position to trade so that unity could be achieved. Though Johnson had expressed no interest in securing the Vice-Presidency, Rayburn wanted to have the strength to bring about harmony if the Convention got out of hand.

The groundwork for putting Johnson in the favorite son position had been laid in the precinct and county conventions. Victory at the May 22 State Convention in Dallas was now assured. While the influence of Rayburn and Johnson was felt, much of the success of the loyal Democrats was due to the keen organizing ability of John B. Connally, who had served a successful apprenticeship in campus politics as a student at the University of Texas, and who was just making his debut into the complicated State picture. His sense of strategy and flair for speech-making were decisive factors in Dallas. Rayburn was unable to remain for more than the rally because of Lucinda Rayburn's illness, as he explained in a letter to Paul Butler (May 24): "I felt that it was my duty to be with my sister rather than to be in a big crowd like that where I would have been unhappy."

Since March the Rayburn family had anxiously watched the progress of sister Lou, who had had a major operation for cancer. After remaining in the hospital for several weeks, she was returned to her home on U.S. Highway 82. On May 16, while he was still in Washington, the Speaker received a telephone call that his sister's condition had taken a turn for the worse. She grew steadily weaker and on May 26 at 4:00 P.M., the end came.

The file cabinet containing the correspondence about her death is only a partial indication of the esteem in which she was held. Up until May 5, when he fought the battle of the conventions, Sam Rayburn felt her encouragement and wisdom. Since the mother's death in 1927 she had been in charge of the home and intermittently had served as his hostess in Washington. Though always assuming a modest role, serving humanity through her brother, she frequently revealed great strength of mind and will. She was both gentle and firm in her relations with the man whom she admired so much that she too referred to him as "Mr. Sam." "Gentle nobility," "Victorian decorum," "unselfish dedication," "Christian worthiness," "a charming lady of the old school"—these were some of the words and phrases written about Miss Lou.

Shortly before her death she said, "I have already had my flowers. Please, no flowers." From time to time, though, a friend will bring a rose bush or shrub to plant in the garden east of the

Sam Rayburn Library. In the years after her death, when Mr. Sam returned to Bonham he could be seen taking a silent stroll around this hallowed plot of ground. Perhaps this ritual partly explained the void and depression of soul as he turned his eyes toward Washington. More and more he felt the need to be near his own kin.

The fact that Mr. Sam did not have a wife and children of his own led him to share the various Rayburn groups. They adopted him—brothers, sisters, nephews, nieces, and cousins as their favorite relative. In exchange he gave a deep love.

Misfortunes seemed to multiply in the Rayburn family. While he was at Miss Lou's bedside, his nephew, Charles Rayburn, underwent an emergency operation and died. When Charles' mother, who was a heart patient, received the news she died the same day. And Mr. Sam's heart was indeed heavy when he picked up the gavel to resume his duties, but he said his friends were all very sympathetic. The House of Representatives had already paid their tribute to Miss Lou on the 28th. He remarked that he sensed their feelings by the "clasp of their hands and the look in their eyes."

On June 4 the graduates of Syracuse University heard two commencement addresses; the first by Speaker Rayburn and the other by Minority Leader Martin. Afterward they saw the two legislative leaders receive honorary Doctor of Law degrees. The Speaker expressed his faith in broad shoulders, young hearts, and alert minds to defend and conserve the greatest form of government ever devised. He cautioned the graduates "not to listen to the moaners and groaners who have, since Washington's day, lacked faith in our representative form of government."

Sam Rayburn's legislative record reveals that he was a winner, not a loser. He remarked many times, "I hate to take a licking." The worst kind of defeat in his estimation was one which stemmed from inadequate planning and fumbling once the battle was joined. On June 7, the tables were turned on him and he tasted defeat. The measure was the Mutual Security Act. Both the President and Speaker made their pleas to Congress. Grass roots sentiment, however, that America could not buy friends spoke more loudly than impassioned oratory from the leadership on both sides of the aisle. The House voted 192 to 112 to cut $1,109,000,000 from the foreign aid allotment. Until this point President Eisenhower had maintained a fairly good legislative record in the second session of the Eighty-fourth Congress.

In discussing this reduction with the President at a White House conference, Rayburn was sharply critical of Administrative strategy. He felt that the President's letter to Joe Martin, which was read to the House just before the vote was taken, was ineffective. Instead of this procedure, he believed a meeting should have been held with the Foreign Affairs Committee long before they voted on the measure. Rayburn was quite abrupt in pointing out Eisenhower's failure to do his part:

"Why your advisors didn't tell you about this legislative rule of thumb is something I can't answer. But it's much easier to influence committee action before damage is done than it is to undo such damage after a committee has acted." "No doubt about that," the President agreed, "but I had no warning. I had no idea the Committee would cut the program so deeply. As I recall, I did call in members of Congress to discuss this matter. I believe Representative Richards, Committee Chairman, was there."

Then came the Rayburn reply which brought into focus one of his principal objections to a military-oriented Administration, with its absence of that democratic quality of give and take:

"That may be so, but it's not what I'm talking about. I was talking about the Democratic leaders of the House such as Mr. McCormack and myself. We weren't asked to this meeting you speak of."

Rayburn's remarks to the President were in much better taste than his off-the-cuff comments to friends. Rayburn was thoroughly disgusted with the performance because it violated the basic principles of legislative procedure. Rayburn could give advice and take advice; hence he could not understand a system which was immune to a similar reciprocity.

The second session of the Eighty-fourth Congress was moving toward the convention season and mid-July adjournment in a quiet manner, never before known in a Presidential election year. Dale Miller, a reporter, observed that ordinarily every quadrennium at this time brought forth the sharpest lines of demarcation between the political programs of the two major Parties. Usually the issues separating the Party platforms set off sensational controversies, designed to excite the home folks and rally them around the standard of their particular political philosophy. Miller also noted that this session was conducted in an environment of political calm, except for flare-ups over legislation such as the natural gas bill and farm measures. He attributed some of this tranquility to the cooperation between a Republican President and the leadership of a Democratic Congress, both exponents of moderation.

Before Rayburn turned his thoughts toward Chicago, he first digested a stack of correspondence which reported on the internal nature of the Party strife back in Texas. Perhaps the most informative letter was one from the Austin attorney, Fagan Dickson on August 7, who expressed the good news that he believed "Senator Daniel would like to go along with the Democratic nominee." He also advised Mr. Sam to "hold the whip hand," for the Shivers influence was still strong and the Governor could give trouble in the September 10 State Convention. Rayburn appreciated friends like Dickson who could separate truth from fancy and tell him in simple language what had to be done.

Remembering the confusion in the 1952 Convention, Rayburn outlined some changes he hoped to make in the rules. He wanted to amend the rule that allowed just one man to demand the poll of a delegation to require one-fifth of the members, as in the House. He feared that too often people asked for these polls just so the home folks could see them on television. He stated also that he hoped to have quarters adjacent to the convention hall where delegations could retire to be polled so that the roll call might proceed. He also wanted to restrict the use of television where it seemed to be interfering with the rapid and orderly movement of the proceedings. Rayburn thought of his job as being similar to that of the driver behind a twenty-mule team. When he cracked the whip he wanted the mules to pull together.

The Permanent Chairman of the Democratic National Convention was the ringmaster in Chicago. He gave an exhibition that was characterized by its professionalism. No one found tactical blunders in his performance.

The same gavel that gave finality to the Eighty-fourth Congress on July 27 banged the Convention into session on August 13. It was a highly polished, two-toned gavel of yew made by Grant B. Freer, a friend of Senator Jackson of Washington, who requested that it be used on both these occasions. (There are more than a hundred gavels in the trophy cases at the Sam Rayburn Library which have special historical background significance. Half a century of good parliamentarianism is connoted by this display.)

However, any type of gavel would have been sufficient at Chicago, even a door knob, with the Rayburn Rules of Order in effect. This much discussed set of regulations is contained in an unwritten manuscript based upon Roberts' Rules but revised by experience and practical politics. This edition reflects a technique and personality. Many will emulate but few will ever duplicate perfectly. He gave the impression of authority when he rapped for order and said "Clear the aisles." He was noted for his ability to cut corners. "Those in favor say aye . . . there are no noes . . . it is unanimous." A quite simple bit of parliamentary procedure! He did not wish to short-circuit a small minority, yet he felt that Democrats were always happier working together. His job was to make the team pull as a unit. When delegates began to show the effects of strain he remained unperturbed. When the more agitated shouted for recognition and charged into the aisles, he sometimes failed to see them. Sam Rayburn was a thoroughgoing Democrat in a convention and his rules of order insisted on "order" as well as party unity, especially with all of America looking on. He followed that type of democracy where harmony prevailed, once the majority had spoken. One spectator, in evaluating the way Rayburn wielded the gavel in 1956 said: "The man who now holds the gavel owns it."

The Platform Committee had a real struggle with the Civil Rights plank, and the Northern and Southern factions braced themselves for a showdown fight on the Convention floor. The chair allowed thirty minutes of debate, a reasonable amount of time for the delegates to exercise the democratic processes. The stage was set for a demand from the floor to have a roll call of delegates. The chairmen of the New York and Georgia delegations were waving their arms and shouting for recognition. Mr. Sam rubbed his gimlet eyes to clear his vision but did not see them, then called for a voice vote. Never changing his expression, he promptly ruled the "ayes" had adopted the platform and it was all over. The insurgents were too stunned to do more than look at one another in bewilderment.

He also followed these same Rayburn Rules of Order in making Adlai Stevenson's nomination unanimous. On the voice vote for the Vice-Presidential nomination, those wanting to vote "no" waited in vain. He had objected to an open convention of the Vice-Presidential choice anyway, knowing that it would take at least three days to resolve the conflicts within the Convention. He believed that the Party could not afford to parade such evidence of disunity before the voters. So Mr. Sam had to "squeeze down on the boys" as he explained the way decisions sometimes have to be reached. As the titular head of the Party he acted in the interest of the whole, well aware that he would offend the vociferous fringe, but not afraid to do so. He knew that some decisions had to be reached quickly before the Convention got out of hand and slipped away from him.

The press tried to make the selection of the Democratic nominee into a battle of giants, between Sam Rayburn and Harry Truman, with the one supporting Stevenson and the other Harriman, but the correspondence speaks to the contrary. Rayburn was for Johnson as long as he had a chance, and Party agreement on Stevenson happened too quickly for the kind of deals implied by the press. A few days before the Convention, however, Truman, without warning, came out for Averell Harriman and was reported as saying that Stevenson could not beat Eisenhower. For two days the Stevenson people were stunned.

Truman telephoned Rayburn asking if he might come to his hotel suite. Sam replied cordially, "Sure, come over, Mr. President." He generally called him "Harry," but this was an occasion requiring greater respect.

The conversation was friendly and satisfactory. Mr. Sam alerted Truman to the fact that he wanted him to address the Convention relative to the troublesome platform. Had there been real personal differences it is unlikely that a man who was not even a delegate would have received such consideration and been put in the public eye where he could serve his own ends, though indirectly. They made only superficial reference to what they had read in the papers, since their concern was primarily Party unity. Rayburn, however, may have been thinking that in the endorsement of Averell Harriman, Truman had "shot from the hip again—and missed this time." Johnson and Rayburn knew Harriman did not have a chance. They had at least one hundred votes in their hip pockets, not to mention others had they foreclosed on some IOU's. They knew also that they could deadlock the Convention and perhaps force the nomination of Stuart Symington, if they had so willed. But they wanted the Convention to agree on a winner and, barring their personal feelings for Harriman, they were compelled to believe that he did not qualify.

Truman appeared in the role of a Party boss to check the Stevenson surge, observed William K. Hutchinson, Chief of the Washington Bureau of the International News Service. To onlookers Truman seemed to be opposed by the "age-wise and cagey Rayburn." This is an assumption, however, which did not do justice to the Speaker's emotions. Those trying to read Rayburn's mind concluded that he feared some ill effects from Truman's remarks because of his stature in the Party. Also he wanted Harry Truman to look good in history, because he thought Truman deserved a high place. Mr. Sam, however, never commented on the fact that Harry's statement to the effect that Stevenson could not beat Eisenhower might have been a bull's-eye.

Mr. Sam heard nearly every conceivable comment TV technicians could think of about bald heads and their absence of photogenic qualities. He had been on the rostrum only fifteen minutes when they started yelling about his cranium looking crimson, and he frankly had no sympathy with them in their frustrations. He did condescend, though, to let them take a little of the gloss off. The viewing audience made many quips about his baldness, but no one joked about it to his face because on this issue he was as touchy as Cyrano de Bergerac was about his long nose. Yet on occasion he would allow a reasonable amount of levity.

Rayburn was the star of the Convention and one of the featured orators. His address may have lacked the rabble-rousing quality of Governor Frank G. Clement's keynoter; but it was both timely and full of substance, forcefully delivered. He said what many felt was needed. The twenty-four congressmen who were either delegates or alternates in the Texas delegation were especially proud of him. Along with others in their delegation, they roared with approval, waved their banners and milled around for five minutes with delegates from other states. When he turned on wit and satire, such as the following, they again exploded:

"When Democrats enact welfare laws, they are 'socialistic,' but when the Republican leadership embraces Democratic welfare laws, it is evidence of their tender concern for individual human dignity."

The "dynamic conservatism" of which the Republicans boast, he said, means "standing still dynamically." He even rebuked the speakers who had preceded him for not fixing the real blame where it belonged; then he raked the Republican Administration hard, from stem to stern, for not handling its job.

Rayburn came back to Bonham with the faith that Stevenson and Kefauver would carry the Democratic standard high. His reply August 24 to Mrs. R. D. Randolph's "gracious note" also contained a ray of optimism:

> I feel the Democrats were in the best humor with each other—North, South, East, and West—than at any convention I have attended in many years. There

were no brawls, no fist fights; there was no pulling and hauling at state standards, and everyone looked to be at their best. It seemed that everyone wanted to get a winning ticket and go home and work to elect it.

Before Mr. Rayburn left Bonham to begin the campaign, he telephoned Lee Simmons, at Texoma, a long-time friend and former head of the Texas Prison System, and Elder H. G. Ball, pastor of the Primitive Baptist Church at Tioga (Grayson County), about his desire to join the church. On September 2, Simmons accompanied Rayburn to Tioga, where the baptismal ceremony was performed. Although it was conducted quietly, with only a few close friends present, the incident attracted the attention of the press and a number of correspondents. Some of Mr. Sam's replies to the more wide-eyed religionists were slightly tinctured with the feeling that his privacy had been violated. As late as December 18, he was explaining his reasons for affiliating with "the same faith to which my father belonged."

"Yes, the Hard Shells are feet-washing Baptist, but just as Jesus washed the feet of his disciples so the members of this sect wash each other's feet," he added about his father's faith.

> I have intended to join the church for many years but have been away so much, and frankly I did not know until recently there was a Primitive Baptist Church in this part of the country. I finally found one and I joined it in the little town of Tioga. It was a very little church and that was what made it more interesting.
>
> My health is good and I am at peace with everyone and everything.

The author of these pages, because of his research on the religion of the South and Rayburnism, was the recipient of many comments from the people in his profession about "the old man's" becoming a "Hard Shell," some of the references being slightly unsympathetic. These were the replies in 1956:

"Mr. Sam on occasion attended the First Baptist Church in Bonham. He had been a superintendent of the Sunday School for years. In Washington, though he was only an occasional church-goer, he did read his Bible, as the phrasing and style of certain speeches reveal. Like Lincoln he did not consider church membership the only prerequisite to the good life."

He worshiped privately and quietly. His church was his apartment, where he held his own service. In the New Testament he found spiritual strength. The social gospel and ethics of the "Man from Galilee," referred to so frequently, influenced his political philosophy and permeated his relations with humanity. He could have lived out his days without affiliation with institutional Christianity because he was endowed with a basic religiousness and affinity toward goodness. However, Mr. Sam wanted to belong to a particular group, as he later explains.

Mr. Rayburn's decision to join the Tioga church was perhaps reached during the week prior to Miss Lou's death. Ball, who had been a frequent visitor to the Rayburn home, was a constant attendant during the illness of Lucinda Rayburn. There was some serious talk, but Mr. Sam was never one to converse about his own piety. He did, however, attempt to translate his parents' teachings into his public life. Those who are familiar with Primitive Baptist doctrines, or the "hard shell" tradition—perhaps an unfortunate nomenclature—will see that any other denomination would have been inconceivable for Mr. Sam. Reverend H. A. Sills of Metter, Georgia, in a letter dated December 15, gives an appropriate summation: "In my way of thinking you are properly identified both religiously and politically."

Rayburn went to the State Convention at Fort Worth on September 10 with the hope of bringing some of the warring factions back into the Party to present a united front in November. Governor Shivers' declaration on September 18, that he would support Eisenhower as in 1952, came as no surprise to Rayburn. Nor was he taken by surprise when he received letters that both praised and condemned his stand at the Fort Worth Convention. The following critical letter hurt but he bore no malice himself. It was written by a Houstonian (September 23):

> I have written you many letters over the past twenty years, all of them couched in language which showed the love and affection which I hold for you. All through the dark ages of the Texas Regulars, Dixiecrats, and Shivercrats, I, along with thousands of other loyal and true Democrats always looked to Sam Rayburn whose very presence in our midst was an inspiration to hold the fort and redouble our efforts for Democracy in our State. Your stature was like the Rock of Gibraltar, even in the most bitter days of defeat.
>
> Now I am heartsick, disillusioned and frustrated, because it is extremely difficult for me to comprehend why you would desert me like you did, both at Chicago

> and Fort Worth. We are the ones who worked our fingers to the bone in 1952 against insurmountable odds, trying to hold Texas in the Democratic column, and, if you don't think it was sickening to see you line up with the very people who were crucifying us in that year you should be in my shoes. Never again can I respect you and love you with the deep affection I held before the Fort Worth Convention.

The gentleman went on to say that Sam Rayburn was safe from retribution within the sanctuary of the Fourth District, but that Lyndon Johnson was not protected and that there would be a day of reckoning here. The "stealing of the Fort Worth Convention," he said, would not be forgotten.

Rayburn's reply to this and similar epistles followed this pattern. He stated that he was satisfied with the results in getting a resolution passed to endorse Adlai Stevenson and Estes Kefauver, and for each senatorial district to have its own representatives on the State Executive Committee, with each one pledged to support the Democratic Party. Except in three or four instances the districts elected the desired people. Rayburn reported that he had no agreements with Senator Daniel or anyone else, but the Senator told Rayburn he would support the nominees of the Party.

About the accusation of theft he wrote:

> Senator Johnson and I did not have anything to do with stalling the Convention. I was not in on the know-how of those who were running the Convention, because they did not consult me about any procedure. . . . My Senatorial District in several Conventions has had their recommendations kicked out but that did not put me out of the Democratic Party or make me less enthusiastic for the Democratic National ticket.

Rayburn said he did not "squeeze down" on anyone, but some believed he did, or that Johnson threw some of his weight around. It appeared to the liberals that the Speaker and Majority Leader had made a play for the Dixiecrats and Shivercrats in Houston, Dallas, and Fort Worth. But Rayburn persisted in maintaining that he merely followed his "middle of the road" beliefs. His later endorsement of the liberal Ralph Yarborough for the Senate did, however, appease some who were offended. Such incidents merely show, among other things, that politics in Texas is complicated and that Mr. Sam was a political warrior with many scars of conflict. He was strong in battle, and one without his intestinal fortitude could not have survived. He never ceased to believe that he always did what was best for the majority. Those splinter groups that do not go along sometimes do not get along, he thought. He bore no animosity toward honest men as individuals who followed their convictions. He proceeded on faith that the work done would bear fruit in the future.

With a heaviness of heart, because many of his friends misunderstood his motives, he proceeded in the fall of 1956 to work for the national ticket. He prepared a basic speech, which contained many of the elements he had stressed at Chicago, and began a strenuous tour. Though he learned that the people still liked Ike, he took comfort in the Democrats winning both Houses. The vote for President showed 35,585,316 (457 electoral) to 26,031,322 (seventy-four electoral) votes.

In a sort of post mortem he wrote a friend in Austin on December 18 the following:

> We told the farmer what had happened to him during Democratic Administrations . . . and what would happen to him under Republican Administrations. It took the Republicans less than four years to reduce the farmer's income by more than four-and-one-half billion dollars.
>
> Small business is in a tight squeeze which is going to put many of them out of business, and the high interest rates endorsed by this Administration is one of the things that is adding to the distress of small business and is getting into business that isn't so small.

Rayburn went further to pick up some loose ends that were bothersome to his friends and had provoked letters which obviously had caused some misunderstanding. About Price Daniel he wrote:

> I did not vote for Price in the primary but I have been on very friendly terms with him ever since he has been in Washington. I think if he would free himself of some of his associations and follow his own trend and views that he would be able to make an outstanding governor.

Rayburn's attitude toward Daniel caused some hostility within Texas Party ranks, but Mr. Sam was trying to see the national problem and pull the splinter groups back together.

Rayburn's method of speaking in broad terms and his use of generalities sometimes led to misunderstandings. During the campaign, he frankly admitted, "I did say some pretty sharp things about some people in the oil industry, which I think they deserved having said about them." In reply to the letters, from his friends among the oil men who seemed dismayed, he wrote:

> I do not put all the people in the oil industry in that class, for there are many of them who have been loyal and have contributed to the Democratic Party in campaigns. I am not speaking about people who contribute in local primary campaigns, or who support the State Democratic ticket.
>
> The national ticket is another thing to me entirely. I was told by an outstanding citizen in Wichita Falls that when many of the men in the oil industry were asked to buy a $10 ticket to a dinner where the principal speaker was Senator Gore of Tennessee, and Lyndon Johnson, Frank Ikard and I were to be there, they changed the subject and talked about something else.

Late in November, Speaker Rayburn and Majority Leader Johnson announced that there would be no precise statement of the Democratic program until the President had first declared his program. Rayburn's caution was prompted by an upsurge of liberalism within the Party. Moderation was sharply challenged by such liberals as Neuberger of Oregon, Douglas of Illinois, McNamara of Michigan, and Humphrey of Minnesota. The pending revolt, however, had its origin with the Averell Harriman campaign to win the nomination. Dale Miller predicted that the liberal forces would first attack Rule 22 of Senate procedure, the rule which provides that closure of debate can be imposed only by a two-thirds majority vote. As long as one-third opposed cloture a filibuster could continue indefinitely if enough senators were willing to talk in relays. The conservative and moderate forces in the Senate had used this rule quite effectively in standing off liberal legislation.

Goaded by the liberal element, Democratic Chairman Paul Butler came up with the idea of a seventeen-man advisory committee, including eleven members of Congress, to help coordinate efforts in behalf of Democratic programs and principles. After consulting their lieutenants, both Rayburn and Johnson declined to serve on the committee, but indicated an initial willingness to consult with the advisory group, though making no promises to follow their suggestions. Butler had hoped that by getting the two leaders on the committee more liberal views might seep across to them. To Mr. Sam the whole idea appeared to be a "Butler Brainstorm." He remarked that congressmen were elected by the people and were responsible to the people and should not be responsible to a busybody group. The more the Speaker thought about the whole idea the less he liked it.

During the month of December, Rayburn showed concern over the political picture in Texas. He wrote a number of letters concerning the effect of Price Daniel's resignation from the Senate seat. Since Daniel was to become Governor, rumors were rampant as to his successor in the Senate. The question was whether the outgoing Shivers would make a temporary appointment or whether Daniel would later make the selection. Shivers' choice of the conservative Democrat William Blakley, however, eased Mr. Sam's mind temporarily on the possibility of a Republican who might have upset the status quo in the Senate, where the Democrats held only a narrow margin.

The topic of the hydrogen bomb and the dangers from "fall-out" was another subject about which he wrote in December. He rephrased Governor Stevenson's views about the need for unilateral controls, and praised the Governor for stimulating Eisenhower's interest in finding a solution, aware that this issue, plus the eruption over the Suez Canal, might have been a contributing factor in the Democratic defeat. He reasoned that because of these world tensions, the people wanted Ike, but not the Republican Party, since they left the Democratic control of both Houses intact. He advanced this thinking as a partial refutation of the arguments that in some metropolitan areas the Party lost many labor and minority votes in order to hold a small segment of conservatives and moderates.

When Stevenson announced that his own political obituary had been written, that he had even read his own epitaph, and that in his will he was making Johnson his heir apparent, for what it was worth, he was giving a subtle hint that Rayburn and Johnson should keep their eyes on 1960. Mr. Sam, however, had already been doing some thinking of his own, as the next four years reveal.

☆ XXI ☆

Mr. Speaker's Next Three Years Under Eisenhower

ON JANUARY 3, 1957, Sam Rayburn was elected to his seventh full term as Speaker with a majority of thirty votes, and the Democrats proceeded to organize the House. In the Senate the issue was temporarily in doubt. Had Senator Frank Lausche (D., Ohio) decided to do what he threatened and switched his vote to the GOP side, Vice-President Nixon could have broken the tie in favor of his Party and the Democrats would have lost that body. Senator Jacob Javits (R., N.Y.) also helped thwart Republican hopes by deciding to finish out his term as Attorney-General before taking his seat. However, Johnson emerged victorious as Majority Leader, and the Democrats continued to control both Houses. With his protégé at the helm, Rayburn felt rather confident.

In presenting Rayburn, Joe Martin used the words "just, with a fierce determination to uphold the fine traditions" of the House. Rayburn responded with the assurance that he came to the rostrum again "with no enemies to punish." "This is no time for acrimony," he reminded them. "This is a time of dedication for every human being who lives within the confines of the United States of America."

Although Speaker Rayburn and Majority Leader Johnson seemed to be sitting high on their respective thrones within the Party, some watched with anticipation the activity of Democratic Chairman Paul M. Butler and his seventeen-member advisory committee, which hoped to inject the voice of the more "progressive" or "liberal" wing into the charting of a program for the Eighty-fifth Congress. Others virtually ignored Butler's optimism believing that someone had underestimated Mr. Sam's behind-the-scenes power through whispered conversations in clockrooms and calm, persuasive conferences in his hideaway. His advancing years had ceased to offer encouragement to political antagonists because of his enormous zest for life. He had already declared, "I want to see a lot of years to come. I feel like a two-year-old colt." So as Congress opened, he lowered his head like a Texas steer and sank his hoofs into the turf of Capitol Hill. Butler soon learned that he had tackled one longhorn that he could not budge, let along brand.

His friends took special pains to make his diamond birthday a memorable one. His own attitude was that of indifference to the passage of time because the doctors had recently told him he was in "fine fettle" and he should live to be a hundred. To such optimism he replied: "I'm willing. My birthdays don't mean anything to me. There's nothing you can do about avoiding 'em."

In point of service Rayburn, at fifty years, had broken all American records for men in public life. The late Senator Carter Glass and Speaker Cannon had forty-six years; Senator Hayden, Senator Hale, and Representative Sabath, forty-five years, also including their years in state legislatures. With an eye on the world record, Rayburn's only competition appeared to be that of Gladstone's sixty years in Parliament; Arthur James Balfour's fifty-six years; Sir Winston Churchill's fifty-four years at the present point, and France's Charles Freycinet's total of forty-four years. With his firm belief that "Life is a great romance—the greatest romance there is" Mr. Sam set his sights on Gladstone's mark. The people of the Fourth had many times stated that they had no objection.

Rayburn knew that he had done a few things deserving of recognition but his modesty forbade any deviation from his normal routine to get it. In fact, Rayburn had been known to say, "Damn the man who is always looking for credit. I have always noticed that if a man does his job, and does it well, he will get more credit than he is really entitled to."

However, he never hesitated to pay tribute to others who deserved it. On each January 12 he had given recognition to FDR with many laudatory comments. As an old political warrior himself, Rayburn particularly liked to remember about Roosevelt that "when he engaged with you in a fight he never turned his back on you. He stood up and fought with you when he gave an indication that he was going to stand by you." This was the type of example he himself had set for others in the House of Representatives.

Sam Rayburn was aware that Mrs. Roosevelt was none too popular among some people of the South because of her unrelenting stand on Civil Rights. So while he was on this subject of the Roosevelts and giving credit, he wanted to remind these Southerners of something they should remember:

> "Roosevelt always had by his side a woman who I think is one of the great if not the greatest woman in the world today. Her great strength of character, her great strength of mind, her great patriotism, are a challenge to me at all times and every time it is my high privilege to meet and converse with her."

He wanted everyone to know that at least a small portion of the success of the New Deal was the result of this woman's influence.

Rayburn's loyalty to the memory of Roosevelt was surpassed only by his support of Eisenhower's foreign policy. Early in the session he gave the President backing on his Middle East doctrine which cleared the way for favorable House action. He left no one in doubt as to his position when he stated firmly:

> "I think we've got to give the President the authority he requested to use American military forces, if necessary, to bar Communist aggression in the Middle East. I lean very strongly toward giving Mr. Eisenhower the power to spend as he sees fit, $200,000,000 by next June 30 to bolster the economies of Mid East nations."

His stand on this issue was contrary to that taken by former Secretary of State Dean Acheson, who described the President's plan as "vague, inadequate, and not very useful." Mr. Sam, though, remained in a bipartisan frame of mind on this issue as he endorsed a program which would strengthen America's hand in an area of the world where the vital commodity of oil was involved. He was a realist, and if President Eisenhower wanted to welcome King Saud of Saudi Arabia shortly after declining to meet with the Prime Ministers of England and France, he believed this was the White House's business.

However, he knew that he could not escape criticism for pushing the Eisenhower doctrine through the House under a "gag rule" forbidding amendment. But Rayburn assumed full responsibility for shutting off debate in the face of accusations that his move was aimed at protecting oil interests and showed fear of the strong lobby from Texas. Mr. Sam, however, said that economics and world politics entered in here, not local politics. He even boasted that some big oil interests had already tried to break him politically back home and had failed; so he said, "I am not afraid as long as I do what seems right. The people are my tribunal." He had already explained to his people the importance of the twenty-seven-and-one-half-per-cent depletion and the importance of oil to American economic development; in fact, he thought the subject had been exhausted. To a constituent he wrote, "You and I have been in politics long enough to know we cannot please everybody, and I have decided to do the right thing and let the chips fall if they want to."

The Fourth District, though an essentially agrarian sector, understood the facts of life. The people acknowledged the hand of oil companies in shaping foreign policy during both war and peace. They were aware, too, that gifts and loans to foreign countries would affect them directly, whether they used the short or long form in making their income tax reports. History and economics had not made them cynical because they treasured their way of life and preferred it to the type of servitude which could be theirs if America should fail to communicate to the world and prove the superiority of its own system. During the many years they had enjoyed the feeling of strength under Mr. Sam's leadership in world affairs, they had learned to appreciate power—that it is of no value unless the majority could be its beneficiaries. They had been listening to Mr. Sam's simple gospel for half a century, and the hard core of indigenous citizenry were in accord with his belief that "A fellow who eats high on the hog can expect to have a few chitlings [chitterlings]." They had their freedom and wanted to keep it, so they were not going to become bitter about taxes and a few hardships. On foreign policies and economics they expected Mr. Sam to use his judgment.

March 4, 1957, was a day of many anniversaries to those on Capitol Hill. Few were around who could even remember that a special session of the Senate was convened on this date in 1913; that the Sixty-third through the Seventy-second Congresses adjourned on the fourth, a fact known to Mr. Sam. He particularly recalled that the Seventy-third session opened on this date, when the wheels of the New Deal began to turn. To Mr. Sam, March 4, 1957, marked his forty-fourth anniversary in Washington.

The man best qualified to indulge in reminiscences about Mr. Sam was Senator Johnson. His account is valuable both to the historian and layman who have frequently inquired as to the time when Mr. Sam became interested in him. The Speaker frequently referred to someone as being "one of his boys," but when he spoke of Lyndon in these terms his words had a deeper meaning. The Senator's tribute gave a part of the explanation:

> "Mr. Speaker is one of the few men in history who occupies at the same time the position of a legend and the position of a living force. His personality is stamped on this nation and on its laws. But at the same time he is still helping to make those laws, and millions of Americans are grateful that he is at the helm.
>
> "To me, however, there is a deep personal significance to this occasion. It arises from the fact that before I had even discovered America, Speaker Rayburn and my father were close friends, serving together in the Texas Legislature. My father stood beside Sam Rayburn in many of his fights in that body.
>
> "When I was a small, but gangling boy whose legs still wobbled like a colt on the range, my daddy impressed upon me that Sam Rayburn is always a friend. I have never forgotten that early lesson.
>
> "I am doubly grateful to Sam Rayburn for what he has done for our country, and for his everlasting friendship to the Johnson family.
>
> "People will come, and people will go, but Speaker Rayburn will always remain as the promise of the eternal youth and the eternal vigor of the institutions of this nation."

Mr. Sam was a practical politician. He knew people. He was loyal to his friends. He had a special devotion to Texas friends and prided himself in being able to recognize their abilities. From time to time he said proudly: "In my estimation Senator Johnson has made the best Majority Leader the Senate has ever known." Mr. Sam believed that history would bear him out in this judgment and prove that his faith in Lyndon was well founded.

The White House also commemorated the anniversary by a dinner, an annual affair for the Speaker, but 1957 was special. There were seventy-nine persons present. The guest list included key people in the Senate and House. Mrs. S. E. Bartley, the Speaker's sister, who served as his hostess after Miss Lou's death, was among the guests. Sarah McClendon reported that the White House dinner table was exceptionally handsome, with red and white carnations and blue iris. The Monroe plateau, purchased by President James Monroe, was on the table. It was used only for the most important dinners. It is a three-sectioned mirror bordered in gold with gold candelabras about three feet high and tall gold épergnes filled with fruits. The gold knives and forks were also included in the service, as well as the new gold and white china recently added to the White House collection by the President. A vocalist and violinist entertained in the East Room after the meal.

Early in March, Rayburn was answering correspondence relative to the Senatorial position in the State, which had to be filled at a special election, where only a plurality was necessary to be elected. He was quite disturbed on March 8 that the Texas Senate had not passed the Pool bill, or some other bill, that would give a double election. Without some such legislation he believed the Democrats would have "to look around and pick out that man we think is strongest and concentrate on him and try to beat the Republican, Thad Hutcheson from Houston." By March 22, he saw Ralph Yarborough and Martin Dies as the "two front runners." He predicted that "Dies would go down and Hutcheson come up" before the election. His thinking on Hutcheson was, of course, not personal, only the views of an unwavering Democrat. He believed "that Hutcheson couldn't be counted out because they are going to spend all the money they think is necessary to put him before the public in the most favorable manner." Later he added, "There are some so-called Democrats in Texas who would like to play this kind of a joke on the Democrats of Texas." He feared that the Democratic vote would be sufficiently split among the several candidates to allow the one Republican a plurality. To circumvent the "joke" he expressed his friendliness toward Yarborough, who on April 3, 1957, emerged as the victor with a plurality of about 73,000 votes. Rayburn was happy.

"I think that if the bad weather had not come just when it

did, keeping a great many of the laboring people away from the polls after their day's work was finished, that Ralph would have had a much bigger plurality. I am glad that I could finally win with him because I lost with him when I voted for him four times before this and he had my vote again this time."

Mr. Sam's peace of mind, however, could be only temporary with the home-front torn into splinter groups as it was. The Democrats for Eisenhower, the Democrats of Texas (DOT), the loyal Democrats (SDEC), the Dixiecrats, and others trying to crystallize their thinking again had the precincts and State convention in a turmoil. They were feuding about either precinct chairmen, committeewomen or basic issues related to Civil Rights. Had his political philosophy not been moored to the "sacred center," he could have been dashed upon the rocks of discord. There were differences of opinion between him and a few long-time associates, yet they seemed to maintain respect for his integrity and sincerity.

He kept telling his friends to achieve harmony first, win the election, and then let Congress thrash out the problems in legislative channels where their collective thinking could be translated into action. He abhorred discord, and always tried to get the Democrats to see the whole picture and not a segment of it.

The Supreme Court decision on segregation, explained Rayburn, "created a great problem for the people of the South." It was the source of some of the internal trouble for the Party. Although his personal evolvement was in advance of that of his section, he recognized that change would now be effected faster than the people could adjust, because, "It is going to be a long pull to re-educate our people to be sure that they will do the just and fair thing." He believed, though, that the majority of those in the North were a "just people" and would be fair, interpreting the "deliberate speed" of the decision as meaning that the pace should be only as fast as the South could be expected to move on an issue so deeply imbedded in its social structure. His moderate position on Civil Rights in the Eighty-fifth Congress, however, drew the rebuke on October 2 of the "Americans for Democratic Action," on the one hand, and the displeasure of conservative Southerners, on the other. When the Civil Rights bill finally passed it was trimmed down to what he called "a rights to vote bill in its fundamental aspects" and was a good beginning.

At a White House conference the last week in March, Eisenhower brought forth his proposal for "temporary presidency" legislation. With his usual bluntness Sam Rayburn said he was against it. Other legislative figures shared his views but guarded their remarks, waiting for him to fire the first shot. Mr. Sam waded into the issue as he told the President that the country had gotten along very well for 168 years without special arrangements for temporary succession, and that if the President should send up a special letter on the subject, people would start talking about his health and possibly his stepping out. The President could not withhold good-natured laughter at the Congressman's abruptness and unadorned method of expressing opposition. Eisenhower tried to dissuade Rayburn from his position but made no impression whatever. Mr. Sam was against the whole concept on principle; and also there was a practical matter, which good Party men did not discuss. Rayburn was never drawn to Nixon, when he was in the House or was Vice-President, and did not want to place him in such a strategic position. Mr. Sam was hopeful that the American people would "see the light of day in 1960."

From time to time during this session of the Eighty-fifth Congress, the Speaker encouraged less Federal spending and ultimate tax reduction, but insisted that the issue should be above the level of partisanship. If clear vision and common sense were not applied to the whole question of taxation, he explained, there could be an eventual national exhaustion. Every time the Government spends, the people must pay, and the more the taxpayer turns back to the Government the more he has reduced his purchasing power in the community. In the long run, consumption and production of new products he believed would be affected. Business could not expand and employment of new labor would be curtailed. These were some rather fundamental economic principles, Rayburn remarked, that were involved in the reduction of taxes.

Mr. Sam's aggressiveness became very much in evidence on June 19, when he called the House Committee on Un-American Activities on the carpet for permitting the filming and televising of some out-of-town hearings. Back in 1952 and again in 1955, the question had arisen, and he believed it had been settled, for as he told the press, "I thought I had interpreted the House rule rather clearly." There was to be no broadcasting of any committee hearings in Washington or anywhere else. The infraction was called to Rayburn's attention when a witness, a biochemist, apparently committed suicide before his appearance at a San Francisco hearing. The individual left a note declaring he had "a fierce resentment of being televised." Frank Eleazer of the Washington *Post* and *Times Herald* interviewed Richard Arens, staff director for the Un-American Activities group, and learned that Arens was of the opinion that the ruling applied only to Washington hearings. "Outside Washington we use the facilities of the Federal courts," Arens explained. "We take the position we are guests of the local Federal judge. We follow whatever rules he applies to the courtrooms we use." Some judges did bar even cameras, others permitted televising, still others allowed only filming.

When Rayburn was interviewed on the subject he merely reiterated what he had said in 1952 and had repeated in 1955—that in the absence of specific rules by the House, the general House rules apply also to its committees. These rules did not permit radio or television broadcasts of House sessions. The House had not voted otherwise, and as the delegated authority, he would carry out its intent.

In reply to a man who wrote on a postcard, asking for his reasons, Mr. Sam gave a full and prompt statement of his objections. Televising will "slow up proceedings of committees and lengthen them and the parts that are put on television are only the so-called 'high lights' that do not give a good demonstration of the committee proceedings or a clear picture of the issues. I do not think it is conducive to decorum or orderly procedure to have flash bulb pictures being taken or television cameras in operation while a committee is in actual hearing. . . . These are disturbing factors." After the sessions had adjourned, he stated, the photographers were free to take their pictures for their stories.

The Chairman of the House Committee, Representative Francis E. Walter (D., Pa.) according to Warren Unna, "curled his lip at the Speaker and Mr. Sam didn't like it one bit." Rayburn minced no words: "There will not be any more [House] committee or subcommittee hearings in Washington, or anywhere else, televised or broadcast by radio. Period."

When Walter received Rayburn's command he defiantly looked straight into the cameras and told a suffering witness, "There is no such rule."

When a United Press teletype of the remark was delivered to Rayburn in the Speaker's outer office, he read each word slowly. The famous bald dome began to light up. He thought a moment, then said, "No comment."

The word spread rapidly through corridors and cloakrooms.

The tension on the House floor on both sides of the aisles led the galleries to feel that another Archduke had been assassinated. Debate on a piece of legislation was temporarily interrupted. Representative Clyde Doyle (D., Calif.), a member of Walter's Committee, who had drafted fair play amendments for the House Committee in 1955, promptly upheld the Speaker's ruling. Representative Roy W. Wier (D., Minn.), who had consistently voted against appropriations for the subcommittee stated:

> "I think I have got the cure for the whole controversy and that is to wipe out the Committee. It assumes to be the investigator, the judge and the jury and even takes over judicial authority in the disposition of its cases. What's more, I do not like the way they are using the Committee to get headlines in the districts of the men running for election."

Rayburn did not get involved in the discussion but quietly cited Chief Justice Earl Warren's remark after the Supreme Court's timely ruling, when he criticized the Un-American Activities Subcommittee for "exposure for the sake of exposure."

Within a few hours both sides of the aisle quickly rallied to Rayburn's support and the accumulated grievances against Walter began to be expressed. Walter, potential Speaker material himself and close advisor to Rayburn, had for the time being at least, some thought, "torn his political breeches." Mr. Sam, however, did not go beyond his original public statement, yet his irritation was clearly obvious. He considered sufficient the general response from the House. He was quite sure that the House could provide its own type of discipline and restraining influences on future infractions of its rules. The Speaker derived a great deal of comfort from the knowledge that he had the support of the House of Representatives and that the body followed his leadership.

On October 9, 1957, Bonham again opened its doors to thousands of Mr. Sam's friends, including such guests as the Trumans, Secretary of the Treasury Robert Anderson, Lyndon Johnson, and hosts of congressmen and prominent citizens. A dream which began years back had now become a reality. When the people arrived they saw first of all a $490,000 white Georgian marble structure.

It was Georgian marble instead of another kind, for reasons which George Dixon learned at the time the specifications were made; Governor Marvin Griffin extracted a half promise from

Sam that it would be Georgian marble. The architect, Roscoe DeWitt of Dallas, telephoned Mr. Sam all excited. "Something has just come up. We've had a better offer of marble from Vermont."

"Hum-m!" said the Speaker. "That's very interesting."

"Shall I accept?"

"NO," declared Rayburn. "Use the Georgia marble."

"For Pete's sake, why?"

"Because," replied Sam, the Southerner, "I have a lot of friends in Georgia, and very few in Vermont." [1]

After the crowds had ceased admiring the exterior, they went inside, where they saw display rooms, reading rooms, the vault containing the documents covering more than half a century of a statesman's life, then the replica of the Speaker's room in Washington.

Like the reputation of the man the Library memorialized, it was built to last. Roscoe DeWitt, the architect, said it contained the finest materials and workmanship of any structure he had ever seen. At the dedication he called attention to certain features which marked it for long life; for example, the "crawl space" under the basement; the foundation resting on sturdy piers with the basement floor off the ground; the marble as a part of the wall itself; the use of copper, including the roof, as protection against the elements; the concrete and steel frame with solid brick walls and the marble bonded to the brick; aluminum windows; the large window of bronze looking out on Miss Lou's garden; concrete floors covered with tile; an interior faced with red antique marble or oak and walnut; doors of mahogany.

It was strictly quality workmanship from start to finish. Clarence C. Sandell, the superintendent of the work, assigned by Carpenter Brothers Construction Company, put his very life into the job. He watched each stone as it was lifted into position and stroked with pride the smooth marble. With deep affection and admiration for Sam Rayburn he went about his daily work as a craftsman of the old school trying to fuse those abstract qualities of the living personality into the edifice which future generations would recognize as a symbol. On May 31, 1957, Sandell was stricken with a heart attack and his dream of finishing the Library faded instantaneously. The standards he set, however, were carried to their fruition by John A. Warrick, Sandell's assistant and a specialist on interiors.

The Speaker's room is an exact replica of that in the nation's Capitol. The desk and furniture were bought by Mr. Rayburn when other furniture for the Speaker's room in Washington was obtained. Along with these came the chandelier, the fireplace mantel, the rug and tables also purchased by foundation funds. Both floor and ceiling were duplicated; the colorful floor-length draperies had been in the House "longer than I have been," Mr. Sam said. The pictures on the mantelpiece and walls are also duplicates of those in his Washington office.

Even the flag at the dedication had been used on several significant occasions. It had flown over the Capitol on December 10, 1955, the day of the ground-breaking ceremonies for the Sam Rayburn Library; on January 3, 1956, the day of the opening of the second session of the Eighty-fourth Congress with Mr. Sam in the Speaker's chair; on January 6, 1956, over the Supreme Court, on his birthday; and on March 30, 1957, over the White House.

As for the research facilities, Karl Trever, special assistant to the Archivist of the United States, who helped organize the books, papers, and mementos preparatory to public use, saw the Library as "an institution of pre-eminence in its chosen field" in the years to come, and the achievement of "a place in the ranks of the outstanding specialized libraries of the Southwest." Wayne C. Grover, third archivist of the United States, in charge of the National Archives and Records Service, also had a major part in arranging books, papers, and mementos.

Mr. Sam had a long-range plan for the development of a regional, and to some extent, even a national center for historical research. The direction of the Library's philosophy was influenced by his own personal interest in history and belief that all Americans should strive to learn more about their country's achievements. With a firm conviction that the American system was the best yet conceived, the dissemination of knowledge about its virtues would, it seemed to him, go a long way toward refuting some of the more competitive and obnoxious ideas in the world, such as Communism.

His plan and concepts were approved by the Sam Rayburn Board of Trustees shortly before the dedication ceremonies. The original personnel of the Board included H. G. Dulaney, Director of the Library; Bernice Newman, Secretarial Assistant to the Board; Buster Cole, Secretary-treasurer; R. M. McCleary; Mrs. John Palmore; Ray Manning; Speaker Rayburn; and H. A. Cunningham, Chairman.

Besides the Speaker's personal library, public documents, personal records, and Americana, there are mementos that reach across more than fifty years of Mr. Sam's life. There are hundreds of pictures, citations, scrolls, certificates and diplomas, plaques, one hundred gavels that have special significance, and gifts from governments and friends. One trophy case contains the honorary degrees that had been conferred upon Mr. Rayburn through the years, including the Doctor of Law from Muhlenberg College, May 30, 1942; East Texas State Teachers College, August 6, 1943; the University of Maryland on June 27, 1945; National University on June 9, 1950; Tusculum College on May 22, 1955; University of West Virginia on May 30, 1955; Syracuse University on June 4, 1956; the Doctor of Humanities from Austin College on May 23, 1950.

In a sense the Memorial Library contains a cross section of American political history since 1913 and the peaks of a man's career that are inseparable from public affairs. His life was so interlocked with his job that there is very little which is strictly personal. Sam Rayburn was a full-time congressman and had little opportunity for his private considerations.

Speaker Rayburn's modesty is clearly expressed in his belief that this was to be a monument to historical research and not to him personally. This same modesty was revealed in his resistance to starting a session of Congress on his birthday to avoid wasting the taxpayers' money with private considerations. However, he loved all the eulogizing despite appearances that he was impatient to get down to business. On his seventy-sixth birthday in 1958, he refused to hold his press conference or allow his picture to be taken, but his colleagues turned the tables on him. When Supreme Court justices, White House staff, top Administration agency heads, Democratic and Republican Senators, House members (including the Texas delegation), took it upon themselves to stage their own gathering to commemorate the day, the Speaker had to yield to everyone's wishes.

President and Mrs. Eisenhower's annual dinner for the Speaker on January 23 followed its usual pattern of splendor. Among the guests were twenty-one Republican members of Congress and only seventeen Democrats; hence Mr. Sam found himself in the minority at one of these White House dinners. The Speaker escorted his sister, Mrs. W. A. Thomas, who shared with Mrs. S. E. Bartley the duties of hostess. The friendly bipartisan gaiety and cordiality gave no evidence of the rancor that was to transpire over pending legislation and the forthcoming attacks upon the Administration, even by Mr. Sam himself.

Men of both Parties sensed on this evening, as they moved

into the spacious dining room of the White House, that they walked with one of the great figures in history. There was an unusual atmosphere of restlessness in Washington—a sad frustration, because the lawmakers were soon to be about the business, not of making life better for humanity but in appropriating money for atomic submarines, missiles, and other materials of war. Their hearts were more inclined toward other pursuits, like the construction of hospitals and schoolrooms. Mr. Sam's simple love for his fellowman, caused him to share this restlessness also, but he refused to abandon, even briefly, his dreams for a better society here and abroad. Security from foreign aggression, though, was one of his prime considerations. There was much boasting and bickering in Washington over the shortcuts to scientific achievement in realms of defense, but Mr. Sam kept his composure amid telephone calls and appointments handled on a mass production basis. He continued to carry his office in his right hip pocket on the back of an old envelope, as several have observed.[2] The pressure of the age never made him deviate from his habit of looking after the smaller details and concerns of his beloved constituents. This was the type of man who was honored at the White House on January 23. This was the figure whom many were already describing as the greatest living figure in American political life.

When asked on February 3 what America needed most, he blurted out in emphatic terms—"It needs leadership." He went on to explain: "I think that the entire political leadership of the country—Congress and the Administration, Democrats and Republicans—is guilty of underestimating the American people." Again he came back to his familiar estimate of people and his faith in them and their desire to know the "cold hard facts of where we stand in the arms race with Russia." He was quite sure that the people were not afraid, but he was aware that they were troubled and humiliated by the reports concerning our lagging behind the Russians in some things. His plea was for Congress to move ahead and even exceed some of the administrative requests.

Such aggressiveness was hardly to be expected from a man of seventy-six who rightfully should have been giving thought to passing the responsibility to someone else so that he could return to his quieter Speaker's office in Bonham, where he might catch up with so many personal pleasures and hobbies that had always been denied him. His course, however, had been set. Unless ill health forced him into retirement, he knew that the only direction he could go, with so much at stake for America and the Party, was forward. He would be compelled to die "with his boots on," as he liked to say. This was the only way for his breed of Texan to go.

Newsmen and closest associates marveled at his ability to keep his perspective and good sense of humor during these most strenuous years. Walter C. Hornaday recalls an incident which occurred just the day before Mr. Sam brought the House to prompt adjournment. He was in the Speaker's office and asked him what he planned to do.

"I am driving back to Texas," answered Mr. Sam.

Thoughtlessly Hornaday asked, "Who's going with you?"

The Speaker looked all around to make certain no one was listening, and leaning forward over his desk, whispered, "A woman."

This was Mr. Sam's way of telling Hornaday that it was none of his business.

Rayburn then chuckled and added, "I am taking two of my office staff with me." [3]

Besides the defense program, one of the most significant measures which he believed needed his attention during this second session of the Eighty-fifth Congress was Reciprocal Trade. The Reciprocal Trade agreement was due to expire on June 30, 1958, unless the bill, calling for a five-year renewal, was approved. For almost twenty years Southern Democrats had found themselves on the defensive in their own Party, given to resisting and blocking whenever possible most legislation which was not complementary to their sectional interests. In the current session these gentlemen found themselves in a more favorable position with the opportunity to take a positive action instead of a negative one on a measure wherein they had both an historic and practical interest—that of reciprocal trade and lowering tariffs to promote world trade and offset Communist gains.

Mr. Sam went to Congress in 1913 dedicated to support lower tariffs, being the product of an agrarian rather than an industrial economy. This was a bill, he said many times, which clearly separated the Jeffersonians from the Hamiltonians. Numbered among the former, and believing that the achievement of prosperity could be realized only by having a strong base —the man on the farm and the man in the shop—he sat about looking for support on a measure which would work to this end. In March of 1958 he counted noses. There were men like Howard Smith, Chairman of the Rules Committee, and Harry Byrd, on whom he could depend as far as this legislation was concerned. When two quiet and calculating men like Rayburn and Byrd shook hands on an issue there was real political professionalism. There was also a temporary realignment of forces.

As a rule where there was so much at stake, Mr. Sam usually did not appear overconfident, but he did not hesitate to solicit the most powerful lobby in America—the people. So he declared in a sad and doleful voice, even as early as February 24, that the important Reciprocal Trade Agreement Act could be defeated.

In 1955 the protectionists, he recalled, had fought against a three-year renewal, but it passed. Since 1934 he had shepherded reciprocal trade, resisting the richest and best organized lobby in America. With President Eisenhower also supporting the measure it had now become bipartisan, and this was the way Rayburn wanted it to be.

Mr. Sam warned against amendments which could kill the effect of the bill by reducing the time limit to one year, or a complete defeat of the measure. He argued that the renewal of the program would benefit many more people and businesses than it would hurt, and that it was a sure way to establish friendly ties with foreign governments whose confidence the United States needed in the world-wide struggle with Communism. If America is to maintain its position, he said: "We must sit down with the other countries of the earth and determine which tariff they can pay to get into this country and how much they are going to charge us. We cannot be in this world and not of it. And if we do not extend this Reciprocal Trade Act and keep up the kind of trade we have now, we will just be out of the world as far as trade and commerce are concerned."

This was his prelude to victory, for this was the message he sent back to the people in areas where congressmen were none too friendly toward renewal. The people got the word back in time to give him the kind of help he needed in the House. But a great deal of compromising had to be done before the Reciprocal Trade Act of 1958 became a reality. At the time the bill passed Mr. Sam sensed an alarming rise of protectionist sentiment which could pose trouble for any future administrative aspirations to reduce tariffs.

In expressing his personal satisfaction over the success of this bill in the House, he mentioned also his pleasure over the passage of the special defense construction bill, debt ceiling increase, price support freeze on agriculture (which the President vetoed on March 31), second supplemental appropriation, supplemental defense appropriation, supplemental Labor Department appropriation, Treasury and Post Office appropriations. In discussing when forthcoming legislation would be debated he always revealed an understanding and an uncanny sense of timing. In a press conference he pointed out that the postal pay increase was in conference and would not come up before Easter. The rivers and harbors authorization and the highway construction bill were likewise in conference, but he stated that the former would be called up on April 1, while the latter was not ready. He affirmed that the big agricultural and appropriation act would pass on April 1 or 2, and in this manner he proceeded to outline the calendar for each day before the Easter recess. This is the kind of precision for which the Speaker was famous. He permitted the House to start slowly but shortly before Easter he began to crack the whip.

In the spring of 1958, with the country on the verge of a depression, he pushed such legislation as the housing bill that would start 200,000 homes and put 500,000 people to work. Some things he believed could not wait: "If we hadn't taken the action that we have taken, I mean this Democratic Congress, and hadn't done it hurriedly I think we could have had a deep depression."

His concern was further revealed when he said:

> "It doesn't make any difference to me what Party gets the credit for it. I want to get out of this thing and to get out as quickly as possible, because when people are unemployed, when they do not have the money to buy the things that are necessary for their livelihoods, they get in a bad humor, and I don't want to see our people in a bad humor."

In response to questions about Eisenhower's foreign aid program, Rayburn was direct. Convinced that the Marshall Plan had saved Western Europe from Communism, he wanted Congress to give the President as much of his $3,900,000,000 as possible. "We have not made as many friends as we should have made, for the simple reason that the aid had not been properly handled. . . . The Russians are beating us on propaganda." Hence he maintained on March 31:

> "I think we have ultimately got to have another Summit Conference because the world must know that we are against war. I have always thought that the ex-

plosion of nuclear bombs must stop. I remember very well Governor Stevenson's saying that he would like to stop it, but he was misunderstood. I don't think he wanted it done unilaterally. . . . But I am not a scientist and I am not an engineer. . . . We might develop something that would be for peaceful uses."

While the Speaker was engaged in legislative controversy there was another type which set off national interest. Eric Sevareid brought the issue into focus as he concluded a thirty-minute interview of the Speaker on March 31, 1958, by asking a question concerning the much discussed remodeling of the east front of the Capitol Building. Both men remembered quite vividly that late in 1957 opposition had developed to the face-lifting plan. The American Institute of Architects, Daughters of the American Revolution, and other groups interested in historic preservation, succeeded in stirring up quite a bit of support on Capitol Hill against changing the much photographed east front porch on which every President since Andrew Jackson had been administered the oath of office. The Senate in August, 1958, however, voted forty-seven to thirty-two for extension at a cost in excess of $21,000,000.

"What is your real reason for wanting to do this?" Sevareid asked.

"Yes, they want to put it 'defacing the Capitol,' " Rayburn snapped. "They want to call it vandalism and so forth." Then he told how the "vandals" took down the hitching post to which Thomas Jefferson tied his horse to make room for expansion of the east, the north, and the south fronts. He told about the rail fence built around a part of the Capitol to please Lincoln and how that got torn down by the "vandals."

"Now I think that the east front should be extended. I think I know from talking to the best engineers I know and the best experts that the east front of the Capitol is beginning to be a hazard."

Then he referred to the chunks of stone that had fallen out and had been replaced with concrete. "Now if thirty-five coats of paint doesn't deface that sandstone that the east front of the Capitol is made out of, I don't see how you could deface it."

Continuing, he said:

". . . for two reasons I think it is time for it to come down. Those beautiful pieces of cornice up there are falling off. They can't be replaced, and a lot of the impression goes out that this would be so far out that it would hide the Senate and House ends. Well, this east front of the Capitol can be extended thirty-two-and-a-half feet and yet be forty feet inside of the distance out east of the east front of the Senate and of the House of Representatives."

He explained that the space would give fifty-four much needed rooms. The Capitol was a place to work as well as a memorial, and his type of "defacement" he believed would satisfy both the practical and beauty angle. The policy would be quite in line with past expansions or "defacements," needed to keep the building abreast of the times and needs.

Mr. Sevareid then made some predictions as he concluded the subject: "Well, my brief reading of history teaches me that Sam Rayburn of Texas usually gets what he wants on this Capitol Hill. I suspect, Mr. Speaker, the east front will be changed."[4]

Rayburn's will did prevail but not until thousands of words had been written editorializing what the critics considered to be "Rayburn's madness." "Vandalism," "barbarous mutilation," "destruction of our heritage," "elimination of the Capitol plaza," "messing up the Nation's superb and unique Capitol," "vandalism and extravagance," an intent "to hack up and deface the historic United States Capitol"—this was some of the most connotative language reported in the Washington *Evening Star* as used in the campaign against carrying out the ninety-four-year-old proposal. The *Star,* however, praised Mr. Sam for his courage and willingness to make a decision when he was being castigated from so many sides by people who did not have access to the facts. However, others showed courage too, for Rayburn was not alone; four of the five members of the committee concurred—Martin, Nixon, Knowland, and George Stewart, the architect of the Capitol.

His most provocative and carefully phrased defense of his decision was an address before the National Press Club on May 27. Here he said, "It boils down to this: The stones we can't save. The design we can. And we can save it better and more safely on a new wall thirty-two-and-one-half feet to the east."

Throughout this whole controversy Rayburn revealed a strong feeling of responsibility. The Capitol Building had become almost as much a part of him as the old homestead back in Bonham. For years he had resisted changes like this but realized he was wrong. It was also his job as Speaker to guard and preserve it. During the war, for example, he had expressed occasional concern about the protection of the property from enemy attack. During the Seventy-eighth Congress (1943) he declared emphatically: "We have on this hill $180,000,000 worth of property. We have a few metropolitan police around here and we have some boys, who are on patronage, wearing police uniforms." He argued for the keeping of soldiers close by because somebody could go into the Capitol and destroy a million dollars worth of property before the very eyes of untrained personnel. He had the country's interest at heart in every decision concerning Capitol Hill.

With no warning to the home folks Mr. Sam showed up for the weekend of July 18. The reason was the Flag Springs homecoming. Two hundred alumni of the now famous little school were enjoying conversation about old times when in walked the most distinguished ex-student.

"There are some who think I should have been in Washington the past three or four days, but I told them I had a very important date to keep at Flag Springs today and I would be back Monday," he told the people. "I love this ground; it is my native heath." After bidding them an affectionate farewell, he left at 2:30 P.M. for Dallas to catch a plane to Washington.

Rayburn had predicted in an interview with Eric Sevareid that this session of the Eighty-fifth Congress would be a record-breaking one from the standpoint of achievements. Roscoe Drummond described the activity and accomplishments of a session of Congress in terms of a six-day bicycle race, because it never looks good until the last few laps, and then the entries finish fast. By the end of July, Rayburn observed that there were only eight or ten major bills left to consider, and several important measures that had been in the air for several sessions had already been approved. The press had commented on the congenial and bipartisan spirit which prevailed, with both Rayburn and Johnson cited as the instruments largely responsible for the harmony. The "Texas Twins" had played brilliant roles in getting some of the more controversial measures through. Johnson with almost an evenly divided Senate had performed several near miracles with a show of sheer finesse, but Rayburn with a wider division in the House, sometimes dominated by a coalition of Southern Democrats and Republicans, had to rely on his popularity and personal resources. Bills pertaining to international affairs, government reorganization, national economy, agriculture, labor welfare—these were the areas where big accomplishments had already been made. Mr. Sam saw all of this as good news for the Democrats in the fall elections.

On the eve of the September 9 State Convention in San Antonio, Governor Price Daniel, Senator Ralph Yarborough, and Mrs. Randolph, National Democratic Committeewoman, commended the Speaker's plea for harmony. The conservatives were headed by Daniel and the liberals (Democrats of Texas) by Mrs. Randolph. Rayburn's plea for good spirit added this:

"I will vote to seat every delegation that is legally elected. I shall advocate allowing each senatorial district to name its two representatives on the State Democratic Executive Committee if they will pledge themselves to support the Democratic nominees of the Party—state and national. It would seem to me that any Democrat could and should agree to this program."

The Democrats scored sweeping victories throughout most of the nation in the general election of November 4, again winning control of both the Senate and House. They held the largest margins since the landslide of 1936 under Roosevelt. The score in the Senate stood 62 to 34 and in the House 282 to 153. On November 5, Mr. Sam had this to say about the results, "We're going to call the turn in the next Congress. But there will be no vindictiveness."

Rayburn's announcement about "calling the turn" was hardly necessary because the Democrats had been doing this for three Congresses already. The reference to vindictiveness was intended to mean that the Democrats would not appear proud and arrogant. They would continue to support the Administration's measures if the country's welfare was seriously involved. His press conference was merely a "business as usual" sort of pronouncement. Also superfluous was the belief that Speaker of the House Sam Rayburn and Senate Majority Leader Lyndon Johnson would guide the Eighty-sixth Congress, for their power was indisputable.

The level of Rayburn's bipartisanship thinking was best illustrated in the non-political tribute paid him on December 29 at Sherman, Texas, when forty Senators who once served under him in the House gathered to show their appreciation to this patriarch. A planeload of Senators, commonly referred to as "his boys," came from Washington and assembled at the Grayson Hotel for a luncheon. Senator Monroney of Oklahoma gave the principal address and E. B. Chapman of Sherman presented the Speaker with a plaque. Several Republicans, like Senator Everett M. Dirksen, Minority Leader, who had holiday commitments, sent telegrams expressing their respect to the man who had served forty-six consecutive years. He had made so many friends during this span of time that the gentlemen on the other side of the aisle would have claimed him on this day, but Mr. Sam thought it was a little late for him to be changing. He was rather well satisfied with being a Democrat.

For the first time in the long history of the Washington Birthday festivities in Sam Rayburn's honor, the atmosphere was not quite right. Some real tears were shed, not from joy but profound sorrow. The Republican Party had, only a few hours earlier, held a caucus in the House chamber to depose Joe Martin, their long-time leader, in favor of Charles Halleck of Indiana. While Mr. Sam tactfully concealed the emotion that was deep within and publicly refrained from taking a stand on the subject, one can surmise how he felt about an older man being deposed after faithful service. However, Joe Martin knew Sam Rayburn's sentiments.

During the noise and fun of the party, which was being held at the Women's National Democratic Club by the Dale Millers, a solitary figure, limping slightly, strolled into the room. While the guests waited to be greeted, Mr. Sam walked over to Joe and put his arm around him. "Do you have a cubby-hole for me anywhere?" Joe Martin asked Mr. Sam.

Mr. Sam replied, "Joe, you can have anything you want." And with this the tears streamed down the face of the dejected-looking Congressman from Massachusetts.

After Rayburn returned to his guests, he remarked, "I hate to see Joe Martin go. I'm sorry to see a great career end in that manner; however, I'm a warm friend of Charlie Halleck."

What was in Rayburn's mind about this incident one can only surmise. It did violate his sense of justice. Dismissing all the intrigue and pettiness, he recognized that his friend Joe Martin had been made the whipping boy for a Party that had become impotent from repeated defeats at the polls. The end of Joe Martin really began on November 3, 1958, when for the third consecutive time his Party lost control of the legislative branch. Eisenhower, however, had won two landslide victories, not because of his Party affiliation, but because of the glamor of his name and the magic in a wand he held in his hand when he returned from the "Great Crusade." He looked clean and free of the political stench that some thought they were beginning to detect in some areas of Washington. Many voters wanted an exterminator rather than an administrator, Rayburn thought. Republican leaders knew that with Democratic control of Congress only a miracle could save them from total defeat again in 1960 since their philosophy had never crystallized. Their Party was so charged with decadence, said Rayburn, that the new look of "modern Republicans" reminded him of "modern antiques."

Sam understood that his friend Joe Martin had become the victim of an Administration that was accustomed in desperation to recalling its generals when the battle did not go according to plan. In Mr. Sam's judgment, though he only inferred it, this was the fallacy of putting a man in the White House who knew only military strategy and little about political maneuvering. Generals command, but statesmen seek the will of the enlightened majority. People in Congress he firmly felt should not be considered expendable, and respect for the principle of seniority was both practical and ethical.

Although the President supposedly maintained a strict neutrality during all the subterfuge, his underlings, like Sherman Adams, were reputed to be quite busy. Martin had regarded some of these men as only lackeys, and they were naturally consumed with wrath when the Republican leadership on the Hill did not recognize them. So in the language of Shakespeare, these Oswalds, upon the command of their Goneril, with hungry swords searched the countryside for an old and faithful Gloucester, having blinded him as punishment for a fidelity to an ancient cause. Figuratively speaking, first they pulled out his eyes and then turned his face toward the cliffs of Dover.

Mr. Sam also realized that Joe's friendship for him had been damaging. Joe frankly admitted that his Republican friends had advocated hostility instead of friendly behavior on many occasions. The Republicans, Mr. Sam said so many times, are haters. They had lost the art of love because their very philosophy removed them from the people. They were the sons' of Mammon and not of Jesse. Rayburn said he and Joe were cooperative, but he also commended Charlie Halleck's friendly approach. "We have to work together in the House if we are going to get anything accomplished. So we have an agreement as to how we are going to do it." Sam and Joe had made an agreement. He and Charlie reached a similar one.

Joe and Charlie watched Sam perform the usual ritual of the birthday cake, a four-tiered white frosted confection with "Happy Birthday," and perhaps only these three sensed the mixed emotions and the significance of "life's little ironies."

Afterward Rayburn had his dinner at the Mayflower with the Ed Connallys of Abilene, Texas. The menu included a somewhat standard course for Mr. Sam's January 6—turkey, turnip greens, and coconut cake.

Before he picked up the gavel the following day to open the Eighty-sixth Congress and begin his eighth term as Speaker, he had suppressed a little revolution within the Democratic ranks that had been fomenting for several sessions. The liberals were plotting to overthrow the conservatives. Rayburn and Johnson were moderates, sitting between the conservative and liberal blocs. The Speaker had no sooner reached his apartment, upon his return to Washington, than he received a telephone call about two imminent battles. He forestalled the first revolt with only one telephone call. There was a movement under way to amend the rules of the House Rules Committee because of the personnel of the Committee, who in the past had held up legislation indefinitely and not permitted some measures to reach the floor for debate.

Rayburn called Chet Holifield (D., Calif.), spokesman for the liberals, and assured him that he would use his influence to see that essential legislation was not permitted to get bottled up. Though Mr. Sam's efforts did not settle anything, he did save "a big fuss." Acceptance of his approach to the problem, however, did show the House's confidence in him. James Reston for the New York *Times* reports the following conversation:

"What shall I tell the others who want these rules changed?"

"Tell 'em everything I've told you," Mr. Sam replied.

"I'll see them if you insist, but I'll just repeat what I've told you; and if we have a meeting the reporters will be ready to blow that Little Rock thing wide open."[5]

This was Mr. Sam's second problem, for the liberals were trying to prevent the seating of Dr. Dale Alford, the segregationist, who had defeated Brooks Hays in the stormy Arkansas primary. Mr. Sam advised Alford not to show up at the Party caucus before the opening of Congress on January 7. He also advised Alford to allow all the other new members to be sworn in and that he be seated only provisionally, waiting the outcome of the investigation of the election in Little Rock. Dr. Alford accepted Rayburn's method of handling the problem and the Eighty-sixth Congress began on a friendly note.

Mr. Sam's success in putting down these two liberal revolts temporarily required no underhanded tactics. He merely collected dividends on a forty-six-year investment of building confidence. He had sowed the seeds of goodwill and was repaid in kind.

At the other end of the Capitol, Senator Johnson had a more complicated picture in dealing with the liberal agitation to change the rules so that a simple majority of the total membership could bring an issue to a vote. Senator William Proxmire (D., Wis.) was urging Party control over Johnson to curtail his power. James Reston observed that Senator Johnson was leading a large Democratic majority (sixty-four–thirty-four) in a Senate studded with potential Democratic Presidential nominees. These performers quite naturally had their eyes on the gallery. Already in January, 1959, several names had been discussed for the 1960 spectacular. Rayburn himself had mentioned Johnson; former Secretary of State Dean Acheson and Truman had proposed either Johnson or Stuart Symington (Mo.); and John F. Kennedy, since 1956, had been working at promoting his own candidacy. Speaker Rayburn was realistic in recognizing that a Majority Leader who handled his job effectively could hardly have the time to promote his own interests, and with the factionalism in the Senate, could hardly escape controversy if he gave a strong leadership. From the very outset, then, he did not conceive of the Senator's active promotion of a campaign for the nomination.

Because of his interest in Johnson, Rayburn followed closely the peregrinations in the Senate, particularly since they were related to the overall Congressional picture. The Majority Leader likewise kept his attention on Mr. Sam's problems. He could foresee that Rayburn's controversial promise to Representative Holifield that the Rules Committee would permit essential legislation to clear was one that set the stage for a showdown. For if the Speaker was denied in this Congress, he would have to find a stronger method than friendly persuasion in the next Congress. The Majority Leader was inclined to be a little more hard-boiled than his benign mentor and perhaps a little more direct in facing the inevitable. He might have advised his friend to fight today and argue about it tomorrow, but Mr. Sam's pattern on the Rules issue was to have the argument first.

Illustrative of the problem was the disposition of the multibillion dollar housing bill sponsored by Albert Raines of Alabama. The twelve member Rules Committee was divided six–six, and Mr. Sam started looking for another vote to break the deadlock. The six opponents, who had resisted such legislation in the previous Congress and were rather strongly committed to their present stand, were Chairman Howard Smith (D., Va.), William Colmer (D., Miss.), Leo Allen (R., Ill.), Clarence Brown (R., Ohio), Carroll Reece (R., Tenn.), Hamer Budge (R., Idaho). The opposition in the previous session had refused to act on the Senate-approved version of a housing bill and had forced the sponsors to attempt a bypass of the Rules Committee. The necessary two-thirds majority, however, was missed by six votes.

Again this year Mr. Sam was faced with the same set of circumstances. When Howard Smith was questioned by the press concerning Rayburn's commitment to the liberal faction, he replied: "I'm not bound by it; I didn't make an agreement with these men or give assurance to anyone." When questioned further concerning the awkward position in which such an attitude placed the Speaker, who was Smith's friend and the Party leader, Smith merely reiterated, "I made no commitments and gave no assurances." The reporter continued to probe, but each time received an identical reply. Thus the stage was set for a showdown with Smith. This was the set of circumstances which the Speaker faced as he turned his thoughts to the business of the session in 1959.

In a speech on February 12 before the National Rural Electric Cooperative Association, Rayburn sounded the word that he favored keeping the rate of interest at two per cent, in opposition to Administration proposals for an increase. Even if a subsidy was necessary to maintain this rate, Rayburn said, he would favor it:

> "Why not a little for the millions who until a few years ago were the underprivileged? We have subsidized shipping, we have subsidized railroads, we have subsidized business, and if a two per cent interest on the money that you borrow is a subsidy then I am for subsidy for that. . . . Every time in the history of the U.S. from the time of Jefferson to now, when some man who came along with great vision and boundless courage had started out to do something with force, they have called him a demagogue, or they have said he was running the country into socialism."

At almost the same moment Rayburn was delivering his address before the convention, Secretary of Agriculture Ezra Taft Benson, in a news conference, was arguing the other side of the question against socialization.

On February 25, Speaker Rayburn turned over two spadesful of historic dirt to initiate the work on the controversial face lifting of the Capitol's east front. The new façade, he stated, would "be the pride and joy of everybody." He announced that the new marble portico would be ready for the next Presidential inauguration in 1961. Three days later in the Sheraton Park Hotel he told Party leaders, at a $100-a-plate dinner, that it would be a Democrat in 1961 who would have the honor of standing in front of this new east wing.

When it came to face lifting on Capitol Hill, Mr. Sam was not one to be satisfied with performing plastic surgery on just one side or portion. George Dixon of the Washington *Post* tells a very interesting story of a fateful visit the elderly gentleman made one evening to the Capitol Hill Club which put other ideas in his head. Joe Martin invited Sam to go with him to the Republican "holy of holies," to see his own life-size portrait which had been hung a few months earlier. Mr. Sam hesitated to go into this type of club but his friend told him he could sneak in with a mask on. Finally, one dark night, says Dixon, Mr. Sam and Joe sneaked in. "In the deep leather seats reposed some of the highest-paid lobbyists in the world, plying costly potables on visiting employers who were so awed they forgot they'd eventually have to pay for the drinks."

Not a drinking man, Joe spent the time merely explaining to Rayburn how the Capitol Hill Club made the "flintiest tycoons generous toward lobbyists." Reports Dixon: "He suggested it might possibly be that the captains of industry met the fairest flower of Republican legislative leadership in the place and decided it was well worth the money."

He also told Mr. Sam that this club "represented the dream of Representative James C. Auchincloss of New Jersey, among whose family—but not political—connections is Mrs. Senator John F. Kennedy." Joe pointed out that Jackie's GOP kin had the idea of expanding this establishment into luxury hotel proportions. Mr. Sam was very quiet, but Joe finally got him to admit that it was a fine place.

Rayburn had little patience with congressmen of either Party who spent time in clubs when they were supposed to be on duty. He had been informed as to the whereabouts of certain Republicans when the House was in session. So he decided to remove temptation. Moving quickly, he pushed through his Democratic controlled House a vote to acquire two square blocks of Capitol Hill land. The Republican Attorney-General was promptly asked to secure a title to the land. Mr. Sam then let everyone know that the buildings on this property would have to come down.[6] He was preparing for expansion and improvements, as the future would unfold.

March 5 began for Mr. Sam as most of the days had since 1913. He entered his office at 9:45 A.M. There were several congressmen waiting for a chance to discuss certain items with him. A few minutes before noon the day became unlike any other because the reporters interrupted the usual conference with the announcement that this was his 16,801 day as a congressman. The moment he stepped into the House he had broken the forty-six year record of old Joe Cannon. To the historian this was significant but to the Speaker it was not unusual, because at the end of the day he stood without emotion as he had so many times before waiting to catch the elevator. His day's work was done.

In the historic old Supreme Court quarters on March 12, forty-five Senators and a Vice-President assembled around a congressman with whom they had served in the House before their moving to the other end of the Capitol. The signatures of all these men were engraved on a silver tray presented to the Speaker. During the ceremony Mr. Sam issued his proclamation on Party loyalty. "The Democratic Party is a many splendored thing," he said, in beginning his analogy which showed one similarity between a Party platform and a church doctrine. Both were sufficiently broad, in his judgment, to include many people of different tastes and interests.

"One doesn't, as a usual thing, quit a particular denominational church because he doesn't like the pastor or feel that some other members are not pious enough to please him. He stays in the church until a new pastor, more to his liking, is named. And the same goes with the fellow members. Unless he dislikes the church itself, it is a wise member who realizes that the church is bigger than its pastor or any given segment of its membership."

When Mr. Sam left Washington for the Easter recess there was one big piece of unfinished business, his pledge to Holifield, which was destined to haunt him for some time to come. The Chairman of the Rules Committee was showing the Speaker a new type of filibuster. Smith had staged a successful delay of action on the Housing bill that 150 liberal Democrats had been assured would receive attention. They felt rather confident, though, that Rayburn would find a way to get this bill out of the

Rules Committee or use the available, but cumbersome, procedures to circumvent the roadblock. The delay on this and other controversial measures left no doubt in the minds of some that eventually these two old Southerners would have to settle their differences, because the House, according to their predictions, was not big enough to contain two men who were growing apart so fast in their political philosophies. After the first six–six tie vote, Smith gave Rayburn little chance to use his friendly persuasion.

While Rayburn was at home during the Easter recess he observed that new construction around Bonham was at a standstill. Carpenters and bricklayers were unemployed. Some were at Texoma fishing, while others were sitting on the south side of the courthouse lawn in the shade swapping knives or whittling their time away. Lyndon Johnson, shortly before Mr. Sam's first-hand indoctrination, had revealed the bitter facts—that there were 260,000 people unemployed who could go back to work if Smith would quit holding up the housing bill. Rayburn knew that without Congressional action the Federal Housing Administration would soon run out of authority to insure mortgages; hence new home construction would be terminated.

Mr. Sam, after seeing the effects of delay and visioning its effect upon the economy, charged back to Washington from his brief rest with a communication to the Rules Committee informing them of what they were doing to the nation's business. He told them that the people knew who the six obstructionists were. When he announced that he would bypass the Committee and that he had the strength to do so, two of the six members, seeing that Sam Rayburn meant business, announced that they would switch their votes to report the bill through the Committee. Since there was a provision in the bill for continuing the public housing program itself and slum clearance these members decided that in the interest of the general welfare they would reconsider. While Mr. Sam was pleased with the immediate turn of events, he could see that he was only temporizing, for this ordeal would have to be relived with every future controversial measure.

Mr. Sam moved a step closer to success on July 4 on another of his pet projects—the construction of the new east front of the Capitol. The Thirty-fourth President of the United States lifted a spade of dirt with the same silver trowel that the first Chief Executive had used in the laying of the original cornerstone for the Capitol on September 18, 1793, a stone which is now missing. President Eisenhower symbolically laid the large pink cornerstone, which resembles the granite of the Texas State Capitol. It is a three-foot cube, with a hollowed-out cavity twenty by twenty by twelve inches in which a copper box is secured for preserving the documents of the ceremony. The overall weight is 4200 pounds. As was the custom of the early days, a new cornerstone was placed below ground level.

Out of respect to Rayburn, chairman of the committee which guided the program through the gauntlet of criticism, Texas granite was selected. When the President looked at the stone he expressed surprise that it was found in Texas. Rayburn promptly reminded him that many public buildings down there were made of this native granite; in fact, he added, "The courthouse in Denison, the place of your birth, is a good example."

The Speaker's concluding remarks at the ceremony, because of deep affections and proprietary feelings toward the Capitol, bear a special significance: "We trust that this whole building will stand throughout the ages and that irresponsible and mad men who are willing to destroy everything will never set foot on this soil. We love this ground. We love this Hill."

When Sam Rayburn returned to the privacy of his office after this ceremony he undoubtedly observed that the Speaker of the House of Representatives in July, 1959, was sitting on a very difficult job. The business of the east front was virtually completed, but there was certain to be further discussion of all the issues involved. He still had the liberal-conservative fight within the Rules Committee which was laden with possibilities of splitting the Democratic Party. There were also two new items—the pending labor legislation and the thinking of National Chairman Paul Butler—which undoubtedly added further wrinkles in the already serious brow of Mr. Speaker. Only one cut along Rayburn's lines could have contemplated the future months without getting ulcers or developing a coronary.

During the summer, Congress was certain to pass some sort of legislation to control labor racketeering. There had been at least three types of bills proposed, reflecting the degrees of irritation with organized labor. They were designed to establish specialists who would function under the Secretary of Labor's Washington headquarters, to deal with the so-called "labor rackets." The extent of the power was something which particularly concerned the top men in the labor movement and quite naturally its lobby had been busy around Washington.

According to Victor Riesel, Walter Reuther and George M.

Harrison of the railroad clerks' union, had called on Mr. Sam on June 9 at 11:00 A.M. They wanted to find out what Congress had in mind. The conference lasted forty minutes. At the outset the two leaders expressed the hope that the House would pass a softer bill than the one approved by the Senate. Mr. Sam in his usual direct manner asked them what kind of bill they had in mind. To be sure, the gentlemen expressed their views, but Rayburn found their suggestions entirely too theoretical. Mr. Sam asked the question "How can you ask me to promise anything in this off-the-record talk when labor itself is unable to offer anything specific?"

Later Rayburn went on to explain that he recognized as many as ten factions within the general labor movement and each wanted something different. He said that there were extremists like John L. Lewis, who did not want any legislation, and the rest of the people could not agree.

Rayburn refused to make any promises to Reuther and Harrison, but left the impression in this June 9 meeting that he thought a middle-of-the-road bill would be about the best thing to discipline the extremists and not hurt the people who behaved themselves.[7]

When Rayburn addressed the nation on August 10, he proposed a "middle-of-the-road" bill, pointing out that there were three bills before the House. The one backed by AFL-CIO, Rayburn considered inadequate; the Republican-backed bill (Griffin-Landrum) was too severe. The best proposal, he thought, was "the committee bill" introduced by Carl Elliott of Alabama. Rayburn explained that the Republican bill and this one contained the same basic weapons against racketeering. The real issue was not that of outlawing racketeering, but clarifying the function of the Federal Government in the whole process. Rayburn did not want to see the Government champion management against labor, because it would upset the balance. A bill must be strong enough and fair to both groups. In defense of the "middle-of-the-road" bill, he pointed out that it "is being shot at from all sides. Jimmy Hoffa violently opposed it; the AFL-CIO is lobbying actively against it, along with the United States Chamber of Commerce; the National Association of Manufacturers will be satisfied with no bill that does not punish unions." When both Hoffa and the labor-haters were against a bill, Mr. Sam declared that this was a good recommendation for it. As evidence of its strength he mentioned several of the provisions: 1) a $10,000 fine and a twenty-year prison sentence for shakedown picketing;

2) a $10,000 fine and five-year prison term for embezzlement of union funds; 3) full financial reports to be made to the secretary of labor, with a $10,000 fine and a year in prison for misrepresentations; 4) election of union officers periodically by secret ballot; 5) "hot cargo" contracts outlawed; 6) organizational picketing regulated.

He recalled the days when Wall Street and the utility people needed to be restrained, and pointed out that the "middle-of-the-road" approach had worked at that time. Now, he said, the other side is getting out of hand. "To cut out the cancer of corruption, we used a surgeon's scalpel instead of a butcher's cleaver." In any age, he affirmed, we must reform without ruining.

His critics were quick to recall that in 1958 he considered labor reform "non-imperative" and had held up the Senate-passed Kennedy-Ives bill for forty days before sending it to the Labor Committee for consideration. They also accused him of finally arranging a parliamentary maneuver which would kill the measure in such a way that some of the blame would go to the Republicans for voting against the only bill they were permitted to discuss. They also called attention to his fight against Taft-Hartley, as an argument that he had only recently become interested in maintaining the balance between labor and management. All of these points annoyed the Speaker no end.

Rayburn's discovery that he was at odds with public sentiment in his own State made him see quite clearly the difficulty of being both congressman and Speaker.

The Texas home front was somewhat disturbed over the findings of the McClellan Committee and the general arrogance of Jimmy Hoffa at the hearings. Lyndon Johnson cautioned Mr. Sam that for Texans to vote for anything less than the toughest possible labor bill under the circumstances would mean their political death back home. Following his advice and their own inclinations, the Texas delegation abandoned Mr. Sam to vote seventeen to four for the Landrum-Griffin bill, which was passed in August. Mr. Sam said they became frightened and began to run. Also of concern to him was the realization that the Southern vote was the deciding factor in the passage of the most severe of the three bills. The failure of his moderate bill to clear the committee for House consideration also bothered him.

Another very difficult rebuff for Rayburn to accept was the behavior of Democratic Executive Committee Chairman Paul Butler, who was pulling against the Democratic leadership in

Congress. While he searched for a solution that would achieve Party harmony, he was reminded of the Saturday afternoon in 1956, following the adjournment of the Convention in Chicago, when according to Jim Mathis, he prevailed on Adali Stevenson to keep Butler. Stevenson had already stated that he would accept Butler's resignation, begrudgingly given. Stevenson wanted Jim Finnegan, who had done such a commendable job for the Party in the State of Pennsylvania. Upon hearing about the anticipated change, Rayburn, fearing that "it was pretty late in the day for such action," went directly to Stevenson's room in the hotel and frankly put it to the nominee: "We have enough differences in the Party now without reopening old wounds." Stevenson yielded but believed he had reason to regret it, after the strife between the National Committee and the campaign staff headed by Finnegan.

Butler had moved into the top echelon of the Party following the 1954 fall Congressional elections, when the Democrats won 232 seats to the Republican's 203. Chairman Stephen Mitchell called a meeting of the National Committee in New Orleans for the month of December, at which time he resigned. Rayburn's efforts to postpone action until 1955 on his replacement were resisted by Stevenson, who succeeded in placing Butler in the top position because of his liberal leanings. Then Butler moved adroitly to pull the liberal groups together, but in so doing led the Party organization farther from Southern conservatism and left Mr. Sam sitting on "high-center."

Rayburn's lukewarm attitude toward the seventeen-member advisory committee was one of the sources of Butler's irritation, because he believed the big Congressional majorities were a mandate from the people for more liberal legislation. Hence he was repelled by the Rayburn and Johnson moderate views.

Down in Texas, National Committeewoman Randolph of Houston had built up quite a following among the liberals, and she was friendly to Butler. She had predicted a showdown in 1960 with the middle-of-the-road conservatives and Lyndon Johnson, whose legislative performance since 1953 had not been pleasing to her groups. While she had enjoyed cordial relations with the Speaker, it would appear that she was beginning to become somewhat irked by his "get-along, go-along" policy, his compromising techniques, and his influence over the Senate. Some of the liberals believed Mr. Sam really preferred to have a Republican in the White House, so that he could enhance his own position by taking credit for victories and by casting blame for failures upon the opposition. A few regarded him as a benevolent dictator who was becoming drunk with power. Others were bothered by his support of Johnson. Later there was also a personal consideration which arose over the choice of the National Committeewoman. And when Butler was invited out to dinner by people with these beliefs, Mr. Sam began to wonder what the National Chairman had in the back part of his mind.

Butler's belief that the Democratic Party would be strong enough to win without the South was also unacceptable to Rayburn and Johnson because they were unwilling to abandon old friends and face the type of platform which would be written by a Butler-inspired committee. On July 5, Butler without calling any names, was critical of Democratic leadership for being soft on Eisenhower, and for deliberately compromising instead of risking a Presidential veto. Butler was receiving encouragement from such figures as James Roosevelt, William Proxmire, Hubert Humphrey, Paul Douglas, and "Soapy" Williams. Rayburn appeared to ignore these rebuffs in the interest of harmony.

However, he quietly asked Butler to come to see him and Johnson. What happened or what was said only the three knew. The meeting lasted for an hour, wrote Robert C. Albright, while newsmen and photographers were packed into the Speaker's outer office. "We had a very friendly meeting," Mr. Sam reported. "There was no loud talk . . . no violent disagreements . . . no fighting and scratching."

Johnson said, "It was a pleasant and constructive meeting; it ought to do a lot of good."

Afterward, the photographers and TV cameras were set to take pictures of the trio, and Butler remarked, "Let's try to look happy together." [8]

Though a facetious comment, it seemed to have some meaning. It implied a truce—that there was to be no further criticism by the National Chairman of this middle-of-the-road course followed by the Democratic Congressional leaders. The Chairman did not appear very happy with the outcome, and he left the meeting with a far-away look in his eyes—toward the selection in 1960 of a liberal who would deal with some of the country's most perplexing problems, Civil Rights being one of them.

Mr. Sam's failure to get a tax measure for highway construction out of the Ways and Means Committee, plus the President's veto of a billion-dollar public works program, helped make the month of August about as disagreeable as July. There was also the rebuke by his own Texas delegation on the Landrum-Griffin bill.

The columnist Drew Pearson called attention to another irritation near the end of August. The Speaker had been hearing a great deal about "secondary boycotts" in labor legislation, says Pearson; so he decided to stage a primary boycott of his own. The retiring Democratic delegate to Congress from Hawaii, John A. Burns, was snubbed by the President and not invited to the White House for the signing of the Statehood Proclamation.

"In that case, I won't go myself," flared up the Speaker. "No one has done more to achieve Statehood for Hawaii than Jack Burns and no one has a better right to be present at the Proclamation signing. Yet he wasn't invited to the White House because he's a Democrat. Well, if they're counting Jack Burns out, they can count me out also."

Burns upon hearing about Rayburn's attitude went promptly to see his old Democratic friend to talk him out of his stand. "I appreciate your friendly support, Mr. Speaker," he pleaded, "but forget about me. I can stand the snub. This thing is bigger than any one personality. In the interest of Hawaii and its people—and for my sake—I am asking you to go to the White House on this occasion."

Rayburn went reluctantly but tried his best to wipe the smile off the President's face when the Chief Executive offered Mr. Sam the pen. "I don't believe I want that," Rayburn replied coolly.

But the new Democratic Congressman-elect from Hawaii, Daniel Inouye, whispered: "Mr. Speaker, maybe Jack Burns would like that pen."

"Maybe he would at that," Rayburn agreed. "He's certainly entitled to it."

Rayburn then stalked back to the President and said, "I'll take that pen, after all. I'd like to give it to Jack Burns."

Afterward, Pearson said he gave Interior Secretary Fred Seaton, who was also present at the ceremony, a "Sam Rayburn bawling out" for the Burns snub:

"I don't know who is responsible and I'm not blaming you personally, but this was inexcusable and pretty small, if you ask me. The White House deliberately ignored the man who had the most right to be here today." [9]

When Sam Rayburn got out of sorts he generally cleared his chest of everything that had been bothering him. He invited the press in to let the Federal Reserve authorities have some of his thoughts also. The champions of the Federal Reserve had rushed in to battle the "sense of Congress" amendment to the bill raising the ceiling on the interest rate the Federal Government can pay. The right of Congress to give these or any other instructions to the Federal Reserve was, in Mr. Sam's judgment, beyond question. His rebuke was heard and heeded:

"I have been forced to the conclusion that the Federal Reserve authorities have reached a point in their thinking where they consider themselves immune to any direction or suggestion by the Congress, let alone a simple expression of the sense of Congress."

A spectator sitting in the gallery could almost ascertain the Speaker's disposition on a given day by the sound of his gavel. During these weeks it fell with a heavy thud. Talking about these moments when he was out of sorts, he said, "I broke the gavel once. A fella kept talking after his time ran out. Wouldn't sit down. Kinda wish I'd hit him over the head." He did not say whether it was a Democrat or Republican.

An explosion which caused many of his colleagues to break forth in laughter came without any ceremony, fanfare or forewarning. The House of Representatives had a full day's session which was devoted entirely to memorials. The outburst occurred when a member rose to memorialize Arthur Fiedler, for thirty years a conductor of the Boston Symphony Orchestra. By the time the congressmen had finished their comments, Mr. Sam's dome had acquired a pink tinge. Then he burst forth:

> "Such things are mighty wasteful of the taxpayer's money. It costs eighty-five dollars a page to print the *Congressional Record* in which these memorials are printed. The bill mounts up if we continue to congratulate everybody in the United States. It's time to stop issuing a memorial every time someone has done a grand deed or lived a good life."

As an indication of Eisenhower's position in his personal relationship with Sam Rayburn and his side of the story is the first paragraph of a letter from the White House dated November 3, 1959, in which the President frowns upon the Speaker's request that an eighty-year-old judge not be retired:

> It is indeed difficult for me to decline to go along with a personal suggestion of yours affecting an individual in government. Indeed, I cannot recall any case of doing so during the past seven years.

Perhaps a most basic irritation to Rayburn at this time was the realization that a Republican President was sitting in the White House being protected from public rebuke by Democratic benevolence in Congress. There was pressure on Mr. Sam to give "Ike the treatment," for the sake of political expediency. The liberal segment implied that the Speaker had been intimidated by the Presidential veto. In a very calm manner he explained about the enormous complexity of the legislation necessary to solve present-day problems, and he reminded the dissenters about the factionalism which existed in the House of Representatives. He added that he and Johnson had pledged their support of the President on issues where the national welfare was involved. However, there was the feeling in some Democratic quarters that the White House did not recognize or appreciate their charities and the Speaker should make him "toe the mark."

Congressman Jim Wright of Texas explained it this way:

"He [Eisenhower] doesn't seem to realize how very well he has been treated. Almost all of his major requests have been granted. He has been accorded greater kindness and more consideration by the Congress than any chief executive in history has been given by a Congress of the other party. Rayburn and Johnson have leaned over backwards to find areas of agreement, avoid criticism of the President merely for the sake of criticism, in short, to be constructive rather than partisan, to create solutions instead of issues. The President needs to yield a bit too and to guard more carefully his remarks about the Congress. . . . But the Chief Executive apparently does not realize that there are heavy pressures within the Democratic Party to stop giving him so much of what he asks and let him stew in his own juice."

Rayburn had been urged to let Congress fail to pass another housing bill and permit home building to stop and to let some of the other measures die. This would awaken the folks back home; then there would be retaliation. Mr. Sam, though, decided that he would swallow his pride, make a few concessions, and try to give the President something he would sign. After all Sam had been around Capitol Hill longer than Ike and he was not going to be provoked into deviation from a well-established code of professional behavior. However, he promised the Democrats to do some talking next year and put a man up for President who would approach administration differently. The name on Rayburn's tongue was Lyndon Baines Johnson.

"Has Lyndon agreed to this?" Harry McCormick asked him.

"We have agreed to it. Johnson has not been consulted."

"What effect will this announcement have on your role as presiding officer for many years over the Democratic National Convention?"

"I'll make an announcement regarding that on January 1," Rayburn replied.

Congress adjourned on August 30 and Mr. Sam went home to begin organizing Texas to make Senator Johnson the favorite son and nominee for President on the Democratic ticket in 1960. Getting an instructed delegation in the Lone Star State was not inconceivable, but would hardly be an achievement without some resistance from the liberal bloc. The States Righters were not completely extinct either, but the more persistent had rallied under the banner of "Freedom in Action" and called themselves the Constitution Party. They were not a strong bloc numerically, but not without influence. When Rayburn looked about and saw the various shades of political thinking he expressed the desire not to have a label attached to his name because of the ambiguity of terms. Some called him a liberal, others, a conservative, and still others, a moderate. He saw himself in 1959 as a plain Democrat.

Those who tried to clarify their affiliation with the Party liked to refer to themselves as "Sam Rayburn Democrats." This was a classification which carried respectability along with an all-embracing philosophy. They liked to use the term "Sam Rayburn Democrat" rather than "conservative Democrat" because it was a way of political thinking which all Americans understood and was intelligible to a great mass of the electorate. It was conceived by a Jeffersonian who could "hear the clamoring of the multitudes," as he defined his own sensitivity to the voices of humanity.

☆ XXII ☆

The Dawn of the New Frontier

BY COINCIDENCE Mr. Sam's seventy-eighth birthday fell once again on the opening day of Congress, the second session of the Eighty-sixth. As the usual anniversary rituals were performed, he was lauded for his attainments, and especially for his long years of service as Congressman and Speaker. In 1960 he outranked all members in the House, but he still trailed Senator Hayden of Arizona. Hayden went to Washington the year before Rayburn, when Arizona was admitted to the Union.

During the January 6 ceremonies someone remembered what General Douglas MacArthur had said on his own seventy-fifth birthday and thought it applied quite well to Rayburn:

> "Youth is not entirely a time of life—it is a state of mind. It is not wholly a matter of ripe cheeks, red lips or supple knees. It is a temper of the will, a quality of the imagination, a vigor of the emotions. Nobody grows old by merely living a number of years. People grow old only by deserting their ideals. You are as young as your faith, as old as your doubt; as young as your self-confidence, as old as your fear; as young as your hope, as old as your despair. In the central place of every heart, there is a recording chamber; so long

> as it receives messages of beauty, hope, cheer, and courage, so long are you young. When the wires are all down and your heart is covered with the snows of pessimism and the ice of cynicism, then and then only are you grown old."

Mr. Sam's friends agreed that there was no better yardstick than this for measuring the youth of the seventy-eight-year-old legend. Sam Rayburn, though, would never have viewed his station in life so poetically. Instead he would have used one of his own favorite expressions: "I feel like a two-year-old colt."

Men of both Parties joined in their commemorations. The President the week before wired early congratulations: "I am proud to have been born in your Congressional District." Charles Halleck in referring to him as a "magnificent Speaker" established the tone of the eulogies.

At his press conference, called to give his predictions for the new session, Rayburn lighted a cigarette, sank back in his red leather swivel chair and told the boys to "Shoot." He ruled out major tax cuts. Since it was election year he thought there would be a boost of the $1 an hour minimum wage to $1.10 or $1.25 and some liberalization of Social Security benefits. He invited the House, but did not urge it, to take some action on a pending Civil Rights bill, which would bolster voting rights in the South and provide new penalties for obstructing school desegregation orders. He referred to the possibility of using a discharge petition, which would need 219 signatures, to get the bill out of the Rules Committee, where it was tied up. The reporters then turned to some personal matters, touching lightly on Mr. Sam's bachelorhood as a possible reason for his long life and good health.

"Bachelorhood? No. Whether a man ought to get married or not is a private question. Anybody ought to get married if he wants to. There's argument on both sides. That question is about as silly as the one going around on practicing birth control. It is not a national issue, but an individual one."

One reporter inquired about his promise back in December to comment on his plans for Lyndon Johnson and his chances of becoming a candidate for President:

"Is he a candidate?" was the final question.

"Well, he's my candidate" was the reply.

When asked whether he had discussed the matter with Truman, he replied, "There never has been any such discussion." Knowing that reporters liked facts rather than fiction he tried to illustrate by telling a story about "old Ezra." Ezra had been poorly, so he went to the doctor. After the examination he was told he would have to stop drinking. On a return visit to his physician, when he was asked whether he had followed the advice, he stated, "No, sir, I like better what I sees, not what I hears." Some of the newsmen missed the point.

When Rayburn announced on January 11 that he would relinquish his post as Permanent Chairman of the Democratic National Convention, the reporters began to understand his intentions. "I have a great desire to see one convention from the floor," he said. He acknowledged that on the floor he would be in a position "to feel the sentiment" and work for the candidate of his choice. They then caught the full import of the "old Ezra" story.

There was one thing Mr. Sam expected and that was loyalty. When he first announced his ambitions for Lyndon Johnson, he somehow thought his friends, who were Democrats, would respond immediately. The junior Senator from Texas, Ralph Yarborough, was at first noncommittal. He refused several invitations to go along with Mr. Sam's plans, not so much for personal as for political reasons. The Speaker was puzzled because he had endorsed Yarborough for the Senate and Yarborough had profited from describing himself as a "Sam Rayburn Democrat." "All of this was worth 100,000 votes," Mr. Sam said privately.

Yarborough was undoubtedly restrained by the liberal faction in the Senate which had tried to curb some of the Majority Leader's power and by his more dedicated followers back home, like Mrs. Randolph, who was the Democratic National Committeewoman and head of the Democrats of Texas clubs. Yarborough's vote for Senator Albert Gore's resolution striking at Johnson's leadership aggravated the Speaker even further. "I couldn't be more disappointed in a man than I am in Mr. Yarborough for what he did." Although Johnson on January 13 was successful by a fifty-one to twelve vote in maintaining his "middle-of-the-road" control over the Policy Committee, Rayburn was still peeved. The Speaker was angry! He sulked! He fumed! And not until after the Los Angeles Convention did he appear to regain some of the former cordiality toward the Senator, although Yarborough had pledged all along that he would support the nominee of the Party.

While Rayburn was nursing his injured pride over Yarborough's defection on the Johnson issue, he was puzzling over the problems in the Rules Committee. The Rules could not be changed before the next session and there he sat trying to live up to his 1959 commitment to Chet Holifield's liberal forces. His position was further complicated by a coalition of Charles Halleck with the Dixiecrats, which had blocked several important bills. The Senate was also feeling the same type of coalition, with Senator Gene McCarthy of Minnesota playing a major role in the strategy. When questioned by the press about the intra-Party squabble, Rayburn tried to put up a good front by quipping, "We're Democrats, you know, and nobody can boss us. And we can fight like hell." However, he was less casual in his communication to the Rules Committee on the Civil Rights bills, holding out the discharge petition as a threat, although he frankly said he had never signed one of these himself. He observed that once successful with this approach, the roadblock could be broken and other important bills could get a hearing.

Rumors were flying fast around Washington and back in the Fourth District during the month of January, that Mr. Sam had planned to lay his gavel down and come home for good. Ambitious young men and older politicians who for years had tried to keep their fences mended began clearing their throats and shaking hands more freely. The Speaker, however, was not responsible for building up any of these false hopes. For on the morning of January 28, Deets Dorough, Chairman of the Fannin County Democratic Executive Committee, walked across the street from his real estate and loan office to the Post Office to get his mail. With his pocket knife he cut into the familiar letter first, and seeing the check for the filing fee, announced to the other men in the lobby the news, "Boys, he's done it again." Then he walked up the street three doors to the *Daily Favorite* office to hand the communication to the press.

The basis for the assumptions about Rayburn's retirement was contained in the fact that his eyes were giving him trouble. He had long since lost his twenty-twenty vision for the printed page, but he still retained better than ten-twenty insight into human nature. John M. Virden, editor of the *American Weekend* magazine, vouched for Mr. Sam's ability to see through people. He had been commissioned to write an article on Carl Albert, Congressman of Oklahoma and, at the time, the Democratic "whip" in the House of Representatives. An interview of thirty minutes with Rayburn at his home had been arranged. Rayburn did not know Virden, but with his usual hospitable, Texas friendliness he said, "Certainly, come down anytime." As the bus neared Ector, Virden moved up to the driver and explained his mission, inquiring if he could get a taxi from the depot out to Mr. Sam's house. The driver nodded, but when he neared the road leading into the Rayburn property he made a right turn and drove up in front of the house, a procedure strictly contrary to regulations. Surprised, Virden got off the bus, stepped up on the front porch, and knocked. Mr. Rayburn answered the knock, stuck out his hand and said, "I am Sam Rayburn. Sit over there. I want to look at you for a while and see what kind of a man you are."

"Maybe it was only a couple of minutes that Mr. Sam 'looked' at me but it seemed a lot longer than that," reports Virden. "If you ain't ever been 'looked at' by Mr. Rayburn, you have no idea how much that man can say with those snapping brown eyes without ever uttering a word. I guess I must have passed inspection. Mr. Rayburn finally leaned back in his chair and put his run-over cowboy boots on the coffee table and said, 'What kind of cigarettes do you smoke?' "

"Camels," I said.

"Well, that shows good sense. So do I, but I'm out; give me one."

When the thirty minutes had passed Virden stated that he had used up his time and prepared to leave. "Sit down," Rayburn said. "I want to talk to you." The interview continued for an additional two and a half hours, the shortest three-hour interview Virden could remember.

About the rest of the experience, the reporter had these impressions.

"He never ducked, never hedged on any question I asked him and he never had to think about the answer. It came right back and all of them made sense. . . . I went away from Mr. Rayburn's home that evening wondering if we still breed men like that. He is indeed a magnificent American. If all politicians had even a few of Sam Rayburn's virtues, that would be the most respected profession in the country, bar none. It is just too bad he never was elected President of the United States and at seventy-eight years old I'd vote for him in preference to anybody else." [1]

Mr. Sam looked squarely at a man when he talked to him and expected the other person to do likewise. John Garner had stressed the importance of such to Sam during the years of his apprenticeship. Once when Rayburn was judging prospective Presidential candidates he remarked as follows about one of them:

"He's a good fellow and I like him, but he can't win, because the folks won't believe him. I have watched him while we have conversed. He has eyes that shift around. He couldn't look a farmer down there at Ivanhoe, for example, in the eye. You can't get a farmer's confidence if you don't look at him. A farmer wouldn't believe a word he said, despite the fact that he's a pretty truthful fellow."

To silence all the rumors about his health, Mr. Sam went to see his doctor in Washington. The physician reported that barring some unforeseen developments he should live to be a hundred. The inability to read for any length of time a *Congressional Record* or letters was not sufficient basis for him to drop out of politics, so long as he could still "judge men."

While the folks at home were rejoicing that their Mr. Sam was planning to "call the turns" for another two years, the Speaker was continuing to make history in Washington. On January 28, he was awarded the Cordell Hull Award in recognition of his long vigilance over foreign trade and his support of a liberal policy. The dinner at which the award was made climaxed a two-day conference for businessmen, economists, government officials, and industrialists. Because Rayburn had followed in the footsteps of America's foremost exponent of reciprocal trade, he was cited for his "vision and statesmanship in the advancement of the United States policy promoting reciprocal trade among nations." In his acceptance Rayburn told 500 guests of his long friendship with Hull, the man who, in his estimation, was the one being honored—"the author of friendship throughout the world, whose ideas could ease the tensions in an age of uneasiness."

Afterward Rayburn reminisced about Hull, stating that he had pleasant memories of those evenings in the lobby of the Cochran Hotel back in 1913 when the men all pulled their chairs around in a circle. "I have often thought that this was the best school of political science I ever attended." Rayburn pointed out that in the Underwood Tariff bill was a provision for the first constitutional income tax plan. Hull was the author of the plan, and it was the debate on this bill, Rayburn said, which inspired "my maiden speech in Congress."

In his February 10 press conference, Rayburn concentrated on aspects of defense. He referred to Chairman Carl Vinson (D., Ga.) of the House Armed Services Committee, who on February 9 had called for drastic sacrifices to get America back in the missiles race. "Vinson," he said, "laid it on the line." Rayburn in expressing his opinion on the progress being made by the Administration said:

"I don't know whether our engineers and scientists have not been turned loose or what, but it doesn't do any good to be second in war, I am not satisfied with the progress that has been made with the money we have appropriated for defense."

This was perhaps the first instance in his forty-seven years in Congress that he had been partisan on foreign and military policy.

It was in a similar press conference shortly afterward that, when Mr. Sam strayed from his well-established pattern of procedure, an attractive lady reporter, observing that the Speaker had finished before the time was up, asked a question completely unrelated to the occasion:

"What does the dignified Speaker of the House of Representatives think about women tourists wearing shorts around the Capitol?"

"Well," he replied, "I haven't examined all of them. I wouldn't say that what women wear comes under the head of my business." With this comment his secretary called time and the meeting adjourned.

Back in Texas on February 20 in the Houston City Auditorium, the liberals within the Democratic Party began beating the war drums over issues that were to become significant in the State Convention, and were to attract Rayburn's attention in the next national campaign. They deplored the "disloyalty" of the 1952 Executive Committee and the "indifference" of the 1956 Committee, denounced all Democrats who abandoned Party ranks, and urged the support of all nominees "regardless of their religion or the section from which they come." In opening the session of the Democrats of Texas, Mrs. Randolph urged participation in precinct conventions and elections so that 1960 would be a year of Democratic victory. Jerry Holleman (State President of the AFL-CIO), State Representative Bill Kilgarlin, Walter G. Hall, Sr. (Dickinson banker), and Senator Wayne Morse were speakers. Senator Yarborough, who could not attend this State-wide Convention, warned, in a letter, against:

> . . . those Judas goats who led us to slaughter in 1952 and 1956 who now tell you they are good, loyal Democrats and your sole organizers for the 1960 national campaign. If we are to win the victory in Texas this year, it must be won by your loyal DOT Democrats.

Mr. Sam could not have expressed the disloyalty motif any better, but he would not have singled out any special type of Democrat, opposed to labels as he was. The Shivercrats and other ultra-conservatives who had bolted the Party in 1952 and 1956 were the "Judas goats."

The purpose of these appeals was to unite all Democrats around a more liberal banner, in an effort to pull slightly to the left of Mr. Sam's "middle-of-the-road." Some of the speakers and leading participants among the DOT's, however, were Mr. Sam's personal friends, who were not too alarmed over his moderate position because they recognized among the issues sponsored by the DOT clubs several ideas acceptable to him. Some of the issues endorsed by the liberal movement follow: the rejection by state and local governments of strategems to evade compliance with the Supreme Court's nonsegregation school decision; a food stamp program for the undernourished, needy, old age pensioners and unemployed; partnership by all Western hemisphere democracies in the Panama Canal, including policing and defense of the Canal Zone; major power and atomic energy projects to be publicly owned and operated; Federal public housing program and an area redevelopment act which includes loans to communities for sewerage systems and other public facilities; expansion of the Social Security program, including medical and hospitalization care for persons retired under Social Security; Federal legislation to provide uniform unemployment standards; Federal minimum wages of $1.25 to include farm workers not covered by the existing $1 per hour minimum wage law; elimination of the oil depletion allowance credit on foreign oil production; repeal of the poll tax as a requirement for voting; a bold, aggressive food for peace program. Of some significance is the fact that this body of recommendations anticipates some of the themes of the "New Frontier," to which Mr. Sam, on the whole, was later to dedicate himself.

The 1960 Convention in Texas promised to bring about a battle over philosophies and control of the State organization. It was not necessarily a clash between youth and age, principle and prejudice, but a tug of war between zealousness and experience, idealism and common sense. Two groups were trying to resolve within a democratic framework certain differences which were to engage nationally the minds of Americans for at least a decade.

During the five months before Sam Rayburn made his trek West to the Los Angeles Convention, he spoke out on several major issues and problems: Civil Rights, the poll tax, natural gas, medical aid and health plans, the summit meeting, opening House expense accounts, Butler's activities as Chairman of the National Democratic Committee, and LBJ's chances for receiving the nomination.

Tensions mounted quickly on Capitol Hill with the Civil Rights problems coming into focus. The Speaker promptly asked for tolerance by Northern proponents toward demands of outnumbered Southerners to air their objections. "These fellows have different problems in their districts," he explained. "You can't just crack down on them." Loaded with amendments, the Southerners came to the House, however, to keep the talk going through the day's session hoping, if a vote were taken, to water down a proposal which would authorize Federal courts to appoint referees to guarantee Negro voting rights. The Southerners were picking up some support from Republicans to limit the plan to elections for Federal officials only, eliminating state and municipal elections. The vigor of Southern objections to the March 16 stiffening of the referee plan appeared to be destroying Rayburn's hopes for a March 18 vote. Rayburn and Johnson's strategy appeared to be to send the House bill over to the Senate, so that body could quickly approve it, a procedure that would avoid adjustment in a conference committee and by-pass perhaps another delaying action from the House Rules Committee. Rayburn's parliamentary skill here was very much in evidence. His technique at compromise was also reflected in the two months of behind-the-scenes activity before he could get a satisfactory bill ready. He had been around long enough to know the voting records of the men at both ends of Capitol Hill on most issues. On Civil Rights he knew just about how far each congressman would be pushed or just how much he would yield. The Speaker recognized that hostility would be greater in the House than in the Senate and that only a compromise bill could possibly pass. Johnson's moderates were in control of the Senate, yet with the famous filibuster a Southern bloc could attempt a stand, but Rayburn knew it would have been only a Thermopylae even on a good compromise bill.

Rayburn had sensed a softening of the opposition to this phase of Civil Rights—that is, the voting rights—because his own Texas delegation, which in 1957 had voted solidly against it, was this time split nine for and eleven against. Of course, Rayburn knew that during an election year some politics got mixed up in national issues. The fact that a resolution in the Senate was passed to keep confidential all names of those who had filibustered against Civil Rights reflected some desire to keep the Majority Leader from using the issue to further his chances at Los Angeles, because Johnson would not have joined this group. Rayburn was always very cautious in handling Civil Rights legislation because he feared that it could be used as a political weapon to penalize a section of the country, or could be exploited to further individual ambitions. Fears of the by-products of the legislation led him to demand careful committee surveillance.

Before the Easter recess the Senate passed the right to vote bill, but, said Mr. Sam, "That doesn't have much bearing in Texas. Everyone who is qualified to vote has been allowed to vote." Rayburn thought the House would probably suspend the joint committee consideration to give the Rights bill quick approval before sending it to the White House.

A side issue of Civil Rights was the poll tax, on which Rayburn had been doing some hard thinking for about four years. An effort to outlaw the poll tax on a national basis was now being made by the Democratic leadership in Washington. In Texas, this effort to abolish the tax met with some opposition on technicalities from the legal subcommittee of the State Democratic Executive Committee. Walter Hall, chairman of the state campaign to abolish this tax, who was among the original Johnson-for-President people, feared that any opposition by this subcommittee would be interpreted outside Texas as a "slap at Senator Johnson," though in reality it would not be, he thought. Rayburn's evolvement on this issue paralleled his changing views on the whole Civil Rights question. Opposition was based on the fear that the question would be linked with disputes over racial segregation and would add fuel to them. While Governor Price Daniel perhaps privately favored the action of Hall's group, he had his fears, and preferred to keep his attention focused on other issues more immediately related to the economy of the State. The poll tax issue appeared to be one on which Rayburn and Johnson found themselves completely compatible with both Mrs. Randolph and DOT's.

In 1956, President Eisenhower had vetoed a bill to relieve natural gas producers of public utility-type regulation. Although he stated at the time that he approved of the principle, the President affirmed that he acted in the aftermath of a charge that some gas interests attempted to use Senatorial campaign contributions to advance the measure. Rayburn and Johnson, who had exercised all the influence at their command to get the bill through at the time, were set back by the White House's communication coming so late in the session, during the third week of March: "I am ready and willing to support this legislation in this session with full vigor if those in control of Congress give some indication that they will join in this effort."

Rayburn replied to the President's request at a news conference in these terms:

"We passed a good gas bill once and he vetoed it. What kind of bill he would sign, I don't know. I would want to see what he proposed—there's no use going up the hill if you have to roll down again."

The Speaker was informed shortly afterward that the President wanted a bill that would exempt producers from direct Federal price regulation at the well. Rayburn promptly informed the Administration that it would have to assume the leadership for the time element and conditions were not favorable. Rayburn was half-way vexed because the suddenness of the request seemed to reflect the kind of action one might expect from a military leadership. To Mr. Sam, legislation was like a good bourbon. It had to age, because most congressmen refused to drink "raw, white lightning."

While Mr. Sam was at home for the Easter recess he talked rather freely about a Social Security-based, medical aid bill for the aged, which he hoped could be passed before the July adjournment for the conventions. At the time he stated that he favored increasing the Social Security tax base from $4800 to $6000. At this stage, however, he had not expressed a preference for any plan to help the aged, that is, the sixty-five-year-old group. He did state, however, that he was against the Forand bill, which would have increased the Social Security tax and furnished hospital and medical care to recipients of Social Security benefits, but the House had already rejected this proposal. The bill which he predicted would meet with success could be a compromise with less than the Forand, that also allowed nursing and surgical benefits, but would be more than the voluntary plan the Administration was examining. He stated that he was trying to get the bill out of the Ways and Means Committee for consideration on the floor. Indicating his feeling that a little speed was needed, he said, "I told the boys that I thought it ought to be out pretty soon." Since this was a controversial measure he was trying to prevent it from getting in the way of other legislation, such as the appropriation for mutual security or foreign aid, which he was going to bring out next. One of Rayburn's special skills was the ability to bring to the floor the right bill at the right time. He resembled the veteran cop at a rush hour in downtown traffic. Rayburn expressed confidence that Congress could work "mighty fast if they want to." But as far as the medical aid bill was concerned he feared "a snarl could develop at any time," because Congress, he affirmed dogmatically, would not pass a measure for the aged that would lead to socialized medicine, as it was conceived in the popular mind.

While President Eisenhower was in Europe at the abortive Summit conference trying to reach some agreement with Soviet Premier Nikita Khrushchev on the arms race, Speaker Rayburn joined with Adlai Stevenson, Senator Johnson, and Senator J. William Fulbright (Chairman of the Foreign Relations Committee) to send a message to express the thinking of the opposition Party. The Russian Premier had suggested that action should be postponed until after the election; hence Rayburn wanted to convey the sentiment that the next President's attitudes would be similar to Eisenhower's. Rayburn wanted Khrushchev to be aware of a united front. The last part of the message conveyed this concept of unity: "All of the American people earnestly desire peace, an end to the arms race and ever-better relations between our countries. We ask you as the leader of this nation to see that these views are conveyed to Mr. Khrushchev." When the conference collapsed, Rayburn said that he had fears such would happen. He believed that this country should now alert its defenses and maintain its military strength. Invited by the White House, he joined a delegation at Andrews Air Base on May 20, to greet the President upon his return and express his personal cooperation.

The relationship between the White House and the Speaker on foreign affairs could not have been improved upon. President Eisenhower's May 14 communication containing his appreciation for the success of the mutual security authorizing legislation is only one example of the bipartisan thinking. Concerning the appropriation, he concluded his letter thus:

> If in your judgment this situation is beginning to go badly during my attendance at the Summit Meeting I hope you will send to me any suggestions you might have as to what I could additionally do to be helpful. America has too much at stake in this program for any of us to avoid doing our utmost in its behalf.

The man who persisted in the statement that the $25 his father handed him when he went to college was the only money ever given him for personal use, and the man who conscientiously used his Government expense account, was upset on June 1 when he learned of apparent irregularities and indiscretions in some congressmen's expenses reported on "official business" trips. Accounts were ordered reopened for public inspection, but he directed that no records could be photographed or physically removed from the files. A representative for the House Clerk was asked to be present during the examination to protect the records.

The week before, the files had been padlocked, upon House Clerk Ralph Roberts' order, not Rayburn's, when pictures of certain documents revealing some embarrassing information were published in a magazine and a number of newspapers. Bar bills, hotel expenses for congressmen's wives, party expenses and such, were some of the exhibits which led to the sensationalism, and the closing of the files. Rayburn's decision to reopen them came when he realized that there might have been some indiscretions. To prevent a recurrence of such abuses, Rayburn afterward told chairmen of committees to scrutinize expense accounts more closely in the future and to abandon the previous habit of accepting reports in a routine fashion.

On February 20 the liberal Democrats of Texas nailed their manifesto on the precinct doors and by early April they were making plans to challenge the moderates under the leadership of Rayburn, Johnson, Governor Daniel, National Committeeman Byron Skelton, and State Chairman Ed Connally. Twice they had failed in their bid to wrest control from the Governor. If Johnson won the nomination the liberals realized they would be at a disadvantage, but if John Kennedy or another liberal gained the top place on the ticket they would recover some of the glory they began losing after 1944. The thing which bothered Mr. Sam was that some Texans had lost State pride. He could never understand people who were not loyal to their group.

Chairman Butler sent Mr. Sam's blood pressure up when he began expressing his personal preference. Butler stated publicly that Kennedy would win the Wisconsin primary on April 5 and the nomination in July, perhaps even on the first ballot. "If the statement attributed to Mr. Butler," stated Rayburn, "is accurate—and I understand it is undenied—I think he has tremendously lessened his influence by making himself a partisan, not only for a candidate but also against other candidates."

Butler had indirectly suggested in his New York University speech that new faces were needed in the Democratic front ranks. Some believed he specifically referred to Mr. Sam as being too old, for example, to preside at the 1960 Convention. Butler's fraternizing with the liberals back in Texas had already aroused Mr. Sam's suspicions and this recent incident led him to reflect on his loss of faith in the Chairman. Although Butler was secure in his post, he was faced with demands from Democrats, including Senator Humphrey, for him to resign, since his partisanship had destroyed party faith in his ability to name committeemen and carry out convention arrangements.

Although preoccupied with keeping legislative machinery moving, Rayburn and Johnson from time to time buttonholed their friends in Congress, who in turn began the spade work back home. The Senator was able to get away from Washington on the weekend of April 23 for a trip into Colorado, Wyoming, Utah, and Nevada; and Mr. Sam visited Richmond, Virginia, on May 7. By May 20, Rayburn was beginning to appear optimistic, believing that Johnson had support all over the country although he seemed strongest in the South and border States. He refused to put too much faith in the Kennedy victories in the six primaries.

Sam Rayburn was also encouraged by the events at the State Convention in Austin, where on June 14 and 15 the Senator was successful in winning 61 pledged delegates. The liberals made a noisy fight of it, but some of them remarked sadly, "This was not our year." Johnson received 2252 votes to 40 on the Party loyalty issue. The liberal labor groups lost in the big city delegations from Harris, Dallas, and El Paso Counties. On the controversial National Committeewoman issue, Mrs. Randolph was replaced by Mrs. Hilda Weinert and Byron Skelton was re-elected National Committeeman without opposition. The arch-conservatives from Houston were also beaten. Mr. Sam stayed around only for the elaborate political dinner the evening before the Convention got down to business, because he was called back to Washington by President Eisenhower to discuss the rebuff he had received upon announcing his plans to visit in the Far East. However, 3000 guests had an opportunity to hear Rayburn set the stage for a Johnson victory the next day. Rayburn received the news in Washington with great rejoicing, and he considered this perhaps his greatest victory in these rowdy State meetings.

He now affirmed that Johnson would carry between 450 and 500 votes to Los Angeles, but he could not state exactly how many ballots it would take to nominate a candidate. The fifth ballot seemed to him to be about the right number. With seventeen of the Texas Democratic congressmen as delegates to Los Angeles, Rayburn believed there could be a great deal of reconnoitering done among congressmen from other states. Congressmen have a way of remembering past favors and are sometimes rather eager to pave the way for some of their favorite legislation.

The promotion of Johnson's interests occupied most of Rayburn's time during the few weeks before Los Angeles, and when questioned about his thinking on the once-vital redistricting he seemed to show a lackadaisical attitude. True, his mind was preoccupied, but he had just about become reconciled to the inevitable. For years at census time the Fourth District showed a loss of population. In 1960 it had dropped 11,968 and was down to 215,767, well under the 370,000 average for Congressional districts in Texas. He could see that the inequity was now conspicuous and that at least two more counties would be needed to make a partial readjustment. Of course, he almost swallowed his cigarette, though tightly held between his lips, when reference was made to bringing in that "silk stocking" section of Dallas County, the northern portion of which was predominantly Republican. Lieutenant Governor Ben Ramsey and Speaker Waggoner Carr in 1959 had appointed committee chairmen who would be sympathetic toward Fourth District problems—Senator Ray Roberts of McKinney, one-time Rayburn assistant, and Representative Charles E. Hughes of Sherman. Rayburn's own expression of a desire for a larger district appeared to take some of the pressure off the committee that would deal with the issue in 1961. He liked the idea of adding Cooke and Denton Counties, because they were "more his kind of folks," that is rural in background. He was bothered, though, by the effect that this reorganization would have on some of the other people in the Texas delegation; but with the population shifting toward the larger cities he could now see there eventually would be considerable reorganization and realignments.

Rayburn usually insisted upon Congress' completing its business before adjourning, but this year he was willing to permit an exception, despite the fact that some major legislation was left hanging in the balance on July 5. Not since 1932, when he entered the name of John Nance Garner in the Presidential Derby, had he felt such an urgency to pull up stakes and go West. The Convention was only six days away and he had advised

Johnson to leave promptly for Los Angeles, since there was a great deal of work still to be done.

Sam Rayburn himself could be a little more leisurely and take off at least two days before leaving for Los Angeles, since Governor LeRoy Collins of Florida was assuming his old familiar role as Permanent Chairman. Though Clarence Cannon, the well-known parliamentarian would be on hand to assist, Rayburn had taken time out to give his successor some coaching. He spent forty-five minutes with Collins and Cannon reviewing the rules and pointing out some of the dangerous places. "A convention can get away from you in a hurry, if you don't watch out," he warned.

To be sure, Rayburn had an indirect part in selecting his replacement. Collins, although without too much experience, had certain qualifications that Rayburn looked for in a year when the Civil Rights issue could produce a schism. Free of Congressional pressures, a moderate from a state which is cosmopolitan in its mores but on the periphery of the South, Collins could command the respect of Northerners and at the same time retain the confidence of Southerners. Rayburn liked men who were on dead center for parliamentary posts.

When the arrangements committee met in New York on May 26 to select a replacement for Mr. Sam as the permanent chairman, the group promptly offered him the honorary chairmanship. In expressing his appreciation he said, "I may accept it, if it gives me an automobile and a chauffeur, a hotel room, meals, and several hundred extra tickets."

The Citizens-for-Johnson Committee, headed by Oscar Chapman, the Interior Secretary under President Truman, and India Evans, had been officially set up in the Ambassador Hotel by Mr. Sam on June 2 and had worked actively until the exodus to Los Angeles. The executive director was John B. Connally. Thousands of Texans, however, long before had been disseminating information and corresponding with groups in other states where the Senator had established beachheads. Large "LBJ" buttons were not an uncommon sight in Texas as early as May. Some wore them with a gusto, others quietly put them in their pockets or gave them to their children, if they were debating between a favorite son or a tenuous liberalism. There were still others, who had left the Democratic fold in 1952 and 1956, who indulged their wit with uncomplimentary parodies and after the National Convention, became quite articulate in their witticism. This form of humor cut Mr. Sam to the quick!

He flinched like one of his white-faced cows tormented with stinging flies in the hot summer time.

Mr. Sam had heard that some of the top labor leaders were not too friendly toward Senator Johnson's efforts to win the nomination because he was too conservative. He was a very direct man, unwilling to take mere hearsay. Victor Riesel wrote that Mr. Sam on an afternoon early in June had a chance to discuss the whole matter when Walter Reuther dropped by the Speaker's office in connection with some labor-backed bills. "Sit down," Mr. Sam said. "I'm glad you're here. I want to talk to you. I'm sick of the labor leaders ganging up on Johnson. In all the years he's been here, he hasn't hit out at any labor people. He didn't vote against them as Minority Leader—nor as Majority Leader, especially as Majority Leader. Why do you fellows go around hitting him?"

Reuther answered quickly: "Look, Mr. Speaker, don't include me in that sentiment. I'm not against Lyndon Johnson. I want a winner. I don't want eight more years of Republican rule. . . . I'll take anybody the Party names. I'm not fighting Johnson."

Riesel believed that Reuther left Rayburn's office in a friendly frame of mind, but not a Johnson man, and still privately but ardently for Kennedy. Riesel also pointed out that labor leaders do not like to get involved in pre-convention fights.[2] Their policy is to wait, accept a Party's decision, and then mobilize all their strength behind the candidate they believe will serve their interests best.

Mr. Sam rarely had any time strictly his own. He was always the public servant and friend to everyone with an honest need. No pomp or ceremony was necessary, no go-between to negotiate. The open sesame to Mr. Sam was an honest face and a problem. His right hand reached across the threshold thousands of times during his twenty-five terms to pull a troubled spirit into the quiet sanctuary of the big white house where obstacles crumbled away under the bombardment of his direct analysis. The troubles melted like the clods in his freshly plowed field after a fall rain. His words were as comforting to the spirit as the moisture to the fertility of the earth.

He also gave of his energy to make many public appearances; for example, such things as riding one of his prized horses in a rodeo parade. In his last event in Bonham in 1960, at the Kueckelhan rodeo, he had to settle for a ride in a pony cart drawn by two Silver Crescent Shetlands. The owner, Sheriff Hoyt

Ivey, did the driving. Three months later, when he was at Pasadena, Texas, on October 10, he had to be content with leading a rodeo parade in a shining convertible. At seventy-eight his strenuous performances were behind him, but on his ranch he was still known to take a few turns in the saddle.

One morning before Mr. Sam took off for the Convention he had some free time to talk. After inspecting Miss Lou's garden and complimenting Jesse Higgs for the way in which he was looking after the grass and beds, he turned to the author of these pages and said, "I believe you wanted to talk politics." It seemed rather ludicrous to pursue any other subject with the most exciting figure in American politics standing there loaded with things to say about forthcoming events. With so much to ask him, and the telephone constantly ringing inside the library, the conversation took place in the shade of an elm tree at the southeast corner of the building.

"Mr. Sam, do you believe Lyndon will win the nomination?"

"Well, if we can get through the first roll call, he has a chance. Jack could win it on the first ballot. He has worked hard and has made many trips. Everywhere he goes he leaves behind an organization. There are some good young fellows working for him too. Lyndon just hasn't had the time to do this."

"Are you against Jack Kennedy?"

"No," he said, "I am for Lyndon Johnson."

"Have you and Harry Truman discussed this Convention?"

"Yes, Harry wrote me, and he said he thought we should get together on this thing. He likes Johnson but also thinks Symington would make a good President."

"Will you support Symington if Lyndon sees he can't win?"

"It may never reach this stage, but we are going to nominate a man who can win."

"You do think, though, that Johnson can win, if he should be nominated?"

"Yes, a Democrat can win. This is our year."

"Do you think Johnson would make a better President than Kennedy?"

"Well, I know more about Lyndon. However, I think I have known Jack all of his life. Johnson, though, has had more experience in Congress than Jack, and I believe he will give us the kind of leadership we need." Rayburn recalled that Johnson only recently had received forty-one out of a possible fifty votes as the most able Democrat in the Senate, to win the balloting in the straw vote taken by Washington's foremost correspondents. He was, of course, too modest to say anything about his own winning of thirty-six votes for the commensurate honor in the House.

"Would you say that Jack Kennedy lacks the ability to be President?"

"No, I wouldn't say that. It's simply that he's young. These are troublesome times, and Lyndon is tested."

"Mr. Sam, what about the religious issue, if Kennedy gets the nomination?"

"It shouldn't enter in at all, but it will. There are some folks, and I don't want to call any names, who will hold it against him. In America this should not be an issue at all."

"What about Stevenson?"

"He does not have the organization. I like Adlai. He's a good fellow, and he makes a good speech, but he can't pull the Party together. He's been beaten twice already."

"Mr. Sam, it would appear that Nixon will win the Republican nomination."

"Maybe, but there are several other fellows who would be harder to beat."

At this point he mentioned Republicans who were his close friends and pointed out that he surely would hate to campaign against a few of them because of his high personal regard. This part of the conversation carried Mr. Sam up to the brink of personalities, but he always had a knack for ducking questions that were designed to lead him on. When he saw these questions coming, he would blow the center out of the strategy by some such remark as, "Yeah, some people have said that, but I have always found him to be a good citizen." A "good citizen" to Rayburn meant a number of things—patriotism, loyalty to his group, devotion to his family and constituents, et cetera. The president of a bank would define "good citizen" as one who "inspires confidence"; the president of the Chamber of Commerce would say, "He's safe." But actually, Rayburn meant, "We can work together." Since Rayburn could work with most people, he spent his time trying to sound the depths of goodness and if there was any evil there, he saw it, but didn't discuss it, and tried to contain it in such a way that it would never do much damage.

The next question almost upset the elder statesman. "Mr. Sam, do you think, if elected, that Nixon would make a good President?"

"In the first place, he's not going to be elected. I have faith in these American people. He's just too light for these dangerous times—a little man on a big horse."

Just before he crawled into his 1955 Plymouth, he was asked this question, which lay between two of the earlier ones. "Whom will the Democrats nominate?"

Squinting his eyes and smiling just a bit, he quipped, "A winner!"

But there was more to follow. "If Johnson should not get the nomination, do you think he would consider the Vice-Presidency?"

"Well, that's what happened to Garner in 1932. I went to the convention to nominate him for President, not for Vice-President. Those are my plans about Lyndon. Garner didn't want that thing. Lyndon knows that his present job is more important than holding a gavel over there in the Senate, that is, with the Vice-Presidency what it has been for so long a time. He wants to work where he can do the most good. We both feel about the same way on this."

The next we hear of the honorary chairman of the Convention he was in Los Angeles, moving from delegation to delegation. Everywhere he heard such salutations as "Hi, Sam," "Howdy, Mr. Sam," "Hello, Mr. Speaker." With such general acclaim and the awareness that he had his pockets full of political IOU's, some Texans reflected optimism. However, one skeptical Texan remarked, "Mr. Sam has thumped and pulled some mighty big watermelons in his day, without even plugging them, but this one looks green to me."

Something of the Speaker's popularity in Los Angeles was revealed on the Monday evening when he made his first appearance on the floor. Seeing him first, the North Carolina delegation started an ovation which disrupted the proceedings. The Texas delegation then applauded so loudly that the Convention's official roll call was temporarily interrupted. Chairman Paul Butler, appearing irritated with the rowdy Texans, but more probably upset by the enthusiasm for Rayburn, took the microphone and demanded that delegates be seated. Mr. Sam looked toward the rostrum and appeared to be enjoying himself with not being in charge, as he circulated on the floor, remarking, "It's not as lonesome as sitting up there, and you can move around and visit."

Sam Rayburn, in the late afternoon of July 13, placed in nomination the name of Lyndon Baines Johnson. Intimately and personally, as a father would recommend his own son, he offered the services of Lyndon to America as a man who "is a winner," belonging to "no class, no section, no faction—a man for all Americans—a leader matured by long experience, a soldier seasoned in many battles, a tall, sun-crowned man who stands ready now to lead America and lovers of freedom everywhere through our most fateful hours."

While the roll call was in progress Mr. Sam sat there in the second seat from the aisle with his eyes closed and hands clasped on his chest. Albert M. Colegrove described him as "looking much like a tired businessman drowsing through an endless night at the opera." He did not bother to keep a tally sheet. When the Kennedy vote mounted he opened his eyes, shrugged his shoulders and lighted a cigarette. He was conditioning himself to what he had sensed, as early as July 1, might happen if the Kennedy bandwagon started rolling. After the first ten delegations had cast their votes he knew that his intuitive judgment had not betrayed him, but those who observed his behavior saw only his exterior optimism. Mr. Sam rarely misjudged the outcome of any political battle. As a leader he could not have afforded to have predicted defeat because of the effect that his pessimism might have had on those with lesser faith and a strong desire to be on the winning side. Hence he kept his own company. Rarely by word or action did he detract from a cause to which he was dedicated by waving the white flag. It was not dishonesty but common sense for Mr. Sam to play his hand out according to his own rules. Many admired his skill but few understood his technique. Hence his spirit was one of the most lonesome in American politics for want of companionship with those who possessed his type of detachment and vision.

But as the roll call continued, the other members of the Texas delegation were full of life, working diligently and efficiently up until the last minute. National Committeeman Byron Skelton and Governor Daniel kept the floor telephone of the delegation busy to other delegations. There were Johnson men sitting with key delegations trying to siphon off stray votes, even one or two. The strategy was to stop Kennedy on the first ballot, but the effort began too late, months too late. The Kennedy forces had overlooked nothing; every delegation's arrival time in Los Angeles was known, and reception committees were waiting to chaperone them to their hotels. They took no chances with Mr. Sam's persuasive power and nailed the lid down before he could drive a wedge into even the tiniest crack.

One of the most gallant, but futile, efforts on the floor was made by Price Daniel when Chairman Collins began calling for vote changes and delegations that had passed during the regular roll call. The Chair began with Kansas, and Governor James T.

Blair of Missouri moved to make the nomination unanimous. Daniel began kicking up a storm. Protesting, he stated, "The Chair said it would call the states alphabetically for changes." Rayburn could see that there was not the remotest chance that another order would have changed the shape of things, but he sympathized with Daniel in his distress over not being given the chance he was pledged.

Wyoming's fifteen votes liquidated Mr. Sam's last hope. The magic 761 had been reached. The TV camera caught him just at the moment. He was described later as the picture of dejection and physical exhaustion. Disappointment would have been a more appropriate portrayal; however, to observers, his physical being seemed to be on the decline shortly before Los Angeles. With tremendous resilience, he promptly declared, "Majority rules, and we've all got to stand by the majority decision. We fought a good fight. Of course we'll support Mr. Kennedy. That's the Democratic way—and I'm a Democrat. Now let's watch the Convention."

Johnson, always more verbose, pledged: "Senator Kennedy has my sincere congratulations and my solemn assurance that in the coming months of this campaign no one will be more dedicated than I—no one will work harder than I to make doubly sure of what all Democrats here and throughout the country know must come for the good of the nation and the free world—that John F. Kennedy will be elected the next President of the United States."

Johnson communicated with Rayburn and reported that he had been told that he was being considered for the second place on the ticket. Mr. Sam thought a moment then blurted out, "Turn it down!" He did not go into any explanation, for Rayburn had already made his position clear about the value of Johnson as Majority Leader. Yet Rayburn undoubtedly saw some logic in it all. Had Johnson won and Kennedy been second, the two Texans would have considered the Massachusetts man.

The press reported that Joe Kennedy, the nominee's father, had earlier approached his son in Johnson's behalf. There were also reports that another close to the nominee had expressed the belief that a Midwesterner, with liberal leanings, would make a stronger ticket. Some of the possibilities suggested around the convention hall were Hubert Humphrey, "Soapy" Williams, or Governor Freeman.

The press also reported that the second place appealed to Mrs. Johnson (Lady Bird) more than it did to the two Texans;

however, wives generally let husbands make men's decisions. Before Mr. Rayburn and the Senator left the convention hall, Johnson assured Mr. Sam that he would keep in touch with him and he would be consulted.

The chronology of the next twelve hours is based upon accounts by Rayburn's administrative assistant, John Holton, journalists' interpretations, and others. When the versions are put together they reveal the following sequence of events.

Mr. Sam and John Holton left the convention hall and went to their hotel. They got off the elevator and walked down the corridor. Just as they made a left turn Mr. Sam, hearing some confusion, asked John what all the commotion was at the far end of the hall. Holton remarked that there were newspapermen, TV cameras, and photographers crowding outside Lyndon Johnson's suite. Mr. Sam remarked, "My God, he's already done it." But then he remembered Johnson's promise, and took comfort in it.

Somewhat dejectedly, he hurried to his room and John followed him in. The telephone had been ringing. This is what the voice on the other end of the line said. "Sam, Jack is here and we are discussing the Vice-Presidency. I told him what you said, but he wants to discuss it with you."

At this point Mr. Kennedy must have asked to speak to Rayburn, for the next thing Rayburn knew he was talking to the nominee.

"Mr. Speaker, I want to talk to you about this."

"All right, I shall be glad to meet you at your room," he replied.

"No, I think it is more appropriate that I should come to you," was the reply.

"All right, I shall wait here."

"Good, I shall be there in twenty minutes," Kennedy answered.

The telephone rang again. This time it was John McCormack, Convention manager for Kennedy. He stated that he had been searching for the Speaker for nearly an hour to seek his help in convincing Johnson that he should take the VP position. McCormack then revealed that Johnson had been Kennedy's choice for months. It was also pointed out that the nominee's father was also aware of the preference. Mr. Sam, though, gave little encouragement to McCormack, since he believed Johnson could render a greater service to his country as Senate Majority Leader.

Then Rayburn turned to his assistant and said, "John, I must find a place where I can be alone and think this thing through."

Holton promptly said, "Take my key and go to my room, for no one can find you there."

Then Mr. Sam slipped away unseen and began wrestling with the problem. But within fifteen minutes he returned to await Mr. Kennedy's visit. The man from Massachusetts, however, did not show up and after about forty minutes Rayburn asked Johnson to telephone Kennedy's room. "Tell him that it will be all right if he has changed his mind. I must get some sleep."

Kennedy answered, "I have been detained but will be there very shortly."

He had been detained by someone who insisted fervently that a Midwesterner or Northern liberal who would appeal to labor and minority groups was needed. The advice was that Johnson could give the ticket strength only in the South and border States. Kennedy had been advised that he should not worry about the South. He was assured that the Democrats could win without the Solid South, that most Southerners would go along regardless of the ticket.

Kennedy did not like or want to accept this generalization. He explained that he was to be the candidate for a united Party, not a divided one. Although he perhaps knew he could count on Mr. Sam's support in the House, he may have realized the Speaker would not be a "rubber stamp." With Johnson as his co-partner, he believed Rayburn would work a little harder at finding good compromises. He no doubt wanted to have Rayburn's name bandied around during the campaign for the confidence it would inspire. He recognized all of the Speaker's values, as would any intelligent candidate.

Finally, Kennedy knocked on Mr. Sam's door. Rayburn could see that he looked a little flustered. Then the two got off in the corner of the room, and Sam Rayburn listened, scarcely taking his peering eyes off the young man's face. Kennedy's humility and sincerity won the older man. The thought that he wanted to unite the Party and make the Vice-Presidency an important job appealed to Mr. Sam, because he came to realize about a year after Eisenhower first brought up the subject of increasing the Vice-President's responsibilities, that some duties of the President's job should be delegated. Kennedy's reference to wanting to use Johnson's finesse in handling people on an international level—to make the job more important—sounded good to Rayburn.

Johnson a bit earlier had talked to the nominee about the greater function of the Vice-Presidency; however, Johnson had stated frankly that he would be against making the assignment a pseudo-legislative post. He called Kennedy's attention to Rayburn's refusal during the early days of the Fair Deal to attend a Cabinet meeting, called by President Truman. Rayburn had stated at that time quite bluntly that he favored the separation of powers between Congress and the executive branch. This Rayburnesque concept had already been planted in Kennedy's mind and he knew of Johnson's loyalty and that the only way to win Johnson was to win Rayburn. Hence in his conversation with Rayburn he very delicately steered around Mr. Sam's hard and fast belief.

Rayburn then asked, "What is Lyndon's desire?"

"He won't commit himself until you have expressed yourself."

"Well," Mr. Sam said, "up until thirty minutes ago I was against it, and I have withheld a final decision until I could really find out what was in your heart. You know, Jack, I am a very old man and sometimes given to being a little selfish, I am sure. I am in the twilight of my life, walking down into the valley. My career is behind me, but Lyndon is only approaching the summit of his. I am afraid I was trying to keep him in the legislative end where he could help me. Now the way you explain it I can see that you need him more. You are looking at the whole. Well, there is always the thought in a fellow's mind that he might get to be President. Lyndon is a good soldier and he will hear the call of duty. I yield on one condition. I make this one request—that you go on the radio or television and tell the people you came to us and asked for this thing." The nominee agreed that if he and Johnson could get together, he would do it.

He had no sooner closed Mr. Sam's door than a reception committee was waiting to repeat the routine which had delayed Kennedy's arrival at the Speaker's room. After Kennedy finally cleared his suite, he went to bed. According to Sarah McLendon, an article written by Jack Knight was instrumental in calling Mr. Sam from his bed. The item reported that Mr. Sam twisted Kennedy's arm to force Lyndon's choice for second place on the ticket. Rayburn at 2:00 A.M. telephoned Kennedy to find out what was going on. He was irritated! It was a surprise to Kennedy, and he assured Mr. Sam that the whole thing was entirely false and would be refuted the next morning. Mr. Sam was not satisfied until the newspaper was telephoned immediately and the story retracted. The newspaper, however, thought it had the story from one who should know what was going on, that is, a lawyer for Stuart Symington. The attorney, some believed, was upset over the turn of events. The greatest damage, however, was done back in Texas, for there were some who preferred to believe otherwise. They were looking for an excuse to yell "double cross" so that they could behave the way they had planned all along. Even Kennedy's statement the next day on TV did not convince them.

While this drama was being enacted, and before the last conference between the nominee and Johnson, according to one account, the elder Kennedy called on the Senator and argued for his accepting the job. The Senator said he really preferred to stay in the Upper House because "a vote is a lot more important than a gavel."

Joe Kennedy replied, "You are not looking at the complete picture and as Vice-President you will have considerably more influence than a single vote."

Johnson terminated the discussion by saying, "Jack should decide what is best for the country and the Party and put it on that basis. Any patriotic American cannot refuse such a call."

Before the final decision was made, Kennedy talked to his headquarters in New York, Pennsylvania, and Ohio. These sources thought Johnson would strengthen the ticket. Some other advice contradicted this conclusion. Kennedy then turned the problem over in his mind again and reached a decision.

The next morning at 8:30, Kennedy put the issue squarely to Johnson in the Senator's hotel suite. The Senator was silent for a moment. Then he stuck out his hand. "All right, Jack. For the good of the country and the Party, I'll accept. You can count me in."

A part of the interview was carried over television, to comply with Rayburn's request, if Johnson were offered the Vice-Presidency. As the program was concluded, Mr. Sam turned off his set with a smile on his face because he believed the voice of Kennedy reflected the will of the people. He thought this combination would make a winning ticket. However, he did not anticipate the bitterness ahead, certainly not the loss of national pride among some Texans.

As Mr. Sam strolled into the convention hall, some of the former fire and enthusiasm seemed restored. However, he appeared fatigued. The nomination of Johnson was really only a formality. When Chairman Collins was about to wrap it all up, he fumbled the gavel briefly and Mr. Sam unconsciously with clenched fist lurched forward in his seat from reflex action, as though he were banging the gavel down. He appeared to shout something to Collins. Then he looked around, grinned, and joined in the excitement of the moment. The television audience perhaps saw more of Mr. Sam than did the press because the cameras followed him when he was on the floor. Off the floor he had a way of vanishing from the reporters' sight.

The game of politics is glamorous as well as brutal. There were rumors of plots to derail the two Texas moderates. Some liberal opposition talked about kicking Johnson upstairs into a sort of ineffective position and then attempting to bring Mr. Sam in tow come January, but this small minority had underestimated the strength of Rayburn and the wisdom and "backbone" of Jack Kennedy. Kennedy wanted to combine his liberalism with the Johnson moderation, a strategy which the experts believed spelled victory for the Democrats. Without Johnson, they maintained, Kennedy would never see the White House save from the iron gates on Pennsylvania Avenue. And without Rayburn he would not get the first stages of the New Frontier off the ground. Kennedy would never have listened to the assassins who later might have whispered in his ear that they purge Caesar, for he knew that there would have been many bloodstains on the carpeting of both Houses. The blood of Caesar would have mingled with that of both Brutus and Cassius, and the New Frontier might have expired in the Forum before reaching the fields of Philippi.

When Mr. Sam failed to carry the field for Lyndon Johnson, and the old men of the South could exercise little influence upon the Platform Committee, many who had followed these conventions for years foresaw some radical changes in American politics. James Reston of the New York *Times* stated that the Democratic Convention looked, sounded, and even smelled like every other one of the past twenty years but it was not the same. Sam Rayburn also recognized that this Convention was different. The major issues were settled back home before the professional politicians could swing into action. The political leaders were powerless to resist the great mass of delegates, many of them young and teeming with a sense of urgency about solving America's problems. Half amused, Reston watched the mob of notorious political peacocks standing around the lobby of the Biltmore Hotel. They smoked cigars as big as ball bats and pretended they were going to stop Kennedy or elect him.[3] The young dandies only laughed at these ghosts of fallen dynasties as they stood rubbing cigar butts and staring out of glassy, bleary eyes.

The men who promoted the Kennedy campaigns during the primaries urged him to make a clean break with the old men of the nineteenth century, most of them born in log cabins and clutching stereotyped beliefs about social, domestic, and international affairs. Some even wanted to derail Mr. Sam and Lyndon Johnson, but Kennedy did not associate these two with the political bosses of bygone days. Their ageless experience was marked by a great fertility of mind and tremendous popularity at the ballot box. With the stigma of religion, and a platform that anticipated a social and economic revolution, he needed the solid maturity of these two Texans during the campaign and the years ahead. They were veterans of change and several times had survived the passing of the old and the dawning of the new.

Kennedy further recognized that there was a difference between winning the primaries and the nomination, and convincing the voters in November. There was also an Eighty-seventh Congress to face. This realization made him solicitous of other old pros similar to Rayburn and Johnson. Young brother Bobby had virtually pulled off a miracle in getting the JFK image transfixed in the Convention's imagination, but it was the head of the clan who helped put across the facts of life. The nominee, however, had a mind of his own and no doubt found in his father's advice a confirmation of his own beliefs. Harry Truman, prevented from attending the Convention because of illness in the family, was asked by Kennedy to help him in the campaign; Stevenson was likewise solicited. Senator Johnson made a beeline for Independence before going to Hyannis Port. Veterans like Chicago's Mayor Richard Daley, California's Governor Pat Brown, Connecticut's Governor Abe Ribicoff, Michigan's Governor "Soapy" Williams, labor leader Walter Reuther, New York's Mayor Wagner and Carmine De Sapio, Ohio's Governor Mike DiSalle, and others of this caliber and vintage were promptly called into service by the young nominee. The old pros, then, were not fading from America's political scene. They were simply moving into the background where they could function more efficiently. This 1960 up-to-date look in the Democratic Party was merely the result of a few streamlined features. The chassis was the same that had been on the road for years. It had proved a durable and satisfactory vehicle, and Kennedy was not ready to trade it in for a new model, when all it really needed was a tune-up.

When Mr. Sam came home to Bonham on July 16 he did not show any evidence of having taken a beating. He was all smiles because he believed the Democrats had picked a winning team. When asked if he thought Johnson scored a Convention victory in accepting second place on the ticket after losing the first place, Rayburn said: "I have never known but one man who ran for President who wouldn't take the Vice-Presidency. That man was Hiram Johnson of California. And it later turned out he made a mistake."

The aftermath of the Convention is best described by reading Mr. Sam's mail and his replies. A great many letters were filled with talk about the platform, about the way Sam's friends had deserted him, and the religious issue. For example, a very prominent congressman wrote, on August 25, about the way some of Sam's friends ran out on him:

> Well, you fought a good fight and imagine you were terribly disappointed, as I was, that certain people did not appreciate what you and Lyndon Johnson had done for them down through the years. You did more than President Franklin D. Roosevelt, Harry Truman and all of the others put together, but when I was watching on the television and saw the very ones that you had helped the most go right square against you, not even giving us one-half of a vote, . . . it was terrible.
>
> The platform is going to be hard to swallow and there is a great deal of criticism about it. It may defeat us. If we are defeated it will be our platform that did it, because, personally, I believe it is very impractical.

In replying to the many complaints, Mr. Sam pursued this line of reasoning:

> The platform does not suit a lot of people, but if you read the platform of the Republicans you will find it as bad or worse. I am telling people that Congress interprets the platform and their interpretation is the law of the land.

To a man at Crowell, Texas, who had parted with the Democrats over the religious question, he wrote as follows on August 4:

> It is natural for people to disagree. I do not think in a country like ours, which is dedicated to freedom of religion, that any man's religion should be held against him in a contest for any office, from the highest to the lowest.
>
> John F. Kennedy willingly offered his life for his country during World War II. His ship was shot from under him in the Pacific Ocean. He swam for safety and rescued five men who could not swim. I cannot believe that any man, who would offer his life for this country, would be untrue to it in any position in which he may be placed.
>
> This country of ours, both domestically and in its foreign relations, needs a change. I know that John F. Kennedy and Lyndon Johnson are able and patriotic men who love their country next to their families. They are both in middle age, vigorous in health, and sound in intellect. I believe they can lead this country in a path of peace better than any Republican.
>
> I am glad, being a Baptist of the hard shell type, that I have no religious prejudices. I have served in Congress with hundreds of Catholics. By no speech they ever made, nor vote they ever cast, did they indicate they were Catholic, Protestant, or Jew. I know this statement is true.
>
> Please think again and vote for the men, regardless of religion, whom you think can best serve our beloved country.

In the Rice Hotel in Houston one evening during the campaign, while waiting to catch an elevator, he brought up this topic of religion. Standing around him at the time were perhaps half a dozen men. "Religious intolerance," said Rayburn, "bothers me. I am a hard shell Baptist, and they say we are just about the most prejudiced people in the whole country on this issue, but look at *me*, I am *not* prejudiced."

Hoping to learn more about his views on religious tolerance, the author at a later date, after the election, quizzed him rather sharply on this and other controversial issues with a tape recorder.

"I just feel terrible when people preach hate for any class or any sect. I want everyone to choose their own way to get to heaven as far as I am concerned. And I have made this prediction about Kennedy's election to all preachers in the pulpits that I think Kennedy's election will do more for religious tolerance in the United States than anything that could possibly happen because in a year or two, after he has been there, they can't tell by his actions and his appointees whether he is a Jew or Presbyterian or Catholic. And he couldn't afford to be otherwise. It would take a silly, ignorant man to take Jack Kennedy as a simple soul. You are on the wrong man here."

Then rather suddenly the Speaker drifted off onto the question of race and spoke somewhat loosely as follows:

"I have never mentioned this race question in public. I feel this way. I feel that the average person around Bonham thinks it's coming, feels sure it is, because it's the law. But they want to give them time enough to kind of get used to it. And, I think the Supreme Court meant that when it said with deliberate speed and that may be slow. But there were a group of people, colored and more whites, who wanted to grab the bits in the teeth and run the whole distance the first dash.

"But it is a progressive thing. You've got to get people used to it. I thank God that I am one human being that has no racial or religious prejudices in my life. A man can't help being a Negro, any more than I can help being born. And they are certainly human beings, because all except for the color, they are like us. And of course, there are radicals in that group, you know, preaching hurry-up and all this stuff."

Rayburn's replies to letters about the platform were brief. In effect he said Congress enacts the laws that put platforms into action.

About Johnson's "double cross," as some persisted in phrasing it, he was equally brief. He affirmed that the call of duty compelled Johnson to follow a course of action which they had not contemplated prior to the Convention.

Rayburn announced formally that he was prepared to hear the call himself but that the candidates themselves should take the lead; however, he stated that he had no intention of sitting around campaign headquarters like some old man. He stated that he had played an active role in nine conventions, missing only one since 1924, that one in 1944. He also reminded his Democratic friends that he had never turned down the opportunity to participate in the campaign tours.

The Speaker's office in Bonham was frequented by reporters before he left for Washington to call the House together on August 15 for its special session. These were interesting times for one collecting data about Sam Rayburn, especially with a front seat and a cooperative private secretary like H. G. Dulaney, who gave his ideas and impressions of Mr. Sam's responses to the more bitter issues and problems that were discussed in the big office. All of Rayburn's mail was made available, daily, immediately after it had been answered.

Rayburn told most of the visitors who inquired about the Convention that "it reflected the seriousness of the times. There were no bitter speeches and the delegates were trying to work together." One day someone asked the rather touchy question, "Do you believe that young men are taking over the Party?"

"NO!" he replied. "William Jennings Bryan was thirty-six when he was nominated for the first time. Kennedy is forty-three. Our ticket does appeal to younger people and the women voters. The Democratic Party is composed of people both young and old. These two young men just happened to come along in 1960. We have done more for the aged than for any other group. Many would not be eating today if it were not for social security and old age assistance."

Continuing, he said: "Kennedy won the same way he will win in November—by strenuous campaigning. He is an organizer with energy and stamina. I heard that he flew out to Utah seven times before the Convention and that he left an organization in every place he visited. This is just an example of the way he works, and this type of campaigning will win. The Party is in fairly good shape financially and this should help, because the Republicans will always have money to spend."

Rayburn explained that the country was "in bad shape" and that the people were going to be shocked when they learned more: "By grabs, they were already learning it, and they will find out about it just as sure as God makes little apples. This disappearance of our gold is a dangerous thing. Somebody told me the other day that statistics showed that the tourists from the United States in Europe alone spent a billion dollars more than all the tourists from all the countries in the world spent in the United States of America. Now, that is a billion dollars gone. That's gold they are spending. Our money is based on gold."

When asked to comment on an article in the *Wall Street Journal* about labor's effort to make the Party more liberal, he replied, "Such a force is apt to have some influence, but it will not be dominating. I am unaware of Walter Reuther's objection to Johnson."

Rayburn's activities, before returning to Washington for the special session, consisted of such things as dedicating a medical clinic at Savoy on July 24, a community youth center at Frisco, Texas, on July 30, and addressing the Annual Rural Electrification meeting in Bonham on August 1. His references to world tensions seemed to anticipate the theme of his fall speeches when the campaign was to be fully launched.

On August 5, some three hundred optimistic Bonhamites turned out at Jones Field to greet the Vice-Presidential nominee, Mrs. Johnson, Lynda Bird, Secretary of State Zollie Steakley, Gerald Mann, and Grover Sellers. Johnson's plane had put down to pick up Mr. Sam to attend Senator Robert S. Kerr's reception in Oklahoma City. Mr. Sam extended a word of welcome and then each dignitary made a few remarks about the Party's chances for victory in November. Among the enthusiastic crowd were twenty-five Negro students in a government class at Booker T. Washington High School.

The reception in Oklahoma City attracted one thousand friends who were instructed not to talk politics because it was intended to honor Senator Kerr for his new book *Land, Wood and Water*. Louisiana Governor Jimmie Davis later led the group in the song fest. However, when the menfolks, except for Rayburn, stripped off their coats and the women pulled out their palm-leaf fans the rules were broken. Barbecue and barrels of lemonade set the stage. After Mr. Sam had spoken for two or three minutes, the gathering turned into a political rally.

He told about his maiden speech in Congress on May 6, 1913, and assured the people that he had been around long enough to recognize the superiority of the American way. Then he spoke feelingly against prejudice and suppression of human rights. At one point Rayburn took the Republicans to task for using the name "Democrat" Party instead of "Democratic" Party. If they did not stop the practice, he said, he was going to begin calling them "Publicans." Johnson circulated through the throng shaking the hands of the people who enveloped him. Working with both hands he overlooked no one, not even those waiting in the hotel lobby and at the airport. A reception which began as a tribute to an author was terminated in an Oklahoma political picnic with Johnson and Rayburn as the stars.

Rayburn gaveled the special session to order on August 15. After he had surveyed the Administration's twenty-one-point request, he proclaimed:

> "It would take Congress from now until Christmas to pass all the legislation President Eisenhower

requested in his message this week. I was utterly amazed that the President would present such a long list of recommendations for major legislation."

It just shows, he said, that the President doesn't know too much about the legislative process because it takes time to do anything. He struck out at the charges that Democrats were bigger spenders than the Republicans:

> "During the last seven years of Mr. Truman's Administration we spent $335 billion and fought the Korean War that cost billions during that time. In seven years of Mr. Eisenhower, beginning in 1954, his Administration has spent $499 billion—$164 billion more than the Democrats spent in the previous seven years."

The Senate had a week's start on the House, and Mr. Sam was watching their progress before making any predictions on the success of the session. When asked how long he would keep the House in session, he leaned back in his large swivel chair and said he could answer the question by an illustration: "A farmer back home got tangled up with a bull that had a rope around his horns. A neighbor came by and asked, 'Where are you going?' The farmer replied, 'Don't ask me. Ask the bull.'" The bull, Rayburn said, was the United States Senate. "Ask them." Labor Day, however, was the target date he had set in his own mind.

Rayburn was outspoken in his desire to get a school construction bill out of the Rules Committee. In some quarters, the thought was expressed that he might have to seek the assistance of Vice-President Nixon, if he expected to get this controversial measure to a conference committee during the session. The minimum wage and housing were other measures which he could see would keep Congress occupied.

Though the years were creeping up on him, Sam Rayburn had not learned to pace himself. During an election year he was the fiery warrior of old. When he opened the Rains County Fair and launched the Kennedy-Johnson campaign at Sherman and Bonham, there were signs that the body was yielding to time but the spirit was filled with the fire of youth. His face was lined and his eyes surrounded by a wrinkled puffiness, yet they sparkled when he projected his imagination into the future prospects of his Party. However, he warned, at the Bonham State Park:

> "The people of the United States and the free world have a rendezvous with destiny in 1960. The question is whether we will survive or perish, and we need most an honest, vigorous, far-reaching, inspiring leader to do the job."

While he continued to add achievement to achievement, the honors likewise rolled in as expressions of his worthiness. He was notified that he was the recipient of the National Committee for a Representative Congress' formal "Award for Outstanding Representative Public Service." The organization is composed of an independent, non-partisan group. The citation summarized qualities and achievements which had been recognized by colleagues, citizens, foreign dignitaries, and people everywhere who knew Sam Rayburn.

The citation made reference to his adherence to the principles of representative government, his championing of democracy, his support of strong national defense, and his half a century of endorsement of sound legislation for the betterment of America. It paid special tribute to his faith in God, in country, fellowman, and self. He was referred to as a symbol of all that makes America great—"a beloved symbol that makes 'Mr. Sam,' 'Mr. Texas,' 'Mr. America,' all one, a living symbol of a good man, a good neighbor, a good citizen, a good public servant, *patiently* dedicated to serving *others* with unselfish disregard of any political consequences."

Even during the waning hours of the campaign Sam Rayburn continued to drive himself and press the fight for his Party. In the tour through Texas he concentrated on the controversial issues which he thought should be honestly aired. He gave the Houston audience the facts "with the bark on." He minced no words on the religious issue and oil depletion. "We are in control of Congress and we are going to be. . . . And if we cared more for vengeance than we do for justice, we'd do something about it." He told some Houstonians that they had not been fair in deserting the Party which had helped them get rich. Later he was privately asked to elaborate upon the political situation to which he had referred—the two types of Democrats. He replied as follows:

"I'll illustrate it this way. There are two breeds of hounds down there in Houston—yours and my kind—and that other type. Well, you have seen our type follow the scent, find the tree, and stay right under it. But take that other type of hound, he'll be going along until he is distracted; maybe a rabbit runs across his path, and off he goes. This type of hound won't tree, and I just don't see how a fellow can hunt with a dog like that. Does that answer your question?"

In Fort Worth on November 1, according to Ed Johnson of the *Star Telegram,* "Mr. Democrat basted the Republicans in general, and Richard Nixon in particular, with hot sauce at a barbecue for Party faithfuls." America has never produced a better chef when the meat over the hot coals was a Republican. He had prepared an enormous bed of hot coals for this night's cookout. After discussing the "socialistic labels," oil depletion, and religious tolerance, he talked about the brand of Communism that was only ninety miles off the Florida Coast: "This Administration has not even tapped Castro on the wrist. If Harry Truman were President he would have had something to say to Mr. Castro before now." Then in a voice full of sarcasm, he added, "I know Richard Milhous Nixon."

Though he did not admit that he was feeling the physical strain, the week following the election he was forced to yield to a bad cold. His doctor, Joe Risser, almost had to hogtie him to get him into the hospital for only two days of rest. Risser feared that pneumonia would develop. Mr. Sam said this was the second time he had ever been in a hospital as a patient, the first time being fifty years ago, when he had his tonsils out. He even affirmed that he had never had a headache, and had always been in perfect health. His weight was almost to a pound what it had been for half a century, and he wore the "same sized breeches he always did." Those who knew him best frankly admitted that Sam Rayburn was correct—"Regardless of fame and honors, he never got too big for his breeches. This was one earmark of his greatness," they explain.

Rayburn was pleased with the prospects under Kennedy's leadership. When asked how he could be so enthusiastic about a man who was Senator Johnson's adversary at Los Angeles, he replied curtly: "That boy grows on you! People everywhere seem to like him." He believed Senator Kennedy had more initiative than President Eisenhower, but that the latter was "just as good a man as an individual, and if he were not in politics, he would be just the kind of fellow you would want to know." His feelings are revealed also in the telegram he sent when he learned that John F. Kennedy, Jr., had been born: "I trust he will grow like his father and look like his mother."

On the morning of December 19, Mr. Sam boarded President-elect Kennedy's private plane at Perrin Air Force Base and flew for a conference at Palm Beach, Florida. Vice-President-elect Lyndon B. Johnson and Senator Mike Mansfield were also invited to the vacation headquarters for a two-day look at the legislative picture facing the new Congress. Mrs. Kennedy discussed housing arrangements with Lady Bird Johnson because she did not know where to put the Speaker. The new baby posed a problem, being housed next door to Mr. Sam. Maxine Cheshire recalls this report: "I hope he'll be quiet" (the reference was to the infant, not to Mr. Sam's snoring, and the possibility of his setting off some disturbance).

While the "big four" were in session, Mr. Sam's eyes kept roaming out the window at the water, when there was a lull in activities. Jacqueline Kennedy read his mind and when he eased out of the room, she followed behind to take a snapshot of Mr. Sam just as he threw his fishing line from the pier. Mr. Sam grinned and the press said he expressed the desire to hook a few little ones today and save the big ones for January. Mrs. Kennedy expressed her faith in a comment on the photograph: "The fish haven't a chance."

Speaking of photographs relative to Mr. Sam's fishing exploits, several very provocative ones were snapped during 1960. Mr. Sam, dressed in his somewhat frayed fishing clothes, was seen loading his fishing gear into his $11,000 limousine for a day of recreation down in Virginia with George, his chauffeur. Mr. Sam had two pertinent comments here. He reminded people that besides his fishing clothes he had two other wardrobes—a formal outfit and several blue suits, which he bought in Baltimore. About the expensive limousine, he stated that it was furnished on a sort of rental basis to the Government at $500 a year. This plan, he said, reduced the Capitol automobile expense by a considerable figure.

About those "big fish," he had these predictions afterward when he went to Washington for a brief meeting. He saw quick action on a depressed areas bill, housing, school construction, and minimum wage. He predicted also some good agricultural legislation, help for the aged, strong defense measures, some thought on closing the tax loopholes (not the twenty-seven-and-one-half-per-cent depletion, which was not a loophole, he insisted), and some consideration for aid to education (but he hoped that paying teachers' salaries did not get involved).

One of the first items of business in Washington was to take a look at the progress being made on the new east front of the Capitol. The workmen were moving around a little more rapidly, putting on the finishing touches for the unveiling ceremony of January 20, which was to have a special significance this time. Mr. Democrat was to be the "Big Daddy," as some of his Mississippi friends visioned him.

Honor and prestige, however, never turned Mr. Sam's head or made him feel superior to his people. They had rewarded him far beyond what he really deserved, he so frequently stated. In return for their confidence he gave a life of dedicated service and grew into an institution, unique in the history of American politics and government.

☆ Epilogue ☆

Americans everywhere have said that there will not be another Mr. Sam. As the President of the United States said, "They don't make them like that any more." His like will perhaps never be seen again. He was the last tie between the frontier concepts and ideals of Thomas Jefferson, Andrew Jackson, Davy Crockett, Sam Houston, and Abraham Lincoln and the New Frontier of science and international understanding. Implanted deep in his nature were those eternal qualities which all men steeped in the democratic tradition revere. Germinated in the mind of John Milton, transplanted to New England soil by his protégé Roger Williams, and diffused through the minds of three centuries, those basic concepts of justice, freedom, and love of fellow man found a firm root in the black waxy soil of the Fourth District. The harvest of this heart and mind blessed both the city and countryside of America. Where men feel free to speak their thoughts in the American tradition, where health and security have replaced poverty and want, where light pierces the darkness of rural homes and people travel in comfort regardless of the weather, the name of one public servant will be upon their lips in gratitude. Though he was born in a log cabin and was a product of the era of homespun, success never made him lose touch with the rock from which he was hewn and the people who gave him inspiration. He established an identity with certain abstract qualities of his country's soul; hence he is ageless. He belongs to yesterday, today, and tomorrow. His immortality is both here and hereafter, in men's minds and their laws. So long as America preserves her ideals and remains on the course charted by the founding fathers will one man remain secure in history—Mr. Sam of the Fourth District.

☆ A Sam Rayburn Chronology ☆

1840. October 22, William Marion Rayburn (father) born in Tennessee.

1846. August 26, Martha Clementine Waller (mother) born.

1868. May 14, William Marion Rayburn and Martha Clementine Waller married.

1869. July 24, John Franklin Rayburn born.

1873. Charles Rayburn born.

1875. January 14, Lucinda Rayburn born.

1877. March 6, Jim and Will Rayburn born.

1882. January 6, Samuel Taliaferro Rayburn born.

1884. June 20, Richard Ashby (Dick) Rayburn born.

1886. October 20, Tom Rayburn born.

1887. William Marion and Martha Waller Rayburn came to Texas with ten children. November 2, bought a farm at Flag Springs.

1890. Sam started to school at Burnett.

1891. Transferred to Flag Springs. January 22, Abner Rayburn born.

1900. Enrolled at the Mayo Normal, Commerce, Texas.

1901. Taught school at Greenwood in Hopkins County. Charles Rayburn (brother) died, buried at Dodd City.

1903. Awarded B.S. degree. Began teaching again—Dial (two years), then Lannius (one year).

1906. Announced for the State Legislature and elected.

1908. Elected to a second term. Passed bar examination after taking courses at the University of Texas.

1910. Elected to a third term.

1911. January 10, elected Speaker of Thirty-second Legislature.

1912. February 2, announced for Congress. Elected over seven opponents July 27. Family moved from Flag Springs to farm west of Bonham, built house, remodeled it in 1937.

1913. February 27, left for Washington. April 7, took the oath of office (Sixty-third Congress). June 3, became a member of the Committee on Interstate and Foreign Commerce. May 6, delivered maiden speech.

1914. Defeated Tom Perkins (Collin) for a second term. July 22, Abner Rayburn (brother) died.

1916. Defeated Andrew Randell (Grayson) for a third term. October 16, William Marion Rayburn (father) died.

1918. Defeated Robert Lovelace (Fannin) for a fourth term.

1920. Defeated Ed Westbrook (Hunt) for a fifth term.

1922. Defeated Ed Westbrook again for a sixth term.

1924. Defeated M. M. Morrison (Grayson) for a seventh term.

1926. Elected to an eighth term without opposition.

1927. February 21, Martha Waller Rayburn (mother) died.

1928. Defeated three opponents for a ninth term. May 19, Dr. John Franklin Rayburn (brother) died.

1930. Defeated C. B. Randell and B. L. Shirley for a tenth term.

1931. Became Chairman of Committee on Interstate and Foreign Commerce.

1932. Defeated Jess Morris (Hunt) and C. B. Randell (Grayson) for an eleventh term.

1934. Defeated Jess Morris for a twelfth term.

1936. Defeated Jess Morris and Will A. Harris for a thirteenth term.

1937. January 4, elected Majority Leader in Democratic caucus (Seventy-fifth Congress).

1938. The $54,000,000 Denison Dam project approved. Elected without opposition to a fourteenth term.

1940. Defeated Dr. Biven R. Galbraith (Fannin) for fifteenth term. Elected Speaker September 16 to fill out Bankhead's term (Seventy-sixth Congress, third session).

1941. January 3, elected to first full term as Speaker (Seventy-seventh Congress). August 12, extension of Selective Service Act approved.

1942. May 30, awarded Doctor of Laws degree by Muhlenberg College. Defeated George Balch (Hunt) for a sixteenth term.

1943. January 6, elected to a second full term as Speaker. August 6, awarded the Doctor of Laws degree by East Texas State Teachers College. March 18, William H. Rayburn (brother) died.

1944. Defeated G. C. Morris (Hunt) and George Balch for a seventeenth term.

1945. Elected to a third full term as Speaker. June 27, awarded the Doctor of Laws degree by the University of Maryland.

1946. Elected without opposition to an eighteenth term.

1947. January 3, elected Minority Leader by Democratic caucus (Eightieth Congress).

1948. Served as Permanent Chairman of Democratic National Convention. Defeated G. C. Morris and David Brown for a nineteenth term.

1949. January 3, elected Speaker for a fourth term. May 3, won the *Collier's* magazine award of $10,000 for distinguished service. November 5, elected honorary member of the Alpha of Texas chapter of Phi Beta Kappa.

1950. May 8, James Lee Rayburn (brother) died, buried at Dodd City. May 23, awarded the Doctor of Humanities degree by Austin College. June 9, awarded Doctor of Laws degree by National University. Elected to twentieth term without opposition.

1951. January 3, elected for fifth full term as Speaker. January 30, surpassed Henry Clay's record of 3056½ days as Speaker.

1952. Served as Permanent Chairman of Democratic National Convention. Defeated Reagan Brown (Kaufman) for a twenty-first term.

1953. January 3, Minority Leader again (Eighty-third Congress).

1954. March 11, bids received for Sam Rayburn Library. May 7, initiated by Phi Delta Phi. Defeated A. G. McRae (Fannin) for a twenty-seond term.

1955. January 6, elected Speaker for sixth full term. April 16, figuratively replaced two presidents at Jefferson-Jackson Day $100-a-plate dinner. May 25, awarded Doctor of Laws degree by Tusculum College. May 30, awarded the Doctor of Laws degree by the University of West Virginia.

1956. April 9, awarded the Order of Sikatuna. May 26, Lucinda Rayburn (sister) died of cancer. June 4, awarded the Doctor of Laws degree by Syracuse University. Served as Permanent Chairman Democratic National Convention. Elected without opposition to twenty-third term.

1957. January 3, elected to a seventh full term as Speaker. October 9, Sam Rayburn Library dedicated.

1958. Elected without opposition to a twenty-fourth term.

1959. January 7, elected to his eighth full term as Speaker. March 5, broke Joe Cannon's forty-six-year record for number of years as Speaker.

1960. January 28, received Cordell Hull award. Elected honorary Permanent Chairman of the Democratic National

Convention. March 1, Tom Rayburn (brother) died. July 13, nominated Senator Lyndon Baines Johnson for President. Elected without opposition to a twenty-fifth term. Received the "Award for Outstanding Representative Public Service."

1961. January 3, elected Speaker for the tenth time, the ninth full term (Eighty-seventh Congress). January 31, won the fight to enlarge the Rules Committee. June 12, doubled Henry Clay's record for service as Speaker. August 31, suffering from what he termed "lumbago" he returned to Bonham. October 2, admitted to Baylor Medical Hospital; October 5, ailment officially diagnosed as cancer. October 31, returned to Bonham to spend last days among his friends. November 16, 6:20 A.M., died at Joe Risser Hospital. November 18, buried Willow Wild Cemetery.

☆ Genealogy of the Rayburn Family ☆

Children of George Waller and Ann Winston Carr, with dates where available, also spouses' names:

1. Elizabeth (born 1762, married Jacob McCraw)
2. Mary Winston (born 1763, married Major John Redd)
3. John (born 1765, married Polly Cooper)
4. Carr (born 1767)
5. Ann (Nancy) (born 1770, married Thomas King, then Thomas C. Morrison)
6. George (born 1773, married Polly Staples)
7. William (born 1775, married Mary Barksdale)
8. Edmund (born 1779, married Maria Dunson)

Children of John Barksdale Waller and Katherine Pickle Waller, with dates where available:

1. William B. Waller (born August 9, 1825; died September 24, 1825)
2. Peggy A. M. Waller (born August 17, 1826)
3. Mary J. Waller (born February 24, 1828)
4. Elizabeth E. Waller (born November 15, 1829)
5. Henry A. Waller (born November 22, 1831)
6. Jacob L. Waller (born November 28, 1834)
7. John W. Waller (born December 6, 1836; died August 4, 1884)
8. Sarah K. Waller (born May 21, 1839; died May 4, 1865)
9. Carr M. Waller (born December 21, 1841)
10. Edmund F. Waller (born June 18, 1844; died November 28, 1862)
11. Martha Clementine Waller (born August 26, 1846; died February 21, 1927)
12. Elizabeth M. Waller (born November 30, 1849)
13. Amanda S. Waller (born January 17, 1852)

☆ Bibliography ☆

I. BOOKS AND ARTICLES ABOUT SAM RAYBURN

A. *Articles or Books (selected)*

BOYD, EDWARD, "Mr. Speaker, the Dynamo of Capitol Hill," *American* magazine, CLIX, April, 1955, pp. 24, 98–99, 102–103.

COHN, DAVID L., "Mr. Speaker," *The Atlantic Monthly*, October, 1942, pp. 73–78.

COUGHLAN, ROBERT, "Proprietors of the House," *Life*, February 14, 1955, pp. 73–94.

FOX, J. DEWITT, "Mr. Speaker," *Life and Health*, Summer, 1959.

HEALY, PAUL F., "They Are Just Crazy About Sam," *Saturday Evening Post*, November 24, 1951, pp. 22–23.

HINGA, DON, "Sam Rayburn: Texas Squire," *Southwest Review*, Summer, 1944, pp. 471–480.

KORNITZER, BELA, "The Untalkative Speaker Talks—About His Father," *American Fathers and Sons*, New York: Hermitage House, 1952.

MALLON, PAUL, "Man in the Shadows," *The Statesman's Corner*, February 3, 1934.

MEYER, KARL E., "Texas Puts Its Brand on Washington," *Harper's*, November, 1960, pp. 40–44.

NASH, WALTER C., "Sam Rayburn the Congressman of the Fourth District" (unpublished Master's Thesis), East Texas State Teachers College, August, 1950.

ROSS, BILL, "Mr. Sam Rayburn of Texas," *Facts*, pp. 89–93.

WHITE, WILLIAM S., "Sam Rayburn, the Untalkative Speaker," New York *Times*, Magazine Section, February 27, 1949.

YOUNG, VALTON J., *The Speaker's Agent*. New York: Vantage Press, 1956.

B. *Authors of other articles or news items cited*

AGRONSKY, MARTIN
ALBRIGHT, ROBERT C.
ALLEN, ROBERT S.
ALSOP, JOSEPH
BECKLER, JOHN
BOLTON, PAUL
BRANDT, RAYMOND P.
BROWN, GEORGE ROTHWELL
CARPENTER, ELIZABETH
CARPENTER, LESLIE
CHEAVENS, DAVE
CHESIRE, MAXINE

Colegrove, Albert M.
Dickson, Cecil B.
Dickson, Fagan
Dixon, George
Drummond, Roscoe
Duckworth, Allen
Easley, Tex
Edwards, Willard
Eleazer, Frank
Hardeman, D. B.
Hornaday, Walter C.
Hutchinson, William K.
Johnson, Ed
Johnson, Ralph
Kiernan, Walter
Kintner, Robert
Lyons, Richard L.
Mathis, Jim
McClendon, Sarah
McCormick, Harry
McNair, Marie
Miller, Dale
Pearson, Drew
Reston, James
Riesel, Victor
Sevareid, Eric
Simmons, Lee
Stimpson, George W.
Timmons, Bascom N.
Unna, Warren
Virden, John M.
Winningham, George W.
Winters, S. R.

II. GENERAL MISCELLANEOUS

A. Proceedings of House of Representatives, Austin, Texas, Thirtieth through Thirty-second Legislatures (1907–1912) and Fifty-seventh Legislature (1961–1962).

B. Congressional Records of Sixty-third Congress (1913) through Eighty-seventh Congress (1962).

C. Sam Rayburn files (1906–1961)—correspondence with family, friends, constituents, colleagues, etc., exclusive of those lost in 1927.

D. Scrapbooks (newspaper clippings, articles, photographs, brochures, campaign literature, etc., exclusive of those lost in Washington).

E. Speech files (addresses and campaign speeches 1913–1961).

F. Exhibits in Sam Rayburn Library (awards, public documents, mementos, pictures, etc., pertaining to significant events in Rayburn's life).

G. Recorded interviews with Mr. Rayburn by the author, reports of interviews by others, interviews with people in his public and private life.

H. Correspondence with about forty congressmen and other people of prominence, motivated by a questionnaire pertaining to Rayburn's life and ideas.

I. Newspaper files of publications in Fourth District, including Bonham *Daily Favorite*, Denison *Herald*, Sherman *Democrat*. Files of Dallas *Morning News*, *Texas Observer*, Washington *Post*, Washington *Evening Star*, and other publications cited. Magazine files, including *Newsweek*, *Time*, *Life*, *U.S. News and World Report*, and other periodicals cited.

J. Other books (selected)

Adams, Samuel Hopkins. *Incredible Era, the Life and*

Times of Warren Gamaliel Harding. Boston: Houghton Mifflin Co., 1939.

ALLEN, FREDERICK LEWIS. *The Big Change, America Transforms Itself.* New York: Harper and Brothers, 1952.

ALSOP, EM BOWLES (ed.). *The Greatness of Woodrow Wilson, 1856–1956.* New York: Rinehart and Co., 1956. Introduction by Dwight D. Eisenhower.

BLUM, JOHN M. *Joe Tumulty and the Wilson Era.* New York: Houghton Mifflin Co., 1951.

COULTER, E. MERTON. *The South During Reconstruction, 1865–1877.* Baton Rouge: Louisiana State University Press, 1947.

DANIELS, JOSEPHUS. *The Wilson Era, Years of Peace—1910–1917, 1917–1923.* Two volumes. Chapel Hill: The University of North Carolina Press, 1946.

DONOVAN, ROBERT J. *Joe Martin, My First Fifty Years in Politics.* New York: McGraw-Hill Book Company, 1960.

FARLEY, JAMES A. *Behind the Ballots, The Personal History of a Politician.* New York: Harcourt, Brace and Co., 1938.

GARWOOD, ELLEN CLAYTON. *Will Clayton. A Short Biography.* Austin: University of Texas Press, 1958.

HINSHAW, DAVID. *Herbert Hoover: American Quaker.* New York: Farrar, Straus and Co., 1950.

HOFSTADTER, RICHARD. *The American Political Tradition and the Men Who Made It.* New York: Vintage Books, 1959.

HULL, CORDELL. *The Memoirs of.* New York: The Macmillan Co., 1948.

JAMES, MARQUIS. *Mr. Garner of Texas.* New York: The Bobbs-Merrill Co., 1939.

KITTRELL, NORMAN G. *Governors Who Have Been, and Other Public Men of Texas.* Houston: Dealy-Asley-Elgin Co., 1921.

LINK, ARTHUR S. *Wilson, the New Freedom.* Princeton: Princeton University Press, 1956.

———. *Woodrow Wilson and the Progressive Era, 1910–1917.* New York: Harper and Brothers, 1954.

McKAY, SETH SHEPARD. *Texas Politics, 1906–1944, with Special Reference to the German Counties.* Lubbock: Texas Tech Press, 1952.

MYERS, WILLIAM STARR and NEWTON, WALTER H. *The Hoover Administration, a Documented Narrative.* New York: Charles Scribner's Sons, 1936.

PATMAN, WRIGHT. *Our American Government. 1001 Questions on How it Works.* Scholastic Magazines, 1958.

STEEN, RALPH W. *Twentieth Century Texas.* Austin: The Steck Co., 1942.

TRUMAN, HARRY S. *Memoirs.* Volume One. *Year of Decisions,* Garden City: Doubleday and Co., Inc., 1955.

———. *Memoirs.* Volume Two. *Years of Trial and Hope,* Garden City: Doubleday and Co., Inc., 1956.

WECTER, DIXON. *The Age of the Great Depression.* New York: The Macmillan Co., 1948.

WHITE, WILLIAM ALLEN. *A Puritan in Babylon.* New York: The Macmillan Co., 1938.

WILBUR, RAY LYMAN and HYDE, ARTHUR MASTICK. *The Hoover Policies.* New York: Charles Scribner's Sons, 1936.

☆ Notes ☆

Chapter I

[1] Robert S. Allen and Paul Scott, "The Allen-Scott Report," January 9, 1961 (Hall Syndicate, Inc.).

[2] John Beckler, Washington Correspondent (AP), March 3, 1961.

[3] George Dixon, "Washington Scene," Houston *Post*, June 20, 1961.

Chapter II

[1] E. Merton Coulter, *The South During Reconstruction, 1865–1877* (Baton Rouge: Louisiana State University Press, 1947), p. 2.

[2] Bela Kornitzer, "The Untalkative Speaker Talks—About His Father," *American Fathers and Sons* (New York: Hermitage House, 1952), p. 214.

[3] *Ibid.*, pp. 219–220.

Chapter III

[1] David L. Cohn, "Mr. Speaker," *The Atlantic Monthly*, October, 1942, p. 76.

Chapter IV

[1] Norman G. Kittrell, *Governors Who Have Been, and Other Public Men of Texas* (Houston: Dealy-Ashley-Elgin Co., 1921), p. 127.

Chapter IX

[1] Samuel Hopkins Adams, *Incredible Era, the Life and Times of Warren Gamaliel Harding* (Boston: Houghton Mifflin Co., 1939), p. 170; quoted from Walter Davenport, *Power and Glory* (New York: G. P. Putnam's Sons, 1931).

Chapter X

[1] William Allen White, *A Puritan in Babylon* (New York: The Macmillan Co., 1938), p. 127.

Chapter XI

[1] James A. Farley, *Behind the Ballots, the Personal History of a Politician* (New York: Harcourt, Brace and Co., 1938), p. 134.

[2] *Ibid.*, pp. 134–135.

[3] *Ibid.*, p. 138.

[4] *Idem.*

[5] *Idem.*

Chapter XII

[1] Valton J. Young, *The Speaker's Agent* (New York: Vantage Press, 1956), pp. 11–12.

[2] *Ibid.*, p. 13.

[3] *Idem.*

[4] *Ibid.*, pp. 13–14.

[5] *Ibid.*, pp. 15–16.

[6] *Ibid.*, p. 17.

[7] *Ibid.*, pp. 19–21.

[8] Dixon Wecter, *The Age of the Great Depression* (New York: The Macmillan Co., 1948), p. 66.

[9] Young, *op. cit.*, p. 56.

[10] *Ibid.*, pp. 58–59.

Chapter XIII

[1] Cf. Young, *The Speaker's Agent*, p. 24.

[2] *Ibid.*, p. 27.

[3] *Ibid.*, p. 28.

[4] *Ibid.*, p. 35.

[5] *Ibid.*, pp. 37–38.

[6] *Ibid.*, pp. 36–37.

[7] *Ibid.*, p. 44.

Chapter XIV

[1] *The Saturday Evening Post*, January 18, 1941, p. 22.

[2] Cf. Cohn, "Mr. Speaker," *The Atlantic Monthly*, October, 1942, p. 77.

[3] *Ibid.*, p. 73.

Chapter XV

[1] Seth Shepard McKay, *Texas Politics, 1906–1944 . . .* (Lubbock: Texas Tech Press, 1952), p. 319.

[2] "A Communication," *The New Republic*, July 10, 1944.

Chapter XVI

[1] William S. White, from a United Feature Syndicate column.

[2] From a filmed interview of Speaker Rayburn by Martin Agronsky (NBC).

[3] Cf. Young, *The Speaker's Agent*, pp. 68–69.

Chapter XVII

[1] Cf. Young, *The Speaker's Agent*, p. 60.

[2] Edward Boyd, "Mr. Speaker, The Dynamo of Capitol Hill," *American* magazine, Vol. CLIX, p. 100.

[3] Young, *op. cit.*, pp. 47–48.

Chapter XVIII

[1] Cf. Boyd, "Mr. Speaker. . . ," *American* magazine, Vol. CLIX, p. 99.

[2] Harry S Truman, *Memoirs*, II (Garden City: Doubleday and Co., Inc., 1956), p. 438.

Chapter XIX

[1] Robert Coughlan, "Proprietors of the House," *Life* magazine, February 14, 1955, p. 75.

Chapter XX

[1] Drew Pearson, "The Washington Merry-Go-Round," March 15, 1955 (Bell Syndicate, Inc.).

Chapter XXI

[1] George Dixon, "Washington Scene" (King Features Syndicate).

[2] Elizabeth Carpenter, " 'Mr. Sam'—A Note on 'the Uncorrupted Man,' " for the *Gazette* Washington Bureau, January 20, 1958.

[3] Walter C. Hornaday, Chief of the *News* Washington Bureau.

[4] Eric Sevareid and Sam Rayburn, "Capitol Cloakroom," Interview (CBS).

[5] James Reston, New York *Times*, January 5, 1959.

[6] George Dixon, "Speaker Rayburn's Fateful Visit," "Washington Scene," Washington *Post*, August 9, 1960 (King Features Syndicate).

[7] Victor Riesel, "Inside Labor," June 9, 1959 (Hall Syndicate, Inc.).

[8] Robert C. Albright, Washington *Post*, July 25, 1959.

[9] Drew Pearson, "Washington Merry-Go-Round," Washington *Post,* August 31, 1959 (Bell Syndicate, Inc.).

Chapter XXII

[1] Colonel John H. Virden, editor *The American Weekend* (Army Times Publishers).

[2] Victor Riesel, "Inside Labor," June 8, 1960 (Hall Syndicate, Inc.).

[3] James Reston, New York *Times,* July 15, 1960.

☆ INDEX ☆

ABOUT THE AUTHOR

C. Dwight Dorough was born in Gober, Texas, near Bonham, in 1912, the year Sam Rayburn was elected to Congress. His family have long been friends of Mr. Rayburn, and his father is chairman of the Democratic Executive Committee of Fannin County. The author took his B.A. and M.A. degrees in 1936 and his Ph.D. in 1946 from the University of Texas. He has been a principal of the Harrison School in Fannin County and an investigator for the Attorney General of Texas. In 1948 he took a teaching position at the University of Houston, was chairman of the English Department from 1954 to 1958, and is now a professor there. Mr. Dorough lives in Houston with his wife and two daughters.